D0897899

EX LIBRIS
PACE COLLEGE
WESTCHESTER

PLEASANTVILLE, NEW YORK

American Participation in the Second Vatican Council

American Participation in the Second Vatican Council

EDITED BY
MONSIGNOR VINCENT A. YZERMANS

SHEED AND WARD : NEW YORK

© Sheed and Ward, Inc., 1967

Library of Congress Catalog Card Number 67–13766

Nihil Obstat: Very Rev. Colman Barry, O.S.B.
          Censor Deputatus

Imprimatur: †Peter W. Bartholome
          Bishop of St. Cloud
          St. Cloud, Minnesota
          February 22, 1967

Manufactured in the United States of America

BX
830.
1962
A514

To PETER W. BARTHOLOME
Bishop of St. Cloud

Acknowledgements

I wish to acknowledge my deep appreciation to the publishers of the following books and periodicals for their kind permission to quote material in this book from works that have previously appeared under their imprint:

United Church Press, for the quotation from Douglas Horton's *Vatican Diary* (Philadelphia-Boston, 1964), p. 57.

Christianity and Crisis, for quotations from Robert McAfee Brown's "In Memoriam: Gustave Weigel, S.J." (February 3, 1964).

Commonweal, for quotations from Gregory A. Baum's "The Council Ends" (January 7, 1966, pp. 404–405).

America, for the quotation from John Courtney Murray's "This Matter of Religious Freedom" (January 9, 1965, p. 43).

The Catholic World, for the quotation from Joseph L. Lichten's "The Council Declaration on the Jews" (August 1964, pp. 275–276).

Chicago Studies, for the quotation from my article on the late Albert Cardinal Meyer.

Paulist Press of Glen Rock, New Jersey, for quotations from *Third Session, Council Speeches of Vatican II,* edited by William K. Leahy and Anthony T. Massimini.

National Catholic News Service of Washington, D.C., for all quotations from the addresses of Pope Paul VI.

Foreword

The Second Vatican Council will be recorded in history as the outstanding religious event of the twentieth century. Under the inspiration of the Holy Spirit and the guidance of Pope John and Pope Paul, the Council's success is attributable not to any particular group of persons, but to all the Fathers and to all the priests, religious and lay people who rendered a variety of services that were necessary for the progress of the event.

A few weeks before the end of the Council, Pope Paul gave public evidence of appreciation of the work of the religious, the *periti* and the pastors at the Council by inviting some of them to concelebrate Mass with him at the public session of November 18, 1965. On the eve of the solemn closing, at a special audience for the young clerics who had distributed and collected ballots and documents, the Holy Father, with grateful appreciation and paternal affection, referred to them as the *lubrificanti*—the lubricants who had ensured the smooth and speedy progress of the Council.

This impressive volume, *American Participation in the Second Vatican Council*, provides an authentic picture of the interest and concerns of many of the United States' bishops at the Council. The author modestly, but properly, refers to his work as an "interim report."

He is modest because the volume contains the actual texts of the 118 addresses made by the United States' bishops in the Council. In addition to these, the author has quoted substantially from many of the written interventions which normally would not see the light of day for many years. This collection of interventions speaks eloquently about the openness of the United States' bishops, about their confidence in Monsignor Yzermans, and it makes this volume singular and historically valuable.

The author calls this an "interim report" because he does not presume to give the full dimensions, nor does he attempt to give a complete evaluation of the impact of the contributions made by the bishops of the United States. He simply reports all that is presently available and certain.

A final and complete report and evaluation must await the date of free access to the Council archives. The records and meetings of all general and particular sessions, of all commissions, subcommissions, and tribunals are preserved in an orderly fashion. These records are being transcribed, and eventually some will appear in printed form.

A complete report would require a careful study of the 350 printed pages of suggested topics submitted by 149 out of 214 United States' bishops in 1959. It would require a culling of the minutes of all meetings of the preparatory commissions and subcommissions for a record of the activity of the 61 United States' bishops and *periti* who served on these commissions. One of the commissions held 66 plenary meetings for a total of 371 hours, and the subcommittees of another commission met 215 times for periods of from two and a half to three hours.

There were 246 United States' bishops who attended all or some part of the Council sessions. About 30 of them served on various conciliar bodies. Many of them responded to the invitation to submit written observations on the *schemata* in the intervals between the four sessions. During the Council, many bishops from the United States followed the pattern of submitting written interventions without requesting an opportunity to speak. Actually, all interventions—in order to receive any consideration—had to be submitted in writing. Of the total of 6,434 written interventions submitted, only 2,205 were delivered orally in the Basilica.

In this "interim report" Monsignor Yzermans provides a historical introduction to each of the conciliar documents. These introductions are laced with quotations from the written observations submitted by our American bishops. He also provides commentaries on all documents. The commentaries are not official interpretations, but they are written by the leading *periti* or consultants from the United States who were at the Council. Some of these were officially attached to conciliar commissions and secretariats and actually participated in drafting and revising conciliar acts. Others served as personal consultants to the bishops, advising them and helping them to draft their interventions. All commentaries provide insights from experts who were on the scene—from first-hand sources—and they attempt to relate the conciliar decisions to the Catholic Church in the United States.

While a full appreciation of the impact of the United States' bishops on the Council must await a study of their interventions in the general sessions and in the meetings of the preparatory and conciliar commissions, Monsignor Yzermans' work traces a pattern of the contributions of the bishops. The pattern shows individual and coordinated actions, a wide divergence of views and an unevenness of utterances. Some may be tempted to regard such a pattern as evidence of disunity and ineffectiveness. I venture to express the belief that the example of freedom of action and expression was one of the significant contributions of the United States' hierarchy and one which earned for them the esteem of others.

From the very opening of the preparatory phase it was evident that bishops of some countries had decided to follow a single line. This approach carried over into the first session. In some circles there was apprehension that our

American bishops would take advantage of their numbers and of their munificence to bishops in other countries to develop a strong bloc of voices and votes.

The reaction of some of the bishops, when they first heard an auxiliary bishop from the United States express a view different from that expressed by a United States' cardinal, was amusing. They agreed that freedom of speech was allowed in the United States and in the Ecumenical Council, but they felt that it was indelicate for bishops from one country to take different views. The Council Fathers soon realized that our bishops could and did act in concert and also individually; that their interest in the universal Church transcended geographic and political boundaries; that they could and did plead as vigorously for the solution of problems in emerging nations and missionary areas as they did for a solution of the problems in their own backyard; and that they were reflecting the different circumstances in which the Church operates in our vast country.

Such genuine concern for the Church in the world and such frankness on the part of the bishops from the United States inspired imitation and admiration. On a number of occasions I was asked whether the views expressed by one or more of our American bishops represented a majority view, because the bishops were anxious to support the majority view of the United States' bishops. A telling evidence of the esteem for the American hierarchy occurred when the membership of the commissions was being increased. The complete list of United States' candidates submitted by their bishops were incorporated into the international list of candidates, and all the United States' candidates proposed and supported by their United States' bishops were elected by the general assembly.

I am very happy to see Monsignor Yzermans' work published at this time. It provides the reader with primary sources and enables him to acquire an insight into the contributions of the United States' bishops as well as an appreciation of the conciliar documents. I congratulate the general editor, the commentators and all who helped in the publication of this work.

This volume is a singular contribution to post-conciliar literature. It merits the widest possible circulation, and it will serve as an added means of promoting the renewal of the Church in the United States along the precise lines and directives of the Second Vatican Council.

✠ John Cardinal Krol
Archbishop of Philadelphia

CONTENTS

American Participation in the Second Vatican Council

Introduction

This work is meant to be a report about the American bishops at the Second Vatican Council, and meant to be nothing more than an interim report—until that day when a professional historian will have ready access to the archives of the Council. This book, then, has no particular thesis to defend. It was written for no other reason than to report that American bishops, present at the Second Vatican Council, exerted an influence upon the course of the Council and that they profited in varying degrees as a result of the Council. I have intended, as a reporter, to record no more and no less than that.

The American bishops were present at the Second Vatican Council both as witnesses of the faith as lived in the United States of America as well as teachers of that faith. I believe that the American hierarchy exerted a definitive influence upon the documents of Vatican II, especially regarding the Declaration on Religious Freedom and the Declaration on the Relationship of the Church to Non-Christian Religions. I believe, further, that Lee E. Dirks, writing from Rome in the November 9, 1964 issue of *The National Observer*, best summarized their role at the Council. He wrote:

> Just as Americans here have influenced the council, the council has influenced these Americans. It has instilled in the American bishops and priests here an alertness toward theology they have never had before. It has quickened their awareness of their common heritage. It has enhanced their sense of a common mission in the United States.

If Mr. Dirk's observation deserves more than passing mention, another observation merits even more reflection. In one of the best articles written on the role of American bishops at the Council, Sidney Hyman, writing in the December 5, 1956 issue of *The Washington Post*, made this observation:

> What happens to a community of 40 million American Catholics should be a subject of sympathetic interest to 160 million of their fellow Americans who are not Catholic. Further, the kind of leverage the bishops of the American Catholic community can exercise in a world Catholic community of 500 million deserves more than a passing glance from us all.

Nor is this work intended to be an evaluation. Only the foolhardy would attempt an evaluation of the American bishops' role at Vatican II at this time. Evaluations can be made only after all the evidence is presented. Vatican procedures prevent the amassing of this evidence at this time; thus we must be content with no more than tentative judgments.

In assessing the role of American bishops at Vatican II, the reader must keep in mind the unique character of their witness which had been conditioned by the pragmatic conditions of their formation. Some aspects of that character can be explained.

First, as bishops of a growing, developing Church, the American bishops had to become builders, administrators and financiers. To shirk these duties would mean a real neglect of interests which are essential for the proper functioning of the Church in their country. Secondly, the American bishops' reluctance to speak, if it can be called reluctance, is best explained by the American character itself. An American prefers action to speech. He finds it embarrassing to create tedium by voicing views which another has already expressed. This national temperament had restrained more than one American bishop from addressing the Council assembly.

There is, however, merit even in the reluctance of the American bishops to speak. Thus, when an American bishop did speak, many other Council Fathers listened with special interest. Aware of the strength of Catholic life in America, aware, too, that American bishops are not given to much talking, the other bishops knew that the speaker felt he had something worth saying and on many occasions gave him their full attention. The interventions submitted by some American bishops were real contributions of the Council and accomplished more than a little in directing the course of the Council.

This leads us to the central theme of this book: the thinking expressed by members of the American hierarchy at the Second Vatican Council. It was by no means an easy task to gather together this information, for some of it had been already buried in the archives of the Second Vatican Council; some had already been lost, with no copies available; and some had been misplaced or destroyed. Nonetheless, the information gathered together in this volume has been possible only through the courtesy and cooperation of the American bishops.

On July 16, 1965, I wrote every member of the American hierarchy asking for "the texts, either in Latin or English, of any and all the written and oral interventions you made during the Council." In response to that letter I received 84 replies, with many of the bishops enclosing copies of their interventions and an almost equal number declaring that they had nothing to submit for my use in a volume of this nature. Some of their replies are of particular interest.

Archbishop William E. Cousins of Milwaukee wrote: "As a matter of policy, many of us agreed that a particular bishop would speak in the names of many. My opinions, therefore, would have been included in the interventions of someone who spoke in my name and that of other bishops." Bishop John L. Paschang of Grand Island, Nebraska, wrote: "The good Lord knows there have been too many interventions and too many long speeches—men talking ten minutes to suggest the change of a single word. We hope things will move along more rapidly this next session." Auxiliary Bishop Joseph Green of Lansing, Michigan, wrote: "Like so many of the American hierarchy, especially during the second and third sessions, I refrained from making personal interventions and incorporated my ideas and opinions with those of other bishops who spoke in the name of several members of the hierarchy. This was done, as you know, to save time and avoid the monotonous repetition of ideas on the Council floor." The late Bishop Jerome D. Hannan of Scranton, Pennsylvania, wrote: "I believe I deserve the thanks of the Fathers of the Council in having refrained from taxing their ears with any such intervention from me."

Other American bishops replied regretfully that they were unable to attend the Council. Archbishop William O'Brien of Hartford, Connecticut, wrote that he "was forced to return home during the first session for reasons of health and has been forbidden by the doctor to return to Rome for the Council." Many other elderly American bishops replied in a similar vein. The then bishop of San Angelo, Texas, Thomas J. Drury, replied: "At the three sessions of Vatican II, I tried, as a freshly consecrated bishop, to be a good listener." Bishop Daniel J. Feeney of Portland, Maine, wrote: "For your records, I was and shall continue to be a 'silent observer' at the Council."

The replies of Bishop Alexander M. Zaleski of Lansing, Michigan, and Bishop Lambert A. Hoch of Sioux Falls, South Dakota, were typical of many. The former regretted "that I have kept no written record of the observations that I presented during the last three sessions of the Council." The latter wrote: "Unhappily, I haven't kept copies of the written interventions that we have made. I did not feel that they were significantly important, since they often followed the tenor of our ghost writers. However, I had my own observations here and there and was glad to see one of them incorporated in the schema on religious liberty." Bishop Marion F. Forst of Dodge City, Kansas, summarized in his reply the interventions that he submitted on eight schemata "in view of the fact that they also serve only as 'seconds' for the proposals of others."

In response to this letter, the present writer received through the mail over a hundred copies of interventions either delivered orally or submitted in writing by members of the American hierarchy. After the closing of the Council, on January 10, 1966, I again wrote every American bishop and major religious superior who was present at the Council. Again I requested "interventions that you have not sent me previously or any interventions you submitted during the fourth session." In reply I received 76 letters, many of them containing interventions either delivered orally or submitted in writing. Again, the responses were similar to those I had received the preceeding year.

Auxiliary Bishop Eldon B. Schuster of Great Falls, Montana, wrote: "I submitted one written intervention stressing the urgency of a declaration on religious liberty. I regret I have not a copy of the text at hand." Many bishops replied in words similar to those penned by Bishop Ignatius J. Strecker of Springfield-Cape Girardeau, Missouri, who wrote: "I regret even now that I cannot assist you by making available to you any interventions made by me for the very simple reason that I have not kept a copy of any of the interventions which I made. All I can now say is—I'm very sorry."

Archbishop John P. Cody of Chicago wrote: "I wish to advise that I made only one intervention 'in aula,' but I did make several others, and perhaps more effectively, 'extra aulam.'" Auxiliary Bishop Cletus F. O'Donnell of Chicago wrote: "I made no oral interventions, but submitted several in writing. I am sorry to say that I do not have copies of them in my file here at home. I think that they must be in Rome at the Chicago House, for I left many things there. However, my interventions would add nothing to the status of your book. They merely followed the same position as those of Cardinal Meyer on religious liberty, ecumenism and the priesthood. . . ."

Bishop Warren L. Boudreaux wrote: "Actually, I would not have sent in any interventions if the American hierarchy had been as active in the fourth session as it was in the others. . . . In the other sessions, I had endorsed several other interventions, a 'group intervention,' as it was often done in the first sessions, especially in the second and third. But, as you know, the American bishops did not meet much during the fourth session, and this was the only way I could say some things I thought should have been said." A typical response was penned by Bishop Floyd L. Begin of Oakland, California:

There was much more participation than the interventions made orally. All of us, throughout the Council, handed in at various times suggestions and amendments which, for the most part, are reflected in the text of the final documents. I did not keep copies of my written interventions. I have a suspicion that might have been the case with many other bishops. We all learned after the first year's experience that written interventions were just as acceptable to the commissions and just as effective as oral interventions. This truth dissuaded many American bishops from talking on the Council floor.

This work bears out the accuracy of Bishop Begin's observations. As the Church invariably suffers from a lack of a sense of history, so the Americans, as other national participants in the Second Vatican Council, failed to keep detailed accounts of their observations. Nor does this work even so much as mention the innumerable *modi*, or suggestions, signed by many American bishops time after time throughout the period of the Council.

The work carried out within the conciliar commissions was essential to the Council. Several observers have already pointed out the inadequate machinery of the Council which left a relatively few Council Fathers with the major task of drafting the text of conciliar documents. Other observers have noted that the structure of the conciliar organization made it so that the real work of the Council was in the hands of less than five per cent of the participants. The work of the commissions remains largely a part of conciliar secrecy locked behind the doors of the Vatican archives. When the files are opened, the work of Americans on these commissions will be recorded more adequately and fully.

The writer did, however, send a questionnaire to all 26 American members of the commissions. The responses to that questionnaire have been incorporated into the text of this work. For the record it should be stated that 43 Americans served as members and consultants to the preparatory commissions, among whom were two American prelates who were claimed by death before the opening of the Council. These were Aloysius Cardinal Muench, former bishop of Fargo, North Dakota, and Archbishop William O. Brady of St. Paul, Minnesota.

Following the election of members to the conciliar commissions, during both the first and second sessions there were 26 members of the American hierarchy either elected by their colleagues or appointed by the Holy Father. This number exceeded the number of representatives on conciliar commissions from all other countries except Italy and France. The Church in the United States was also represented in the persons of the three score and more consultants, or *periti*, who were appointed either before or in the early stages of the Council.

In the first session alone there were 19 American Protestant observer-delegates and guests of the Secretariat for the Promotion of Christian Unity out of a total of 52 representatives. In the succeeding sessions the number of American observer-delegates increased, and their influence upon the conciliar proceedings will never be adequately recorded. One of them claims a distinction which only very few Council Fathers or consultants can claim. Dr. Douglas Horton of Randolph, New Hampshire, never missed a single working congregation of the Council. The American laity were also represented in the persons of Martin H. Work, James Norris and Mrs. Catherine McCarthy, as were the American sisterhoods by Sister M. Luke, president of the Conference of the Major Superiors of Women.

Three American prelates served on the Presidency of the Council. They were Francis Cardinal Spellman, Albert Cardinal Meyer, and Lawrence Cardinal Shehan who succeeded the Archbishop of Chicago in the last session. Cardinal Spellman was recognized early in the Council as the titular leader of the American hierarchy. He spoke on the floor of the Council more frequently than any other American, and his 131 oral and written interventions on every conciliar schemata were considered in more than one commission.

Cardinal Meyer emerged during the time of the Council as "the reluctant leader" of the American hierarchy. More and more, as the Council proceeded, his colleagues turned to him for leadership and recognized in him the splendid qualities that he had brought to the Archdiocese of Chicago as well as to the Church throughout the United States. His untimely death was a great loss both to the Church in our country as well as to American leadership for the remainder of the Council.

Cardinal Meyer's oral interventions are indications of his leadership and, at the same time, assure him a respected place in the history of the Second Vatican Council. This observation is made neither because he spoke the most frequently (Ernesto Cardinal Ruffini lays claim to that distinction) nor most eloquently (in my opinion, Josef Cardinal Frings merits that honor). Cardinal Meyer, however, deserves a niche of honor because repeatedly and consistently he voiced the most representative and theologically progressive thoughts evident in the Second Vatican Council. Another writer, on another occasion, must examine how effective his interventions were in the ultimate formulation of the conciliar constitutions, decrees or declarations. That remains outside the scope of this work.

It was, nonetheless, quite generally recognized that Cardinal Meyer was a voice to be heeded. On more than one occasion members of other hierarchies approached him after his intervention to ask for copies of his address. In one commission meeting an American consultant overheard a group of French bishops remark, as they were discussing a crucial issue: "We had better consult Meyer on this. His judgment would be most valuable." It is a known fact among those closely associated with the Council that both Cardinal Suenens and Cardinal Alfrink diligently made efforts to cultivate the friendship and the subtle influence of Cardinal Meyer among the Americans.

Cardinal Ottaviani, too, was a friend of the Chicago cardinal, even though he referred to the latter as *uomo freddo* (a cold man). Cardinal Meyer's actions, however, in no way deserved the epithet. During the first session the Cardinal-Secretary of the Holy Office was quite anxious to have Cardinal Meyer speak. It must be remembered that Cardinal Meyer had great respect for Ottaviani. One night they were both dinner guests in the apartments of Cardinal Cicognani. At the end of the dinner, Meyer drew Cardinal Ottaviani aside and said, "Your Eminence, I have decided to speak in the Council and have handed in my name." He referred to his intervention of November 19, 1962 on the sources of revelation.

"That is fine," said Cardinal Ottaviani, "I am glad to hear it."

"But, Your Eminence," replied Cardinal Meyer, "I do not think you will like what I am going to say concerning divine revelation. In conscience I cannot accept the position of the schema as it is."

The reply came fast. "That is all right with me, Your Eminence. Just as long as you speak."

Cardinal Meyer, in his usual charity, went on: "But I want you to realize, Your Eminence, that nothing I shall say tomorrow should ever be interpreted by you as indicating any reflection on you, either personally or on your dignity as a cardinal."

On the occasion when Cardinal Meyer related this incident, he went on to quote this passage from the prayer to the Holy Spirit recited at the opening of every working congregation at the Council: "Let us not disturb order, You who love absolute justice. Let not our ignorance betray us into evil, nor let favoritism influence us, nor respect for high office or persons corrupt us." This opening Council prayer, incidentally, had a deep effect on him. He referred to it frequently. In a way, he felt it was almost a divine seal of approval on his actions. It did not really matter much to him who liked or disliked what he would say. Once he was convinced, under the assurance of the Spirit as he saw it, he was absolutely fearless.

The Cardinal's interventions were, in the final analysis, respectfully received because they were from the very depths of his own soul. He strove mightily to give honest expression to his deepest convictions. He worked diligently over each intervention. His work made him seek out the best minds he could assemble in drafting his interventions. Those who worked with him estimate that he spent at least five intense hours in the actual drafting of each intervention. This in no way takes into consideration the many hours of remote preparation and thought he gave to each subject between and during the session of the Council. In his presentations, Cardinal Meyer was always concerned with the positive approach. In this sense he followed Pope John's admonition to the letter. He was not concerned with condemnations. He wanted the Church to speak to the modern world in a language modern man would understand.

Archbishop John J. Krol of Philadelphia was, perhaps, the most effective as well as the busiest American at the Council. He served as a member of the preparatory commission on bishops and the government of dioceses and, at the very beginning of the first session, was appointed the English-speaking under-secretary of the Council and a member of the central coordinating commission. His work entailed incalculable hours both at home and in Rome and, between 1961 and the close of the Council, necessitated a dozen journeys to Rome. His specific duty as the under-secretary of the Council was to keep a record of all the voting and to coordinate the announcements of the votes, the distribution, collection and tabulation of the ballots.

In the absence of Archbishop Pericle Felici for two days during the fourth session, Archbishop Krol acted as substitute for the General Secretary. "Archbishop Felici," wrote the Archbishop of Philadelphia, "had the most difficult, delicate and demanding assignment in the Council. I can speak of his work and his many responsibilities only in superlatives." As a member of the central coordinating commission, Archbishop Krol shared the responsibility of coordinating the work of all the conciliar commissions, keeping the progress of the Council on a projected time schedule and reducing to a minimum the objections of those who favored or opposed the passage of decrees.

In a significant intervention written on July 5, 1963, Archbishop Krol suggested various means that could be adopted in order to increase the efficiency of the conciliar program. He was of the opinion that the right to speak in the Council should be emphasized rather as a right of presenting one's ideas in writing. He wrote: "The right of speaking in general congregation is an individual right and, as such, it should not impede the right of the community." He also suggested that a definite time limit be announced so that the Council Fathers would submit their interventions early enough for the commissions to examine them, and that the commissions, in turn, submit the emended text to the office of the General Secretary to present to the assembly.

He further suggested "that the commissions be given the same authority which they enjoyed during the First Vatican Council, namely, the authority to accept or reject changes of lesser consequence and of presenting only those of greater importance to a vote of the Fathers." Many subjects, Archbishop Krol felt, could be much better treated by the commission for the revision of the Code of Canon Law than on the floor of the Council. In order to avoid annoyances, he suggested "that an automatic warning be given each speaker two minutes before the end of his assigned time." Finally, he felt that some of the voting "with reservations" could be eliminated in order to save time, and he suggested the inauguration of some kind of open meeting for the conciliar commissions. "In this way," he concluded, "the Council Fathers would have the opportunity to present arguments directly to the members of a commission rather than directly to the general assembly."

Another unique American contribution was the American Bishops' Press Panel, established midway in the first session as a response to complaints from American newsmen. It proved to be one of the most successful press operations of the Council, with its sometimes hearty and sometimes tense exchanges between the panel of experts and the members of the working press. The fellowship experienced at these almost daily afternoon sessions was one thoroughly appreciated by the American bishops (some of whom were frequent visitors), the observer-delegates, the clerical experts and the members of the working press.

The American priests who were appointed consultants performed notable service to the Council Fathers. They were not employed to the extent other national hierarchies employed their consultants, and this remains a question for future speculations: if the American hierarchy had made better use of their services, would its participation in the Council been markedly different? Nonetheless, it is already known that many of the American consultants did, in fact, assist in the drafting of several interventions submitted by American Council Fathers. Nor can it be denied that the American consultants performed a service by keeping the American public informed about the issues, developments and meaning of the Second Vatican Council.

Throughout the four sessions of the Council there were 4,229 written and 2,205 spoken interventions delivered by the Council Fathers. Of this number there were 118 spoken interventions delivered by American bishops. The Americans constituted approximately ten per cent of the total number of Council Fathers. The interventions submitted by Americans in this work represent approximately five per cent of the total number of all interventions. However the reader must bear in mind that not all the American interventions are contained in this work, but only those that were given to this writer for publication. More than a few American bishops no longer had copies of their interventions.

Again, the writer must stress that this work is in the nature of a preliminary report. He can hardly be expected to pass judgment on various issues and statements, both because almost all the participants are still numbered among the living and because all the facts cannot possibly be known at this time.

For the sake of the record we should mention several other items concerning the interventions that are contained in this work. First of all, in response to my letters to the American bishops, I received the texts of 341 interventions which they either delivered orally or submitted in writing. Cardinal Spellman proved that he was the *de facto* spokesman for the Church in the United States by the fact that, of this number, 131 interventions were submitted by him. On many occasions the Archbishop of New York submitted the identical or similar intervention to one, two or three different conciliar commissions. In so doing, Cardinal Spellman recognized the nature of the conciliar process and thus assured himself that his opinions would receive a broader hearing.

It is impossible at this time to record the number of interventions submitted by other American bishops. We do know that Cardinal Ritter delivered 16 interventions and Cardinal Meyer delivered 15, but these are only their oral interventions. What they submitted in writing must be left to the analysis of a future historian. We know also that Cardinal McIntyre spoke six times, Cardinal Shehan seven times and Cardinal Cushing three times on the floor of the Council. All told, we know as a result of this study that 56 American bishops submitted their observations orally or in writing on the various subjects discussed during the Second Vatican Council. Breaking down the number of interventions of American bishops (and the one religious superior, the Very Reverend Joseph Buckley, S.M.) according to the number of interventions on each of the Council's sixteen documents (and bearing in mind that this is merely an interim report), we are able to present the following table:

DOCUMENT	INTERVENTIONS		
	Oral	*Written*	*Cardinal Spellman*
The Church	18	20	15
Revelation	8	8	4
Liturgy	18	13	11
Modern World	14	34	13
Communications	1	6	7
Ecumenism	8	13	6
Eastern Churches	2	8	7
Bishops	11	21	20
Seminaries	1	10	6
Religious	2	6	5
Laity	2	11	6
Priesthood	6	12	6
Missions	1	16	9
Education	4	10	7
Non-Christians	5	5	2
Freedom	14	26	6
Marriage	3	4	1
Total	118	223	131

This work does not even propose to include all of the interventions of the American bishops that the author has received. It contains only the complete text of the interventions of American bishops who spoke on the floor of the Council. The written interventions are quoted and summarized in the historical introductions that treat each of the conciliar documents. It is this writer's intention to publish, in another volume at a later date, the complete text of the written interventions.

The historical introductions are the work of the writer and he, perhaps more than most others, realize that they await the correction of future historians who have readier access to the complete archives of the Council. He does, however, hope that this work will enable a future historian to find his work that much easier because this author labored under the disadvantages of being a reporter of events that deserve to be the subject of a more careful scrutiny by subsequent scholars.

Apart from the contribution that the American bishops made to the Council (which must be determined tentatively by the reader), there remains the related subject of how much the Council contributed to the American bishops. This subject falls outside the limits that were established for this work. Nonetheless, it remains a subject that another writer might pursue with great profit, for even the most casual observer must remark upon the change that has taken place in the Church in the United States during and after the time of the Council. While most observers would be reluctant to attribute this wholesome change to the influence of the bishops, a keen historian would readily admit the sometimes dominant, sometimes permissive and sometimes reluctant, but always necessary, role played by the American bishops in the transportation of *aggiornamento* to American shores.

This important fact remains. Although the structures of the past which produced a certain degree of confidence are changing, the promises offered by the advocates of change are still in a formulative stage, and this can only offer a certain degree of hope. Many American bishops have manifested a sufficient degree of Christian hope by more clearly understanding the nature of the pilgrim, servant Church as enunciated by the Council. This realization would prompt more than a few—in fact, in the writer's judgment, the majority—of the American bishops to subscribe to the observation made by a prominent theologian: "The present crisis of authority which is so dangerous to the Church, will be overcome only when these two principles—of dialogue and authority—are stressed simultaneously. Dialogue will be the context in which authority is exercised and obedience is bestowed."

I should be not only remiss, but also ungrateful if I did not publicly acknowledge my appreciation to those who have assisted me in the preparation of this work. First of all, I am grateful to my Ordinary, the Most Reverend Peter W. Bartholome, D.D., Bishop of St. Cloud, who not only afforded me the opportunity to attend the Second Vatican Council, but also encouraged and supported me in the preparation of this book. I acknowledge my appreciation to the members of the American hierarchy who graciously and generously cooperated in allowing me to make use of their written and oral interventions as well as to those who answered questionnaires (a tedious, thankless task!) and offered suggestions. I am grateful, too, to the American priests and laymen who gave of their time and talents to contribute commentaries to this work; to Mr. Michael Dick of the North American College who assisted me in translating many of the American bishops' interventions; to Miss Mira Luy who typed the manuscript and Mr. Gerald Renner, associate director of the United States Catholic Conference Bureau of Information. Finally, I acknowledge my gratitude to the Most Reverend James P. Shannon, Auxiliary Bishop of St. Paul and my priestly friends and associates of the United States Catholic Conference who offered innumerable and valuable suggestions. What merit this work will have in many ways is a result of their assistance and advice; its shortcomings must be attributed to this writer's limitations.

Vincent A. Yzermans

Feast of the Ascension
May 4, 1967

I/DOGMATIC CONSTITUTION ON THE CHURCH

Dogmatic Constitution on the Church

✠ HISTORICAL INTRODUCTION

When the Fathers of the Second Vatican Council returned to the second session, they were greeted by a new supreme pontiff. Pope Paul VI, in his opening address, September 29, 1963, let his brother bishops know that his desires were those of his beloved predecessor. He then set the stage for the work of this session when he said:

> The time has now come, we believe, when the truth regarding the Church of Christ should be examined, coordinated and expressed. The expression should not, perhaps, take the form of a solemn dogmatic definition, but of declarations making known by means of the Church's magisterium, in a more explicit and authoritative form, what the Church considers herself to be. This self-awareness of the Church is clarified by faithful adherence to the words and thought of Christ, by respectful attention to the teaching of ecclesiastical tradition and by docility to the interior illumination of the Holy Spirit, who seems to be requiring of the Church today that she should do all she can to make known what she really is.

The document on the Church was to be, in the words of Albert Cardinal Meyer, "the most important contribution of the Second Vatican Council." The 16,200 words of the Dogmatic Constitution on the Church are already recognized by all as the most impressive work of the Council. It is central to other acts of the Council, and apart from it many other conciliar documents would be incomplete. The Dogmatic Constitution *Lumen Gentium* looks to the future, and Christians in the years ahead will hopefully experience its theological wealth even more than those of the present day. The Church of the future should be shaped to a major degree by the teaching of this keystone document.

The Constitution on the Church began its long and sometimes perilous journey on July 2, 1960 when the Central Preparatory Commission issued a list of subjects to be prepared by the Theological Commission. In that instruction the Central Preparatory Commission noted: "The Constitution on the Catholic Church, which was prepared by the First Vatican Council, should be completed and perfected, especially concerning a) the Mystical Body of Christ,

b) the episcopacy and c) the laity." The Central Preparatory Commission's directive echoed the wishes expressed by the bishops who submitted their ideas on what should be discussed at the Council. The bishops' suggestions concerning the Church were summarized in 367 brief propositions which filled 65 large printed pages and were categorized under 42 general sections.

Two subjects which were especially stressed in this collection of propositions were, first, a better presentation of the sacramentality of the episcopacy and its collegial nature and, secondly, a proper presentation of the Church's teachings concerning the Blessed Virgin Mary.

Two years later the preparatory Theological Commission had completed its work on the schema. At this time it consisted of eleven chapters, the last being a discussion of ecumenism. This chapter, however, was later separated from the schema and committed to the Secretariat for the Promotion of Christian Unity. The ten chapters of the schema were examined by the Central Preparatory Commission during its final two meetings, on May 8 and 9 and again on June 19, 1962. The eleven chapters were:

1) The Nature of the Church Militant
2) The Members of the Church Militant and its Necessity for Salvation
3) The Episcopacy and the Plentitude of the Sacrament of Orders and the Priesthood
4) Residential Bishops
5) The States for Acquiring Evangelical Perfection
6) The Laity
7) The Magisterium of the Church
8) Authority and Obedience in the Church
9) The Relations between Church and State, and Religious Tolerance
10) The Need to Announce the Gospel to All Peoples and Nations
11) Ecumenism

The preparatory Theological Commission prepared also a schema on the Blessed Virgin Mary, the Mother of God and Mother of Men, which consisted of seven pages of text and 31 pages of notes. This was also examined by the Central Preparatory Commission during its last meeting in June, 1962.

Cardinal Spellman, as a member of the Central Preparatory Commission, submitted his observations on the ten chapters of this original schema. He said, first of all, that the schema was "of the utmost importance" so that both clergy and laity would come to understand the Church better and "in such a way love and devotion to the Church [would] increase for all from day to day." He then suggested:

Perhaps the Holy Council has a fitting and convenient opportunity to explain certain questions more clearly, namely: that our union with Christ is not merely ideal, which has been established only by a mental consideration, but truly it is objectively real through relations or real bonds which are independent from a consideration of the mind. This union is a truly moral one with the moral relationships to Christ of fidelity, gratitude and imitation. It is also moral insofar as it is not completed by relations of this type. However, these moral relationships also presuppose a union between Christ and us which is in some sense physical, with a basis in physical realities. Such a physical union is in no way of the natural order, but rather it belongs to the order of the mystical and supernatural.

The Archbishop of New York welcomed what the schema stated concerning the episcopacy and priesthood, "especially since quite recently there has been too much confusion spread around on these questions both among the clergy and the people." He felt, too, that what was stated concerning the dignity and primacy of bishops, their relation to the universal Church and conference of bishops was "extremely beautiful." He approved also the schema's statements on the universal priesthood, the rights and duties of the laity and the importance and position of the states of perfection in the Church. The schema's remarks concerning the magisterium of the Church were well stated and also most beneficial for the Church since "even many modern Catholics quite easily fall into great difficulties and false opinions." He thought the eighth chapter, on authority and obedience in the Church, was "completely acceptable." He then made this observation:

> Since, with modern men, there is no lack of those who hold that Christian obedience is incompatible with the dignity of man and the rights of the free person, the statements on the origin and nature of authority in the Church and of the relation between those placed in authority and those placed under it are of great help. It is of great value that those in authority in the Church, put in office for the good of the community and of souls, should know that they ought to clothe themselves in the image of the Good Pastor, and they should be mindful that there is no regard for persons with the Lord in Heaven. It will also be valuable since healthy public opinion can promote the good of the Church. This opinion not only should be tolerated, but it must be valued by pastors of the Church in the exercise of their rule.

The Cardinal did not completely agree with the ninth chapter on the relations between Church and State, for, as he wrote, "Although, perhaps, principles as principles cannot be controverted, nevertheless, at times a doubt arises as to the application of the principles to present historical circumstances." His chief reservation concerning this chapter was stated in these words:

> Certain statements of the theological commission on the religious duties of the civil power and on the moderation by the civil power of the public displays of different religions little agree with the statements of the Secretariat for Promoting Christian Unity in the schema on the Constitution on

Religious Liberty. The principles of this secretariat are better suited for today's pastoral goal and for true ecumenism.

He then accepted the tenth chapter because "everything is proposed in a kind of pastoral style, nor does the dogmatic text appear too juridical."

With the formal inauguration of the Council, the preparatory commissions gave way to the conciliar commissions. Alfredo Cardinal Ottaviani remained the president of the Doctrinal Commission on Faith and Practices, generally referred to as the Theological Commission. Three American prelates were elected to serve as members of this Commission by their colleagues. They were Archbishop John Dearden of Detroit, Bishop John Wright of Pittsburgh and Auxiliary Bishop James Griffiths of New York. Unfortunately, death claimed Bishop Griffiths before the beginning of the second session.

The tireless work of the members of the Theological Commission can never be adequately recorded. Archbishop Dearden made at least ten trips to Rome to take part in at least two hundred meetings of the Commission. The meetings he attended averaged at least three hours, and thus at least six hundred hours were spent in this work, not to mention the countless hours of study and consultation that the Commission work also demanded. Bishop John Wright made 32 trips to Rome and took part in about 160 plenary and 80 subcommission meetings. Archbishop Dearden was assigned the chairmanship of the subcommission that was charged with the schema's second chapter dealing with the people of God, and Bishop Wright was chairman of the schema's fourth chapter concerning the laity.

Commenting on the work of the Commission, Bishop Wright said, "In the Theological Commission the issue was repeatedly joined between the 'open' approach to Council issues and a more 'closed' approach. The most 'crucial' work of the Commission was the winnowing of the wheat from the chaff in both approaches." Archbishop Dearden said that he felt "the great preoccupation of the Commission was to try to reflect the mind of the Fathers of the Council in redrafting documents of particular sensitivity. At times it called for painstaking, precise and measured effort. The redrafting," he continued, "in a form that differed so markedly from the original and finally reflected the spirit of the Council was a major task."

When asked what they thought to be the most satisfying work of the Commission, Archbishop Dearden said, first, that even though the work "demanded long, arduous, painstaking effort, it was amply compensated for by the final results." Bishop Wright said that his most satisfying experience on the Commission was "the opportunity to share the thinking of men from other 'worlds' within the modern Church, from France and Belgium and especially from the Iron Curtain countries." He added, "In terms of schema 13, the opportunity to discover Africa."

Bishop Wright said that he felt the great leaders of the Theological Commission were Archbishop Gabriel Garrone of Toulouse, France; Bishop André

Charue of Namur, Belgium; Archbishop Pietro Parente of the Roman Curia; Bishop Mark McGrath of Santiago, Panama; Bishop Joseph Schröffer of Eichstatt, Germany; Archbishop Franjo Šeper of Zagreb, Yugoslavia; and Abbot Christopher Butler, O.S.B., of Downside Abbey, England. Among the experts who worked with the members of the Commission he singled out Monsignor Gerard Philips of the University of Louvain and Canon Charles Moehler, the Reverend Henri de Lubac, S.J., the Reverend Jean Daniélou, S.J., and the Reverend Karl Rahner, S.J.

When asked what he felt might be the most lasting fruits of the Commission's work, Archbishop Dearden replied:

> The direction of the renewal that is taking place in the Church has been set by the conciliar documents that were worked on by our commission. While other documents reached certain more specific areas of concern, in many instances they drew upon one or several of the documents for which we were responsible. In a more removed sense, we like to feel that the insights that are given in the Constitution on the Church do throw their light on so many of the good things that are taking place in the Church today.

Answering the same question, Bishop Wright declared:

> I am convinced that the Church is faced, as is the world, with the long "winter" that must follow the rise of atheistic humanism and "technologism." It is a chapter of history foretold by prophetic spirits: Newman, Soloviev, among many. During that "winter" the seed-ideas sifted chiefly in our Commission will "incubate" under the soil against the inevitable "second spring." The "seed-ideas" of the chapter on collegiality, the chapter on the laity and the chapter on the Blessed Virgin in the Constitution on the Church as well as the "seed-ideas" of the sections on the person, Christian anthropology, dialogue with atheism, marriage and peace and war in the Constitution on the Church in the Modern World will be vitally important in regard to the confrontation with atheistic humanism or "scientism."

The schema on the Church was distributed to the Council Fathers during the closing days of November, 1962. During the thirty-first general congregation, on December 1, Cardinal Ottaviani introduced the schema on the floor of the Council. It was discussed by 78 Fathers throughout six congregations, almost all of whom expressed displeasure with the text. Forty-four other Fathers, unable to voice their observations because time had run out, submitted the texts of their speeches to the Theological Commission. The Fathers criticized this text because it was too dry, too juridical, too scholastic and lacking in ecumenical approach.

Shortly after the first session, the Central Coordinating Commission charged the Theological Commission to prepare a new schema on the Church and, specifically, to include the following points: 1) the connection between Vatican Council I and Vatican Council II concerning the doctrine of papal primacy; 2) an explanation of the meaning and extent of episcopal collegiality; 3) a fuller treatment of the nature of the episcopacy; 4) a more detailed statement on the relationship between the episcopacy and the presbyterate; 5) a stronger affirmation of the role of the laity in the Church.

The Theological Commission followed these guidelines as well as the observations that the Council Fathers made during the first session. By the end of March the first part of its work was completed, and the schema was sent to the Central Coordinating Commission for approval. The first part of the schema, approved by Pope John on April 22 and transmitted to the Council Fathers through the office of the papal Secretary of State, consisted of a brief introduction and two chapters. The first chapter discussed the mystery of the Church; the second chapter examined the hierarchical constitution of the Church and, specifically, the episcopacy.

The second half of the schema waited for approval until after the coronation of Pope Paul. On July 19, Pope Paul approved the final two chapters of the schema, one dealing with the people of God and especially the laity, the other dealing with the vocation to holiness in the Church. Before discussion could begin during the second session, however, the Central Coordinating Commission accepted Cardinal Suenens' suggestion that greater stress should be placed upon the notion of the Church as the People of God. Thus, even before debate began in the Council hall, the Fathers were presented a booklet of corrections on the printed text which were made in accord with subsequent suggestions from the Council Fathers. This booklet stated also the new arrangement of the schema's chapters. Its five chapters were:

1) The Mystery of the Church
2) The People of God in General
3) The Hierarchical Constitution of the Church
4) The Laity in Particular
5) The Vocation to Sanctity in the Church

The revised schema was the first item on the agenda of the second session. It was again introduced by Cardinal Ottaviani, followed by Michael Cardinal Browne, during the thirty-seventh congregation. Throughout the next month, until October 31, and throughout 23 congregations, 323 Council Fathers made their views known on the floor of the Council. The debates were at times lively, but, for the most part, were repetitious and monotonous. The issues at all times, however, were vital, and their significance escaped only a very few. The central issue, of course, was collegiality. Other issues, such as the concept of the pilgrim Church, the Church of the poor, the Roman curia, the restoration of a permanent diaconate and the relation of the Blessed Virgin Mary to the Church, although of lesser importance, were nonetheless essential to the drafting of an adequate constitution on the Church. For this entire month the Roman air was charged with as much excitement as expectancy. October 29, the day of the fifty-seventh congregation, would mark the turning of the tide.

Throughout the debates of this month, those who represented a conservative position on these and related issues were given more than enough time to present their point of view. If one would attempt to measure the thinking of Church leaders from the opinions of the minority voiced during this period on the floor of the Council, he would have a most distorted view of the Church's thinking. The majority, who shared a progressive position in varying degrees, bided its time. It did not voice its sentiments, precisely because it was sure of its ground. On the other hand, the minority was most vociferous in enunciating its position, possibly because it subconsciously realized it was trying to save a sinking ship.

In seeking the self-awareness of the Church, the Council Fathers returned to Sacred Scripture. They were determined to make the document on the Church reflect the words which Pope Paul had spoken in his opening address of the session:

> There can be no doubt whatever on the Church's desire and need and duty to give a more thorough definition of herself. We are all familiar with the magnificent images by which Holy Scripture describes the nature of the Church: the building raised up by Christ, the house of God, the temple and tabernacle of God, His people, His flock, His vine, His field, His city, the pillar of Truth and, finally, the Bride of Christ, His Mystical Body.

The majority view supported Pope Paul, and this biblical orientation found its way into the first and second chapters of the final constitution.

Collegiality was a more difficult concept. The obstructionists had made this the main thrust of their attack. On October 16 the Secretary General, Archbishop Felici, announced that the Fathers would be asked to vote on four propositions in order to enable the Theological Commission to ascertain the mind of the Fathers on certain key ideas expressed in chapter two of the schema. Thirteen days passed before the Council Fathers received a copy of these propositions—which were now five, instead of the previously announced four. The five propositions and the result of the voting on each of them were published by the Council press office in its bulletin dated October 30. It read as follows:

> 1) Is it agreeable to the Fathers that the schema be so drawn up as to state that episcopal consecration constitutes the peak of the Sacrament of Orders?—Votes cast, 2,157; favorable, 2,123; negative, 34.
>
> 2) Is it agreeable to the Fathers that the schema be so drawn up as to state that every bishop legitimately consecrated in communion with other bishops and the Roman Pontiff, as their Head and principle of unity, is a

member of the episcopal body?—Votes cast, 2,154; favorable, 2,049; negative, 104; null, 1.

3) Is it agreeable to the Fathers that the schema be so drawn up as to state that, in its task of evangelizing, sanctifying and feeding, the body or college of bishops succeeds the college of the apostles, and that, in union with its Head, the Roman Pontiff, and never without this Head (whose primatial rights over all pastors and faithful remain intact) this body enjoys full and supreme power over the universal Church?—Votes cast, 2,148; favorable, 1,808; negative, 336.

4 Is it agreeable to the Fathers that the schema be so drawn up as to state that the aforesaid power belongs to the episcopal college, united with its Head, by divine right?—Votes cast, 2,138; favorable, 1,717; negative, 408; null, 13.

5) Is it agreeable to the Fathers that the schema be so drawn up as to consider the opportuneness of restoring the diaconate as a distinct and permanent rank of the sacred ministry, according to the needs of the Church in different localities?—Votes cast, 2,120; favorable, 1,588; negative, 525; null, 7.

October 29 presented a high-water mark for yet another reason. On that date the Council Fathers voted also to make the schema on the Blessed Virgin Mary a special chapter in the schema on the Church. On October 24, two of the Council Fathers presented their views on whether there should be a special schema concerning the Blessed Virgin Mary or whether it should become a part of the schema on the Church. Rufino Cardinal Santos, Archbishop of Manila, Philippines, argued that Mary's special dignity demanded a special recognition.

The dignity of the Mother of God and her role in the divine economy of salvation deserve to be given special treatment, and not to be simply inserted into an already long schema on the Church, or put into a brief appendix, as if it were something of only secondary importance. Nor should it be forgotten that cutting down this schema on the Blessed Virgin Mary, which was already announced and after approval by the coordinating commission, would cause wonderment and might be interpreted as a lessening of the honor due to the Blessed Virgin, and would also call attention to controversies existing among Catholics which seem imprudent.

Franziskus Cardinal König, Archbishop of Vienna, took the opposition stand. He recalled that the majority vote of the Theological Commission on October 9 had already favored including the schema on the Blessed Virgin Mary in the one on the Church. He argued that, since the Church is the central theme of the Council, the doctrine concerning the Blessed Virgin Mary belonged here in order to show the close relationship between Mary and the Church. His argument from pastoral reasons was most cogent.

A pastoral consideration is that this method of treatment would help to instruct the faithful correctly on the mystery of the Incarnation and the part played by the Blessed Virgin therein. Popular devotion needs to be guided and directed lest it neglect essentials and get lost in secondary and accidental things. This is why, not rarely, devotion to the Blessed Virgin is separated from the mystery of Christ and His Church. Thus, our Mariological teaching should not stand out as something separate, but as a teaching united with the Church. The result will be an enrichment of both doctrines.

Following this presentation of both views by Cardinals Santos and König, the Council Fathers were asked to vote on the following propositions: "Is it agreeable to the Fathers that the schema on the Blessed Virgin Mary, Mother of the Church, be so modified as to become chapter six of the schema on the Church?" The response was the closest of any in the Council: 1,074 were in favor of a separate schema; 1,114 preferred to incorporate the schema into the schema on the Church; five cast null votes.

Observers attributed the results of this vote to the presentation which four American scholars had made before the regular weekly meeting of the American hierarchy on October 28. Their presentation succeeded in convincing a good part of the American hierarchy to vote in favor of incorporating the Marian schema into the schema on the Church. If they had not had the opportunity of making this presentation, perhaps the forty-vote difference in the voting would have resulted in favor of a special Marian decree. During that meeting the Reverend Barnabas Ahern, C.P., addressed the bishops on the background of the present schema; the Reverend Eugene Maly on the scriptural basis of the schema; the Reverend Godfrey Diekmann, O.S.B., on its patristic background; and the Reverend Thomas W. Coyle, C.Ss.R., on the treatment of Mary in the theological manuals.

One American bishop called the presentation made by this panel "a masterful job." Another American prelate, commenting on the closeness of this vote, made this observation:

One factor which saved the situation was the fact that a goodly number of Latin American bishops have become frightened by the fact that a great many of their people have little religion left except a distorted form of a cult of the Blessed Mother which in many cases is material, if not formal, idolatry. They want to get the devotion to Our Lady into its proper perspective; hence they supported our point of view. Another factor in the successful vote was the excellent job done by the panel at the meeting of the United States bishops yesterday afternoon. I am convinced that a number of the United States bishops would have voted with the conservatives if they had not had the benefit of the presentation made by this panel on the subject of Mariology. A switch of only twenty votes would have defeated the project. I feel quite sure that at least twenty votes of the United States bishops were switched as a result of that meeting.

One of the strangest stories of the Council was recorded by another American bishop. On the best authority he learned that the Secretary of State himself, Cardinal Cicognani, had approached Cardinal König (after the latter had delivered his speech in favor of incorporating the Marian schema into the schema on the Church) and asked him to support and actively promote a negative vote—this, after Cardinal Ottaviani personally had asked Cardinal König to make an intervention in support of the proposition. Naturally, Cardinal König refused without hesitation, but he did not pass this bit of information around. "If he had," said this American prelate, "there certainly would have been a reaction that would have had many repercussions not only on this vote, but on future developments in the Council." The same bishop expressed surprise that Cardinal Cicognani was a party to this matter, for he had never expected that the Cardinal Secretary of State would be a partner in this type of action.

The reform of the Roman curia was a recurrent theme during these days. No single intervention, perhaps, was as pointed and vehement as the one delivered by titular Archbishop Joachim Ammann of Petnelisso, a retired bishop of Tanganyika. He caught the Council Fathers by surprise on October 15 when he suggested that the entire institution of papal delegates and nuncios should be abolished. The concept of collegiality, he said, calls into question the whole notion of intermediaries between the Holy Father and his brother bishops.

The subject of the restoration of a permanent diaconate was also a thorny one. Opinion was divided and, generally speaking, Fathers from the established Church opposed it as vehemently as Fathers from the "third world" supported it. The vote of October 30, however, revealed the mind of the majority of the Council Fathers, for at that time only 525 of the 2,120 Fathers who voted were opposed to restoring a permanent diaconate, and even a married diaconate, where the hierarchy deemed it necessary. Cardinal Spellman was vehemently opposed to the restoration of the diaconate. At least three of his interventions opposed its restoration. Auxiliary Bishop Fulton J. Sheen of New York, however, was very much in favor of a restored diaconate. In his written intervention on the missionary schema in 1965, Bishop Sheen raised the following question and proposed the following solution:

Why—after so many eloquent speeches in the Council hall by missionary bishops and after the declaration of November 21, 1964, in the Constitution on the Church—why is there no full section dealing with the diaconate in this schema? The vague mention is not enough. Therefore, we propose a new article on the diaconate, which can be inserted either before or after the article on the local clergy.

The second session closed. The Theological Commission went to work collating and considering the amendments and suggestions offered by the Council Fathers both in writing and in public discussion on the floor of the Council. On July 3, 1964, Pope Paul VI approved the revised text that had been previously approved by the Theological Commission and the Central Coordinating Commission. By this time the text of the schema had achieved its final structure. It now consisted of the following chapters:

1) The Mystery of the Church
2) The People of God
3) The Hierarchical Constitution of the Church and Especially the Episcopacy
4) The Laity
5) The Universal Call to Holiness in the Church
6) The Religious
7) The Eschatological Nature of Our Vocation and Our Union with the Heavenly Church
8) The Blessed Virgin Mary, Mother of God, in the Mystery of Christ and the Church.

The third session began immediately with a discussion, lasting throughout three congregations, of the last two chapters of the revised schema on the Church. Fifty Council Fathers expressed their opinions regarding the text on the floor of the Council, and even more than that number submitted their opinions in writing. On September 16 the Council Fathers began voting on the schema, section by section. The voting on each chapter of the schema was as follows:

Chapter	Total	Affirmative	Negative	Reservations	Null
One	2,189	2,114	11	63	1
Two	2,190	1,615	19	553	3
Three 18–23	2,242	1,624	42	572	4
Three 24–29	2,240	1,704	53	481	2
Four	2,236	2,152	8	76	–
Five	2,177	1,856	17	302	2
Six	2,189	1,736	12	438	3
Seven	2,184	1,921	29	233	1
Eight	2,091	1,559	10	521	1

These figures reveal the moral consensus that was achieved by the alchemy of the Council. The Fathers, who may have been divided in their opinions when the discussions on each chapter began, had by now arrived at a moral unanimity. Chapter three, concerning the episcopacy and collegiality, was the most delicate. Thus a series of 27 votes were taken on the contents of this chapter, not only number by number, but, in some cases, sentence by sentence. Nonetheless, each vote revealed the unanimity of opinion that prevailed among the Council Fathers. By the time they came to vote their approval of the final text, on November 19 during the 126th general congregation, that moral unanimity had reached the proportions of a practical consensus. On that day, of the 2,145 Council Fathers who cast their ballots, 2,134 were in favor of the text, and only ten were opposed, with one Father casting an invalid ballot. Two days later, casting their votes during the public session immediately before the promulgation of the Dogmatic Constitution on the Church, only five Fathers voted negatively. A consensus had been achieved.

During the voting on each chapter of the schema, one of the members of the Theological Commission was called upon to present the revised chapter. On September 30, Bishop John Wright, as chairman of the subcommission charged with chapter four on the laity, presented the Commission's report. He first summarized the suggestions offered by the Council Fathers on the previous text. These three principal types of observations, he said, were as follows:

1) Some Fathers regarded the proposed notion of the *laity* or of *laymen* as too negative;

2) Some Fathers felt that our exposition on laymen had been insufficiently or even inexactly related to customary Catholic teaching on the hierarchy and on the constitution of the hierarchy of the Church;

3) Some preferred a more explicit exposition of the concept of that royal priesthood, about which St. Peter spoke, and concerning the part of the laity in the works of Christ and precisely with regard to the consecration of the world.

Bishop Wright's concluding words were these:

We ask for approval or a consensus of the Council Fathers for our chapter, in the hope that these things which we now propose correspond to the mind of the Fathers expressed in the debate. We are so much the more hopeful on this account since the importance of this part of the entire task of the Council can scarcely be exaggerated. Each man speaks either good or bad about the race track or the horse race according to the luck of his own horse. Wherefore, for the greatest part of the members of the Church, namely the Christian laymen, the image of the Second Vatican Council, as it is termed today, depends on the nature of the declaration of the Council on the laity in the Church of Christ.

The bishop's reference to the race track—"Each man speaks either good or bad about the race track or the horse race according to the luck of his own horse"—caused two reactions. Dr. Douglas Horton was amused; another Council Father was bewildered and wrote the Bishop of Pittsburgh to inquire about the nature of clerical interest in horse racing! Dr. Horton wrote in his diary of the third session:

> To justify his own belief that the chapter on which he and his aids had labored so tirelessly was critically important for the Council, he quoted a proverb I had never heard before: "Everyone judges a horse race by the success of his own horse." The lay mind is evidently making itself felt in the Church already.

At the beginning of the second session, the Reverend John Courtney Murray, S.J., penned the following words in *America:*

> One might think it would be highly congenial to American Catholics to look on themselves as the People of God. A fact of our history could be of some importance here. We were largely an immigrant Church. The Catholic faithful flocked to our shores from almost all the nations of the earth. The people were here first, in a fashion, and upon the people the Church has been built in a very real sense.
>
> The American Church has produced some great pastors, but they were great precisely because the people were great in numbers and because their needs were great. Moreover, the American Church has always been noted for the closeness that historically and most blessedly has obtained between pastors and people. It may be that in recent generations the self-awareness expressed in the image of the Church as the People of God has been somewhat dimmed or obscured. It would promise well for the renewal of the Church in our midst—the renewal that is also among the aims of the Council —if this consciousness of being the People of God through Christ and in the Holy Spirit were to be aroused and newly quickened among us—among the faithful, our priests and our bishops.

Father Murray's comments, written at that date, were echoed, as a matter of fact, in the observations that members of the American hierarchy expressed concerning the schema on the Church.

The first American to speak on this schema was Joseph Cardinal Ritter who said, on December 1, 1962, that "there is much missing which must be treated." He said that the concept of the Church as expressed in this first schema was "entirely inadequate and, so to speak, closed." He cited three items which reveal how insufficient was the schema. First, he said, almost nothing is stated about the sanctity of the Church; secondly, it neglects the duty of the entire Church, including the laity, in preserving, guarding and explaining the deposit of faith; thirdly, the section dealing with relations between Church and State enunciates principles which "now are of no value for the whole age, even in particulars." Finally, he stated his own concept of the Church in these words:

> The Church is Christ Himself mystically living and working in all the members, in whom the Holy Spirit—the Spirit of Christ—dwells and operates. Only through such a concept can we understand the Church and her "operation in the measure of each member" by which the Church grows in its structure and in love. In Christ, through Christ and with Christ, the Church teaches, offers worship, sanctifies and is sanctified, and in some way rules and reigns. Every member has a part in activities of this sort and in the life of the Church—each according to his own talents.

During the first session, on December 3, James Cardinal McIntyre expressed what he felt was a lack in the schema concerning those who are not members of the Church.

> There does not seem to be a complete separation among the orders of persons. There is a gap because infants dying without Baptism are not included in these classes of persons. Since these infants are persons, it seems to me both reasonable and useful for the Holy Vatican Council, in this place, to concern itself with the eternal lot of these infants. This is most certainly an involved question, one that has been disputed for a long time among theologians.
>
> Perhaps the question does not pertain directly to this schema; but there is no treatment of this thing in any place of the schemata.

On the same day Cardinal Spellman issued a warning concerning the schema's treatment of the laity. He felt "there is too little insistence on Catholic Action" in the schema because "it is a form of the apostolate of the laity established by the Holy See itself and constantly propounded by it." Then, speaking on the relation that should exist between the hierarchy and laity, he said:

> As much as possible, it should be noted that lay people, although they are endowed with neither sacred power nor authority, are nonetheless expected to cooperate in a fitting way with those who have power and authority in order to fulfill the mission of the Church. It is a mistake to think that they are incorporated in the Church only to work out their own salvation; they should cooperate in the work of the Church in their own way and order. From their very Baptism they share in a certain way a common priesthood and, while through it they are fit to worship in the Church, they are also called to communicate to others the benefits of the Redemption in a way suited to them. They are strengthened through the sacrament of Confirmation in order that they may profess, spread and defend the Catholic faith before the world.

The Very Reverend Joseph Buckley, Superior General of the Marists and a native of St. Paul, Minnesota, directed his remarks on December 6 to the recent crisis in obedience in the Church. "For many Catholics," he said, "the crisis of obedience is not merely to obey or not to obey. For them the crisis of authority is a question of reason and method." He then explained his reason for making this observation:

Liberty, insofar as it is individual choice, chosen among many true goods, is a pure perfection, a perfection pure and simple, as theologians say, which as such can also be attributed to God. It is not without reason that men down the ages have fought and died for liberty, thinking that it was most dear and precious. Obedience is a virtue, truly necessary, but it is not pure perfection. It is a perfection only in creatures. God is free, not obedient. Christ was obedient, but in His human nature. Since obedience is in itself a perfection inferior to liberty, overemphasis of obedience and authority on the limiting of liberty should not be made without proportionate reason. I do not hold that every precept presented to one's subjects is to be bolstered by explanations. I do think, however, that the doctrine of authority and obedience should be presented by beginning with the liberty of the individual and not with the State and Church.

Father Buckley's words struck at the very philosophic foundations of the Council.

This priority of the individual person and the personal conscience seem to offer some keys to a solution of the problems on the relation between Church and State in our modern pluralistic societies. The schema on the Church, which is pastoral and ecumenical, must in its structure insert the notion of the liberty of the individual person.

During the second session, 13 Amercans spoke on the floor of the Council, expressing their opinions concerning the schema on the Church. The first was Bishop Ernest J. Primeau of Manchester, New Hampshire. The moderator, Cardinal Döpfner, introduced him as the Bishop of Manchester, England. Bishop Primeau replied: "First of all, I want to make a brief change in the words of introduction by our eminent moderator. I am the Bishop of Manchester in the United States. The Bishop of Manchester in England is one of our separated brothers and up until now has not had an active part in this Council!"

Bishop Primeau had two observations to make. First, he said, he felt that the schema did not sufficiently distinguish "between participation in or incorporation before God or in His judgment, and the same incorporation or participation before the Church or in her judgment." He stressed the distinction between the Church as a community and the Church as a society. The former includes all members of the Church militant, suffering and triumphant; the latter consists of only those who are striving here on earth to attain heaven. Explaining this last notion more fully, he said:

> In fact, before God, "who searches our hearts," the Church or the Mystical Body is the congregation only of the just, those namely who share in sanctifying grace, and thus does not include those sinners who by their fault do not live in faith or hope or charity. But in the face of the Church or its judgment, "which does not judge hidden matters," the ecclesiastical communion or community simply includes all those on earth who externally profess the true faith, show themselves submissive to legitimate authority and are not excommunicated from the communion of the faithful on account of evident sins or censures.

Secondly, Bishop Primeau asked for a fuller explanation of the relations between the Church and the state, or political society. He pointed out that previously this subject had been discussed in the original chapter nine of the schema, but was not now incorporated into the first chapter. He felt the schema should include "an explanation which considers men not only as individuals, but also as members of civil societies." Thus he concluded: "In the voting, many bishops of the United States definitely want the general principles of this question treated, if not here, then in another schema."

Cardinal Ritter's intervention on the following day, October 3, was critical of the schema as "very deficient, almost silent, about the way in which the Church is a sign and sacrament of unity, about the means of sanctification which the Church has and about the actions the ministry exercises and fulfills as its mission." He then made this appeal:

> Here there should be found especially a theology of the Word of God, living and efficaciously working in the Church of Christ. Word and sacrament, with ruling power, comprise the salvific and sanctifying ministry and activity of the Church.
>
> "To preach" and "to teach"—conceptually these activities are almost synonymous with the Church. Nonetheless, in reality in many areas of the Church they are scarcely exercised and in others only poorly. They receive the esteem and reverence due them in very few places.
>
> The causality of the sacraments has been clearly and perfectly explained in detail in the Council of Trent, while the efficacy of the Word preached in the Church has remained in the shadows. Liturgical reform, the renewal of the Church, the doctrinal and disciplinary *aggiornamento*—all these cannot be conceived of without the restoration of preaching to its pristine dignity.

His concluding words were a summary of some of the best thinking in contemporary theology.

By Word and Work, God reveals and communicates Himself to men. This is the history of human salvation. In Christ, God brought forth for men the ultimate Word and the perfect Work of salvation. Both Word and Work, signs of the divine love lacking nothing, perdure, operate and are manifested in the Church and through the Church which is itself the Sacrament of that same love. The Word and Sacramental Work are essential to the Church; without a clear perception of this Work and this Word an adequate concept of the Church is neither given nor can be given.

On October 4, Bishop Joseph Marling of Jefferson City, Missouri, struck an ecumenical note in his comments on the section concerning "The relations of the Church with non-Catholic Christians." For this section he proposed the following addition to the text:

> With all those who glory in the Christian name, even though they do not profess the whole faith or unity of communion with the Roman Pontiff, the Church, the holy Mother of all, knows itself to be joined with them for many reasons.
>
> For she acknowledges that many outside her communion satisfy the conditions given by Christ, and therefore are worthy of His promise: "If anyone love me . . . and my Father will love him, and we will come to him and make our abode with him" (Jn. 14:23). With those adorned by sanctifying grace, the Church has some union in the Holy Spirit. Holy Mother Church also asserts that our separated brothers are adorned in the face as in the heart with the most glorious name of Christ, because they have put on Christ through Baptism (Gal. 3:28), and are buried with him in death (Rom. 6:4). The Church acknowledges a firmer and stronger bond when, as in the case of the separated Orientals, all the other sacraments are received, especially the Eucharist, the sacrament of unity; the apostolic succession is preserved in a certain way; and devotion to the Virgin Mother of God is fostered.

In the opinion he delivered on the Council floor on the same day, Cardinal Spellman reiterated his opposition to the establishment of the permanent diaconate. He felt the Council should neither "discuss an institution which may perhaps be established in the future with no practical trial" nor "establish and praise in a solemn constitution an institution of this type which can give rise to great inconvenience for the Church." He then cited the following three reasons, among others, why he was opposed to the establishment of the permanent diaconate:

> The permanent or stable diaconate has not thrived through the ages in the Latin Church. If this institution, which once flourished, grew obsolete in the passage of time, then it should not be reestablished before we diligently

seek the reasons why it has become obsolete. Further, we ought to inquire about the difficulties which can arise from this renewal.

Thus, the permanent deacons should conduct themselves as ministers of the Church with the faithful and non-Catholics. To perform this duty, the permanent deacons should be sufficiently prepared. In many areas it is hardly possible to build and maintain seminaries for candidates for the priesthood. How can these other obligations regarding a house of formation for deacons now also be assumed?

Besides, permanent deacons, especially if they are not bound by the sacred laws of celibacy, can cause great astonishment and confusion with Catholics as well as non-Catholics.

Earlier, in March, 1963, Cardinal Spellman had expressed his opposition to the permanent diaconate in a written observation to the central coordinating commission. He reminded his colleagues that this was a schema of "a *dogmatic* constitution" (at a time, as a matter of fact, when the title page referred to the text simply as "A Schema of a Constitution on the Church"), and thus he did not see any reason why an explicit mention about a stable diaconate should be added. He concluded this intervention with the flat statement: "I strenuously and firmly object to any mention in the acts of the Council about reestablishing a permanent or stable diaconate." In another intervention, submitted again to the Central Coordinating Commission, Cardinal Spellman reiterated his opposition to the establishment of a permanent diaconate. In this document he made his own comments on the five proposals that the Council Fathers would be asked to vote upon during the congregation of October 29. In this intervention he repeated what he had stated on the floor of the Council on October 4. He said:

> . . . the proposal should be kept in mind that the renewal of a permanent diaconate for the most part seems to come from those liturgists who would wish to revive the usages of the ancient Church without examining present actually existing circumstances. In this matter it helps to recall the declaration of Pius XII: "Old usage should not be thought wiser and better in itself or for following times or for what pertains to new circumstances just because of the fact that it smacks of antiquity . . . for it is neither wise nor laudable to reduce everything in some way to antiquity" (*Mediator Dei*, AAS XXXIX, vol. XIV, p. 545). These words indeed pertain to the proposed reestablishment of a permanent diaconate.

Archbishop Lawrence Shehan of Baltimore, during his intervention on October 10, expressed his approval about the matter in the second chapter concerning the presbytery. He did propose, however, two changes in the text. He admitted that all Catholics accept the doctrine of papal infallibility, but felt that the statement of the definition in the schema was a source of difficulty, especially to Protestants. This difficulty arose, he said, both because of "the false concepts about the nature and fullness of the infallibility of the Roman Pontiff and about the relationship between the definition and the consensus of the Church." In support of his position, he quoted from the words of Bishop Vincent Gasser, an Austrian prelate who had attended the First Vatican Council and who had said:

> We cannot separate the Pope from the consensus of the Church because this consensus is never able to be made without him. Since we believe the Pope to be infallible through the help of God, we also believe that these definitions are not lacking in the assent of the Church, for it is not possible that the body of the bishops be separated from its head, and because the universal Church cannot be mistaken.

Secondly, Archbishop Shehan disapproved of the sentence stating that "since either the Roman Pontiff or a Council defines an opinion, they offer it according to that Revelation to which all must conform and which was written or handed down through the legal succession of bishops. . . ." The Archbishop of Baltimore stated his reason for the change he advocated (and at the same time recounted a frequently-told Council story) in these words:

> The Fathers of the Council of Trent, as is evident from the actions of that Sacred Synod, after a long and lively discussion, in the decree about the sacred books and tradition, rejected such words as "partly . . . partly," "either . . . or," "one or the other," and accepted the word "and." To avoid a long and fruitless discussion, I propose that we follow the good example of the Fathers of the Council of Trent in using their words regarding the relation between the Sacred Scripture and Tradition.
> All of us have heard about certain Fathers who were coming to the Council in a taxi and, good grief, found themselves far from Rome, on the Via Flaminia hurrying towards the city of Trent. It seems to me, that whenever we talk about the relation between Sacred Scripture and Tradition, we would do well to return to the Council of Trent.
> Therefore, I propose the word "and" in place of the word "or."

Auxiliary Bishop Philip Hannan spoke on October 17 concerning the relation between Church and State, thus being the first American prelate on the floor of St. Peter's to direct the Council's attention specifically to this problem. He felt that the Council's task was "to give an exposition of the principles which can be applied to those conditions which, because of the very nature of civil society, are found today in so many nations." He went on to say that, in any discussion of the relation between Church and State, both the nature of the State as it exists today and the nature of the role of the citizenry must be considered. Concerning the nature of the State he said:

The State considers itself neither to be a guardian of morals nor obliged to profess a religion. Indeed, because of the multitude of religions which are professed, or pluralism, very often the State feels that it cannot be the guardian of morals, in the traditional sense. In fact, it would be very dangerous for the Church today to depend upon a particular State as the guardian of morals. Furthermore, heads of modern States do not have as much power as did the kings in the past.

Historical reasons, he continued, have helped to make citizens consider that they are themselves the source of power. Thus they elect their rulers, choose their type of government and establish laws that direct their lives. Citizens also prefer the Church to be completely separated from the State. Bishop Hannan then cited four reasons to show the benefits the Church enjoys when it is entirely independent of the State. He said:

a) The Holy See has full liberty to create dioceses solely according to the spiritual needs of the faithful, without seeking the permission of the State.

b) The Supreme Pontiff can name bishops without consulting the State in any way.

c) Bishops can explain the laws of Christ and deal with social justice without any fear of the State.

d) The laity, knowing that the temporal good of the Church has been laid upon their shoulders, have a great and actual part in its life. They frequently take part in Mass and the reception of sacraments, and liberally provide money. This most faithful devotion not only leads many young people, boys and girls, to a religious vocation, but also persuades the faithful to provide money so liberally that many charitable institutions of all kinds, as well as school systems, may be erected. In these schools, from elementary through the university, religious instruction is given not only at certain hours, but the spirit of religion is always and everywhere felt by the students who study in these schools, under the guidance of religious. This most profound devotion of Catholics, aided by the grace of God, brings about a great number of conversions.

Bishop John Wright of Pittsburgh, the chairman of the subcommission charged with drafting the chapter on the laity, spoke on October 17 concerning the chapter then under discussion. His remarks were summarized by the Vatican Council news bulletin for that day as follows:

We cannot emphasize too much the historical and theological import of this chapter on the laity. After the discussion has ended and all necessary amendments have been introduced into the text, it is to be hoped that the schema will retain the basic principles set forth here and also the very words of the text, unless even stronger words to express these same truths can be found.

The schema expresses positively the mind and the will of Christ on the laity. It will thus lay a solid foundation for authentic Catholic Action and will dissipate the prevailing erroneous impression that the Church is exclusively "clerical." This will be taken care of by formulating a genuinely adequate definition of the laity.

The Bishop's personal views on the role of the laity were expounded in an article he penned for his diocesan newspaper, the *Pittsburgh Catholic*. Writing in its October 24, 1963 issue, Bishop Wright made these observations:

One of the corniest jokes in the modern Church is the story (usually attributed, appropriately enough, to Cardinal Gasquet) of a nineteenth-century cleric who was asked the position of the layman in the Church. The cleric—good straight man—replied that the layman had two positions: he kneels before the altar and he sits beneath the pulpit.

A developed version of the witticism adds that the layman is also invited to *stand* in order *to put his hands* into his billfold.

There is in the yarn the truth of caricature; however, it is a caricature of a caricature and, as a result, farther from the truth. It is twice removed from the theological truth (the only norm ultimately pertinent in a discussion of the Church) and is therefore far from the essential image of Catholicism on which Pope John hoped his Council would focus attention.

That image presents, to be sure, a people on its knees at prayer, but a prayer in corporate unity of one with all and all with one, across all diversities of members and functions, in a liturgical action which, while presupposing differences of orders and ministries, subordinates and synthesizes such differences in the organic unity of the one and unique person in whom, with whom and through whom all differences and dignities fade, Christ the Eternal Priest.

The theologically accurate image of the Church reveals, too, a people seated at attention, eager to be enlightened, but, again in a corporate unity such that differences of offices do not alter the basic fact that all, the teachers and the taught, are under the necessity of being taught by God; all, individually and as a body, are subject to God's judgment and dependent on His mercy.

This is the condition of all within the Church, of all without exception, and it is so much of the essence that any differences, even those arising from the divine ordinance or special consecration, are, even when real and substantial, necessarily secondary. It is more important to be part of the people of God than to hold a specific post among them.

Albert Cardinal Meyer of Chicago, speaking on October 21 during the discussion dealing with the idea of the Church as the People of God, called the schema "incomplete and thus not realistic." He admitted that the schema contained an excellent presentation of the positive teaching on the graces, privileges and prerogatives which all receive who are baptized in Christ. Nevertheless, he said, the schema fails to recall two facts that are basic:

> First: all of us who are called by Christ into the Church are sinners, members of a fallen race. Second: even after our entrance into the Church we remain ever conscious of our weakness, our moral feebleness and, on occasion, our falling into sin. For, as the Council of Trent states: "Those words of the just are both humble and truthful: Forgive us our trespasses."

The Cardinal said the difficulties in leading a full Christian life arise internally because "there abides in us that tendency to sin which is called concupiscence," and externally because there is a devil who "roams around like a lion seeking whom he may devour." The Cardinal concluded his remarks with this suggestion:

> In order that our schema may reach the hearts of men today—men who are burdened by a sense both of sin and of their own moral weakness—I am emboldened to propose this emendation of the chapter on the People of God. My preference is that before the People of God is described as being without stain or wrinkle, we preface this by a paragraph in which we proclaim to all men, in so many words, that the Church is the household of the Father of mercies in which the failings of prodigal sons are forgiven, their wounds are bound up, their weaknesses are cured, and their needs are answered.
>
> In this way, our contemporary world will echo once more with a clear statement of those words once spoken by God: "I have not come to summon the just, but sinners" (Mk. 2:17). And the truth proclaimed in the First Vatican Council will be made abundantly clear: "The Eternal Pastor and shepherd of our souls, in order to render the saving work of redemption a lasting thing, determined to erect holy Church."

Archbishop Shehan rose again on October 23 to take exception to the phrase "unfortunate separation" that the schema used in treating the relations between Church and State. He said he was speaking "in the name of the American bishops, who in their session this week charged me with the duty of expressing their thoughts." He minced no words:

> That part of the text in which the words "unfortunate separation" appear seems to us to need a complete revision. From what has already been said, both inside and outside this hall, it seems perfectly evident that the present text lacks clarity. Some assume that the text treats the relations between Church and State, which to us seems to be entirely false.

He recalled also that this third chapter treats of the duty that the Catholic lay apostolate has in the sanctification of the world and, in this task, in avoiding two extremes. The one extreme, cited in the schema, is the undue mixing of religion and the Church in purely civic matters, and the other is the absolute separation of these things into two distinct categories. He then forcefully expressed the sentiment of the American hierarchy in these words:

> The whole question about the relations between the Church and State is of the utmost importance and requires diligence and prudence. The question of the laity is pertinent, and especially pertinent to the whole Church. In this chapter, however, it seems to us that it [the separation of Church and State] should not have a place and, especially, it should not be introduced as an aside.

On the same day Bishop Ernest Primeau spoke on the relations that should exist between the hierarchy and laity. He reminded his colleagues that "we have to keep before our eyes the growing concern which the laity has about its proper status in the apostolate of the Church. Lay people today," he continued, "are conscious of their capabilities and will not allow themselves to be treated, as in past times, as merely passive members of the Church, blindly bowing to authority as mute sheep." He then entered into this description of the caliber of laity in the Church today:

> There are many well-educated faithful who ask to be heard on questions of undertakings in which they have a competence that clerics more often than not lack. They want to share in the apostolic work of the Church, and they certainly intend to do this under the direction of the hierarchy, but not without previously being heard by the hierarchy concerning matters within their competence. They expect the confidence of the hierarchy.
>
> They have a great love for holy Mother Church and manifest great reverence and confidence towards legitimate authority. They are also aware of their own dignity and competence, however, not only in temporal affairs, but also in the internal life of the Church. Above all, they consider dialogue between themselves and the hierarchy as absolutely necessary for promoting the common good of the Church and for defining the special role of the laity in the apostolate. By divine providence this Ecumenical Council has done a lot to make this dialogue possible. It has given the laity great hope and the opportunity for raising many questions.

The schema, Bishop Primeau said, must define the roles of freedom and authority in the Church and, if it does not, we can expect three results: a growing bitterness toward the Church's authority; a growing indifference among laymen "who passively keep the laws, but never share in the life and mission of the Church"; and finally, defections from the faith and the Church. Bishop Primeau continued:

> The Church needs the help of the laity, especially those who are called "intellectuals," in order to grow. The Church can never use their help and advice unless it acknowledges their legitimate freedom of action, the meaning of "initiative" and is ready to consult them with due respect about matters within their competence. . . .
>
> The text insists too much on the need of obedience, reverence, and subjection and does not sufficiently emphasize proper responsibility and freedom of action, as the proper possession of laity who are true members of the Mystical Body of Christ. Let this constant talk of their duty of subjection and reverence cease—as if their only duty be stated in these terms: believe, pray, pay and obey.

In concluding his remarks, Bishop Primeau offered two final suggestions. He said that the bishops must seek out ways and means "so that in each diocese there would be a structure by which the laity, especially the more educated laity, could communicate with the bishop and pastors." Secondly, like other bishops, he was speaking on behalf of the laity, but, he added, "I also ask the Fathers to hear the laity, namely, that the auditors here in the aula would speak in the name of all the laity."

On October 24, Bishop Robert E. Tracy of Baton Rouge, Louisiana, spoke on racial discrimination. Many observers have cited his brief intervention as one of the most pointed and direct of all the interventions delivered during this discussion of the schema on the Church. He asked that the section concerning the people of God "put clearer emphasis on the equality of everyone in the Church with no distinction on account of race." He added six reasons why he felt this should be done. His third reason concerned the United States. He said:

> Because of the present situation in the United States and also, *mutatis mutandis,* in other areas, the Council Fathers are often faced with this problem of race prejudice. The bishops of the United States have repeatedly issued public statements explaining this doctrine in an effort to teach the people social justice and love. Now, if the Council issues a solemn and concrete affirmation of the equality of all races, it will greatly help the bishops to teach their people more effectively.

Bishop John J. Russell, speaking on October 30 in the name of many North American bishops, directed his remarks to the chapter dealing with holiness in the Church. He criticized this part of the schema because he felt something about the holiness of the Church itself should be stated "before it considered the vocation of the faithful in the Church to holiness." This consideration, he said, was necessary because many people today ask "How and in what sense is the Church holy, since there are in it also sinners?" Answering the question he had posed, Bishop Russell continued:

> The Church is holy because it is the Body of Christ. Its author is God. It is consecrated to God who is peculiarly present to it and in it. The proper work of the Church is salvation, the union of man with God in Christ, the communication of grace through the sacraments, through preaching of the Word and through the presence of Christ in it.
>
> Finally, just as Christ Himself in His holy humanity was an instrument joined to divinity for the sanctifying of men, so the Church, as the true continuation of Christ in the world, is the salutary instrument of the sanctification of the faithful and their union with God.

Bishop Russell next asked that the "true sense of the vocation of the perfection of holiness" should be defined more clearly. He wanted to see the distinction between absolute and relative perfection more clearly stated. "Absolute perfection," he said, "signifies the actual acquisition of that very end which, for the Christian, is achieved only in heaven where God is possessed through pure love. The perfection of holiness in this life, therefore, is a relative perfection, that is, something not static and completed, but dynamic and perfectible." He then cited three degrees of holiness in these words:

> However, in practice and in a rather ancient tradition, holiness seems to be understood in a threefold manner, namely, of those among whom, perhaps, very many of the faithful would be numbered who live in the state of grace and hence united with God, fulfilling that precept of Christ, "Who has my commandments and serves them, he it is who loves me."
>
> There is another part of the faithful who not only do not want to offend God, but also wish to serve and please Him, and who in their own way can say with Christ: "I always do those things which are pleasing to Him [the Father]."
>
> Finally, there are those relatively few—for example, St. John Leonard, St. John Vianney and the newly beatified John Nepomucene Neumann, a bishop in the United States—who choose to dedicate themselves wholly and totally to the love of God through heroic charity, through heroic holiness.

Three other American prelates submitted their observations on the schema in writing. In July, 1963, Archbishop John J. Krol wrote that "each chapter of this first part of the schema expresses the best synthesis of both the traditional and recent doctrine on the Church." He did, however, make ten specific suggestions for changes in the text, most of them being grammatical corrections. Two of them, however, were of more than passing significance. First, he felt, the word "sacrament" should be clarified, and thus wrote:

The word *sacrament* carries with it a technical meaning in Catholic theology. Thus, confusion can arise if this concept is used to designate the Church as such. However, it should be noticed that note five cites some sayings of the Fathers which use the word *sacrament* in this broad connotation. If it is expedient to restrict this word to the seven sacraments, another word, e.g., temple, mystery, mother, could be substituted.

Secondly, Archbishop Krol felt, the second chapter of the schema, dealing with bishops as successors to the college of the Apostles, was obscure. "The universal jurisdiction in the Church," he wrote, "as it is given to the college of bishops is clearly affirmed; but, perhaps, the power of each of the bishops to teach should be stated with greater clarity." He thus proposed the following sentences to be incorporated into the text in order to declare explicitly the doctrine of the Church concerning the episcopacy:

"We teach that the bishops, united in college with their head, the successor of Peter, succeed to the college of Apostles with a divine mandate."

"We teach that the bishops alone, in conformity with the divine establishment of the Church, exercise immediately and completely the apostolic ministry of doctrine, sacred worship, and government of the faithful, since it is the source of all the power and sanctification in the Church."

Bishop Charles B. Greco of Alexandria, Louisiana, submitted his observations concerning the schema's third chapter on the laity. First, he wanted to see the term "Mystical Body of Christ" employed in the schema rather than what in most references is simply called the "Body of Christ." He offered this reason for suggesting the change:

It seems to me that in such important constitutions of this great Synod that, when there is mention of the Church, it would be more correctly and accurately called not the *Body of Christ,* but the *Mystical Body of Christ,* in order to eliminate the confusion which already exists in the minds of the faithful on this matter. For many writers and speakers confuse the true Body of Christ, which is real, physical, born from the Virgin Mary, and which has suffered, died, and been raised, sitting at the right hand of the Father and present in the Sacred Eucharist, with His *mystical* Body, which is the Church constituted from many members. Many books and many writings in periodicals and religious papers use these and similar expressions: "Christ is the Church" or, vice versa, "the Church is Christ"; "The parish is Christ" or "Christ is the parish." According to these people who write and speak inaccurately and incautiously and thus confuse the true Body of Christ present in the Sacred Eucharist with the Mystical Body of Christ, that is, the Church, the logical but absurd conclusion could be drawn that when anyone receives the Eucharistic Body of Christ, he receives the whole Church. It seems to me that these expressions are not accurate and thus they can be causes of confusion and error, and I think that this Council should take away any opportunity for error.

Bishop Greco was further pleased with the schema's insistence on the layman's obligation to participate in the salvific mission of the Church. He wanted, moreover, even a stronger statement in this regard and thus wrote:

> Under the guidance of experience, it must be said that laymen generally, since they have a firm faith and an ardent love for Christ and the Church—and very many of these are found in almost every land, especially where they receive encouragement and stimulus from the leaders of the Church—freely, even most freely, give themselves to participation in the works of the Church. It is wonderful what and how many things the laymen can do and, as a matter of fact, do perform on behalf of the Church under the guidance of ecclesiastical authority, where opportunities are presented to them.
>
> But it often happens that laymen, for various reasons, are impeded from perfecting the gifts proper to laymen. There are many ruling in the Church who fear the laymen as if they wished to govern the Church or teach false doctrine. Unless I am mistaken, heresies in the Church have never begun with laymen, and rarely have the Christian faithful tried to take over the government of the Church. Thus it seems best to me that the constitution of this section (page nine, line eight), after it has discerned the obligation and duty, affirm the right of laymen to cooperate in religious works with these words: "And so these people (laymen) have the *right*, with their resources, actively and in their own way, to participate in the salvific work of the Church."

He then adduced four reasons to show more clearly the laymen's obligation and right to participate in the apostolate of the Church: 1) Laymen are members of the Mystical Body of Christ; 2) Laymen share in the royal and universal priesthood of Christ through Baptism and Confirmation; 3) The Church greatly needs the assistance of the laity; 4) Laymen actually sanctify themselves and the world in which they live through sharing in this salvific work of the Church. Bishop Greco concluded with a stirring plea: "It is said that this is the golden age for laymen in the Church. It should rather be said that this is the golden age—even the millennium—for the Church if she uses laymen in all her works according to the ability and desires of the laity."

Bishop Fulton J. Sheen also submitted his observations on this schema in an intervention he entitled "On the Locked Doors." He began by asking two questions: "Does it not seem to you that this schema on the Church has been written with the doors locked? Should it not be stated that this schema is more some sort of colloquy with ourselves than with the men of our times?" Providing an answer to his own questions, Bishop Sheen pointed out that the Church is not "a detached traveler through the world," that she is not to be defined as "the formed Church, but also as the forming Church; not only as the Church already called, but also as the Church now calling." He suggested that the word *dialogue* (which Pope Paul used 57 times in his encyclical *Ecclesiam Suam*) should be used to describe the Church today. He wrote:

> Dialogue takes in every relationship between the Church and the world. In the words of the Sovereign Pontiff, dialogue, rather than merely *external* mission, is *total* mission. Dialogue takes in the responsibility of priests, the faithful, religious and bishops not only towards members of the Church, but also towards atheists, Jews, Christians, men of good will; towards the community, the State, the nation, the world. In this sense the Sovereign Pontiff affirms: What is the apostolate except dialogue? We know, to be sure, that there is another schema in which the specific problems of the Church in the world today are treated.

Bishop Sheen then criticized the schema because it considered too exclusively the Church internally and observed that "the Church is not complete if it is described only from within and not from without." He suggested that the schema should also stress the dialogue that the Church should carry on with the nations of the world, with atheistic, unbelieving people, with the poor and the starving. On this last point he added:

> The Council of Trent reminded the Church of the evangelical counsel of chastity. The First Vatican Council, of the evangelical counsel of obedience. In this Second Ecumenical Vatican Council, there is set upon our shoulders the evangelical counsel of poverty.

In conclusion, Bishop Sheen stressed that dialogue enables the Church to have access to the world, and the world to have approach to the Church; the closer the Church draws near to the world, the more the world gives itself in dialogue with the Church. His final words contained all the drama of a conclusion of one of his television appearances. He said:

> In the First Ecumenical Vatican Council, practically all the bishops came from Europe. There was no bishop from Asia or Africa.
> Today, of the Fathers of this Council, 62 per cent come from Asia, Africa, England, and North and Central America. The world is pouring into the Church a new blood, a new order of things: John's *aggiornamento*.
> Would that Christ would once again appear to us, we who are protected by locked doors, and admonish us with those words of the Apocalypse: "See, I have put before you an open door, that no one can close."

In another written intervention dealing chiefly with the schema on the missionary activity of the Church, Bishop Sheen touched upon the doctrine of collegiality as it applied to the Church's missionary efforts.

The Church is missionary because Christ sent His Apostles into the world (Mt. 16: 16–20). The bishops, under the authority of Peter, since they are the successors of the Apostles by their episcopal consecration, have responsibility for the world. Individual bishops are bound, by the institution and command of Christ, to be concerned for the whole Church.

The episcopal role can only be exercised in communion with all the other bishops of the world, because apostolicity cannot be exercised without catholicity. The diocese is not only a certain separate administrative entity, but rather an integral part of the mission of Christ to the world. Mission is not some "pious extra," but the expression of the very nature of the Church. "The missionary spirit and the catholic spirit are to be considered one and the same" (Pius XI).

In the Acts of the Apostles there is no distinction made between the Church and missions. With great care does the Spirit force the Church into giving testimony, and the Church incessantly rises from that mission.

In the amendments to the original schema on the Blessed Virgin Mary the Mother of the Church, the suggestions of two American prelates were cited. Archbishop Krol asked that the title of the schema be changed to read: "On the Blessed Virgin Mary, Mother of the Redeemer." He also felt that the expression "Daughter of the Father" should be omitted from the schema. Auxiliary Bishop John Whealon of Cleveland, together with the bishops of Indonesia, some French bishops and others, stated that the term "Mediatrix of Graces" should be removed from the schema. Archbishop Krol's position was spelled out in an intervention he submitted on July 19, 1963.

One can oppose the title of the Blessed Virgin "Mother of the Church" for the same reason that he objects to the title "Exemplar of the Church" and "Daughter of the Father," about which there will be a treatment further on (page seven, line 22; page ten, line thirty-six). The title "Mother of the Redeemer" seems to express better the essential position of Mary in the economy of salvation, while at the same time it contains the meaning of the other prerogatives which follow that position.

Archbishop Krol also praised the schema on the Blessed Virgin Mary for "its brevity, clarity, its derivation solely from Sacred Scripture and the previous declarations of the Church's magisterium." He thought, too, that the schema was notable "because it rejects the errors of both the maximalists and of the minimalists and also because throughout all of this it breathes charity, a spirit which is maintained with difficulty against the opinions of some of the separated brethren."

Cardinal Spellman submitted one intervention concerning the Blessed Virgin Mary when the schema was a distinct document, and another after it had been incorporated into the schema on the Church. Concerning the original schema, he wrote:

> I am quite pleased with the admonition that theologians and heralds of the divine word beware of such a false hyperbole of the truth and of an excessive narrowmindedness in considering the dignity of the Mother of God. Likewise, among the very beautiful statements made on the limited association of the Blessed Virgin Mary with Christ in the economy of salvation and on the singular privileges of the Mother of God and men, it has been usefully and most truly noted that she was redeemed in a more sublime way and that in no way is the Mother of God to be equated with Christ.

In his later intervention the Cardinal realized "that Catholics as well as non-Catholics justly and deservedly await a clear word on what the Catholic Church as such really believes, holds and teaches concerning the tribute, privileges and cult of Mary." He found the revised schema such a type of statement and believed it would be of great pastoral and doctrinal assistance. In this same brief intervention Cardinal Spellman expressed a reservation about the title of the seventh chapter of the schema on the Church. He felt that many contemporaries did not understand the word "eschatological" in the title and, therefore, for pastoral reasons the word should be avoided.

Shortly before the Dogmatic Constitution on the Church was promulgated, the Reverend Gustave Weigel, S.J., hailed it as "the keystone which will determine the direction of all the other schemas to be considered." As the distinguished professor of ecclesiology at Woodstock College, and a member of the American Bishops' Press Panel, he followed the conciliar discussions on the schema with great interest. Two months before his untimely death in January, 1964, Father Weigel had written:

> What the Council Fathers have achieved is a highly significant piece of work. It will be a source of orientation for theologians and preachers for years to come. . . . Ecclesiology, the theological study of the Church, has many questions to ask. The Council did not answer all or even many of them. However, it did solve problems for men of our day, living in a world that challenges Christian endeavor. The days and the years will bring out many facets of the Council's teaching which its new appearance cannot yet reveal.

The promulgation of the Dogmatic Constitution on the Church, during the fifth public session of the Second Vatican Council on November 21, 1964, will be long remembered by Christians everywhere. It marked the completion and fulfillment of the First Vatican Council; it pointed out the direction the Church would take as a pilgrim, a servant, a witness in the world of tomorrow. In his address following the promulgation of the Constitution, Pope Paul VI summarized the thoughts of the Council Fathers on that day in these words:

From now on we can enjoy greater understanding of divine thought relative to the Mystical Body of Christ, and from this we can draw clear and safer rules for the life of the Church, greater energy for her incessant effort to lead men to salvation, further hope for the progress of the reign of Christ in the world. Let us bless the Lord.

Dogmatic Constitution on the Church

✠ INTERVENTIONS

JOSEPH CARDINAL RITTER, *1 December, 1962*

All parts of the Dogmatic Constitution on the Church treat well—and, for the most part, adequately—their own matter. However, the totality only in a minimal way gives us an adequate doctrine concerning the nature and life of the Church. The schema has much to say, and says it well. But there is much missing which must be treated. Nevertheless, this defect is not found in a single absence which can easily be fulfilled, but it is found in the very method and system in which the tract is advanced.

The powers of the magisterium, jurisdiction, orders, or whatever is of importance are not principles of the whole, but of only a part of the activity and life of the Church. And so they are insufficient, and a doctrine of the Church cannot be construed or deducted from them. Because the schema follows this method, the concept of the Church which it furnishes is entirely inadequate and, so to speak, closed. Allow me to illustrate the insufficiency of this method by indicating some defects in the doctrine of the schema.

The schema considers the sanctity of the Church as consisting principally— I do not mean totally—in the causality of the instrument related to the sanctity of the members. Almost nothing is said about the formal sanctity of the Church, about which St. Paul wrote: "Christ loved the Church and he handed himself over for it, that he might sanctify it."

The second example that I give: The schema considers the duty of preserving, guarding and explaining the deposit of the faith only in terms of the magisterium, who, we may conclude, have this office and right exclusively. On the other hand, this is a duty of the entire Church; the magisterium exercises only a part of this function. All the members of the Church, yes even the simple faithful, most certainly have a part in preserving, in guarding and probably even in explaining the deposit of faith. The faithful are capable of this not because of a favor or a special indult of the magisterium, but because of their Christian character.

The third example includes the whole of chapter nine which speaks about the relation between Church and State. Awaiting a doctrine suited to modern

48

necessity, we find only an application of principles to circumstances which, *never* universal, *now* are of no value for the whole age, even in particulars. Moreover, it seems to me, in order to remove this matter from all useless controversy, the Council ought to give public law with a decree on the liberty which must be accorded conscience and all religions—setting aside a dogmatic constitution.

There are also some things lacking; for example, the absence of a consideration of the worship of the Church. All these flow from an insufficient rooting and foundation. The Church is Christ Himself mystically living and working in all the members, in whom the Holy Spirit—the Spirit of Christ—dwells and operates. Only through such a concept can we understand the Church and her "operation in the measure of each member" by which the Church grows in its structure and in love. In Christ, through Christ and with Christ, the Church teaches, offers worship, sanctifies and is sanctified, and in some way rules and reigns. Every member has a part in activities of this sort and in the life of the Church—each according to his own talents.

In these propositions, it seems to me, is the foreshadowing whereby the schema can be more clearly and more adequately composed. If not the greatest, it is at least one of the more pleasant duties of this Council to indicate what the Church understands about herself and what she says she is.

And we must indicate how the Church understands herself today. We cannot, by reverting to the partial concepts of Trent and Vatican I, bypass the theological works of more recent times which render such perfection to the understanding of the Church, the Mystical Body of Christ.

For myself, I wish that the schema of the Dogmatic Constitution on the Church be revised and studied again in the light of the proffered suggestions.

FRANCIS CARDINAL SPELLMAN, *3 December, 1962*

The schema of the Dogmatic Constitution on the Church pleases me. But I would like to proffer a warning on chapter six, on the laity.

Every baptized person has certain real relations with the true Church of Christ in the sacramental and juridic order. Nonetheless, only those fully belong to the Church whom the Church, according to the institution of Christ, brings together in the unity of faith, worship and rule. Only those, therefore, are truly and properly called members of the Church who, cleansed by the water of regeneration, profess the true Catholic faith, acknowledge the authority of the Church in her bishops and in the Vicar of Christ, and perform divine worship according to the institution of Christ. Among the members of the Church a distinction between clerics and laymen must be made: that is, between those who share the priesthood of Christ from sacramental ordination and are endowed either from their office or from legitimate delegation with the authority of the Church and those who do not share power of this sort, but are subject to priestly ministers (prelates) and are ruled according to the common norms of the Christian life.

As much as possible, it should be noted that lay people, although they are endowed with neither sacred power nor authority, are nonetheless expected to cooperate in a fitting way with those who have power and authority in order to fulfill the mission of the Church. It is a mistake to think that they are incorporated in the Church only to work out their own salvation; they should cooperate in the work of the Church in their own way and order. From their very Baptism they share, in a certain way, a common priesthood and, while through it they are fit to worship in the Church, they are also called to communicate to others the benefits of the Redemption in a way suited to them. They are strengthened through the sacrament of Confirmation in order that they may profess, spread and defend the Catholic faith before the world. This has already been said by St. Paul: "Doing the truth in love, let us increase through all in him who is the head, Christ: from whom the whole body makes an addition to the body compact and connected through every joining of service according to operation in the measure of each member in the building up of itself in charity."

This duty is the layman's according to his state. It can be performed individually or collectively. According to the circumstances of time and place, it can embrace strictly religious works or social or economic ones, provided that it be ordered to the good of persons and society and promotes the mission of the Church. By its very nature, this work of the laity enjoys a special effectiveness insofar as they act in the world, converse among their fellow citizens and share their conditions.

In our age a new form of the apostolate of the laity has evolved which answers its intended purpose very well. It is called Catholic Action by which the laity are associated in the apostolate of the hierarchy by a true canonical mission from their proper ordinary. It includes religious, apostolic, charitable, social and economic associations of the laity and can be directed to any work which, according to circumstances and necessities, promotes the mission of the Church. It is a form of the apostolate of the laity set up by the Holy See itself and constantly propounded by it. Where it has been well organized and skillfully directed, it is the greatest help to the hierarchy in advancing the mission of the Church, especially in those things in which the laity are more fit.

In this schema, however, there is too little insistence on Catholic Action. It should be brought into the light because of its great importance and its great ability to deal with present-day conditions.

JAMES CARDINAL McINTYRE, *3 December, 1962*

In chapter two, paragraph nine of the schema on the Church, mention is made of those who are members of the Church in the proper sense.

There does not seem to be complete separation among the orders of persons. There is a gap because infants dying without Baptism are not included in these classes of persons. Since these infants are persons it seems to me both reasonable and useful for the Holy Vatican Council, in this place, to concern itself with the eternal lot of these infants. This is most certainly an involved question, one that has been disputed for a long time among theologians.

Perhaps the question does not pertain directly to this schema; but there is no treatment of this thing in any place of the schemas.

Therefore, I propose that the consideration of this question be added to paragraph nine, at least in an implicit manner, because there seems to be some connection with the material treated in this paragraph.

The solution of the question may, nevertheless, be a thing hidden in the eternal plan of the providence of God.

VERY REV. JOSEPH BUCKLEY, S.M., *6 December, 1962*

In the present discussion about the approval of the schema on the Church in general, it seems that something should be said about the way the question of authority and obedience should be treated.

This matter is touched upon in chapter five in relation to the religious vow of obedience, hinted at in chapter seven on the magisterium of the Church, suggested in chapter nine on the relations between Church and State, and it forms the direct object of chapter eight on the authority and obedience in the Church. This last chapter treats of the recent crisis in obedience, but seems to prescind completely from the psychological conditions and the very basis of the crisis which is always present.

Authority and obedience are equally necessary. As a Superior General, I certainly do not want to diminish authority, ecclesiastical or any other legitimate authority. With the authors of the schema I reject the errors mentioned on pages 60–62. If the schema is left as it is now, namely, that it should assert (apart from any adequate distinction and explanation) that one should obey civil authority because it is from God, and also the same for obedience to ecclesiastical authority because it is from God, many sons and daughters of the Church would deduce that the nature of this crisis of authority in the Church is scarcely understood by the Council Fathers.

For many Catholics, among whom are many religious, the crisis of obedience is not merely to obey or not to obey. For them the crisis of authority is a question of reason and method.

1) *Reason.* The schema proposed to us is founded on authority, whether civil or religious, as coming from God. To others, however, it seems that the foundation should rest rather on the individual person, with his liberty, obligations and consequent rights. Because, note well, all rights of men flow from obligations.

Liberty, insofar as it is individual choice, chosen among many true goods, is a pure perfection, a perfection pure and simple as theologians say, which as such can also be attributed to God. It is not without reason that men down the ages have fought and died for liberty, thinking that it was most dear and precious. Obedience is a virtue, truly necessary, but it is not pure perfection. It is a perfection only in creatures. God is free, not obedient. Christ was obedient, but in His human nature. Since obedience is, in itself, a perfection inferior to liberty, overemphasis of obedience and authority on the limiting of liberty should not be made without proportionate reason. I do not hold that every precept presented to one's subjects is to be bolstered up by explanations. I do think, however, that the doctrine of authority and obedience should be presented by beginning with the liberty of the individual and not with the State and Church, as it is done in the schema.

2) *Method.* Here it is also necessary to lay a good foundation. The authority of the Church and its hierarchy was established by Christ. But many are interested in making a distinction between the different grades of authority and the reciprocal grades of obedience, e.g., between a solemn definition of faith by the Holy Father and, on the other hand, a precept handed down by a religious superior to his subjects. This distinction is somewhat seen in the schema, but in the schema it appears as a tendency covering all of these things by asserting that the will of the superior is the will of God. On the contrary, the will of the superior has no necessary connection with the object of decision as does the will of God. It is true that it is the general will of God that we obey when we obey superiors, but by this it does not mean that obedience is removed from the realm of prudence and mature conscience.

In the Middle Ages, emperors and kings founded their power in the authority of the pope and bishops, simply saying that their authority was from God and was, therefore, the will of God.

The authority of the Church is really from God in Christ. But the authority of the State is from God in the sense only that God created man as a social being and, therefore, he must act in society. For this reason the authority of the leaders of the people comes from the consent of the people. They err when they say that they never have to give account to the people, but only to God and history.

The truth is rather that not only civil authority, but also ecclesiastical authority, even if the latter comes directly from God, is exercised by men in a fallible and human way, except, of course, *ex cathedra* statements and the like.

In both cases, Church and State, in addition to the principle of authority, there must be considered also the principle of autonomy formulated by Pope Pius XI and approved by John XXIII in his encyclical letter *Mater et Magistra* under the name of the principle of subsidiarity: ". . . it is wrong to take away and transfer to an organization those things which can be performed by individual men by their own powers and industry."

This priority of the individual person and the personal conscience seems to offer some keys to a solution of the problems on the relation between Church and State in our modern pluralistic societies.

The schema on the Church which is pastoral and ecumenical must in its structure insert the notion of the liberty of the individual person.

BISHOP ERNEST PRIMEAU, 2 *October, 1963*

First of all, I want to make a brief change in the words of introduction by our eminent moderator. I am the bishop of Manchester in the United States. The bishop of Manchester in England is one of our separated brothers and up to now has not had an active part in this Council!

It helps to note some things which bear on the nature of the Church and especially about those who are incorporated into the Church or participate in it (cf. numbers eight and nine of the schema). As it stands, the text of the schema is somewhat confusing. On the one hand it does not, or not sufficiently, distinguish between participation in or incorporation *before* God or in His judgment, and the same incorporation or participation *before the Church* or in her judgment. On the other hand it does not distinguish between the Church as a community or communion which includes all the just or justified (that is, not only men living on earth who share in the same revealed truth and grace, but also the saints in heaven and the souls in purgatory) and the Church *as a society* whose members can only be baptized men on earth, namely those alone who are capable of reaching their end. For this reason there does not exist a *division* between the Church-community and the Church-society, but only a distinction of *two aspects* of the same reality, the Church. A community is the sum of all those who actually share in the same notes or properties. A society is the union of many for a common action (St. Thomas, *Contra Impugnantes Dei cultum et religionem, c. 3*), namely, in attaining a common end. The Church is both a community and, as regards those here on earth, a society. They are two aspects of the same Church.

Therefore certain changes in the text of the schema should be made:

1) On page seven, line 22: "This congregation of the just is called the universal Church by the Fathers." This congregation is later, on page nine, rightly called (and is) the Mystical Body of Christ. But on page twelve, line 8:

"Though they pertain to the Church, those who do not live in faith, hope and charity are not saved; for the sinner remains in the Church 'in body,' but not 'in heart.'" This is said in an obscure and indistinct way.

In fact, before God "who searches our hearts" (Rom. 8:27; I Cor. 2:10), the Church or the Mystical Body is the congregation only of the just, those namely who share in sanctifying grace, and thus does not include those sinners who by their fault do not live in faith or hope or charity. But in the face of the Church or its judgment, "which does not judge hidden matters" (Innocent III, in c. 33, X, V, 3), the ecclesial communion or community simply includes all those on earth who externally profess the true faith, show themselves submissive to legitimate authority and are not excommunicated from the communion of the faithful on account of evident sins or censures.

2) Furthermore, confer page twelve, line 3 and following: "Really and simply speaking, only those are incorporated into the society of the Church who acknowledge its total structure and all the means of salvation instituted in it, . . ." In fact, by the judgment of the Church, they and only they share fully and simply in the communion of the Church when they verify what constitutes the specific character of the communion or the full communion. Furthermore, they alone share simply and actively here on earth in the Church as society when they are baptized and participate in the social life of the Church.

Therefore: 1) On page twelve, line 3, I offer this text:

"Really and simply, i.e., only those share fully in the communion of the Church, only those are simply and actively members of the society of the Church who . . . etc.," or the simpler text: "Really and simply only those are incorporated into the Church who . . . etc.," without mentioning the distinction between community and society.

3) On page twelve, number nine, line 24, in place of "With all those who, baptized, are given the name of Christian. . . . The Church, loving Mother of all men, knows for various reason that they are joined to her. . . ." is proposed: "All those who are baptized, bear the name of Christian, but, adults, do not profess the whole faith or unity of faith or unity of community under the Roman Pontiff, the Church, loving mother of men, for various reasons holds them as joined to her and calls them, with reason, sons."

Finally, let me add another comment to my preceding ones. In this schema we seek an explanation of the relations between the Church and the State or the political society, which was to have been dealt with in chapter nine of the first schema. In chapter one, now, since we consider the relation between the Church and people, an explanation should be given which sees men not only as individuals, but also as joined in civil societies. In the voting, many bishops of the United States definitely want the general principles of this question treated, if not here, then in another schema.

JOSEPH CARDINAL RITTER, *3 October, 1963*

"The Church is a sacrament of the intimate unity of the whole human race and of its union with God." Thus the introduction of the schema on the Church speaks well and most aptly. It further says a sacrament is both a sign and instrument of this unity and union. Therefore, in the seventh paragraph the schema puts it well in saying, "The Church . . . on this earth remains true to the connection of the means of sanctification."

Almost all the other propositions or opinions of the schema speak of the Church as a community of faith, love and grace. In this sense, the Church is identified with men already united to God; it is an effect of the divine action of sanctification and unification. Therefore the schema is very deficient, almost silent, about the way in which the Church is a sign and sacrament of union, about the means of sanctification which the Church has and about the actions the ministry exercises and fulfills as its mission.

In my judgment, paragraph seven, immediately after the words *constat et sustentur* in the seventh line, ought to contain at least a generic treatment of the dynamism and the salvific ministry of the Church, "The Church as a pilgrim in the world." Here there should be found especially a theology of the Word of God, living and efficaciously working in the Church of Christ. Word and sacrament, with ruling power, comprise the salvific and sanctifying ministry and activity of the Church.

"To preach" and "to teach"—conceptually these activities are almost synonymous with the Church. Nonetheless, in reality in many areas of the Church they are scarcely exercised and in others only poorly. They receive the esteem and reverence due them in very few places.

The causality of the sacraments has been clearly and perfectly explained in detail by the Council of Trent while the efficacy of the Word preached in the Church has remained in the shadows. Liturgical reform, the renewal of the Church, the doctrinal and disciplinary *aggiornamento*—all these cannot be conceived of without the restoration of preaching to its pristine dignity.

Nor may it be said that this matter pertains to some other schema or to another commission. Last year, with great joy we accepted the schema on the Word of God from the Secretariat for Promoting Christian Unity. Who knows where, when, or how it has been lost, passed over or rejected? But it does not matter. The theology of the Word of God in the schema on the Church ought to be set forth in the very beginning because the Word of God lives, illumines and gives life only in the Church of Christ.

By Word and Work, God reveals and communicates Himself to men. This is the history of human salvation. In Christ, God brought forth for men the perfect Work of salvation. Both Word and Work, signs of the divine love lacking nothing, perdure, operate and are manifested in the Church and through the Church which is itself the sacrament of that same love. The Word and

Sacramental Work are essential to the Church; without a clear perception of this Work and this Word an adequate concept of the Church is neither given nor can be given.

BISHOP JOSEPH MARLING, C.PP.S, *4 October, 1963*

It is my proposition to emend paragraph nine, page 12, the title of which is "On the Relations of the Church with non-Catholic Christians," because the doctrinal basis of ecumenism, and especially the invitation to fervent ecumenism, seems poorly expressed and certainly lacks order.

If paragraph eight is retained and non-Catholic Christians are saved not as members of Christ's Body, but in a somewhat imperfect manner, I propose the following in paragraph nine. I offer it without comment or explanation.

> With all those who glory in the Christian name, even though they do not profess the whole faith or unity of communion with the Roman Pontiff, the Church, the holy Mother of all, knows itself to be joined for many reasons.
>
> For she acknowledges that many outside her communion satisfy the condition given by Christ, and therefore are worthy of His promise: "If anyone love me . . . and my Father will love him, and we will come to him and make our abode with him" (Jn. 14:23). With those adorned by sanctifying grace, the Church has some union in the Holy Spirit. Holy Mother Church also asserts that our separated brothers are adorned in the face as in the heart with the most glorious name of Christ, because they have put on Christ through baptism (Gal. 3:28), and are buried with him in death (Rom. 6:4). The Church acknowledges a firmer and stronger bond when, as in the case of the separated Orientals, all the other sacraments are received, especially the Eucharist, the sacrament of unity; the apostolic succession is preserved in a certain way; and devotion to the Virgin Mother of God is fostered.

May the last sentence be a grave exhortation to all, in and out of the Church's communion, to pray and cooperate that the desire of Christ may soon be fulfilled: one flock and one Shepherd.

FRANCIS CARDINAL SPELLMAN, *4 October, 1963*

I am amazed that in the second chapter we still find, in number 15, lines 33–41, page 26, the suggestion of restoring the permanent or stable diaconate. This is a *dogmatic* Constitution. Therefore, in this place the diaconate and its office in general is to be treated dogmatically. Enough has already been stated in lines 28–33 of this paragraph concerning the diaconate inasmuch as it is an inferior grade in the hierarchical ministry of the Church. Why, therefore, is there such an explicit mention of a permanent diaconate? Without a doubt, the subject of a permanent diaconate is not dogmatic but disciplinary. Therefore, I believe that in a dogmatic Constitution it should not in the least be found.

Another question arises, namely, whether this and similar subjects should be treated by the Second Vatican Council. In my opinion, the response to this question should be negative. It is not the function of an Ecumenical Council to deal without any practical experience with a certain institution which could be restored, perhaps, in the future. Furthermore, it is not the task of an Ecumenical Council to institute or, in a solemn Constitution of this kind, approve what can bring about a great hardship to the Church.

The permanent or stable diaconate has not been practiced in the Latin Church already for many centuries. Since this institution, that formerly was practiced, has become obsolete in the course of the years, it should not be restored before we diligently inquire into the reasons why it became obsolete. Furthermore, we should also inquire into the difficulties which can arise from this restoration.

Furthermore, permanent deacons should conduct themselves as ministers of the Church both in the eyes of the faithful as well as non-Catholics. In order to perform their task they should be sufficiently prepared. Nonetheless, in many regions it is scarcely possible to build and sustain seminaries for candidates to the priesthood. How, therefore, can we now assume other obligations towards a house of formation for deacons?

Finally, the necessity of a permanent diaconate is a gratuitous assumption. Religion and members of secular institutions labor magnificently for the good of souls in those places where the necessities of the Church are the greatest. Furthermore, in recent years the number of lay people who devote themselves to the service of the Church in those places for a certain number of years is increasing more and more.

ALBERT CARDINAL MEYER, 7 *October, 1963*

What I have to say concerns especially the contents of the chapter on the collegiality of the Apostles and its transmission to the bishops.

The things already stated in the schema on this subject please me. My intention is to offer certain observations which seem to me useful both to strengthen those things which are already contained in the schema and to amplify the scriptural foundation of this collegiality and its transmission to the bishops.

Our schema shows clearly in paragraph twelve that Our Lord Jesus Christ entrusted His Church to a college of the twelve Apostles. The schema's doing this pleases me because of the testimony of the New Testament showing that (1) the New Testament contains sayings and actions of Christ which cannot permit any other interpretation, and that (2) the sayings and actions of Christ were interpreted in favor of collegiality by the primitive Church.

It is also worthy of note that the New Testament is not a legal code and that, therefore, it does not express its truths in juridic terminology.

If we look at those actions and sayings of Christ, we see that He Himself chose the twelve Apostles. No more, no less. The Twelve in His mind represented the whole of the New Israel. Moreover, the unity of the New People of Israel required that they be represented in the Twelve not as individuals, but as a body.

Along this line, the special instruction of Christ about the Kingdom was given to each and every one of the Twelve.

Also, to the Twelve were given all the means of salvation along with the command that they administer these means to others.

Finally, after the resurrection the Lord ordered that the body of Apostles be witness to Him unto the ends of the earth.

Now it seems to me, however, that another truth ought to be more clearly introduced into the schema, a truth which is also evident in the New Testament. This truth is that the Lord wished that the body of the Twelve endure in the Church until the end of the world. For He explicitly said to the body of Apostles: "All power on heaven and earth has been given to me. Go therefore and teach all nations [note the task and, therefore, the power to teach], baptizing them in the name of the Father and of the Son and of the Holy Spirit [note the office and thus the power of sanctifying], teaching them to observe all things which I have commanded you [note the office and thus the power to promulgate the law of Christ], and I am with you all days until the consummation of the world [note the explicit will of Christ that the body of Apostles perdure in the Church]."

This will of Christ is strengthened by those words which He said to the Twelve at the Last Supper: "And I will ask the Father and He will give you another advocate to remain with you forever."

These words, as all others in this context, are expressed in the plural form: you (pl.), to you (pl.) teach (pl.) baptizing (pl.), and so forth. Let us also note in passing the phrases: "until the consummation of the world" and "forever."

It is of great importance that we understand how the primitive Church interpreted these sayings and acts of Christ. We find this interpretation in the Acts of the Apostles. I offer three cases of it:

1) The first act of the Apostles after ascension of the Lord was to restore

the sacred number twelve by choosing Matthias for the dignity of apostleship. Why did they do so? The text itself gives the reason: "It is fitting therefore," said Peter, "that from these men who are gathered with us, a witness of His resurrection be made one of us." It is fitting therefore that not eleven, but twelve, Apostles be witnesses of His resurrection. And Luke closes his narration by saying, "Matthias who was chosen was numbered with the eleven apostles."

2) Of particular importance in those first days after Christ's ascension was the birth of the Church on Pentecost Sunday. Sacred Scripture indicates how this happened, for it says, "Standing with the eleven, Peter raised his voice," thus showing the importance of the breathing of the Holy Spirit on the Twelve. Therefore the Church was constituted through the wonderful Petrine revelation and the collegial experience of the Twelve on Pentecost Sunday. For the text continues: "When these things were heard, the hearers were moved deeply and said to Peter and the rest of the Apostles: 'Brothers, what shall we men do?'"

The Church, therefore, was born through the collegial action of the twelve Apostles.

3) When temporal necessities demanded that there be a new and special ministry in the Church, this was done by the action of the Apostles, as Luke narrates: "The Twelve, gathering together a multitude of disciples, said: 'It is not fitting for us to abandon the word of God and wait on tables. Therefore consider seven men from among you whom we will appoint for this work.'" We must note again the words in the plural form: "the Twelve calling together," and "we will appoint." Thus also Luke closes his narrative: "These seven stood before the Apostles and praying they [the Apostles] imposed their hands upon them."

Therefore, just as no Catholic denies that the Church is based in a singular manner on Peter according to the testimony of the New Testament, so I believe that, on account of the testimony of the same source, we ought to admit also that the Church was founded by Christ on the college of the twelve Apostles, and, according to the will of Christ, always ought to rest on this college.

LAWRENCE CARDINAL SHEHAN, *10 October, 1963*

First of all, I wish to approve the second chapter which speaks about the necessity of including the paragraph about the presbytery. This paragraph, however, ought to take note of chapter one of the schema on clerics, especially about the perfection or the sanctity of the priestly life, and it should agree with it.

Furthermore, besides those things which have already been proposed, I wish to propose two other changes.

1) On page 30, line 3 we read: "Already Vatican Council I has rightly stated that the definitions of the Roman Pontiff are unchangeable, so that it is never permitted to replace his judgment for another." All Catholics without distinction or restriction accept this clear and complete definition with their whole heart.

However, this definition, because of the false concepts about the nature and the fullness of the infallibility of the Roman Pontiff and about the connection between the definition and the consensus of the Church, is a source of difficulty, perhaps the principal difficulty, on the part of our separated brothers. Therefore, I ask whether in this constitution we should not include a fuller explanation of this definition.

In his speech, after celebrating Solemn Mass which opened the second session, Pope Paul VI, happily reigning, said: "It seems perfectly clear that the time has now come, in which the truth about the Church must be explored, digested, expressed, perhaps not by solemn proclamations, which are called dogmatic definitions, but rather by employing declarations, by means of which the Church, using a greater and more dignified magisterium, declares what it thinks about itself."

Such a declaration about the definition of infallibility and about the connection between the definition in general and about the consensus of the Church seems to be found on page 42 in note 52, where the words of Gasser, which he spoke in Vatican Council I are given: "We cannot separate the Pope from the consensus of the Church, because this consensus is never able to be made without him. Since we believe the Pope to be infallible through the help of God, we also believe that these definitions are not lacking the assent of the Church, for it is not possible that the body of the bishops be separated from its head, and because the universal Church cannot be mistaken. For when . . . etc."

Without a doubt, a declaration or an explanation is possible which uses more exact and more suitable words than that selected from the words of Gasser.

2) On page 30, line 12, we read: "However, since either the Roman Pontiff or a Council defines an opinion, they offer it according to that Revelation to which all must conform and which, written or oral, is handed down integrally through the legitimate succession of bishops and in the first place is in charge of the Roman Pontiff . . . etc."

The emendation I propose is that in place of the word "or" we add the word "and."

The reason for the change: The Fathers of the Council of Trent, as is evident from the actions of that Sacred Synod, after a long and lively discussion, in the decree about the sacred books and tradition, rejected such words as "partly . . . partly," "either . . . or," "one or the other," and accepted the word "and." To avoid a long and fruitless discussion, I propose that we follow the good example of the Fathers of the Council of Trent in using the words which consider the relation between the Sacred Scriptures and Tradition.

All of us have heard about certain Fathers who were coming to the Council in a taxi, and, good grief, found themselves far from Rome, on the Via Flaminia hurrying towards the city of Trent. It seems to me, that whenever we talk about the relation between Sacred Scripture and Tradition, we would do well to return to the Council of Trent.

Therefore, I propose the word "and" in place of the word "or."

JOSEPH CARDINAL RITTER, *14 October, 1963*

I should like to say a very few words on the second chapter of the schema concerning the Church. Since episcopal collegiality and the restoration of the permanent diaconate are of great importance, they deserve a very clear and mature deliberation. But the discussion on both of them, at least in my judgment, is obscured by a certain confusion.

There are two questions concerning episcopal collegiality—one speculative or dogmatic, the other practical. In this schema on the Church, only the dogmatic question is treated—concerning the essential structure of the Church and, therefore, the nature of the episcopate. At this point in the Council the debate is concerned with whether the episcopate is collegial according to its institution; what Sacred Scripture and Tradition teach about collegiality must be considered. As to the rest, concerning the when and how and what sort of college might exercise episcopal authority, there will be discussion in the schema on bishops and the administration of dioceses.

With the necessary changes, the same things are to be said concerning the restoration of the diaconate. At this point in the Council the discussion is concerned with whether the permanent diaconate ought to be restored. It must be considered whether this will be useful for the building, renewal and increase of the Church. The question of how many and of what variety are the difficulties concerning the restoration of the diaconate, whether married or unmarried, may be left for discussion in its proper time and place.

BISHOP JOHN WRIGHT, *17 October, 1963*

I am expressing some thoughts of great import, both historical and theological, on the chapter concerning the laity, hoping that, after the Council discussions and whatever emendations are necessary to correct individual matters, there will remain both the principles and, in those things which are positive, also the words of this chapter. However, stronger words might be found to state more strongly the positive values of the schema as, for example, those which are now proposed on page ten and eleven of the revision of the fascicle.

In truth, I can say that the Christian faithful have been waiting four hundred years for such a positive conciliar exposition, such as is now presented by the Council, on the place, dignity and vocation of the laity in the Church of Christ. Indeed, the Roman pontiffs, who in recent times have given such impetus to the apostolate of like to like, especially Pius XI and in another manner and more recently Pius XII, have spoken strongly to us and the world about the lay apostolate and vocation. Many theologians, among whom the French, Germans and Italians are first at least in time, have written about such an apostolate both in ascetical and dogmatic theology. Very many bishops scattered throughout the world have favored Catholic Action and have echoed the voice of the Roman pontiffs concerning the cooperation of the laity in individual dioceses.

Now, however, by Divine Providence an opportunity is presented the whole teaching Church speaking together in Council to establish a theological and organic basis for Catholic Action in the true and full sense of the term. The schema now before us intends to do this by at least beginning the huge labor of showing in a positive manner the mind and will of Christ in regard to the Christian faithful who are called the laity.

In my judgment, the present chapter is a hopeful beginning. Many, however, hope that the Council will more explicitly remember the expectations of Pius XI in regard to the Catholic Action of the laity, and also the prophetic vision of Pius XII about supernatural forces and the admirable role of the laity in the consecration of the world.

Deeply realizing how greatly the general priesthood of the people of God and the sacerdotal priesthood of their shepherds differ, our faithful rejoice that the Catholic Church is a priestly Church in many senses. But they also will rejoice when, through a teaching of the Council which is especially positive on the laity, the very hierarchy of the Church begins to put a happy end to the false and theologically unfounded notion that the Catholic Church is, so to speak, "clerical," whereas the so-called reformed churches are somehow more suitable to the laity.

There will be joy and excitement or cause for more profound love toward the Church and her works for all the Christian faithful everywhere if the Council will clearly and explicitly teach what the Christian laity is, with positive ideas about the dignity of the lay Christian in the Church and their vocation before God, even though they are lay. Teaching thus, this third chapter of the schema on the Church will be a cornerstone not only for today's lay apostolate, but for constructing a Christian society in the world of tomorrow.

The traditional notion or canonical description of the lay person is negative: a layman is not a cleric, not a religious, and the like. Such a notion will hardly suffice for a juridical society suitably organized for effectively carrying out the work of Christ in our times. The Church, inasmuch as it is an organic society and somehow Christ Himself working in our world, obviously needs, with contradiction to no one, a positive notion of the Christian laity. And, indeed, if the ontological, organic and, therefore, theological nature of the laity is declared by the Council, then the juridical structure of the Church will be made alive in theological flesh and blood, and thus the work of the Church, as whole and integral in Christ, will be fully and duly perfected.

ARCHBISHOP PHILIP HANNAN, *17 October, 1963*

In certain parts of this schema on the Church there is wanting, in my humble judgment, a consideration of the "non-ideal" conditions in many places in which the greater part of the population is non-Catholic.

For example, in chapter nine on the relation between Church and State, principles are described which are effective when the condition of the relation between Church and State is best, indeed even perfect. However, these conditions, because of causes flowing from the vicissitudes of history, are found only in a very few nations. Our task, therefore, is to give an exposition of the principles which can be applied to those conditions which, because of the very nature of civil society, are found today in so many nations.

In discussing the relation between Church and State, the following circumstances of civil society must be considered:

1) *The nature of the State today.* The State considers itself neither to be a guardian of morals nor obliged to profess a religion. Indeed, because of the multitude of religions which are professed, or pluralism, very often the State feels that it cannot be the guardian of morals, in the traditional sense. In fact, it would be very dangerous for the Church today to depend upon a particular State as the guardian of morals. Furthermore, heads of modern States do not have as much power as did the kings in the past.

2) *The nature of the role of citizens.* Because of historical reasons, citizens consider themselves to be the source of power. They consider themselves able to elect this or that form of government to rule them and to establish the laws which direct their lives. By no means is it rare that the State, or whatever public power there is, will hardly attempt to regulate morals, unless the public order or the common good demands it. This clearly shows that the citizens want the Church completely separated from the State.

3) Nevertheless, under those conditions in which the Church is entirely

independent of the State, the Church enjoys greater benefits, among which the following can be numbered:

a) The Holy See has full liberty to create dioceses solely according to the spiritual needs of the faithful, without seeking the permission of the State.

b) The Supreme Pontiff can name bishops without consulting the State in any way.

c) Bishops can explain the laws of Christ and deal with social justice without any fear of the State.

d) The laity, knowing that the temporal good of the Church has been laid upon their shoulders, have a great and actual part in its life. They frequently take part in the Mass and the reception of sacraments, and liberally provide money. This most faithful devotion not only leads many young people, boys and girls, to a religious vocation, but also persuades the faithful to provide money so liberally that many charitable institutions of all kinds, as well as school systems, may be erected. In these schools, from elementary through the university, religious instruction is given not only at certain hours, but the spirit of religion is always and everywhere felt by the students who study in these schools under the guidance of religious. This most profound devotion of Catholics, aided by the grace of God, brings about a great number of conversions.

It will also be helpful in this matter to recall the words of Pope Pius XII in his allocution, *Si riesce,* and especially the words of Christ: "A bad tree does not bear good fruit."

Most certainly very grave evils result when there is separation of Church and State, but a free Church can overcome these evils.

From this the need is apparent, in my humble judgment, of proposing principles pertinent to the conditions present between Church and State in many nations so that the kingdom of Christ may more quickly arrive.

ALBERT CARDINAL MEYER, *21 October, 1963*

This chapter on the schema which treats of the People of God makes an excellent presentation of positive teaching on the graces, privileges and prerogatives which all receive who are baptized in Christ.

Nevertheless, this picture of Christian life, though true, is not complete and thus is not realistic. It is incomplete, in my belief, for it fails to recall two facts that are basic in this matter. First: all of us who are called by Christ into the Church are sinners, members of a fallen race. Second: even after our entrance into the Church we remain ever conscious of our weakness, our moral feebleness and, on occasion, our falling into sin. For, as the

Council of Trent states (DB 804): "Those words of the just are both humble and truthful: Forgive us our trespasses."

It is not sufficient, therefore, that our schema limit itself to the privileges conferred on us by God, unless there is a clear exposition also of their relationship to the very grave difficulties involved in leading a truly Christian life while on this earth.

Someone may put the question: "What is this difficulty involved in leading a Christian life?" The difficulty, as we know from experience, is twofold: *Internal:* because there abides in us that tendency to sin which is called concupiscence. Experience furnishes the evidence that it usually does not remain a mere tendency, but translates itself into action. Thus Sacred Scripture insists, "We all offend in many things" (James 3:2). *External:* because there is a devil who, according to the words of St. Peter, "roams around like a lion seeking whom he may devour" (I Peter 5:8).

It is on this account that God in the New Testament always reveals the two contrary aspects of the Christian life, namely, the heavenly and the human. The Christian life, on the one hand, is a sharing in the ineffable richness of Christ; on the other, however, it is a constant struggle against the powers of darkness, "for our wrestling is not against the flesh and blood: but against principalities and powers, against the rulers of the world of this darkness, against the spirits of wickedness in the high places" (Ephesians 6:12).

For this reason the Epistle to the Hebrews portrays Christ to us as a high priest living in the Church, not only in order positively to bestow graces on us, but also in order to share in our weaknesses and to sympathize with those who are in ignorance or error. "For we have not a high priest, who cannot have compassion on our infirmities: but one tempted in all things like as we are, without sin" (Hebrews 4:15).

This awareness of the grave difficulty involved in living the Christian life is evident in the liturgy of the Church. For when the priest celebrates the Sacrifice of the Mass, he asks divine forgiveness for the countless sins, offenses and failings of himself and of all Christian believers. Again, before the Communion, the celebrant likewise asks, unworthy as he is to receive the Body of Christ, that this reception may not work to his judgment and damnation, but may benefit him in soul and body through the loving mindfulness of Christ. And all of this is ratified in the prayer we make each day at the start of a general congregation when we say: "We are at hand, Lord Holy Spirit; we stand here enchained by the dread evil of sin."

The same awareness of the difficulty involved in leading the Christian life in worthy fashion has moved saintly men in the Church to look on themselves as sinners rather than as saints. The words of St. John of the Cross, as he lay on his deathbed, are well known. When his confrères endeavored to comfort him by recalling all his good deeds, he replied, "Don't remind me of my good deeds, for there is no deed of mine which does not now stand witness against me before God."

Wherefore, in order that our schema may reach the hearts of men today —men who are burdened by a sense both of sin and of their own moral weakness—I am emboldened to propose this emendation of the chapter on the People of God. My preference is that before the People of God is described as being without stain or wrinkle, we preface this by a paragraph in which we proclaim to all men, in so many words, that the Church is the household of the Father of mercies in which the failings of prodigal sons are forgiven, their wounds are bound up, their weaknesses are cured and their needs are answered.

In this way, our contemporary world will echo once more with a clear statement of those words once spoken by God: "I have not come to summon the just, but sinners" (Mark 2:17). And the truth proclaimed in the First Vatican Council will be made abundantly clear: "The Eternal Pastor and Shepherd of our souls, in order to render the saving work of redemption a lasting thing, determined to erect holy Church" (DB 1821).

LAWRENCE CARDINAL SHEHAN, *23 October, 1963*

I shall speak in the name of the American bishops who, in their session this week, charged me with the duty of expressing their thoughts about that part of chapter three of the schema on the Church which is found under number 25, page 10, from line 7 to line 22 inclusive.

That part of the text in which the words "unfortunate separation" appear seems to us to need a complete revision. From what has already been said, both inside and outside this hall, it seems perfectly evident that the present text lacks clarity. Some assume that the text treats the relations between Church and State, which to us seems to be entirely false.

First of all, in the third chapter, the duty of the Catholic lay apostolate in the world is treated, the duty, namely, of sanctifying the world and, in this work of sanctification, of avoiding two extremes namely: "on the one hand, confusion or undue mixing of religion and the Church with merely civic matters" and, on the other hand, the separation of these things into two distinct categories, completely separated and profoundly opposed.

The whole question about the relations between the Church and State is of the utmost importance and requires diligence and prudence. The question of the laity is pertinent, and especially pertinent to the whole Church. In this chapter, however, it seems to us that it (the question of Church and State) should not have a place and, especially, it should not be introduced as an aside.

We are convinced, in brief, that the lines cited above on page ten must be revised so that the question about the relation between Church and State may be completely put aside. Otherwise, we think it would be better if the text, or rather that part of the text about which I have spoken, be removed.

As far as I am concerned, moreover, I wish to propose one change. On page six, from line 30 to line 40, the matter about the faithful Christian exercising his own particular mission in the world is discussed.

The word "world" is indeed clarified in the fourth note, which begins in the second last line on page eleven.

I think, however, that it is necessary that the word "world" be even further clarified in this text. Therefore, I propose this change in line forty after the words "they make holy," namely: "For the world must be regarded by Christians under two aspects, just as it was regarded by Christ who saw the world under the command of sin and the hatred of Satan, but He loved the men living in the world and He wished the world to be saved through faith; so also must Christians act. All according to the operation . . . etc."

The reasons for this change are:

1) Thus are clarified both the antithesis of the Christian so much ensnared in the secular life and the mission of the laity in the Church and the end, or aim, of Catholic Action which is that, by the labor of Catholics, everything which surrounds them and which they touch may become Christianized.

2) This change is very . . .

MODERATOR: (11:12 A.M.) Venerable Fathers, please listen for a short time so that I may give an explanation to the Fathers. The change which must be voted on is the change which is indicated on page 7a, number 12, in article 77. In the text, it appears as the last change, but now it must be noted as it is on page 7a, change 12a, which was read by the Secretary General.

SHEHAN: I am finished speaking.

MODERATOR: I beg your pardon, Father; continue to speak, Father. You may speak now, . . .

BISHOP ERNEST PRIMEAU, 23 October, 1963

This concerns the relation between the hierarchy and the laity in the schema on page 10, number 26. In the splendid address which the Supreme Pontiff uttered at the opening of this Council he stressed its pastoral importance.

To reach this goal, in dealing with the laity we have to keep before our eyes the growing concern which the laity has about its proper status in the apostolate of the Church. If this were not done, everything the Council has proposed or established would be spoken to deaf ears. Certainly we must avoid the danger of generalization; nonetheless we can affirm that lay people today, conscious of their capabilities, will not allow themselves to be treated as in past times as merely passive members of the Church, blindly bowing to authority, or as mute sheep.

On the contrary, there are many well-educated faithful who ask to be heard on questions of undertakings in which they have a competence that clerics more often than not lack.

They want to share in the apostolic work of the Church and they certainly intend to do this under the direction of the hierarchy, but not without previously being heard by the hierarchy concerning matters within their competence. They expect the confidence of the hierarchy.

They have a great love for Holy Mother Church and manifest great reverence and confidence towards legitimate authority. They are also aware of their own dignity and competence, however, not only in temporal affairs, but also in the internal life of the Church. Above all, they consider dialogue between themselves and the hierarchy as absolutely necessary for promoting the common good of the Church and for defining the special role of the laity in the apostolate. By divine providence this Ecumenical Council has done a lot to make this dialogue possible. It has given the laity great hope and the opportunity for raising many questions. One important question concerns the definition of the roles of freedom and authority. If the Council does not give an answer to this question, we can doubtless expect 1) a growing bitterness among the laity towards the Church's authority; 2) the growing indifference of laymen who passively keep the laws, but never share in the life and mission of the Church; 3) finally, sad to say, defections from the faith and the Church. The Church needs the help of the laity, especially those who are called "intellectuals," in order to grow. The Church can never use their help and advice unless it acknowledges their legitimate freedom of action, the meaning of "initiative" and is ready to consult them with due respect about matters within their competence.

If we keep all this in mind, it seems that some parts of chapter three hinder more than help the vital apostolate of the laity; for example, especially number 26, page 10. The text is too negative, perhaps too cautious, and too clerical.

The text insists too much on the need of obedience, reverence and subjection and does not sufficiently emphasize proper responsibility and freedom of action, as the proper possession of laity who are true members of the Mystical Body of Christ. Let this constant talk of their duty of subjection and reverence cease—as if their only duty be stated in these terms: believe, pray, pay and obey.

Let us not forget that the faithful laity honor and love the Church just as we do. However, they also yearn to share actively in the mission of the

Church, to be known not as mere representatives of the clergy and hierarchy, but as having their own unique part in the mission of the Church as laity whose proper role is defined and approved by the Church.

All this would have little value unless in this fundamental schema we affirm our sincere acknowledgment of the competency of the laity, show our readiness to hear them, and, above all, acknowledge clearly their right to exercise their proper spiritual activity in freedom and mutual confidence with hierarchical authority. In this sense, we, the bishops, must further expand and evolve the directives mentioned in number 26, so that in each diocese there would be a structure by which the laity, especially the more educated laity, could communicate with the bishop and pastors. Today I speak for the laity, and in the same way some other bishops have spoken for them, presenting their desires to the Council. But I also ask the Fathers to hear the laity, namely, that the auditors here in the aula would speak in the name of all the laity.

BISHOP ROBERT TRACY, 24 *October*, 1963

In the name of the bishops of the United States of North America, I want to suggest that in speaking of the People of God, we put clearer emphasis on the equality of everyone in the Church with no distinction on account of race.

Here are the reasons for the suggestion.

1) If the Council does this, it will more concretely and explicitly show that equality which all the members of the People of God rightfully possess. Furthermore, all discrimination based on race alone is completely irreconcilable with the truth which we believe, namely, that God has created all men with equal rights and dignity.

2) In this way we shall be more fully in harmony with that text of St. Paul where he wants to insist that all opposition between "Jew" and "Greek" has now disappeared. For it is more accurate to understand the terms "Jew" and "Greek" here as referring to distinction on the basis of religion, culture and race, rather than nation.

3) Because of the present situation in the United States and also, *mutatis mutandis*, in other areas, the Council Fathers are often faced with this problem of race prejudice. The bishops of the United States have repeatedly issued public statements explaining this doctrine in an effort to teach the people social justice and love. Now, if the Council issues a solemn and concrete affirmation of the equality of all races, it will greatly help the bishops to teach their people more effectively.

4) Even though these problems are confined to certain geographical

areas, their echo and effect make this an international problem worthy of action by the Council.

5) Such a statement by the Council would bring great consolation to all those who are deprived of equal liberty and humiliated and oppressed under the yoke of prejudice for no other reason than their race.

6) A statement of this kind from the Council will also provide the doctrinal basis for future decrees which will perhaps apply the principle of equality of all peoples more fully and in greater detail to modern needs. Therefore, for these reasons which concern a problem which is pastoral in a very special way and is urgent in our times, we ask that a solemn dogmatic declaration of the equality of all men, of whatever people or race, be included in the chapter on the People of God.

BISHOP JOHN RUSSELL, *30 October, 1963*

May it be permitted to me briefly to speak in the name of many North American bishops in regard to the introduction of article 28, "The Vocation to Holiness in the Church," and article 29, "The Universal Vocation to Sanctity."

First. It seems to me that it would have been better if the Council had said something about the holiness of the Church itself before it considered the vocation of the faithful in the Church to holiness.

The reason is because in today's world it is asked how and in what sense the Church is holy, since there are in it also sinners, a fact well-known to many, especially those who do not acknowledge the Church.

Many believe that the Church has an ambiguous and double norm, embracing within its bosom, for example, those who preach about austerity, but who are in no way austere; Christians who do not even exercise the virtues of the pagans; members who, at least in practice, seem to profess a faith separated from charity; scandals among those who have vowed themselves to perfection; social discrimination and many other things similar to these.

And all these things are found in that Church which says that it is divine and which, in the First Vatican Council, asserted of itself, "to the Catholic Church alone do all those things pertain which, so many and so wondrous, have been divinely disposed for the evident credibility of the Christian faith. And indeed the Church itself, because of its high degree of holiness and fecundity, unexhausted in all good things, is a great and perpetual motive of credibility and an irrefutable witness of its divine mission."

I would speak of the holiness of the Church not only as a motive of credibility, but precisely about the essential holiness in the Church itself which is an institution, indeed is Christ Himself.

The Church is holy because it is the Body of Christ. Its author is God. It is consecrated to God who is peculiarly present to it and in it. The proper work of the Church is salvation, the union of man with God in Christ, the communication of grace through the Sacraments, through preaching of the Word and through the presence of Christ in it.

Finally, just as Christ Himself in His holy humanity was an instrument joined to divinity for the sanctifying of men, so the Church, as the true continuation of Christ in the world, is the salutary instrument of the sanctification of the faithful and their union with God.

Therefore, it seems to me that, in the twenty-eighth article of the introduction, the holiness of the Church ought briefly to be explained before there is discussion of the vocation on the part of its members to holiness.

Second. In article 29 there ought to be defined more clearly and more accurately the true sense of the vocation to the perfection of holiness of the faithful who are pilgrims in this life. For the very concept of perfection involves some difficulty which also, unless I am mistaken, is found in the description of perfection in note one, page 23, where one reads: "That one is perfect who lacks nothing in the moral order; of whose fullness God Himself is the exemplar."

According to Origen, "perfection is similitude with Christ when someone has so adapted himself in all things to the Word and Wisdom of God, that there is nothing in him which would detract from this similitude." According to Marcion, perfection signifies a full and absolute purity from evil affections. According to St. Thomas in the *Summa Theologica,* perfection *per se* and essentially consists in charity which, according to all its fullness, is a precept. According to those authors, it seems that perfection is a simple and absolute quality.

We know well, however, from those who have written on ascetical matters, that it is common doctrine that no human creature living on earth, with the unique exception, because of special privilege, of the Blessed Virgin Mary, has attained absolute perfection, that is, that no one has been able to keep himself immune from all imperfections before perfect union with God in the beatific vision.

Every creature must be perfected and, indeed, is perfect inasmuch as it attains its end. Hence, absolute perfection signifies the actual acquisition of that very end which for the Christian is had only in heaven where God is possessed through pure love.

The perfection of holiness in this life, therefore, is a relative perfection, that is, something not static and already completed, but dynamic and perfectible. Since it is relative, it can have increase. All the faithful can progress in holiness and, indeed, must. But, in line 24, holiness is represented as the very same thing as a life fully Christian with perfect charity. Page 20, line 20, speaks of the *vocation* to perfect holiness, but now in this place there is introduced an *obligation* to the highest holiness—perfect charity.

However, in practice and in a rather ancient tradition, holiness seems to be understood in a threefold manner, namely, of those among whom, perhaps, very many of the faithful would be numbered who live in the state of grace and hence united with God, fulfilling that precept of Christ: "Who has my commandments and keeps them, he it is who loves me."

There is another part of the faithful which not only does not want to offend God, but also wishes to serve and please Him, and who in their own way can say with Christ: "I always do those things which are pleasing to Him [the Father]."

Finally, there are those relatively few—for example, St. John Leonard, St. John Vianney, and the newly beatified John Nepomucene Neumann, a bishop in the United States—who choose to dedicate themselves wholly and totally to the love of God through heroic charity, through heroic holiness.

If it is inferred that the obligation to perfect holiness is demanded of all, it will seem that those who do not strive for perfect and heroic holiness are violating a grave obligation and, therefore, are sinning.

The possibility of such confusion should be eliminated from the schema. The sentence, "May all the faithful extend the powers which they have received according to the measure of the gift of Christ to perfect charity" in line 31 of page 18, is to be more clearly and more fully explained.

I propose that line 23 of page 18 be so amended: "Wherefore it is known to all that the Lord has called all disciples to seek the holiness of a Christian life in charity."

In this way, I think, the words placed in the end will be in better harmony: "Therefore, may all the faithful extend the powers which they have received according to the measure of the gift of Christ to perfect charity, so that, following His image, they will devote themselves to the glory of God and the service of their neighbor with all their heart."

Dogmatic Constitution on the Church

✠ COMMENTARY by Rev. Godfrey L. Diekmann, O.S.B.

Whatever the judgment of history about the relative priorities of importance to be attached to the 16 documents promulgated by Vatican II, there can be no question that the Fathers of the Council themselves viewed the Constitution on the Church as central to as well as ideologically normative for all the rest.

By the second session in the fall of 1963, after the floundering start of the first session when the very vastness of the proposed agenda had threatened to suffocate hope of significant accomplishment, it had become clear to all that the Church itself was to be the principal theme of the Council's concern. Pope Paul VI, in his opening speech to the second session on September 29, gave this general conviction point.

> There can be no doubt whatever of the Church's need and duty to give a more thorough definition of herself. . . . The Council, therefore, has four objectives: the knowledge, or if you prefer, the awareness of the Church; its reform; the bringing together of all Christians in unity; the dialogue of the Church with the contemporary world.

As a matter of fact, all 16 documents issued by the Council do fit into one or the other of these four categories: all are ecclesiological.

This decision to concentrate attention on the Church was, in itself, already a heartening evidence of *aggiornamento*, for ecclesiology had easily been topic number one in Catholic theological thought of the twentieth century. Because it had likewise been to the fore in Protestant theology, the pronouncement of the highest Catholic magisterium on the subject would inevitably prove of ecumenical significance.

The Constitution on the Church was, therefore, deliberately intended as the foundation-document of Vatican II. In the words of Paul VI, its purpose is

> to examine the intimate nature of the Church and to express in human language, so far as possible, a definition which will best reveal the Church's

real, fundamental constitution and manifest its manifold mission of salvation.

The Pope thereupon referred explicitly to "the magnificent developments" of the theological doctrine on the Church

which merit the attentive consideration also of our separated brethren, and which, as we ardently hope, may make the path toward common agreement easier. (Opening address to Session II, September 29, 1963)

To appreciate the breadth of these developments, one need but compare the Constitution with Pope Pius XII's encyclical on the Mystical Body (1943). The contrast, both in approach and content, is so striking that one is apt to forget what a remarkable breakthrough the encyclical had been for its day, only two short decades previously. Although it reflected all too closely the ecclesiology of Bellarmine, conditioned by the sixteenth-century polemical anti-Protestant concern to stress the visible structure of the Church and the necessary role of the hierarchy—above all, the Roman Pontiff—it had, at the same time, given official voice and sanction to the rediscovery of a Pauline concept of the Church as the Body of Christ which for nearly a generation had characterized and given new vitality to theological and apostolic circles in the Roman Catholic communion.

Even more significant is the fact that these "magnificent developments" took visible shape in the space of two years of conciliar work. Nothing the Council has done so vividly illustrates the reality of the "new Pentecost" as the progressive transformation of its text on the Church. The first draft did not even do justice to some of the advances embodied in Pius XII's encyclical, but seemed rather a throwback to the "*De Ecclesia*" treatment customarily found in manuals of apologetics. Its eleven chapters, beginning with "On the Nature of the Militant Church," deserved the charge of ecclesiastical "triumphalism" which Bishop De Smedt of Bruges, in a ringing speech which echoed around the world, lodged against it.

Nevertheless, in all fairness it must be asked whether the theological commission which produced the first text, while admittedly not representative of the more progressive theological thought of our times, did not, by and large, mirror the initial mind of the majority of the Council Fathers. It is the profound reorientation of thinking of the bishops of the world during the Council itself which constitutes "the miracle of Vatican II"; and this found its most remarkable witness in the Constitution on the Church.

Four factors (besides, of course, the Holy Spirit to whom we look first of all when there is question of a "new Pentecost") may be cited as contributory to the change of outlook resulting in the final version of the Constitution.

1) The bishops of the world discovered at Vatican II the catholicity of

the Church. They experienced the living, existential Church, with its staggeringly diversified problems and needs and hopes. Ecclesiology could never again be for them a schoolbook abstraction, described in neat categories. The living Church, in the person of its bishops, had, as never before in its history, become aware of itself, its nature and mission, and each succeeding week of common effort and personal contacts brought new disclosures. The Council itself was, in effect, the most potent catalyst for a truly contemporary ecclesiology.

2) This experience of the living Church and consequent disenchantment with some of the traditional textbook formulations led to increasing openness to present-day theological and biblical developments. This was noticeable not only in the growing influence of competent exponents of modern ecclesiological scholarship among the bishops in the hall of the Council, but also in a change of attitude toward the *periti*. Rahner, Ratzinger, Congar, Philips and others talked to packed auditoriums. Their lectures, plus the numerous and eagerly read memoranda that appeared whenever major matters came up for conciliar discussion, amounted to a crash program of theological formation.

3) Likewise effective of reorientation of ecclesiological thought during the Council itself was the felt presence of the Protestant and Orthodox observers. Thus Dr. Kristen Skydsgaard of Copenhagen, of the Lutheran World Federation, in response to the Holy Father's words of welcome to the observers on October 17, 1963, declared, "The doctrine of the Church is the point at which all our divisions culminate, so that it is precisely here that they seem unsurmountable, despite our sincere efforts to understand each other." He went on to plead for "a biblical theology which concentrates on the study of the history of salvation in the Old as well as in the New Testament . . . a concrete and historical theology nourished by the Bible and the teaching of the Fathers." His talk, widely publicized, had acknowledged impact. It was, in substance, echoed repeatedly on the Council floor in criticism of the proposed schema.

4) A fourth factor, of more immediate influence, was the ecclesiology implicit in the schema on the liturgy whose protracted discussion preceded the discussion of the schema on the Church. Already Pius XII, in his encyclical on the Mystical Body, had given credit to the liturgical movement for having brought the doctrine of the Church as the Body of Christ to the fore of Catholic consciousness. It had been in the communal action of eucharistic celebration, in common prayer and song at the tables of the Word and Bread that insights were gained and convictions firmed which were then written into the schema by the preparatory liturgical commission composed of representative leaders of the liturgical renewal throughout the world.

Among instances of such ecclesiological themes in the liturgy text, the following are perhaps most pertinent. The importance of community celebration—the entire body, and each of its members, is to be actively engaged. This underscores the dignity of responsible Christian personhood, based on the sacraments of Baptism and Confirmation, whereby the person has a true share in the priesthood of Christ. The liturgy is not the preserve of the clergy, but the action of the whole body to whom the priest *ministers* the mysteries. Christ is present in the worshipping assembly, in the proclaimed word, in the sacramental action. It is in the liturgy, above all, that the priestly work of Christ is continued, His paschal mysteries become operative. The Eucharist— Bread *and Word*—is the sign of the Church's unity, and effects it: at the tables of the Word and Bread, Christ wills to create His people into a brotherhood of faith and love. The local community gathered around its bishop or his priest-representative for eucharistic worship is, therefore, the preeminent self-manifestation of the Church: diocese and parish are representative of and, pastorally speaking, the most important realization of the universal visible Church. As a consequence, while substantial unity must be maintained, reasonable diversity in rite and adaptation to given cultural structures are imperative. Territorial groups of bishops can best judge about such needs, and therefore some degree of decentralization of liturgical legislative powers is a precondition of meaningful reform.

Because the liturgy schema was discussed so thoroughly and at such great length prior to the debate on the Church, the Council Fathers not only were bound to become aware of this implicit ecclesiology, but, by accepting the schema, they approved it. Hence the decisive intervention of Archbishop Martin of Rouen, voicing the discontent of many, that the ecclesiology of the original text on the Church was inferior to and not in harmony with the understanding of the Church already adopted in the schema on the liturgy.

And, in all this, one needs to keep constantly in mind that these new insights into the nature of the Church and its mission, which were embodied in the Constitution on the Sacred Liturgy and subsequently in the Constitution on the Church, were not the product primarily of abstract theological speculations, but rather of grass-roots spiritual or pastoral renewal, guided by the close collaboration of its leaders with the live contemporary biblical and patristic movements. The Church had indeed come to life in the heart of men in the table-community of the Word and Sacrament. It was a presently lived, experiential and developing ecclesiology, though channeled by deliberate and competent reference to its sources in Bible and Tradition, that gained authoritative sanction at Vatican II.

We might say, therefore, that one of the most significant features of the Constitution on the Church is its predominantly inductive approach (except, perhaps, in its third chapter) in contrast to the more destructive method that had characterized theology ever since scholastic times. God's mystery of love, taking visible form in history, in the experiences not least of all of our own day, furnishes the outlines of the ground plan which the document attempts to describe. The fact of adopting this approach merits praise, but a certain quality of fluidity that inevitably attaches to it does make a summary analysis such as the present more difficult. Rather than systematically examine chapter after chapter, I shall, therefore, limit myself to sketching the remarkable new synthesis which the Constitution achieves between a number of ecclesiological aspects and elements which, for all too long, have seemed not only disparate, but to a greater or lesser degree in factual opposition to each other.

Communion of Divine Life and Society

First and foremost, and basic to the understanding of the document and all its parts, is the priority which the Constitution gives to the innermost nature of the Church as a communion of divine love and life. Pius XII's encyclical had begun with a chapter on the nature of the Church militant. The Constitution heads its first chapter "The Mystery of the Church." That is to say, the Church itself is, above all, the *mysterium* of which St. Paul speaks, the reflection and realization in time of that mystery of fellowship that exists in the trinity of divine persons. Boldly reverting to an earlier usage of the term, the Constitution speaks of the Church as "the sacrament," the sign or instrument of God's loving and life-giving action among men. It is not, in the first place, a visible structure with divine content, not a *societas perfecta*, the "perfect society" that by Christ's ordinance is able to dispense grace, but a communion of human persons united by the Father in faith, hope and love through the indwelling of the Spirit who communicates to them a sharing in the saving death and resurrection of the Son. God's love, creative of communion, made visible historically in the person of Christ, continues to be made visible through Christ's actions in visible sacraments, initially and incorporatively by Baptism, and most fully by the Eucharist which is the sacrament of unity, formative of Christ's Mystical Body. By His sacrament of Holy Orders, Christ chooses some members of that body as deacons, priests and bishops, to minister to the community—more specifically, to be the chief visible representatives of His own teaching, governing and sanctifying activity in and through His Spirit in His body, the Church, until His return in glory. They do not constitute the unifying element of the Church. Rather, He who unifies is the Spirit of Love who is constantly creating the community of love through the eucharistic sacrament of love, at which priest and bishop preside as symbols of that unity which is effected by the Spirit through their ministry.

In a word, the Constitution gives emphatic priority to what Père Congar calls the ontology of grace over its organizational structures and hierarchical offices. The Church is an event; it is God's plan of salvation now taking place. Structure, the distinction into laity and hierarchy, however essential because willed by Christ and demanded by the interrelation of a community of persons, is secondary to and at the service of the interior communion of love and truth and shared divine life. "For Christ has bought it [the Church] for Himself with His blood, has filled it with the Spirit *and* provided it with those means that befit it as a visible and social union" (n. 9). The Church is a society, hierarchically structured; but it is the communion of grace that gives the structure meaning and spells its purpose and enriches it with life.

The prior significance of the Church's nature as communion over her outward structuring as society, seems to be suggested even in the arrangement of the chapters of the Constitution. If this is an accident, it can only be called a happy one. The first two and the final two chapters, beginning and end, as well as the fifth chapter in the central part, speak of the Church as the Mystery of grace in its various dimensions. As it were, they surround and help interpret the third, fourth and sixth chapters which deal more specifically with the Church's component members and their social relations to each other. But even in these three chapters the primacy of grace and the interior structuring through Christ's action in the sacraments underlies all.

These are not mere academic matters nor a question of juggling theological concepts into proper sequence. Attaching practical priority to juridical structures and hierarchical government has been, through history, the chief temptation of the Church and surrendering to that temptation in greater or less degree is the chief reason why the "holy" Church has always been "in need of being purified" (n. 8). It should give us pause that the majority of heresies through the centuries were "spiritualist" in purpose, that is, provoked by what its leaders considered an imbalance in favor of the outward, juridical and hierarchical structures on the part of the contemporary Church. It is one of the great tragedies of history that the Protestant Reformers' stress on the "pneumatic" of inner and spiritual nature of the Church (because not recognized soon enough for the sound Catholic doctrine that it is) led to their severance from the structure of the Church, which, of course, is equally essential, but nevertheless in a subsidiary role. Vatican II at long last is trying to make amends and redress the balance.

Structure has gained primacy when, for instance, the image which our faithful have of their bishops is more associated with his desk at the chancery than with the altar of sacrifice; or when the predominant image which those outside the Church have of it is in terms of affluence and institutions and power structure. Not thus, especially not in our times, is the Church "a sign to the nations." As in the case of all symbols, the institutional nature of the Church both reveals and veils its inner reality. By our giving it priority, the veiling has becoming an obscuring, often beyond possibility of recognition by men of good will. By condemning such ecclesial materialism and by restoring primacy to the community of love—thereby effectively substituting the ideal of the "Church that serves" for the "Church that reigns"—the Council has perhaps taken its most momentous step toward the renewal of the Church according to the image of Christ "the Servant." One of the most moving phenomena of the Council was the constantly swelling chorus pleading for more decisive identification of the Church with the poor, God's *anawim*. One must be grateful that this found expression in the very first chapter of our document. The Church that not merely serves the poor, but is poor will not likely be bothered much by temptations to triumphalism—or the second temptation of Christ.

The People of God and Mankind

After several decades of concentration on the image of the Church as the Body of Christ, or the Mystical Body, theologians toward the end of the thirties began to exploit in earnest the biblical data on the people of God. As Pius XII, in his encyclical, gave authoritative voice to the understanding of the former, so the Council reflected contemporary emphasis on the latter. Scripture uses multiple images to suggest the inexhaustible riches of the Mystery which is the Church, the more important of which are enumerated by the Constitution. By giving preferential treatment to the concept of the People of God, the Council, in effect, tells us that this image proclaims aspects of the Church which deserve more explicit attention on our part today. To cite but several: The Church as the People of God of the New Testament underscores the Church's continuity with the People of God in the Old Dispensation. The People of God are a pilgrim people, a people on the march, whose full citizenship and goal are in heaven: that is to say, the eschatological nature of the Church comes clearer. Most importantly, People of God, by comparison to Mystical Body, demands a more personalist emphasis: a people is constituted of persons, each of whom has an active and specific function for the well-being of the whole. The expanded description of the Church as the People of God enabled the Council to underscore the dignity and critical value of free and responsible personhood of every son of God—and perhaps this may, in the long run, prove the most significant single contribution of the entire Vatican II. "The status of this people is that of the dignity and freedom of the sons of God, in whose hearts the Holy Spirit dwells as in His temple, and whose new commandment is to love as Christ loved us" (n. 9).

This people is a "messianic people" (the term is completely new in official Church documents) which, although it "does not actually include all men . . . is nonetheless a most certain seed of unity, hope and salvation for the whole human race . . . an instrument for the redemption of all" (n. 9).

As is well known, Pius XII, in his encyclical on the Mystical Body, starting from the premise of the Church as a visible society, identified that body with the Church Militant and enumerated three conditions of "really" (*reapse*) being a member of the Church: regeneration in the waters of Baptism; profession of the true faith; submission to legitimate authority. A person is either a member or a non-member. The latter, without distinction as to whether he is a baptized Christian or a pagan, is at best "directed to" (*ordinari ad*) the Mystical Body if, namely, he has a desire (at least implicit) of belonging to the Church.

By starting from a different premise, not primarily from the Church as a visible society but as a communion of life and love, the Council could bring long-overdue nuances into this harsh exclusivism, which smacked so embarrassingly of spiritual triumphalism. It deliberately avoided the word "member" since this had contributed to the sorry impasse. In what is doubtless the most important single textual change of the whole document, it states that "the one Church of Christ . . . *subsists in* the Catholic Church, which is governed by the successor of Peter and by the bishops in his communion." (The earlier text had read: "The one Church of Christ . . . *is* the Catholic Church. . . .") And it goes on to say that "Many elements of sanctification and truth may be found outside of its visible structure, which, as gifts belonging to the Church of Christ, are forces impelling toward Catholic unity" (n. 8). The Church of Christ is, therefore, a broader concept than the historical "Roman Catholic Church," which latter is its visibly concrete realization, its "sacrament," or sign.

While Catholics are said to be "fully incorporated"—although, if they lack charity, only "bodily" so—"all who believe in Christ, and indeed the whole of mankind belong to it or are related to it in various ways, for all men are called by the grace of God to salvation" (n. 13). The Constitution then proceeds to specify some of the "elements of sanctification and truth" which are found in other Christian communions. These latter are called, again for the first time in official Catholic statements, "Churches or ecclesial communities" (n. 15), since it is in and through them that their communicants possess the "elements of sanctification and truth" by which they are "united" to the Catholic Church. Non-Christians—Jews, Moslems, and all who, through no fault of their own, do not know the Gospel of Christ or His Church—all in varying degrees have some "elements of salvation and truth" which "are looked upon by the Church as a preparation for the Gospel" (n. 16) and by which they belong in some way to the Church and can be saved.

The Decree on Ecumenism was to spell out in greater detail this more positive understanding of "outside the Church there is no salvation." But neither it nor the Constitution on the Church purports to solve the difficult problem of how those who have not even heard of Christ can be said to have "the faith that justifies." They have left that for future theologians to wrestle with, and already theological journals are echoing merrily with the din of battle. Perhaps the entire question can ultimately be better clarified if the Church be not taken as the point of departure—with consequent evaluation of which of the Church's "elements of sanctification and truth" are found outside her visible communion—but rather Christ Himself, who by His incarnation became the second Adam, the first fruit, and the first "of many brethren."

In any event, the Constitution has achieved the beginning of a "synthesis" between People of God and all mankind, which future development of doctrine can bring to ecumenical fruition. In the meanwhile, we can rejoice to know that we no longer have to feel secretly guilty about regarding our

Christian and even non-Christian neighbor as truly our "brother." The danger of indifferentism, which a large minority of Council Fathers feared, will be non-existent if we pay full value to the Council's further statement, that "whosoever, knowing that the Catholic Church was made necessary by Christ, would refuse to enter it or to remain in it, can not be saved" (n. 14). Moreover, as Auxiliary Bishop Stephen Leven of San Antonio pointedly remarked, it is not in those countries in which religious pluralism prevails that one finds large Catholic membership in the Communist party or a tradition of Sunday church absenteeism. Be that as it may, our history of friendly coexistence among the churches challenges America, more perhaps than any other country, now to carry forward the ecumenical potentialities opened up officially for the first time in this theme on the Constitution.

Laity and Clergy

There seems to be a growing consensus, Catholic as well as Protestant and Orthodox, that the turning point of the entire Council was its decision, contrary to the earlier text of the schema, to insert the chapter on the People of God before that on the hierarchy. Methodologically, of course, this was unexceptionable, for it is logical to treat first of all what a group has in common before describing what distinguishes them one from another. Besides, Christ instructed all His disciples before He chose from among their number the Twelve. But the inversion of the proposed order involved the profoundest ideological orientation as well. It meant, above all, the definite avowal of the priority of the inner nature of the Church as a communion in the spirit of life, truth and love over its external, though essential, structure of government. And it meant, consequently, that government itself can rightly be interpreted only as a function of love. Authority in the Church is itself a gift of the spirit of love; "It is a true service, which in sacred literature is significantly called *diakonia,* ministry"(n. 24).

Centuries-old emphasis on the structural organization of the Church had resulted in a thoroughgoing clericalization which had found its clearest manifestation in the liturgy. It was, therefore, very important that the Council radically abrogated it, first of all, in its Constitution on the Sacred Liturgy. How thoroughly this clericalization, not only in the liturgy but also sociologically, had triumphed can be gathered from its classic expression in the Decree of Gratian (twelfth century): "There are two kinds of Christians. One is consecrated to divine service, contemplation and prayer, the clerics and religious. But there is likewise another type of Christian, the lay man, who is permitted [!] to marry and till the earth." Some of the most lively interventions on the floor of the Council dealt, therefore, with clergy-lay relations. When the full history of the Council will be available, the laity will, no doubt, be heartened to learn of the repeated bursts of applause that greeted the numerous episcopal denunciations of clericalism, "that error which is the source of so much harm," as Bishop Charbonneau of Canada called it. The issue had been squarely set, at length and forthrightly. The second and fourth chapters of the Constitution, expanded further in the subsequent Decree on the Apostolate of the Laity, met it head-on. It must be admitted, however, that the fourth chapter, taken by itself, is disappointingly weak. For when the second chapter, on the people of God, was decided upon, the core of the former treatment of the laity was transferred to it, leaving for chapter four only odds and ends which, because in themselves brief, were then given quantitative padding.

We must therefore look chiefly to chapter two, dealing with the people of God, for the Council's mind on the layman and his role; what is contained in the chapter four presupposes it. Thus, when the Constitution, in chapter four, declares that "what specifically characterizes the laity is their secular nature . . . the engaging in temporal affairs and ordering them according to the plan of God" (n. 31), one could easily, and falsely, conclude that the layman's essential work is limited to the secular field by contrast to the clergy whose work is the ecclesiastical ministry—and we would be right back to Gratian. Chapter two, however, teaches that the entire people of God, laity and clergy, by virtue of their common baptismal consecration have the common essential task of witnessing, sanctifying and ministering. Moreover, "the entire body of the faithful, anointed as they are by the Holy One, cannot err in matters of belief" (n. 12). Sharing in the offering of the Eucharist is the greatest privilege and duty of the layman as well as of the priest, each according to his rank. Layman and priest truly share in the one priesthood of Christ, although in essentially diverse degrees. The essential *generic* work of the layman, too, is therefore ecclesial; it is his essential *specific* task to engage in temporal affairs. And even in the latter capacity his task is ecclesial insofar as, by the competence of his professional engagement, he witnesses to the Church's high regard for the autonomy and goodness of the secular order of values (n. 36). The layman of today, more than ever before, *is* the Church in the world.

> What is to be completely avoided is that the hierarchical structure of the Church appear as an administrative apparatus with no intimate connection with the charismatic gifts of the Holy Spirit which are spread throughout the life of the Church. . . . Each and every Christian has his charism in his daily life for the upbuilding of the Church.

When Cardinal Suenens spoke thus in the second session, few seem to have understood him, for the term "charism" had been traditionally limited to the extraordinary gifts of the Spirit which characterized the early Church. It is a measure of the Council Fathers' willingness to learn that, within a short time, the substance of Suenens' intervention was embodied in the conciliar text, thus opening (by going back to the sources) another rich vein of doctrine conducive to Christian action (n. 12).

Since the charismatic "manifestation of the Spirit is given to everyone for profit," the personal importance and free responsibility of each baptized person must loom large in the over-all task of the "renewal and building up of the Church" (n. 12). The normal apostolate of the laity can no longer be viewed as "a sharing in the apostolate of the hierarchy" (surely, a clericalized notion); it is the rightful obligatory participation in the total mission of the Church. The layman may no longer be defined, as was usually done, by reference to the clergy—"The layman is a non-cleric"—but vice versa. The layman is a baptized Christian; and the hierarchy by divine choice are selected from among the laity, as a pattern to the flock, to lead and serve them so that they may mature unto the full stature of Christ and worthily be called a Church (n. 28).

After all these principles have been clearly established, article 37 gets down to some basic application in practice. The laymen's strengthened sense of personal responsibility, exercised under the leadership of the ordained priest who must willingly employ his "brothers'" prudent advice, allow them "freedom and room for action," and encourage their initiative—this, in the concrete, adds up to the imperative necessity of "familiar dialogue between the laity and their pastors" (n. 37). The key concept, it becomes even clearer, is communication. The highly publicized conciliar declaration about collegiality as applied to bishops must find its analagous counterpart in the diocese and in the parish. But precisely because this goes contrary to the structures of a thousand and more years of predominantly vertical-line procedure, mere words and even optimum good will are insufficient. Structures for dialogue are of the essence: "Let this be done through the organs erected by the Church for this purpose" (n. 37).

Our country, far from suffering the "scandal of the nineteenth century"— the loss of the working man to the Church—was, on the contrary, uniquely fortunate in retaining the loyalty of the millions of immigrant poor who flocked to our shores, and of their sons and grandsons. No doubt, one of the reasons for this grace has been and is their generous involvement in the material upbuilding of the Church. We might say that up to the present they have been engaged largely in the offertory of the sacrifice, in preparing the gifts enabling the Church to accomplish her great work. Their right to engage actively in that work themselves, to enter what had been marked off as the clerical "holy of holies," has now been proclaimed and enjoined by the Constitution. Implementation will, of necessity, vary from country to country, according to prevailing educational, cultural and sociological—and even political—conditions. The word "democratic" does not appear in the document, but neither does "monarchical." And there can be no gainsaying that "the familiar dialogue" it calls for between pastor and people, and its stress on free responsible collaboration, are of democratic rather than monarchical vintage.

Moreover, because of an unparalleled general level of education, the

American Church can now draw upon an abundance of schooled talents among the laity. As a matter of fact, they have long been ready. Had the Council not taken action, one may even speculate whether "the scandal of the nineteenth century" in Europe would not have been succeeded in the twentieth century by the scandal in America of the loss of the educated Catholic. All too often, the spectre of the "trustee system" has been conjured up out of the closet of our past to frighten lay initiative back into his submissive groove. Just possibly, it may, like all "heresies," have had some positive and needed insights that could be of help to us today.

In any case, a tradition of practicing sacramental life, our democratic milieu and an educated laity add up to what appears a uniquely favorable testing ground for translating article 37 into a new structure of clergy-lay collaboration. One can sympathize with the impatience of the laity in dioceses and parishes that, to all intents and purposes, have remained pre-conciliar. Yet the over-all national picture does give ground for optimism. Almost every week the press reports some initiative. And the very variety of the experiments begun or announced—little councils, diocesan synods with lay participation, diocesan and parish senates—is an encouraging sign of creative thought and good will.

Perhaps, also, another "return to the sources," not mentioned by the Constitution, may in time be allowed to furnish yet firmer foundation to familiar clergy-lay dialogue. In the rite of ordination of priests we read: "Not without reason did our Fathers establish that the people, too, be consulted in the choice of those who are to serve at the altar. . . . *This is necessary*, in order that the laity may more readily show obedience to the ordained, since they had assented to his ordination."

Bishops and Pope

The new synthesis effected by the Constitution in the interrelations of pope and bishops has been given the name of collegiality. Chapter three of the Constitution, which treats of it, was intended by the Council Fathers to complete the unfinished business of the First Vatican Council which had defined only the role of the pope. "Continuing in that same undertaking, this Council is resolved to declare and proclaim the doctrine concerning bishops, the successors of the apostles, who together with the successor of Peter, the vicar of Christ, the visible head of the whole Church, govern the house of the living God" (n. 18).

Christ appointed the twelve Apostles, "formed them after the manner of a college or a fixed group" (n. 19), and, in order that this college remain one and undivided, He placed Peter over the other Apostles "as a permanent and visible source and foundation of unity of faith and communion" (n. 18). The bishops of the world, by divine institution, are the successors of this college (n. 20), just as the pope is the personal successor of Peter. With the Roman

Pontiff at its head, the college of bishops has "supreme and full power over the universal Church" (n. 22), the identical supreme and full power which the pope has as the successor of Peter, head of the college of apostles. The pope's leadership, although exercised personally and not dependent on the expressed approval of the college of bishops, is never exercised in isolation from that college. Rather, by the very nature of its divine institution, it "personifies" the college, "personifies" the teaching and ruling Church. Implicitly it is the entire college of bishops which acts through its head, the pope, whenever the latter teaches and rules the Church authoritatively; the head of the college cannot act in isolation from the body, nor can the body of the college act in isolation from its head.

However important these considerations for eventual righting of the excessive centralization that has long characterized the Catholic Church, it is the Council's teaching that "by episcopal consecration, the fullness of the sacrament of Holy Orders is conferred . . . the high priesthood, the supreme power of the sacred ministry" (n. 29), which will effectively eliminate the priority of jurisdictional emphasis that had been largely responsible for the imbalance. Not through a jurisdictional grant from the Holy See, but through the episcopal consecration of the sacrament of Holy Orders—that is, directly as a gift from Christ—does each bishop receive "the fullness of power"—the supreme power of the sacred ministry, together with the office of teaching and governing. Jurisdiction is no more than a function of episcopal Holy Orders, a specification of where and over whom "the fullness of power" may be exercised. By virtue of episcopal Holy Orders, all bishops, whether auxiliary bishops or the Bishop of Rome, have identical "fullness of power." But by Christ's disposition, that fullness of power" is exercised by the successor of Peter, the Bishop of Rome, over the whole Church; his jurisdiction extends over the entire Body; other members of the episcopal college exercise more limited jurisdiction over determined "particular churches" (n. 23) or dioceses.

"In the bishops, for whom priests are assistants, our Lord Jesus Christ, the supreme high priest, is present in the midst of those who believe" (n. 21). Because his consecration makes him a member of the college of bishops, successors of the Apostles, each bishop is obliged not merely to exercise pastoral government over the portion of the people of God committed to him, but "to be solicitous for the whole Church . . . and to instruct his faithful to love the whole mystical body, especially its poor and suffering members" (n. 23). The bishop must be "*in communion* with the head and the members of the college" (n. 21). The diocesan (or parish) boundary lines are not walls of separation. The deepest bond of the college is love, deriving from the Eucharist, "by which the Church lives and grows" (n. 26), and to preside at whose celebration is the chief exercise of the bishop's "stewardship of the grace of the supreme priesthood" (*ibid.*). It is through the Mass, above all, that the entire People of God, as well as each member of the college of bishops, is established in the communion of love with "Your servant, our pope, N., . . .

and with all [bishops] who faithfully teach the Catholic apostolic faith" (Canon of the Mass). A wealthy diocese or parish which has little or no concern for a poor neighboring community, or for the missions or for its city slums, celebrates the Eucharist unworthily. It is guilty of the Body and the Blood of the Lord.

Through its legislation in this same chapter three, the Council also wrote another new chapter of history by restoring the diaconate as "a proper and permanent rank of the hierarchy" (n. 29). It has been, perhaps, too much taken for granted that the functional diaconate will be needed only in mission areas. I venture to think that in less than a generation it will be precisely in our own huge city parishes that the apostolic contribution of the deacon, whether married or no, will be found indispensable.

Local Church and Church Universal

The Constitution on the Sacred Liturgy had, in what are among its most important ecclesiological articles, stated clearly that "the preeminent manifestation of the Church" consists in the local assembly, most especially the eucharistic assembly, in which God's holy people gather around their bishop or his representative, the priest, and thereby "in some manner represent the visible Church throughout the world" (Art. 41, 42). Diocese (or parish) is not merely an administrative division of the Church: it is the Church; it realizes, fully in the case of the diocese, less perfectly in case of a parish (or its equivalent), the concept of the Church. The Church universal is a communion of Churches. Pastorally speaking, however, the local Church is "preeminent."

It must be said that the Constitution on the Church fails to exploit either the theological or the pastoral potentialities of this Pauline and early Christian understanding of Church. Apart from an occasional reference to "local Churches" and a sentence or two in article 28, it devotes only one paragraph explicitly to the subject (n. 26). What it does say is excellent and compelling. It compels us to rethink the structuring of most of our parishes, whose very vastness makes it impossible even for the Eucharist to create of them true communities. As a territorial entity, the parish may be no more than of ecclesiastical origin. But as a *"brotherhood joined together* by the food and blood of the Lord," as a *"community* of the altar" (n. 26), the "parish" (or whatever name the local assembly may have) is of the Lord's institution. The people of God in the New Testament is meant to be, and specifically through the Eucharist is meant to become, *familia tua,* as the Roman Missal in some dozen prayers attests. In the breaking of bread we are to "recognize" Christ and likewise our brothers in Christ. We do not honor the right of every baptized Catholic to participate fully in the Sacrifice-Meal that creates a brotherhood if all we can normally confront him with is "brother anonymous."

Laymen and Religious

The reason I have used these two groups to illustrate a new synthesis achieved by the Constitution should be clear from chapter five, "The Universal Call to Holiness in the Church." As a religious myself, I regret deeply that chapter six, "On Religious," falls short of presenting a really convincing and inspiring rationale of the meaning of religious life and of the role of religious in the world of today (and priests may echo this regret in regard to the Council's treatment of the priesthood, whereas the laity and bishops have been better served). This weakness of chapter six, carried over, it seems to me, into the Decree on the Appropriate Renewal of the Religious Life, furnishes at least partial explanation of the current unrest and uncertainties in many of our religious communities.

Nevertheless, I believe most religious will rejoice that the spiritual arrogance connoted by the term "the state of perfection" or "the state of perfection to be acquired" can no longer be laid to their charge. "In the various classes and differing duties of life, one and the same holiness is cultivated by all" (n. 41). "All the faithful of Christ, of whatever rank or status, are called to the fullness of the Christian life and the perfection of charity" (n. 40). Even poverty, chastity, and obedience are not ideals limited to religious: it is only the means or manner of striving for these ideals that vary and thus give rise to distinctions. In fact, the Constitution hesitates to call this trilogy of virtues "evangelical." It speaks cautiously of "the counsels customarily called 'evangelical'" (n. 39). This caution was primarily due to the warning by exegetes that obedience has not the same warranty from the Sermon on the Mount as the other two. But it would be encouraging to discover that the caution derived also from the conviction of the framers of the text that, in the striving for perfection, justice, humility, truthfulness, sincerity and, above all, charity, are equally "evangelical" and important.

In the enumeration of "classes of people" a last-minute addition, highly welcome, is the mention of "single people" living in the world (n. 41). Again and again, too—and likewise highly welcome—is the clear statement that, by means precisely of their daily professional work, Christians can and should achieve sanctity. This likewise represents a needed synthesis. Sacraments, prayers *and work* are means of holiness.

Heaven and Earth

One of the objections voiced on the floor of the Council against chapter seven was that few Catholics have ever heard of "eschatology," to which, perhaps, the only appropriate reply is: It's about time they learned. But over and above introducing a new term which will sound new to many faithful, this chapter in its contents also strikes a note that had not been clearly heard for centuries, although it sounded with unmistakable clarity in Scripture and patristic writings.

The eschatology to which we have been accustomed is an individualistic one. The treatment of "the four last things" dealt predominantly with an individual's fate in death and the hereafter. Chapter seven wonderfully widens our vision. The Church is the People of God. This people is a pilgrim people. But not only are they on the march to heaven, their true home of the future: "The promised restoration that we are awaiting has already begun in Christ . . . already the final age of the world has come upon us" (n. 48). The Church on earth and the Church in heaven are the identical Church; the new creation has already begun, but will find its full perfection in the glory of heaven. The Church on earth is the Body of the risen and glorious Christ. Already now, therefore, it is an integral part of the heavenly Jerusalem.

The entire chapter is a joyous *sursum corda*—"lift up your hearts." This phrase of the Mass can all the more appropriately be cited because the chapter repeatedly reminds us that it is in and through the Eucharist that the pilgrim people are now already the heavenly race. Christ makes them "partake of His glorious life by nourishing them with His own body and blood" (n. 48). Our every partaking of the Eucharist is a "viaticum," our food for the journey. "Celebrating the eucharistic sacrifice, we are most closely united to the Church in heaven . . . with all the saints" (n. 50).

The people of God on earth must, therefore, be united in love with the saints in glory, must honor them as models pointing us to Christ, and avoid "any abuses, excesses or defects that have crept in here and there" which would detract from "restoring all things to a fuller praise of Christ" (n. 51; cf. article 125 of the Constitution on the Sacred Liturgy).

While thus widening the horizons from an individualistic eschatology to an ecclesial one, the chapter unfortunately does not fulfill the promise inherent in its first paragraph; it does not adequately widen our view to the cosmic eschatology, the restoration of *all* things in Christ, of the entire world as well as the human race. Had it done so more forcefully, the possibility of an escapist interpretation of Christian existence in the world, and even of this chapter—and angelism is an alluring as well as enduring temptation—would have been more effectively forestalled. The scriptural insistence that all things are to be reestablished in Christ faces us squarely with the obligation of our collaborating in that transformation of all things. Though pilgrims in the world, we work also in and for the world. For the cosmos, too, is on pilgrimage, and we are to give it a helping hand until the new heaven and the new earth shall appear.

Mary and the Church

The decision to include the Council's teaching on Mary within the Constitution on the Church rests on the closest vote recorded in Vatican II: 1,114 for;

1,074 against. The opposition feared that failure to devote a separate document to Mary would be interpreted as a downgrading of Catholic devotion to her. Those in favor were equally convinced that only by treating of Mary in the context of the Church would Catholic veneration of her be properly understood and authentically fostered. I am among those who believe that the decision was not only right in itself, but will indeed further a synthesis of Catholic thought that will deepen true devotion to the Mother of God. Moreover, it seems beyond dispute that our past teaching concerning Mary, precisely because it was carried on in too great isolation from its doctrinal matrix, contributed substantially to the criticism (and misunderstandings) on the part of our separated brethren. A new synthesis has, therefore, significant ecumenical bearing.

The text represents a conscious effort at biblical theology. Mary's role is an integral part of God's plan of salvation for the entire People of God. The earliest and consistent patristic theme of Mary as a second Eve supplements this approach. As Eve collaborated in the sin of Adam, so Mary is the "woman" who, in God's plan of restoration, was associated with the saving work of Christ, the second Adam, but always in total subordination to Him, the only source of all grace. "Mary was on earth Christ's generous associate and humble handmaid" (n. 61). Seen in this light, Mary, like the Church itself, can be called our mother, Mother of Men, particularly of the faithful" (n. 54)—a parallelism first expressed by Ambrose and then eloquently developed by Augustine. In Catholic popular devotion, as well as in the more recent theological speculation of those who have been called Marian "maximalists," it was this understanding of Mary— her collaborating in the work of redemption, and her intercessory role—which had predominated to the point of dangerous imbalance.

Our chapter adds the needed complementary emphasis on Mary as the "type" of the Church being herself sanctified. She, too, was redeemed, although in a uniquely special manner as befitted the mother of the Redeemer. By divine disposition free of all sin, she, too, is a daughter of Eve; she, too, can be called a daughter of the Church, the Body of Christ, and its most important member. She is the exemplar of all other members of that body by her receptivity to God's love, above all by her *faith* and *obedience*. Here again the patristic theme of the second Eve applies, this time by contrast. "The knot of Eve's disobedience was untied by Mary's obedience; what the virgin Eve bound through her unbelief, Mary loosened by her faith" (n. 56, quoting Irenaeus). Faith and obedience: these are the virtues by which Mary most perfectly imaged Christ and for which Scripture and the Fathers extol her. These, too, are the chief reasons the liturgy has praised her through the centuries: for she, far surpassing all others, heard the word of God (faith) and kept it (obedience).

Strong criticism was voiced by Council Fathers (among the strongest, to the surprise of many, by several bishops of Latin America) for the excesses that actually obtain in popular devotion to Mary. While urging right devotion, based on Scripture and modelled on the Church's own devotion expressed in her liturgy, our chapter takes cognizance of the fact and underscores the ecumenical harm which such abuses engender. "Let them [theologians and preachers of the divine Word] assiduously keep away from whatever, either by word or deed, could lead separated brethren or any others into error regarding the true doctrine of the Church" (n. 67). Rigorous opposition also developed against employing the term "mediatrix," lest it occasion even the appearance of any diminution of the central Christian belief in the unique mediatorship of Christ. The word, nevertheless, was retained, with an explanation that must be unexceptionable to anyone who accepts the basic Catholic premise of the possibility of human cooperation with divine grace, "which is but a sharing in this one source" (n. 62). There remain those, however, who fear that such contextual explanation will not always be forthcoming in all speaking of Mary as mediatrix. And certainly one may in all loyalty continue to regret that the usage of a word was approved which so easily gives rise to misunderstanding of the quintessence of the Christian message.

Conclusion

Dr. George Lindbeck, a Lutheran observer at the Council, has called the Constitution on the Church "the fullest dogmatic statement on the nature of the Church which has ever been formulated by any Christian body." There is general agreement that it is a good statement. Few question that it could be improved. As a matter of fact, the Decree on Ecumenism and the Pastoral Constitution on the Church in the Modern World have already developed into teaching on specific issues. Many, especially from the Eastern tradition, have pointed out that the role of the Holy Spirit in the life of the Church is not sufficiently stressed or integrated into the total presentation. Others are disappointed that its sacramental emphasis, while sound, was not more explicitly complemented by stress on the Church-formative power of the Word. One might add the regret that, in exploiting the scriptural images of the Church, no attention was paid to what is certainly one of the richest biblical themes of anthropological import: that of *eikon,* or image.

Granting the validity of these criticisms, one must nevertheless be humbly grateful that so much was accomplished by so many, that such a profound reorientation of ecclesiological thought took place in such a short time. The test of the document's potential for renewal consists, however, in whether or not the Constitution will convince the teaching authority of the Church of the need of continued and progressive openness to whatever reorientation may be called for in the future. The document's stress on the image of the pilgrim people should help in this respect. Not enough will have been gained if the post-Trent era will now be matched by a post-Vatican II era. Whatever the excellence of the letter of the Constitution, its spirit demands that it be interpreted as threshold rather than as terminus. A reason for optimism (besides our faith) is the fact that the new orientations embodied in the Constitution, as mentioned earlier, are not so much the product of deductive, abstract speculation, but of a lived experience of the Church. This convinced the Council Fathers that given structures in the Church, however ancient, are not all optimum or immutable. Seeing the Church in a changing world, as they never had seen it before, they realized that willingness to engage in reasonable experiment, to tolerate a certain state of fluidity, is the necessary condition for serving the world—and its men. Genuine essentials must remain, but, even in their case, their relations to each other may have to be varied to meet new challenges.

In effect, therefore, the bishops of the world in the Constitution on the Church have asked us to make an act of faith in the one, holy, catholic, apostolic and changing Church.

II/DOGMATIC CONSTITUTION ON DIVINE REVELATION

Dogmatic Constitution on Divine Revelation
✠ HISTORICAL INTRODUCTION

During the fourteenth congregation, November 7, 1962, the Secretary General announced that, upon completing the discussions concerning the sacred liturgy, the next schema to be introduced would be on the sources of Revelation. Accordingly, Cardinal Ottaviani, president of the theological commission, presented the schema to the Council Fathers at the beginning of the nineteenth congregation, November 14. In his introductory remarks the Cardinal-Secretary of the Holy Office recognized the controversy over the schema that was already raging in the Eternal City. He said, "There are a number of schemata in circulation which oppose that which I am about to introduce."

The debate over the schema proved to be divisive throughout the six working congregations that followed. A total of 105 Council Fathers spoke on the subject. It soon became apparent that on this subject, as in the case of the vernacular in the liturgy, positions were being polarized. Abbot Christopher Butler, O.S.B., called these days "the central drama of the first session." One group, whose members defended the schema, held fast to a somewhat narrow, scholastic and manualistic attitude concerning the study and interpretation of Sacred Scripture and Tradition. The other group proved to reflect a majority opinion and this group, according to Bishop André Charue, one of the vice presidents of the theological commission, regarded the schema as "couched in unduly scholastic terminology and as being not very ecumenical in its tone."

After a somewhat heated discussion on the schema in general throughout five congregations, most observers realized that the schema was in trouble, despite the admonition of Cardinal Ottaviani that "here we have the right to propose amendments, and then only on the schema proposed, not on any other." Modern biblical scholarship, quietly at work within the Church since Pius XII's masterful encyclical *Divino Afflante Spiritu*, issued in 1943, was carrying the day. Leaders such as Cardinals Léger, König, Alfrink, Suenens and Bea all reflected the blunt conclusion voiced by Cardinal Ritter: The schema must be rejected. Bishop James Griffiths added the adverb: It must be rejected *radicaliter*.

During the twenty-third congregation the Council of Presidents asked the Council Fathers to vote on the schema as a whole. The result was a confirmation of Pope John's *aggiornamento:* 1,368 voted against the text, and 822 voted in favor of keeping it as a document for further debate. Although the majority failed to muster the necessary two-thirds majority, it was obvious to all that a stalemate had been reached. Accordingly, on the following day Pope John stepped into the impasse. The Secretary General announced that the Holy Father had turned the schema on the sources of Revelation over to a mixed commission made up of members from both the Theological Commission and the Secretariat for Promoting Christian Unity. The co-presidents of this mixed commission would be Cardinals Bea and Ottaviani.

This mixed commission went to work immediately. It held an organizational meeting at five o'clock in the afternoon of November 25 and agreed to meet every Tuesday, Thursday and Saturday evening throughout the remainder of the session. The subcommission consisted of 12 cardinals, 25 bishops and 7 *periti,* one of them being Father Karl Rahner, S.J. The most significant decision that came out of this meeting was the agreement to change the name of the schema from "On the Sources of Revelation" to simply "On Divine Revelation." This was interpreted at the time by one American bishop as a "very definite concession to the viewpoint of the Unity Secretariat and the 'liberal' group generally."

The revised schema was approved by the Central Coordinating Commission on April 22, 1963, and distributed to the Council Fathers. However, it was never introduced on the Council floor during the second session because of the press of other schemata. Nonetheless, it was not a "forgotten" matter. In his closing address at the end of that session, Pope Paul VI noted that "other questions are still subject to further studies and discussions" and expressed the hope "that the third session in the autumn of next year will bring them to completion." In regard to this schema, Pope Paul went on to say:

> Such, for example, is the question of divine revelation to which the Council will give a reply which, while defending the sacred deposit of divine truth against errors, abuses and doubts that endanger its objective validity, at the same time will provide directives to guide biblical, patristic and theological studies which Catholic thought, faithful to ecclesiastical teaching and vitalized by every good modern scientific tool, will want to promote earnestly, prudently and with confidence.

Between the sessions the Council Fathers again submitted their observations on the second schema which resulted in the Central Coordinating Commission requesting another draft of the text. This text was approved on July 3, 1964, and distributed to the Council Fathers through the mails. Commenting on the three drafts of the text, the German theologian, Father I. Neuner, S.J., observed that the schema on divine revelation "in the first draft, became a symbol of disagreement; in the second, an attempt at reconciliation; in its third form, a positive exposition of the nature of revelation and its presence in the Church."

This third draft was in the hands of the Council Fathers when it was introduced on the floor during the ninety-first congregation of the third session, September 30, 1964. Two members of the mixed commission which drafted the schema made introductions. Bishop Franjo Franić presented the minority report, assuring the audience that theological conservatives die hard, and Archbishop Ermenegildo Florit offered the majority report, reflecting an ability to accept change when it is presented on the firm foundation of scholarship.

Throughout the next five congregations, 69 Fathers rose to speak on the new schema. Their remarks were in striking contrast to the previous debate on the subject. A few, to be sure, continued to oppose the schema, but this time they were the conservatives rather than the liberals. By and large, most of the speakers (who obviously had done considerable homework on the subject) asked that the "open" approach of the schema be strengthened rather than weakened. The venerable and lovable old Scripture professor, Ernesto Cardinal Ruffini, did not in the least modify his position of opposition to the schema. Again the session closed without a vote on the schema concerning divine revelation. There was to be a fourth session, and again promises were given that the schema would be brought back for a vote.

During the first session, four American prelates spoke in the Council hall on the subject of revelation. On the day the schema was introduced, November 14, Cardinal Ritter declared that it must be rejected. He offered three reasons. First, he said, the schema lacked any evident usefulness, containing "nothing new, no accommodation which renders either Christian doctrine or Christian life of greater significance or efficacy for modern man." Secondly, he felt, ambiguity abounded in the schema, observing that "nothing is said that is clear and determined." Finally, he urged, the greatest weakness was the fact that "the whole schema is clouded in pessimism and a negative spirit. Stating nothing explicitly, it seems to affix doubt and undue suspicion on a great part of the more recent New Testament exegesis." He concluded with the following admonition:

> If there are no solutions, indeed, let the Council say so or remain quiet. If errors exist, let the Council remonstrate and even condemn them. But let the Council abstain from statements that lack any use, imperil unity and engender suspicions. Such things can only implant fear and disgust toward Scripture and theology in the faithful, rather than love and reverence.

Two days later the Cardinal of Los Angeles rose to state a position similar to the one enunciated by Cardinal Ruffini. Cardinal McIntyre came out strongly in defense of the schema.

> . . . this schema really contains positive action aimed at correcting new theories which are not acceptable—and action against scientific theories

which should be considered only as theories. Therefore, the schema should be accepted. The intention of the Council certainly is not to introduce new theology. Not only are [new theories] numerous, but they also exceed the present state of human understanding, which is extremely limited in things divine.

The Cardinal thereupon launched into a discussion on the value of faith, explaining its nature and importance for the Christian theologian and philosopher. His closing remarks, readily accepted by one and all, had little relation to the subject under discussion. "Faith," he said, "must hold some place in our investigation of truth. Gladly, with patience and serenity, we must accept in faith divinely revealed mysteries and dogmas of the Church."

In a written intervention on the same schema, Cardinal McIntyre brilliantly summarized the Church's teaching on the two sources of revelation as contained in most of the manuals of the seventeenth, eighteenth and nineteenth centuries. He seemed to argue for the preservation of the two sources by giving a historical synopsis of their development in the apostolic Church. His own deep respect for the law is reflected in the following words he penned concerning the relationship between the two sources and the natural law:

Let us recognize that Tradition and the written word contain some principles of the natural law. The law itself prescribed and instituted the order of nature. Law and order of nature were instituted by God for the common good of men. The basis or font of the order of nature is the natural law— the law according to which God created nature. By this law or order we, in turn, distinguish good from evil, that is, conformity or nonconformity with the divine will. Obedient to this law, we fulfill the obligation of grace due to God and conform our mind to the law of the natural order. Therefore, it follows that the divine disposition, that is, the antecedents of Tradition and Scripture in the natural law, constitute a law binding all men, even the mental errors and the voluntary faults which history has incited.

In his observations, stated in the aula on November 19, Cardinal Meyer took cognizance of the two opposing views and said he felt that they were "the cause of very great anxiety to many Fathers." He went on to say that this difference "has its root in the fact that many believe the method of setting forth the teaching employed in this schema does not adequately correspond to the aim of the Council." He agreed with Abbot Butler that the Council "ought to display to the world unanimity in so serious a matter." He agreed, too, with Cardinal Bea that "a new schema be drafted with the assistance of theologians and exegetes of various nations and tendencies." Finally, he said, he would ask the Council to do these three things:

First: Express confidence in Catholic exegetical endeavors. Second: Recommend to exegetes their duty to follow the teaching set forth by supreme pontiffs up to the present on the interpretation of Sacred Scripture. Third: Make special mention, in referring to the supreme pontiffs, of Pius XII of happy memory, who is recognized as the architect and promoter of biblical renewal in our century.

Auxiliary Bishop James Griffiths of New York spoke the same day. He pleaded for "clarity, charity and, above all, truth." He asked that the Council meet its responsibility to prevent excess by those who are not biblical and theological scholars, but who are second-rate teachers in colleges and seminaries and "popularizers" of various theories. He maintained that difficulties and scandals arise not from real scholars, but from these "popularizers."

The following April, after the revised second draft of the schema was presented to the Central Coordinating Commission, Cardinal Spellman voted his approval of the new text. He wrote:

The discussion of the things contained in the first chapter about the mutual relationship of Sacred Scripture and Tradition has already been extended more than enough. In the present version nothing is pressed too strongly. Specifically, the statements on the relationship of both is a great help to the magisterium in placing a quasi-mediator between Sacred Scripture and Sacred Tradition.

In July, 1963, Archbishop John Krol submitted his observations on the revelation schema. He felt it would be impossible "to have any form of expression which of itself would be immediately clear to all non-Catholics." Explaining his observation, he went on to state:

Revelation often designates one of the following: whatever can be learned about God from any source; whatever can be learned about man from any source; the action of the Spirit under any form; God's continuous manifestation of Himself in nature or in the mind and heart of men; the actual manifestation of divine providence. The "Word of God" is used more or less in the same way.

Archbishop Krol accordingly made the following suggestion:

It should be made clear, although not necessarily in the Constitution itself, that revelation is understood as a special manifestation of God Himself given by God in ancient Israel and in the person, in the works and in the doctrine of Jesus, as well as in the first years of the Church.

In a written intervention submitted July 29, 1963, Bishop Albert Fletcher requested that "commentaries pertaining to the completion of instructions ought to be approved by the Holy See through a motion made by the national conferences of bishops." He cited the following three reasons for making this observation:

1) So that no interpretation might be made of passages of the Old and New Testament in Sacred Scripture "which at present require a certain and definite exposition" (cf. number 19), such as might cause wonderment or scandal of the faithful by imprudent men.

2) So that the faithful might not be deceived by certain non-Catholic exegetes who reduce the Old Testament to fables by a rationalistic method.

3) So that Catholic authors might execute their pastoral work truly "under the guidance of the Church's magisterium."

In July, 1964, before the schema was brought back to the floor of the

Council for discussion, Cardinal Spellman submitted another written observation. He thought again that the third revision of the schema was "very acceptable." In this intervention he proposed two amendments. His first amendment was as follows:

For at one time the truth is expressed and proposed in historical texts in various ways, while at another time in didactic or prophetic texts. And so it is necessary that the exegete inquire after the sense which the holy writer expressly intended and expressed in his determined circumstances, given the conditions of his time, by means of the types of literature used at that time.

The Cardinal's second amendment was proposed in these words:

However, the four holy writers wrote the Gospels, selecting certain things from the things which had been handed down both by mouth and in writing, synthesizing some things and explaining things with attention to the conditions of the churches. This, however, does not prevent the evangelists from having somewhat modified and elaborated the words and deeds of Christ the Lord. For these men wrote out the Gospels under the inspiration of that Spirit of truth who was promised to the Apostles by Christ, that He might lead them to the path of all truth. Otherwise they did not discharge the magisterium of the earliest Church, whose responsibility is to enlighten and clarify what is implicitly contained within the deposit.

When the schema was brought back for discussion during the third session, three Americans rose and addressed themselves to the third, and final, revised schema. On September 30, 1964, Cardinal Meyer stated that the revised text was acceptable, even though it needed to be amended in several points. He felt also that the nature of revelation should be clarified in the light of recent research. He thought, too, that faith should not be described in such a way as to make it too intellectual, as this would be contrary to the spirit of St. Paul.

Six days later, Cardinal Meyer rose again to discuss certain aspects of chapter two, especially that section which described "Sacred Tradition as something living, dynamic, all-embracing, that is, that it consists not only in doctrinal propositions, but also in the worship and practice of the entire Church." He felt, however, that tradition should be so stated in this section that it is clear that "it is also subject to the limits and defects of the pilgrim Church, which is the Church of sinners and which knows divine matters in a mirror darkly." He therefore suggested the following addition to the text:

Nevertheless, this living tradition does not always and in all things advance and grow. For when the Pilgrim Church contemplates divine matters, it can fail in some respects and actually has failed. For this reason, it carries within itself Sacred Scripture as an abiding norm, one against which it can measure its own life and thus unceasingly correct and improve itself.

On October 1, Archbishop Shehan of Baltimore rose and also approved the revised schema. He then went on to propose the following change in chapter one of the text, concerning the nature and object of revelation:

. . . supernatural revelation truly is the communication of God with man by which God reveals Himself. This communication, *in an active and, indeed, dynamic sense,* is rightly called the speaking of God, not, however, necessarily as a formal speech of God, but rather as a salvific action of God toward men *along with a divine selection and movement of the witnesses,* who, by the goodness of God and the action of the Holy Spirit, understanding what had been revealed to them, gave their interpretation in the historical context of the people of God and put it into human words. The witnesses of the Old Testament are, first of all, the Patriarchs and the Prophets; in the New Testament, Christ Himself gives the most outstanding witness and, after Him, the Apostles called by Him. Revelation, however, *in a passive and static sense,* is regarded as that interpretation of the witnesses, accomplished by the Spirit of God, from which arise doctrines and revealed truths.

Bishop Charles Maloney, the auxiliary of Louisville, directed his remarks on October 5 to chapter three of the schema. He praised the text for recognizing that "literary genres were known to the Church from the beginning, and had to be known." He also regretted "popular authors" who "have written much and imperfectly about the newness of the method and thus have disturbed the minds of the faithful and sometimes of the leaders." Then praising the May 14, 1964 instruction of the Biblical Commission, Bishop Maloney recalled that "the historical method as a whole is called 'a new help to exegesis if properly used.' The technology involved in *formgeschichte*, or the history of literary forms, is carefully distinguished from the false principles with which it is mixed." He thereupon requested that the directives of this instruction "be reflected in chapter three on interpretation." Finally, he concluded on a humorous note with these words: "I thank our angel, rather our great archangel, and the moderators for such a smooth pronunciation of the name of the archdiocese of *Ludovico-politanae* [Louisville]!"

During the 131st congregation, on September 20, 1965, the Council Fathers finally began voting on the schema concerning divine revelation. Throughout the following three congregations they continued to vote on the schema. In contrast with the heated discussions of the first session, the voting that took place during these three days reflected the open mind of a Church that had already accepted the open door policy of Pope John.

This revised schema now consisted of an introduction and six chapters. During this period twenty votes were cast on the entire schema. The voting on the introduction and six chapters is noteworthy:

Chapter	Approval	Disapproval	Qualified Approval
Introduction and Chapter One	1,822	3	248
Chapter Two	1,874	9	354
Chapter Three	1,777	6	324
Chapter Four	2,183	–	47
Chapter Five	1,850	–	313
Chapter Six	1,915	1	212

The transformation that took place, both in the text of the schema and in the thinking of the Council Fathers in the relatively brief period of three years, was a tribute to the authentic conciliar experience.

On October 25, during the 152nd congregation, the Council Fathers received the suggestions for improvement submitted in favor of the schema. At that time the General Secretary announced that the final vote on the schema would be taken on October 29. During the 155th congregation, on that date, the Archbishop of Florence, now Ermenegildo Cardinal Florit, introduced the revisions to the introduction and first two chapters of the schema made by the Council Fathers. During the same congregation Bishop André Charue, representing the absent Bishop Jan Van Dodewaard who had worked so diligently in preparing the schema, presented the suggestions for emendation on the other five chapters of the schema. The final votes on the schema revealed these results:

Chapter	Approval	Non-Approval	Null
Introduction & Chapter One	2,169	23	2
Chapter Two	2,123	55	7
Chapter Three	2,154	31	4
Chapter Four	2,178	8	2
Chapter Five	2,115	19	5
Chapter Six	2,126	14	6

The vote of approval of the complete text was an overwhelming victory for those who had labored on its behalf since those dark, distressing days of 1962. Of the 2,115 Council Fathers who voted their final approval, 2,081 were in favor, 27 were opposed, and seven cast invalid ballots. The vote was immediately recognized as a victory of recent biblical scholarship at work in the Church for the past generation.

As the liturgy schema had two American experts who gave it a gentle assist, so also did the schema on divine revelation have its guardian angels. They were Reverend Francis McCool, S.J., a Brooklynite transplanted to the Pontifical Biblical Institute, and Reverend Barnabas Mary Ahern, C.P., of Louisville's Passionist Seminary. At the American Bishops' Press Panel, Father McCool addressed the press corps on September 24, even though he knew at the time that their principal interests centered about the Declaration on Religious Liberty. He called the voting on divine revelation "three historic days" in which "the Second Vatican Council has placed its seal of approval on several doctrinal points which theologians have seen with new clarity in the course of the last hundred years." In the same prepared statement, Father McCool underscored the ecumenical significance of the approved schema in these words:

> The ecumenical nature of the schema, however, is shown most clearly in what it deliberately did not say. Ever since the Protestant Revolt, the assertion of the Reformers that Scripture was the only vehicle which transmitted God's revelation to man offended Catholic sensibilities. The Council of Trent insisted in reply that divine revelation came to us in both Scripture and Apostolic Tradition. After Trent, some Catholic theologians developed the theory that Scripture and Tradition were complementary sources and that, therefore, Scripture alone was an incomplete source. Though this view won a certain predominance in the manuals of the nineteenth century, other Catholic theologians more recently have proposed another explanation of the relation between Scripture and Tradition. All of divine revelation is contained in both, though, naturally, in different ways. When Vatican II began, this draft, then entitled "On the Sources of Revelation," presupposed as established the first of these two positions—which caused the turmoil in which that draft was rejected. Now, two sessions later, the Council is content to reaffirm the position of Trent—revelation comes to us in both Scripture

and Tradition. It asserts that both are intimately related, indeed intertwined with each other. But it has reserved for a future Council the exact determination of what these relations are.

No individual, perhaps, did more to promote biblical scholarship among the American hierarchy than Father Barnabas Ahern. He was, before the Council opened, the leading American biblical scholar. Throughout the time of the Council, even though opted by the Secretariat for the Promotion of Christian Unity, his was the personal apostolate of leading the American intellectual community toward a fuller appreciation of the biblical advances made during the past twenty years. He was the second American *peritus* to address the American hierarchy, speaking to the group at their weekly meeting on November 19, 1962. An American bishop, present at the meeting, gave the following account of Father Ahern's presentation:

> Father Barnabas Mary Ahern spoke on the question of modern exegesis. He gave a quick run-down of the matter of literary forms and their various effects on the interpretation of the New Testament as they have been applied to the Old Testament for some years. He gave an excellent speech, keeping his audience completely spellbound. . . . The Apostolic Delegate took the floor at the end of the meeting, speaking very critically, even patronizingly, of the things Father Ahern had said. Since time was up, Archbishop Boland was going to close the meeting; but there was a general protest from the floor, so Father Ahern was given opportunity to answer the Delegate's questions. This he did with utmost tactfullness and with devastating effect. It was very obvious that Ahern is a master in his field. . . .

During the eighth public session of the Council, on November 18, 1965, Pope Paul VI solemnly promulgated the Dogmatic Constitution on Divine Revelation after a conciliar vote of 2,344 in favor and six opposed. The Council and the Church and the separated brethren and the world had come a long, long way since that "black Wednesday," as Monsignor Rudolph Bandas described it, in 1962 when Pope John established the mixed commission. As a matter of fact, however, Catholic theological and biblical scholarship had come a long way since that date.

Dogmatic Constitution on Divine Revelation

✠ INTERVENTIONS

JOSEPH CARDINAL RITTER, *14 November, 1962*

In my opinion, my humble opinion, the schema on the fonts of revelation must be rejected so that another may be proposed, and for the following reasons.

First, it lacks any evident usefulness. It contains nothing new, no accommodations which render either Christian doctrine or Christian life of greater significance or efficacy for modern man. It presents only again—sometimes less clear than before—the doctrine of the Councils of Trent and Vatican I. This mere repetition, it seems to me, is neither necessary nor useful.

Second, this is more important—ambiguity abounds in the schema. Perhaps indirectly and yet openly the schema touches actual problems both theological and spiritual. Thus, the propositions are arranged as to seem to proffer solutions; in actual fact, however, nothing is said that is clear and determined.

Then—and this of the greatest importance it seems to me—the whole schema is clouded in pessimism and a negative spirit. Saying nothing explicit, it seems to affix doubt and undue suspicion on a great part of the more recent neo-testamental exegesis.

Venerable Fathers! Students, the faithful and the experts as well want and expect sustenance and especially positive illumination from this Council. We must help and direct, not reprimand and dissuade. If the Council has solutions to actual problems, let it show them as clearly, as distinctly as possible. If there are no solutions, indeed, let the Council say so or remain quiet. If errors exist, let the Council remonstrate and even condemn them. But let the Council abstain from statements that lack any use, imperil unity and engender suspicions. Such things can only implant fear and disgust toward Scripture and theology in the faithful, rather than love and reverence.

JAMES CARDINAL McINTYRE, *16 November, 1962*

This schema has given to the modern world a summary and explicit confirmation of the truths relating to the sources of revelation. In a special way our attention is drawn to the points which deal with present-day scientific investigations and theories. Allow me to indicate some things of major importance concerning these points:

On page ten, paragraph five, it is clearly indicated: "No one should dare make little of tradition or deny fidelity to it." On page twelve, paragraph eight, is given the definition of biblical inspiration: "Namely, that certain special charism for writing by which God, operating in and through the writer, speaks to men in writing, and consequently He is said to be and truly is the principal author of the entire sacred text." The Church unrestrictedly objects to any effort at reducing the nature of inspiration in any way to a merely natural impulse. In paragraph nine, it is stated: "Of each and every book of the Old and New Testament written in any period, there is only one primary author, namely, God."

On page thirteen, paragraph ten, it is declared: ". . . the charism of sacred inspiration was for the writers elected and led by God proper and personal, it was not a charism common or communicated to the assembly of the faithful."

On page seventeen, paragraph nineteen, ecclesiastical tradition is definitively confirmed: "The Church of God . . . has constantly held and holds that the human authors were those who in the canon of the Sacred Books are called Matthew, Mark, Luke and John."

In paragraph twenty-one the following errors are condemned: "Those who deny or extenuate in any way or for any reason the genuine historical and objective truth of the facts of life of Our Lord Jesus Christ as they are narrated in those Gospels." Today we find many pernicious errors against this historical truth.

In paragraph twenty-two is condemned the error which asserts that the words attributed to Our Lord by the Gospels, at least regarding the very thing signified by the words, are most often not those of Christ himself, but rather refer to the mind of the Evangelist. The words "at least regarding the very thing signified by the words" ought to be examined with care.

Therefore, it seems to me that this schema really contains positive action aimed at correcting new theories which are not acceptable—and action against scientific theories, and against scientific theories *which should be considered only as theories*. Therefore, the schema should be accepted. The intention of the Council certainly is not to introduce new theology. Not only are [new theories] numerous, but they also exceed the present state of human understanding which is extremely limited in things divine. The necessity of faith must be admitted and professed.

The knowledge of God, the knowledge of man's relation to God, and the knowledge of the wonderful ordering of human things is near at hand for men inasmuch as they are able and have need of it; but our knowledge always remains within the limits of natural intellect when we consider the perception and assimilation of truth.

Gradually and at diverse historical moments, God granted to men's minds other and transcendent truths concerning himself and the order of nature. Man, when he became aware that these truths were divinely revealed, according to his ability and need gave his assent because of the authority of God revealing. This assent is called faith, which faith is the most precious human treasure.

Human reason, by reason of rational speculation and simultaneous illumination of the Holy Spirit, seeks and reaches some understanding of divine mysteries. These human speculations, inasmuch as they had been accepted in the course of centuries, also received the approval of Holy Mother Church. The Christian faithful recognize this understanding of mysteries as the valid expression of the dogmas of faith.

Nevertheless, it is at the same time evident that God has not given to men the possibility in this life—in our days—of reaching perfect and comprehensive understanding of the divine mysteries and of the nature of things.

God granted to His theologians and philosophers the faculty of exercising their more excellent rational powers in investigating all intelligible things, even in the order of possible things; but many things remain unknown. The acceptance in faith of truths not understood by us is rewarded by God.

Therefore, faith must hold some place in our investigation of truth. Gladly, with patience and serenity, we must accept in faith divinely revealed mysteries and dogmas of the Church.

It is also necessary in this Ecumenical Council that we should be contented —accepting in faith and confirming the truths which God revealed to us. We must expect, with anticipation and trust, progress in the understanding of dogmas. But it is not the purpose of this Council to solve every current problem.

ALBERT CARDINAL MEYER, *19 November 1962*

In the debate thus far on the schema "On the Fonts of Revelation," two opposing views have been expressed by the Council Fathers on a matter of the gravest importance. In my view, this difference has its root in the fact that many, among whom I count myself, believe that the method of setting forth the teaching employed in this schema does not adequately correspond to the aim of the Council as it was expressed both in the opening address of the Supreme Pontiff and in our message sent to all mankind.

This opposition of views, in my opinion, is the cause of very great anxiety to many Fathers. Their uneasiness consists in this, that much study is demanded to make a proper judgment on this matter. Undoubtedly, as Fathers gathered in Council, we have the promised help of the Holy Spirit. Nevertheless, we are not dispensed on this account from the grave duty of proceeding with caution, prudence and great care. But here we find precisely the source of our difficulty. For many of the Fathers fear that they do not have sufficient learning.

Another wise observation, one made by the Right Reverend Lord Abbot Butler, is of the greatest significance, namely, that "we ought to display to the world unanimity in so serious a matter." As a matter of fact, whatever we may decide in this matter will appear to the world as the judgment of the entire Council. But, in order that this appearance may have a foundation in reality, there is demanded of us a satisfactory agreement of judgment, according to the rules of the Council. In the debate held thus far, however, it is clearly evident that such an agreement can scarcely, if ever, be obtained so long as this schema stands.

Having thought the matter over before God, therefore, I must express my own view in accord with what Cardinal Bea has said. I wish, therefore, as he does, that a new schema be drafted, following the general lines sketched by him, and retaining from the present schema all those points that correspond to the aim of this Council, while adding others that are presently lacking. Moreover, it is my desire that this new schema be drafted with the help of theologians and exegetes of various nations and tendencies.

In a special way I desire that the Council do three things. First: Express confidence in Catholic exegetical endeavors. Second: Recommend to exegetes their duty to follow the teaching set forth by supreme pontiffs up to the present on the interpretation of Sacred Scripture. Third: Make special mention, in referring to the supreme pontiffs, of Pius XII of happy memory who is recognized as the architect and promoter of biblical renewal in our century.

BISHOP JAMES GRIFFITHS, *19 November, 1962*

After so many more learned and eloquent speakers, it seems to me that I ought to begin by saying, "Remain with us, Lord, evening is coming!" lest I should say more cynically, "Lord, we have labored all night and have accomplished nothing, but in Your Name we will safely relax."

In dealing, in this Council hall, with the schema entitled "On the Fonts of Revelation," do we not have, and shall have, but one end, that of detecting the truth not only in the substance of the schema, but even, and perhaps especially, of the best method of expounding it? Many Fathers have already spoken wisely and learnedly on this schema, not merely to give their opinions, but to find, if it be possible, the most suitable method of teaching and exposing the most important truth of divine revelation, first to the Catholic world and then to all men of good will. There have been some, as you now know well, who have felt that the schema should be completely rejected. There were others who thought that this schema (which all, even the more hostile recognize, has been prepared with the greatest diligence and expert advice of many scholars of many nations) should be retained if it could be notably shortened and corrected from the common opinions of the Fathers.

As to the first proposition, it hardly seems prudent to reject a document completely which we have read and scrutinized and which we candidly admit could be corrected in some parts, and now accept something else which we have not examined—indeed, which not many of us have even seen.

However, on the other hand, since clerics and many of the faithful throughout the world are waiting and hoping that this Second Vatican Council will say and teach something about the fonts or, if you prefer, font of revelation and other questions which have been under discussion for very many years, in my humble opinion, we Fathers cannot remain silent on these controversies.

We have heard opinions not only diverse, but very often radically contradictory, not without censure and, unfortunately, bitter accusations coming from either side, that our clergy and faithful—especially the laity who are sort of cut off and left in confusion—strongly desire to know from us, their pastors, what in good faith and fidelity to the teaching of the Church they can accept and hold in this matter. Therefore, it seems to me that we Council Fathers, in the performance of our true pastoral office, cannot pass over something of such great importance or leave it till the end of the Council or some indefinite time, for we are like Paul to whom the Athenians said, "Let us hear what you have to say on this matter."

Even if some have said that the matter is not yet sufficiently developed, it is clear to all and hidden to none that this controversy is something real and actual in the Church. It can be stated without exaggeration that, at least in some sense, there will be scandal not only among the faithful (whose spiritual good is our serious concern and, in sacred matters, is our especial intellectual interest), but also among our separated brethren (whom we paternally call to unity) when they see such a division in the Church of God over such a fundamental matter.

Therefore, under the guidance of the Holy Spirit the Paraclete, for the good of the People of God, let us faithfully take up the discussion of this matter, with the advice of experts from both sides and from widely diverse schools, considering the schema not necessarily entirely as it was proposed in the beginning, but emending, abbreviating and polishing it where we can, going into and correcting it in its very essence. Unless I am mistaken, even those who oppose the schema admit that it is not all bad. His Eminence, Cardinal Meyer, has told us that we ought to retain everything good in the present schema and incorporate it in some new schema. I ask, why should we not keep these good things until we can place them in a new schema? This seems to me to be a sufficiently fundamental distinction. And, in deliberating on the schema, let it be that each Father enjoys full liberty to open his mind before God, as we have done up until now in every discussion in this Holy Synod, to the applause and admiration of the whole world, both Catholic and non-Catholic, free of any fear.

Therefore, following the truth in charity, it will not be impossible that, with the aid of the Spirit, we can come to some acceptable form or find, as I have said, a middle way, so that we can hand over to the clergy and people some sort of rule, even if minimal, that is sane and secure. This, however, means that should we not all be prepared to give and take, not, of course, in essentials, but in those little things which are doubtful and open? Let us use as a guide that wise saying which His Eminence the Cardinal Relator [Ottaviani] has cited and which has been praised by many authors: "In essential things, unity; in doubtful things, liberty; in all things, charity."

Finally, it is right for me to say something about the form, Venerable Fathers, of redrafting our schema, if at last, if ever, it is conceived.

The discussion still goes on, and it has been said that the present schema does not adequately show that ecumenical spirit with which the acts and declarations of this Holy Synod should be imbued. We candidly admit that, although we have only applause for the notable progress in the area of this very important type of ecumenism which has already been made and will be made in the future. Still we have not found clear examples of that ecumenical style, as it is called. Perhaps it is intended that the Constitutions and decrees should be written with the utmost charity and with concern for the mind of the great number of good non-Catholics spread throughout the world, who anxiously await solace for the soul from this ecumenical assembly. If this is the way in which it is understood, then we gladly and sincerely approve and recommend the proposal.

But I would like to add that we have the duty to speak not only with charity, but also with clearness and agreeableness, most certainly not only about these things which we hold in common with our separated brothers, but even about those things which—sad to say—we do not yet admit in common! It is well known that the separated brothers themselves want this to be done in this wise. Is it not true that we shall not be able to deal with our separated brothers who seek ardently after the mind of the Church and are most deserving of our estimation, unless we, the promoters of unity, act in this way with sincerity and veracity? If we shall have acted otherwise, there would be a great danger of some type of false irenical theology (irenism), about which, some months ago, His Eminence Cardinal Bea warned so opportunely and wisely.

I have not said all these things that I may ask from you Constitutions and decrees of a more durable quality. Far from it! I ask only that the acts and decrees of this Holy Synod be composed not by using weighty legalistic terms, but simply and smoothly, even clearly and candidly, according to the general norm of conciliar style which has been used for such a long time without any harm.

Therefore, let us constantly keep these three things before our mind: charity, clarity and, above all, truth. The most provident God Himself will show us these three things, if we recognize them, and, what is better, if we bring them into action without fear. God will open the way of light and peace which we all, as successors of the Apostles, seek here under the shadow of Peter.

ALBERT CARDINAL MEYER, *30 September, 1964*

Chapter II in its entirety is very acceptable—particularly the manner in which it presents sacred tradition as being something alive, dynamic and whole, i.e., consisting not only of doctrinal declarations, but also the cult and practice of the entire Church.

That section is likewise acceptable which shows how tradition is enlarged not only through the definitions of the magisterium, but also through the contemplation of the faithful and through their interior experience of spiritual realities.

The paragraph's reference to the Blessed Virgin Mary also is acceptable— in which it states that the Church imitates her by considering in its heart the things and words handed down to it.

Nevertheless, this paragraph—if I have understood it correctly, even after the report given today—presents the life and cult of the Church entirely under a positive aspect. Tradition in this paragraph is extended, in my opinion, beyond the limits of the infallible magisterium. If this interpretation is true, then such tradition is subject to the limitations and defects of the Church Militant, which is the Church of sinners and which knows divine realities through a mirror darkly.

The history of the Church amply attests to these defects, e.g., the long, obscure theological doctrine concerning the resurrection of Christ, moralism with exaggerated casuistry, non-liturgical piety and the neglect of Sacred Scripture. There are many other similar instances.

This paragraph, therefore, must be augmented with the addition of words which point out both these defects, which are always possible in this state of life, and their remedy.

LAWRENCE CARDINAL SHEHAN, *1 October, 1964*

Chapters one and two of this schema in general are very acceptable.

My intervention concerns number two of chapter one, on page five concerning the nature and the object of revelation.

There is no one who does not see the necessity, at this time, of presenting a complete, and the fullest, notion of divine revelation. The evolution of the text, which we have before us, to which so many Fathers have lent their support, demonstrates the consciousness of the necessity of presenting a fuller and more precise notion than that which is found in the theological manuals and in the text of the previous schema. A notion is desired which coincides with both scriptural and theological studies and one which responds to modern needs.

As was noted yesterday by His Eminence Cardinal Döpfner, the role of the human author is very much neglected in our text.

The improved text of chapter one, in number two, from line fifteen on page five to line fourteen on page six is clear and farsighted. I believe, however, that it labors under this defect: it does not express explicitly enough that which is accomplished by the subject of revelation, that is, by the human mind which receives revelation from God, interprets and transmits it to the people of God. Therefore, it does not express why revelation, given by God, is expressed by such and such precise words; why he uses this particular and specific form. This question very much interests the mind of modern man.

Therefore, I propose the following change: immediately after the word "may admit," which is found in line three on page six, these words should be added in the text, namely;

> And so supernatural revelation truly is the communication of God with man by which God reveals Himself. This communication, *in an active and, indeed, dynamic sense*, is rightly called the speaking of God, not however necessarily as a formal speech of God, but rather as a salvific action of God toward men *along with a divine selection and movement of the witnesses*, who, by the goodness of God and the action of the Holy Spirit, understanding what had been revealed to them, gave their interpretation in the historical context of the People of God, and put it into human words. The witnesses of the Old Testament are, first of all, the Patriarchs and the Prophets; in the New Testament, Christ Himself gives the most outstanding witness and, after Him, the Apostles called by Him. Revelation, however, *in a passive and static sense*, is regarded as that interpretation of the witnesses, accomplished by the Spirit of God, from which arise doctrines and revealed truth.

The improved text next proceeds from the words "This economy of revelation . . ." in line three on page six.

Reason for the change

This change which is proposed shows the two parts of the process of revelation, i.e., *the action of God* or *the kindness of God* (which indeed constitutes a fuller category than the doctrinal proposition), and the *perception* and the *experience* of these kindnesses of God and their *interpretation*. This interpretation, indeed, is in no way the interpretation and the subjective experience of the Modernists, because the Spirit of God actually moves the subject of revelation to perceive and to interpret, and because the cognitive interpretation really depends on the true, objective acts which are accomplished history—especially in the history of the people selected by God; which acts, indeed, reveal the intimate reality of God.

Further reasons for a change in the text

First, a theological reason: The treatment of divine revelation in many theological manuals seems to indicate that divine revelation is accomplished through the words properly spoken, i.e., through a formal speaking—which, indeed, in an exclusive sense, does not at all agree with the mode of communication of personal knowledge, excluding certain experiences of life and treating only the words, almost never is accomplished nor, most certainly, is the communication between God and men thus carried out. For human communication, words are certainly needed and through words communication is ordinarily carried out, but words almost always arise from thinking and reflecting on the experience. In the process of revelation, words are most certainly helpful; but words have arisen from reflection or thought on the true, objective *praereflexive* experience. Thus revelation is an action on the part of God and an interpretation under the influence of the Holy Spirit on the part of the subject.

Second, a pastoral reason: From this fuller notion of revelation, men will be able to understand better the human role and, among the human words, to find the truth, which is collected in human words.

An ecumenical reason and other reasons have been written out and handed in to the Secretary General.

ALBERT CARDINAL MEYER, 5 October, 1964

My remarks, in this brief intervention, refer especially to number eight in chapter two of our schema. I shall submit further observations in writing.

The whole of chapter two is most satisfactory, particularly the manner in which number eight shows that sacred tradition is something living, dynamic, all-embracing, i.e., that it consists not only in doctrinal propositions, but also in the worship and practice of the entire Church.

I find it equally satisfactory that part of this paragraph which shows how tradition grows not only through definitions of the magisterium, but also "through the contemplation and intimate spiritual experience of the believers."

The reference to the Church's imitation of the Blessed Virgin Mary by pondering in its heart those things and statements that have been handed down is likewise satisfactory.

Nevertheless, this paragraph, if I have understood it properly, even after today's *relatio,* sets forth the life and worship of the Church only in a positive light. Tradition, however, it seems to me, in this paragraph reaches beyond the limits of the infallible Magisterium. If this interpretation is correct, then tradition in this sense is also subject to the limits and defects of the Pilgrim Church, which is the Church of sinners and which knows divine matters in a mirror darkly (1 Cor. 13:12).

Church history contains abundant evidence of failings: for example, the prolonged overshadowing of theological doctrine on Church's resurrection, the moralizing with its exaggerated casuistry which has prevailed from the eighteenth century; non-liturgical piety thrrough the centuries, which had so often been sentimental in the century past; neglect of Sacred Scripture, and other things of that sort.

Thus, this paragraph ought to be rounded out by the addition of a passage setting forth these failings—which are always possible in this life on earth—and their remedies. I suggest to the Fathers, therefore, that the following formulation be inserted after the phrase "intimate spiritual experience" in line 16:

> Nevertheless, this living tradition does not always and in all things advance and grow. For when the Pilgrim Church contemplates divine matters, it can fail in some respects and actually has failed. For this reason, it carries within itself Sacred Scripture as an abiding norm, one against which it can measure its own life and thus unceasingly correct and improve itself.

By this brief insertion, which fits in with what went before and what comes after it, paragraph eight can, I hope, achieve proper balance and completeness.

In this manner, it seems to me, this paragraph will better harmonize with what is contained in the second chapter of the schema "On the Church" (number ten, toward the end, page 30, 11. 28–35), where it is stated:

> The Church, passing through trials and tribulations, is strengthened by the power of the grace promised it by the Lord, so that it may not depart from perfect fidelity despite the weakness of the flesh, but may remain

a spouse worthy of its Lord, and, under the movement of the Holy Spirit, it may not cease to renew itself until by the cross it arrives at the light which knows no dimming.

BISHOP CHARLES MALONEY, 5 *October, 1964*

I thought we were to speak only about chapter three, so I shall not say anything about the other chapters.

In chapter three, the Council, teaching both old and new matter, should indicate certain things held by all and should mention what will be clarified by free, yet prudent, investigation and discussion. With this in mind, the harshness of the arguments and disagreements would decrease, and the way would be cleared for that internal unity of the Church which would cleanse the blemishes of the Bride of Christ and would make her wrinkles disappear.

The method is, in a way, new but the doctrine is old. For, as was noted in this aula a few days ago, literary genres were known to the Church from the beginning, and had to be known. This is clear from the writings of the Fathers. To quote only two: St. Augustine's *The Agreement of the Gospels* and St. Chrysostom's *Homilies on the Epistles of St. Paul.* These occur also in documents, in the encyclicals of the popes, especially in our time. And now the Church is given wider instruments—archeological, historical and others of that kind, so that, with the expansion of the sciences, they would corroborate what the Church had been teaching. Other things would likewise be made more explicit.

Sad to say, popular authors have written much and imperfectly about the newness of the method, and thus they disturb the minds of the faithful and sometimes of the leaders.

On the so-called historical method, the Instruction of the Pontifical Biblical Commission, issued last May 14, is noteworthy. It is published in the *Acta Apostolicae Sedis,* volume 56, page 712. For there the historical method as a whole is called "a new help to exegesis if properly used." The technology involved in *formgeschichte,* or the history of literary forms, is carefully distinguished from the false principles with which it is mixed. Note the words of the Instruction:

> Where necessary, the investigator can study what solid elements are found in *formgeschichte* which may be used for a fuller, correct understanding of the Gospels. This must be done carefully, because unverified philosophical and theological principles are often mixed with the method, often disparaging both the method and the literary conclusions involved.

These statements can be accepted by all, if I am not mistaken. Insofar as the Instruction treats of interpretation, it should be reflected in chapter three on interpretation.

Now, briefly, I propose the following emendations in order to render the text clearer and more precise, if so it would seem fitting to the Fathers.

The first change affects only the one word "all" in number eleven, line 13. I do not know if a poet or hagiographer uses all his faculties under the influence of inspiration or not, and so I propose "human" in place of "all." Thus: ". . . whom he uses acting with their *human* faculties and power."

Then, after line 17, before 18, I propose an insertion to satisfy both opinions, namely, the phrase "in the way in which it is asserted." Then it reads: "When therefore all that the inspired author or hagiographer asserts, *in the way in which it asserted,* must be retained as asserted by the Holy Spirit. . . ." Maybe this middle path would satisfy objections to the text and the genuine notion of inerrancy would be preserved.

I think another change would perfect the text, in the first part of number twelve on the same page, line 28, where what the hagiographer must investigate is considered. In the relation (D) it is stated: "We abstract from solving the question of *sensus plenior* in Scripture." This is good, but the question is whether this abstraction is apparent enough in the text, since the *relations* are not a part of the text of the Constitution.

For me, at least, the distinction of a disjunctive conjunction is not enough. Thus I propose the repetition of the word *quid* so that line 27 would read: "[The interpreter] . . . must investigate what the hagiographer really meant and *what* God wished to manifest by his words."

I think this is enough. I thank our angel, rather our great archangel, and the moderators for such a smooth pronunciation of the name of the archdiocese of *Ludovicopolitanae* [Louisville]!

Dogmatic Constitution on Divine Revelation

✠ COMMENTARY *by Rev. Barnabas Mary Ahern, C.P.*

The Dogmatic Constitution on Divine Revelation is one of the most memorable acts of Vatican Council II. Apart from the intrinsic worth of the Constitution solemnly promulgated by the Council, the history of its formation presents a revealing insight into the process of maturation which gradually developed through the successive stages of Vatican II.

The preparation of the Constitution was co-terminous with the Council itself. Introduced as the second schema to be discussed in the first session of the Council, in October 1962, the document was constantly worked over until its final promulgation at the end of the last session of the Council, in November, 1965.

The schema first presented was the work of a preparatory theological commission which drafted a summa of theses drawn almost verbatim from typical early twentieth-century theology manuals. Dissident voices in the commission were not numerous enough to force a re-thinking of conventional formulations which modern scholarship has rendered suspect. Members of the commission who recognized the inadequacy and even falsity of many statements in the schema and who winced before its inquisitorial and repressive spirit could do nothing but wait for the time when the Fathers of the Council themselves would use the scalpel on this seminary *vademecum* of a time long past.

The Council did not disappoint their expectancy. The discussion of the schema on revelation in the first session was devastating. Bishops freely criticized its spirit, style and contents. At the end of the discussion, so large a number voted against the schema that Pope John XXIII ordered its complete rewriting by the newly formed Theological Commission and the Secretariate for Promoting Christian Unity. When this combined group finished drafting a basic document, the schema was carefully reviewed and reworked by the members of the Theological Commission. The emergent draft was discussed in the third session of the Council. Because it showed such marked improvement over the discarded first schema, it received the Fathers' vote of general acceptance. By this time, however, the bishops had so grown in awareness of their freedom and competence and were so firmly committed to a policy of realistic appraisal that they did not hesitate to ask for further perfecting of many features which would have passed muster at an earlier period of conciliar discussion.

The schema, therefore, went back to the Theological Commission for more improvements. Many changes were introduced in the light of emendations submitted by the Council Fathers. Later discussion of the resultant fourth draft called for still more changes of minor importance. When, at last, a fifth document came to the floor of the Council for final vote, it represented a long history of Vatican II's change from the bastioned enclosure of fixed and outmoded formulae to the vast terrain of truth illumined by the light of God and wide open to life-giving perspectives. The document finally approved by the Council is rich with the insights of modern theological scholarship. Its style is clear and balanced, with each word carefully weighed and each phrase delicately chiseled to the exact measure of truth.

Even a casual reading of the Constitution brings an impression of luminous focal points which will serve as points of departure for more dynamic Catholic life and for further theological research. Whatever there is of time-honored doctrine in this document has been re-thought and re-stated; whatever is new in conciliar teaching marks an advance in the Church's understanding of and response to the revealing word of God. It may be of help to indicate in the contents of each chapter the principles which will mark new guidelines in the teaching and life of the Church.

Chapter 1

This chapter on the nature of revelation emphasizes its perennial vitality. Only too often have Catholics looked upon the truth of God's teaching as a collection of conceptual formulations which have come down in a hermetically sealed box from that ancient past when Christ first uttered them. The least suggestion of development and of new tonalities in the voice of God was intransigently rejected by some as unwarranted tampering with the supposed monolithic integrity of dogma. In harmony with this attitude, the response of faith to God's revelation was often presented as an inflexibly univocal act of intellect and will accepting God's words as true.

The present Constitution, while stressing the divine origin of revelation and the human intellectual assent to it through faith, lays emphasis also on another aspect which, though equally important, has not always been to the fore in catechetical teaching or in common Catholic thinking. This new stress calls attention to the fact that God is always speaking to His children through the truths of revelation. These truths, therefore, are not merely a voice from the past; they are a living communication from God who speaks here and now to all those who hear His voice. This theme, which recurs frequently in the Constitution, is pointedly expressed in its first chapter: "Through this revelation the invisible God out of the abundance of His love speaks to men as friends and lives among them, so that He may invite and receive them into fellowship with Himself" (paragraph 2).

The divine communication is richly personal. It lays bare the heart of God, His thoughts, His love, His saving plan. This dynamically personal element in revelation flows from a simple truth which the Constitution repeats again and again. All revelation is but an echo of the Word who is God's own Son, Christ Jesus. As St. John of the Cross has aptly observed, "God speaks only one Word; and this Word is His Son." Revelation in its created expression is but a spectrum refracting into multifarious colors the pure white light which is Christ. Every truth, therefore, which God speaks, He speaks here and now in Christ. As the Constitution expresses it, "By this revelation the deepest truth about God and the salvation of man shines out for our sake in Christ who is both the mediator and the fulness of all revelation" (paragraph 2).

Once a Christian grasps this vital and personal quality of revelation, his faith becomes not merely an intellectual *credo,* but a fervent response of his whole being. Christian life is seen as a loving dialogue between the Father who speaks through His Son and the child who in Christ Jesus responds with complete self-committal.

This concept of revelation spells a new depth and a new intensity for Christian life. Following upon the necessary emphasis of Trent on the intellectual quality of faith, many in the Church have narrowed the vast Pauline perspective of *pistis* as a committal involving the whole man. In common teaching, faith was drained of its eminently vital quality; men spoke of "living faith" and "dead faith" simply because they thought of faith as so totally intellectual that it could be verified equally in saints and sinners. The Council has restored Paul's wider concept of faith as something eminently vital, alive with the gifts of the Holy Spirit, always growing and embracing the whole man. This chapter speaks of faith as "an obedience by which man commits his whole self freely to God, offering the full submission of intellect and will to God" who speaks to him here and now as a Father with His son. (Cf. paragraph 5.)

Chapter 2

This quality of dialogue between God who communicates Himself personally and man who lovingly responds continues as a *leitmotiv* in the second chapter's treatment of the transmission of revelation. For this first time in a conciliar Constitution the whole Church is identified as the living voice of tradition. Previous teaching has drawn sharp lines of demarcation between the *donnée* given to the Apostles and the *donnée* received by the Church, between the teaching magisterium and the quiescently receptive disciples. Although the Constitution preserves all that is true in such distinctions, it deliberately avoids the nomenclature and formulations which have served to deaden in the consciousness of many the full, rich reality of life in the Church.

Once one accepts the truth emphasized in the first chapter that every Christian is caught up in an I-and-Thou dialogue with the revealing God, he must also recognize that every Christian is himself a living echo of the words of God. With a mind enlightened by the truths which God now speaks and with conduct modeled on these truths, the whole personality of the Christian is resonant with the voice of God. The transmission of divine truth, therefore, although entrusted primarily to the bishops as successors of the Apostles, forms also an integral part of every Christian life. In the words of the Constitution, the tradition which comes from the Apostles and develops with the help of the Holy Spirit is "a living tradition whose wealth is poured into the practice and life of the believing and praying Church" (paragraph 8).

The life of every real Catholic, therefore, is rich with inherent and dynamic power to make the living word of God vocal among all those with whom he associates. Even more, every Catholic who is truly living by the Holy Spirit has power to advance the Church in its understanding of the word of God and in loving response to His voice. By reason of their office, pope and bishops alone are competent to test and to formulate authoritatively; but the actual momentum of response can come from any quarter. Our own century has seen the marked contribution of priests, religious and laity to the Church's understanding of God's word. Catholic doctrine and life owe a great deal to the meditation and writings of Dom Marmion and Dom Beaudouin, St. Thérèse of Lisieux and Elizabeth of the Trinity. How much, too, the Church's apostolate has gained from the Spirit-inspired activities of Pauline Jaricot and Yvonne Poncelet, Frank Duff and Frederic Ozanam, the Ladies of the Grail and the Auxiliaries of the Missions—all of them lay people.

This living quality of tradition which is borne out by every page of history has now received formal conciliar recognition. In one of its most beautiful paragraphs the Constitution affirms:

> This Tradition which comes from the Apostles develops in the Church with the help of the Holy Spirit. For there is growth in the understanding of the realities and the words which have been handed down. This happens through the contemplation and study of believers who treasure these things in their hearts, through a penetrating understanding of these spiritual things which they experience, and through the preaching of those who with episcopal succession have received the sure gift of truth. For as the centuries succeed one another, the Church constantly moves forward towards the fullness of divine truth until the words of God reach their complete fulfillment in her. (paragraph 8)

The voice of God, therefore, is always growing more and more resonant in the Church. "The apostolic teaching, which is expressed in a special way in the inspired books, was to be preserved in continuous succession until the end of time"—through Scripture and Tradition (paragraph 83). What is the exact relation between these two, what is the measure of the divine word which each contains—this thorny question the Council has deliberately avoided answering. The Fathers were content simply to reaffirm the teaching of Trent and Vatican I. God's word is the only source of revelation, and this is contained in the Bible and in the Church's Tradition: "Both of them, flowing from the same divine wellspring, in a certain way merge into unity and tend toward the same end" (paragraph 8).

Previously, Catholics found it convenient to meet the queries of non-Catholics about the scriptural source of our teaching by affirming that many revealed truths are found only in Tradition. This conviction was widespread among the Fathers at Trent; it was popularized in the polemic catechism of St. Peter Canisius; later it became a common theological cliché. Dom Christopher Butler, however, pointed out in the Council that this common teaching does not bear the compelling authority of ordinary magisterium. Today, in fact, historical studies have convinced many that this conviction was not to the fore in the centuries which preceded Trent. Even at Trent itself this position was so competently challenged by two of the Fathers that the Council refrained from any apodictic pronouncement. Continuing doubts after Trent, specially among English theologians, persuaded the Fathers of Vatican I to use the same discretion in leaving the question open. In Vatican II the opposition to the supposed common teaching was so well argued that the members of the Theological Commission studiously avoided using any expression which would limit liberty in discussing the relation between Scripture and Tradition in their respective transmissions of the word of God.

Chapter 3

The Constitution devotes four of its six chapters to the Bible. The fact that this book contains the message of salvation written under the inspiration of the Holy Spirit makes it "the word of God in a very special way" (paragraphs 7, 8).

The third chapter which opens the formal discussion of Scripture treats of its inspiration and interpretation. The dogma of inspiration, already defined by Vatican I, is succinctly repeated (paragraph 11). While thus emphasizing God's authorship of the sacred books, the Council also takes cognizance of the full authorship of the human writers: "In composing the sacred books, God chose men and made use of their powers and abilities while employed by Him, so that with Him acting in them and through them, they, as true authors, consigned to writing everything and only those things which He wanted" (paragraph 11). The Fathers of the Council, however, have made no effort to show how these two activities, divine and human, were combined. It was decided that theological thought on the nature of inspiration was not yet mature enough for the Council to venture a definitive statement on this delicate question.

On the other hand, the Fathers were fully outspoken when inerrancy, the natural emergent of inspiration, came under discussion. That the Bible is free of error has always been taught by the Church. Since, however, it is not the function of ordinary magisterium to define doctrine, it often happens (as in the present case of inerrancy) that the exact truth to be believed is obscured by exaggeration or distorted by faulty perspective. Fundamentalists, for example, relying on their concept of inerrancy, have sought to draw exact natural science from the sacred text. Others, more enlightened, still cling to the conviction that, with certain reservations and qualifications, exact factual truth could be found in Scripture in the same way in which it is found in modern scientific history.

Cardinal Meyer of Chicago was the first to point out that such widespread concepts of inerrancy which appeared even in the third draft of the schema were contrary to the nature and purpose of biblical writing. His criticism was seconded and amplified by Cardinal König of Vienna. Bishop Simons of Indore (India) struck the *coup de grâce* when he asked for a forthright rejection of all faulty notions and for a clear, correct presentation of what inerrancy really means.

As a result of these well-founded criticisms the Fathers of the Council have given to the Church an authoritative statement. They have made clear that the Bible, a religious book, must be judged free of error in accord with its purpose to teach the historic and doctrinal way of salvation: "The books of Scripture must be acknowledged as teaching solidly, faithfully and without error that truth which *for our salvation* God wanted put into the Sacred Writings" (paragraph 11).[1]

Seen in this light, inerrancy is a richly positive doctrine. Based on God's authorship of Scripture it strengthens man with the certainty that the divine communication presented in the Scriptures truly reveals all the elements of God's saving plan. It was within this luminous and positive scope that St. Paul himself saw the full meaning of biblical inerrancy, and so this paragraph of the third chapter concludes with the Apostle's own words: "All Scripture is divinely inspired and has its use for teaching the truth and refuting error, for reformation of manners and discipline in right living, so that the man

---

[1] The Italian translation of the Dogmatic Constitution on the Church which appeared in *L'Osservatore Romano*, Nov. 22–23, 1965, mistranslated the important phrase, *"quam Deus nostrae salutis causa."* Whereas the members of the Theological Commission and the Conciliar Fathers used *"causa"* as an ablative ("for the sake of our salvation"), the *L'Osservatore Romano* translation, unlike the other vernacular translations, understood *"causa"* as a nominative, so that the Italian version became *"che Dio cause della nostra salvezz."* This mistranslation completely distorts the meaning of this essential phrase and thus nullifies the conciliar clarification of inerrancy.

of God may be efficient and equipped for good work of every kind. (2 Tim 3:16–17).

In its second half the third chapter lays down sound principles to guide the Church in its understanding of the sacred text. This section, which will be of special interest to professional students of the Bible, incorporates all that is best in the principles of modern biblical scholarship. It makes very clear that if Scripture is to be rightly understood, it must be read in the spirit in which it was written. Only too often in the past men have tried to read the Scripture as a modern book of western culture. They have identified its words and phrases with their own thought-patterns, and so have silted the true meaning of God's words with their own interpretation. This was pardonable in an age when men did not have access to the world of the ancient Near East. Today, however, when excavation and research have uncovered the land and the literature, the imagery and background of the biblical world, it is needful to utilize these new helps in understanding the sacred text.

The section on interpretation re-presents in summary form the well-known directives which Pope Pius XII developed at length in his memorable encyclical *Divino Afflante Spiritu*. Because "God spoke in Sacred Scripture through men in human fashion" (paragraph 12), the meaning of His message requires careful attention to the purpose, the style of writing and the whole literary, social and conceptual background of the human writer who has presented the inspired word of God with the imagery and thought patterns of his own time. God still speaks to men from the pages of Sacred Scripture, but in the language of ancient Israel.

Chapter 4

Although this chapter is the briefest in the whole Constitution, it is also vital with the spirit which unifies the whole document. Two new elements, emergents of modern scholarship, are conspicuous. First, the Old Testament is presented not as history in the modern sense of the word, written in the style of Mommsen-Von Ranke historiographers, but rather as a theologized narrative intended to trace the course and to unfold the involvement of God's saving action in Israel and through Israel in the world. The first sentence of this chapter focuses attention on that character of Old Testament history which modern scholars have called *Heilsgeschichte*, the theologized recountal of God's saving deeds which have power to save every man if only he responds with faith: "In carefully planning and preparing the salvation of the whole human race the God of infinite love, by a special dispensation, chose for himself a people to whom He would entrust His promise" (paragraph 14).

History in the Old Testament, therefore, is seen as the working out of God's plan of salvation. Through the gradual unfolding of His plan, God reveals Himself not merely by a conceptual communication of words and ideas, as some have thought, but also by dynamic self-manifestation in deeds. This recognition of the revelatory function of God's deeds is already found in the writings of St. Augustine: "The deeds of the Word are themselves words." But emphasis on this fact is the second contribution which modern scholarship has made to this part of the Constitution which gives it pointed and felicitous expression: "The plan of revelation is realized by deeds and words having an inner unity: the deeds wrought by God in the history of salvation manifest and confirm the teaching and realities signified by the words, while the words themselves proclaim the deeds and clarify the mystery contained in them" (paragraph 2).

In accord with this perspective, the opening paragraph of the fourth chapter describes in lapidary phrases the whole development of God's dealings with the chosen people. Dominant motifs of Old Testament theology are singled out to linger in the memory as guiding insights into the mystery of God and of His plans for men. His one concern was to give Himself to men through word and work that they might know Him and enter into fellowship with Him. Although centered in Israel, this revelation was intended for all time, since the living God never changes.

But there is no history of salvation or manifestation of God which does not center in Christ. The second paragraph of this chapter (paragraph 15), therefore, points out that all divine activity in the period of the Old Testament was intended to prepare for the full execution of God's saving plan in Christ. In the earlier drafts of the Constitution, this Christocentric tenor of the Old Testament was validated only by allusions to the prophecies and types which are found in its pages. In the Constitution as finally promulgated, the work of preparation is seen to be as vast as the Old Testament itself. All the wondrous elements of Israel's life—its living sense of God, its clear knowledge of the ways of God with men, its inspired treasury of prayers— all the perennial values of the Old Testament are now seen to have their full meaning as a positive preparation of God's people to hear and answer the perfect Word of God, Christ Jesus. (Cf. paragraph 15).

Chapter 5

In its fifth chapter, the theme of fulfillment pervades and integrates the Constitution's treatment of the New Testament. The first sentence of the opening paragraph sums up all that can be said: "The word of God, which is the power of God for the saving of all who believe, is set forth and shows its power in a most excellent way in the writings of the New Testament" (paragraph 17). These books treat directly of the redemptive mystery of Christ, and so they orchestrate the consummate revelation of God.

This thought naturally turns the development of the chapter to the Gospels. Their apostolic origin is affirmed, although detailed problems of actual authorship are carefully avoided, for in this matter scholarship has not yet reached final conclusions. To establish the fact that the fourfold gospel is the foundation of faith, the Conciliar Fathers thought it sufficient to affirm that, humanly, the Gospels are of apostolic origin and, divinely, they are of God's inspiration.

The Gospels, however, provide the foundation of faith precisely because they relate the saving realities of Christ's life, death and resurrection. It is imperative, then, that men be assured of their truly historical value. To do so is clearly the purpose of the second paragraph. Here the Constitution clearly states that the Gospels "faithfully hand on what Jesus Christ, while living among men, really did and taught for their eternal salvation until the day he was taken up into heaven" (paragraph 19).

But an important qualification is necessary. The history of Jesus, like salvation history in the Old Testament, was not written to meet the norms of historiographers of our century. The Gospels, instead, were composed according to the patterns of the ancient world where "history" was often enough an amalgam of earlier oral traditions and where an interpretative philosophy of history was quite as important as the facts themselves. Utilizing with competence the emergents of Gospel study in our present century, this paragraph of the Constitution recognizes the validity of the sound and proven methods which have emerged from the study of literary forms and redaction techniques.

A precedent for this approach to the Gospels was already provided by the instruction of the Pontifical Biblical Commission, *Sancta Mater Ecclesia,* published in April, 1964. This letter, while safeguarding the reliable historicity of the Gospels, pointed out the significant fact that both the early apostolic community and the evangelists themselves have shaped the story of Jesus according to their own Spirit-guided understanding of its profound significance and have also given to the materials of this history the literary forms required to adapt the words and deeds of Jesus to the preaching of the early Church, to its liturgy, doctrinal instruction, controversy and other activities. The words of the Pontifical Biblical Commission's instruction are incorporated verbatim into the text of the Constitution.

The last paragraph of this chapter (paragraph 20) may seem to treat rather summarily the rest of the New Testament writings. Nevertheless this treatment, although brief, succinctly presents the precise nature of their rich contribution. Through the mystery of Christ, fully set forth in the Gospels, God speaks His perfect word and gives Himself totally to men. Whatever else is written in the New Testament is but the clarification and unfolding of the consummate mystery of Christ.

Chapter 6

This last chapter is best described as the practical and pastoral conclusion of the light-giving truths which the Constitution has developed. Because Sacred Scripture is everywhere resonant with the living voice of God and because the people of God must respond to His voice with the self-committal of living faith, the Council Fathers have voiced their concordant appeal that the Scriptures should become once more for all men "the bread of life" (paragraph 21). No matter how or under what pretext many have neglected it in the past, it must now assume a primary role in the Church's spiritual life; for if religion means anything, it is a loving communication between God and man, a continuing I-and-Thou dialogue between a devoted Father who speaks and an attentive child who faithfully responds.

If only the recommendations of this final chapter of the Constitution are followed, a renewal of love for the Scriptures will bring fresh and dynamic power into the lives of all the people of God. At the same time, this renewal will forge a new bond with those sincere Christians who, although not members of the Church, have always cherished the Sacred Scriptures and have often expressed wonderment that Catholics in general have so little familiarity with its pages.

To strengthen this ecumenical rapport with those outside the Church, the Constitution endorses collaboration between Catholics and non-Catholics in translating the Scriptures. This measure removes forever the wall of separation which has kept Catholics and Protestants apart in their reading of that divine word which belongs to every true child of God.

Every chapter of this wondrous Constitution, therefore, serves to emphasize the life-giving truth that God is always speaking to the Church. It is for the Church, then, to listen attentively to His voice and to respond with living faith. Only the years to come will show what this means for the deepening and enriching of Christian life. It is certain, however, that if only every Christian takes to heart the message of the Constitution, the promise of St. Paul, which is the very spirit of this document, will be certainly realized: "The Gospel is the power of God for salvation to everyone who has faith" (Rom. 1:16).

III/DOGMATIC CONSTITUTION ON THE SACRED LITURGY

Dogmatic Constitution on the Sacred Liturgy

⚜ HISTORICAL INTRODUCTION

When the American bishops entered St. Peter's basilica on October 22, 1962, their sentiments were quite naturally similar to those of their episcopal colleagues from other nations. The electrifying excitement of the previous week, sparked by Achille Cardinal Liénart's statement demanding more time to elect the members of conciliar commissions, had subsided. Those nine days served as the initiation of most Fathers into the ways of the Romans, the democratic process of a Council and the importance of international representation on the vitally important commissions. If they had been up until then "like novices singing in a choir," as Pope John remarked, these first nine days of the Council proved to be the crucial time of their novitiate.

Quite naturally, the members of the Council's Commission on the Liturgy were happy to learn on October 16, during the second congregation, that their schema would be the first discussed on the floor of the Council. As *La Croix* observed, the subject was important both theologically and pastorally, and thus in accord with Pope John's inaugural address; while it would not cause dissension in the ranks, it would serve as a catalyst and allow the advocates of renewal to establish the *leitmotiv* of the entire Council. In florid, curial tones, the Vatican Council Press Office explained the papal decision to make the sacred liturgy the first item on the agenda. It announced on October 16:

> The work of Redemption, pre-announced by God in the Sacred Scripture and fulfilled by Christ, is continued in the Church chiefly through the liturgy, through the Sacrifice of the Cross perpetually renewed on the altar, through the sacraments and through daily tribute of public prayer.

No one, perhaps, better than Pope John himself expressed the reason for his choosing the sacred liturgy as the first topic for discussion. Speaking to the members of the central preparatory commission in June, 1961, he said:

> To put it all very briefly, the aim of the Council is to make the clergy on every level shine with a new holiness; to bring the main points and

129

precepts of Christian doctrine to the people of God in the best possible way; to give young people, the fresh seeds whose growth holds the hope of a better age, sound training in how to live as they should; to foster the activities of the social apostolate; and to nourish a deep missionary spirit, the kind of spirit that will make it clear to everyone that each and every person is our brother and our friend.

This, in fact, was precisely what liturgical scholars had been saying since the days of Dom Lambert Beauduin in 1909.

Many of the Fathers felt that an atmosphere of peace and tranquility would descend upon the gathering. Who could possibly imagine anything divisive about the sacred liturgy? So they took their assigned seats in the aula, with the schema on the sacred liturgy before them.

The liturgical schema was, from its very beginning, the best of the original 73 and subsequent 17 presented for discussion. It was a tribute to the excellent work performed by the members of the preparatory and conciliar commissions. It was the only schema not to be rejected or returned for complete revision. Its acceptance by the Council Fathers, with only emendations, was a profound recognition of the sound scholarship produced by the two commissions directly, as well as indirectly by the previous fifty years of liturgical activity and scholarship. The schema itself was a triumph over those seemingly distant days when Dom Lambert Beauduin, one of the founders of the "movement," asked to speak at the Belgium Catholic Congress in 1909 on the subject of the liturgy. His speech was assigned to the section discussing "Art and Archeology"! Indirectly, too, the schema was a tribute to the activity taking place on American shores among such liturgical pioneers as Father Virgil Michel, O.S.B., Father Michael Ducey, O.S.B., Monsignor Martin Hellriegel, Monsignor William Busch and Monsignor Reynold Hillen-brand in the late twenties, thirties and early forties. They could have well spoken the same words their European counterpart, Father Joseph Jung-mann, S.J., uttered when the preparatory commission had finished its work: "If the Council accepts this statement, I shall be happy to sing my *Nunc Dimittis.*"

The preparatory Commission on the Liturgy, established by Pope John XXIII, was formed with Gaetano Cardinal Cicognani as chairman and Father Annibale Bugnini, C.M., as secretary. The only American member of this Commission was Reverend John Quasten of The Catholic University of America. Consultants to the Commission were Reverend Frederick McManus of the Catholic University of America and Reverend Godfrey Diek-mann, O.S.B., of St. John's Abbey in Minnesota. Shortly after Cardinal Cicognani's death on February 5, 1962, Arcadio Cardinal Larraona, C.M.F., was named chairman.

Pope John officially opened the preparatory phase of the Council on June

5, 1960. The formal beginning of the work of the preparatory commissions began with a solemn papal audience in St. Peter's basilica on November 14 of the same year. The preparatory Commission on the Liturgy numbered in its ranks, as members and consultants, first-class scholars from throughout the world. Among them from other countries were Martimort and Roguet from France, Jungmann from Austria, Wagner and Fischer from Germany, Schmidt from Holland, Bugnini and Vaggagini from Italy.

The work of the preparatory Commission on the Liturgy was immense. Between November, 1960, and the summer of 1962 it held 4 plenary meetings, the shortest lasting 7 days and the longest, 15 days. At the November, 1960 meeting the material submitted by the world's bishops was examined and sifted down to essential proposals. Since, at this time, no member of the Commission had any conciliar experience, it was the general feeling of the Commission to include every item submitted by any bishop. At this meeting, too, subcommissions were already appointed to examine various specific suggestions more minutely. A record of these meetings would be impossible to obtain at this time. Most of them were held informally, and their findings were presented to the general commission meetings.

In January, 1962, the preparatory Commission on the Liturgy met for its final meeting in Rome. At this time the material had been collated and presented in a completed form. The members of the Commission thereupon accepted the material and, in turn, presented it to the Central Preparatory Commission. At that stage the members of the Commission were under the impression that its schema would be submitted intact to the Fathers of the Council. As it turned out, however, the contents of the schema had been "somewhat amended" by a subcommission of the Central Preparatory Commission. The principal emendation, at this point, consisted of the ommission of a great deal of explanatory material that had been appended to the document. This, however, was not done with the schema submitted by the Theological Commission. This material had been deleted, much to the surprise of many bishops upon receiving the text of the liturgy schema from the office of the Secretariat of State in the summer of 1962. During the first session, however, the Liturgical Commission succeeded in distributing much of this material to the Council Fathers in booklets.

According to Father Frederick McManus, the meetings of the preparatory Commission on the Liturgy were "very open," that is, both members and consultors spoke frequently and openly. In this aspect of its work it differed considerably from other preparatory commissions where, generally, only the members had a voice. In both cases, however, only the members of the Commission cast a vote. The last meeting of the preparatory Commission occurred in January, 1962, and culminated in Cardinal Larraona presenting its completed work, in the form of a schema, to the Central Preparatory Commission some three months later.

Even before the introduction of the liturgical schema to the deliberations of the Council Fathers, the conciliar Commission on the Liturgy had begun its work. On October 21, 1962, the Commission met under the presidency of Cardinal Larraona with all twenty-four members and consultors present. At that time the Cardinal-president appointed Paolo Cardinal Giobbe and Andrea Cardinal Jullien as vice presidents and Father Ferdinando Antonelli, O.F.M., as secretary.

Throughout the first session, members of the Commission on the Liturgy met almost daily. As soon as interventions were uttered on the floor of the Council or submitted in writing, the Commission examined them, word for word. The work was so immense that the Commission was subdivided into 13 working subcommissions consisting of both conciliar Fathers and consultants.

After the liturgical schema was voted upon and accepted for discussion, the Commission members continually returned to a principle: Since the schema is in possession, we cannot weaken it, but must strengthen it according to the suggestions of the majority. Time after time during its meetings, this principle was recalled either to strengthen the fainthearted or to overcome the obstructionists. The Commission felt it to be its duty to reject the note published on the title page of the original schema, namely: "The purpose of this Constitution is to propose only general norms and the fundamental principles for bringing about a universal liturgical renewal; it is left to the Holy See to spell out particular directives." Some members felt this note was drafted by an "enemy" of the schema, actually working within the Commission! The Commission's concern was the 46 pages and 105 numbers of the original schema. Fourteen months later, after literally countless hours of work, the Commission members witnessed the promulgation of a constitution consisting of 37 pages and 130 numbers, to the intense joy of almost the entire Commission.

According to Archbishop Hallinan, the conciliar commission charged with examining the observations made during the Council discussions divided them into four groups. He explained:

First there are the proposals already covered in the schema itself or by previous amendments to the schema. Then there are the proposals which our liturgical commission has passed on to the other commissions of the Council where the matter in question is treated more directly. The third category contains proposals considered by the liturgical commission to be too detailed, and these have been referred to a post-conciliar commission to be set up after the Council ends, as provided for in the papal document of 6 December. The final category includes all real amendments to the liturgy schema, and these are what we have processed in our subcommission and commission meetings.

On another occasion, when asked what took place during an average meeting of the Commission on the Liturgy, Father Godfrey Diekmann, O.S.B., replied:

> Our present task, as distinguished from the role of the preparatory commission, consists in studying and coordinating all the recommendations of the conciliar Fathers. We must consider their verbal and oral suggestions and incorporate them into the schema which will ultimately be presented to them for their final approval or rejection. This, of course, entails a great detail of work, and consequently we meet now every day for about two hours in order to prepare these corrections and emendations for the votes of the Fathers of the Council.

Most important, too, was the actual program of liturgical education that continued throughout the first and second sessions that members and consultants of the Commission carried out in the Eternal City. Meetings of episcopal conferences, press conferences, lectures in seminaries and religious houses, articles, background pieces, pamphlets, private conversations in the side aisles of St. Peter's, at a coffee table along the Via dellà Conciliazione, a dinner meeting in some small, out-of-the-way Roman restaurant—every educational technique available was used.

In this work two Americans were outstanding. Without a doubt, they contributed more than any other Americans to the formulation, understanding and final acceptance of the liturgical schema. They were Archbishop Paul J. Hallinan of Atlanta and Father Frederick McManus of The Catholic University of America.

The educational efforts of the American hierarchy did not lag. Its committee, established along with the eleven others in the latter part of October, 1962, at least attempted an educational program within its own ranks concerning matters liturgical. Members of the committee were: Bishops Vincent S. Waters, Raleigh, North Carolina, Chairman; Leo F. Dworschak, Fargo, North Dakota; Charles A. Buswell, Pueblo, Colorado; Victor J. Reed, Oklahoma City-Tulsa, Oklahoma; Clarence G. Issenman, Columbus, Ohio; Gerald V. McDevitt, auxiliary of Philadelphia, Pennsylvania; and John J. Russell, Richmond, Virginia. One of their efforts was to secure Father Frederick McManus to address the body of American bishops at one of their earliest Sunday morning meetings, October 28, held at the North American College. Father McManus thus held the distinction of being the first American consultant to address his own hierarchy during the time of the Council.

Although two Americans, Archbishop Hallinan and Bishop Leo Dworschak, were proposed on the Americans' list for Commission members, only the former received the necessary number of votes. Nonetheless, Bishop Dworschak, as a member of the American committee, played an important role in the liturgical education of the American hierarchy. First of all, he was the one who suggested that Father McManus be approached to address the body of American bishops. On several occasions during those first weeks he also served as a liaison between the French and German hierarchies and the Americans. In some respects he was in the perfect position to fulfill this important role these opening weeks of the Council, both because he was living at Salvator Mundi Hospital and had formed many important contacts in previous years through his relationships with Aloysius Cardinal Muench, his predecessor in the Fargo see.

On October 21, the American bishops met at the North American College to establish a working arrangement of holding regular meetings during the Council sessions. It was proposed at this meeting to set up a presidency of five members, a secretariat of three members and a committee of seven members corresponding to the existing conciliar commissions. At this meeting Bishop Ernest J. Primeau of Manchester, New Hampshire, was designated the executive assistant to the presidency. At this meeting, too, there was a certain degree of urgency to elect members of the American bishops' liturgical commission since it was known that the Council would begin discussion on the liturgy schema the next day.

According to one observer, Cardinal Spellman who was then presiding, was most reluctant to permit an election of members to this committee because he felt that the nominees were "stacked," to use his own expression. After more than half an hour of wrangling, the Cardinal finally read the names of the nominees, and finally the American bishops voted these members of the American bishops' liturgical commission: Bishops Leo F. Dworschak, Charles Buswell, Victor Reed, Clarence Issenman, Vincent Waters, John Russell and Gerald McDevitt. Bishop Waters was subsequently chosen chairman of the committee.

Throughout most of the first session the American bishops' committee on the liturgy met frequently, at first in the Rome offices of the National Catholic Welfare Conference and later, following the regular Monday-evening meetings of the American bishops, at the North American College.

Another example of the educational program embarked upon was the explanations given daily at the American Bishops' Press Panel by Father McManus. He literally conducted, for the benefit of some forty representatives of the press, one of the best postgraduate courses in the liturgy available anywhere. Several times Archbishop Hallinan appeared as a guest at the press panel. On October 26 he appeared and told the press that, in his opinion, "there have been very few extremists in the debate. Every one of the speakers has conceded the merits of the other side." When asked how he would describe the debate on the liturgy taking place in the Council hall, he said, "The words 'wide open' would describe it best."

The debate was, in fact, "wide open." It lasted throughout fifteen congregations, from October 22 until November 13.*

Early in the Council deliberations the question of the vernacular became its symbol. It was the rallying point for the two general positions taken by the Fathers, including the Americans. Those in favor of its most extensive use were called in the daily press the "progressives"; those adamantly opposed to any use of the vernacular whatever were labeled "conservatives." Admittedly there were many degrees of opinion between poles. Generally speaking, the majority of the American bishops preferred to be called "moderates." By the time of the voting, however, the vast majority of them cast their ballots in favor of the progressives.

Even on the floor of the Council the advocates of wider use of the vernacular carried the day precisely because their reasons were more cogent. For this reason the Vatican Council press-bulletin report on the seventh congregation did not accurately relate the actual situation in the aula (a discrepancy immediately recognized by the working press and which was to be repeated, time after time, during the first session). The report that day stated:

> Another point on which the Fathers spoke was that of the language which should be used in the liturgy. There are reasons which militate in favor of Latin, inasmuch as its adoption has not only traditional values, but has also a truly unifying effect. Furthermore, because of its logical precision, because of its concrete phraseology of legal terms, it is particularly suited for theology and dogma.
>
> Latin also has considerable psychological and ascetical values since it tends to make one speak in a logical and rational manner and prevents abandonment to sentimentalities and romantic evasions. It tends to give its user discipline of expression and of life.

Some speakers, to be sure, did utter these thoughts, somewhat to the amusement and consternation of the majority of listeners. However, most speakers on the subject presented arguments more pertinent to the discussion of the liturgy and the pastoral needs of people. The dispatch correctly stated that "the Council Fathers' discussion on these points was done with mutual exchange of each one's learning and experience." It could hardly have been further from the truth, however, when it went on to state: "It is not a matter of opposing positions, but of a common and fraternal research through the free expression of different points of view. . . ." On the contrary. It was quite definitely "a matter of opposing positions."

The American bishops fulfilled their obligations as teachers and witnesses

* For a more extensive account of the entire discussion concerning the liturgy, the reader is referred to: Rynne, Xavier, *Letters from Vatican City*, Farrar, Straus & Company, New York, 1963, pp. 68–139.

during the discussion on the sacred liturgy. Of the 329 interventions concerning the liturgy delivered on the floor of the Council, 19 were uttered by Americans. Only a future historian will know exactly how many interventions were submitted in writing. At this time we know of at least seven written interventions by American prelates, not to mention the numerous *modi* signed individually.

It seemed no more than fitting that the first American to speak in the Council would be Francis Cardinal Spellman of New York. He was, after all, the leader of the American hierarchy. He took, as was expected, a hold-the-line position and approached every change with something more than caution. His attitude toward the vernacular was clearly enunciated: "The Latin language, which is truly the Catholic language, is unchangeable, is not vulgar, and has been for many centuries the guardian of the unity of the Western Church." His words were, for the most part, exactly what members of other hierarchies expected an American to say. His position remained unchanged throughout the other three interventions he delivered on the liturgy schema. Again he cautioned "the greatest prudence and circumspection in introducing innovations" and warned about "an exaggerated 'historicism' and a zeal for novelties." His approach was pastoral, to be sure, but a pastoral approach that seemed to many, even as he spoke, completely out of tune with the current needs.

In his intervention during the sixteenth congregation, Cardinal Spellman came out strongly in favor of the use of the vernacular in the private recitation of the Divine Office. There was a bit of consternation in the minds of many at this point. Here, they thought, is the same man who two weeks ago spoke against introducing the vernacular into the Mass, and now he is in favor of making use of the vernacular in the breviary! He argued: "If there are innovations, they should be such that the Office becomes better accommodated to the condition of today's busy life, especially of the pastor of souls." His final intervention on the liturgy, delivered during the sixteenth congregation, was his briefest, lasting only two minutes. He agreed that the liturgical calendar should be so reformed as to coincide with the civil calendar.

No American prelate devoted more written attention to the Dogmatic Constitution on the Sacred Liturgy than Cardinal Spellman. His written interventions, which number more than a dozen, reflect, by and large, the same opinions that he stated on the floor of the Council.

If Cardinal Spellman took a position which most observers and participants at the Council expected *at that time,* Cardinal Ritter offered them a complete surprise on the second day of the liturgy discussion, during the fifth congregation. He spoke Latin as a mid-Westerner would, and his ideas, to a large extent, reflected the liturgical thinking that had been developing for a generation in the heartland of the United States. He spoke, too, as a representative of the "new" kind of thinking taking place within the minds of many younger members of the American hierarchy who had only a small voice on the national scene. As one consultant put it, he was "wide open for reform." His position could not have been stated more directly: "The very nature of the liturgy and the Church," he said, "strongly persuades and even demonstrates the need for reform." By his speech and demeanor, Cardinal Ritter revealed to the other bishops of the world that the American hierarchy was by no means a monolith.

The Cardinal of Los Angeles, who spoke during the same congregation, dramatically highlighted the divergent views among the Americans on the liturgy. Cardinal McIntyre delivered an eloquent defense of the Latin language when he said:

> The Latin language . . . gave rise to wonderful effects. Its severity overcame nationalities. In politics it was neutral. With great constancy its efficiency perdured into our epoch. Once adopted, Latin became truly universal, especially among educated and literary men. Having a mathematical rather than vulgar structure, Latin attained a continuous primacy and perdured through the centuries. It is very outstanding in intellectual, literary and scientific matters.

Cardinal McIntyre's position was crystal clear. No one was surprised, then, and, for that matter, rather expected the same statement of principle when he rose again to speak during the twelfth congregation on the Holy Sacrifice of the Mass. He took pains to explain how Holy Mass was celebrated in the parishes of the United States. "Changes are not needed," he said, and went on to cite the 1958 Instruction of the Sacred Congregation of Rites which declared that the primary intention in hearing Mass is internal. "This internal intention," he concluded, "is frequently practiced by those whose intellectual capacity is not great. Furthermore, active participation is frequently a distraction."

Cardinal McIntyre was the first American, and one of the first of all the Council Fathers, to salute the observer-delegates. He did so in this intervention when he addressed them as "Brother Observers."

The next day the Council Fathers had the opportunity to hear a man they had been waiting to observe. Cardinal Meyer, with quiet dignity, presented two points for consideration. He commended the "true middle path" concerning the liturgical language by leaving the decision to the National Episcopal Conference and the approval of the Holy See. Secondly, he opposed giving a national liturgical commission too much authority. Stating his deep-seated conviction, he said, "Let it *always* be the bishop in his own diocese who is the moderator of liturgical, pastoral action under the rule of the Holy See, and not under the rule of some national commission." At that point he won the respect of his colleagues, even though, during the second session he somewhat modified his stand on the role of the bishop in his own diocese.

The humility and prudence of Cardinal Meyer were disarming. When he spoke again on November 9, his words carried even more weight. He was opposed to any "insistence on the carrying out of various parts of the Divine Office at fixed hours of the day," for he knew how difficult of fulfillment the ideal would be for those engaged in the active ministry. Secondly, he suggested that "for the sake of greater piety, it be permitted in private recitation to use an approved translation in the vernacular."

One of the finest interventions on the sacred liturgy was delivered during the eleventh congregation by Archbishop Hallinan. He was the first American who began by saying, "I speak for many bishops, although not for all, of the United States of America." He favored renewal, advocating more active and intelligent participation through the use of the vernacular and a restructuring of the liturgical rites. He then introduced an ecumenical dimension to the sacred liturgy:

> The more that we can do to render the Mass understandable to all, not just to those equipped by learning or formed by habit, the more we open new avenues to the minds and hearts of Christians who are not Catholic. The Church is the loving mother of *all*.

By this time Council Fathers from other nations were beginning to realize that the American hierarchy was not a monolith. At first, many of them believed that American bishops quite generally followed the leadership of Cardinals Spellman and McIntyre. Archbishop Halinan's observations, as well as those presented by other Americans in the succeeding days, brought about the realization that, rather than one, there were several, and even opposing, intellectual and pastoral positions among the American hierarchy.

As the discussion continued, more American bishops rose to state their opinions. The conciliar experience was beginning to take hold. The Americans were beginning to understand the full import of the words Bishop Ullathorne had written in his diary at the First Vatican Council:

> In the General Council the office of the bishops is twofold: they are witnesses and judges. As a witness, each bishop bears testimony to the traditions, teachings and customs of the church over which he presides; and so, when all the bishops have given their testimony, the doctrine and practice of the Universal Church becomes manifest.

Bishop Charles Helmsing undoubtedly has the distinction of delivering the shortest speech on the Council floor, much to the pleasure of his colleagues. On October 30 he rose and candidly stated: "After receiving the schema, I took care to send my observations and emendations to the Secretary of State to His Holiness. Since I have been informed that these observations have been sent to the proper commission, in order to accelerate the work of the Council, I freely cede the occasion to speak." For this he received the hearty applause of the assembly.

During the last four congregations devoted to the liturgy schema, six other Americans delivered interventions. Bishop William Connare spoke "in the name of many priests of my diocese and other dioceses as well." He argued in favor of giving priests the option of reciting the Divine Office in either Latin or the vernacular.

Speaking on the same day, Bishop Francis Reh proposed a change in the structure of the Divine Office. He argued for "a form of the breviary which is better suited for the use of clerics who, in fact, are almost always forced to recite the canonical hours alone." While he conceded the great splendor and beauty of choral recitation and singing of the Divine Office, he defended "the true and efficacious representation" of the Church performed by a person reciting the breviary alone.

On the following day, November 10, Bishop Stephen Leven stated his approval of the same concession. "My argument," he said, "is neither against the Latin language nor concerning the ignorance of some, but is based only on pastoral practices, so that the priest may become 'a man approved, a worker that cannot be ashamed, rightly handling the word of truth.'" Bishop Victor Reed, in the same congregation, made three proposals for the reform of the liturgical calendar. He asked, first, that a greater variety of scriptural texts be employed in the Sunday and daily Masses; secondly, that ferial Masses be formulated for every day of the year when first- and second-class feasts are not celebrated; that votive Masses of a more determined nature be formulated. Speaking for his people, he concluded:

> I wish to say that the people of my diocese have accepted with enthusiasm the recent liturgical reforms. Not only do they need liturgical participation in the Mass and in the sacraments, but they also longed for this participation because today they are better educated and therefore seek a fuller understanding and appreciation of the riches and the fullness of the sacred liturgy.

During this same congregation Bishop Joseph Marling, C.PP.S., pleaded that the feast of St. Gaspar, the founder of the Congregation of the Most Precious Blood, be extended to the universal Church. His reason: "In the calendar of the universal Church the feast of those saints have a place who are acknowledged by official authority as apostles, that is, the principal promoters of major and universal devotions which have importance in the Church."

The last American to speak on the subject of the sacred liturgy was Bishop Russell McVinney who centered his remarks around article 83, on "the penitential practice of Lent usefully undertaken." He proposed a stricter observance of the Lenten season and made the following observation:

The faithful are hardly strengthened if the exercise of the faith is rendered easier. Just as the muscles of the body are hardened by exercise and not by indulgence, so also the "muscles" of the spirit. Look around you and see where the strong faith is found, and there you will find a radical conviction about the necessity of penitential reparation.

Seven written interventions on the sacred liturgy by American prelates are known to have been submitted for the consideration of the committee. Two were submitted by Archbishop Philip Hannan, one by Archbishop John Krol and Bishops Aloysius Willinger, C.Ss.R., John Russell, John Franz and Robert Tracy. The last-mentioned asked that it be permitted to recite the Divine Office in the vernacular. His reasons were, first, that "the recitation of the breviary be attentive, devout and fruitful"; secondly, that "priests spontaneously think and speak in the vernacular"; thirdly, that it "will help their spiritual life and devotion"; fourthly, that it "will also help them in preaching, catechizing and in instructing the faithful." For the first time an American bishop, John Russell, cited a specific number of his colleagues who agreed with his position:

At least 150 bishops of the United States of America agree with this opinion because they feel that the recitation of the breviary in the vernacular every day will bear fruit and foster spiritual growth both for priests and for the faithful.

Bishop Willinger submitted a most learned and scholarly intervention on the sacred liturgy. He centered his observations around number 41 of the schema which states: "The bishop is to be considered as the high priest of his flock, from whom the life in Christ of his faithful is in some way derived and dependent." His lengthy intervention revealed an understanding of the most recent liturgical scholarship, and every statement proposed was documented by a reference to one or another recent liturgical work. After citing the need of intelligent participation by a brief explanation of every part of the fore-Mass, Bishop Willinger concluded:

This introduction of the vernacular into the sacred liturgy of the Mass will implement the present yearning for and insistence on the participation of the laity in the liturgical function, contribute to the interest, understanding and fervor of the faithful, center their minds and hearts on the essence and dignity of the mystery of the grand sacrifice that is to follow, and even appeal to the religious sense of our separated brethren.

Bishop Franz reflected the prevailing sentiment among the Americans by asking in his intervention for a greater use of the vernacular in the Mass and administration of the sacraments. Bishop Robert Tracy requested a dispensation from reciting the Divine Office for priests who assist at Masses celebrated on special occasions, such as weddings, funerals, anniversaries and forty-hours devotions. He wrote:

> With the granting of this dispensation, the priests themselves would enter freely and readily into a fuller participation in the liturgy and, at the same time, be a more fitting and efficacious example of that active participation in the Mass to which the priests, as their teachers and leaders in the liturgy, constantly urge the faithful.

In his written intervention on the liturgy, submitted a month before the Council opened, Archbishop Krol had recommended the homily as part of the very liturgy. He wrote: "It is proposed that a homily, or talk or sermon be given in those Masses which are publicly celebrated on Sundays and, if possible, also on required feasts."

Archbishop Hannan's interventions concerned the use of the vernacular in the Divine Office and the practice of concelebration. His reasons for favoring the first practice were the same as those expressed on the Council floor by other American bishops. His advocacy of the practice of concelebration, however, is the only intervention on the subject presented by an American, excluding the disapproval voiced by Cardinal Spellman in the course of his intervention of October 29. On this subject, it should also be noted, Archbishop Hannan spoke also in the name of "certain other bishops of the United States of America." He asked, first, that the faculty of permitting concelebration be granted to the local ordinary. Passing over the reasons derived from the nature of the Mass and episcopacy, he suggested that "concelebration by its very nature acts to unite souls in Christ, especially when the bishop celebrates the Mass. For when the bishop, as the chief pastor of the diocese," he continued, "concelebrates together with his priests, it presents to the faithful a great sign of the unity in Christ which is most favorable for fostering piety." He cited likewise the experience derived from the concelebrated Masses in the National Shrine of the Immaculate Conception in Washington, D.C., where "the sacred liturgy according to the venerable Oriental rites is celebrated, especially in the January novena devotions called the 'Chair of Unity.'"

During this time, which seemed interminable to many American participants, 329 Fathers expressed their opinions on the Council floor. On November 14, Archbishop Pericle Felici, the General Secretary, in the name of Cardinal Tisserant proposed the vote on whether the liturgy schema should be approved in principle and whether, after the proposed amendments had been acted upon by the Commission on the Liturgy, the schema should be submitted to a later vote by the Fathers. The result of the vote was joy to the heart of most members of the Commission: 2,162 approved; 46 disapproved; 7 abstained.

By this time many Americans became impatient. They had spent a month in Rome and had nothing concrete to show for it. They were looking to that day, less than a month away, when they would return home with no concrete legislation, no promulgated decree, no definitive pronouncement to relay to their priests and people. The conciliar experience demanded time. In mid-November the Americans and others were only beginning to realize the chemistry of a Council. Nonetheless, they were elated during the thirtieth congregation, on November 30, when the voting on the introduction and first chapter of the schema began. During the next six congregations, 22 votes on individual points in the introduction and first chapter of the liturgy schema were cast, all with overwhelming majorities. The crucial vote came on December 7, during the thirty-sixth congregation, when a vote on the entire introduction and first chapter was called for. The result was 1,922 in favor, 11 opposed, 180 in favor with reservations, and 5 null votes.

The American bishops now had their definite, black-on-white result of the first session. More than that, they had grown wiser in the course of the past two months. None of them, as many remarked at this time, could ever be the same. In so many ways so difficult to describe, they had "discovered" the Church. The liturgy, for them, had been the weathervane. The "new Pentecost" to which Pope John had referred in his closing address was almost felt by the bishops as they prepared to return home. There was a definite sense of accomplishment, for the direction of the future had been charted out.

The Church had opted for change. The Church had made its own that principle of Cardinal Newman which Archbishop Shehan would stress in his intervention during the next session: "A power of development is a proof of life." Cardinal Montini had reflected this same spirit during the first session. Before the opening of the next session, he was to be Pope Paul VI and would state the same principle in his first encyclical letter in these words: "The Church . . . advances more and more in the awareness of its duty, of the nature of its mysteries, of its doctrines. . . ." Cardinal Newman had himself prophetically stated what was actually taking place during this first session of Vatican II:

> There will be general agitation of thought, and an action of mind upon mind. There will be a time of confusion, when conceptions and misconceptions are in conflict. . . . New lights will be brought to bear upon the original statements of the doctrine put forward; judgments and aspects will accumulate. After a while some definite teaching emerges. . . . It will be interrogated and criticized by enemies and defended by well wishers. . . . This process, whether it be longer or shorter in time . . . I call it development.

This process in this precise way was taking place during these closing days of 1962, not only within the Council hall, but also among the American bishops. Their interventions, above all, reflected a "development."

The next session began September 29, 1963. Its discussions centered around the Church, bishops and ecumenism. It produced its fruits, tangible and real, in the voting on the schemata concerning sacred liturgy and the media of social communications. It also came face to face with a new pontiff, Paul VI. His address, opening the second session, was equal to Pope John's inaugural address. He chartered the remaining sessions of the Council by enunciating four objectives: self-awareness of the Church; renewal of the Church; encounter with the separated brothers; dialogue with the world. The last was an echo of his profoundly significant, although somewhat enigmatic, inaugural encyclical *Ecclesiam Suam.*

The Fathers present for the second session were concerned now more with a legislative than an educational aspect of the sacred liturgy. The discussions were finished. They now acted, and fully consciously so, as the divinely appointed judges and rulers of the Church of God. Electronic computers, to be sure, assisted a great deal. Ushers who distributed and gathered ballots were likewise useful. Yet only a bishop or his religious counterpart could pick up the electronic pen and write his *placet, non placet* or *placet juxta modum.* The Americans had experienced the conciliar alchemy. They had given testimony, as they knew it, to the liturgical experience in the United States. In many areas they had manifestly experienced a metamorphosis. Now they were called upon to be judges and rulers. Admittedly, this was a new experience, tasted only slightly in the first session.

The voting on the schema concerning the sacred liturgy was important for several reasons. First, it established a pattern that was to be followed in every other conciliar discussion. More than that, it revealed a democratic spirit at work within the Church because of confidence in the guiding influence of the Holy Spirit that no other parliamentary assembly enjoys. It likewise demonstrated the complete autonomy (with a concomitant and almost paradoxical unanimity) of each conciliar Father. For these reasons, among others, the voting on the schema concerning the sacred liturgy deserves a closer scrutiny.

Every schema was subjected to five basic votes, excluding those that were cast on individual amendments. First of all, there was the vote to accept the schema as a basis for discussion. This was followed by a vote to accept the schema, chapter by chapter, and, finally, as a whole after the observations of the conciliar Fathers had been made a part of the schema. The third vote was cast upon each of the amendments after the *modi* had been considered by the Commission. The fourth vote was given on the entire schema after, literally, every word and every phrase had been given due consideration by the conciliar Commission. The fifth vote was cast on the very day of promulgation, immediately preceding the conciliar promulgation.

During the forty-fifth congregation, on October 10, 1963, the Secretary General announced that voting would begin on chapter two of the liturgy schema, on the mystery of the Holy Eucharist. During the forty-seventh congregation, on October 14, the chapter was voted on. Of the 2,242 present, only 1,417 voted approval, 36 voted non-approval, and 781 cast an approval-with-reservations ballot. Thus the Commission took under consideration the suggestions offered by those who voted "with reservations." On November 20, during the seventy-first congregation, the same chapter was returned to the floor of the Council with slight revisions and was approved again by a vote of 2,112 to 40.

The third chapter of the liturgy schema on the sacraments and sacramentals was presented for the vote of the Council Fathers by Archbishop Paul J. Hallinan during the fifty-first congregation on October 18. The vote on the chapter was 1,130 in favor, 30 against, and 1,054 favorable with reservations. Again the Commission went to work examining and heeding the *modi*. When Bishop Otto Spülbeck of Meissen brought the chapter back to the Council floor during the seventy-second congregation, on November 21, the vote was 2,107 favorable, 35 negative and 1 null.

The chapter on the Divine Office, about which many Americans had voiced their opinions, was introduced to the Fathers by Bishop Joseph Martin of Nicolet, Canada, on October 21 during the fifty-second congregation. After voting on 13 individual amendments, the Fathers approved the entire fourth chapter by a vote of 1,638 to 43, with 552 disapprovals "with reservations." When the chapter was returned to the floor for a vote, it won overwhelming approval by 2,131 in favor, 50 against and 2 null.

The fifth chapter of the liturgy schema concerned the liturgical year. In this case the Fathers were asked to vote on ten propositions. The voting continued through the fifty-fifth and fifty-sixth congregations. On October 29, during the fifty-seventh congregation, the Fathers voted approval of the entire chapter by 2,154 to 21. At this point the weariness of the Fathers began to show itself. During the fifty-ninth congregation, on October 31, Bishop Carlo Rossi read a report from the Liturgical Commission in which he stated that chapter six, on sacred art, and chapter eight, on church furnishings, would become a single chapter. During the same congregation, the moderator, Cardinal Döpfner, suggested with the approval of the Fathers that, rather than have the various points within the chapters voted on, they be voted on in their entirety. Accordingly, the vote was 1,838 in favor, 9 opposed and 94 favorable "with reservations." When the three chapters were returned to the Council floor during the seventy-third congregation on November 22, the vote turned out to be 2,149 in favor, 5 against and 2 null.

This day, the Feast of St. Cecilia, became for many of those who had worked with the schema on the liturgy a great day of jubilation. During the morning congregation the Secretary General asked for a vote of acceptance on the entire schema. The response was overwhelming: 2,158 in favor of it, 19 against it and 1 null vote. The announcement of the vote was greeted with enthusiastic and prolonged applause in St. Peter's.

Archbishop Hallinan was delighted, as was also Father McManus; both had given their best toward the realization of this day. No one, perhaps, was quite so expressive as Father Godfrey Diekmann. He was, on every count, the successor of the pioneers. As editor of *Worship,* he had carried on the work of the Benedictines of Germany, France and Belgium (not to mention his own predecessor, Father Virgil Michel, O.S.B.). For two decades he and his community had dared to enter where angels feared to tread.

The "victory" celebration that evening in the dining room of the Cavalieri Hilton was meant to be precisely a moment of sweet triumph. Seated about the table were Bishop Leonard Hagarty, O.S.B. (also a member of the St. John's community), Father Diekmann, Father William Leonard, S.J., and this writer. The celebration turned into tragedy when Archbishop John P. Cody walked into the room, approached our table and solemnly announced, "I have just heard on the radio that our President John Kennedy has been shot in Dallas." At that moment the victory celebration went sour. We hailed a cab and joined the thousands of misty-eyed Americans and Italians in front of the American Embassy on the Via Veneto.

On the evening of November 22, one American bishop returned to his room and, summarizing the sentiments of many Americans in Rome that day, made the following entry in his diary:

> This was one of the really historic congregations of the entire Council so far. It was the first time that a final vote on a completed schema was taken! This occasion will long be remembered not only by those who were trying to promote the apostolate of the liturgy since its beginnings, but also by many of the Council Fathers who came here last year with little understanding and less interest in the subject. Even the most optimistic of the promoters of the liturgy who came a year ago never dreamed that we would get half of what was contained in the original schema, to say nothing about an end result which went far beyond the original schema proposed! And that with a vote which, for all practical purposes, could be considered *unanimous.* The nineteen negative votes in the last ballot really represented a tattered remnant of the hard core of resistance. I could hardly believe my eyes when I read the *L'Osservatore Romano* for November 23. The headline was as follows: "*Approviazione Quasi Unanime dellà schema sull Liturgia.*" A year ago such a headline would have been unthinkable; during the progress of the debate the official reports in *L'Osservatore* were such as to lead people to believe that there was only a half-hearted interest in the subject! While the hard-core resistance is still as hard as ever, if not hardening, the feeling in the Council as a whole has certainly taken off in the direction of bringing the Church more into contact with the modern world. . . . The thrill with which I witnessed the proceedings today is something I will never forget.

At this stage, the words which Archbishop Hallinan had spoken during the press panel on October 15 were fulfilled: "Another step has been taken in the forward movement of the Church as the liturgy progresses to that 'happy conclusion' of which Pope Paul spoke in his opening address."

In his own closing address at the end of the session, Pope Paul himself summarized the purpose of the liturgy decree in these words:

> If we now wish to simplify our liturgical rites, if we wish to render them more intelligible to the people and accommodated to the language they speak, by so doing we certainly do not wish to lessen the importance of prayer, or to give it less importance than other forms of the sacred ministry of pastoral activity, or to impoverish its expressive force and artistic charm. On the contrary, we wish to render the liturgy more pure, more genuine, more in agreement with the source of truth and grace, more suitable to be transformed into a spiritual patrimony of the people.

The American hierarchy was among the first to act on the concessions formulated in the Dogmatic Constitution on the Sacred Liturgy. On December 4, the very day the Constitution was promulgated, the American bishops issued a joint statement announcing their formal agreement "to make full use of the vernacular concessions made by the Council." In the same statement the bishops of the United States authorized the Bishops' Commission on the Liturgical Apostolate "to propose English translations for the consideration of all the Bishops." Members of this Commission were Archbishop John F. Dearden of Detroit, Archbishop Paul J. Hallinan of Atlanta, Auxiliary Bishop James H. Griffiths of New York, Bishop Vincent S. Waters of Raleigh and Bishop Victor J. Reed of Oklahoma City-Tulsa. The text of the bishops' statement is as follows:

> The Constitution on the Sacred Liturgy promulgated on Dec. 4 is the first achievement of Vatican Council II. It will affect the spiritual life of prayer and worship of all Catholics. It will make the Church more comprehensible to all men.
>
> Thus it is the first great step in the Church's inner renewal begun by Pope John XXIII and now being carried out by all the bishops in union with the chief bishop, Pope Paul VI.
>
> The Bishops of the United States, having taken part fully in the discussion, amendment and acceptance of this document, welcome it wholeheartedly and dedicate themselves to fulfill its purposes.
>
> On the one hand the Constitution is a statement of the Church's doctrine and discipline. It explains the meaning of public worship. It gives a clear mandate to deepen the liturgical understanding and activity of the people. "This full and active participation by all the people is the aim to be considered before all else."
>
> At the same time the Constitution is a document of change and revision. In broad terms it directs a reform of rites and texts so that they may be

simpler and clearer. Putting such changes into effect must await specific action by a commission set up by the Holy Father.

One important change, however, has become the immediate concern of the bodies of bishops in the different countries or regions. This is the concession of the vernacular languages in the liturgy for the sake of the people's understanding, piety and easier participation.

Such concessions are possible without waiting for the revision of rites, but depend upon the action of the bodies of bishops for the respective regions. For the Mass the Council has allowed the vernacular for the lessons and for the parts of the people, in effect for most of the parts said aloud or sung up to the Canon and for such parts as the Sanctus, Our Father, etc. For the sacraments and sacramentals the vernacular is allowed throughout. For the Divine Office the clergy must receive permission from the individual bishops or Ordinaries.

The Bishops of the United States, assembled in Rome, have formally agreed to make full use of the vernacular concessions made by the Council. They have directed the Bishops' Commission in the Liturgical Apostolate to propose English translations for the consideration of all the Bishops.

At a meeting of the Bishops, now proposed for the spring of 1964, formal decrees will be drawn up and sent to the Apostolic See in Rome for confirmation. At the same time official translations will be approved by the Bishops for publication. Only then can a date be determined by the Bishops for the actual use of English in the liturgy.

This prompt action ensures the introduction of English into public worship during the interim period while the revision of the missal, ritual, breviary, etc., is awaited. In addition, the Bishops of the United States authorized their representatives to work with an international committee. This committee will ultimately propose translations based upon the reformed rites for the consideration of the respective hierarchies of the English-speaking world.

The significance of the Constitution on the Sacred Liturgy was recognized throughout the nation. Three comments by people closely associated with its formation and eventual promulgation suffice. Wrote Father McManus: "The Second Vatican Council may be remembered in history as the Council that brought the people back into the public worship of the Church." Writing in the pages of *America* shortly after the promulgation of the Constitution, Father William J. Leonard, S.J., stated:

. . . perhaps we should not dwell so much on the labor of the undertaking as on the magnificent prospects that open before us. Think, for instance, of a Sunday congregation that will hear the word of God copiously and in its mother tongue; that will sing its praises, weep for its sins and beg for its necessities consciously and together; that will know, as the Council says, how to offer the spotless Victim not only by the hands of the priest, but even with him, and to offer themselves as well.

Taking a broad, historical view of the document, Father Godfrey Diekmann said a year after its promulgation:

> I am convinced that, after the inspired word of Holy Scripture, there has appeared no writing of an official public character in the entire history of the Catholic Church which is the peer of this document in containing the potentialities of spiritual revitalization. It is the Magna Carta of the Catholic Church's hoped-for second spring. And it is such because, above all else, it represents a deliberate return to the sources, to the fresh waters of the saving paschal mystery of Christ, His death and resurrection.

Yet much more was accomplished by the promulgation of the Constitution on the Sacred Liturgy than a renewal of the Church's acts of worship. The many hours of labor in the Commission, the comparable hours of discussion on the floor of the Council and the numerous votes taken were all indications as well of the Church's desire to change. The Church of the mid-twentieth century had, to be sure, bowed respectfully and reverently to the past. At the same time the leaders of the Church looked to the future. The winds of change blowing through a restless world had entered the holy temple of the Church. Significantly the opening paragraph to the Constitution remained basically unchanged from the day it had been presented to the Central Preparatory Commission until it was finally promulgated by Pope Paul. That paragraph set the tone for every conciliar document; it helped to launch Peter's barque upon the high waters of the modern world:

> This Sacred Council has several aims in view: it desires to impart an ever increasing vigor to the Christian life of the faithful; to adapt more suitably to the needs of our own times those institutions which are subject to change; to foster whatever can promote union among all who believe in Christ; to strengthen whatever can help to call the whole of mankind into the household of the Church. The Council therefore sees particularly cogent reasons for undertaking the reform and promotion of the liturgy.

Dogmatic Constitution on the Sacred Liturgy

✠ INTERVENTIONS

FRANCIS CARDINAL SPELLMAN, *22 October, 1962*

Concerning general principles for instituting and fostering the sacred liturgy, there is well set forth, in numbers one and two, the nature and importance of the sacred liturgy in the life of the Church, namely, liturgical institutions and active participation. Without a doubt, no effort should be spared in fostering both in the clergy and in the Christian people a conscious, active and fruitful participation in the sacred celebrations. Mere popularization and purely external participation (which, perhaps, has the appearance of the true liturgical life, but which is far from adoration in the spirit and truth) should be avoided.

Number three deals with the renewal of the liturgy. It must be kept firmly in mind that the liturgy is made up of an unchangeable part, as it is divinely instituted, and parts easily changeable, which in the course of time can or even must be changed. Thus, changes can be admitted insofar as they are necessary for legitimate progress, and they are of real use to the Church. In order that this may be attained, there must be retained a sane tradition, and an accurate investigation be established, not only theologically and historically, but also pastorally. There are, indeed, many among the clergy and laity who, imbued with historicism, rather than with true pastoral sense, look for great changes without sufficiently considering their usefulness to the faithful.

In these matters, pastors of souls do not always feel the same as those who have only an historical and speculative outlook. For example, a pastor must always have a care for the many millions of the faithful who attend the Holy Sacrifice on Sundays and holy days. We must be careful lest we impose on the whole world a liturgical structure which would perhaps be suitable in a monastery, in religious houses or even in small parishes to the detriment of the faithful. Wherefore, there should be no innovations unless the true good of the Church demands it, and care should be taken that new liturgical forms in some way grow organically from those already existing.

The same things should be kept in mind in investigating liturgical books. Great care should be taken that the rubrics cover even the parts of the faithful, especially since many of the Christian people are accustomed to follow the Roman missal when they assist at Mass.

The Church, in those things which do not touch the faith or the good of the whole community, does not wish to impose a rigid liturgical form of only one type. Therefore, in the substantial unity of the Roman rite, there may be legitimate variations and adaptations of place, for various groups, regions and peoples, especially in the missions. Neither, however, should new variations be imposed on places where the accustomed forms are best suited to the character of the people and traditions always rooted there. Thus, for example, the desired unity between the faithful and the celebrant may be more efficaciously obtained in some regions by the use of the missal than by the use of the so-called dialogue Mass. In these matters, the greatest prudence must be used lest the faith and devotion of the people be weakened rather than strengthened.

Even if promoting the unity of the faith cannot be admitted as the only principle in the ordering of the liturgy, it is, in general, a very great norm. Therefore it does not seem possible to approve of previous experiments offered to certain groups, as they are likely to bring about confusion, astonishment and injury among the Christian people. Especially the more simple among the faithful can easily be scandalized when they see the unchangeable Church changing her rites. On the other hand, our soldiers and others traveling through various parts of the world, often admire the wonderful unity of the Church in her language and rites from which they profit a great deal. Even non-Catholics admire the outstanding doctrinal and ritual unity of the Catholic Church. It must also be noted that as experiments and innovations increase, so also do great difficulties, which are already found among many both of the faithful and of the clergy. For the same reason, if certain innovations and adaptations of rites and liturgical books are deemed necessary, it is very important that they not be promulgated individually, one after another, but rather many at a time.

As to the question of the liturgical language, we must distinguish. On the one hand there is the Eucharistic Sacrifice and, on the other, the sacraments, sacramentals and other liturgical actions.

As to the Sacrifice of the Mass, the words of this Constitution must be applied: "The use of the Latin language is to be preserved in the western liturgy."

For the Latin language, which is truly the Catholic language, is unchangeable, is not vulgar and has been for many centuries the guardian of the unity of the western Church. Thus now it can form a very strong bond between Christian peoples, especially when it is retained in the celebration of the Holy Sacrifice, which is the center of the whole liturgy, and it is essentially that action which requires active participation. Those who do not understand Latin may have at hand missals with a version in the vernacular; in this way they can easily follow the action of the Holy Sacrifice.

In the same Constitution it is proposed that an appropriate place be assigned to the vernacular in the celebration of the Mass with the people.

This, however, is to be understood in the sense of readings, of common prayers and some songs, not of rites pertaining to the Mass itself. Moreover, it is stated that the use of the vernacular be according to the norm of article 24 of this Constitution, according to which it will be the task of the Episcopal Conference to propose to the Holy See the limits and methods of admitting the vernacular into the liturgy.

As to the sacraments, it must be kept in mind that they are ordered for the sanctification of man and, by means of words and actions, to instruct and nurture his faith. Therefore, in their administration a wider place can be given to the vernacular so that they may more fully attain their pastoral end. In this Constitution it is stated: "In the new 'typical' edition of the Roman ritual there should be clearly indicated the parts which in the particular rituals can be said in the vernacular."

The rite of Baptism, the first sacrament of initiation in Christ and the Church, is now, for the most part, performed in the vernacular. For the same reason, the vernacular can be used in the administration of the sacrament of Confirmation by which this mystical initiation is perfected. The sacrament of the Anointing of the Sick, given its particular end, is well suited for administration in the vernacular. The sacrament of Matrimony is universally administered in the vernacular, as it could hardly be otherwise, since the spouses themselves mutually administer the sacrament. Therefore it is proper that there be offered for them, in the same language, instructions, exhortations and prayers. In this Constitution it is proposed that the prayer over the bride should be so fittingly emended that it can be recited over both spouses and in the vernacular.

As for the sacramentals, blessings of things can be retained in Latin, but sacramentals which are performed with the faithful present or are administered to them, when they have the same pastoral end, can fittingly be performed in the vernacular: for example, the blessing of a woman after childbirth.

Thus, in liturgical actions other than the Mass, a wider place can be given to the vernacular in readings and exhortations and in some prayers and songs.

In all these matters the norm of article 24 is to be preserved, that is, that the limits and methods of admitting the vernacular into the liturgy is to be proposed to the Holy See by the Episcopal Conference.

JOSEPH CARDINAL RITTER, *23 October, 1962*

With the necessity or usefulness of the Church's renewal now accepted, nothing has been *a priori* excluded from scrutiny and change except the essence of the Mystical Body and the precepts of the same divine origin. On the other hand, the methods and other human precepts of past centuries have been very thoroughly examined under the light of modern usefulness and necessity.

For this reason, the most holy Synod cannot remain indifferent to the question of whether the liturgy should be reformed or renewed. The question is proposed openly and sincerely, and it must be responded to either affirmatively or negatively. It seems to me that such a reform is not only desirable, but highly necessary. The very nature of the liturgy and the Church strongly persuades and even demonstrates the need for reform.

Let us consider, first, the nature and one function of the liturgy. The most holy Ecumenical Synod of Trent taught: "Since the nature of man is such that it cannot easily be drawn to meditation on divine things without external support, Holy Mother Church has instituted certain rites and ceremonies that the majesty of such a sacrifice would be preserved and the minds of the faithful would be inspired through these visible signs of religion and piety which conceal the contemplation of these august mysteries in this sacrifice."

The same Synod taught also that "this power was always in the Church, to legislate and change those things in the dispensation of the sacraments, except in their substance, which she judged to be more expedient in the acceptance or usefulness or veneration of the very sacraments for a variety of situations, times and places." At least in part, the function or end of the liturgy is thus logically to influence the minds of the faithful, to cause, to nourish, to perfect internal devotion and cult in them. Therefore, the psychological and mental dispositions of our contemporary men should be the normative and determining element of any liturgical decree. The difference between modern man and sixteenth-century man is such that there is a strong indication of the need for liturgical reform.

The same thing is known from the nature of the Church itself, whose law of life is "unity in necessity, freedom in the rest." Human perfection of the highest kind, which is called civilization or culture and is possible only in a society expressing unity in the fundamentals, nevertheless consists of a variety of partial and complementary perfections. And so the Church, whose highest office is not to destroy, but to bring all natural perfections to Christ who renders them to the Father, ought to encourage and promote the private and public seeking of these diverse perfections. Therefore, also in the liturgy, uniformity without necessity and without the greatest usefulness contradicts the very end and function of the Church. For only a liturgy which exists in the greatest conformity with the daily life of man is able to work as an integral element and integrate that same life.

The *a posteriori* arguments also clearly and firmly demonstrate the same need. The request for reform, clamorously and insistently arising from all regions, even if empty and irrational in some cases, nevertheless manifests an urgent need on the part of Christ's faithful and a useless hindrance and restriction to the efficacy of pastors. The vain requests of a few should not exclude our solicitude for the genuine needs of the many. In this century we have come a long way toward recognizing the practice of the rights and offices of Christ's faithful as members of the Mystical Body of Christ. It does not suffice to acknowledge this only in regard to the apostolate, but it is also necessary in regard to the priestly ministry of the Church. And so, according to that which is proper to each, we must render possible this fuller participation which is the right and office of the laity and accommodate the liturgical decrees to actual conditions. Indeed, Christ gave himself over to death "that he might bring forth in himself a Church not having spot or wrinkle, but that it might be holy and spotless." And He gave the sacraments as signs and the fonts of grace to effect and more widely suffuse it. If the Church does not yet approximate such a condition, in every way we ought to call for a fuller, more profound and more perfect sacramental life. Nor should we exclude the changes of the liturgical decrees which, according to the Council of Trent, are ordered "for the variety of situations, times and places," so that "the majesty of such a sacrifice would be preserved and the minds of the faithful would be inspired to contemplation of the august mysteries" and "the reception of the very sacraments in effectiveness and veneration" would be fostered.

Venerable Brothers, it seems to me that the schema on the sacred liturgy is admirable for its aptitude, rectitude and prudence. It acknowledges the need for accommodation; it offers the end and direction to this accommodation. Certain things remain to the prudence of ordinaries who, in conjunction with the Apostolic See, would accommodate the liturgical decrees, at least in part, to the pastoral needs of their dioceses. This being so, to reject this schema, in my opinion and, I believe, in the opinion of many of the bishops of the United States—again I say, to reject this schema is to reject an accommodation so great that it would, in fact, negate the very great changes which, through all the ages, obtain a place in the life of both the world and the Church. This we must not, we cannot, even contemplate. I recommend, therefore, the acceptance of this schema in general, not intending, however, to preclude the discussion of particulars.

JAMES CARDINAL McINTYRE, *23 October, 1962*

In the United States of America the Holy Sacrifice of the Mass is offered with great fidelity and devotion according to the Roman rite and the rubrics of the Roman missal.

By dogmatic and catechetical instruction the distinction between the Mass of the Catechumens and the "preparatory part" of the Canon and the Consecration are clearly shown and well understood by the faithful. Very many of the faithful read the whole Mass assiduously and privately with the help of missals. These missals are written either in the vernacular or with the Latin on the same page.

For that reason Holy Mass is one in intention and action for all, and every part tends toward the Consecration. The Mass is an act of worship and a divine sacrifice. Thus it absorbs the attention of all the bystanders.

On Sundays and feast days, the Mass is interrupted after the Gospel of the Mass in Latin. The celebrant or another priest explains, from the pulpit, the Epistle and the Gospel with a brief commentary or gives an instruction from the catechism. Then the Mass resumes in Latin with the *Credo*.

In this ordering, the integrity of the Mass in Latin is kept. The vernacular used is separated from the action of the Mass, and it is not employed in all Masses.

The schema on page 175 proposes confusion and complication. If it is adopted, it would be an immediate scandal for our people.

The continuity of the Mass must be kept. The tradition of the sacred ceremonies must be preserved. The instructions on Sacred Scripture, dogma and on the catechism can be kept in the vernacular without offense to Latin. All these are kept in the present system; changes are not needed. In the schema on the liturgy, chapter two, paragraph 41 and following, there is not sufficient consideration given to this chief principle.

The Instructions of the Sacred Congregation of Rites, given in September, 1958, state that the primary attention in hearing the Mass is internal, the contemplation of the mystery of the Eucharist. Therefore, it seems to me, in these discussions active participation is receiving more consideration than needed.

This internal attention is frequently practiced by those whose intellectual capacity is not great. Furthermore, active participation is frequently a distraction.

ALBERT CARDINAL MEYER, *24 October, 1962*

There are two observations I have to offer on this first chapter of this schema.

In the first place, with respect to the liturgical language, in number 23, page 167. The norm laid down here seems to me to be very good. It expresses, as I admit, the true middle path between various opposing opinions. This norm speaks of "granting wider scope" to "the popular tongue," leaving the decision, first, in the way of recommendation, to the National Episcopal Conference and, secondly—and indeed definitively—to the Holy See.

Certainly, indeed, many of the faithful expect *something* on this matter from the Council. The minimum that would satisfy the wishes of many, it seems to me, would be wider use of the popular speech or vernacular in the administration of the sacraments and sacramentals. Many, in addition, express ardent desires with respect to certain parts of the Mass, those especially that concern the readings, the common prayer and some hymns, hoping that these parts may in some way be available in the vernacular. Nevertheless, among those people, as among their pastors, there exists a sometimes great variety of opinions. Hence, a middle path must be found for reconciling all of these views in some better pastoral manner. The norm set down in number 24 seems to me to be such a middle path.

In the second place, I would prefer that number 34, page 170, where there is a question of national commissions, be reconciled with number 24. The breadth of power which number 34 seems to attribute to a national liturgical commission does not please me; specifically these words—"to moderate liturgical pastoral action in the entire nation"—are too extensive. Let it always be the bishop in his own diocese who is the moderator of liturgical pastoral action under the rule of the Holy See, and not under the rule of some national commission! Let there be such commissions, certainly, for carrying out appropriate studies and for suggesting proper means. However, in my opinion, it is better for us not to speak of power on the part of such commissions to regulate for the entire nation.

FRANCIS CARDINAL SPELLMAN, *29 October, 1962*

In chapter two "On the Most Holy Mystery of the Eucharist" there is enunciated the highest pastoral goal to be attained in the liturgy, namely, that the faithful be present at this mystery of faith not as inert and mute spectators, but that they participate in the rites and prayers consciously, actively and piously.

The question that arises is only about the means most appropriate to attain this end, and not about the end itself. Therefore in this regard, it must be accurately recalled what was said in chapter one about true pastoral usefulness as the highest norm, about the greatest prudence and circumspection in introducing innovations and about avoiding an exaggerated "historicism" and a zeal for novelties.

In this Constitution it is proposed: "The rite of the Mass is to be so revised . . . that it may be more clearly understood and that it may render easier the active participation of the faithful." This principle, as such, cannot be disputed. It is asked, however, what does "to revise the rite of Mass" mean? It does not seem that it should be admitted as the only or primary principle that those rites which first appeared in the Roman missal in the sixteenth century are to be renewed. Such a principle, if admitted and rigidly applied, would easily lead to revivifying only rites already obsolete. In the fifth or sixteenth or twentieth century, the Church, always the same, lives and grows with the mission divinely given her and forms her liturgical structure, at least in part, in every age from her experience of the necessities and benefit of the faithful.

In the same article it is proposed: "The rite of Mass is to be so revised . . . in each of its parts." This seems to leave the way wide open for every sort of innovation. There are those who would wish that there be fewer signs of the Cross, kisses of the altar, genuflections and bows during the Mass. Again it is asked whether these innovations would be made for the true benefit of the faithful? Sometimes there is talk of a shorter formula for the distribution of Holy Communion, for example, "The Body of Christ. Amen." But we must be on our guard lest reverence for the Most Holy Sacrament be lessened. On the other hand, they can do away with all restrictions by which the faithful are kept from receiving Holy Communion at certain Masses. This would be a truly pastoral consideration.

A fuller reading of the Holy Scriptures is to be commended in principle. In practice, however, we must beware lest the Mass be drawn out too long and the time for a beneficial homily be too greatly restricted. If the Mass be drawn out too long, where a great number of the faithful assist at Mass, attendance will be burdensome for some or almost impossible for others because of their necessary daily work. Communion under both species, as is mentioned in the schema, "with danger to the faithful removed," would be a great practical inconvenience and would not be truly useful for the Church. Concessions, as again mentioned in the schema, "for certain cases well determined by the Holy See," would bring about great confusion and disquiet among the faithful. As regards extending concelebration of the Mass, it is asked: Is there sufficient reason to abrogate the prevailing law and also whether it would be truly to the benefit of the faithful?

It is often desired, because of the scarcity of priests in so many places, that the ordinary's faculty to permit bination or trination be extended. For the same cause, it is also desired that the ordinary's power to designate fitting places to celebrate Mass be extended.

BISHOP CHARLES HELMSING, *30 October, 1962*

After receiving the schema, I took care to send my observations and emendations to the Secretary of State to His Holiness. Since I have been informed that these observations have been sent to the proper commission, in order to accelerate the work of the Council, I freely cede the occasion to speak.

ARCHBISHOP PAUL HALLINAN, *31 October, 1962*

I speak for many bishops (although not for all) of the United States of America who hope for the more vital, conscious and fruitful participation of our people in the Mass. We urge the adoption by the Council of the propositions and adaptations of chapter two as necessary. We also strongly petition the use of the vernacular language, but since enough has already been said on that, I shall add nothing more.

The duty of a bishop is the care of souls. These souls are not inactive and mute, but conscious and intelligent. For centuries the pastors of souls have preached the Gospel to their people—and this is good. In recent years we have opened for the faithful a path to a more intimate participation in the liturgy by responses made in Latin—and this is better. But—and this is far better—the acceptance by the Council of the articles of chapter two will draw our people even closer to a truly fruitful participation in the unity of Christ. If the order of the Mass is arranged more clearly and made more intelligible, this will render our people more conscious and knowing, more truly prepared for the sacred action which follows.

In the United States, as in the rest of the world, our Christian people and others, too, live in an atmosphere of isolation. They are the victims of an excessive spirit of individualism. This is the very antithesis of universal Christianity: of the Gospel for all men, of Christ Our King whose rule extends to all creatures. The liturgy of the Church must be public, but this can have real meaning for our people only if they understand enough of it to be a part of it. They must be united to God not alone as in private prayer, but together with the whole Church in our Head who is Christ. But the articles of chapter two are especially efficacious in leading our Catholic people to this full concept of the liturgy.

Our Holy Father, Pope John XXIII, fervently desires, and with him all the Fathers of the Council, that, the custody of the faith being safeguarded, we open new avenues of return to our brothers who are separated from the unity of the Mystical Body of Christ. In a particular manner this is desired by the bishops of those regions in which there are few Catholics. For example, in my own Archdiocese of Atlanta scarcely two per cent of the population is Catholic. The more that we can do to render the Mass understandable to all, not just to those equipped by learning or formed by habit, the more we open new avenues to the minds and hearts of Christians who are not Catholic. The Church is the loving Mother of all. Should not this Mother open her treasures of the Scriptures to all? Should she not beseech God for all in a common prayer, especially in an order made more clear, and in the mother-tongue which her children (whether in her embrace or not yet in it) can understand, love and cherish? Summing up, then, I conclude: The adaptation of the form of the Sacrifice of the Mass, in the parts noted in chapter two is urged for this threefold reason:

1) That the faithful may better understand what they hear and what they say;

2) That they may understand and accept the public nature of divine worship;

3) That the Church may open new avenues of return to our brothers separated from the unity of the Mystical Body of Christ.

JAMES CARDINAL McINTYRE, 5 *November, 1962*

These comments on the language of the liturgy refer to page 167 and paragraph 24.

With the growth of the Roman Empire, the universal use of the Latin language in the holy Church's liturgy was correctly ascribed to human and more than human wisdom. Divine Providence showed a clear path in this matter. In the fourth century the Councils of the Church formulated doctrines and dogmas of the Church in precise Latin terminology. The events of the fourth century show a very serious reason for retaining the use of the Latin language in the holy liturgy and in sacred theology. The consideration of historical facts is very worthwhile at the present time. Attempts at weakening the solidity of the tradition of the Latin language in these matters involves a catastrophe. Fundamentally, the Latin language was adopted because our fathers understood well the truly apostolic nature of Holy Mother Church and her universality as extending itself to all nations. They correctly believed that such a universality would be best served by a common means of communication. Certainly the Latin language wonderfully showed itself useful for such a common medium. Therefore, the doctrines of the Church were made precise through the events of the fourth century. Doctrines so defined required formulation in an exact, clear, immutable, easily understood language which could at least be grasped by many and understood by all when it was interpreted to them.

The Latin language showed itself just such a medium of communication. It gave rise to wonderful effects. Its severity overcame nationalities. In politics it was neutral. With great constancy its efficiency perdured into our epoch.

Once adopted, Latin became truly universal, especially among educated and literary men. Having a mathematical rather than vulgar structure, Latin attained a continuous primacy and perdured through the centuries. It is very outstanding in intellectual, literary and scientific matters.

The Councils of the first centuries formulated dogmas of the Church in Latin even to the point of accommodating and transcribing in Latin disputed Greek vocabulary. Latin was always the vehicle of dogma because it was an apt means of thinking and establishing principles accurately, definitively and in a determined fashion. It served faithfully not only ecclesiastical disciplines, but also civil law and philosophy. If this instrument, so fit for restraining and fixing, is removed from the sacred liturgy, the stability of dogma is jeopardized. Protestant sects turned to the vernacular and dissolved into numerous factions.

Throughout many centuries Latin showed a magnificent stability under the guidance of the Church. It is the basis of immutability and offers educated men a precious means of speaking and writing.

By the fact that Latin never evolved into a vulgar language, its stability and immutability grew. Clearly at all times it is the classical language, especially of erudite men.

Recalling both the history of early centuries and contemporary necessities, where is the justification of the opinion which wants to change the venerable language of the sacred liturgy at will? An attack on Latin in the liturgy is indirectly but truly an attack upon the stability of sacred doctrines because the liturgy necessarily involves dogma.

In recent times, even in materialistic North America, the growth of the Church was magnificent with the liturgy being kept in Latin. The attempts of Protestants have failed, and Protestantism uses the vernacular. We ask again: Why the change, especially since changes in this matter involve many difficulties and great dangers? All of us here at the Council can recall the fundamental changes in the meaning of words in common use. Thus it follows that if the sacred liturgy were in the vernacular, the immutability of doctrine would be endangered. Finally, in recent years unknown nations have come to the fore and many new languages, both of nations and of tribes, have become known through the United Nations.

If the vernacular is introduced, we foresee many interpretations of sacred dogmas. To express the eternal truth of doctrine, let sacred dogmas immutably retain their pristine meaning and form!

The introduction of the vernacular should be separated from the action of the Mass. The Mass must remain as it is. Grave changes in the liturgy introduce grave changes in dogmas.

FRANCIS CARDINAL SPELLMAN, 9 *November, 1962*

Concerning chapter four on the Divine Office, that the recitation of the Divine Office in today's circumstances should be made easier and more perfect, this is an end greatly to be desired. Everyone, however, should avoid experiments both because of confusion and because of great difficulties. If there are innovations, they should be such that the Office becomes better accommodated to the condition of today's busy life, especially of the pastor of souls. We must beware lest the innovations favor historicism and obsolete things rather than the true needs of clerics.

Above all else, since in all parts of the world there are clerics praying the breviary in Latin who scarcely understand what they are saying, this Most Holy Synod can properly decide to allow all praying privately the right to choose either Latin or the vernacular. The words of the present schema, "In the Divine Office the Latin language is to be preserved by clerics," do not sufficiently consider the needs of the Church today.

Internal spiritual devotion—scarcely present when only words without understanding are recited—is necessary for clerics not only to fulfill rightly the obligation of the whole Church of publicly praising God (for the good of the whole Church), but also to live soberly and piously among so many worldly dangers. The reasons proposed elsewhere against the use of the vernacular because of confusion and danger to the faithful do not pertain here because we are speaking only of clerics praying alone.

ALBERT CARDINAL MEYER, 9 *November, 1962*

I speak concerning numbers 68 and 76 of this chapter, where there is question of the cycle of hours and of the time for recitation of the Divine Office.

In these numbers, it seems to me, there is manifested too great an insistence on the carrying out of various parts of the Divine Office at fixed hours of the day. Though this is proposed in the new code of rubrics (n. 142) as an ideal, if I may so put it, nevertheless it must be admitted that more often than not, this ideal can scarcely be attained by priests engaged in the active ministry despite their very best intentions.

Thus, in order that their consciences will not be unnecessarily strained, it seems to me better that the Council refrain from approving number 76. This question, indeed, is linked closely with the whole question of reform of the Divine Office. An excellent principle to guide this reform is set forth in the words of number 68, where it is said: "Taking into account the diverse circumstances of daily life." This principle seems to be neglected, however, if the Divine Office is reformed with too much insistence on the cycle of hours and on the time for reciting various hours of the Divine Office.

With respect to number 77 where there is question of the language to be used in reciting the Divine Office:

Out of the greatest reverence for that venerable "age-old tradition" spoken about in line five of this number, I confess I find myself somewhat divided in mind about saying something to the contrary. Nevertheless, because I am convinced that it is a question of the greatest importance for the spiritual life of a very great many priests, I propose the following observation.

I strongly wished that the Council Fathers would have an opportunity to cast a ballot on the question of permissive use of the vernacular in private recitation of the Divine Office.

This proposition was already contained in some fashion in the preparatory schema. Although the precise manner in which it was then proposed did not satisfy me, nevertheless I think the proposition ought to be contained in some way in our schema.

I propose, therefore, that the Council Fathers have at least the opportunity of voting whether or not some modification of this number 77a, allowing for use of the vernacular, ought not to be proposed.

What form this modification ought to take will probably better appear in the light of what other Fathers may say on this matter. Perhaps it could be proposed in this way: "In accord with the age-old tradition of the western Church, Latin is to be preserved by clerics in the Divine Office. Nevertheless, for the sake of greater piety, it is permitted in private recitation to use an approved translation in the vernacular."

I say "for the sake of greater piety" and *not on account of a lack of knowledge of the Latin language,* for I think that there are also many priests who have an excellent knowledge of Latin who would receive this permission with great joy. I bow to better judgment! In addition, such a permission in my opinion ought in no way to depend upon any action whatever of some episcopal conference, but, if it be granted, ought to be granted directly to all priests by this Sacred Synod or by the Holy See itself to be used under such conditions as should be determined. Again, I bow to better judgment!

BISHOP WILLIAM CONNARE, *9 November, 1962*

In page 185 toward the end of the schema, it states that "the Divine Office be performed easier and more perfectly by the priests and other members of the Church."

For this reason I would like to say something in the name of many priests of my diocese and other dioceses as well. These loyal and eager co-workers and friends of mine are asking that they be able to enjoy the privilege of reciting the Divine Office privately in the vernacular. I have willingly consented to this request, and ninety per cent of the bishops of the United States are with me on this as is indicated by the remarks of Cardinals Spellman and Meyer.

It is therefore desired that the obligation mentioned be expressed rather by way of free choice, so that the priests reciting the Divine Office privately may be given the option of reciting it in Latin or in the vernacular.

The recitation of the breviary in Latin, the traditional language of the western Church, is to be praised and should be commended. However, when it is recited privately, by those who are not, strictly speaking, connected with choral recitation, the choice of saying it in the vernacular should be granted to the individual priests.

Of course, such a vernacular edition of the breviary would be edited by the experts of the various areas under the guidance of the bishops of the region and would not be put into use without the approval of the Holy See.

The reason for this proposition is twofold: First, such a privilege would be a great advantage to the spiritual life of these priests for whom the riches of the breviary are hidden under the veil of the Latin usage. Nor would it make sense to say that after reading the breviary in Latin, they would be able to read it in the vernacular. In these busy days zealous priests in America and everywhere in the world cannot take the time for this.

In this Council the voice of these loyal priests is heard through the voice of the bishops. This voice asks the privilege that "the Divine Office be performed easier and more perfectly."

Secondly, such a privilege would be a great advantage to the pastoral life of these priests, which the Supreme Pontiff, Pope John XXIII, had in mind when he called this Council. The pastoral obligation first of all demands that the priest foster in the faithful a constant growth in the knowledge and love of Christ, so that, one with Christ, they may ever more faithfully serve God. Certainly, if this obligation is to be better carried out, it would help greatly if the priest could assimilate the sacred riches from the breviary in the same language in which he preaches them to the people.

Readings from Scripture and the Fathers, lives of the saints, hymns and orations—all these can bear great fruit in homilies, addresses and teaching catechism—in the total ministry of the Word of God to the people—if they are not only read, but also understood.

It is quickly conceded that all priests should know Latin. As a matter of fact, however, many priests throughout the world are unable to speak or read this venerable language, or at least only with difficulty. For these priests, therefore, the private recitation of the breviary becomes merely mechanical and scarcely intelligible.

For this reason I propose that the obligation mentioned in the schema be expressed rather by free choice, so that priests reciting the Divine Office privately be given the option of reciting it in Latin or the vernacular.

BISHOP FRANCIS REH, 9 *November, 1962*

I humbly offer an argument concerning the form of the breviary which should be better revised for the use of clerics who, as a matter of fact, are forced almost always to recite the canonical hours alone. In the proposed schema a form of this kind is not only not accepted, but it is even positively rejected, as we saw in the fifth note found at the end of page 188.

Although I *de facto* speak only in my own name, nevertheless I dare to think that I also propose this argument in the name of others, since, as we read in note five, many more favored some form of the breviary which had been accommodated for solitary recitation.

The opposing argument which is explained in the same note, namely that "the Church has never admitted a form of breviary which would exclude community recitation," seems to me to be of rather small importance. Cannot we also object that the Church has never admitted other adaptations which have now been proposed for us here and elsewhere in this very schema?

I propose to the judgment of the Fathers the fact that the choir or community recitation of the canonical hours is not strictly according to their nature or essence, which would rather consist in their recitation by a person delegated by the Church. All in all, I grant that the praying Church is better represented by a community recital, more beautifully still by the splendor of a choir's chant. The better representation of the Church, however, hardly excludes the true and efficacious representation read alone,—true and efficacious apart from any need for some choir or community which is totally absent, though imagined by the modern form of the breviary.

Already an historical fact long ago, it certainly is the case today that very many priests weighed down by pastoral work are almost always forced by circumstances to recite the breviary alone. How many priests there are in the world, parish priests, who—with the exception of the annual spiritual exercises—live alone in parishes! Is it any benefit for them to have at hand a breviary which has always been set up for the community recital of his brother priests, which in fact they recite alone for almost the whole year?

On the other hand, the almost daily solitary recitation of the breviary, whose nature is for the most part choral, seems to impose such an undesired fiction on so many priests without proportionate reason. The priest on his knees before the Blessed Sacrament piously praying in the name of the Church, reciting the invitatory, the antiphons and psalms, the verses with responsories, the short responsories and verses, pardoning and even blessing himself, completes the wonderful skipping from one choir to the other, without even neglecting the place of the hebdomadary—an effort quite difficult for a parish priest already worn out by his pastoral work.

Therefore, the legitimate progress of the liturgy demands that the Church allow a form of the breviary which is more adjusted to private recitation.

Humbly, therefore, I propose, in the name of many priests, that to section 73, page 187, under the letter "b" on line 19, after the word *persolvere,* another sentence be added composed of the following words or words quite similar:

Not having changed the regulation arising from a communitarian nature, which is established in section 26 of this Constitution, the faculty is granted to those clergy reciting alone to recite the canonical hours according to a form of the breviary revised for their use.

BISHOP JOSEPH MARLING, C.PP.S., *10 November, 1962*

It seems to me that number 77 should be changed to permit both priests and those in major orders who are not bound to choir or communal recitation to recite the Divine Office in the vernacular when they fulfill their obligation in private. In support of this recommendation, I give the following reasons which, I confess, I did not always adhere to, but which I firmly believe now.

The usual arguments that are offered favoring the preservation of Latin in the Mass (which I myself hold very sacred) do not apply in this case. Here Latin does not necessarily seem to create the same bond of unity (as in the Mass), nor, if the Latin is missing, must we fear scandalizing the people.

Furthermore, the new Psalter makes the recitation of the breviary in Latin easier and more intelligible, but the difficulty is not removed. For prayer *is* communication or talking with God. But who would say that such an intimate and familiar dialogue or talk can even take place in language other than one's own? I think we have to keep in mind that among the greatest problems this Sacred Council must face is the scarcity of priests throughout the world. Very often it is a source of wonderment for those whose work it is to teach in seminaries that, while God calls many men to the priesthood, they are not always endowed with a great deal of ability. In order to provide for a sufficient number of priests for those places in need and at the same time to help those other areas where there is a notable, perhaps acute scarcity of priests, we must remove as many obstacles as possible before ordination rather than, after that, face those men called to the priesthood, but whose abilities are limited. In order to understand what I have said, I am seeking not a watered-down plan or course of studies for candidates to the priesthood, but simply the recognition of an indisputably studied fact and also a practical approach, as they say, to today's situation which is both real and very serious.

Indeed, it is much easier to be able to enter into the spirit of the Latin prayers of the Mass than those of the Divine Office. For at Mass the prayers for the greatest part are the same from day to day. Plus the fact that the celebration of Mass is always surrounded with a certain special reverence which greatly aids concentration and attention. But things are different in the recitation of the breviary. If the Divine Office can be recited in the vernacular, much more weight will be given to the consideration of the proposal to broaden and expand the order of the Psalms to be introduced.

Priests will more easily instill in the hearts of the laity an admiration of the Divine Office and the Psalms, something to be hoped for, if the Divine Office and the Psalms become a more intimate part of the prayer life of priests through familiarity with a language they themselves understand perfectly.

I am convinced that priests all over the world would welcome permission to recite the breviary in the vernacular, not because they would be giving in to laziness, but because they would have a real stimulus to reverence and devotion.

BISHOP STEPHEN LEVEN, *10 November, 1962*

To paragraph 77, page 188, I propose the addition of a new paragraph, namely, "Everyone bound to the sacred office may by his proper Ordinary be granted permission to recite the Divine Office in the vernacular."

My argument is neither against the Latin language nor concerning the ignorance of some, but based only on pastoral practice so that the priest may become "a man approved, a worker that cannot be ashamed, rightly handling the word of truth" (2 Tim 2:15).

In order to accomplish this, a continuous, laborious and daily use of the very words of Sacred Scripture in the vernacular is necessary. For 27 years I have preached to our separated brethren in the streets and market places of cities and towns and little villages in the United States of North America. From this practice I learned that nothing touches the hearts of men so surely as the very words of Sacred Scripture. This is true not only of our separated brethren, but also of our faithful Catholics.

The words of Sacred Scripture enjoy a special assistance of the Holy Spirit; they were inspired by the Holy Spirit. It is the experience of all preachers that the citation of the very words of Sacred Scripture gives beauty of expression, strength of persuasion and warmth and conviction to one's preaching. Well did St. Paul say, "All Scripture is inspired by God and useful for teaching, for reproving, for correcting, for instructing in justice" (2 Tim. 3:16).

This familiarity with the words of Sacred Scripture is not easily acquired. Daily application and daily exercise are necessary, and it is not easy to transfer this exercise in one language to use in another language.

Since, therefore, the priest is already bound to the daily recitation of the breviary, and thus already holds and handles the sacred pages every day, he could from the same reading done in the vernacular have a very great help in perfecting himself in a pastoral work so useful and so necessary. Practically, if the proficient use of Sacred Scripture in daily pastoral action is not learned in this way, it will never be possessed.

Consequently, for all bound to the sacred office, especially for priests in pastoral practice, I consider the recitation of the divine office in the vernacular to be very useful. I propose this and ask this of the conciliar Fathers.

FRANCIS CARDINAL SPELLMAN, *10 November, 1962*

In regard to chapter five on the liturgical year, it is again proposed that those things and only those things be recognized which will truly assist pastoral activity.

To assign the Feast of Easter to a certain Sunday is contrary to Church tradition of many centuries, and there does not appear to be sufficient reason to change this tradition.

BISHOP JOSEPH MARLING, C.PP.S., *12 November, 1962*

Please excuse me for speaking on a matter already decided, but my words require only two moments. It is no wonder that each wishes his proper saint proclaimed. For this reason, in my opinion, the rule in number 84 was established for selecting saints whose feasts would be celebrated in the universal Church.

I propose this as a norm:

In the calender of the universal Church the feast of those saints have a place who are acknowledged by official authority as apostles, that is, the principal promoters of major and universal devotions which have importance in the Church. So there should be assigned a universal feast to the most illustrious author of devotion to the Most Blessed Sacrament, Peter Eymard, when he will be added to the catalogue of saints. My example also applies to St. Gaspar.

The Supreme Pontiff, John XXIII, in his apostolic letter *Inde a primis* said that the devotion to the Most Precious Blood, along with the devotion to the Most Sacred Name and the Most Sacred Heart of Jesus, pertains to those forms of piety which in the universal Church "are thought altogether outstanding and more suitable for seeking holiness." In the same document he declares that St. Gaspar, a priest of the Roman clergy, had been an admirable promoter of the cult of the Most Precious Blood.

St. Gaspar was placed among the saints nine years ago, but his feast is not yet celebrated in the universal Church. Thus I am compelled to commend this addition to number 84.

BISHOP RUSSELL McVINNEY, *12 November, 1962*

Invoking your indulgence and benevolence, I would comment briefly on two sections of Chapter Five, that is number 82 and number 83 found on page 191, and specifically on number 83—*Praxis paenitentialis quadragesimae opportuna restituenda*—line 35, page 191 and lines 1 and 2, page 192. I quote: *Instauretur, proinde, juxta nostrae aetatis et diversarum regionum possibilitates necnon fidelium condiciones, opportuna praxis paenitentialis.*

I think the last words—*opportuna praxis paenitentialis*—to be too vague. It would seem desirable to specify the practices of penance, v.g. fast as spelled out in the Canons or at least more frequent spiritual exercises. And it should be stressed that all of Lent is a preparation for Easter. The Easter fast as set forth in the following lines mentioning Good Friday and Holy Saturday might be interpreted as restricting that fast to those days. The directives of these two paragraphs are highly commendable, and should be seriously considered by all in their profound significance. They point the obligation incumbent on all, priests and people, to understand thoroughly the reason for Lenten penances and to practice them assiduously.

Sin committed by a member of the Mystical Body is not just a personal dereliction. It has a social impact. There is scarcely any sin which does not affect society adversely. Society, then—our own Catholic population in this instance—should be brought to realize the enormity of sin, not only vis-a-vis one's own personal sanctification, but with respect to the community of which one is a member. Hence the need for reparation by the individual, as individual and as member of society or his particular community.

It seems to me, therefore, imperative that we impress upon our people the need for penance in reparation for personal sins and the sins of society.

I feel it most important in our day, when the conviction of the need of penance is being widely disregarded. One may note an ever widening tendency toward softness of life. The people constantly ask for the relaxation of the disciplines made sacred by the strict observance of our more sturdy forebears. Even we bishops, moved by paternal sympathy, give dispensations from the law of fast and abstinence for the slightest reason, and thus unwittingly contribute to the spread of this philosophy of ease.

We should not forget the scriptural injunction: "The kingdom of heaven suffers violence, and the violent take it." The faith of our people is not going to be enhanced by making its practice easy. Spiritual muscles, as well as physical ones, are developed by exercise, not by indulgence. Look about and see where the faith is strong, and you will find a deeply rooted conviction of the need for penance. Conversely, where luxury and ease are cultivated the faith is moribund. The kind of devil that besets our world today can be driven out only by prayers and fasting. Let us not forget the influence in his world of the Poverello. Our age needs another Francis. This era needs to be made conscious that heaven belongs to the strong. *"Per aspera ad astra."*

BISHOP VICTOR REED, *12 November, 1962*

In chapter five concerning the established liturgical year, on page 191, article 81, we read: "The souls of the faithful are directed to the feast days of the Lord. . . ."

Concerning this article I wish to propose three things:

First: That a greater variety of scriptural texts be employed in the Sunday and daily Masses.

Second: That ferial Masses be formulated for every day of the year besides first and second class feasts, and especially particular Masses for the days on which the Mass either of the Sunday or of the feast is actually repeated.

Third: That votive Masses of a more determined nature be formulated.

In regard to the first point: People are prevented from a fuller knowledge of the words and acts of Our Savior because of the multitude of saints' feastdays and because of the frequent repetition of Sunday Masses during the week days.

Many have already spoken about the multitude of saints' feastdays in the calendar of the universal Church which is now in use. I wish to add only this, namely: I hope to retain in the calendar only the feasts of the saints which truly lay claim to a universal significance; and in regional calendars only those feasts which enjoy particular historical and devotional reasons.

Furthermore, because of deficiencies of apt texts for the instruction of the people about the life of Christ, we often repeat the text from the Mass of the Sunday during the time of Advent and during the other times of the liturgical year. For example, last week we repeated the Mass of last Sunday three or four times.

Likewise, the Mass for the Feast of the Epiphany of the Lord in general is repeated without change throughout the days following that feast, except on the Feast of the Holy Family and, lately, on the Feast of the Baptism of Christ.

In regard to the second point: Ferial Masses should be formulated for all the days of the year, besides first- and second-class feasts, and, indeed, Masses should be formulated for those days on which the Mass of the Sunday or of the feast is actually repeated. After such Masses have been formulated, we shall be able to see with greater clarity during the liturgical year the perfect example of Christ Our Lord shining forth through the words of Sacred Scripture, and we shall obtain a greater variety of texts as sources of homilies for the instruction of the people.

In regard to the third point: Votive Masses of a more determined nature should be formulated. I wish to point out that certain occasions which frequently occur in particular regions seem to require votive Masses more specifically accommodated for those occasions. For example: The votive Mass of the Holy Spirit is widely used in America for the opening of the school year and also for the opening of diocesan or provincial meetings, as well as for other meetings of the clergy and of the laity. For this reason, it seems to me that we ought to have not only one Mass of the Holy Spirit, but many which are suited for such specific occasions.

My priestly experience of 33 years in the same diocese has been concerned almost totally with the pastoral care of souls. I wish to say that the people of my diocese have accepted with enthusiasm the recent liturgical reforms. Not only do they need liturgical participation in the Mass and in the sacraments, but they also longed for this participation because today they are better educated and therefore seek a fuller understanding and appreciation of the riches and the fullness of the sacred liturgy.

In my judgment, this end will be more efficaciously obtained through a fuller use of the vernacular and a greater application of Scripture in the sacred liturgy.

Dogmatic Constitution on the Sacred Liturgy

✠ COMMENTARY *by Rev. Frederick R. McManus*

Like the other documents of the Ecumenical Council, the Constitution on the Sacred Liturgy must be read for itself. No outline, commentary or interpretation can substitute for the Constitution.

This must be said because of the truism that the Council is only a starting point. It would be a total misunderstanding to think of the progress achieved by the Council or the pronouncements uttered by the Council as representing a plateau on which we may smugly rest for the next generation. Whether in liturgical revision or in the total reform of the Church, the Council can only offer insights and open doors. The progress lies ahead.

Yet the opposite danger is as great, that, to the disparagement of the Council's decisions, we should stumble into the future without chart or guide. We cannot praise the Council for its spirit of openness and blithely neglect the words it spoke.

More to the point, the vast majority of the Church's members have not as yet comprehended either the need for the Council or the Council's achievements and decisions, even though these are merely a beginning and are surely limited and partial. Until the words have been digested and the gain consolidated, the renewal of the Church's life will be gravely defective. And the chief failure of the past two decades in the matter of liturgical renewal—the failure to prepare the people of the Church for change—will only be compounded.

Perhaps this is the principal justification for commentaries and expositions, to offer background and to propose a way to study and reflect upon the Council's own teachings.

For the Constitution on the Sacred Liturgy, the background is suggested by the initial distinction in its text between the promotion and the reform of the Roman liturgy. The promotion of the liturgy—for which the Council gives the strongest impetus to date—consists of a broad range of study and action of liturgical promoters, clergy and laity. It includes all the endeavors to explore the meaning of the liturgy as the celebration of the Christian community and to communicate this meaning as widely as possible. It includes equally, on the level of action, all the endeavors to stimulate and develop the

170

full involvement or participation of the whole Christian community in the celebrations of public worship.

This species of liturgical promotion, embracing education and participation, was made official by Pope Pius XII in 1947, but with relatively little success, in fact not much more success than had attended the efforts of the teachers and pastors concerned with the liturgical movement since early in the twentieth century. It now remains to be seen whether this on-going task will become the mass movement of liturgical involvement expected by the Council. Such promotion is essential if the faith and devotion reflected by external forms and rites are to be profound and authentic.

The great hope and stimulus may, in fact, rest with the other aspect of the Council's liturgical decisions. The spread of understanding and participation has been inextricably tied to the need of liturgical revision or reform. Every major step in liturgical promotion during the past thirty or forty years has had to face the obstacle of defective liturgical forms which were substantially unchanged since the sixteenth century.

Because there was this background of promotion and clamor for revision, the Constitution on the Sacred Liturgy was accepted by the Council in substantially the same form in which it had been proposed by the liturgical specialists—and this in spite of the stormy debate of the Council on the subject in 1962 and the gloomy hesitations of a strong minority.

In fact, liturgical revision was already under way in the latter years of Pope Pius XII, and it remained for Pope John to seek from the Council a mandate for the continuance and enlargement of this reform of the Roman rite.

This liturgical reform—already at hand in the provisional forms of the "new liturgy"—is, in part, a recognition of defects and limitations. If the signs and symbols of existing rites cannot be made comprehensible, they must be changed; if the language is unintelligible, it must give way to the language of the people. As in every facet of Church life and discipline, the contemporary situation demands accommodation and adaptation. And—perhaps most important of all—each age and culture must add its own form and spirit to the liturgical celebration, a principle explicitly recognized by the Council in its provisions for regional adaptability of the Roman liturgy.

If we turn to the document itself, we find that in quantity it is principally a matter of revisions and change, all the way from the concelebration of Mass to the new stress on the paschal character of Christian death. Yet the decrees and directives are actually secondary to the doctrine, and the Constitution on the Sacred Liturgy cannot be understood unless it is seen first as a doctrinal pronouncement at the basis of specific decisions. No matter what the fate of liturgical revision, the doctrine remains valid.

Not long after the Constitution on the Sacred Liturgy was promulgated by the Council, there were various attempts to downgrade its doctrinal and theological significance, largely by those who feared its style and method. The latter reflect the biblical, catechetical and patristic studies of the past few decades, while they canonize the liturgical movement. The doctrine, however, is basic. It provides the whole motive for action, as, indeed, such motive should be offered in the publication of any sound decrees for the Church's life and growth.

The doctrine is that of God's ultimate revelation of Himself in Jesus Christ, the redemptive act in the paschal mystery of the Lord's passion and resurrection, and the continuation of Christ's priestly ministry in the Church, which is called together by God as a community and assembly of faith and love. The liturgy is seen as the work of Christ, the Priest and Head acting in His members, Christ now made present in signs and sacraments.

The Fathers of the Council present this teaching principally in the opening paragraphs of the first chapter of the Constitution; it is developed in the opening paragraphs of succeeding chapters. As an explanation of the community's public act of worship, it represents marked progress from the teaching of Pius XII: the liturgy is not seen almost exclusively as man's act of worship, but rather as the dialogue of God's action and man's response. The Council takes up the teaching of Pius XII that the liturgy is Christ's act and develops this eloquently and succinctly.

The Constitution sees the liturgy—and especially the eucharistic celebration—as the high point toward which all the activities of the Church are directed, so that all the endeavors of the members lead to that moment when the community is assembled by God to hear His word and to respond in prayer, praise and sacrifice.

The liturgy is seen, too, as the source of all the Church's strength and other activity. This means that the liturgy is the moment of commitment and pledge, the starting point for all apostolic activities, the call to the Church's total mission.

The liturgy is the present celebration of the Lord's death, resurrection and ascension—the central and single mystery which the Constitution repeatedly calls the paschal mystery. This is evidently far removed from any concept of liturgics or of merely external rites and observances formalized in routine services. And, because this doctrine pervades the Constitution, it is possible for the practical norms and decrees of the Council to be more than up-dated legislation.

The opening chapter of the Constitution is noteworthy on several counts, in addition to the dozen paragraphs of doctrinal introduction already mentioned. Its concern for liturgical education extends from seminary to religious house, from priests in the ministry to the whole congregation of the faithful. It is concrete and practical in its dealing with liturgical commissions of nations and dioceses. Its central article of reform decrees that all the liturgical books of the Roman rite should be thoroughly revised with the help of bishops and specialists from all parts of the world.

The happy marriage of theory and practice can be seen in the two articles which are respectively the most authoritarian and the most theological of the Constitution.

One article speaks of the Eucharist as the preeminent manifestation of the Church and insists that it is in the one celebration under the presidency of the bishop that this sign is most perfectly realized. The Church is, in fact, the assembly of God's holy people gathered and ordered under the bishops.

In the concrete terms of ecclesiastical law this is reflected by the breaking down of the former reservation of liturgical norms to the Holy See. Instead, the direction and regulation of the liturgy pertain both to the Holy See and, within the limits of Church law, to the bishop of the local church.

The full meaning of episcopal collegiality had to wait the promulgation of the Constitution on the Church at a session following that in which the Constitution on the Sacred Liturgy was issued. But the earlier document speaks also of the regional reflection of that collegiality and initiates the process of decentralization in the Church by recognizing the rights of the conferences of bishops in the different countries.

The celebration of the liturgy is always dependent upon the presidency and guidance of the local bishop. Lest there be too great divergence from local church to local church, however, the Constitution establishes a pattern of liturgical direction vested in the conferences of bishops for the respective countries or territories.

For the Constitution's principal contribution in the practical order, we have to look to the mandate which it provides for the post-conciliar liturgical commission—a body set up by Pope Paul VI a few weeks after the issuance of the conciliar document. In its desire to make the liturgical celebrations the authentic expression of the praying people of God, in its desire to make the signs signify, the Council laid down broad guidelines for revision. They come under three headings and represent a restoration of balance and a recovery of emphasis.

The first broad mandate is that the liturgy should recover its community and hierarchical nature. This is another way of saying that the liturgy should reflect the true nature of the Church itself.

It is possible to look at this decision of the Council negatively and to see it as aimed at the correction of two crucial areas of imbalance.

One imbalance is the loss of community sense and the corresponding emphasis upon an individualistic piety even in the midst of the Christian assembly. For evidence it is enough to cite the tremendous if understandable resistance to common song at the common eucharistic banquet. This only suggests the need for the Council to insist upon recovery of a community sense, especially in the Eucharist and especially in the parish celebration of the Sunday Mass.

The other disproportion, again practical and not necessarily theoretical, has been the assumption by the priest of almost all the roles in the liturgy. The ordinary Mass celebration of the recent past has had the priest taking the role of celebrant, deacon, lector, choir and cantor, and a good portion of the congregation's role, the remainder being taken by a server.

To correct these weaknesses demands more than a change in the mechanics and techniques of liturgical celebration. They go to the heart of what is meant by the Church as a community of worshipers, what is meant by roles and ranks and orders, functions and responsibilities within the Church.

The recovery or restoration of the lay role in the Church is not simply a liturgical phenomenon. But the liturgy should reflect this recovery of responsibility by laymen and laywomen in the total mission and apostolate of the Church. Liturgically, this is represented by the word "participation," now so easily and casually tossed about.

Participation, once again, is not a matter of external techniques merely, not simply a question of more congregational singing, common recitation and response, and the like. It is a matter of the most profound and inward involvement of each member of the community, the inner purpose and intent of each one to be a complete member of the praying people. The ritual and liturgical side, since the liturgy is signs, demands that this interior act be manifest outwardly to the community and for the community.

The social and corporate manifestation inflicts no wound on personal commitment. On the contrary, it demands the personal relationship of the members of the praying community one to the other, and of the whole body to God through Christ the Head and Mediator.

In the concrete terms of liturgical renewal, as experienced in the ordinary American parish, participation means a greater or less measure of common song and the regular response of the whole body, in a dialogue of prayer, to its leading member, the celebrating and presiding priest. And the experience of this achieves more than any theory: in a few months it has become normal and natural for the whole congregation to pray the Our Father before Communion and thus to be led to the table of the Lord by the Lord's own prayer.

The techniques are, in fact, often imperfect, but the experience should gradually achieve the purposes of the Council and show, by the preference given to the community manner of celebration, that the liturgy is never a private matter, but a celebration of the whole Church, which is the sacrament of unity.

Liturgical participation, active and aware, internal and external, will be pressed home in every development of ritual change, if only because of the Constitution's principle that this participation is the aim to be considered above all others. Neither this participation of the people nor the attention to pastoral and contemporary needs can really be in conflict with the sound liturgical traditions of the past, which the Council insisted upon retaining. A balance is to be sought between past traditions and the progress to current understanding and real meaning. In point of fact, the concern for organic growth out of the past will itself prompt a concentration on community participation.

The matter of the distribution and apportionment of roles is somewhat more complex. The Constitution on the Sacred Liturgy puts it in these terms: "In liturgical celebrations each person, minister or layman, who has an office to perform, should do all of, but only, those parts which pertain to his office by the nature of the rite and the principles of liturgy."

The full steps toward this new awareness of the different functions and responsibilities in the Church, as reflected in the liturgical assembly, have been taken in the documents implementing the Constitution. An obvious instance is the restoration of the lector's office, especially the lector's office as filled by a layman. This gives a distinct responsibility in the liturgy, the responsibility of announcing God's word, to someone other than the celebrating priest. The same is true of the restoration or innovation of the commentator's role. He is, in fact, the cantor, leader of song, guide to common praying and singing, and the like; in some ways his office is related to that of deacon.

This breaking down of the liturgical celebration, especially the rite of Mass, into the parts assigned to different participants—whether individuals or members of the singing choir or the whole congregation—has the effect of clarifying and enhancing the priest's part. Instead of being indiscriminately the reader or reciter of prayers, hymns, psalms, scriptural passage, etc., the priest has become or is becoming the true leader and presiding officer of the community. He is the one who directs and guides, the one who is the spokesman for the assembly in its prayers of petition, the one who, above all, proclaims the eucharistic and sacrificial prayer on behalf of the community.

In some places this recovery of a community sense and this hierarchical apportionment in roles of celebration have been quickly understood. The achievement is largely due to preparation by priests in consultation with lectors and commentators, choir directors and leaders, parish liturgy committees and so on. In the United States, at least, even where the preparation has been defective, even where the leaflets, booklets or books in the hands of the congregation have been poorly designed, still the very inclusion of a rubric directing the people to make this response or say that prayer has begun the revolution of attitudes.

If the recovery of community consciousness and sense in liturgical celebration is important, even broader results can be expected from the second heading of liturgical change: what the Council calls the pastoral and didactic nature of the liturgy.

Apart from the most patently didactic elements of the liturgy (biblical readings and preaching, although preaching often enough was looked upon as an interruption of the liturgy rather than an integral part of it), in recent tradition this side of the liturgy has been neglected or woefully subordinated. In fact, the nature of liturgy as forming man—indeed as God's saving action in man—has been almost lost in the rigid definitions of liturgy as cult or worship due to the Almighty.

The word "pastoral," although overused and overworked, has in this case an appropriate breadth. It recalls that the pastoral concern of the shepherd for the flock has been the key to liturgical evolution—both the forward progress, to suit the needs of the Church's people, and the retrogression, whenever in history the liturgy was divorced from the understanding of the people.

The word "didactic" is not the happiest expression in English. The purpose of the liturgy as teacher goes beyond indoctrination or instruction in the sense of communicating a series of truths. What is meant can best be expressed by paraphrase. The liturgy, in all its moments and in all its parts and elements, is teacher; it has, or should have, the power to deepen faith and understanding, to build up, to form and change. Its nature is to be formative as well as informative; it is educative in the best and fullest sense.

Even the use of these terms suggests that the experience of liturgical celebration is at the heart of the proclamation of God's message. The point is made in different terms at the beginning of the third chapter of the Constitution where, speaking of sacraments, the Council adds the building up of the Body of Christ to the notion of liturgy as the cult of God and as sanctification of the individual.

The prayers, the sacred song, the response, the gestures, the deeds and signs—all the elements instruct, again in the most profound sense of instruction. Because the liturgy is sacramental, it consists of signs—including the sign of language—which must be intelligible and comprehensible to the participants.

The principal implementation of the Constitution on the Sacred Liturgy in the immediate period following its promulgation falls under this heading. It is the development of the vernacular as a substitute for the sacrosanct but unintelligible Latin in the Roman and other rites of the Western Church. Its introduction, at least in the case of Mass, was to be limited and gradual, since in this regard the Constitution was drawn to satisfy those who found it hard to tolerate the change of language even for countries other than their own.

The development was actually accepted in almost every country by authority of the conferences of bishops to which the initiative and the decision have been left. In the United States there was a twofold decision by the episcopate: in the spring of 1964, to permit English in the biblical readings and in the people's parts of Mass, as well as in all the sacramental rites outside of Mass; in the fall of 1965, to extend the English to the celebrant's "public prayers" at Mass. Most other countries combined the two stages and acted more quickly.

The pastoral and didactic purpose of this development needs no explanation. Almost as obviously related to this purpose is the Constitution's attitude—page after page—toward the Scriptures in the liturgy.

The Scriptures permeate the liturgy, not only in the passages formally read or quoted, but in the whole context of prayer and song. The conciliar decision is to improve the formal use of Scripture, make it a part of services other than the Mass and Office of prayer, improve the selection of passages for public proclamation, and increase the variety of such choices. Under this heading, too, fall the Bible services proposed in the first chapter of the Constitution in the formal limits of the prescribed liturgical services.

Here, too, we find the preaching of the word of God. The purpose of the restoration—in this case almost a revolution—is twofold: to integrate preaching into the liturgy and the liturgical context, and to make it an authentic and concrete proclamation of the mystery of Christ. The Constitution's tone is a good illustration of the influence of recent liturgical thinking from the proclaimed word of God in the setting of the liturgical assembly.

This matter, which is dealt with broadly in the first chapter, is taken up again in connection with the Eucharist, in which the preaching of the word is an integral part. Desirable on all occasions of community celebration, the homily is demanded in the Sunday Mass. By implication all the schemes of occasional preaching and catechetical lessons, artificially contrived without regard for the scriptural proclamation, are rejected. And, because the liturgy's words are so often impersonal and abstract and too generalized, the preaching must make the concrete application and draw forth the response of the community in its everyday life if the liturgy is to fulfill its pastoral function.

The place of biblical proclamation and preaching in the liturgy has been restored in some degree through the very first provisional implementations of the Constitution. The structure of the Mass rite has already been revised—as of Lent, 1965—to give a proper and distinctive setting for the liturgy of the word in the eucharistic celebration, Physically, this is reflected in the decision to remove the celebrant from the altar during the service of God's word, reserving the altar for the sacrificial banquet. It is represented as well by the prominence of the distinctive place for the biblical reading: the pulpit, ambo or lectern. Similarly, the quick spread of the prayer of the faithful, which completes the liturgy of the word and flows from the biblical reading and preaching, serves to express the needs of the whole Church and of the particular assembly in the language of petition to God.

Still under the heading of achieving the pastoral and formative purposes of the liturgy, the conciliar document speaks in terms of a noble simplicity to be attempted in the revision of rites. This is easier to decree than to achieve, but even the first steps in this direction suggest the possibilities. The confusing and the complex, the additions which now have no meaning, all must now be stripped from the liturgy so that its structure and outlines are clear. Neither iconoclasm nor philistinism is intended: the noble simplicity must not turn its back on past or present beauty. But the primacy must go to intelligibility in forms, with no obscurity for obscurity's sake. The sacred is not necessarily the mysterious; the mystery is to be revealed and proclaimed in human language and deeds.

What the Council says about the liturgy's teaching function has direct application to liturgical revision. Like the stress on the community sense and consciousness, or on the liturgy's adaptability (which comes next), it has significance also for every effort to understand the liturgy's true meaning and to communicate it to others. The Council's purpose can be achieved, more or less perfectly, as the liturgical externals are revised. The principle of the liturgy's pastoral function goes deeper and is a guide to all teachers and preachers.

These two concerns of the Council in liturgical revision—a recovery of community sense and the didactic nature of worship—are important correctives to past imbalance. The implications of the final heading of reform—liturgical adaptation—are even broader.

The immediate purpose of these norms, found toward the end of the first chapter of the Constitution on the Sacred Liturgy, is to provide for a regional adaptation of the liturgy to the cultures and traditions of different nations and peoples. It rejects the rigid uniformity of the past and the imposition of alien forms, symbols and expression.

It works both ways. The Christian revelation stands in judgment on human culture; it must reject anything that is superstitious or meretricious, no matter how traditional in the religious usage of peoples. Human culture also has its imprint to impose upon liturgical celebration, and this third directive for revision is a recognition of the positive goodness of diversity in the liturgy.

One misconception has already arisen, largely because of the expression "particularly in mission lands," which appears occasionally in certain parts of the Constitution. The use of this expression in no way limits the reforms—or the adaptability mentioned here—to those territories which are popularly or technically known as mission lands. The principles are everywhere valid, even if the questions have arisen first in mission lands because of greater pastoral understanding or progress.

The decision of the Council to admit flexibility and diversity on a scale never permitted in modern times for the Roman liturgy is in sharp contrast to the static approach of liturgical uniformity. Since the beauty of diversity in Oriental rites has had little practical impact on Roman usage, uniformity of liturgical usage has become a false ideal in the Western Church, increasingly so since the sixteenth century.

Breaking up this pattern of almost absolute uniformity is not an easy task, since the Council did not for a moment contemplate liturgical chaos or free experimentation.

Basic to the plan is the revision of the Roman liturgy, whose service books are to afford concrete opportunities for addition, subtraction and variation at the discretion of the conferences of bishops. More radical and creative adaptations or developments are also envisioned. Again, the details are left to the conferences of bishops which may obtain permission from the Holy See to conduct "necessary preliminary experiments over a determined period of time among certain groups suited for the purpose."

The line between the "substantial unity of the Roman rite" and the wealth of variations and new forms and texts will probably be difficult to draw. And the openness to adaptation has to be balanced against the Council's strong words against private innovations. In practice, the possibilities of variations, without upsetting the existing norms of liturgical books, are rather generous and become more generous with each step in the implementation of the Constitution, whether through the structural changes in the Mass rite or such concessions as Communion under both kinds.

Some may object that the Constitution, in this treatment of liturgical adaptation, is concerned only with regional or territorial diversities. If the text is looked at rigidly, one might think that the thorough revision of the Roman liturgy, together with a subsequent regional adaptation, country by country, could provide a fixed liturgy for generations or centuries to come.

The opposite is true. The principle of liturgical diversity, flexibility and adaptability means that no reform of the liturgy can be permanent or even definitive except in a relative sense. A measure of stability can be achieved and is highly desirable each time the liturgical books are revised, but no future revision can ever forget the principle of continuing evolution of liturgical forms.

The need of flexibility and openness runs through the entire Constitution on the Sacred Liturgy, with all its reference to pastoral needs, accommodation to contemporary understanding, recognition of past weaknesses and defects. It also underlies each individual decision of the Council in liturgical matters, because the very failure of the Roman liturgy to evolve since the late Middle Ages created the impasse which the Council seeks to break.

All this—community sense expressed in liturgical forms, pastoral consequences of liturgical celebration, adaptability and flexibility—is directed toward a more authentic and living liturgy. Anything artificial or routine must be replaced by the genuine and the personal. Each rite, and each part of each rite, must have genuine meaning for all the participants as they take their full and conscious part.

In effect, the general principles of the Constitution's first chapter, dealing as they do with the whole liturgical promotion and restoration, might be considered quite sufficient by themselves. Although the succeeding chapters have their expression of principles and doctrine, their development is implied in the first chapter, and the specific decisions which occupy them flow from the first chapter.

All this is another way of saying the broad doctrine and plan of the Constitution on the Sacred Liturgy should be kept in mind in the reading of the whole document. Yet the other six chapters—on the Eucharist, the other sacraments, the public prayer, the Church year and the arts of the liturgy— were and are necessary. In the matter-of-fact world of ecclesiastical renewal, even the measured steps of reforms since 1963 would not have been taken if the Council had failed to be specific. The broad principles concerning the vernacular, as worked out in the first chapter, might have been left hanging in unhappy suspense except for the clear terms of the second and third chapters concerning the vernacular in the Mass and in the other sacraments. The admirable and eloquent doctrine of the first chapter concerning the fullness of communal celebration of the Eucharist would hardly have led to the speedy introduction of concelebration were it not for the explicit decree of the Council contained in the chapter on the Eucharist.

Some of the norms and some of the language of the other six chapters will pass into history when the decisions are implemented. But the principles and the point of view will remain valid, and all deserve reflection.

In the chapter, "The Most Sacred Mystery of the Eucharist," for example, the dramatic developments are the extension of Communion under both kinds, in specified cases, to the laity, religious, and the clergy, other than the celebrant of Mass, and the restoration of the concelebrated Eucharist in the Western Church. These developments are directed toward the fuller appreciation of the eucharistic sign or sacrament, so that the meaning of Eucharist as banquet and as food and drink may be evident to all the worshipers and—in the case of concelebration—so that the collegiate and corporate nature of the ordained priesthood may be understood in the act of the whole community at worship. The Eucharist should signify what it truly is, the memorial and celebration of the redemptive event in the form of a fraternal banquet, the communal act of the whole Christian body in union with its head.

Just as significant, although less revolutionary, is the Council's determination that the liturgy of the word and the eucharistic liturgy should be appreciated as the two integral parts of the one celebration. Of all the detailed revisions of the Mass rite implicit in the second chapter of the Constitution on the Sacred Liturgy, none is more important than the fresh emphasis upon the service of God's word as part of the Eucharist in the fullest sense. Nor is it necessary to dwell on the ecumenical importance of this restoration which can have the deepest meaning to other Christians by relating and unifying word and sacrament.

The third chapter of the Constitution on the Sacred Liturgy deals with the whole sacramental system of other sacraments and sacramentals—apart from, but in complete dependence upon, the central Eucharist. The details are too many for comment. The high points range from a clear interpretation of the sequence of Christian initiation—Baptism, Confirmation, and Eucharist—to a recovery of the paschal character of Christian death as expressed in liturgical rites. Repeatedly the major celebrations of the liturgy are given a clearer relationship to the Eucharist, with Baptism, Confirmation, Matrimony, and religious profession inserted in the eucharistic rite. The treatment of the anointing of the sick restores that sacrament to its role as the prayer of faith that saves the sick man and, by this very fact, confirms the Eucharist as the ultimate sacrament of the Christian life, as the sacrament of Christian death.

The revision of the Church's Office of prayer was a difficult matter for the Council to undertake, complicated by the desire to relate the forms of popular devotions and public services, especially Bible services, to an official morning and evening prayer. At least the principles, laid down in the fourth chapter of the Constitution, explain the specific demands of this reform. The Office is the prayer of the whole Church; it must be accommodated to the needs of all and provide at least a basic and common prayer. Actually, it stands in greater need of revision than perhaps any other liturgical rite. Now its essential structure must shine forth more evidently, basically as the morning prayer of Lauds and the evening prayer of Vespers, with a period or hour of scriptural and patristic readings.

The fifth chapter of the Constitution, dealing with the Church year of feasts and seasons, is, in part, a profound meditation upon the centrality of the Paschal mystery, the Lord's death and resurrection, His passion and glorification.

Concretely this chapter calls for a fresh understanding of Sunday as the day of the Lord, as the basic celebration of the Church year because it is primarily the observance of the Paschal mystery itself. A revision of the Church calendar demands, above all else, the proper relation and subordination of feasts, so that first place is given—after the Sunday observance—to the fundamental aspects of the mystery of Christ, beginning with the Easter observance. Only then can a greatly reduced list of saints' days and observances take their proper place in relationship to the mystery of Christ.

The last two chapters of the Constitution deal in turn with music and the other arts of the Church. The chapter on music is marked by a radical departure from earlier concentration upon art-music in favor of congregational participation. Even the paragraph insisting upon the preservation of the liturgical treasury of music provides an immediate corrective by its insistence upon popular participation in the singing of acclamations, responses, psalmody, antiphons and psalms. The integration of diverse musical traditions of various cultures into validity is urged, as formal operation is given to "all forms of true art having the qualities needed" for the Christian liturgy.

The same point of view prevails in the final chapter on sacred art, including the important matter of church architecture. No form or style of art is or can be canonized as ecclesiastical or liturgical. The chapter's key statement is that churches should be "suitable for the celebration of liturgical services and for the active participation of the faithful."

This bare enumeration of a few high points in the Constitution does suggest one way to read it as a pronouncement of the Ecumenical Council. Another is to approach its specific provisions from the point of view of the goals of liturgical reform which look outward from the Roman liturgy itself.

The first of these is, of course, the ecumenical aim, expressed at the beginning of the Constitution on the Sacred Liturgy as "fostering whatever can promote union among all who believe in Christ." Anything that makes the Roman liturgy more comprehensible and attractive can serve the cause of ecumenism. Anything in the Roman liturgy that can reflect more surely or more evidently the values preserved in other Christian liturgies will help bridge gaps and provide points of discussion.

One of these has already been mentioned repeatedly: the stress upon Sacred Scripture. Another is the doctrine of the Church found in the Constitution. This is expressed in words in the first introductory paragraphs of the document; it is expressed in liturgical practice by the restoration of communal celebration which is the sign of what the Church truly is. It will be possible to go through the Constitution, paragraph by paragraph, and see the impact or potential impact of the conciliar decision upon the ecumenical dialogue.

Nevertheless, as the Council's Decree on Ecumenism is quick to point out, the manifold endeavors looking to Christian unity are not introspective. They are certainly not aimed at setting up a closed and institutionalized Christian community.

No more is the liturgy, as promoted and reformed by decree of the Second Vatican Council, to be closed or introspective. On the contrary, the aim of the Constitution is that the liturgy—and, above all, the Eucharist—should be in actual fact the means of manifesting to others the mystery of Christ and the Church's real nature. This question of involvement and concern, explained at length in the Pastoral Constitution on the Church in the Modern World, expresses the Constitution's view that the liturgy "shows forth the Church to those who are outside as a sign lifted up among the nations under which the scattered children of God may be gathered together . . ."

The dangers of excessive ritualism are a kind of escapism in the liturgy and are only too apparent. The promotion and reform of the liturgy determined by the Council must follow different patterns and must lead to an ever deeper involvement and commitment of the Christian to the needs of this life, even as he "looks forward to the resurrection of the dead and the life of the world to come." If the liturgy is the source of all the Church's strength, it is the starting point of every apostolic activity in the Church's total mission of witness, service and communion. If the liturgy is the high point of the Church's action, it is indeed because the Eucharist makes the Christian community. If this community is not conscious of God's universal call, the liturgy is words and sham.

Happily, both the liturgical movement of recent decades and the intent of the Council are quite the contrary. The response to God's call, uttered and proclaimed in the Eucharistic assembly, must be one of complete and willing dedication. It is the response expressed in the words of prayer, but necessarily expressed in life and action as well.

When the Constitution on the Sacred Liturgy is read in terms of these broad purposes, looking to Christian unity and to the oneness of the human family in Christ, it falls into place as the starting point of the conciliar renewal of the Church. Christ calls the Church to an unending reform, which must begin with the constant conversion of heart, the inner turning to God as this is expressed and manifest in the assembly gathered together in faith and love.

IV/PASTORAL CONSTITUTION ON THE CHURCH IN THE MODERN WORLD

Pastoral Constitution on the Church in the Modern World

☦ HISTORICAL INTRODUCTION

No document of the Council captured the imagination of the world so much as the Pastoral Constitution *Gaudium et Spes*. At the same time, no conciliar document has so dramatically answered Pope John's desire for updating the Church. Paradoxically, no conciliar document will be so readily outmoded, for as Archbishop John F. Dearden of Detroit has pointed out, although it "has historic significance, it is inevitably dated." Bishop Mark McGrath, C.S.C., of Panama, who played a key role in the formulation of the text, asserted the same in his final presentation of the first chapter of the Constitution when he said:

> . . . the very newness of many of the questions proposed and their diversity . . . impose limits on our document. General principles, either doctrinal or moral, are proposed, which principles frequently do not touch upon completely concrete solutions either because the problems involved require more mature examination or because they must be considered by the faithful in a particular way in each region, under the guidance of their pastors.

Many factors, nonetheless, combine to make this Constitution the most unique of all conciliar documents. First of all, it is the longest, consisting of 23,335 words. Secondly, it is specifically addressed to all men of good will and thus is not simply a "Catholic" document. It represents the first time the Catholic Church in a Council has undertaken to address itself to the searing practical problems of the world. Finally, it is entitled a "pastoral" constitution both to distinguish it from a dogmatic constitution and to reveal the Church's heightened concern with the real problems facing mankind today. The Constitution was an experience for both the Church and the world. It might well be judged by future historians as a high-water mark in ecclesiastical history because of its unique conciliar endeavor to build a bridge between the sanctuary of religion and the marketplace of the world.

The Constitution, as such, was not even discussed during the preparatory phase of the Council. It might best be described as a written testimony of Pope John's open approach to the world. Its origins can be traced to the common desire of the Council Fathers to enter into dialogue with the world. This desire was expressed in the Council's message to humanity issued on October 20, 1962. In it the Fathers declared their common desire "that the light of faith will shine more clearly and more vigorously as a result of this Council's efforts." They added that they "look forward to a spiritual renewal from which will also flow a happy impulse on behalf of human values such as scientific discoveries, technological advances and a wider discussion of knowledge."

In the closing days of the first session, Leo Cardinal Suenens of Malines-Brussels, Belgium, delivered an intervention which most commentators admit was instrumental in the formation of this Constitution. On December 4, during the thirty-third congregation, Cardinal Suenens presented his observations for the revision of the schemata. The official press bulletin summarized his remarks in these words:

One of the speakers recalled that the Holy Father, in his discourse of September 11, had expressed the hope that the Council would present the Church to the world as the light of the nations. He said that if the theme treated in these days is to be a kind of central point of the Council, from which the general directives are to be taken for all the other future discussions, it would be advisable to coordinate all the work of revision on the different projects with the study of the Church considered from within and considered from without: that is, the Church in herself, in her nature and in her mission as Mother and Teacher; then the Church in the face of the great problems which trouble today's world, beginning with those concerning the human person and going on to those referring to society with its demands of justice and peace.

The following day the then-Archbishop of Milan, Giovanni Battista Montini, wholeheartedly approved of the Belgian cardinal's proposal. He said the Church does not exist for itself, but as a servant of all mankind. It is, in fact, Christ Himself using His members as instruments in bringing salvation to mankind. The official press release did not even mention Cardinal Montini's intervention.

The Central Coordinating Commission, following the directives of Pope John, began work in January, 1963, to reduce the number of schemata. At this time the 73 schemata originally prepared were reduced to 17. The last of these, for some time simply called "Schema 17" and later known as "Schema 13," was entitled "The Efficacious Presence of the Church in the World." The schema was entrusted to a mixed commission composed of members from the Doctrinal Commission and the Commission on the Apostolate of the Laity. The mixed commission met in Rome the following month. According to Bishop McGrath, the mixed commission was presented with the task of coordinating four schemata originally prepared by the Doctrinal Commission, namely, "On the Moral Order," "On Marriage and the Family," "On the Social Order" and "On the Community of Nations"; two schemata originally prepared by the Commission on the Discipline of the Clergy and Christian People, namely, "On the Care of Souls" and "On Communism"; and one schema originally prepared by the Commission on the Apostolate of the Laity, namely, "On the Apostolate of the Laity."

During the preparatory phase of the Council many Fathers had submitted suggestions that dealt specifically with the topics discussed in this Constitution. Such suggestions dealt with the relationship between the Church and science, the relationship between the Church and international society, and the social doctrine of the Church, especially discrimination, totalitarianism, genocide, immigration, liberalism and communism. Other Fathers submitted suggestions concerning marriage, recreation and the dignity of the human person.

Another factor behind the formulation of this schema was Pope John's radio message of September 11, 1962. Discussing the innate vitality of the Church, Pope John spoke about what the Council should say concerning the real needs of people. He enumerated these as the needs of love, of bread, of peace, of education, of freedom, of justice, of brotherhood and of respect of one's own dignity.

The mixed commission began to work early in 1963 under the presidency of Alfredo Cardinal Ottaviani and Fernando Cardinal Cento. By the following May the Commission had prepared a text consisting of six chapters. The first of these treated "The Admirable Vocation of Man." This was followed by five specific chapters dealing with the person and personal rights, marriage and the family, culture and its diffusion, the socio-economic order and the community of nations and peace. The Central Coordinating Commission examined this draft on July 4, 1963, and decided to call for a revision that would develop more fully the doctrinal sections of the first chapter and relegate the material contained in the other five chapters to the status of appendices to the text.

During the summer months Cardinal Suenens called together a group of theologians in Malines, Belgium, to redraft the text according to the instructions of the Central Coordinating Commission. This text was presented to the mixed commission charged with drafting what was at that time known as "the famous schema 17." The Commission, however, did not accept it, judging it to be too abstract and imprecise. At its meeting on November 29 the mixed commission realized that the "unwieldy number of participants" was causing an impasse and thereupon established a small steering committee with the unwieldy title of the Central Mixed Subcommission. This steering committee, under the chairmanship of Bishop Emilio Guano of Livorno, Italy, originally consisted of three members from the Doctrinal commission and three from the Commission on the Apostolate of the Laity. They were Bishop Bernhard Schröffer of Eichstätt, Germany, Bishop Alfred Ancel of Mirina, France, and Bishop Mark McGrath, C.S.C., of Santiago di Veraguas, Panama, from the Doctrinal Commission, and Bishop Franz Hengsbach of Essen, Germany,

Bishop Jacques Ménager of Meaux, France, and Bishop Guano from the Commission on the Apostolate of the Laity. Shortly afterward Bishop John Wright of Pittsburgh and Bishop Joseph Blomjous of Mwanza, Tanganyika, were added to the group.

This steering committee called together clerical and lay experts to meet with it in Zurich, Switzerland, during February, 1964. The text prepared during this meeting was approved by the mixed commission during the two plenary sessions of March 4–9. The steering committee examined the oral and written suggestions offered by the mixed commission and presented a new revision of the text during another meeting of the mixed commission in early June. This text was finally approved by the Central Coordinating Commission and, with the approval of Pope Paul, was mailed to the Council Fathers in July, with the assurance that it would be the basis of a discussion during the third session. This text, called by the Reverend R. A. Sigmond, O.P., "the Zurich text," consisted of an introduction, four chapters, and a conclusion—in all, twenty-five paragraphs. The material contained in the original final five chapters was rearranged and published in a 64-page booklet and called the *adnexa*. Both the contents of the *adnexa* as well as their manner of presentation caused John Cardinal Heenan of Westminster to coin the colorful phrase, "*Timeo peritos adnexa ferentes*" ("I fear the experts bearing *adnexa*.").

On October 20, during the 105th general congregation, Cardinal Cento and Bishop Guano introduced the schema to the Council Fathers. "It is obvious to everyone," declared Bishop Guano, "that this Constitution is awaited with high hopes by many, both within and outside the Church. A great deal is expected from this document." The Council Fathers discussed the schema throughout 13 congregations, with 169 Fathers making oral interventions, and 830 pages of written observations being submitted. Commenting on the suggestions made during this period, Bishop McGrath wrote: "All in all, it took the pressure of debate on the Council floor, to which was quickly added the mounting interest of the press and of the listening world, to give this Constitution its due importance in the full perspective of the Council."

During this third session two lay auditors also addressed the Council Fathers on the material contained in the schema. Mr. Juan Vazquez of Argentina addressed the Fathers on the closing day of the discussion, November 10. The other lay auditor was Mr. James Norris, assistant director of N.C.W.C. Catholic Relief Services and president of the International Catholic Migration Commission. He addressed the assembly on the subject of world hunger and was warmly applauded at the conclusion of his address.

At the very outset of his remarks, Mr. Norris reminded the Fathers of the global dimension of poverty:

> In this lopsided community, one small group of nations have become immensely wealthy. These nations represent sixteen per cent of the world's peoples, and they own seventy per cent of its wealth. They are the nations

grouped around the North Atlantic, which are Christian by tradition, if not always in practice. For the first time in history they foresee rising prosperity —rich today, they will be richer tomorrow. Meanwhile, three-quarters of the human race live in a state of poverty bordering on or below the subsistence level.

Mr. Norris did not foresee any speedy, simple solution to the problem of world poverty, and he urged Christian people not to become weary of doing good. The goal, however, can be reached, he felt, if "a strong, committed, well-informed and courageous group of men of good will" is prepared in wealthy nations to consider world poverty as one of the greatest concerns of our time. He then proposed the following consideration to the Council Fathers:

> From this Ecumenical Council could come a clarion call for action which would involve the creation of a structure that would devise the kind of institutions, contracts, forms of cooperation and policy which the Church can adopt, to secure full Catholic participation in the worldwide attack on poverty. This great gathering of bishops represents every continent and every country on earth. Since world poverty affects all humanity, the great contribution of our universal Church can be a world-encircling manifestation of brotherly love, bringing effectively to bear the social teaching of the Church.

During the fourth session Mr. Norris and his colleagues, deeply concerned with the problem of world hunger were busy, night and day, making known to Council Fathers a proposal for the establishment of a papal Secretariat for the Promotion of World Justice and Development. Other Americans who joined actively with him and his associates from other nations were Auxiliary Bishop Edward Swanstrom of New York, Monsignor Luigi Ligutti, Monsignor Joseph Gremillion and Mr. Martin Work. The inclusion of the concluding paragraph in number ninety of the Constitution is a tribute to the zeal and creativity of the men who had successfully directed the universal Church's attention to the demands of world justice and development.

The discussion on the floor of the Council, as well as the continuous flow of written observations, greatly assisted the steering committee in its revision of the text according to the recommendations of the Fathers. As a result of these suggestions, greater prominence was given to the problem of atheism in the first part of the schema, and the chapters on marriage, culture and war underwent substantial changes. The steering committee worked from November 17 to 20 and made four proposals which were accepted by the Plenary Mixed Commission. These proposals were: 1) that eight more members be added to the steering committee, giving the "third world" greater representation; 2) that six experts be appointed to do further drafting and editing; 3) that an expository introduction, considering "the signs of the times" be added; 4) that the *adnexa* be incorporated into the text.

From January 31 to February 6 the enlarged steering committee worked on the revised text in Ariccia, near Rome. It enlisted the aid of 21 other Council Fathers, 39 experts, and 20 laymen and laywomen. Bishop McGrath has called this meeting "a breakthrough" because "the presence of laymen, most of them specifically competent in one or other area touched upon by the schema, was most comforting." During this meeting Archbishop Gabriel Garrone of Toulouse, France, who was charged with the entire doctrinal section of the schema, emerged as a leading figure. From the discussions at this meeting and under the leadership of Archbishop Garrone, a new ordering of the chapters in the schema was introduced. "The most striking difference between the texts of Ariccia and Zurich," wrote the Reverend R. A. Sigmond, O.P., "was demonstrated in the attitude of the first part: the next text began with a long introduction on the modern world; it then sought to develop a Christian anthropology; only thirdly did it outline the position of the Church in relation to the world."

The Ariccia text was presented to the steering committee during the week of February 8–13 where it was discussed at length and finally approved. The Plenary Mixed Commission, composed now of 67 members of the Doctrinal Commission and the Commission on the Apostolate of the Laity, reviewed the text during its meeting from March 29 to April 6 and approved it almost unanimously. The Central Coordinating Commission approved it on May 11, and Pope Paul, on May 29, authorized that it be mailed to all the Council Fathers. This text now consisted of 80 pages and 106 paragraphs. It was to be submitted for discussion on the floor of the Council during the fourth session.

From the 133rd to the 145th congregations, September 22 to October 8, some 163 Fathers delivered oral interventions on the floor of the Council. Even at this stage many Fathers still felt the document was "immature." Again the steering committee returned to the work of examining more than 20,000 suggestions submitted by the Council Fathers. In an almost unbelievably short time, the committee prepared two large booklets containing the *textus recognitus* which incorporated the suggestions of the Fathers in the text. These were distributed to the Fathers on November 12 and 13. On November 15 the Council Fathers began a series of 33 votes on the schema which continued until November 17.

At this point the schema was returned to the almost completely exhausted steering committee. "Amid difficulties of every kind," wrote the Reverend Giovanni Caprile, S.J., "not the least among them was the very short time at their disposal; those in charge of the schema worked literally in a race with the clock, night and day, in evaluating the numerous *modi* proposed during the previous voting." Nonetheless, the steering committee was able to return the *textus denuo recognitus* to the Council Fathers for another series of 12 votes on the amended passages in the text. During the final general congregation, with 2,373 Fathers voting, the text received 2,111 affirmative, 251 negative and 11 null votes. During the ninth public session, December 7, the Pastoral Constitution on the Church in the Modern World" received 2,309 affirmative votes, 75 negative votes and 10 null votes. Thereupon Pope Paul, "joined with the Venerable Fathers," solemnly promulgated the Pastoral Constitution on the Church in the Modern World which opens with the words *Gaudium et Spes.*

Two American prelates played a very important role in the formulation of this Pastoral Constitution. Archbishop John F. Dearden of Detroit served as president of the mixed subcommission responsible for the chapter on "Marriage and the Family." Bishop John Wright of Pittsburgh served on several subcommissions charged with drafting the document. He was president of the subcommission on "The Human Person" and a member of the subcommission on "The Signs of the Times" and "The Church of the Poor." Both, too, introduced their specific chapters on the floor of the Council: Bishop Wright on October 28, 1964, during the 111th congregation, and Archbishop Dearden on the following day.

Bishop Wright introduced the fourth chapter of the schema, at that time entitled "The Principal Duties of Christians at the Present Time," by stating that the discussion would concern "some of the major themes and problems which just about everywhere and almost always are a source of human preoccupation because of the obstacles they sometimes place in the way of man's attainment of his vocation." He declared that the Commission's intention was not "to attempt easy and over-ready answers." He expressed the hope that there would be "specialists, religious and lay, to help us in the future, as they have in the past, to proceed securely in the work of determining which are the 'signs of the times' which best guide us." Explaining why the chapter was by no means meant to be the last word on the subject, he said:

> . . . this chapter should not be the *final* word in the Council's dialogue with the world, but the *first;* indeed, on our side, it should be but the beginning of the presentation of the case for the teachings of the Church. It represents our desire to open new doors to new contacts in order to accomplish immediately some first objective, to set up the guidelines for the dialogue, to dispose of certain prejudices and to set up protections against false tendencies. The dialogue on these basic problems which begins in this aspect of the Council should, if it gets well underway, be long and carefully kept up by the Church, both by the hierarchy as a matter of official duty and by all the faithful as they do their work in the world with motivation at once Christian and humane.

Bishop Wright concluded his remarks by saying that the members of the subcommission charged with drafting the chapter "modestly seek to present some general principles and introductory observations about the responsibility of Christians in restoring and helping to nourish the concept of personal dignity." He asked for a discussion which he called "indispensable" in developing the contents of the chapter so that it might arrive at eventual perfection.

Archbishop Dearden's introductory remarks on the following day, concerning "Marriage and the Family," were no less significant. They introduced a discussion on the floor of the Council that would occupy the attention of millions throughout the world in the coming months. "No one," he said, "is unaware of the importance of the subject of marriage and the family." He admitted that his subcommission did not intend to propose a full treatment of the doctrine on matrimony. Its statement was to be nothing more than "a certain doctrinal synthesis which can help Christians of our day to arrive at a deeper understanding of the nature and dignity of married and domestic life." He explained the fundamental lines of the text in these words:

Matrimony is a sacred institution; more so in the Christian dispensation because it is a sacrament. By a stable and permanent union the married couple share the work of God, bear and instruct offspring, and sustain each other in grace. Marriage thus involves a sacred origin and end, and ordering to God's glorification a very specific community of love and essential relation to offspring. Moreover, a firm basis of family spirituality and morality is found in Christian matrimony.

True conjugal love must be understood in this context. It is a very profound union which perfects and ennobles the marital and familial community. That love, sustained by faith and charity, is clearly, above all, based on affection. The more the nature of conjugal love is considered, the more its importance in married life is understood.

From the nature of conjugal love, its ordination to fecundity not only for this world, but also for eternal life is made clear, and the essential ordination of matrimony to rearing and education of children becomes manifest.

Concerning the delicate question of family planning, Archbishop Dearden minced no words. He continued:

In treating of the fecundity of marriage, the principle of generous and conscious procreation is opportunely elucidated. From this there arises a very crucial question, if I may say so, about which the text cannot be silent —the question of the formation of conscience in regard to the problems of conscious responsibility in the vocation of fatherhood and motherhood. First of all, it is asserted that for grave enough reasons the couple can form its own conscience on the number of children. Judgment in this matter belongs to the couple, who are bound to make a judgment, moved by true conjugal love, in the light of a correctly formed conscience and with Christian prudence. But the methods or means to attain this end—and this must be noted —the methods for reaching this end must be judged according to the doctrine and mind of the Church. From the fact that the couple themselves must judge on the number of children they will rear, by no means does it follow that the couple can choose for themselves any means whatsoever for the act of regulating offspring. Thus any intervention which opposes the natural order of the conjugal act or the very expression of conjugal love, or corrupts or vitiates the conjugal act as the work of a person cannot in any way be admitted. There is no room here for subjectivism.

On the subject of anovulant pills, he said that the schema deliberately avoided the question because "the Holy Father wisely reserved judgment to himself. This problem," he insisted, "certainly will not be solved by discussions in the Council hall."

On the preceding day the moderator, Cardinal Agagianian, had already informed the Fathers that there would be no public discussion in the aula on "certain points" contained in the chapter. He did, however, urge the Council Fathers to submit their observations on these matters in writing and assured them that their suggestions would be given full consideration by the subcommission.

This admonition, however, did not prevent a large number of prominent Catholic intellectuals from making their own intervention. In a pamphlet entitled "Address to the Second Vatican Council on the Subject of the Problem of the Family," this distinguished group of medical men, university professors and journalists asked that the Council Fathers seriously consider the many worldwide problems that the rising world population is creating. They questioned whether the "particular conception and understanding of the natural law," upon which Christian morality in this area is based, is still applicable. "It seems," this international group of lay Catholics argued, "that there could be no possible conflict between a natural law based on respect for human values and a control of human fecundity—or the means employed to attain it—oriented toward man's total well-being." Other arguments they presented were of a physiological and psychological nature. Their address concluded with the following suggestion:

> In view of the complexity of the question involved, and the importance of these factors in the lives of millions of human beings, we are disposed to believe that the spiritual task to be accomplished needs a period of maturation, which will be profitable both for the reflection on the teaching of the Church and for the formation of the conscience of married people.

Among these signers, eighteen were from the United States. They were: Thomas K. Burch, Joseph L. Caulfield, André J. de Bethune, Louis Dupré, Joseph T. English, Alden L. Fisher, Rosemary F. Fisher, Frederick Flynn, John W. Higgins, Robert G. Hoyt, John Latendresse, David L. McManus, Michael Novak, Robert A. Preston, John Rock, Philip J. Scharper, Joseph Deuel Sullivan and Raymond L. VandeWiele. Another American, Dr. John T. Noonan, Jr., played a significant role in the conciliar treatment of this question. His impressive historical study, *Contraception*, was of great value to the work of Archbishop Dearden's subcommission. He came to Rome during the fourth session and served as an unofficial consultant to many of the Council Fathers. His subsequent study, entitled "Contraception and the Council," is one of the best to appear to date.*

As members of the Doctrinal Commission, both Archbishop Dearden and Bishop Wright played their respective roles in the drafting of the Dogmatic Constitution on the Church and the Dogmatic Constitution on Divine Revelation. This matter was treated more fully in the chapter concerning the Constitution on the Church. Suffice it to say at this point that Archbishop Dearden, according to many American experts, emerged as the great American leader during the fourth session because of his crucial role as chairman of the subcommission charged with handling the chapter on marriage and the family. His courage and prudence caused him to be considered as a giant among his peers during the difficult closing days of the final session.

Bishop John Wright presented to his colleagues from other nations an image of the American bishop they were not quite prepared to expect. "I conceived it our duty as American bishops," said Bishop Wright, "to welcome opportunities for the presentation to European audiences of seminarians, priests and laity the Catholic American understanding of the Council and its agenda." Throughout the time of the Council he lectured at 11 seminaries in Rome, addressed 7 meetings of national hierarchies, traveled to 4 countries to speak with 6 groups of university professors and students, attended 4 general congresses and conventions in 3 different countries, granted 15 European press interviews to representatives from 5 different countries and appeared in 4 radio and television interviews over European stations.

Other American bishops were deeply concerned with the Pastoral Constitution. Thirteen of them delivered their observations on the floor of the Council, and others submitted 27 observations in writing. Many of them submitted numerous *modi* either individually or collectively. The activities of Archbishop Philip Hannan of New Orleans, which will be discussed later, also evidenced the keen interest of the Americans in this document.

The observations submitted by members of the American hierarchy, either orally or in writing, deal with almost every aspect of the Constitution. In the early stages they discussed the nature of the schema in general terms; they later made their observations on specific articles of the schema. Their suggestions centered on three major areas: the dignity of the human person and the related issues of socio-economic life and the fostering of peace. Their observations on the last two problems may have been stimulated by Bishop Guano's request for more Americans to make their voices heard in these areas where presumably they have had the most experience. The Americans also submitted observations concerning marriage and family life. These will be treated together with the observations that were submitted relative to the one-day discussion on the *votum* on matrimony.

* Noonan, John T., "Contraception and the Council," *Commonweal*, 83 (March 11, 1966), no. 22, pp. 657–62.

1. *The Schema in General*

In 1963, Cardinal Spellman had already submitted his observations concerning the schema then entitled "on the Efficacious Presence of the Church in the Modern World." He declared that the pastoral aims and the particular spirit of the Council presented "the opportunity—indeed, the necessity—for such a schema." He then asked for a clear delineation of three items within the text.

First, he wanted the text clarified in order to forestall the possibility that "some men might be able to twist unjustly the words of the Council in condemnation of the so-called doctrine of segregation, the doctrine according to which men of one race and color ought to live apart from men of another race and color." Secondly, he felt that an explicit mention should be made concerning "the obedience owed the magisterium of the Church, by which the faithful might learn to respond to their Christian vocation perfectly and effectively. Today," he continued, "sad to say, there is a tendency, even among some Christians, to limit the extent of the Church's magisterium too much." Finally, he made the following comment concerning sacred virginity:

> I was surprised that almost nothing was said about *virginity* or about chastity for those in the single state. In the schema on matrimony, the family and virginity prepared by the theological commission (about which I have previously brought up questions in our commission meetings), there is a very beautiful treatment of virginity specifically insofar as it is a witness to the fruitful union of Christ and His Church. Considering the sufficiently false opinions of the present day, I do not see how the Ecumenical Council can at this point silently pass over the social import of Christian virginity. Furthermore, the purpose of the Second Vatican Council is essentially pastoral. No one with a care for souls can ignore the pastoral problems which arise from the spirit of secularism and the exaggerated opinions about an excessively diminished responsibility concerning chastity and modesty. It is very opportune that the Council should briefly but clearly set forth the teaching of the Church on these matters to enlighten and strengthen the souls of all men.

During the following year, the Archbishop of New York submitted another observation, taking his cue from the encyclical of Pope Paul VI, *Ecclesiam Suam*. In this written suggestion he asked that all the faithful enter into a "dialogue or exchange of views with all men of good will." He felt that a condition of this dialogue was the genuine spirit of Christian obedience and wrote:

> In this connection, it is greatly to be desired that the words of our Holy Father Paul VI in his encyclical *Ecclesiam Suam* concerning the necessity of the virtue of obedience will be included in the schema on the Church in the present world. For, on the part of the Christian, an essential condition for

any dialogue is a spirit of obedience toward that power "which in the Church has been established by Christ; acts as His Vicar; is, as it were, the public instrument of His voice and represents the love of so great a Shepherd" (Encyclical *Ecclesiam Suam*). It is most necessary, in my opinion, both for the sake of the children of the Church and for all our fellowmen that we explain the substance and meaning of freely given Christian filial obedience. All too often it appears to some that the Catholic Church greatly favors an obedience that is merely legalistic, somewhat unreflective, rooted perhaps in an excessive authoritarianism. The precisely Christian orientation of obedience is in complete harmony with Christian freedom, and its direction is toward the effectiveness of our ministry of service to mankind.

In his only observation on this schema Albert Cardinal Meyer of Chicago expressed the opinion that the schema was "too fearful of infection from the world and too strong in urging the Christian to pass his life 'as one departing and about to pass on.' He criticized the schema for its failure to recognize that "the whole world is not only the means by which redeemed man perfects himself, but is itself the object of redemption, just as our own bodies are."

The Archbishop of Chicago cited many passages from St. Paul attesting to the universal redemption of all creation. His words echoed the writings of Teilhard de Chardin. 'Christian salvation,' he said, "includes, first of all, the resurrection of our bodies, and then that mysterious transformation of the whole material universe to which our bodies belong. . . . We cannot imagine the condition of that transformed world; we cannot, however, call into doubt the fact." At the end of his oral intervention he drew this conclusion:

> This is, moreover, of the greatest concern to us here and now. For if this is really the way it is, then the work by which man leads the universe to the perfection God intends it to have does not belong to a mere temporal order, an order of things profane and contingent, but to a lasting order. For in his work with temporal things, man in some way prepares that consummation by which God will transform our world into a new heaven and a new earth.
>
> In light of this, all our attempts and successes in the cultural arena, in economics, science and social life—all these are understood to contribute positively to the realization of that plan in which God will restore all things in Christ (Eph. 1:10).

In what was, perhaps, one of the most philosophically profound of all American observations, Archbishop Lawrence Shehan, in his oral intervention of October 22, 1964, echoed Cardinal Newman's theory on the development of doctrine. He said:

> Indeed, the Church cannot change the deposit of Faith in which resides its main treasure; nor, at the same time, can it change its fundamental struc-

ture which was given to it by Christ the Lord. Nor are those doctrines changeable which have been defined under the influence of the Holy Spirit. Nevertheless, the Church has progressed and has to continue to progress in regard to its doctrine and its structure, so that it may respond to the problems of the world by adapting itself, and especially to those problems which arise from the relationships between those things and men who are always becoming their originators.

More than one hundred years ago, John Henry Newman, who afterwards was named a cardinal of the holy Roman Church, wrote a great work *Essay on the Development of Christian Doctrine,* in which is found the sentence, repeated in various ways: "a power of development is a proof of life." This same truth, which is of great importance for our schema, is sketched, I believe, in various places and in diverse ways, if not openly expressed, in the encyclical *Ecclesiam Suam* of Pope Paul VI—especially on page 12 of the copy of that encyclical distributed in this hall—where it states: 'The Church . . . advances more and more in the awareness of its duty, of the nature of its mysteries, of its doctrines. . . ."

In my humble opinion, this sentence should be explained in detail so that it might constitute a part of the schema that we are now talking about.

His concluding words echo the same sentiment. "Authentic tradition," he observed, "has to be preserved; but, at the same time, progress has to be admitted for a fuller knowledge and a stronger awareness of the Word of God or Gospel and its application to the 'signs of the times.' " His final sentence was a quotation from Pope Paul's *Ecclesiam Suam:* "The Church more and more advances in the awareness of its duty, of the nature of its mysteries, of its doctrines."

The Archbishop of Baltimore also submitted a written observation concerning the style and the method of the schema. He felt that the drafters of the text, although striving to reject an undue separation between the natural and supernatural orders, had not completely succeeded. "Such a separation of these two orders," he wrote, "can be best avoided by a presentation of the facts and truths of both orders in what is called a *synthesis.*" In the final session the newly created Archbishop of Baltimore spelled out in detail the nature of the synthesis he advocated. Speaking on September 23, 1964, during the 134th congregation, he explained his reason for advocating a Christian synthesis in these words:

The matter treated in these chapters offers an opportunity to adumbrate a truly Christian anthropology, accommodated to the progress of the teaching of the Church for these times. For the truths and deeds of the natural and supernatural orders consider one and the same thing, namely man in the real and concrete realm, and they find in him the proper principle of unity or synthesis. For man, existing in the real and concrete order, can be taken as follows:

1) as an *individual,* one and unique among others, from whom he is inwardly distinct;

2) as a spiritual *person:* on the one hand he is capable of infinite reality by reason of his intelligence and love, and, on the other hand, he is capable of the communion of the community with other persons by reason of that same intelligence and love;

3) as *a son of God,* to whom God Himself has given power to enter into a communion of community with the Blessed Trinity.

Since these three orders, essentially different from each other, are found in the one individual person of the man who is redeemed or capable of redemption, they manifest in the concrete and real order a deep unity of these orders and make a synthesis possible. But these orders are in contact with reality and the concrete existing order only within a union interiorly contracted. And so, man is a member of the human race because he is an individual; of the human community because he is a person; and a member of the Church united with Christ because he is a redeemed person.

Archbishop Shehan concluded by answering the fears of those who might feel that such a synthesis would be contrary to the traditional teaching of the Church. He distinguished between compromise and synthesis in these words:

There should not be any fear of a realistic and strong synthesis in the matter of this schema. Rather we must expect a progress in doctrine brought on by a change in circumstances and the rise of new problems. A synthesis is totally different from a compromise. The solutions in a compromise are reached by mutual concessions. However, the solutions of a synthesis seek truths by completing those things which actually complement one another. This method, namely synthesis, is prominent in this Most Holy Synod from the very beginning in its renewal of the Church in its life, teaching, and institutions.

Therefore, the Church faithfully fulfills its mission in searching after a synthesis.

2. The Dignity of the Human Person

In a world that seemingly had lost sight of the value of life and the dignity of the individual, it seemed imperative for the Second Vatican Council to devote a sizable portion of this document to a theological discussion of the dignity of the human person. American prelates were among the many who offered suggestions on this section of the text. Three Americans spoke on October 28, 1964, concerning this aspect of the schema: Joseph Cardinal Ritter, Archbishop Patrick A. O'Boyle of Washington, D.C., and Bishop Andrew Grutka of Gary, Indiana.

"The dignity of the human person and its recognition in practice," said

Cardinal Ritter, "are the necessary bases for all human life, whether individual or social." He insisted that the text be more emphatic in recognizing the dignity of man and said:

> Such an acknowledgment can take root only in the mind and heart of each man: it is necessary that each and every man first perceive and then recognize in practice his own dignity. If the Christian faithful desire to communicate the Christian concept of human worth to the world, then they will have to enlighten this concept not merely in words, but in all of life's activities. Accordingly, the schema should enumerate in this place those qualities which describe the life which is truly Christian and congruent with the dignity of man.

Cardinal Ritter then enumerated the principles that he felt would help underline this dignity. These two principles, he said, were the practical recognition that each man's dignity required his total dedication to the honor of God and that each live in such a way that he manifest a concern for his intimate union with God. He then concluded with the following observation concerning the passivity on the part of many individual Christians:

> Regrettably, Christians often substitute collective activity and responsibility for their own personal conscience: too often it is rather the case that the world molds the Christian than the Christian the world. In this age, when crimes against the human person are being increased, Christians either hesitate to exercise their own responsibility or even deny it. By their silence, if not by their activity, they are guilty of infidelity towards God. The concepts of personal responsibility and rational obedience should be made clear in the schema so that all Christian faithful, aware of their relationship to God and of their worth, may show the world the transcendent value of human life and the true dignity of the human person.

Bishop Grutka delivered one of the strongest attacks against racial discrimination heard on the floor of the Council. His remarks echoed the sentiment expressed the previous year by Bishop Robert Tracy of Baton Rouge, Louisiana. In his opening sentences Bishop Grutka declared: "Discrimination and segregation because of color, country of origin, or creed must not be condoned for any reason; to despise a man for his color, his origin, or his belief is a challenge to Divine Providence." The Bishop of Gary, however, was not content merely with enunciating principles. He made application in these words:

> Proper housing is essential because it promotes and enhances good family life—the foundation of society. Poor housing deteriorates into slums which become the breeding place for every form of crime and vice. Just as no one

looks for beauty on a garbage dump, neither should one expect virtue from the slums.

It is a deplorable fact that discrimination and segregation do exist in many parts of the world. In many instances the image of the Church has been tarnished and the pastoral labors of priests initiated in the apostolic work of missionaries stymied as the result of parishioners abandoning their neighborhoods when people of another color attempted to settle in this same area.

We know that the Church of Christ is the hope and salvation of all men, but this truth is not always reflected very clearly in actual practice. In view of the signs of the times, the emphasis on personal human dignity and rights is not strong enough. It behooves the Fathers of this Council—gathered here from all parts of the world and representing in themselves all colors and races —to voice their opposition to every form of segregation and discrimination with the force of the trumpets of Jericho and proclaim the dignity and rights of human persons everywhere with the utmost clarity.

The next speaker, Archbishop Patrick A. O'Boyle, chairman of the administration board of the National Catholic Welfare Conference, spoke "in the name of all the bishops of the United States gathered in Rome." He praised the schema for emphasizing the need for continuing the religious dialogue, which "can be carried on more effectively not only by the hierarchy, but, even more importantly, by the faithful." The principal reason for this intervention was, he said, "to propose the addition of a separate section in chapter four on the problem of racial discrimination and other forms of racial injustice." In this proposal he echoed the previous speech of Bishop Grutka. Speaking in language that would be especially heartening to all civil-rights workers in the United States, he said:

Our treatment of this problem in Schema 13 need not be very long, nor should it attempt to offer detailed solutions to specific problems in particular countries or regions of the world. At the very least, however, it should include a forthright and unequivocal condemnation of racism in all its forms and should outline, if only in general terms, the theological basis for this condemnation. It should also emphasize the obligation which rests upon all members of the Church to do everything within their power to eliminate the cancerous evil of racial injustice and to advance, through all available means, the cause of interracial brotherhood under the fatherhood of God. I might add, in this connection, that our own experience in the United States suggests that this is one area of social action which calls for the closest possible cooperation among Catholics, Protestants, and Jews and all other men of good will.

In our judgment, racism is one of the most serious moral and religious problems of our times. If we fail to give it separate and adequate treatment, I fear that the world will conclude that we are poorly informed about the signs of the time or, worse than that, that we are insensitive to the tragic plight of the millions of innocent men and women all over the world who are the victims of racial pride and racial injustice.

In closing, permit me to quote, in my own native language, a brief excerpt from an address delivered in that language by Pope Pius XII, of happy memory, to a group of Negro publishers from the United States: "All men are brothers in Jesus Christ; for He, though God, became also man, became a member of the human family, a brother of all. This fact, the expression of infinite universal love, is the true bond of fraternal charity which unites men and nations. May it be welded even more firmly through the efforts of all men of good will."

Another intervention on the subject of racial discrimination was submitted in writing by Archbishop Paul J. Hallinan of Atlanta, Georgia, on October 11, 1965. Even after the revision in the light of previous interventions, the Archbishop of Atlanta felt that the subject of racial discrimination "is not given the clear and forceful treatment for which injustice cries out today." He then argued that a conciliar statement against racial discrimination

> would strengthen the hands of bishops, priests, religious and laity as they earnestly try to remove this moral offense from mankind's catalog of sins. It would ennoble the difficult efforts of those governments that are concerned with the social evils in inequality. With justice and compassion, this statement would publicly accord to the victims of these evils the dignity that is inalienably theirs. And, finally, it would assure the world that the Church will constantly proclaim God's law of justice and love, constantly act upon it, and lead its members to live in that true harmony that only equality and fraternity can provide.

In another written intervention, dated the following day, Archbishop Hallinan praised the schema for citing three important points concerning the Church's teaching on the role of woman, namely, her present condition, her origin according to the book of Genesis and the contemporary abuses she suffers. He felt, however, that the schema failed to come to grips with the "urgent problems" which the world faces in this regard. He said that "the Church has been slow in denouncing the degradation of women in slavery and in claiming for them the right of suffrage and economic equality." Surveying the present situation, he said that

> women in many places and in many respects still bear the marks of inequality. This is evident in working conditions, wages and hours of work, and in marriage and property laws. Above all, it is present in that gradualism, bordering on inaction, which limits their presence in the tremendous forces now working for universal education, for peace, for the rehabilitation of the

deprived, the just and the compassionate care of the young, the aged and the needy, the dispossessed and the victims of human injustice and weakness. Certain nations have led the way, but even in these the ideal and complementary role of man and woman has not yet become the basis and norm of our social order.

In order to strengthen the text of the schema, Archbishop Hallinan then proposed these four practical suggestions:

> That the Church define the liturgical functions of women so that they could serve as lectors and acoyltes, and, when properly prepared, also, as they once did, in the apostolic office of deaconess. They could thus, as deacons do, administer certain sacraments.
>
> That the schema should include them in the instruments to be set up after the Council to further the lay apostolate.
>
> That women religious should have representation in those matters which concern their interests, especially in the present and post-conciliar agencies.
>
> That every opportunity should be given to women, both as Sisters and as lay women, to offer their special talents to the ministry of the Church. Mention should also be made of women who are not married. Because of the universal call to women (in *De Ecclesia*), they also promote family values by witnessing in their own way to this universal vocation.

Another lengthy observation on woman's role in the Church was submitted in writing by Auxiliary Bishop Fulton J. Sheen of New York. He pointed out the role of women in the New Testament in his opening words:

> It was to a woman that the promise of salvation was given. The news of the Incarnation was given to a woman. Christ first appeared to a woman after his Resurrection. A woman spoke for humanity when humble Mary's *fiat* responded to the creative *fiat* of the Heavenly Father. Women were to a great extent responsible for giving food and sustenance to Christ and His Apostles. Women were present at the burial and entombing of Our Lord. Peter went to the house of a certain woman where he met many disciples after his miraculous escape from prison (Acts 12). In Joppe, Tabitha, a woman disciple of the Church was honored as "one who filled her days with acts of kindness and charity" (Acts 9:36).
>
> The first convert St. Paul made in Europe is related to be a woman (Acts 16: 14–15), and Paul calls her "his joy and crown" (Phil. 4:1). At Philippi, where this happened, we find women working together with the Apostles (*ibid.* 4: 2–3). The faith of Timothy is stirred up by a reference of Paul: "I am reminded of the sincerity of your faith, a faith which was alive in Lois your grandmother, and Eunice your mother before you" (2 Tim. 1:5). St. Paul committed to Priscilla and Aquila his apostolic labors in Ephesus

(Acts 18: 18–19), and, returning after a year to the city, found a well-organized Christian community. The catechist Priscilla of that same community developed the instructions of the learned Apollo. The name of her husband is mentioned first in the Acts, but, shortly afterwards, the name of the wife is placed first. In the Epistle to the Romans (Rom. 16: 1–2), Phoebe is described by Paul as "she who has been a good friend to many, including myself."

The Blessed Virgin Mary is rightly said to be the center and heart of the College of Apostles (Acts 1:14).

He admitted that woman's role today is rapidly changing, but insisted that true civilization demanded certain qualities which only women can give. "These," said Bishop Sheen, "can be characterized as purity, protection of the weak, sacrifice, procreation, the sustaining and care of human life." He then developed the threefold aspect of motherhood as physical, spiritual and social. In defending the professional woman, he observed that social motherhood offers a woman the occasion to fulfill her maternal instincts fruitfully. "These jobs demand a concentration of heart and strength which physical mothers could not have," he added. "These women would be able to give this service since they are free and held down by no one responsibility." In conclusion he cited the specific gifts that the Christian woman can contribute to society:

In the economic, civil, social and cultural order she will be associated with men, and she should exercise prudence, tenderness and the motherly instinct which is so necessary to compensate for administrative rigidness.

In the sphere of law she should point out the importance of equality and mercy in considering those circumstances which lie outside the strict interpretation of the law. In the area of communication, radio and television, she can become the safeguard of the public morality and also family life. In the line of industry she can moderate the value of material things by pointing out the importance of the dignity of the person and basic human qualities. In the search for peace, insofar as she recognizes the growth and formation which a person must experience, she will try to ward off for other nations the ruinous consequences of war. It is not by chance, but in the providence of God, that a woman, given the capacity to give herself totally to others, be placed in the middle of a world which has forgotten its soul. Every woman without exception is morally obligated according to her capacity and condition in life to realize one of these forms of motherhood.

Concerning that part of the schema dealing with the cooperation that should exist among all Christians in building up the Kingdom of God, Auxiliary Bishop John F. Whealon of Cleveland held a reservation. If the entire paragraph could not be changed, he proposed that the following addition be inserted: "No baptized person or assembly of baptized persons might hold in the name of the

Christian religion a faith or morality inimical to Christ or might be complacent in their error." He praised the positive and ecumenical nature of the paragraph since "these words refer to non-Catholic Christians who maintain a sincere Christian faith and a true Christian morality." His reasons for inserting the proposed sentence were as follows:

> At home, in the United States of America, many non-Catholics have forsaken a full Christian morality; for example, they tolerate and maintain divorce, repeated marriages and even contraception.
>
> These positive statements about these people, which are stated in paragraph nine, accordingly, can be very acceptable to them in their error. These words can easily be cited as approving of their present status, a state which is certainly unfortunate.
>
> Already the number of conversions to the Catholic faith at home has declined. Perhaps, in the future, Catholics with difficulties in moral matters, for this reason or for others, would change over to non-Catholic religions with a calm conscience.

Bishop Russell McVinney of Providence, Rhode Island, delivered his observations on the dignity of the human person on September 22, 1965. He felt that the Council Fathers had a duty to impress upon an amoral world its duty to recognize a properly constituted authority; he warned against "an epidemic of cynicism" afflicting the world today and urged vigilance against "the infiltration of the philosophy of ease into our own ranks." He was wary of "the new-breed theologians" among whom, he felt, are some "searching for insights, enlightenment and interpretation of divine truth," not in Thomas Aquinas, the doctors of the Church or in papal pronouncements, but in writings of non-Catholics. These dangers must be met by insisting upon "the necessity of obedience toward properly constituted authority." He then underscored the relationship between obedience and authority:

> The much vaunted "crisis of obedience" in the Church will disappear when our young people fully understand that obedience and freedom are not contradictory and incompatible, when they see that true freedom can be found only in obedience. It is only by freely subjecting himself to authority that man reaches his perfection in society and in God. The question is not whether we shall obey, but rather how we shall obey . . . in a grudging, reluctant, mean-spirited manner . . . or, as St. Augustine says, "Obey . . . not as slaves under the bondage of the law, but as children, free in the liberty of divine grace."

Two Americans addressed themselves to the issue of dialectical materialism. As early as 1962, Cardinal Spellman had submitted his observations concerning communism as treated in the discarded schema on communism. He rightly observed that the communications media would pay particular attention to what the Council would say concerning communism. He said that what the schema stated about pastors admonishing their people not to vote for communist candidates should be carefully worded. "There should be added to these words," he said, "an explicit warning to bishops and pastors not to mix in affairs of a purely political nature." He further suggested that the contents of this schema should be incorporated in other schemata lest some would think "that these statutes have been set up only because of the danger of communism."

Bishop Nicholas Elko of Pittsburgh also submitted an intervention on the subject of atheism. He argued that the presentation concerning the dignity of the human person should be "more forceful, not so gentle and evasive, but rather clarified in a determinate sense with militant opposition to the evil of dialectical materialism." He asked that "dialectical materialism be named in specific words as the actual pestilence of modern human society." He then proposed the following remedies which he would like to see included in the text.

1) Errors and omissions of Christians who have failed to live up to basic Christian standards should be indicated and Christian criteria that are to be lived up to must be clearly stated.

2) The faithful must be taught to know that this problem of atheism is the enemy of God and there must be education for more profound knowledge of this enemy of God.

3) Social justice, we must admit, needs strenuous and fearless defense without timidity.

4) We must be demonstrative in lifting the cherished value of the supernatural order against the practical materialism and theoretical atheism. We must indicate that poverty does not justify a militancy against God in God's world.

5) Education about atheism should be obligatory in schools and in families; only by knowing the enemies of God and their methods can we cooperate in bringing about a victory for God and His Kingdom.

6) Special books forcefully and profoundly treating the subject of dialectic materialism must be made available.

7) Priests and religious must be instructed in the seminaries about the inevitable confrontation with dialectic materialism in their mission in the entire world.

8) The lay apostolate must have available special modes of instruction on this subject.

9) The theoretical teaching of the Church must be brought to a focal point of attention and vitality by exemplary Christian living, especially the basic charity that is a sign of unity for all men. It must be practiced assiduously.

3. Socio-economic Life

Under the inspiration of Bishop Edward Swanstrom, who had been director of the Catholic Relief Services—National Catholic Welfare Conference for many years, the Americans made their voices heard and their influence felt during the discussion on poverty and international development. Bishop Swanstrom himself delivered two oral interventions and three written interventions on the subject. Eight other Americans submitted observations on this and related subjects.

In his intervention delivered on November 5, 1964, Bishop Swanstrom spoke "as the director of the American bishops' foreign relief program which now encompasses 73 countries of the world." He admitted that "life in America is in sharp contrast to all the unrest, the homelessness, the hunger and anguish that I have witnessed all over the world in the past several years." He then related the story of Lazarus and the rich man as he had personally seen it.

As I have traveled about the world—to its misery-scourged corners—I have seen Lazarus in my mind's eye over and over again.

I have seen him most obviously in the leprous beggar dragged in a cart on a begging journey around the streets of Calcutta, a city whose streets teem with millions of people, many of them refugees. I saw him, too, in the refugee who had escaped from the mainland of China in 1961 and who had been caught up and deposited in the Fan Ling transit camp.

I went up to this camp and saw thousands of unfortunates who had risked their lives to escape, but were allowed to sit at the gates of the free world for a few days, then were herded into trucks to be returned to China. There was no inn for them in the towns and cities of our western civilization.

In the giant slums which have mushroomed around Latin America's proudest cities—Rio de Janeiro, Santiago, Lima, Bogota—I have seen countless men waiting at the gate of the world for the opportunity to take part in productive life and waiting in vain.

Bishop Swanstrom also admitted that the problems of poverty, hunger and disease are not new, but new are the hopes and expectations of the future that all men share. "If men's hopes are not obtainable by a peaceful revolution," he warned, "a violent revolution is inevitable." He suggested that bishops should encourage and support governmental efforts in alleviating the problems of world hunger. Finally, he suggested that the schema should be rewritten to stress "the tremendous responsibility placed upon bishops and priests in our day and age to participate most actively in programs to assist the people of God to raise themselves out of the abyss and poverty and degradation."

Addressing the Council Fathers again on October 4, 1965, Bishop Swanstrom was even more direct in his suggestions. He praised the schema for what it stated concerning "an obvious and ever increasing discrepancy of wealth between the richer and the poorer nations" as well as the "precepts of justice which should be applied to this question. However," he added, "I am deeply concerned about the implementation of this beautiful doctrine of the universal common good and international social justice." For this reason he proposed that "the Church launch a deep and long-term campaign of education, inspiration and moral influence to promote among Christians and all men of good will a live understanding and concern for world poverty and to promote world justice and development in all their facets." He also proposed that "a secretariat be established within the Church to carry on this long-term process of education and inspiration, motivation and moral influence." Finally, he suggested that the following paragraph be inserted into the text:

In order to call with persistence the attention of the People of God and, in fact, all men of the human family to the sad plight of a majority of God's children, and to teach the message of Christ's love for the poor and His justice in and out of season, this Sacred Synod proposes that a secretariat of the Holy See for promoting world justice and development be established. It also urges that national conferences of bishops [*coetus*], religious orders and other appropriate bodies including those composed of laymen, set up suitable means for opening the minds and hearts of all to the cries of the poor over the whole world wherever possible. These educational and inspirational efforts should be carried on in close concert with our separated brothers, with groups inspired by other religions and with all men of good will.

The New York Auxiliary Bishop's other three interventions considered the same problem from different aspects. In one intervention he traced the history of almsgiving from the early days of the Church and suggested how the practice should continue in our day. "However," he pointed out, "the mere distribution of alms itself does not solve the problem because it is uncivil to treat men as beggars constantly. The purpose of material help ought to be to help men to help themselves and to raise them to the dignity of human sufficiency through their own efforts and labors."

In another observation he discussed voluntary poverty and effective charity as "a sign of the spiritual life of the Church." Referring to the practices of the primitive Church as recorded in the New Testament, he recalled how "the first Christians put at least a part of their possessions in common to help the poor." He asked that the practice of active charity as an example on the part of the whole Church be more strongly emphasized so that "it will more clearly and more efficaciously be seen that the intention on the part of the Church today is to imitate the voluntary poverty of Christ."

In his third intervention Bishop Swanstrom quoted Pope Paul VI who had said, "It has been proven scientifically that more than half of the human race is without sufficient food. Also, today entire generations of children, on account of a need which we cannot describe, either die or live in extreme poverty." He argued that this situation demands that the Church adopt new methods by which "we might care for our brothers in this world of ours." He then described the situation in the world today:

> From the conditions of daily present-day life there has arisen throughout the whole world so great a supply of earthly goods that men now speak of a new age in which they will have those things which they never before dreamed possible. All people now desire for themselves what they know other people have; the same things which we wish to give to our loved ones, friends and children. We see happening what is called "a revolution of rising expectations."
>
> All families wish to have the occasion of meriting those things by which they can sustain themselves and live according to the dignity of the human person. They wish that their children be taught to read and write, that the hungry be filled and the sick be cured. They wish today to become participants and have an equal share of the things that are now being produced.
>
> It should not happen that these just desires are ever held back from them. All people of this progressing world are proceeding to better things. We who represent the people of the whole Catholic Church must proceed with them.

Other Americans presented practical suggestions to meet this problem. Bishop Floyd Begin of Oakland, California, spoke about tithing, and Auxiliary Bishop George Speltz of Winona about investments. Bishop Begin asked that the Council Fathers "spend a little time in recalling the economic system instituted by God Himself" because it "offers a solution to the problem of poverty and destitution in this world, while, at the same time, it will promote great sanctity." After tracing the teaching on tithing from the Old and New Testament, the Church Fathers and the liturgy, he said:

> God in the Old Testament demanded from everyone, including the poorest, the firstfruits and the tenth part of any fruits, revenue, gain or profit for the support of worship, the clergy and the works of charity. But He also promised to tithers an abundance of temporal goods and other blessings.
>
> God has never withdrawn this promise. Therefore, if anyone, even the poor, or the poorest, would willingly give to God the first tenth part of his income, he would receive the promised reward and bid farewell to poverty. "Try me in this," says the Lord. A man renders tribute to God by contributing to the works of religion and charity. Since a man in paying the tithe and firstfruits would really be seeking first "the kingdom of God and His justice," he would deserve to hear, "All these things will be given to you besides" (Lk. 12:31).

In conclusion Bishop Begin asked that the following sentence be inserted into the text:

> Finally, this Holy Synod, mindful of the divine institution of tithes and firstfruits revealed to us in the Old Testament and never repealed, mindful also of the rewards promised by God and those who observe this practice, rewards for the spiritual and temporal welfare of the individual and the whole Church and the whole human race—the Holy Synod emphatically approves those Christians and all others who return to God by contributing to works of religion and charity, the first ten per cent of their incomes, salary, profits or gain.

Bishop George Speltz suggested that the schema speak more specifically to the rich since "the spirit of poverty does not prevent us from making lawful use of economic reality which has assumed an enormous and far-reaching importance in the development of modern civilization." He felt that by directing its words to the wealthy, the schema could "more adequately translate the spirit of poverty into language and conduct relevant to their condition and opportunities and in keeping with their status." He concluded by suggesting that the following sentence be included in the schema:

> Let the rich, to whose stewardship much is entrusted and to whom, therefore, the Sacred Synod most urgently addresses herself, give thought how they may most opportunely invest their wealth for the production of goods that will relieve this distress, give employment and restore human dignity. Thus shall the rich, through their sensitivity to the needs of the poor, also be poor in spirit and, at the same time, make an invaluable contribution toward the building up of a fraternal city. And besides, this will be for *all* a pledge of the freedom of the sons of God and the mainstay of freedom and peace in the world.

On June 23, 1965, Archbishop Karl Alter of Cincinnati submitted his observations on the subject of aid to underdeveloped countries and world peace directly to Bishop Emilio Guano, chairman of the steering committee charged with drafting the text. Concerning aid to underdeveloped countries he made the following seven suggestions:

> The needs of many underdeveloped countries are so vast and require such extensive resources in terms of money, capital investment and in terms of highly trained personnel that only governments and an organized international effort can cope adequately with the problems. The duty of the individual Christian is to foster such action, and the development of such organizations in his capacity as a citizen and as a member of society.
> 2) The existing organizations. such as the United Nations and others of

a quasi-governmental nature, should be fostered, improved and made more efficient.

3) The agencies providing aid to underdeveloped countries should be international in their formation and character so as to avoid the danger or charge of pursuing selfish national interests or the exploitation of the under-developed countries.

4) Contributions of money, material, personnel, technical humanitarian and professional education services should be made by individual nations through their governments in proportion to their resources.

5) Voluntary organizations, fostered by the Church, should assist especially in areas where governmental action is inappropriate or less effective, but should not duplicate the international program. The function of the Church is to inspire, encourage and give the human and personal touch to the total effort.

6) There is need of a person-to-person relationship in any program of aid for underdeveloped countries over and beyond the government-to-government relationship.

7) The missionary program of the Church, while directed necessarily to spiritual ends and to the ultimate purpose of extending God's kingdom on earth, should be concerned necessarily also with the exercise of the virtues of social justice and charity. The practical programs adopted should always conform to the native culture, habits, attitudes and traditions of the local people and should avoid the importation of a foreign culture, no matter how superior it may appear to be in the eyes of the missionaries of the Church.

Bishop Fulton J. Sheen also submitted a lengthy written intervention on the socio-economic order. He urged that Catholics cooperate with Protestants, Jews and all men of good will because, as he wrote, " 'Toleration' of other religious groups in social action should give way to 'cooperation.' Toleration has bred indifference; toleration did not have as its basis brotherhood through charity, but deadlock through exhaustion." Urging this cooperation with other groups he wrote:

All religions as moral groups must unite to apply the principles of justice to mass civilization. As communism unites with non-communists, secularists, agencies to further revolution, so Catholic Action should unite with non-Catholic groups to make the principles of justice distributive as well as personal.

The major reforms in the economic order (labor unions, higher wages, shorter working hours) have *for the most part* come from non-religious and purely secular forces and organizations.

Catholic Action must show that the *principles* which guided these agencies were *borrowed* from the Christian tradition. Only in the Christian tradition will they flourish; outside of that soil they wither and die. History proves that the exile of God ends in the tyrannization of man.

Bishop Sheen insisted, secondly, that Catholic endeavors in the economic order never descend to being merely anti-communistic. Catholic activity in the economic order, he said, "must not be *merely* a defense of high wages, the right to organize, shorter hours, greater social benefits, etc., however laudable these be. It must start with a complete philosophy of life which will show the fallacy of communist principles." Nor will there be any identification of the Kingdom of God either with labor unions or private property. "No economic class is *always* right," he observed, "simply because it is a class. Right may at times be on the side of labor, sometimes on the side of capital, and more often on the side of the common good or the public good." He also pointed out that the traditional concept of property has changed and this factor must be taken into consideration in any economic solution the Church proposes. He also advocated the establishment of chaplains in the industrial world similar to chaplains serving the armed forces. "Since five days a week those who serve industry enter into a new *relationship*," he said, "they should be spiritually ministered to *in* that relationship and not apart from it." Catholics, too, must recognize that "industrial civilization is passing from the market-principle to the state-principle." Bishop Sheen cited three reasons for this shift in emphasis:

a) The world is trying to recover the sense of *community* or common purpose which was lost (1) by irreligion, (2) individualism and egotism of the profit-economy.

b) Socialism is the forcible organization of the chaos created by the *laissez-faire* of the old capitalism.

c) As individuals surrender responsibility, the State takes it over. When the family gives up its right to educate, the State educates. When other loyalties fail, the State becomes the object of devotion. Socialism fills the void of *vocational emptiness* occasioned by the loss of a Christian purpose of life.

Bishop Sheen felt that the State-principle, or socialism, would be counteracted only by the establishment of a vast network of professional groups "in which citizens are bound together on the basis of the function or role they play in society." Catholic schools, he said, must educate students to apply Christian principles to the economic order. He also suggested that in underprivileged countries the Church organize "mobile schools" which would move from diocese to diocese to instruct both clergy and laity in the economic and social doctrine of the Church. And he felt that Catholics with a surplus of the world's wealth should be encouraged to surrender voluntarily some of their land and wealth to the underprivileged. In concluding, he made an observation that is all too obvious, but too often overlooked: "The economic order will not be reformed and remade by priests, lawyers, doctors who are outside it, but by capitalists, management and labor who are *within* it."

Auxiliary Bishop Warren Boudreaux of Lafayette, Louisiana, approved of this section of the schema in general, but with a reservation. He desired to see a better balance in the text "to remove the tendency of some to abuse social welfare and to accept it to the decline of their own personalities and human dignity." He described this abuse as follows:

> It is well known by all that the "welfare state" intends to relieve the needy, the poor and those who have not had the opportunity to find work, or who, because of some handicap, are unable to work, or who are temporarily in need, etc. And yet it is common knowledge that large numbers, once they have begun to receive help either from government or private agencies, find it the simplest and easiest way to survive, and abandon themselves to public or private welfare as a way of life. Not only is this unjust (St. Paul said that if a man did not work, neither should he eat) to those who contribute their means to such abused assistance, but the habit is destructive to the recipient himself and creates in his family the mentality that the world owes it a living, so that the vice grows and becomes part of a family mentality. What is said of individuals may well apply to nations.

To offset this abuse, Bishop Boudreaux suggested that the schema incorporate in some way these two observations:

> A. These means of social welfare should be considered by the recipients as temporary, so that as soon as possible they have the obligation to obtain jobs and means of livelihood, since this is required for human dignity and their own spiritual and emotional growth.
>
> B. Recipients of such help, understanding its benefits, should all the more strive to improve their condition through personal initiative, so that they themselves, through the fruits of their labors, may contribute to the help of others. Thus by constant efforts and personal responsibility of individuals, the common lot of man may be improved and the standards of living of all mankind may reach that norm and apex as befits one made in the image and likeness of God.

Auxiliary Bishop John F. Whealon of Cleveland, in his written intervention of October 8, 1965, felt that the schema's teaching concerning labor's right to organize, although traditional, "is a little too simplistic." He suggested, therefore,

> that something should be mentioned about the responsibility of those who administer labor unions and business to consider the common good of the whole country. In the U.S.A., where these labor unions are well established,

both the administrators of business and the heads of labor unions proceed a little too unilaterally, with no concern for the total economic life of the country.

Bishop Frederick Freking of La Crosse, Wisconsin, and president of the National Catholic Rural Life Conference, submitted his written observations on economic determinism and rural life. He said he spoke for several bishops who are members of the National Catholic Rural Life Conference and many farmers and rural people of other nations. He regretted that the schema had so little to say about the people who labor on the land and who "constitute at least forty per cent of all Catholics in the world." He asked, "What is offered those rural people who do not wish to join the endless tide toward urbanization and giant industrialization, but are forced to do so by the sheer weight of economic determination?" These people, he said, are asking for guidance and direction from the Church to help them overcome the economic conditions forcing them to leave the land for the cities. These people, he said,

tell us that the overcostly mechanization of modern agriculture, the exorbitant costs of processing and marketing food, the speculation in food commodities, and the amassing of land by purely capital investment which has no interest in the rural community are forcing them to send their sons to the city to find a livelihood. Seemingly in the underdeveloped nations we fight against the evils of absentee landlords of one kind, and in the nations of greater economic growth we are already encouraging the same evils in a different form of absentee landlords caused by economic determinism.

Bishop Freking then cited papal teaching for the last century that "consistently pointed out that economic forces alone should not control human life to such an extent that men's lives become very impersonal and man is considered simply as part of a mass." He referred also to the policy-statement of the National Catholic Rural Life Conference as declaring "that the individual human being finds conditions more suitable for the development of his physical well-being within the framework of Christian family life, associated in the environment of the natural surroundings of God's natural creation." For these and other reasons, Bishop Freking then suggested that, among others, the following four additions be incorporated into the text:

The increasing migration of families from the country to the city creates many problems in the city and often causes great harm to the family itself. It also upsets and destroys the stability and prosperity of many rural communities, parishes, and civil and ecclesiastical institutions.

Recognizing the Church's traditional principle of subsidiarity, it may sometimes be necessary for public authority to establish programs to assist families who wish to live in the countryside. Investment capital at long-term amortization and low interest, taxation benefits, etc., should be given to families seeking home ownership and especially ownership of land for family use.

Of all production, the growing of food to feed the human race should receive primary consideration. Those who produce from the soil must realize that they have a noble duty and obligation to produce food that is most nutritious and healthful for man's use. Ease of shipment, packaging and marketing of food products, while beneficial, must remain as a secondary consideration of man's vital health and sustenance. Nor should exorbitant prices for processing and marketing be allowed to interfere with man's possibility to obtain food.

Man has a moral obligation to preserve and enrich this national heritage entrusted to him. Of all the material gifts of God to mankind, land for the production of food and fiber is primary. To allow its fertility to become depleted through greed or careless stewardship is a sin against the future generations of mankind.

Bishop Freking concluded his intervention with this plea: "May I suggest that forty per cent of our people deserve more and better consideration and guidance from this Council!"

In October, 1965, Auxiliary Bishop Charles Maloney of Louisville submitted an intervention on the life of the political community. He approved the schema, but suggested that "a note of vitality is missing which might inspire people to seek out a better public administration." He portrayed the present political situation in this way:

There is never any lack of candidates who wish to exercise public office. Often, however, it is difficult to find citizens who are simultaneously prepared and qualified to assume public responsibility.

In part, the cause for this deficiency is found in the fact that citizens of all kinds offer their leaders more criticism than cooperation. Similarly, very often public administration is unjustly represented as an element separate from the people, even as a danger to the common good. On the other hand, officials are not corrupted without the criminal cooperation of some of the citizens.

It is desirable that we conduct ourselves with greater responsibility in our discussions and publications. We should promote the concept in which public government is presented as *our own;* in which those who exercise the coercive power are understood to act on our *behalf.* As all in the Church are the People of God, so all in the State are members of the earthly kingdom. With this understanding, everything works together more harmoniously for political peace.

Then, feeling that the chapter would generate greater inspiration "if some concrete axiom were incorporated into it which might be easily remembered," he suggested these words from President John F. Kennedy's inaugural address: "Ask not what your country can do for you; ask, rather, what you can do for your country."

4. The Fostering of Peace

When Pope John XXIII met, on October 12, 1962, in the Sistine Chapel, with representatives from 85 nations who were present for the solemn opening of the Council, he told them that the Council "wants to show the world how to put into practice the doctrine of its divine founder, the Prince of Peace. Whoever conforms his life to these teachings helps establish peace and foster true prosperity." World peace, in Pope John's heart, was to be one of the fruits of the Council.

One of the 73 original drafts prepared by the preparatory commission was "On Peace and War." Its preface contained these words:

> Even if it is not the place of the Church to engage itself in the political questions of the century, she should nevertheless confront governments with their terrible responsibilities and warn them against violations of human and divine law, infringements of the most solemn treaties, and an attitude which would scorn the precepts of justice.

Even before the schema was dropped and its material assigned to schema 17 by the Central Preparatory Commission, there was considerable activity among the Council Fathers on behalf of a conciliar statement concerning peace. In the closing days of the first session, an eleven-point schema was being privately circulated among the Council Fathers. Maurice Cardinal Feltin, Archbishop of Paris, told a group of newsmen that he was "favorably impressed" with it. The eleven points of this unofficial, privately circulated schema were:

> 1) Even though it is divided into peoples, nations and states, the human race preserves its natural unity. Each man, as a matter of right, is a member of the immense family of humanity. When the order willed by God is undisturbed, the peace of Christ reigns in the Kingdom of Christ.
>
> 2) There is no dispute among nations which cannot be settled by negotiation.
>
> 3) Today, any war would bring about evils infinitely greater than those it would pretend to abolish.
>
> 4) For this reason, the only possible excuse which could be offered by a belligerent would be that it was defending its people against an unjust aggressor.

5) It is not permissible to plead ignorance and to side with an aggressor on the supposition that he is actually the one being attacked.

6) Lawyers have an obligation to propose to the governments of the world a definition of aggression which is clear and universal.

7) Not all methods of making war are justifiable. The destruction of an entire geographic area with all of the population is a crime which cries to Heaven for vengeance.

8) Even though the crime of war remains a threat to humanity, governments have no right to crush their people with taxation or require of their youth a military service longer than is strictly necessary for the defense of their territory.

9) Every man who is injured or captured during hostilities is sacred. He cannot be massacred, tortured, or subjected to any sort of indignity.

10) All of these rules which apply to wars between nations apply also to civil wars among citizens.

11) Civil and military authorities who give orders contrary to these supreme laws of humanity must expect to see their orders disobeyed. Such directives come not from authority, but from simple force.

American bishops, too, made their voices heard on the subject of war and peace during the third session. Speaking on November 10, 1964, on the floor of the Council, Auxiliary Bishop Philip M. Hannan of Washington, D.C., was opposed to the paragraph in the schema dealing with the subject. He felt it "should be corrected and rewritten so that it clearly distinguishes between the aspirations of the Church for the establishment of peace and the requirements of moral theology of the Church on conducting a just war." He continued:

If there is a treatment of the moral theology of conducting warfare, it should be written by very competent moral theologians; these theologians must be acquainted with the facts about modern weapons, including nuclear weapons, or they must be willing to secure the facts. With all our heart we desire peace—peace with justice and complete liberty. Certainly we hold that war is horror, but we must state with precision what is prohibited in waging war to those who justly and laudably defend liberty.

He likewise took exception to that section in the schema concerning nuclear weapons which stated that "their effects are greater than can be imagined" and "must be judged before God and man as most wicked." Contrary to this statement, he said,

there now exist nuclear weapons which have a very precise limit of destruction. Some of these weapons are mobile; obviously, if they did not have a limited field of destruction, they would kill the soldiers who fired them. There is a weapon now in use which has a range of 1.3 to 2.5 miles, whose missile has a force of 40 tons of TNT. These weapons were developed to avoid the huge destruction of larger nuclear explosions and to destroy individual military targets.

Although even a low-yield nuclear weapon inflicts great damage, still it cannot be said that its "effects are greater than what can be imagined (or estimated)." Its effects are very well calculated and can be foreseen. Furthermore, it may be permitted to use these arms, with their limited effects, against military objectives in a just war according to theological principles.

In conclusion, Bishop Hannan wanted to see a positive statement in the schema praising those who have striven to defend liberty. He said:

> The whole paragraph would seem to imply that all nations have been equally negligent in securing international peace. This is a cruel injustice to many nations and heads of governments who have expended great efforts toward securing peace; it is especially cruel to the nations which are now suffering invasion and unjust aggression from that force which has so far prevented peace. The whole world knows the source of aggression.
>
> The question of the greatest importance, now and for the future, is to avoid war and to defend liberty, both national and personal. We must have complete and actual liberty to carry on a dialogue with militant atheists. No dialogue is possible if we fall into slavery. Because liberty is the foundation of human life, those who defend liberty should be praised.
>
> Therefore, since this schema deals with practical matters, we should at least say a word about the defense of liberty and a word of praise in favor of those who defend liberty as well as those who freely offered their lives so that we may enjoy the freedom of the sons of God.

Bishop Hannan's reservations were echoed in the interventions of five other American prelates. Cardinal Spellman, in his oral intervention of September 21, 1965, directed his remarks specifically to the subject of military service and the citizen's obligation to defend his country. Even though every man of good will desires to see wars peacefully avoided and quickly terminated, he said, at times and with good faith "certain governments have reached the decision that military force is absolutely necessary." Cardinal Spellman presented the following argument:

> Even today government leaders can judge that no international organization yet offers a sufficiently strong guarantee of peace and that, as a result, military preparedness is necessary in order to provide a just peace. The presumption in such cases is that those who are called to military service do intend true peace.
>
> As St. Thomas says (*Summa Theologica*, II–II. q 188, a 3 and 2), a

person can resist evil in two ways. First, by enduring any injury done to himself, and this is a perfection when it is done for the welfare of others. Secondly, by patiently tolerating injuries done to others, and this is an imperfection or even a vice if one can resist the aggressor in a suitable manner.

Without doubt, it is difficult to decide on the more perfect way of resisting evil in the world today. But if the leaders of a nation decide in good faith and after mature deliberation that military service by their citizens is absolutely necessary for the defense of peace and justice, how can the individual citizen justly refuse military service? As it is said in the same section of the schema: the legitimate authority is presumed to be acting within its competency, and its laws are to be obeyed except in those cases in which there is a manifest violation of the law of God.

The Cardinal's observations concerning military service had been submitted previously on May 22, 1965 to the Central Coordinating Commission.

Auxiliary Bishop Stanislaus J. Brzana of Buffalo, New York, also disagreed with the schema's statement that the effects of nuclear weapons are not able to be estimated or controlled. "This is false," he wrote. "This section should be revised according to the most up-to-date science." Bishop Albert Fletcher of Little Rock, Arkansas, felt also that the man who defends his country against an aggressor should be praised. He wrote in his intervention of September 29, 1965:

> Anyone can refuse violent action to vindicate his own proper rights, but, in the given circumstances, he can and must vindicate the rights of others, either out of justice or out of charity. So we must love our enemies, but not more than our family and friends. In the legitimate protection of serious rights against an unjust and evil aggressor, someone can laudably use such action, even violent action, as is necessary for maintaining those rights, so long as there is no legitimate authority which will protect and vindicate his rights.

Auxiliary Bishop John F. Whealon also stated in his intervention of October 9, 1965 that the statement concerning war and peace offered him "sufficiently great difficulties." Regarding the rights of conscientious objectors, he felt that the sentence was confusing. He wrote:

> If it refers to pacifists—I am not praising them—I admit their rights while I am dubious about their reasons. Some are pacifists for truly religious reasons; and some are pacifists for political reasons, who often render a simplistic judgment about greatly complex matters. This sentence should certainly be clearer. Does the Church now praise these men, and for what reason?

With regard to nuclear weapons, he felt the passage in the schema "does not agree with present military knowledge." He then added: "This sentence is a military judgment and is non-moral and outside the jurisdiction of this Council. As Bishop Hannan said last year, there are small atomic weapons which have a relatively limited effect."

Bishop Charles Maloney also spoke on the subject of war and peace. He admitted that there were many in the Council who wished to declare unilateral disarmament as obligatory, but he stated that the Council cannot affirm the proposition "however much it should desire bilateral disarmament." Then, with his characteristic penchant for epigrams, Bishop Maloney concluded with these words:

> As for the fifth chapter, I add this word: There are those who would wish to say that unilateral disarmament is obligatory even under the natural law. However, the Council cannot affirm this proposition however much it should desire bilateral disarmament.
>
> I propose to those who are receptive that in the text the Council show forth more openly its abhorrence for war, its great compassion on behalf of war's victims, its true solidarity with those threatened by war, and, finally, the clearer obligation to wage peace in order that, upon the destruction of damnable greed, all men of good will may generously devote their materials, their human activity, and likewise their sacred honor to the quest for means by which that most desired peace may be fostered. In a word, let the Council be willing to advance the proposition, however common, which is understood on both sides of the Iron and Bamboo Curtains: "It is said everywhere simply: War is hell."

In the same intervention cited above, Archbishop Karl Alter presented nine recommendations for international peace: He wrote:

> 1) Since international peace is the work of justice, one of the chief requirements is the faithful observance of international agreements—"*Pacta sunt servanda.*"
>
> 2) International courts of justice should be established and universally recognized by the nations for the adjudication of disputes and definitive interpretation of treaties.
>
> 3) Codes of international law should be formulated and accepted by the United Nations, but with the right of veto by any one nation suppressed. A two-thirds vote or three-fourths vote might be required.
>
> 4) The United Nations should be reorganized to provide voting rights according to respective populations of member states and their financial contributions (without the right of veto). This latter proposition need not be made specific; but greater equity is desired.
>
> 5) Military disarmament should be undertaken by commission studies

and ratified by subsequent international agreement—the progress should be gradual but persistent and guaranteed by inspection. Unilateral action alone can never be effective.

6) Military aggression should be defined, denounced and repudiated by international agreements. Whichever nation first crosses the frontiers of another nation with military force should be held to be the aggressor.

7) The atom bomb should be outlawed, and the first nation to use it, except in self-defense when under attack, should be denounced as the enemy of civilization and human society.

8) Saturation bombing of cities or civilian population should be outlawed by international agreements.

9) The terms such as imperialism, colonization, aggression, self-defense should be carefully defined and then incorporated in international agreements.

During the closing days of the final session, Archbishop Philip Hannan made an effort to change the schema's treatment of modern warfare in the fifth chapter. He succeeded in persuading nine other distinguished prelates to co-sign a letter, dated December 2, 1965, urging a *non placet* vote on the entire chapter. The other Americans who signed the letter were Cardinal Spellman, Cardinal Shehan, Archbishop Patrick A. O'Boyle and Archbishop James Davis of Santa Fe, New Mexico. Later, at the American Bishops' press panel, Cardinal Shehan authorized the Reverend Francis McCool, S.J., of the Pontifical Biblical Institute and a member of the panel to repudiate his endorsement of the letter.

The letter suggested that unless "the errors" in the text be corrected, the entire schema should be given a negative vote and returned to the Synod of Bishops for further study and emendation. The letter contained three reasons for objecting to the schema's statement that the possession of nuclear arms is immoral. They were:

1) . . . the possession of nuclear arms has preserved freedom in a large part of the world. The defense of a large part of the world against aggression is not a crime, but a great service. . . .

2) We also deny that "the recent popes" have condemned total war in a manner as categorical as it is condemned in this section. . . .

3) The Council should not make a decision on this matter about which there is still no consensus of opinions among theologians who are most competent in the matter.

Most observers realized the futility of the gesture because of the timing, and the attempt to correct the schema on the topic of modern warfare failed. The attempt was effective only in confirming the opinion of those who felt that a certain segment of the hierarchy of the United States approved of its country's military position. Repudiating this interpretation of the letter, Auxiliary Bishop Gerald V. McDevitt of Philadelphia expressed concern during the press panel of December 4 that the letter had been "mistakenly assumed to be backed by the American hierarchy, as several bishops of other countries have indicated to me. It is not backed by the American hierarchy at all," he continued. "It is the opinion of the individuals who signed the petition, and they represent only themselves. I am not saying anything against Archbishop Hannan, however. He had a perfect right to campaign as he did, and he did it on his own."

At the same press-panel meeting, Monsignor George G. Higgins, director of the Social Action Department of the National Catholic Welfare Conference, said, "I think the petition was most inopportune because it left itself open to grave misunderstanding on the part of bishops of other countries. The Council's statement will not be as strong as even the Pope's United Nations speech regarding the possession of nuclear weapons: 'Let weapons fall from your hands . . . one cannot love, holding weapons of war.'" During the same panel meeting, Archbishop Dearden declared that his commission had "oriented its statement toward peace, and it is in this context that war has been dealt with. In this context," he said, Archbishop Hannan's "criticism does not have validity."

5. *Marriage and the Family*

Two American bishops submitted their observations in writing concerning the schema's chapter on marriage and the family. In one intervention, dated November 1, 1964, Bishop Albert Fletcher insisted that the law of nature should always be preserved in solving difficulties in marriage because, he wrote, this law "prohibits artificial contraception as is firmly resolved from the ordinary infallible and therefore immutable magisterium of the Church." He offered this reason for desiring to see this point stressed in the schema:

> Besides what has been said by the Most Holy Pontiffs, *all* the books of moral theology employed in seminaries, under the vigilance of the Holy See and approved by the *whole* episcopacy, prove that artificial contraception is against natural law and that not only in a speculative matter but in a practical matter, affects the souls of all the faithful. Thus over the years *all* shepherds of souls and confessors, believing that they were in accord with the Church, have taught the faithful that that act is intrinsically evil and gravely sinful. They have denied sacramental absolution to innumerable impenitent people over this matter.
>
> How can the Church say that any principle of natural law is immutable, if human nature is conceived of as "evolving" in such a way that an immutable law becomes inane and empty?
>
> Perhaps the use of that contraceptive pill can be declared licit in certain cases by the principle of double effect. But the authority of the magisterium

of the Church would be totally lacking in matters of morality unless this authority affirms her traditional teaching again without delay.

In another written intervention of October 22, 1964, Bishop Fletcher said that he would prefer to leave unaltered the present legislation concerning the signing of promises by both parties in a mixed marriage. He wrote:

> In my opinion, the divine law for the universal baptism and education of offspring in the Catholic Church will be safely preserved only if those things which are proposed in the present Code of Canon Law and in the earlier schema of this Council are established anew in the Council. I am speaking of the Church in the West.
>
> It is conceded that a member of the Catholic Church does not have to persuade a separated brother, or sister, to give up his obligations in opposition to the voice of his own conscience. Therefore, if some non-Catholic party sincerely feels obligated to bring up his children in his own religion, a marriage must not take place at all.
>
> But in the United States, non-Catholics for the most part do not think that they are so obligated and freely accept the prescribed cautions; and, what is more important, they faithfully fulfill them.
>
> It seems to me that they give offense who say that non-Catholics who have contracted marriage with a Catholic have accepted the cautions insincerely or are not faithfully fulfilling them.

Bishop John Whealon, in his written intervention of October 24, 1964, felt that the schema's "teaching on marriage morality seems to me so ideal and subjective and uncertain as to open the door to subjectivism, doubts and even sins." He also felt that the schema should direct its attention to the obligation that Christians have to marry only after reaching psychological and economic maturity. Citing statistics from the United States, he wrote:

> At the present time in the United States, one fourth of all children are brought up without their own fathers. Divorce, infidelity, contraception, that psychological instability which affects future generations, an excessive population explosion—the primary and evident remedy for these evils is the obligation of each man not to marry until he is mature and ready to accept the obligations of marriage and parenthood. Perhaps the greatest manifestation of human pride is shown by the man who enters upon marriage or procreates children when he is unable to educate these children with any stability. The responsibility not to marry is evident by natural law. So many recent writings deal with the population explosion; it is strange, however, that nothing is written on such a responsibility. It is the assumption of our age that every man has the right to enter upon marriage and to have children without regard to the considerations of immaturity, lack of pru-

dence, etc. For example, when a boy and girl of the age of fifteen or sixteen associate with one another constantly, when they marry at the age of eighteen (the most common age now in the United States for women to marry), they will most probably find sufficient psychological and economic difficulties, and they will think that the teaching of *Casti Conubii* is too harsh—but the primary trouble lies in their improvident marriage.

The subject of Christian marriage had been previously treated in its canonical aspects during the two-day discussion of the Council's *votum* on matrimony. Between the first and second session, the Commission for the Discipline of the Sacraments had prepared this *votum*, or directive, consisting of only a little more than two pages of printed text. It contained three parts; the first enunciated certain fundamental principles concerning the sacredness of marriage; the second listed certain directives for the revision of Canon Law in accord with the needs of the present time; the third stressed the importance of preparation for marriage as a serious duty of those entering into holy wedlock as well as pastors of souls. This schema also pointed out that future legislation concerning the impediments of mixed religion and disparity of worship should be guided by the provisions set forth in the Decree on Ecumenism.

On November 19, 1964, during the 126th congregation, Benedict Cardinal Masella, president of the Commission for the Discipline of the Sacraments, and Archbishop Josef Schneider of Bamburg, Germany, introduced the *votum* to the Council Fathers. On that and the following day, 14 Fathers delivered observations on the schema. Then the Secretary General, Archbishop Felici, called for a vote on whether or not the *votum* should be transmitted to the Holy Father for subsequent action. Of the 2,024 Fathers who cast ballots, 1,592 voted in the affirmative, 427 in the negative. The Fathers were further informed that those who wished to submit written observations on the schema should do so before November 30.

During the closing congregation of the second session on November 20, three American prelates, however, did speak on the subject. Four other Americans submitted their observations in writing. Joseph Cardinal Ritter said he was pleased with the *votum* and especially with "the suggested dispositions affecting interconfessional marriages." Concerning the premarital guarantees and the canonical form, he said:

The new approach to the guarantees, it seems to me, is particularly praiseworthy in that it serves both truth and charity. Herein the Church is concerned with the observance of divine law and the safeguarding of personal right. It is evident that the new disposition would safeguard the right to marry more realistically than the present law. Moreover, the new approach would more effectively secure respect for the divine law. The norms of the

Code of Canon Law often enough obscure the existence of divine law, and by insisting overmuch on juridical procedure, emphasize ecclesiastical law beyond measure. Adoption of the suggested proposal would strengthen respect for divine law by stressing more emphatically the role of personal responsibility. Responsibility for the security of his own faith, as well as for the Catholic education of children, is rightly placed on the Catholic party. In this way we can lessen the possibility of offense to the consciences of our separated brethren.

The schema proceeds wisely and prudently in its approach to the canonical form. It offers a middle course between the extremes of inflexible retention and complete relaxation of the form. Although each extreme has its adherents, I believe that this compromise affords the best response to the needs of our time. On the side the schema supports the general retention of the canonical form of marriage for validity in such cases. Not a few Fathers will find this displeasing, and they can point out that the clandestinity of marriage, which the Tridentine legislation was intended to counteract, is no longer a problem. However, a new pastoral problem has presented itself in some countries—the high incidence of early and hasty marriage with a probability of subsequent divorce—which recommends the retention of the form for validity.

Nonetheless, to demonstrate our respect for human dignity and to reduce the principles of ecumenism to practice, it is apparent that in some cases the ordinary must be empowered to grant dispensation from the form. This disposition is closer to the spirit of Trent than the existing norms.

Cardinal Spellman, who had already returned to New York, was heard through the voice of Auxiliary Bishop John Fearns of New York who read the Cardinal's intervention. He said that he spoke in the name of more than a hundred American bishops who objected to the schema because its directives would mean that "certain things in our current laws on marriage would be so changed as to injure gravely the spiritual good of our country." He felt that the schema contained so many defects and inconsistencies that "it ought to be revised by the commission." He then pointed out five proposals in the schema that he considered would "lessen the responsibility of pastors" and "inflict grave spiritual harm." The proposed dispensation from the form of marriage for mixed marriages, he said,

would bring it about in our "pluralistic" society that the honor or reverence in which marriage and the sacred ministry of the pastor are held would be lessened. For our Catholic people receive the sacred character of marriage because it is demanded that it be celebrated before a priest either in some Catholic Church or in the rectory, not however in any non-Catholic church or in any civic chamber. This practice so pertains to our religious life that the civil law recognizes it; our civil authority does not require that any civil official assist at a marriage.

Archbishop John J. Krol of Philadelphia, one of the undersecretaries of the Council, also expressed his opinion concerning this schema. He admitted the difficulties involved in formulating a common discipline for so many different areas, accommodating matrimonial discipline to the new circumstances and according to the mind of the Decree on Ecumenism and the Decree on Religious Liberty. He was opposed to the schema's suggestion that the existing form in a mixed marriage be changed and offered these reasons:

> Is it not the duty of the Church to inspire these men [of no religious persuasion] so that at least their children be raised in a religious way? Should not positive cooperation be required of them for the religious formation of children? Finally, should they not be invited by the Church not only to permit but to promise the religious education of their children? The Church can hardly perpetuate indifferentism among those who do not believe and do not practice religion.
>
> The schema of the *votum* on matrimony makes no distinction between men who are truly religious illiterates and those who practice religion from the heart. It is clear from pastoral experience that these areligious men pledge their prenuptial promises in full freedom, hold them sacred and frequently come to the faith themselves. Thus there is a clear necessity of warning all non-Catholics in charity about the promises which the Catholic party has assumed and of demanding some positive affirmation by which their willingness to consent to this matter with the Catholic party would be proved.
>
> Moved by these motives, we earnestly ask that the discipline of the promises be kept even if, by exception, the ordinary would be granted the faculty of sometimes dispensing in cases of non-Catholics who have a religious sentiment and profess a religious life. This mode of acting would keep intact due respect for the freedom of conscience and would promote ecumenical activity and, at the same time, keep in mind the duty of preaching evangelical truth to non-believers, a duty binding on the Church.

In his concluding remarks, Archbishop Krol noted that the schema was not a conciliar decree, but, if approved, would take on the nature of a directive of the Council Fathers. He then asked that these three aspects of the present marriage legislation remain in force:

> *First:* that the general norms still in effect on promises in mixed marriages remain, maintaining the ordinary's faculty of dispensing them in some cases of non-Catholics who have a religious sense and profess a religious life.

Secondly: that the canonical form of marriage remain firm, and the ordinary be given the faculty of allowing, for example, a couple to come before even a non-Catholic minister for truly ecumenical reasons.

Finally: that for a priest's valid assistance at matrimony there be required his approbation by the ordinary of the place or the pastor.

On October 6, 1965, Bishop Joseph Marling of Jefferson City, Missouri, delivered an intervention concerning the population problem. He asserted that "the rapid increase of people in the world today constitutes a grave problem." Lack of food or fertile land, he continued, although a grave aspect of this problem, is not the most serious. "Of graver concern," he added, "is the growth of investment and of all means of production in such wise that they outdistance population increase." He then made this criticism of the schema:

When there is question of food or mere subsistence, recourse can indeed be had to the wealthier nations, as our schema observes. But when there is question of raising, or even of maintaining, a certain standard of living in the face of rapid population growth, this suggestion loses value. All of which directs our thoughts anew to the enormous disparity between the wealthier and poorer nations, toward the solution of which nothing has as yet been proposed that is sufficiently bold to be efficacious. We must not be surprised, then, if, in order to meet the situation occasioned by population pressures, nations turn to means which are extreme and which our schema terms "solutions not in keeping with the moral law."

Our schema rightly states that the decision with regard to the number of offspring rests upon the correct judgment of the parents, and not with public authority. This, however, cannot mean that public authority is prohibited from planning and deciding with regard to population growth. This is quite probably the meaning of the words in the schema, that men be informed, if the situation demand it, of those scientific advances where sufficient moral certainty has been established. Perhaps it would be better, however, for the Council to go farther, and sincerely to advise public authority to make efforts with regard to medical investigation concerning the limitation of births, and to spread knowledge of these findings, especially when there is grave need, and nothing is presented that is in conflict with moral law.

In the second part of his intervention, Bishop Marling suggested that the spiritual approach should not be overlooked altogether, and he recalled the Savior's admonition that His disciples be not inordinately concerned about their future material needs. This promise, he said, does not mean that all human medical, sociological and economic efforts should not be employed in solving the problem, but is, rather, a supplement and stimulus to these efforts.

He concluded his intervention, the last to be delivered by an American on the floor of the Second Vatican Council, with this appeal:

> We are not recommending lethargy or a species of Oriental passivity. It was Christ's thought that men must use their talents to the fullest both for their own advantage and that of others. But when we have done this, we have a right to approach our Heavenly Father with confidence and to seek the help that has been promised. Do we not manifest to some degree at least the secularistic spirit of our times, the prevailing divorce between spiritual and mundane concerns, if we fail to speak out about these words of Christ?
>
> Moreover, our good faithful have a right to the solace which flows from the promise of Christ. And, finally, by proclaiming that Christ's words are an integral part of the discussion concerning the present population growth—but not indeed a substitute for what our schema calls "the most sweeping social changes that must be introduced"—we shall teach all nations (as is surely our commission) that to seek first the Kingdom of God is to have all the things besides added unto us. And we shall thus show that we are sincere when we write: "The Spirit of God who guides the course of history . . . is no stranger to such a decisive turn of events."

As early as March 22, 1963, Archbishop Joseph McGucken of San Francisco had submitted his observations on this *votum*. He was a member of the Commission on the Discipline of the Sacraments, but was unable to attend the Commission's meeting. Thus he submitted his observations directly to the president of the Commission. His intervention pointed out that originally the Commission was charged with drafting six schemata. These were concerned with the preparation for marriage, the form of celebrating marriage, mixed marriages, matrimonial consent, impediments to marriage and the method of dealing with marriage cases. He made observations concerning each of these *schemata*, among which was one concerning the necessary preparation for marriage. He wrote:

> We are most impressed with the schema dealing with preparation for marriage. We hope that this will be adopted and made obligatory in all the dioceses of the world. Of particular import is the recommendation that a series of instructions, and an *examination* on those instructions, be made mandatory prior to all marriages, mixed and Catholic, the nature and scope of which are to be determined by the individual local ordinary. We realize that this places an additional burden on parish priests, but are of the opinion that the burden can be much lightened by enlisting the aid of good Catholic lay couples. We believe that this would be an excellent means of employing the lay apostolate in a very practical way in the parish.

His over-all impression of the Commission's material prompted Archbishop McGucken to make this general observation:

> I feel that the technicalities of Canon Law cannot be fruitfully discussed in the plenary session of the Council. Consequently, I favor sending the proposals of the Commission pertaining to changes in the Canon Law to the Commission for the Code of Canon Law, with strong recommendations that they be considered and implemented as rapidly as possible.

Three other Americans submitted their observations on the *votum* in writing. Auxiliary Bishop Stanislaus J. Brzana of Buffalo made eleven suggestions "for processing cases of marriage nullity and dispensation with the hope of aiding more persons toward the solution of their marital status." His suggestions centered on five juridical aspects, namely, tribunal procedure, Roman cases, impediments to marriage, defects in marriage consent and marriages of prospective converts. Under the last heading he made this suggestion: "Many non-Catholics who wish to join the Church have been involved in former marriages. Ways and means should be sought to give them greater relief than exists at present in order to allow them to marry again in the Catholic Church." Concerning marriage cases that now must be sent to Rome, Bishop Brzana wrote:

> Cases of Privilege of the Faith, involving one non-baptized party, and cases of non-consummation of marriage should be reviewed by a board of assessors or consultors, to be established in appropriate ecclesiastical territories around the world. These boards could be regarded as branches of the Congregation of the Holy Office and Congregation of the Sacraments. . . . The boards could review cases and, in affirmative decisions, could, without further review, petition the Holy Father for dispensation. The great advantage of such a system would be that the marriage cases in question would be greatly expedited.

On November 29, 1965, Bishop Leo T. Maher of Santa Rosa submitted his observations concerning the *votum*. He was, first of all, in favor of retaining the form of marriage as it is now, but of granting the ordinary of the place powers of dispensation in special cases. Then, concerning the precautions, or promises, demanded in the case of mixed marriage, he wrote:

> It is not fitting that the Catholic spouse should be obliged concerning the conversion of the non-Catholic spouse *in writing*, nor should it be required. It is sufficient that only the expression of faith and of conscience on the part of the Catholic member regarding the baptism and education of the children only in the Catholic religion and regarding the fulfillment of his own faith be expressed in writing. Only the Catholic party regularly

should have to sign this expression of faith. The non-Catholic party should act as an official witness of the expression of faith of the Catholic party.

This above-mentioned process has three advantages: 1) it will force the Catholic spouse to recognize the obligation of his faith; 2) the non-Catholic party, in the capacity of an official witness, will understand the mind and conscience of the Catholic spouse; 3) the conscience of the non-Catholic spouse is preserved. The energy and commitment of conscience emanate from *interior* pressure, and not from *exterior*.

Bishop John King Mussio of Stuebenville, Ohio, was also in favor of the schema's provision "that in mixed marriages the non-Catholic party is not required to sign the usual marital promises." In his written observations of January, 1965, he called this "a very realistic and ecumenical provision." He then offered these two considerations as reasons for his position.

First of all, the responsibility should be placed on the Catholic party to the marriage. It is here where it primarily belongs. He should stand on his own feet, understand his duty, and be prepared to do it. It is a false presumption to consider the non-Catholic party always as the danger to the faith of the Catholic. It is rarely that a non-Catholic enters such a marriage with the intention to destroy the faith of the partner. Too often it is the Catholic himself who is the cause of the marital difficulties due to his own lax religious habits and to his failure to give a good example of upright living.

Then, again, to force the non-Catholic party to sign such promises is resented as an unjust encroachment on his own religious liberty. As a result, he looks upon the signed pledge as void, having been obtained, as he claims, under duress. He can marry only if he signs. So he signs without the intention to observe. And very often he is so advised by his pastor. This kind of pressure moves the non-Catholic partner to take a hostile view of the entire proceeding. Instead of helping the marriage, this practice adds another roadblock to its success. I know of no one single practice in the Church which represents a greater obstacle to the exercise of true ecumenism than this outdated and ineffectual practice of signed pledges by a non-Catholic party to a mixed marriage.

Bishop Mussio felt, in conclusion, that a process of conference and explanation between the couple to be married and the priest would prepare both spouses to make a reasonable decision. This method, he said, "is far better suited to our times and circumstances than a system which is resented by the non-Catholic and oftentimes accepted by the Catholic without a true understanding of his own responsibilities in the matter."

Many commentators have already pointed out that the Pastoral Constitution on the Church in the Modern World will stimulate a continuing discussion within and without the Church for many years to come. If it does so, this might be precisely the greatest effect the document will have on the Church and the world. It points a direction; it does not offer all the answers.

During a press conference on October 17, 1964, Bishop Emilio Guano, one of the guiding spirits of the Constitution, made an observation that deserves repeating, now that the Constitution has been promulgated.

Everyone should be on his guard against expecting from the schema what it does not intend to give and cannot give, that is to say, the solution of all the practical problems confronting us every day. No one should be deceived into thinking that the schema can give men everything they desire. The text will necessarily be brief in its explanations, but already in itself it will stand out as an important witness and a noteworthy step of the Church among men, along the path being trod by the human family.

Pastoral Constitution on the Church in the Modern World

✠ INTERVENTIONS

FRANCIS CARDINAL SPELLMAN, *20 October, 1964*

There is no doubt that the schema on the Church in the world today is that which contains the fundamental hope of the Second Vatican Council. Therefore, it is a fine, clear and most sincere affirmation of the position which the Church sees as her own in this age. In preparing the present text, the Commission has done admirably. The text should not be weakened. Our task is to provide some quality or method of expression that very clearly signifies what this schema teaches. It is a public re-dedication, solemn and official—and, at the same time, simple, candid and humble—of the Catholic Church to the service of humanity. It has the purpose of clearly proposing to all men everywhere that, just as Our Lord, we also always consider ourselves in their service. We desire to enter into dialogue, so that we can hear and be heard, so that we may be invited to expound and present our thoughts. First we desire that we be given aid for practically the whole human race, so that all men may be brought to a fuller life.

It is to the perpetual glory of the Second Vatican Council that up until now it has made progress in openly declaring its observations concerning the good in these times. An essential condition of any dialogue on the part of the Christian faithful is a strong spirit of obedience to the authority which is "constituted by Christ" in the Church, and which "is exercised in His place, is like the public instrument of His word, and represents the love of the great Shepherd." It seems to me to be truly necessary, both for the good of the children of the Church and for that of all our brothers, that we openly explain the meaning and substance of Christian filial obedience. Very often it seems to some that the Catholic Church fosters merely a juridical obedience which is indeliberate and founded, perhaps, upon an immoderate authoritarianism. Christian obedience is perfectly consonant with our ministry in the service of the human race.

All of us, with the Holy Father, "strongly desire that that dialogue which up till now has grown in the very midst of the Church, be inflamed with a new ardor, take up new causes to deal with, call forth new dialoguers: so that the sanctity and vigor of the Church may clearly be increased in the living world." Our task in this schema will be to make this saving dialogue even more efficacious, if we are to deal in a truly pastoral way with the necessity both of the virtue of obedience and with the spirit of true Christian liberty in all the faithful who come to this dialogue in a spirit of charity and humility.

The schema on the Church in the world today should humbly direct our thoughts and our hope to the remote future. We see that it is not necessary that the Council try to deal with absolutely every aspect of the dialogue of the Church with the world today. What is necessary, however, is that the Council and the schema clearly and openly manifest the quality of this dialogue. There come to mind the shining words of Pius XII, spoken some twenty years ago:

> Supernatural charity yearns for the salvation of souls, for their eternal salvation, for their sanctification from above, but also for universal love, which, on our part, for all our brothers, is to be embraced: for everyone throughout the whole world is our brother, without any condition or reservation.

It is this shining love, this spirit, this ministry of love toward all men that this schema sets out to instill in us.

ALBERT CARDINAL MEYER, *20 October, 1964*

The schema explains in different ways why the Christian living in the world ought to work for the advancement of the temporal order. Yet it does not adequately explain why man's daily work constitutes an integral part of the economy of salvation. We should not forget that God offers the hope of glory not just to man's soul, but to his whole person and to the entire world. No one denies that, along the way, man fairly often misuses the world and the good things that make it up. But the schema is too preoccupied with this danger. It is too fearful of infection from the world and too strong in urging the Christian to pass his life "as one departing and about to pass on." This preoccupation, which seems excessive to me, is the result (unless I am mistaken) of a certain omission, and not an insignificant one, in the schema. For nowhere does the schema plainly make known that element of Christian revelation which every kind of false dualism denies: namely, that the whole world is not only the means by which redeemed man perfects himself, but is itself the object of redemption, just as our bodies are.

To balance this partial treatment, it seems recourse should be had to St.

Paul's teaching on the economy of salvation. Time and again the Apostle teaches that God the Father handed over to His Son the cosmic work which will not be completed before the final glorification of the world:

1) "Through the Son of his love, God created both man and the entire world: because in him everything in heaven and on earth was created, not only things visible but also invisible. . . . all have been created through him and for him (Col. 1:16–17)." So the Son gives the world its meaning, its value, and thus, in some true way, reality.

2) "The same Son supports man and the whole world: all things are held together in him" (Col. 1:17).

3) "Through the Son, the Father redeems not only the human race, but the whole universe; for it pleased the Father that . . . through him God should reconcile to himself every being, and make peace both on earth and in heaven through the blood shed on the cross" (Col. 1:20). Later tradition would often recall this truth: Christ gave meaning to everything in the world by His cross, as we see in the hymn we recite in Passiontide: "The earth, the sea, the stars, the world are washed in this flood."

Yet we shall not understand the full scope of Christ's cosmic work until we consider the last scene of this divine comedy. As the Apostle says, "For he is destined to reign until God has put all enemies under his feet" (I Cor. 15:25). "And when all things are thus subject to him . . ." (v.28), "he will deliver up the kingdom to the Father" (v.24) "and thus God will be all in all" (v.28).

This subjection of all things also brings with it many other things besides the salvation of our souls. We really will save our souls. But, besides this, Christian salvation includes, first of all, the resurrection of our bodies, and then that mysterious transformation of the whole material universe to which our bodies belong. Paul brings out this truth in such a way that he does not hesitate to speak of a certain sure hope for the world: "The created universe awaits with eager longing the revelation of the children of God . . . because creation itself will be freed from its slavery to corruption to enjoy the freedom and glory of the children of God" (Rom. 8, 19, 21).

We ought to notice the terminology Paul uses to describe this Christian salvation, especially in his Epistle to the Romans. He proposes to us the Spirit who dwells in us, so rich in life that He gives life to our bodies. On account of this, we will be as Christ is now in His risen body. The same glory which, on the day of His Passover, was revealed not only in the soul, but also in the body of Christ will likewise be revealed in us. Wherefore, the Apostle called Christian salvation the redemption of our body. Paul, therefore, does not encourage men to sacrifice the body for the soul; rather, they should free both body and soul from the slavery of sin and thus, while still alive, prepare for the glorification of both.

But the body is part of a wider universe. According to the Apostle and all of Christian tradition, that universe is also destined to become a participant in its own way in the freedom and glory of the children of God. For, as St. Thomas taught, on the day of the *parousia,* "because men will be freed from corruption and will put on glory, it will be necessary for even the bodily creation to take on in its own way a certain bright glory" (*Contra Gentiles, ultima verba*). We cannot imagine the condition of that transformed world; we can not, however, call into doubt the fact. Just as the body, the universe also at the end of time will not be destroyed, but rather redeemed and will shine forth. Just as the body, the universe itself is the object of redemption.

This is, moreover, of the greatest concern to us here and now. For if this is really the way it is, then the work by which man leads the universe to the perfection God intends it to have does not belong to a mere temporal order, an order of things profane and contingent, but to a lasting order. For, in his work with temporal things, man in some way prepares that consummation by which God will transform our world into a new heaven and a new earth.

In light of this, all our attempts and successes in the cultural arena, in economics, science and social life—all these are understood to contribute positively to the realization of that plan in which God will restore all things in Christ (cf. Eph. 1:10).

BISHOP JOSEPH MARLING, C.PP.S, 20 *October, 1964*

Fortunately our schema does take notice of the fact that men of today really want and are sincerely seeking the recognition of the dignity of the human person and that opposed to this are other reasons which, indeed, we list as among the evils of today. There are other things which militate against the dignity of man that spring from the very nature of our age and, in order to overcome them, we must go to the aid of our world. They are born out of progress, and often the individual naturally and without anyone's fault becomes only a very tiny part of a huge crowd or anomymous mass. Among these problems are today's immense productivity, the growth in the mechanization of former manual tasks, the capability of destroying life in one fell swoop, the incredibly swift population growth, the rapid population migration to large cities, the tendency toward a paternalistic government. Our schema must reflect an understanding of this in order to explain it for so many men affected by the drudgery of life today as it strips them of any idea of their supernatural and, indeed, of even their natural destiny.

If there are men today who unhesitatingly exaggerate the population explosion and hence are deprived of seeing the flagrant social injustice in our world, nevertheless, we must admit that it is a real problem in our time and, indeed, something entirely new which endangers the ability of many thousands of men to secure not only the physical necessities (food, clothes and housing), but even the cultural (educational opportunity, recreation, rearing of a family in some kind of dignity). We may ask whether it is, indeed, premature to admit that in the future the population explosion could obligate marriage to be contracted at a more mature age and further obligate the limitation of births by periodic continence. In establishing this principle which would not be implemented at present, but rather in the future (if ever), we are forging a dialogue with the men of today about a problem which, indeed, threatens them.

We are firmly convinced however of the much more fundamentally important issues of the social economic way of life. We must forthrightly and firmly condemn the major part of these issues. If sorrow and sympathy today do not move us to take a stand which many will designate as radical, we shall break faith with many men, especially the poor. Regardless of a few learned opinions, it seems that our schema is too weak in treating these issues. Following the lead of our recent popes, we must call for a complete restoration of the social and economic way of life, without which men cannot achieve their personal dignity, the dignity of their families, the welfare of marriage and peace in our times.

The schema should pay particular attention to farmers. Even farmers in more developed areas are burdened by very great problems which affect the economic structure in such a way that the alleviation of the hunger of thousands of men becomes daily more difficult. Because John XXIII understood the gravity of the problem, he devoted a considerable part of his encyclical *Mater et Magistra* to this very situation. Fortunately, at least a few words in our schema seem to deal with this problem. It is superfluous to list all the specific problems of today, since they are well known by all who have devoted some study to our world today.

In conclusion, I hope that what is treated in chapters one, two and three will be condensed and that it will become an introduction to the topics which are treated in chapter four and in the *Adnexa*.

LAWRENCE CARDINAL SHEHAN, *22 October, 1964*

Although this schema is fine in general, it should be changed in many places. In carrying out these changes, it is very necessary for us to keep before us both the Directions for the Future Elaboration of The Text of our schema, distributed in this hall last month, and the document which is called the *Adnexa*. In these appendices the figure of the Church in the modern world is more realistic and more to the point than that which is found in the schema.

Allow me to propose the following brief observations about revising the schema:

1) In our schema, I propose that the encylical letter of the Holy Father,

Ecclesiam Suam, be referred to. In certain parts of our schema, the ideas are too generally and obscurely expressed, and those ideas are described by means of very lofty and pompous language. In the encyclical, however, we have a document whose suitable riches, precisely because of its depth, are still not fully valued. Since in the encyclical are found not a few sketches of the problems of our times, which are directly and deeply treated, these are most apt for the revision of the schema. Next, it is necessary that the schema specifically refer to those things which were written in the encyclical and which concern the matter at hand, and especially those things which concern the origin of the Church in regard to doctrines and institutions.

Indeed, the Church cannot change the deposit of Faith in which its main treasure resides, nor, at the same time, can it change its fundamental structure which was given to it by Christ the Lord. Nor are those doctrines changeable which have been defined under the influence of the Holy Spirit. Nevertheless, the Church has progressed and has to continue to progress in regard to its doctrine and its structure, so that it may respond to the problems of the world by adapting itself, and especially to those problems which arise from the relationships between those things and men who are always becoming their originators.

More than one hundred years ago, John Henry Newman, who afterwards was named a cardinal of the holy Roman Church, wrote a great work, *Essay on the Development of Christian Doctrine*, in which is found the sentence, repeated in various ways: "a power of development is a proof of life." This same truth, which is of great importance for our schema, is sketched, I believe, in various places and in diverse ways, if not openly expressed, in the encyclical *Ecclesiam Suam* of Pope Paul VI—especially on page 12 of the copy of that encyclical distributed in this hall—where it states: "The Church . . . advances more and more in the awareness of its duty, of the nature of its mysteries, of its doctrines. . . ."

In my humble opinion, this sentence should be explained in detail so that it might constitute a part of the schema that we are now talking about.

2) Precisely because they agree with the matter and the spirit of the encyclical, The Directions for the Future Elaboration of the Text seem to be of the greatest importance for our schema. I have already mentioned the necessity for a greater clarity of expression, which, indeed, is referred to in the first direction.

I also give my assent to those things which have been written in the other directions about the necessity of speaking in a clearer manner, *whether about the object of this schema, or about the relationships with the material in the other conciliar schemata which have already been treated.* It seems to me that from the very beginning of the schema the Ecumenical Council should openly say that it regards the nature of man and his end *under a religious aspect,* indeed, under that aspect which God revealed through Christ the Lord who is Himself really the revelation of God. The biblical renewal, which is referred to primarily in the schema on divine revelation, the liturgical renewal prescribed by the Constitution on the Sacred Liturgy, and also the ecumenical movement commended in the schema on ecumenism, and also ordained for Catholics— all these things have exalted the Word of God according to the propositions found in the schema on the Church. The Word of God remains in the Church, for it was made flesh in Christ the Lord who works in the modern world through the Church, His Mystical Body.

3) What is said in the directions, specifically about the necessity for a clarification of the theological sense of the word "world," is very pleasing. Also, at this point, the schema rightly follows that which was said in the encyclical on page 33 and on the following pages of the copy which was distributed, where the *difference* between the Church and the world is so explained that this *difference* is not to be confused with an *estrangement*.

I also give my assent to those things said in the directions about making changes in some of the chapters. I have handed in to the Secretary General some written observations related to these points.

In conclusion, may I sincerely and humbly say that we must not fear, nor may it be said, that we are perverting the doctrine of the Church because of our attempts at dialogue between the Church and the modern world. Authentic tradition has to be preserved; but, at the same time, *progress* has to be admitted for a fuller knowledge and a stronger awareness of the Word of God or Gospel and its application to the "signs of the times." Such a progress is often indicated by Pope Paul VI in his encyclical *Ecclesiam Suam,* but most clearly stated on page 12, which was cited above, where it is stated: "The Church more and more advances in the awareness of its duty, of the nature of its mysteries, of its doctrines."

JOSEPH CARDINAL RITTER, *28 October, 1964*

The dignity of the human person and its recognition in practice are the necessary bases for all human life, whether individual or social. It is laudable that the schema places these things among the first objects to be discussed. But the way in which the schema treats of them is not pleasing. It seems to me that the twentieth paragraph needs corrections as to content, order and end.

In the first place, with regard to *content:* With the exception of the last five lines, the entire paragraph lists those things which will be considered in the following. Almost nothing is mentioned precisely about the necessity for understanding human dignity and for encouraging its recognition. On the contrary, the schema deals with the effects and signs of such understanding and recognition. I propose that everything said in the paragraph (although somewhat shortened), with the exception of the last lines, be so ordered in the introduction that the whole chapter be adumbrated and the intimate relations among the parts be shown.

Secondly, with regard to *order:* All other paragraphs in the chapter follow the same order: after the problem or matter has been concluded with a few lines, those principles are listed which direct the Christian activity in order to reach its specific goal. The twentieth paragraph is a singular exception out of the entire chapter. I propose that the schema also impose the same order upon this paragraph.

Thirdly, and of the greatest importance, with regard to *end:* The goal of this paragraph should be to assist in recognizing the dignity of man. Such an acknowledgement can take root only in the mind and heart of each man: it is necessary that each and every man first perceive and then recognize in practice his own dignity. If the Christian faithful desire to communicate the Christian concept of human worth to the world, then they will have to enlighten this concept not merely in words, but in all of life's activities. Accordingly, the schema should enumerate in this place those qualities which describe the life which is truly Christian and congruent with the dignity of man. I suggest the following enumeration not as a formal arrangement, but more as an illustration.

First principle: The practical recognition of each man's dignity requires his total dedication to the honoring and possession of God. Either to want or to accept anything less is to disparage and slight human life. The life of the Christian should offer a testimony to the world: a witness to the reality and transcendence of God, to the redemption of the world accomplished by God in Christ, a witness to the permanent and loving presence of God in the world.

Second principle: The practical recognition of each man's dignity requires that Christians in their lives have concern for their intimate union with God. No person, no society is able to interpose itself in this relationship except as a medium for greater familiarity. The value of the human person demands that man form his own conscience in order to overcome natural passivity, to exercise his responsibility in private and public life and to promote the good and conquer the evil.

This last point, Venerable Fathers, seems to me to be of the greatest importance. Regrettably, Christians often substitute collective activity and responsibility for their own personal conscience: too often it is rather the case that the world molds the Christian rather than the Christian the world. In this age, when crimes against the human person are being increased, Christians either hesitate to exercise their own responsibility or even deny it. By their silence, if not by their activity, they are guilty of the greatest injury to human dignity, a scandal to the world and guilty of infidelity towards God. The concepts of personal responsibility and rational obedience should be made clear in the schema so that all Christian faithful, aware of their relationship to God and of their worth, may show the world the transcendent value of human life and the true dignity of the human person.

BISHOP ANDREW GRUTKA, *28 October, 1964*

The pastoral and ecumenical aspects of the deliberations of this Council should make a defense of human dignity and human rights as strong and solid as a mountain of granite. Disadvantaged people everywhere in the world are hopefully looking for a solution to their problems from the generals of the Church Militant gathered in Council on the Rock of Peter.

Discrimination and segregation because of color, country of origin, or creed must not be condoned for any reason. To despise a man for his color, his origin or his belief is a challenge to Divine Providence. No man has any choice in respect to his appearance or the country of his origin. Personal human dignity, human rights, will always suffer as long as segregation and discrimination are practiced. Some form of degradation, some form of hate, some form of disrespect is invariably involved in every act of segregation and discrimination. Every human being, regardless of color, origin or creed should be afforded equal opportunities for housing, education, culture and employment.

Proper housing is essential because it promotes and enhances good family life—the foundation of society. Poor housing deteriorates into slums which become the breeding places for every form of crime and vice. Just as no one looks for beauty on a garbage dump, neither should one expect virtue from the slums.

It is a deplorable fact that discrimination and segregation do exist in many parts of the world. In many instances the image of the Church has been tarnished and the pastoral labors of priests initiated in the apostolic work of missionaries stymied as the result of parishioners abandoning their neighborhoods when people of another color attempted to settle in this same area.

We know that the Church of Christ is the hope and salvation of all men, but this truth is not always reflected very clearly in actual practice. In view of the signs of the times, the emphasis on personal human dignity and rights is not strong enough. It behooves the Fathers of this Council—gathered here from all the parts of the world and representing in themselves all colors and races—to voice their opposition to every form of segregation and discrimination with the force of the trumpets of Jericho and proclaim the dignity and rights of human persons everywhere with the utmost clarity.

ARCHBISHOP PATRICK O'BOYLE, *28 October, 1964*

I speak in the name of all the bishops of the United States gathered in Rome for the present session of the Council.

Schema 13 in general I accept. Indeed, the general spirit or tone of the schema pleases me very much. Its spirit or tone is very positive and constructive. It reflects the same sympathetic interest in and concern for true human values which characterized the two great social encyclicals of Pope John XXIII, of happy memory—*Mater et Magistra* and *Pacem in Terris*. Like the more recent encyclical of Pope Paul VI, *Ecclesiam Suam*, it also emphasizes the need for a continuing dialogue between the Church and the world and indicates a number of ways in which this dialogue, so rich with promise for the future, can be carried on more effectively not only by the hierarchy, but, even more importantly, by the faithful ["*ad quos uti Caput 'De Laicis' in Schemate 'De Ecclesia' bene notat, 'peculiari modo spectat res temporales omnes, quibus arce conjunguntur, ita illuminare et ordinare, ut secundum Christum jugiter fiat et crescant et sint in laudem Creatoris et Redemptoris*"] referred to especially by the chapter on the laity in the schema on the nature of the Church when it says that the layman, looking in a special way at all temporal things with which he is involved, should so clarify and order them that all things may have their beginning, their growth and existence according to Christ in the praise of the Creator and the Redeemer.

In a word, Schema 13, if adopted with whatever changes the Fathers may desire to make in the present text, will do much to advance the *aggiornamento* which good Pope John so auspiciously and so providentially inaugurated in convening this historic Council.

In this intervention I do not intend to suggest any specific changes in the text of the schema or any deletions. Rather, I wish to propose the addition of a separate section in Chapter IV on the problem of racial discrimination and other forms of racial injustice. Racism, which, in various forms and in varying degrees, is to be found in almost every region of the world, is not merely a social or cultural or political problem. It is, first and foremost, a moral and religious problem and one of staggering proportions.

The present text of Schema 13 refers to the problem two or three times, but only incidentally and in passing. What I am proposing is that it be treated formally and explicitly as a separate problem, not merely from the sociological point of view, but from the point of view of morality and religion. Our treatment of this problem in Schema 13 need not be very long, nor should it attempt to offer detailed solutions to specific social problems in particular countries or regions of the world. At the very least, however, it should include a forthright and unequivocal condemnation of racism in all its forms and should outline, if only in general terms, the theological basis for this condemnation. It should also emphasize the obligation which rests upon all the members of the Church to do everything within their power to eliminate the cancerous evil of racial injustice and to advance, through all available means, the cause of interracial brotherhood under the fatherhood of God. I might add, in this connection, that our own experience in the United States suggests that this is one area of social action which calls for the closest possible cooperation among Catholics, Protestants, and Jews and all other men of good will.

In our judgment, racism is one of the most serious moral and religious problems of our times. If we fail to give it separate and adequate treatment, I fear that the world will conclude that we are very poorly informed about the signs of the time or, worse than that, that we are insensitive to the tragic plight of the millions of innocent men and women all over the world who are the victims of racial pride and racial injustice.

In closing, permit me to quote, in my own native language, a brief excerpt from an address delivered in that language by Pope Pius XII, of happy memory, to a group of Negro publishers from the United States:

All men are brothers in Jesus Christ; for He, though God, became also man, became a member of the human family, a brother of all. This fact, the expression of infinite universal love, is the true bond of fraternal charity which unites men and nations. May it be welded even more firmly through the efforts of all men of good will.

Unless I am mistaken, the whole world is looking to us to reaffirm this simple, but very profound truth in a solemn conciliar statement and to do so unequivocally and with all the clarity, precision and forcefulness at our command.

BISHOP EDWARD SWANSTROM, *4 November, 1964*

As the director of the American bishops' foreign relief program which now encompasses 73 countries of the world, I have the privilege of cooperating with many of you in your efforts to assist the poor and afflicted in your areas. In carrying out that responsibility, I have naturally had occasion to visit most of the countries of Europe, the Middle East, Africa, Asia and the Far East, and Latin America.

For those of us who live in America, the world still presents a face of some calm and orderliness. Our lives have not been caught up in the incessant upheavals that have afflicted so many human beings whose fate it was to be thrust over frontiers as refugees or to be part of the post-colonial areas battling their way into freedom and struggling for some semblance of stability.

Even though there are some very threatening clouds on our own horizons, life in America is in sharp contrast to all the unrest, the homelessness, the hunger and anguish that I have witnessed all over the world in the past several years.

We all remember with poignant clarity the Gospel stories of need and suffering that were taught to us even in the years of our childhood. The story of Lazarus and the rich man has always retained a special poignancy for me.

As I have traveled about the world—to its misery-scourged corners—I have seen Lazarus in my mind's eye over and over again.

I have seen him most obviously in the leprous beggar dragged in a cart on a begging journey around the streets of Calcutta, a city whose streets teem with millions of people, many of them refugees. I saw him, too, in the refugee who had escaped from the mainland of China in 1961 and who had been caught up and deposited in the Fan Ling transit camp.

I went up to this camp and saw thousands of unfortunates who had risked their lives to escape, but were allowed to sit at the gates of the free world for a few days, then were herded into trucks to be returned to China. There was no inn for them in the towns and cities of our western civilization.

In the giant slums which have mushroomed around Latin America's proudest cities—Rio de Janeiro, Santiago, Lima, Bogota—I have seen countless men waiting at the gate of the world for the opportunity to take part in productive life and waiting in vain.

The Lazarus of the Gospel sat at the gate longing for "the crumbs that fell from the rich man's table." But the rich man "who used to clothe himself in purple and fine linen, and who feasted every day in fine fashion," turned away from Lazarus and gave him no aid. Poor Lazarus died, and went from the gate where "the dogs licked his sores" to the peace of Abraham's bosom in heaven. When the rich man died, he went to—well, somewhere else—and he cried for Lazarus to come down and put a drop of water on his tongue in his place of torment.

But, as the Gospel tells us, "a great gulf" had been placed between them. The gulf that the rich man had chosen to maintain between him and the poor while on earth was continued for all eternity. It gives us pause to realize that no other sin is imputed to the rich man, merely that he did not perform the works of mercy in his power. He did not feed the hungry.

It is in such Gospel stories as this that we see the real meaning of Pope Paul's message of last Christmas when he told us that world hunger was the most urgent of the world's problems. In talking about the needs of the world— "a question that makes one dizzy," said our Holy Father, "Because the needs are so vast, so manifold, so immeasurable"—he states very definitely that "the first is hunger."

We know that hunger existed, he went on to say, "but today it has been recognized. It has now been scientifically proven to us that more than half the human race has not enough food. Entire generations of children, even today, are dying or suffering because of indescribable poverty." How true are his words!

The great gulf that exists between the hungry and the well-fed, between the rich and poor nations, is one that is dangerous not only in the temporal order, but quite clearly in the eternal order.

If we are our brother's keeper, we must bear witness to this fact. It is not as simple any more as leaving our home and finding a Lazarus at our gate.

Since Vatican Council II is concerned with updating every aspect of the Church's mission to make the Gospel of Christ relevant to twentieth-century life, we must update our expression of concern for our brother in the world in which we find ourselves. In our day and age, the social mission of the Church must be our great concern, perhaps for some of us a primary concern.

How, for example, are we to meet the critical problem of native priests in many areas until we help lift the social and economic status of our people to a point where there is adequate provision for a decent standard of living and for the primary and secondary education of their children, so essential for candidates for the priesthood?

It is not that there is anything new about the situation we find in the world today. Poverty, hunger and disease are afflictions as old as man himself. But in our time and in this age there has been a change. The change is not so much in the realities of life, but in the hopes and expectations of the future. If men's hopes are not obtainable by a peaceful revolution, a violent revolution is inevitable.

The present world situation has created a worldwide boom of vast portent which has come to be known as the "revolution of rising expectations." The meaning of this revolution is very simple. It means that people all over the world want for themselves the same things that they know others have and which all of us want for our loved ones, for our friends, and for our children—and which many of us have already.

They intend that their families shall live a decent life and that they shall have a job that gives them survival and dignity. They intend that their children shall be taught to read and write; they intend that the hungry shall be fed and the sick shall be treated. They intend to take their place in the great movement of modern society, to take their share in the benefits of that society.

These just desires, once unleashed, can never again be stifled. The people in the developing world are on the march, and certainly we, as the leaders of the Catholic Church throughout the world, must be beside them on that march.

In his great encyclical *Mater et Magistra*, which Pope John of blessed memory issued shortly before this Ecumenical Council convened, he states, "we are all equally responsible for the undernourished peoples," and again, "now justice and humanity require that these richer countries come to the aid of those in need."

I am sure we all realize that in the encyclical *Mater et Magistra* our Holy Father is simply making an effort to apply the teaching of Our Lord and Savior, Jesus Christ, to our own times. Christ says He is the light of the world. He makes plain His concern also for the earthly needs of men not only by His words, but also in the deeds of His life, as when, to alleviate the hunger of a crowd, He more than once miraculously multiplies bread.

Every man created by God has a right to the indispensable means of human subsistence, to sufficient food and clothing for his body, to housing, to employment, to suitable leisure and even to decent recreation. What our Holy Father tries to make clear to us is that, if our brothers in any land are lacking any such necessities, they are our responsibility as much as anyone else's.

In our modern civilization, it is worthy of note that many governments have now turned their full attention to the tragic problems of poverty and destitution in the world. Even though their motivation may be largely political and their chief desire is to prevent revolution and war, it is the charity in the hearts of most of their people that is behind this endeavor to spread the world's wealth and goods among all nations. Surely it is our function, as the bishops of the Church established by Christ Himself, to exhort, stimulate and encourage our governments in this endeavor, to assist them in shaping policies and to join with them in distributing food and clothing and the means of earning a livelihood among those less fortunate than ourselves, and most particularly among the destitute and the starving.

Paragraph 24 talks largely about what governments and laity should do. It should be rewritten to emphasize also the tremendous responsibility placed upon bishops and priests in our day and age to participate most actively in programs to assist the people of God to raise themselves out of the abyss of poverty and degradation. Since we are other Christs, like Christ Himself we must carry out our social as well as our spiritual mission.

We, too, must stand before the judgment seat of God and we will want Him to say to us, "Amen, I say to you, when you did this to one of the least of my brethren, you did it unto me."

BISHOP FLOYD BEGIN, 9 *November, 1964*

By reason of the solidarity of the human family, I am most certainly in accord with what has been said by other Council Fathers and even by a layman concerning the necessity of solving, if possible, even on a worldwide and effective level, the problem of poverty and misery in this world. I should like to propose a solution of this problem, a solution which could be adopted here and now by all people of good will, with an effect that would be practically immediate and infallible.

Therefore, I humbly ask that this Holy Synod spend a little time in recalling the economic system instituted by God Himself not only for the economic good, but for the health and welfare of anyone in the world and of the whole human society. This economic system, divinely revealed to us, offers a solution to the problem of poverty and destitution in this world while, at the same time, it will promote great sanctity.

Staggering numbers of the poor and destitute are found in this world. They are needy, however, not because there is any shortage of the goods necessary to sustain human life. An almighty and provident God, who creates all temporal and economic goods out of nothing, created an abundance of them, even a superabundance of them. We are aware that Christ, Our Lord, warned us: "The poor you will always have with you" (Matt. 26: 2). But why do the poor remain with us always? For two reasons, I believe: on the one hand, there are those, who under divine inspiration, embrace voluntary poverty. But with these there is no problem. They are the blessed ones—"*Beati sunt*"—"Blessed are the poor." On the other hand, however, a great number of people experience poverty because they either are ignorant of or fail to accept the economic system revealed by God, the system known as "tithes and first fruits."

Frequently in the Old and also in the New Testament, God speaks of "tithes and firstfruits." Recall the words found in the book of Malachias:

> "Come back to me and I will return to you," says the Lord of Hosts—and you said, "In what should we come back to you?" "In tithes and firstfruits, and in your want you are cursed. Bring into my barn the total tithe, and let there be food in my home, and try me in this," said the Lord. "See if I do not open to you the cataracts of heaven and pour out upon you a blessing unto abundance. I will punish anyone devouring you. The fruits of your field will not corrupt, nor will your vine be sterile in the field—and all nations will call you blessed." (Malach. 3:6–12)

Christ approved the tithing of the Pharisees while He condemned their injustice.

St. Thomas Aquinas treated the law and the moral obligation of the tithe in his *Summa Theologica* (II-II. q. 86, 87).

The *fontes,* or sources, of Canon Law demonstrate that for centuries this practice was a Christian practice and not merely a Judaic practice. Even the present Code of Canon Law (Canon 1502) still praises the practice.

We read in the Roman Pontifical, in use up to the present, an instruction to be given by the bishop on the occasion of the dedication of a church. These are the words of the Pontifical:

> Furthermore, beloved brethren, I admonish you that you pay integrally to the churches and to the priests the tithes which are a divine tribute. The Lord reserves this to Himself as a symbol of His universal dominion.

Then the Roman Pontifical cites the beautiful words of St. Augustine:

> The tithes are the tributes of needy souls. If you will but give the tithe, you will not only receive an abundance of fruit, but also a health of body and soul will be yours. The Lord is not seeking a reward, but honor, recognition,

for God, our God, who has deigned to give us everything, has deigned to receive in return the tenth part or the tithe, not for His profit, but, without doubt, for ours.

God in the Old Testament demanded from everyone, including the poorest, the firstfruits and the tenth part of any fruits, revenue, gain or profit, for the support of worship, the clergy and the works of charity. But He also promised to tithers an abundance of temporal goods and other blessings.

God has never withdrawn this promise. Therefore, if anyone, even the poor, or the poorest, would willingly give to God the first tenth part of his income, he would receive the promised reward and bid farewell to poverty. "Try me in this," says the Lord. A man renders tribute to God by contributing to the works of religion and charity. Since a man, in paying the tithe and firstfruits, would really be seeking first "the kingdom of God and His justice," he would deserve to hear that "all these things will be given to you besides" (Lk. 12:31).

By the practice of giving God the "first ten per cent," a man would

1) Recognize the supreme dominion and the infinite goodness of his Creator.

2) He would express supreme trust and confidence in the promise of God.

3) He would learn in an efficacious and practical manner the necessary virtues of penance, mortification and abnegation.

4) He would find a remedy against the spirit of materialism and the weakness of faith, hope and charity.

5) He would diminish or even remove from his heart inordinate adherence to creatures and temporal goods.

6) He would make the first step in the virtue of poverty.

7) He would remove from his life many of the impediments to perfection.

Unless I am mistaken, we prophets of the will of God, teachers on earth about the life of man, we Fathers of the poor—we could hardly keep from our people a practice so effective for the temporal and spiritual good of men everywhere in the world.

The same practice of tithes and firstfruits would have another effect as a kind of by-product—I mean the better support of the Church, local and universal, about which thus far we have heard not a single word in the Second Vatican Council.

This practice, unless I am mistaken, would amply provide for the missions, for the works of charity, for the clergy and for divine worship. It would make the Church independent not only with religious liberty, but with freedom of religion.

Nevertheless, in favor of the poor and their security, I forego the development of the subject of ecclesiastic temporal welfare. I pass up this question.

What, then, do I ask of the Council Fathers? A new law concerning tithes and firstfruits? Not at all! Even though the single and unique minimum standard established by God for the contributions of the faithful is the tithe, I don't request a law—either local or universal in this matter. I ask only praise—well deserved praise and approval of those who support the works of God by voluntary and generous contributions and especially of those who return to God the first ten per cent of their income through their contributions to religion and charity.

Wherefore, I ask for the approval of the following amendment to chapter four, page 28, number 23 after the twelfth line of the text by adding a new paragraph thus:

> Finally, this Holy Synod, mindful of the divine institution of tithes and firstfruits revealed to us in the Old Testament and never repealed, mindful also of the rewards promised by God to those who observe this practice, rewards for the spiritual and temporal welfare of the individual and the whole Church and the whole human race—the Holy Synod emphatically approves those Christians and all others who return to God by contributing to works of religion and charity, the first ten per cent of their incomes, salary, profits or gain.

May this amendment, praising and approving this practice, be inserted in no. 23 of chapter four or elsewhere in this document.

Thanks be to God.

ARCHBISHOP PHILIP HANNAN, *10 November, 1964*

Paragraph 25 should be corrected and rewritten so that it clearly distinguishes between the aspirations of the Church for the establishment of peace and the requirements of the moral theology of the Church on conducting a just war. If there is a treatment of the moral theology of conducting warfare, it should be written by very competent moral theologians; these theologians must be acquainted with the facts about modern weapons, including nuclear weapons, or they must be willing to secure the facts. With all our heart we desire peace—peace with justice and complete liberty. Certainly we hold that war is horror, but we must state with precision what is prohibited in waging war to those who justly and laudably defend liberty.

1) In Section 1 the first sentence fails to mention the most important foundation of peace, namely, justice—"peace, the work of justice" (the motto of Pius XII). Thus, the first sentence ignores the definition of peace in Paragraph two where it rightly defines peace.

2) In Section 1 the following erroneous sentence occurs: "Therefore, everything that unfortunately divides rather than unites must be adjudged as opposed to peace. . . ." Injustice is the cause of divisions.

3) In Section 2 there is a grave mistake of fact in regard to nuclear weapons, and, therefore, a false conclusion is reached. In the second sentence of this section it is stated, ". . . the use of arms, especially nuclear weapons, whose effects are greater than can be imagined and therefore cannot be reasonably regulated by men, exceeds all just proportion and therefore must be judged before God and man as most wicked." Contrary to this statement, there now exist nuclear weapons which have a very precise limit of destruction. Some of these weapons are mobile; obviously, if they did not have a limited field of destruction, they would kill the soldiers who fired them. There is a weapon now in use which has a range of 1.3 to 2.5 miles whose missile has a force of 40 tons of TNT. These weapons were developed to avoid the huge destruction of larger nuclear explosions and to destroy individual military targets.

Although even a low-yield nuclear weapon inflicts great damage, still it cannot be said that its "effects are greater than what can be imagined (or estimated)." Its effects are very well calculated and can be foreseen. Furthermore, it may be permitted to use these arms, with their limited effect, against military objectives in a just war according to theological principles.

The whole paragraph, therefore, seems to ignore the common teaching of the Church and the norms to be applied to the conduct of a just war.

4) The whole paragraph would seem to imply that all nations have been equally negligent in securing international peace. This is a cruel injustice to many nations and heads of governments who have expended great efforts toward securing peace; it is especially cruel to the nations which are now suffering invasion and unjust aggression from that force which has so far prevented peace. The whole world knows the source of aggression.

The question of the greatest importance, now and for the future, is to avoid war and to defend liberty, both national and personal. We must have complete and actual liberty to carry on a dialogue with militant atheists. No dialogue is possible if we fall into slavery. Because liberty is the foundation of human life, those who defend liberty should be praised.

Therefore, since this schema deals with practical matters, we should at least say a word about the defense of liberty and a word of praise in favor of those who defend liberty as well as those who freely offered their lives so that we may enjoy the freedom of the sons of God.

Therefore, in my humble judgment, the whole paragraph should be completely revised.

JOSEPH CARDINAL RITTER, *20 November, 1964*

I am highly pleased by the *votum* "On the Sacrament of Matrimony" and more particularly on the suggested dispositions affecting interconfessional marriages.

In its fifth paragraph the proposed votum would introduce two very important departures from the present legislation: the one concerns the premarital guarantees, the other the canonical form.

The new approach to the guarantees, it seems to me, is particularly praiseworthy in that it serves both truth and charity. Herein the Church is concerned with the observance of divine law and the safeguarding of personal right. It is evident that the new disposition would safeguard the right to marry more realistically than the present law. Moreover, the new approach would more effectively secure respect for the divine law. The norms of the Code of Canon Law often enough obscure the existence of divine law, and by insisting overmuch on juridical procedure, emphasize ecclesiastical law beyond measure. Adoption of the suggested proposal would strengthen respect for divine law, by stressing more emphatically the role of personal responsibility. Responsibility for the security of his own faith as well as for the Catholic education of children is rightly placed on the Catholic party. In this way we can lessen the possibility of offense to the consciences of our separated brethren.

The schema proceeds wisely and prudently in its approach to the canonical form. It offers a middle course between the extremes of inflexible retention and complete relaxation of the form. Although each extreme has its adherents, I believe that this compromise affords the best response to the needs of our time. On the side the schema supports the general retention of the canonical form of marriage for validity in such cases. Not a few Fathers will find this displeasing, and they can point out that the clandestinity of marriage, which the Tridentine legislation was intended to counteract, is no longer a problem. However, a new pastoral problem has presented itself in some countries—the high incidence of early and hasty marriage with a probability of subsequent divorce—which recommends the retention of the form for validity.

Nonetheless, to demonstrate our respect for human dignity and to reduce the principles of ecumenism to practice, it is apparent that in some cases the ordinary must be empowered to grant dispensation from the form. This disposition is closer to the spirit of Trent than the existing norms. It would be well to remember that, in the Decree *Tametsi*, the Council of Trent, treating of clandestine marriages already contracted, stated: "Inasmuch as we must not doubt that clandestine marriages contracted by the consent of the parties are true marriages as long as the Church did not make them invalid; they are rightly condemned who deny that these are true and valid marriages and this Sacred Synod so condemns them. . . ." (Denz. 990).

Finally, for the sake of honesty and justice, those baptized in the Catholic Church who have been reared without Catholic education, must not be bound by the canonical form of marriage nor restricted by any impediments of merely ecclesiastical law.

I conclude by asking that these norms which answer so well the pressing needs of many persons be enacted and promulgated without delay. In serving the cause of truth and charity, we must transcend considerations of our own convenience and procedural efficiency.

BISHOP JOHN FEARNS, *20 November, 1964*

This is the intervention of Francis Cardinal Spellman, Archbishop of New York in the United States.

I speak in the name of more than one hundred bishops of the United States who are present at the Council.

The Commission on the Discipline of the Sacraments deserves our thanks and praise which we wholeheartedly give, because of its arduous and involved labors and its effect which is shown in the schema on the sacrament of Matrimony. With a joyous spirit we greet every effort which enhances the dignity and sanctity of marriage which in the world today are so openly attacked and so often denied.

This proposed schema contains, however, things which truly prescribe that certain things in our current laws on marriage would be so changed as to injure gravely the spiritual good of our country. Even if these changes, perhaps, are of advantage for some countries, there is no reason why they should be imposed upon other nations. Moreover, it would have been most fitting to grant us enough time so that we might consult our pastors in pastoral matters of such importance. I am convinced that the Commission also should consult pastors from various nations on the changes, especially pastors from nations in which the society, as regards religion, is "pluralistic."

The schema labors under so many defects and inconsistencies that it ought to be revised by the Commission. These most obvious defects should be avoided:

1) Dispensation from the form of marriage for mixed marriages which is mentioned in number five, paragraph b, would bring it about in our "pluralistic" society that the honor or reverence in which marriage and the sacred ministry of the pastor are held would be lessened. For our Catholic people receive the sacred character of marriage because it is demanded that it be celebrated before a priest either in some Catholic church or in the rectory, not however in any non-Catholic church or in any civic chamber. This practice so pertains to our religious life that the civil law recognizes it; our civil authority does not require that any civil official assist at a marriage.

2) The reasons brought forth in the cited paragraph in order that a dis-

pensation from the form of marriage be granted, namely "grave difficulties," are so ambiguous that a new law of this sort would destroy the form required up to now in a mixed marriage. If, then, the spouses refuse to celebrate their marriage before a priest, this is already a sufficient reason to grant dispensation. Therefore, a new law of this sort would put an end to the form now observed in mixed marriages and thus would prevent the pastor from giving to the spouses that very necessary spiritual counsel. Furthermore, it would not provide that the spouses promise to educate their children, if they have any, in their religion. If, therefore, there are regions where such dispensations are necessary, it is fitting that those bishops, having explained the reason, seek the faculty of this sort from the Holy See.

3) The proposed new law passes over the good for which the laws now in force provide very well, the religious state of the children born of mixed marriages. It also passes over both psychological truths to be observed in marriages and principles of the first importance of the pastoral ministry which concern such marriages.

4) Difficulties which can be foreseen in marriage, especially religious difficulties, ought to be solved before the wedding, not afterwards, as all matrimonial counsels warn. The proposed law, indeed, does not sufficiently stress that difficulties of this sort ought to be avoided with wise and prudent care before the wedding.

5) The law proposed in number six, paragraph b, would dangerously lessen the responsibility of the pastor in the affairs of marriage. As a matter of fact, the law would endanger the power the ordinary has over the marriages of his diocese, for any priest (unless he be obviously kept from it) could validly sanction a marriage, even against the requirements of the law.

It ought to be obvious in the schema that these proposals be intended to direct and guide the Commission on the revision of the Code of Canon Law.

To be sure, there are reasons why we should carefully weigh changes in matrimonial law. Changes of this sort, however, ought neither lessen the responsibility of pastors nor inflict grave spiritual harm on any nation without necessity.

ARCHBISHOP JOHN KROL, 20 *November*, 1964

Well-deserved appreciation must be given to the Commission on the Discipline of the Sacraments. It is not easy to coordinate the common discipline of the whole Church with what is variously done in different areas; it is not easy to accommodate matrimonial discipline to the new circumstances of the times and according to the mind of the Decree on Ecumenism and the Declaration on Religious Liberty (when it will have been approved). Therefore, the emendations which I propose in the name of many are offered with the hope of emending rather than rejecting the schema prepared by the Commission.

The goal of the Council is both pastoral and ecumenical. Rightly are we concerned about ecumenical needs. But to no lesser extent must we devote attention to pastoral care of those (and there are many) who are in danger of indifferentism and secularism; those who have practically no religious principles and adhere to no religious persuasion. These men are rarely publicly opposed to the Church and, because of ignorance concerning religious matters, are not suitable for ecumenical dialogue. Thus we can expect almost no ecumenical response from them.

For example: in the United States of America more than sixty million people—almost a third of the population—go to no Church and belong to no religion. These people manifest practically no external sign of religious faith and remain (at least partially) ignorant of their spiritual nature and the noble end of man. Their condition is well described in the schema on the Church in the contemporary world: "They are ignorant of the vocation and proper meaning of their own lives."

Is it not the duty of the Church to inspire these men so that at least their children be raised in a religious way? Should not positive cooperation be required of them for the religious formation of children? Finally, should they not be invited by the Church not only to permit but to promise the religious education of their children? The Church can hardly perpetuate indifferentism among those who do not believe and do not practice religion.

The schema of the *votum* on matrimony makes no distinction between men who are truly religious illiterates and those who practice religion from the heart. It is clear from pastoral experience that these areligious men pledge their prenuptial promises in full freedom, hold them sacred and frequently come to the faith themselves. Thus there is a clear necessity of warning all non-Catholics in charity about the promises which the Catholic party has assumed and of demanding some positive affirmation by which their willingness to consent in this matter with the Catholic party would be proved.

Moved by these motives, we earnestly ask that the discipline of the promises be kept even if, by exception, the ordinary would be granted the faculty of sometimes dispensing in cases of non-Catholics who have religious sentiment and profess a religious life. This mode of acting would keep intact due respect for the freedom of conscience and would promote ecumenical activity and, at the same time, keep in mind the duty of preaching evangelical truth to non-believers, a duty binding on the Church.

The schema of the *votum* proposes that ordinaries be granted the faculty of dispensing from canonical form in mixed marriages "if there are grave difficulties in carrying out the form." Experience teaches that a facility in dispensing, when it becomes known by all, offers an invitation to seek a dispensation, and both parties would present so called "grave difficulties" based on subjective and thoughtless reasons. Thereby the dispensation itself, not to mention diverse practices in conceding it, would be a cause of scandal and confusion. Such a proposition cannot, therefore, be introduced into the Church without previous mature consideration of the very serious disadvantages which it could cause.

The schema of the *votum* penetratingly indicates the conditions necessary for valid and licit assistance at matrimony on the part of the priest. In the following paragraph however, it proposes that, for valid assistance, the presence of any priest would suffice, as long as he is free from excommunication, interdict or suspension. Is this not an invalidation—not to say contradiction—of the law? Does this not encourage "vagabond" clerics? How can one be sure that a strange and possibly unknown priest is free from all censure? Further, how can one be sure that he is a true priest?

In some countries, civil law requires that a competent minister or preacher be acknowledged by some official of the locality before he may assist at the wedding.

Pastoral prudence demands, for valid assistance, that the priest be at least known to competent authority.

Moreover, pastoral discipline demands the suppression of paragraph 6b because it invalidates the disposition of 6a.

Although the schema of the *votum* is not a conciliar decree, by our approbation it would acquire the force of a quasi-order of the Sacred Council. Wherefore we earnestly ask:

First: that the general norms still in effect on promises in mixed marriages remain, maintaining the ordinary's faculty of dispensing them in some cases of non-Catholics who have a religious sense and profess a religious life.

Secondly: that the canonical form of marriage remain firm, and the ordinary be given the faculty of allowing, for example, a couple to come before even a non-Catholic minister for truly ecumenical reasons.

Finally: that for a priest's valid assistance at matrimony there be required his approbation by the ordinary of the place or the pastor.

FRANCIS CARDINAL SPELLMAN, *21 September, 1965*

As I said during the last session of the Council, this pastoral constitution should be a lucid and a totally sincere affirmation of the role which the Church sees as her own in the world. It should be a solemn, yet simple, frank and humble rededication of the Catholic Church to the service of mankind. To accomplish this end, we wish to listen and be listened to; to be asked to state—even to explain—our positions. Above all, we ask that we may be allowed to cooperate in the work of helping all men to achieve a fuller life.

If this constitution is to accomplish its purpose, the substance of the present text must not be weakened in any way. Nevertheless, I believe that the task remains to provide—especially in the first pages of the schema—a certain tone or mode of expression which would signify without any doubt precisely what this schema means to achieve. For in this schema the Church does not intend to give simple and definitive solutions for all the problems of the modern world; rather, she desires to enter into a dialogue with all men of good will to build together a better world.

The essential condition of this dialogue on the part of the Christian faithful is the spirit and virtue of obedience toward that power in the Church "which has been established by Christ, acts in His place, is as it were His visible instrument, and represents the love of so noble a Shepherd." I think it most necessary that we explain the essence and significance of filial Christian obedience generously given. On the one hand, it often appears to some that the Catholic Church especially encourages an obedience which is merely juridical and unreflecting. On the other hand, there are some today who speak as if obedience and reverence toward the magisterium of the Church were somehow opposed to the freedom of the sons of God. Therefore, in a truly pastoral manner we must explain how Christian obedience is in perfect harmony with the freedom of the Christian faithful and how it leads to a better discharge of our ministry of service to mankind.

In particular, let me say that chapter five, on the community of nations and the promotion of peace, has been wisely revised in line with the suggestions of many Fathers. In the text, as it now stands, there shines forth the ardent desire of all men of good will for a peace truly founded in justice and charity.

Nevertheless, I do object to one section. From the wording of number 101 of this schema the notion could arise that military service can never be obligatory or at least that it can be an obligation only for those who do not desire the more perfect Christian life.

Nations, legitimately concerned about their own existence, must consider the concrete conditions in which they find themselves (cf. number 99). Even today government leaders can judge that no international organization yet offers a sufficiently strong guarantee of peace and that, as a result, military preparedness is necessary in order to provide a just peace. The presumption in such cases is that those who are called to military service do intend true peace.

As St. Thomas says (*Summa Theologica*, II–II. q 188, a 3, ad 2) a person can resist evil in two ways. First, by enduring any injury done to himself, and this is a perfection when it is done for the welfare of others. Secondly, by patiently tolerating injuries done to others and this is an imperfection or even a vice if one can resist the aggressor in a suitable manner.

Without doubt, it is difficult to decide on the more perfect way of resisting evil in the world today. But if the leaders of a nation decide in good faith and after mature deliberation that military service by their citizens is absolutely necessary for the defense of peace and justice, how can the individual citizen justly refuse military service? As it is said in the same section of the schema:

the legitimate authority is presumed to be acting within its competency and its laws are to be obeyed except in those cases in which there is a manifest violation of the law of God.

Every man of good will desires that all regional and internal wars should be peacefully prevented or quickly terminated. Nevertheless, certain governments in good faith have reached the decision that military force is absolutely necessary for preserving true peace in the present world situation. We neither wish nor are we able to make a definitive moral judgment on the circumstances which have led to these decisions. Lest this constitution be twisted for political ends—which is contrary to our intention—I strongly urge that number 101 be entirely revised.

BISHOP RUSSELL McVINNEY, *22 September, 1965*

The declaration of intent as spelled out in the first paragraphs of the schema is concise and most laudable. But when the schema attempts to set out guidelines for the cure of specific ills, by an incomprehensible shift of emphasis it lapses into questionable compromise with the purveyors of those ills. We are clothed with the mission to guide the world unfailingly toward God. We shall not accomplish our purpose or fulfill our mission by pampering the wayward or the lukewarm. "I would that you were hot or cold" (Apoc. 3: 15).

At this crucial time in the Church's history, there is a great need for zeal. It is a momentous and critical fight to which we are summoned, and there is need for ardent and wholehearted enthusiasm. "Labor as a good soldier of Christ Jesus . . . for he also that striveth for the mastery is not crowned except he strived lawfully" (2 Tim. 2: 3,5).

Unfortunately, the contrary tepidity characterizes this age. This lethargy of the soul brings with it indifference to virtue and carelessness in respect to sin. The lukewarm Christian is patient only so long as he has nothing to endure, gentle so long as he is not contradicted, willing to be good provided it costs him no trouble; he would like to be virtuous, but not mortified, to be possessed of heaven, but without doing violence to himself.

Nor should we beguile ourselves about the moral condition of the world that we are to redeem. Scarcely a day passes without newspapers announcing an increase in crime, indictments, convictions and scandals. Misdeeds uncovered in government, business, labor, entertainment, education and the family induce an impression of moral hollowness in our most vital institutions. The sense of laxity and moral callousness is heightened by figures on alcoholism and dope addiction, juvenile delinquency, mental disorder.

There are many historical reasons for a steady lowering of standards of behavior. First and foremost, there has been a weakening of authority, both religious and secular. It is incumbent on us to impress on our amoral world the duty to recognize a properly constituted authority.

This cynical age has adopted the attitude that "moral principles are for suckers"; that "everyone has his price and is out to get his"; that "if you don't take the bribe or pay-off, someone else will," that "the big-shots run everything" and that individuals are helpless; that consequently the only effective rule is to "look out for number one" and "keep your nose clean." Cynicism is not, of course, a new attitude, nor are the types of crime and swindling arising from it: the payola, program- and price-rigging, cheating at school, at work and on contracts. What is new, however, is that today there seems to be an epidemic of cynicism.

The unceasing attacks, the endless calumnies, the oppression and persecution to which the Church has been subjected through the ages—all point out the foolhardiness of trying to adjust to the world. The world, the flesh and the devil are still our prime enemies, and all conspire to destroy the solid faith of our people and to lure them to the false gods of their vain waywardness. We are in the world to redeem it, not to be deceived by its pretense or beguiled by its blandishments.

We need, then, to be watchful against the infiltration of the philosophy of ease into our own ranks. Great changes are taking place within the Church today, and we welcome them. The Church is changing because the Church is alive. Change and life go together. Fossils are impervious to change, but fossils became fossils because they could not renew their life. But we should keep in mind that change can be for the worse as well as for the better; and, to my mind, some of the current changes reveal the encroachment of secularism in our thinking and laxity in our conduct.

Nowhere is this spirit of compromise and slackness more clearly evident than in the area of authority. Everywhere today—in essays, articles, pamphlets and books, in discussions and dialogues—there is a great deal of emphasis on liberty, the open Church and freedom within the Church. Seldom do we find a word spoken in favor of authority. Indeed, the word "authority" has become, in some quarters, a term of opprobrium—something which we should be against—rather than being the bedrock of Christ's Church.

The "new breed" theologian is showing a great deal of interest in Protestant scholars and theologians. This may be good and profitable, but it is easy to get the impression that some are searching for insights, enlightenment and interpretation of divine truth, not in Thomas Aquinas, the doctors of the Church, or in papal pronouncements, but in writings of non-Catholics.

Amid all our enthusiasm for liturgical renewal, lay participation, etc., it is well to remember that there is no "kerygma" without authority; there is no "People of God" without the hierarchial institution founded by Jesus Christ; and that the positive faith which our divine Redeemer has given for authentic interpretation has not been given, says Pope Pius XII, "to each of the faithful, not even to theologians, but only to the teaching authority of the Church."

The criticism of the Church prompted by the Vatican Council started out constructively, but has recently deteriorated into carping diatribes against the very authority of the Church and those who wield it. Proponents of the "new look" in Church affairs clamor for a maximum of freedom for themselves and a minimum of so-called "interference" from ecclesiastical authority.

The spirit of the age reflects man's burning desire for greater and greater freedom. It would be tragic, however, if, in the course of fighting for freedom, legitimate authority was undermined. Both freedom and authority have their responsibilities, and one should not be expanded at the expense of the other. Authority is so essential, St. Thomas Aquinas observes, that even in a society of saints it would be necessary.

But the most disturbing element found among our young people, yes, and even among our young priests today, is their lack of understanding or appreciation of the virtue of obedience. Perhaps this is because they fail to see the supreme importance of this virtue in the life of our divine Master, Jesus Christ. The entire course of Our Lord's life on earth was but a living-out of obedience. The Passion, with all its bitter sufferings, was continually before Christ's eyes, but He drew near to it with ardent desire, unflinching and unhesitating, obedient and yet free, because the spring of His obedience was love.

Some would have us believe that obedience is a confession of inferiority. They give us a picture of a weak and submissive Mr. Milquetoast—indecisive, cringing, unaggressive, unwilling and unable to face life except in parasitic dependence upon another who is stronger. But nothing could be farther from the truth. The weakling submits because he is a weakling, because of inner compulsion and need; he does not have the psychological independence or strength of will to resist. The truly obedient man, on the other hand, submits freely and deliberately. He obeys because he chooses to obey and has the strength to overcome whatever impulses would urge him to rebellion.

The much vaunted "crisis of obedience" in the Church will disappear when our young people fully understand that obedience and freedom are not contradictory and incompatible, when they see that true freedom can be found only in obedience. It is only by freely subjecting himself to authority that man reaches his perfection in society and in God. The question is not whether we shall obey, but rather how we shall obey—in a grudging reluctant, mean spirited manner or, as St. Augustine says, "Obey . . . not as slaves under the bondage of the law, but as children, free in the liberty of divine grace."

Our Lord Jesus Christ has promised us that He will be with the Church until the end of time. This does not absolve us, however, from the effort demanded by Christ to promote His Kingdom on earth. We do not have to fear communists, fascists or atheistic dictators. The Church is not weakened by such enemies. She is, however, stricken gravely when the spiritual forces which make men righteous and brave shrivel in the hearts of the faithful.

Finally, I propose that the schema put greater emphasis on problems that concern the tepidity and mediocrity of Catholics and on the necessity of obedience toward properly constituted authority.

LAWRENCE CARDINAL SHEHAN, *23 September, 1965*

The text of this proposed constitution is generally acceptable. But it should be perfected in many aspects, about two of which I wished to say a few words: 1) on style; 2) on method. Since everything which should be said on style has already been mentioned, I will immediately pass on to method.

According to the things which are read in the general report (pages 91 ff.), the drafters of the schema proposed that they express the truths and deeds of the natural order and the truths and deeds of the supernatural order; *however this unfortunate distinction has been rejected.*

An unfortunate separation of this type, in my humble opinion, would be better and more safely avoided if there were a treatment in the schema of the truths of both orders in a truly synthetic method. Those who express these truths (which, on first observation, seem to disagree with one another) in such a way that it is clearly understood that they complement one another in some type of real unity, use such a method properly.

For example, the truths and deeds which are said to be of the natural order can be *conceived* as if they were totally opposed to the supernatural order. However, in the real and concrete order, this is not true at all. For these orders, although they should be distinguished from one another in the mind, nevertheless, on the part of the object, they complement one another since they are actually found in one and the same subject. Thus it is clear why this schema, whose purpose is to consider the real and concrete order, should claim this method as its own, that is, the method of true synthesis.

That synthetic method would have been more happily used, especially in the first, second and third chapters.

The matter treated in these chapters offers an opportunity to adumbrate a truly Christian anthropology, accommodated to the progress of the teaching of the Church for these times. For the truths and deeds of the natural and supernatural orders consider one and the same thing, namely man in the real and concrete realm, and they find in him the proper principle of the unity or synthesis. For man, existing in the real and concrete order, can be taken as follows:

1) as an *individual,* one and unique among others, from whom he is inwardly distinct;

2) as a spiritual *person:* on the one hand he is capable of infinite reality by reason of his intelligence and love, and, on the other hand, he is capable

of the community with other persons by reason of that same intelligence and love.

3) as *a son of God,* to whom God Himself has given power to enter into a communion of community with the Blessed Trinity.

Since these three orders, essentially different from each other, are found in the one individual person of the man who is redeemed or capable of redemption, they manifest in the concrete and real order a deep unity of these orders and make a synthesis possible. But these orders are in contact with reality in the concrete existing order only within a union interiorly contracted. And so, man is a member of the human race because he is an individual; of the human community because he is a person; and a member of the Church united with Christ because he is a redeemed person.

A synthesis of this kind, such as has been indicated above, would enjoin progress in doctrine according to the immutable laws of every progress: continuity and progress; old truths in new forms which have been adjusted to the signs of our time.

In my humble opinion, a happy and realistic synthesis has not yet been obtained: for example, where (page 5) there is a discussion of the influence of Satan in the world; where (page 16) there is a consideration of man's knowledge of God and of the problem of atheism; where (page 48) it deals with conjugal love and its relation to the institute of matrimony.

Finally, Venerable Fathers, let me say a few words about such a comprehensive synthesis.

There should not be any fear of a realistic and strong synthesis in the matter of this schema. Rather we must expect a progress in doctrine brought on by a change in circumstances and the rise of new problems. A synthesis is totally different from a compromise. The solutions in a compromise are reached by mutual concessions. However, the solutions of a synthesis seek truths by completing those things which actually complement one another. This method, namely synthesis, is prominent in this Most Holy Synod from the very beginning in its renewal of the Church in its life, teaching and institutions.

Therefore, the Church faithfully fulfills its mission in searching after a synthesis.

BISHOP EDWARD SWANSTROM, *4 October, 1965*

The schema on the Church in the world of our time treats in admirable manner the searing issue of hunger, disease, ignorance and over-all misery within our human family. This is particularly true of the manner in which the subject is treated in chapter three, paragraphs 81, 84 and 85, and in chapter five, paragraphs 93, 94 and 95.

In these places the schema first states that there exists an obvious and ever-increasing discrepancy of wealth between the richer and the poorer nations. Then it describes these precepts of justice which should be applied to this question. Finally, it says that the wealthier nations should come to the aid of the poorer ones. I am in full agreement with all these things.

However, I am deeply concerned about the implementation of this beautiful doctrine of the universal common good and international social justice.

Although it springs directly from Christ's concern for the poor, the Church's teaching on social and economic justice among all the peoples of the human family sometimes appears to be new and strange to many Christians, especially if they have a sufficiency themselves. There is not only a great gulf between the rich and the poor, but there is a great gulf between our accepting and putting these principles into practice, a great gulf between our words and deeds.

From the dawn of the industrial revolution and beginning particularly with Leo XIII, the Church began to champion the cause of the proletariat and to insist that her children put into practice the principles of social justice and love within our respective nations. International social justice requires still a much deeper grasp of the Christian imperative to reach the much wider dimensions of the whole family of nations, crossing the barriers of race and culture which enclose our national consciences.

For these reasons, I propose concretely that the Church launch a deep and long-term campaign of education, inspiration and moral influence to promote among Christians and all men of good will a live understanding and concern for world poverty, and to promote world justice and development in all their facets.

Since human poverty will be foremost among world issues for the next decade and generation, the remedies already well outlined in the schema will require long-term stamina and persistence, rooted in deep convictions. As the People of God, we must acquire these convictions ourselves and share them with all men of good will, particularly within the richer nations. In this way, their citizens will be more willing to control their own cupidity, to pay taxes in support of aid and loan programs, and to make the other changes necessary for world justice and the development of the poorer peoples.

I propose that a secretariat be established within the Church to carry on this long-term process of education and inspiration, motivation and moral influence.

In a few months this Council will be closed. But our concern for the world's poor, so often voiced in this aula by the college of bishops, led by our chief shepherd the Holy Father, should continue to ring out, to teach and exhort. This would be the role of the secretariat, functioning perhaps under a permanent commission of bishops, appointed by the Holy Father.

This effort would not hinder in any way, but would rather strengthen, the works of social assistance and development now carried on by several national conferences of bishops and by other Church organizations. These raise and distribute funds and are engaged in concrete operations. The new secretariat, I repeat, would be educational and inspirational.

With these purposes in view, I respectfully offer to the Fathers the following addition to the schema. In chapter five, at the end of number 95, entitled "The Role of Christians," add the following new paragraph.

In order to call with persistence the attention of the People of God and, in fact, all men of the human family to the sad plight of a majority of God's children, and to teach the message of Christ's love for the poor and His justice in and out of season, this Sacred Synod proposes that a secretariat of the Holy See for promoting world justice and development be established. It also urges that national conferences of bishops [*coetus*], religious orders and other appropriate bodies including those composed of laymen, set up suitable means for opening the minds and hearts of all to the cries of the poor over the whole world wherever possible. These educational and inspirational efforts should be carried on in close concert with our separated brothers, with groups inspired by other religions and with all men of good will.

Pastoral Constitution on the Church in the Modern World

✠ COMMENTARY *by Rt. Rev. Monsignor George G. Higgins*

Father Robert Tucci, S.J., the distinguished editor of *Civiltá Cattolica* and one of the Vatican II's most gifted and most versatile *periti*, has summarized the work of the Council in terms which, at first glance, might appear to have been borrowed, quite unexpectedly, from the lexicon of the advertising profession. Tucci says that the Church's sustained effort, during the four years of the Council, to reflect on herself, her nature, and her mission in the world, has produced "an image of the Church which has an air of novelty, a new vision of the Church." In point of fact, however, Tucci is using the word "image" in this context to suggest a very profound transformation or change which, upon examination, will be seen to bear no resemblance whatsoever to the superficial, not to say meretricious image-changing or image-making which, rightly or wrongly, has made so many sensitive observers rather cynical about the lucrative arts which are practiced on the Madison Avenues of the world. He says,

> Clearly, there is no question of newness in any absolute sense: in the Church what is new is always old, original. Rather it is a rediscovery of elements which the Church already possessed, but which, in the course of centuries and under the pressure of given historical circumstances, had not been lost, but had become blurred in her consciousness, or else of elements implicitly possessed by the Church in the treasure of her unchanging faith, potentialities which were able to become explicit and to rise to the surface of consciousness through the action of the Holy Spirit on the other hand, and on the other, as a result of the new problems which history is ever again raising for the Church and of the consequent increase in her historical experience.

The new "image" of the Church which Tucci sees emerging from the Council is to be found more or less, he says, in all of the conciliar texts, but mainly in the two constitutions, *Lumen Gentium* and *Gaudium et Spes*. In the case of the latter document, one is inclined to suggest that, if anything, Father Tucci has underestimated the newness of its approach to the Church's role in the contemporary world or, if you will, the newness of the "image" of the Church which it so dramatically projects. Whereas for generations—if not for centuries—the Church, however understandably, had been mistrustful and suspicious of the "others," who were looked upon as actual or potential enemies, and had systematically deprecated other peoples' values as potentially danger-ous, she did an almost complete about-face during the Council. In *Gaudium et Spes* she "broke the siege, took one leap across the chasm, and became open for dialogue with the contemporary world."

Father Tucci is not alone in attributing this radical transformation, in large measure, to the seminal influence of Pope John XXIII. Indeed it has become commonplace to say in the words of the British historian, E.E.Y. Hales, that the optimism of the latter's encyclicals and other public pronouncements— an optimism which was classically recapitulated in his opening address at the first session of the Council—was *sui generis*. "The note of alarm and admoni-tion," says Hales, "is scarcely audible" in John's pronouncements on the problems of the contemporary world. Instead, he continues, "Roncalli turns to those movements which are deserving of praise and commends them; he picks out those bodies which need encouragement . . . and encourages them. . . . He is, by his own admission, an optimist; he is glad to point to what is good; he thinks in many ways the world is a better place than it was; he thinks there have been enough admonitions, and they have not been very effective. He is shocked only by the prophets of gloom."

Pope John himself said as much in his opening address at the first session of the Council, and, happily, the Fathers of the Council took his words to heart, particularly in *Gaudium et Spes,* thus substituting "the medicine of mercy," as prescribed by John, for the unrelieved severity which, a century ago, had prompted the Holy See, in the last of eighty condemned propositions in the Syllabus of Errors, to reject out of hand any suggestion that "the Roman Pontiff can and ought to reconcile and harmonize himself with progress, with liberalism, and with modern civilization."

Thus to contrast *Gaudium et Spes* with the Syllabus of Errors as dramatic symbols of their respective eras in the modern history of the Church, is not to make light of the problems which bedeviled the reign of Pius IX and ultimately prompted him, with his back to the wall, to fulminate against the world of 1864 in the latter document, nor is it to ignore the providential changes which made it not only possible, but absolutely necessary for Vatican II to take a much more conciliatory approach in the former document a century later. Whatever of that, it is fair to say, in the words of Ernesto Balducci, that, with Pope John's opening address at the Council,

a whole era of the history of the Church is solemnly . . . declared closed, and that from that moment the Church has achieved a new consciousness of herself. The Conciliar assembly, receiving such a peremptory warning (against undue severity in its judgment of the contemporary world), far from feeling dismay, rejoiced to hear itself thus freed from a fear complex, and from perplexities concerning possible schemes for the future . . . The voice of her Head . . . brought to the light of day her unconscious intuitions and turned the inarticulate depths of her aspirations into an explicit idea. And in this way there began to take shape, in the most fitting place and manner, a new era of Christianity, which we might call the ecumenical era.

Father Balducci, who is one of Pope John's more perceptive biographers, is using the word ecumenical here, not in the limited sense of Catholic-Protestant relations, but in the much broader sense of a continuing and completely open-ended dialogue between the Church and the contemporary world.

Balducci's emphasis on the crucial importance of Pope John's keynote address at the opening session of the Council is well taken, but, as he himself has pointed out, too little attention has been paid thus far to John's Apostolic Constitution, *Humanae Salutis*, which antedated the Council by almost a year. It was in this earlier document that John not only formally convoked the Council, but quite explicitly noted that, in his judgment, it should proceed according to the methodology recommended to the Church by Christ Himself. "Indeed," he said, "we make ours the recommendation of Jesus that one should know how to distinguish the 'signs of the times' (Mt. 16:4), and we seem to see now, in the midst of so much darkness, a few indications which augur well for the fate of the Church and of humanity."

Again it can be said that the Fathers of the Council took Pope John's words to heart and willingly adopted his recommendation to proceed, not deductively —as their own philosophical and theological training might have tempted them to do—but inductively, if you will, carefully striving, under the guidance of the Holy Spirit, to read and to decipher the hidden meaning of the principal signs of the times. It was to be expected, of course, that they would take particular pains to employ this methodology in *Gaudium et Spes*. The Church's task, they pointed out in the preface to the Constitution, is to give witness to the truth, to love and not to sit in judgement on the world, to serve and not to be served. "To carry out such a task," they hastened to add in a special Introductory Statement on the situation of mankind in the contemporary world, "the Church has always had the duty of scrutinizing the signs of the times and of interpreting them in the light of the Gospel. Thus, in language intelligible to each generation, she can respond to the perennial questions which men ask about this present life and the life to come, and about the relationship of the one to the other. We must therefore recognize and understand the world in which we live, its expectations, its longings and its often dramatic characteristics." Immediately thereafter they sketched some of the main features of the modern world, and then—and only then—did they begin their "conversation" with the world about its problems and its hopes and aspirations.

The specifics of this conversation are too numerous even to list, much less to analyze, in this brief commentary. Moreover, for present purposes, they are perhaps less important than the tone or the spirit of the conversation and the methodology which underlies it. The tone and the spirit of the conversation, as suggested above, are, after the example of Pope John, consistently positive and constructive and—in the best sense of a word which can easily be misunderstood—optimistic. Indeed there are those who feel that *Gaudium et Spes* is theologically too optimistic, in the sense that it fails to give due weight to the "mystery of iniquity" and the continuing power of evil in the world. This point was made several times by some of the Protestant participants in the University of Notre Dame's Spring, 1966, International Theological Conference.

Meanwhile, by coincidence, Pope Paul VI has addressed himself to this problem in one of his weekly audiences. "The Church," His Holiness pointed out, "knows that in the world—that is to say, in our human reality—there are many faults and many evils. It does not ignore all the arguments for modern pessimism. . . . But we cannot forget the optimism—we should say the love— with which the Church of the Council looks to the world in which it finds itself."

Pope Paul's meditation on Christian optimism brings to mind a similar statement made by Pope John XXIII at the end of the first session of the Council.

On Christmas day, 1962, Pope John, who may have had a premonition that death was close upon him and that he was celebrating what was to be his last Christmas on earth, remarked in a public audience that "All days are good for being born, all days are good for dying." The truth of these very simple and characteristically tranquil words, which tell us so much about the inner life of one of the truly great men of our times, will be admitted without argument, not only by Christians, but likewise, presumably, by all those who, though not professing the Christian faith, nevertheless believe in the reality of life everlasting. Pope John, then, was perfectly correct. Obviously all days are good for being born, all days are good for dying.

Yet, from the purely human point of view, we of this generation are fortunate beyond measure to have been born in this particular era and, more specifically, to have lived long enough to witness the Council which John himself was inspired by God to convene and which future historians will undoubtedly look back upon as one of the most important events in the history of Christianity.

If Pope Pius XI—in spite of the fact that he witnessed the rise of both communism and fascism—could say that he thanked God every day for the privilege of having lived in this century, with all of its problems, achievements, and opportunities, surely we can say the same thing with even greater reason.

Pope John remarked in his historic address at the opening session of Vatican Council II,

In the present order of things kind Providence is leading us to a new order of human relationships which, through the work of men, and for the most part in excess of the hopes, is directed toward the fulfillment of their noblest and most unhoped for plans. . . . In our times (he continued) the Bride of Christ prefers to make use of the medicine of mercy rather than of more severe remedies; she thinks that rather than issue condemnations she should try to satisfy the needs of today by proving the truth of her teachings.

As noted above, more than one qualified observer has remarked that with these words of Pope John—which set the tone of Vatican Council II and were faithfully reflected in its deliberations and in the style and content of all its official documents—a whole era in the history of the Church was declared closed, and a new era was ushered in. Some have described this new era as the age of dialogue: dialogue within the Church, dialogue between the Church and other religious bodies, and, last but not least, dialogue between the Church and the modern world.

The dialogue between the Church and the modern world, as we know, was treated in *Gaudium et Spes*. This Constitution was commonly referred to during the last two sessions of the council as Schema 13, although, in point of fact, it was really Schema 16, the last of the Council documents. Superstition has it that 13 is an unlucky number, but I venture to suggest that in the case of the Council it was a very lucky number indeed. History will undoubtedly say that the Council's decision to adopt the so-called Schema 13 on the Church in the Modern World—a decision which was not easily arrived at—was truly providential.

My reason for saying this is that, had the Fathers decided to concentrate exclusively on the internal reform of the Church and to say nothing at all about the Church's relation to the modern world, the Council would have been, not a failure, to be sure, but, at best, only a partial success. It also would have been a grave disappointment to the world, which is probably more eager today than ever before in modern times to begin a fruitful dialogue with the Church.

What a tragedy it would have been if the Church had failed to take advantage of this long-awaited opportunity to engage in fraternal conversation with mankind, which, in the words of the Council, "though stricken with wonder at its own discoveries and its power . . . often raises anxious questions about the current trend of the world, about the place and role of man in the universe, about the meaning of its individual and collective strivings, and about the ultimate destiny of reality and of humanity."

Thanks be to God, the Council not only elected to begin this belated dialogue with the modern world, but did so, as Pope Paul VI remarked on the closing day of the Council, "with the accommodating friendly voice of pastoral charity." Its desire, His Holiness pointed out, "has been to be heard and understood by everyone; it has not merely concentrated on intellectual understanding but has also sought to express itself in simple, up-to-date, conversational style, derived from actual experience and a cordial approach which make it more vital, attractive and persuasive; it has spoken to modern man as he is."

"The Council," as His Holiness remarked in a more recent statement on *Gaudium et Spes,* "considers the world in all its realities with loving attention, capable of discovering everywhere traces of God and therefore of goodness, beauty and truth." This is not only its philosophy, but also its theology—a theology of profound Christian optimism.

Given the optimistic tone and the forward-looking spirit of the Constitution, why, it might be asked, are so many optimistic and forward-looking Catholics somewhat disappointed with the document? One reason is, I suspect, that they do not fully understand its purpose and the methodology employed by the Commission which was responsible for drafting it. This particular conciliar document is, by definition, a "Pastoral" Constitution. Its purpose is not to say the last word on current problems from the point of view of Catholic theology, but rather to call attention to certain practical steps that men of good will can take to make the world a better place in which to live.

Bishop Mark McGrath of Panama who played a prominent role on the Commission which drafted the Constitution, explained all this to the Council Fathers when he presented his "relatio" or introductory statement on the first part of the Constitution. Because of the very nature of the document, he pointed out, it was necessary that the real condition of today's world be described, at least in a general way, before any judgements were made about it. This inductive or descriptive methodology, he said, was set forth in the introductory chapter of the Constitution and was followed throughout the entire document. Finally, the Bishop noted, "the very newness of many of the questions proposed and their diversity . . . impose limits on our document. General principles, either doctrinal or moral, are proposed, which principles frequently do not touch upon completely concrete solutions either because the problems involved require more mature examination, or because they must be considered by the faithful in a particular way in each region, under the guidance of their pastors."

The same point is made in the text of the Constitution itself. It is specifically stated that the program outlined in the Constitution is a very general one and deliberately so, given the immense variety of situations and forms of human culture in the world. "Indeed," we are told, "while it presents teaching already accepted in the Church, the program will have to be followed up and amplified since it sometimes deals with matters in a constant state of development. Still, we have relied on the word of God and the spirit of the Gospel. Hence we entertain the hope that many of our proposals will prove to be of substantial benefit to everyone, especially after they have been adapted to individual nations and mentalities by the faithful under the guidance of their pastors."

The Constitution's explicit reference to the fact that mankind must search for answers to the complex questions of the modern world and that the Church wishes only to be of service to mankind in carrying out this search was echoed in Bishop McGrath's introductory statement on the methodology of the document. Thus, the Bishop stated, the introductory chapter of the Constitution "ought to serve the purpose of the entire schema: namely, to speak to the entire world, with a serious study of the problems which now concern its peoples, so that we may enter into a sincere dialogue with them, bringing forth the light of Christ, for the solace, strength, peace, and more abundant life of all men in God."

The tone of the entire Constitution, then, derives from this purpose, namely, to enter into a dialogue with the modern world, which is quite a different thing from telling the modern world how to "solve" all of the specific problems with which it is confronted. Faithful to the spirit of Pope John XXIII, the document refrains from sterile criticism of individuals and institutions and concentrates singlemindedly on its pastoral task of encouraging and motivating men of good will to move not from A to Z but from A to B to C.

In closing, I would add a further word about the spirit of charity which permeates the Constitution and which, hopefully, will characterize our common efforts to implement its recommendations in the practical order. The Fathers did more than write about charity in *Gaudium et Spes* and various other conciliar documents; they exemplified it by their conduct in the Council. Specifically, they scrupulously avoided anything even remotely resembling chauvinism or exaggerated nationalism, and also kept completely clear of divisive political issues.

As a matter of fact, I do not recall having heard a single political speech either on the council floor in St. Peter's basilica or in any of the pre-conciliar or conciliar commission meetings which I was privileged to attend.

The Fathers made every effort to preserve the unity of the Council and, while on a number of issues they could not help but reflect their own cultural values and their own national and even political loyalties and traditions, they scrupulously refrained from saying or doing anything that smacked of cultural intolerance or narrow-minded nationalism. In a word, they conducted themselves in Rome as they rightly expect the clergy and the faithful to conduct themselves at home—i.e., with sincere respect for legitimate difference of opinion, not only in economic and political life, but also within the life of the Church itself.

Their advice to the clergy and the faithful in this regard is to be found in several different sections of the Pastoral Constitution on the Church in the Modern World. In the chapter on "The Life of the Political Community," the Fathers remind us that legitimate differences of opinion with regard to temporal affairs are to be acknowledged and that those citizens who, either as individuals or as members of groups, honestly defend their own legitimate opinions in the temporal order are to be respected.

Similarly, in the chapter on "The Community of Men," they state that "reverence and charity are to be extended to those who, in social and political matters or even in religious matters, think and act differently than we do; the more intimately, in reverence and charity, we come to understand their way of thinking, the more easily will we be able to enter into dialogue with them."

Finally, in the round-up chapter of the schema, we are told that "above all in the Church itself we are to promote mutual esteem, reverence, and harmony, acknowledging every legitimate difference of opinion . . ." We are to do this for the purpose of developing "an ever more fruitful dialogue among all those who make up the People of God, whether they be pastors (bishops and priests) or members of the faithful. The things which unite the faithful are stronger than those which divide them. Let there be unity in essentials, freedom in those matters which are doubtful, and in all things charity."

This last injunction, referring, as it does, to the particular problem of unity within the Church itself, is most timely in view of the controversy which arose towards the end of the Council over the decision of the Council Fathers not to condemn, or even to identify, Marxist or Communist atheism by name in its general treatment, in *Gaudium et Spes,* of modern atheism. Some 450 Council Fathers signed a petition calling upon the Council to reverse this decision. They were of the opinion that Communism should be clearly identified in the Constitution, and they drafted an amendment which would have put the Council on record as solemnly rejecting Communism by name "not only because it is contaminated by atheism, but also because it has been declared intrinsically perverse by the magisterium (official teaching authority) of the Church on account of the . . . most serious errors with which it is indissolubly connected."

The overwhelming majority of the Council Fathers were convinced that it was unnecessary and would be unwise for the Council to adopt this amendment. I happen to share this opinion, but I hasten to add that I respect the sincerity of those who drafted the amendment. Surely they had a perfect right to push for its adoption by every legitimate parliamentary means at their disposal. On the other hand, I think they ought to dissociate themselves unequivocally from the intemperate extremists who have predictably jumped on their bandwagon and are saying pointblank that the council's decision not to condemn Communism in *Gaudium et Spes* or in any of its other official documents is proof that the "heresy" of neo-modernism (in Italian, "progressismo") is widespread throughout the Church and even seems to have had a stranglehold on the Council itself.

Thus far, thanks be to God, this sort of heresy-hunting, which could simply be laughed off as a bad joke if it were not so vicious in tone—has been confined to a relatively small group of fanatics. Let us hope and pray that it will not become contagious. God help us all if it ever catches on among ordinary Catholics. The post-conciliar Church is going to have enough trouble without being torn asunder by internal hatred and strife. What she will need more than almost anything else for the indefinite future is "unity in essentials, freedom in those matters which are doubtful, and in all things charity."

V/DECREE ON THE INSTRUMENTS OF SOCIAL COMMUNICATION

Decree on the Instruments of Social Communication

✠ HISTORICAL INTRODUCTION

The history of the Decree on the Instruments of Social Communication, promulgated in the public session of December 4, 1963, has been considered by most American conciliar participants and observers as something just a little short of tragedy. Its defenders point with a degree of justifiable pride to the sentence in paragraph five which states: "Therefore, in society men have a right to information, in accord with the circumstances in each case, about matters concerning individuals or the community."

Those who think less kindly about the Decree, however, see in it a great danger of misinterpretation. They fear that it might well be considered as a means of imposing ecclesiastical censorship, as an instruction imposing impossible conditions upon Catholics involved in the communications industry and a weapon to be used by some narrow-minded cleric who wishes to resurrect at some present or future date the most virulent type of puritanism in the realm of the arts. These fears have already been expressed elsewhere, and their discussion is beyond the scope of this essay.*

Cardinal Cento introduced the schema concerning the instruments of social communication on November 23, 1962 during the twenty-fifth general congregation. In his introductory remarks he mentioned that the schema had been drafted by a special secretariat presided over by Archbishop Martin O'Connor, at that time rector of Rome's North American College and for fourteen years president of the Pontifical Commission for Motion Pictures, Radio and Television. The original schema consisted of 45 pages and 114 paragraphs which would, by the time of its promulgation, be reduced to 13 pages and 24 paragraphs.

It consisted of an introduction, four parts and eleven chapters which represented what at that time was considered by many as the worst possible attitude of the Catholic Church toward the communications industry. It reflected, perhaps more than any other schemata presented to the Council Fathers, the epitome of the siege mentality that had dominated the Catholic Church for

---

* For a detailed account confer: Novak, Michael, *The Open Church,* The Macmillan Company, New York, 1962, pp. 260–65; and Brown, Robert McAfee, *Observer in Rome,* Doubleday & Company, Inc., Garden City, New York, pp. 168–172.

almost four hundred years. From the moment that it was introduced on the Council floor it was evident that it would be in for serious trouble. The fact that it was changed from a constitution to a decree is significant. Even more significant is the fact that it survived at all. A future historian might very easily prove that even the Decree would not have survived if the Council Fathers were allowed sufficient time to reflect upon the ramifications their votes would have for future generations.

During the next three congregations, 56 Fathers made their observations on the communications schema. Their general remarks were directed against the schema because it was too long, too clerical and restrictive. Bishop Sanschagrin of Amos, Canada, used the occasion to complain about directives of the Holy See being released to the news media before local bishops had received any communications about them. In this respect he received a great deal of sympathy from the American bishops. The Archbishop of Siena, Ismaele Mario Castellano, saw fit to use the occasion to launch an attack against the Index of Forbidden Books. He was, however, the only prelate to broach the subject on the Council floor. Perhaps the finest address on the subject was delivered by Cardinal Léger. He said:

> The power of modern means of communication is so great that it is ridiculous to try to insulate people against it; rather we must adopt it fearlessly, putting an end to the negative type of criticism characteristic of so many churchmen in the past.

Cardinal Spellman is the only American known to have delivered and submitted observations on this schema. As the ordinary of the city which is the heart of a world-wide communications industry, it seemed only fitting that he should speak on the subject. In his address on the floor of the Council, Cardinal Spellman approved the schema:

> This schema is pleasing insofar as it points out the right of the Church to use these instruments and gives the reasons for it, especially the propagation and explanation of the truth and Christian teaching. It is also satisfactory insofar as it affirms the grave duty of civil authority of recognizing the nature of the common good and setting up just laws, lest, by the base use of these instruments, public morals be damaged.

The Cardinal of New York also reflected in his remarks his own native desire to leave the details of the Church's communications efforts "to that particular organ of the Roman Curia established by Pius XII and enlarged by John XXIII." As the best publicized American prelate, he undoubtedly spoke from personal experience when he concluded his remarks by saying, "Our experience in the United States of America teaches that wise men, Catholics and non-Catholics, can collaborate so that these new inventions are put to the service of men as well as the common good of society."

Cardinal Spellman also submitted six written interventions on the subject of the mass media. In one intervention he approved the positive approach of the original schema's preface which "acknowledges that these means are the best helps furnished humanity, since they contribute greatly, if correctly used, to the development of each man and to the enrichment of human society intellectually and morally, and especially to the propagation and strengthening of the kingdom of God." In another intervention he urged the discussion of principles needed to solve such questions that arise concerning the right to information, freedom of art and the treatment of moral evil. In the same piece he objected to the "negative formulae," such as, "If anyone should say . . . he is at variance with Catholic teaching." The Cardinal bluntly stated, "I do not accept these formulations. . . . For Catholics who listen to the words of the Council Fathers as sons hear the words of their Holy Mother, these formulations—too negative and juridical—are not necessary. These formulations could obscure the obligations which are primarily positive and which all Catholics have to strive especially to channel these new discoveries toward the use of mankind and the good of society."

The Cardinal again showed his respect for the proper office of the Holy See when he took exception, in another written intervention, to one of the directives of the schema. He wrote:

> . . . it is not the proper responsibility of the Ecumenical Council of the Universal Church to treat of the particular and temporary rules which have been adapted with precision to the various situations in the modern world. For example, the order establishing a "day" of education and prayer on this behalf, which is to be observed throughout the world, and the collecting of a fund for this same purpose, should have been directed by the competent office of the Holy See rather than by the Ecumenical Council.

In another intervention Cardinal Spellman suggested that the press be given more consideration by the commission responsible for this schema. At the same time he felt "an innovation is neither necessary nor useful" by establishing another office for motion pictures, radio and television. He praised the work of Archbishop O'Connor's pontifical commission and felt it was especially suitable because it was so intimately related through its membership with the other congregations of the Curia. He further singled out for praise the existing offices concerned with motion pictures, radio, television and decent reading in the United States and felt that, if further norms and instructions were necessary, they "should better be promulgated by the competent office of the Holy See."

The questions of freedom of information, freedom of art and the description of moral evil were also mentioned in another of the Cardinal's interventions. He penned the following warning:

> . . . let the Council Fathers beware lest they forget the contingent and transitory character of these means which are easily modified, evolved and transformed and which even at times pass into obsolesence, while previously unknown new means spring up and come into prominence. It is not the task of the Ecumenical Council to elaborate upon these exceedingly particular circumstances of today so that the instructions of the Council could be interpreted differently in different regions and that the statutes of the Council would not last long into the future.

In his concluding written observation, Cardinal Spellman again suggested that the conclusion of the schema should repeat "the invitation to all men of good will to strive with the Christian faithful in turning these new inventions toward the use of men and the good of society."

The Council Fathers, however, were not very much interested in the schema. The confrontation of liberal and conservative forces, as well as the Pope's personal intervention, during the debates on divine revelation were still very much the talk of the town. At the time, that issue seemed much more important than the present discussion concerning the mass media. The stories and rumors—and counter-rumors—issuing from the Lateran University and the Pontifical Biblical Institute were more exciting than any serious discussion on the right to information, the role of public opinion in the Church and the presentation of evil as a valid art form. At the time few Council participants felt that these latter questions were of much value for the Church's confrontation with the world, compared with the comparatively intramural discussions concerning the sources of revelation. The Bible was a subject with which they had some familiarity, whereas most of them knew and seemed to care even less about the broader issue of communications in a pluralistic world. The distribution of the schemata on the Blessed Virgin Mary and the Church on the same day on which the discussion on social communications was inaugurated proved to be too much of a distraction to many of the Council Fathers. Many of them spent a good deal of the next two and a half congregations examining these schemata rather than reflecting upon the schema under discussion.

The sentiment of many American bishops was expressed by one of them who commented on the congregation which discussed the subject of communications. "As I sat there," he said, "my mind went back to the opening line of Cicero against Cataline, and a paraphrase seemed appropriate: 'How long, O Council Fathers, will you try our patience?' Maybe there was mental telepathy, but a few minutes later a speaker began his remarks, not with the customary "Patres Conciliares," but "Patres Patientissimi!"

An American bishop, commenting on the same congregation stated simply, "It was very dull today. That fact was reflected by the number of Fathers who left their places. At 11:30 less than half of the seats in the aula were occupied! I am sure it was the boredom of the meeting as much as the expresso at the coffee bar which caused this mass movement."

When a vote on the communications schema was asked for by the General Secretary during the twenty-seventh congregation, its outcome was predictable. The proposal submitted to vote stipulated that the schema would be sent back to the commission to be shortened and to be more clearly delineated, separating the principles from practical matters. The latter would be left to the Pontifical Commission on Communications to incorporate into a pastoral instruction to be issued after the Council. The results of the preliminary vote were 2,138 favorable, 15 unfavorable and 7 invalid ballots.

The schema was revised between the first and second session and brought back to the Council floor during the seventy-fourth congregation, November 25, 1963. Previous to that date two incidents occurred which were significant inasmuch as they did not accompany the voting of any other conciliar vote. On November 16, three American journalists, John Cogley, Robert Kaiser and Michael Novak, issued a statement of objections to the schema. Their statement was given added weight by the counter-signature of four prominent theologians, one being Father John Courtney Murray, S.J. Their statement of protest received wide distribution among the conciliar Fathers. The second incident occurred on the steps of St. Peter's basilica on the morning of November 25. Several priests, under the direction of Auxiliary Bishop Joseph Reuss of Mainz, Germany, were distributing a petition signed by twenty-five Council Fathers, urging a negative vote on the acceptance of the communications schema. This resulted in a rather unseemly confrontation between the Secretary General, Archbishop Felici, and Bishop Reuss as well as a subsequent confusing announcement by Cardinal Tisserant within the Council hall. He denounced this action as unworthy of the Council, but, unfortunately, most of the Fathers did not even know what he was talking about.

Nonetheless, the final vote of approval was taken during this congregation with 1,598 voting approval and 503 disapproval. The vote taken during the public session in which the Pope promulgated the decree was 1,960 against 164. Thus the Decree on the Instruments of Social Communications has the distinction of being the document of the Second Vatican Council receiving the largest negative vote both within a working congregation as well as in the public session of promulgation.

At that public session one American journalist summed up the sentiments of many. "The damage is done," he said. "Now we live with a tragedy."

Decree on the Instruments of Social Communication

✠ INTERVENTION

FRANCIS CARDINAL SPELLMAN, 23 *November, 1962*

The instruments of social communication are rightly and justly dealt with in the holy Vatican Council. All wise men recognize their very great power either for good or for evil. This schema is pleasing insofar as it points out the right of the Church to use these instruments, and gives the reasons for it, especially the propagation and explanation of the truth and the Christian teaching. It is also satisfactory insofar as it affirms the grave duty of civil authority of recognizing the nature of the common good and setting up just laws, lest, by the base use of these instruments, public morals be damaged.

The instruments of social communication, because of the inventions of the technical arts, make daily progress: they evolve and are easily changed and transformed. It is not the task of the Ecumenical Council to treat of overly particular questions in these matters, lest the decrees of the Council have no value later on.

The schema deals with ecclesiastical discipline and order in the use of the instruments of social communication. The greater part of this should be left to that particular organ of the Roman Curia established by Pius XII and enlarged by John XXIII into a stable and permanent office with increased authority. The schema deals with certain instruments of social communication considered singly, namely the press, the cinema, radio, television and the rest; this seems to be too drawn out, overly particular things are developed and repetitions abound.

In the prologue to this schema an invitation to all men of good will is very well presented. Our experience in the United States of America teaches that wise men, Catholics and non-Catholics, can collaborate so that these new inventions are put to the service of men as well as the common good of society. It seems to be most opportune to repeat this invitation in the text of this constitution.

Decree on the Instruments of Social Communication
✠ COMMENTARY *by Rev. Edward Duff, S.J.*

No one can choose the time of his birth nor escape the consequences of its cir-cumstances. The Decree on the Instruments of Social Communications was discussed and promulgated before the Council began to address itself to the schema on the role of the Church in the contemporary world, before it con-sidered the nature and scope of the lay apostolate, before, indeed, it had clari-fied its understanding of the inner reality of the Church itself. The Decree, then, represents a stage in Catholicism's evolving attitude toward the secular order and its institutions.

Lacking the affirmative attitude toward the modern world of Pope John XXIII, one developed and deepened by Pope Paul VI, the Decree's orientation is ambivalent and ambiguous. It views the instruments of communication of an industrialized society (one, incidentally, which developed outside the inspira-tion of Christianity), with awe and, perhaps, envy. Mindful of their vast in-fluence, its misgivings yield often to a minatory tone. Moreover, a consciousness of the divine missionary imperative of spreading the Gospel produces a sense of proprietorship over these techniques. In short, the viewpoint of the Decree was not notably affected by the hope of Pope Paul: "Let the world know this: the Church looks to the world with profound understanding, with sincere admira-tion and with a sincere intention not of conquering it, but of serving it, not of despising it, but of appreciating it, not of condemning it, but of strengthening and serving it."

It is important to remember, however, that the Decree, as promulgated, is only one-fourth the length of the document originally presented to the Council Fathers. It may be argued, then, that completeness of exposition was sacrificed to brevity. That the schema was prepared exclusively by ecclesiastics is not contested; that these clerics were, for the most part, representatives of national offices for the moral surveillance of motion pictures is often revealed by the text itself as it is demonstrated by the successive plaques outside the office in charge of the Decree: Pontificia Commissione per la Cinematographia, Ponti-ficia Commissione per la Cinematographia, la Radio et la Televisione, and (currently) Pontificia Commissione per le Communicationi Sociali. The Decree on the Instruments of Social Communication is palpably a continuation of the encyclical *Vigilante Cura* of June 29, 1936, and of *Miranda Prorsus* of September 8, 1957, neither of which concerned itself with the press.

Finally, it should be noted that the Church herself has learned much in the course of the Council about the world of mass media. Reviewing the N.C.W.C. *Council Daybook*, Bishop Thomas K. Gorman of Dallas-Fort Worth, former episcopal chairman of the N.C.W.C. Press Department, spoke of "the progress from an almost stupid and impossible official attempt at secrecy to a wise opening of the door to honest, complete reporting." The salutary influence of the mass media in spotlighting, for hundreds of millions, an internationally significant event has become as evident as the perils of a lubricious movie seen in a darkened theater. On November 25, 1963, the day the Decree received its definite vote, the funeral of President Kennedy was televised. "Never in the history of humanity," observed Père Emile Gabel, A.A., Secretary of the International Union of the Catholic Press, "were so many nations at the same moment called to question themselves on the future of a people and the peace of the world. Never before have so many followed the body of a man to his grave and shared the grief of his widow." Perhaps even more significant was the minute-by-minute television coverage of Pope Paul's historic visit to the United Nations and the subsequent special spreads in the pictorial magazines of at least the Western world. There was in ecclesiastical circles no diffidence before the possibilities of the mass media on this occasion.

Structurally, the Decree is divided into an introduction (indicating the possibilities for good and evil of the instruments of communication), two chapters (one dogmatic, the other pastoral) and a two-paragraph appendix which promises that the "Secretariat for the Supervision of Publications and Entertainments" will issue a pastoral instruction covering the points of the Decree and inviting the collaboration of all in order that the instruments of communications may serve solely the good of society.

"The Teaching of the Church," as the first chapter is entitled, asserts the missionary mandate of the Church and its consequent "inherent right to have at its disposal and to employ any of these media insofar as they are necessary or useful for the instruction of Christians and all its efforts for the welfare of souls." The moral norms controlling the functioning and utilization of the mass media are listed. Three questions are considered.

The right to information is vindicated with the notation that "what is communicated should always be true and complete, within the bounds of justice and charity" with "full respect for the laws of morality and for the legitimate rights and dignity of the individual." That "the right to freedom in searching for truth and in expressing and communicating his opinion" is, as *Pacem in Terris* had declared, a natural right and, therefore, "universal, inviolable and inalienable" is not indicated in the Decree. Nor is any allusion made to freedom of information within the Church, although Pope Pius XII had mentioned the topic in his address to the Third International Congress of the Catholic Press, declaring that the Church is "a living body, and something would be lacking in its life were public opinion to be missing in it, a deficiency for which both pastors and the faithful would be to blame."

The relationship of art and morality is dispatched in a paragraph: ". . . the Council proclaims that all must hold the absolute primacy of the objective moral order, that is, this order by itself surpasses and fittingly coordinates all other spheres of human affairs—the arts not excepted—even though they be endowed with notable dignity." The following paragraph, perhaps significantly, discusses the portrayal of moral evil and counsels moral restraint lest "base desires" be aroused. Nowhere in the Decree is there advertence to advertising with its blatant appeal to covetousness, also a moral evil.

Public opinion is to be guided and controlled through a multiplicity of forces. The choice of the consumer, alerted by the "judgments of authorities competent in these matters," is mentioned first. Parents and teachers have a duty of vigilance. "The principal moral responsibility" is assigned to the producers and sellers, the newsmen, film directors, magazine editors, critics, etc.; self-policing of the professions through the adoption of a code of "sound moral practice" is urged. The role of "protecting and safeguarding true and just freedom of information," of encouraging "spiritual values, culture and the fine arts," as well as of "protecting the rights of those who wish to use the media" is assigned to "the public authority," a conception of a welfare State unfamiliar to Americans, but conceivably pertinent for countries with *Ministres des Beaux Arts* and State-operated radio and television.

The Decree's second chapter is devoted to pastoral implications. It is an earnest exhortation to "all the children of the Church" at every level for a great and common effort to exploit the immense possibilities of the media of communication for the apostolate. The Catholic press should be fostered, decent films are to be supported, Catholics even joining in their production and distribution. Catholic television programs and even Catholic stations, "where it may be necessary," are to be promoted. All of this supposes a considerable financial outlay, but the Decree does not hesitate to speak of an obligation "to maintain and assist Catholic newspapers, periodicals and film projects, radio and television programs and stations whose principal objective is to spread and defend the truth and foster Christian influence in human society."

To emphasize the importance of the issue, one day a year is to be set aside by the national hierarchies when "the faithful are to be instructed in this regard." And to assure a more permanent concern, national offices, to be affiliated with the Roman secretariat, are to be organized in each country "to see to it that the consciences of the faithful are properly instructed with respect to these media." The succeeding sentence raised questions in the minds of some lay Catholic journalists as to their professional independence and their loyalty to their employers: "Likewise they should foster and guide whatever is done by Catholics in these areas."

In these affirmative, even aggressive, declarations on the use of the instruments of social communication, the Church has clearly come out from behind the battlements. The retreat from the modern world which characterized much of the nineteenth century is reversed. And yet some of the cultural conditioning of that combat underlies parts of the Decree. The emphasis on Catholic newspapers and even Catholic television stations seems of a piece with Catholic trade unions, created to protect the institutional interests of the Church in its struggle with continental liberalism and the ideology of Marx. It risks turning the means of communication into instruments of a Catholic *agitprop* and of suggesting a Catholic "party line" on all topics. The authors of the Decree would presumably be uncomfortable on reading the heading over the editorial page of an American diocesan weekly: "A" Catholic, not "The" Catholic, Viewpoint. But, then, the contribution of an American expert in the elaboration of the Decree is not known.

The most noteworthy feature of the Decree is its recognition of the importance of technical competence for anyone hoping to be useful in the general field of communications. Earnestness, good will, ecclesiastical mandate, none of these are adequate substitutes.

And if the whole picture of the Church's involvement, as a writer in the September, 1965, *American Ecclesiastical Review* declared, "is one of confusion and paradox," the causes "are intimately ours." For as Monsignor Francis J. Lally, editor of the Boston *Pilot* told the Pittsburgh convention of the Catholic Press Association in May, 1964, we have not thought about the theology of the matter. The Decree on the Instruments of Social Communications is a beginning and an invitation.

VI/DECREE ON ECUMENISM

VI/DEGREE ON ECUMENISM

Decree on Ecumenism

✠ HISTORICAL INTRODUCTION

"The Church of the Council no longer wants to be an impregnable fortress with slits in its walls for observing the enemy, but a spacious house with large windows from which one can look out into all the areas of human living." So wrote Father Karl Rahner, S.J., shortly after the Council had opened.

No single group of men achieved that change in ecclesiastical mentality more than the members of the Secretariat for the Promotion of Christian Unity. The Decree on Ecumenism is as much a tribute to the diligence of these men, under the leadership of Augustin Cardinal Bea, S.J., as it is to the transformation that took place in the thinking of the Council Fathers as a group in the relatively brief period of four years.

This is not to say that there was no ecumenical spirit at work in the Catholic Church before this time. Pope John, by the force of his own winning personality, had unleashed the spirit of Christian love and brotherhood from the very first day he ascended the throne of Peter. A few brave Catholic theologians, such as Fathers Yves Congar, Thomas Sartory and Gustave Weigel, had been the Catholic precursors in the ecumenical field.

When the Council Fathers converged on Rome in the autumn of 1962, they had only two documents, and the promise of a third, that treated ecumenism. The first document was the 16-page schema concerning the unity of the Church entitled "That All May Be One"; the second was chapter eleven in the proposed schema on the Church. The first was drafted by the Commission for Eastern Churches and was concerned mostly with the Catholic churches of the Oriental rites. The second, although containing much valuable material, failed to grasp the existential demands of ecumenism. A third document, the schema prepared by the Secretariat for Promoting Christian Unity, had not yet been printed or distributed to the Council Fathers.

This schema "That All May Be One" was introduced during the closing days of the first session and was discussed on the floor during four congregations by 53 speakers. Finally the schema was voted upon by the assembly after the Presidency proposed the following recommendation:

285

Having finished the examination of the draft decree on the unity of the Church, the Fathers approve the draft as a document containing the universal truths of the faith and as a sign of respect and good will towards the separated brethren of the East. In accordance with the remarks and proposals made in the Council hall, however, this decree is to be welded into a single document together with the Decree on Ecumenism and the chapter on the same subject contained in the schema on the Dogmatic Constitution on the Church.

The Fathers approved the motion by a vote of 2,068 to 36. Thus the schema on ecumenism became a document drafted by the unity secretariat in collaboration with the Oriental and theological commissions the first three months of 1963.

American prelates, however, even before and during this first session, had expressed their observations on the subject of ecumenism. In a written intervention submitted as early as August 18, 1959, Archbishop Karl Alter urged the establishment of a permanent commission "whose duty it shall be to study the question of the unity of the Church and, at the same time, propose means by which a reconciliation of the churches which are not in agreement with the Holy See might be accomplished." Taking cognizance of the work of the World Council of Churches, he continued:

Recent meetings held by these groups—which are even called "ecumenical" —have tried to arrive at some kind of unity which arises from merely human ingenuity. They did this by thinking out, either for the common good or for their own, the ways and procedures which would produce some order. Therefore, the unity of the Church, as conceived by them, is something not yet existing, which at this time must be produced. Since this is true, it is fitting to explain again, in new decrees, that the unity of the Church as established by the will of Christ is an organic and supernatural unity which gathers in all the members of the Church of Christ through Christ's grace, which has been communicated with His Mystical Body; and that, further, the true unity of the Church demands as an essential point a unity of doctrine, sacraments and discipline under the divinely constituted authority.

In the same intervention Archbishop Alter urged the discussion of religious liberty, thus being the first American to suggest this issue as one for conciliar action. He wrote:

Not a few non-Catholics fear lest the freedom, which today has been granted to Catholics by certain secular governments for the propagation of their religion, be restricted for the non-Catholics should the Catholics ever become a majority. In order to prove the reasonableness of this fear, these non-Catholics cite the mode of operation in some so-called Catholic countries, where freedom of religious expression is restricted by law. Since this matter has hardly been understood correctly, it appears that we must seek a more accurate definition of the nature of doctrinal tolerance in religious matters, which is different from political or civil tolerance. Further, the Catholic notion of freedom of conscience should have been explained more lucidly. In a country where either many religions or none exist, it would seem better if a religion were altogether free and immune from any force on the part of the government, whether it be physical or legal.

In 1962, Cardinal Spellman offered his suggestions concerning the need of prayer on behalf of Christian unity. His suggestion was well stated in the following words:

> Without a doubt, it seems very desirable that the Holy Synod encourage all Christians to pray more frequently and fervently for Christian unity; let this exhortation be drafted in language imbued with the spirit of evangelical humility and genuine charity, lest—as is well pointed out in the Decree— that which was designed for the promotion of unity be turned away to the destruction of brotherly reconciliation. Above all, there is a need that God's grace increase and multiply the efficacious desire for unity among our separated brothers as well as among ourselves, and thus that the way may be opened for that perfect unity for which Christ our Savior always prayed.

During discussions of unity in the first session, two American bishops of the Eastern rites delivered oral interventions. On November 27, Archbishop Ambrose Senyshyn of the Ukrainian Catholic Archeparchy of Philadelphia said he was generally pleased with the schema, although he wished to make two proposals. He suggested that in the first place, the schema "be placed as a corollary of the Constitution on the Church since this is actually its logical consequence." His second recommendation concerned the means to be employed in seeking unity with the separated brethren. Speaking of the close relationship between the Orthodox churches and the Roman Catholic Church, he said:

> There is no mention in the schema about communication in religious worship (*communicatio in sacris*), specifically with the separated brethren who often feel themselves offended since the same rigid norms for communication in worship are applied to them as to the Protestants. My observation, Venerable Fathers, concerns the sacramentology of the Orthodox which differs greatly from that of the Protestants—and I mean this with no offense. For the Orthodox have a true hierarchy, a true priesthood, they offer a true Mass, they recognize and have the same seven sacraments as we do. Thus it does not seem fitting that we should equate them with Protestants in this respect, as is very often done.

On November 30, Bishop Nicholas Elko of the Diocese of Pittsburgh (Byzantine Rite) also approved the schema generally. He felt it was acceptable because it gave "the fundamental principles on the visibility, indivisibility and unity of the Church with and under Peter" and that it "clearly shows a sense of reverence and sincere and fraternal charity toward our separated brothers." Commenting from personal experience on the keystone of the schema, Bishop Elko stated:

> . . . the schema proposes the basic principle of the jurisdictional power of the successor of Peter. This seems to me the basic principle in the entire schema. Bound to this are pastors and faithful of any rank and dignity, individually and together, by the duty of hierarchical subordination and true obedience not only in matters of faith and morals, but also in matters of universal discipline for the whole Church throughout the world.

> Thus, those who say this schema wants to deceive the good will of our separated brothers are seriously wrong. No. I know from experience. What experience? My experience of a few years ago in talking with the monks of Mount Athos. From them I gathered that today the obstacle to unity is not so much the doctrine of purgatory, or the doctrine concerning the *Filioque*, or the Immaculate Conception, or the Assumption of the Holy Virgin Mary as the dogma of the infallibility and primacy of the Roman Pontiff.

In his oral intervention during the congregation of November 28, the Cardinal of New York added his comments on the schema. He felt that in this schema "the Fathers of the sacred Second Vatican Council invite everyone who assists in the reestablishment of Christian unity to revert to supernatural means." He also asked that all Christians invoke the Virgin Mary's assistance in bringing to fulfillment Christ's prayer "that all may be one."

On April 22, 1963, Pope John XXIII approved the schema on ecumenism as it had been drafted by the Secretariat for Promoting Christian Unity in collaboration with members of the Oriental and theological commissions. Pope John had also ordered that it be distributed through the mails to the Council Fathers. From this point on, the schema was chiefly in the hands of the unity secretariat. Strangely enough, during these early days of work on the schema there was not a single American prelate serving as a member of the Secretariat.

However, one American priest, Father James Cunningham, C.S.P., was a member of the Secretariat, and three other priests from the United States were named consultors: Monsignor John Oesterreicher; Father George Tavard, A.A.; Father Edward Hanahoe, S.A. During the second session two American bishops were elected members of the Secretariat: Bishop Ernest J. Primeau of Manchester and Bishop Charles Helmsing of Kansas City–St. Joseph. Shortly afterwards, Archbishop Lawrence Shehan was appointed to the Secretariat by Pope Paul.

Two Americans served as secretaries: Father John Long, S.J., and Father

Thomas Stransky, C.S.P. Both priests did more, perhaps, than any other Americans to promote a proper understanding of the secretariat and its schema among the American bishops and public through their conferences and individual meetings as well as by their patient, useful and exhausting contacts with the American press corps in Rome. Father Stransky was the second American priest to address the American bishops at their regular weekly meetings during the first session. He spoke to them on November 5, explaining the purpose and work of the Secretariat. One American bishop made the following observation after Father Stransky's speech: "He is young, energetic and extremely well informed on the whole history of ecumenism. His speech was very well received, and he was kept on his feet for quite a while answering questions. It is very obvious that the bishops generally are very much interested in this topic."

On Monday, November 18, during the sixty-ninth congregation of the second session, the schema on ecumenism was introduced on the Council floor by Cardinal Amleto Cicognani, president of the mixed commission that had drafted the document. He was followed immediately by Archbishop Joseph Martin of Rouen who commented on the first three chapters of the schema: the first dealing with the principle of Catholic ecumenism; the second with the practical aspects of ecumenism; and the third with the Christians separated from the Catholic Church. On the following day, plans were changed. Instead of beginning with debates on these chapters, the fourth chapter—concerning the Church's relations with non-Christians and especially the Jews—was introduced by the venerable Cardinal Bea. Immediately the fifth chapter on religious liberty was introduced in one of the inspiring speeches of the Council by Bishop Emile de Smedt who observed: "We hope that it will be possible to complete the discussion and the approbation of this very brief, but very important, decree before the end of this second session." It would be a full two years of intense work and two more sessions before his hope was realized.

The Council Fathers discussed the schema on ecumenism throughout the following eleven congregations, that is, until the end of the second session. Five American bishops were among the 165 speakers on the subject.

The Cardinal of St. Louis was the first American to speak during the sixty-ninth congregation. He said he spoke not only for himself, but for many other American bishops. He was very much pleased with the schema "because it responded well to the necessity of expressing the practical consequences of the *aggiornamento* of the Church." He called it "the final end of the counter-Reformation with its unfortunate polemics" and welcomed it because "it urges us to hasten that day in which all will be one in Christ through prayer, study, dialogue and action." Although Cardinal Ritter had made five distinct observations in his intervention, the one that seemed most pertinent was his observation concerning religious liberty.

Joyfully we received the news of chapter five, namely, on religious liberty, and we await tomorrow's distribution. Without such a declaration, mutual faithfulness would be impossible and a serious dialogue would be precluded. Since we consider religious liberty to be the foundation and prerequisite for ecumenical relations with other Christians, we strongly urge that the tract on this subject be incorporated into the schema before a consideration of the practices of ecumenism. Merely expedient motives should not prompt such a text as being worthy of Council deliberation and ecumenical value. Our declaration is solidly founded on theological principles. We must incorporate considerations on the freedom of the act of faith, on the dignity of the human person and his inviolable conscience, on the total incompetence of civil laws in passing judgment on the Gospel of Christ and its interpretation. Thus this declaration reaffirms the complete independence of the Church from any government in fulfilling her mission.

In another suggestion, Cardinal Ritter sounded a request that would be repeated frequently before the Decree was finally promulgated. "Terminology which is perhaps offensive to our separated brethren," he said, "should be removed in the emendations to be made by the Secretariat. Without a judgment about their Orders and Eucharistic celebration, we strenuously ask that the term 'Church' not be denied these Christian groups which in the text are called 'communities.'"

The first speaker on November 20 was Cardinal Meyer. He stated his approval of the schema, even though acknowledging that it could be strengthened by the observations of the Fathers. He was particularly pleased that chapters four and five remained an integral part, and he added this observation:

There might be some difference of opinion on their place in this schema or another, but it is the opinion of numerous Council Fathers that the subjects of these two chapters are intimately connected with the whole question of ecumenism. Although the text can and should be perfected, it is to be hoped that the entire schema will be approved as it stands.

Bishop Stephen Leven rose on November 26 and delivered the "blast" that occasioned the following limerick:

> A bishop from Texas named Leven
> Pulled out a six-shooter or seven.
> He slipped in a clip
> And shot from the hip,
> Sending numerous colleagues to Heaven.

His address was the most electrifying of all those delivered by Americans. He began by stating that "every day it becomes clearer that we need a dialogue not only with Protestants, but also among us bishops." From that point on, he launched into an all-out attack against the conservative voices in and around the

Council. He said they act as if "the only text in the Holy Bible were 'Thou art Peter' and that they never heard the expression of St. Augustine that 'They are our brothers; they will not cease to be our brothers until they cease saying Our Father;' that the doctrine of freedom of conscience is one that is offensive to pious ears; that they prefer to blame non-Catholics rather than to instruct children in their own parishes." On the other hand, he said, "the prelates who seek a sincere and fruitful dialogue with non-Catholics are not the ones who show disaffection and disloyalty to the Holy Father." He concluded, almost passionately, with the following exhortation:

> Venerable Council brothers, I pray you, let us put an end to the scandal of mutual recrimination. Let us proceed in an orderly way with the examination and study of this providential movement called ecumenism so that with patience and humility we may achieve that unity for which the Lord Christ prayed at the Last Supper.

During the seventy-fourth congregation Cardinal Ritter again rose to make further observations on the first chapter of the schema. His remarks were summarized by the Council press office in these words:

> It should be pointed out how the unity which is the goal of all ecumenism is a fundamental principle of the ecumenical movement. For this reason the schema should work out a real concept of unity. Our basic inspiration must be pastoral. We are not only issuing a decree, but are also expected to provide it with effective stimulus for action. The goal to be achieved is the principle of all motion. We have, with our separated brethren, common desires and common activities. We should present unity not merely as a goal of inestimable value, but in such a way as to show disunity as an evil of equal magnitude. Chapter one presents a concept of unity which only Catholics can recognize. In her present state the Church is far from the realization of the full perfection which belongs to her by nature. Separation and division in the ranks of Christians are a scandal to the world. The text tells us that such divisions retard the coming of the Kingdom of God. We shall, of course, be united in perfect union only when we all share together in the Lord's table. We should all pray for unity in the recognition of one and the same truth.

The final American to speak on the ecumenism schema was Bishop Helmsing who was elected by his colleagues on the same day, November 29, as a member of the unity Secretariat. His intervention was one of the most decisive ones of the session. He began by praising the third chapter of the text, but he felt that, by calling other religious groups merely "communities," the text would pose "a grave impediment to dialogue with the Anglicans and many other Protestants." The gist of his intervention was tightly stated in one sentence:

"We strongly hope that, in the place of reading 'communities which have sprung up since the sixteenth century,' the word 'church' or the words 'other Christian churches' might be inserted, both for practical reasons and especially for theological reasons." Then Bishop Helmsing adduced an argument derived from the Old Testament in these words:

> . . . in Holy Scripture we learn that at one time a type of schism happened within the Kingdom of the People of God. At that time the Israelites of the Northern Kingdom, although these were in schism from the seat of David which was subject to the privilege of the Divine Promise, *still* belonged to the *People of God*. And the Spirit of God never stopped inspiring them. Let us not forget that He appointed prophets and sent them word that they correct the abuses of the Kingdom of the South. As it was then, so it is now. Regardless of the sad break of the ecclesiastical union with the chair of Peter, these Christian communities belong to the People of God, and they should also be called churches without violating all the rights of the one true Catholic Church.

Although the words were not written into his prepared text, Bishop Helmsing concluded his observation with an earnest request that chapters four and five be brought to a vote before this session closed, in order to determine their acceptability for debate. He said he spoke in the name of many Council Fathers.

However, the die had already been cast. On the preceding day, Father Weigel had said privately that there was not a chance in the world of getting the two chapters on the floor for a vote. He said that, during a meeting of the Secretariat for Promoting Christian Unity on November 27, Cardinal Bea had conceded that he had no hope for a vote on the chapters. Another consultant to the Secretariat explained that the failure was really a compromise agreed upon by Cardinal Bea in order to secure the approval of the first three chapters of the schema. The Cardinal felt also that separating the two chapters from the schema (a decision handed down during the intersession by the Central Coordinating Commission) would assure a better hearing on the two subjects. Although, at this stage, these were only two of the countless rumors floating through the Council, both subsequently proved to be well founded. .

Before this session closed, the American bishops devoted another of their weekly meetings, on November 18, to a discussion of the schema on ecumenism. Father Weigel spoke to them concerning the religious dialogue and approached the subject chiefly from a strictly theological point of view. He was followed by Father Stransky who rounded out Father Weigel's remarks by stating that dialogue merely provided the intellectual basis for real ecumenism. This, he said, must be preceded by prayer so that the action of the Holy Spirit in the souls of the participants will prepare them for the blessings of the Holy Spirit.

The second session closed with the Eternal City draped in a cloud of pessimism over the proponents of ecumenism. The chapters on religious liberty and the Church's relation with non-Christians and the Jews never even so much as came up for discussion on the floor. Only one ray of hope did show through, and that was Cardinal Bea's summation of the ecumenism debate on December 2. He said, *"Quod defertur non aufertur"* ("What is put off is not put away."). However, what seemed to many at that time as defeat was, in the end, a victory. At that point the schema on ecumenism was affected by that conciliar principle already formulated during the debates on the liturgy: The longer a schema is under discussion, the better it becomes through the conciliar process.

Even though most Americans were dejected by the obvious stalling tactics in the closing days of the session, in retrospect it is also evident that a great deal of work was being accomplished behind the scenes. The vote of November 21 was overlooked by most observers. On that day the Fathers voted by 2,046 to 80 that the schema on ecumenism should be accepted. As Father Stransky observed, "this was a surprise even to the chief drafter, Cardinal Bea's Secretariat for Promoting Christian unity."

Monsignor William Baum, executive secretary of the American Bishops' Secretariat for Ecumenical Affairs, subsequently observed that this vote assured the Vatican Secretariat that it could proceed even more boldly in redrafting the schema than it had done in the early days of the Council. In such a spirit the Secretariat entered upon the examination of the 1,063 pages of interventions which the bishops had submitted, both orally and in writing, as a response to Cardinal Bea's request.

From February 3 to February 24, a committee of experts from the Secretariat, meeting with experts from the Oriental and theological commissions, examined 143 oral and 156 written interventions. On March 7, at Ariccia near Rome, the suggestions of the Fathers were incorporated in a much strengthened document, and the second version of the ecumenism schema was completed.

Several American prelates were among those who submitted interventions in writing to the Secretariat. In March, 1963, Cardinal Spellman had written that "the true ecumenical spirit found in this schema is based in the truth and charity of Christ." Therefore, he felt, it should "be proposed for the debate of the Council Fathers." At the same time, however, Cardinal Spellman stated that "either in the text or in the notes, there should be a reference made to those numbers of the Dogmatic Constitution on the Church which dealt with the relation of non-Catholics to the mystical and visible Body of Christ."

In July and August, Bishop Albert Fletcher submitted two observations on the schema. In the first observation he suggested what actually became reality, namely, an ecumenical commission established by every national conference of bishops. However, Bishop Fletcher had one reservation which he stated in the following words:

> If priests habitually speak about the true faith in the churches of the separated brethren, will not the ministers of the separated brethren want likewise to speak about their doctrine in our churches? What then? Will we

not give offense to our brothers if we do not grant this? And if they preach their doctrine in our edifices, will not the danger of indifferentism arise?

In his second written intervention, Bishop Fletcher continued to raise questions concerning the delicate problem of *communicatio in sacris*. In this intervention he raised, among others, the following questions:

Should a place in our sanctuary be offered to non-Catholic ministers during the celebration of a liturgical rite? Or should a place in a sanctuary or some other place be allowed for priests when non-Catholic rites are being carried on in their churches? Also, in prayers in ecumenical gatherings, ought not the proper precautions be taken so that no "official ecumenical worship" might arise as a kind of "rite of indifferentism"?

Cardinal McIntyre of Los Angeles also submitted his written observations on the subject. He felt that in this matter, above all, it was necessary "to discuss dogma in positive words" and that "the stimulus to amend the schema has not arisen from the Christian faithful, but rather from some modern *periti*— so-called *periti*." He expressed his own attitude toward ecumenism in the concluding words of his intervention:

We have always dealt with great charity toward our truly Christian brothers who are not united to us in full faith or in the unity of obedience, and have shown these same brothers, without doubt or ambiguity, the objective and genuine doctrine which the Catholic Church has always held, knowing that they disagree among themselves in many areas. Neither have I accepted from them all the new things which are taught by some modern Catholic theologians. We strive to elevate and perfect the edifice of the Church which has been handed down to us by our spiritual and temporal fathers without destroying or weakening those things which are solid and remain apt for solving contemporary problems. Allow us to recall the words of St. Paul, "Do not be misled by various and passing doctrines," as well as the words read in St. Vincent of Lerins: "We must have great care to hold that which has been believed everywhere, always, and by all, for this is properly catholic."

On July 19, 1963, Archbishop John Krol submitted his observations on the schema which he called "the briefest and the most succinct." In his observations he raised a question which was to have a direct bearing on the entire philosophic stance of the Council in these words:

Ecumenism, according to the modern concept, is clearly defined and approved as a matter of the highest importance for the Church and all the faithful; for ecumenism exists in the world by the "breath of the Holy Spirit." Its goals and obstacles are unequivocally stated, but the different aspects for the fulfillment of the necessary movement are given in only a schematic way and not concretely. A clear example of this type is found in the discussion, "About the method of expressing and exposing the doctrine of faith" where the statement of a principle will be able to cause the experiences of difficulties and arguments, namely: "At the same time, however, our faith should be explained in such a way that it can also be understood by our separated brothers, who very often use a theological method, culture, history and psychology quite different from our own." This statement contains the expression of a desire, widespread throughout the world, that doctrines of the faith be presented in a more biblical and patristic fashion. Is this, however, to admit the possibility of proclaiming Catholic truths in terms taken from existentialist and Kantian philosophy which are predominant in the theological writings of Protestants? If this is the case, how and to what extent is the traditional presentation of Thomistic Catholic theology affected by this principle?

Secondly, the Archbishop of Philadelphia realized that the schema was not dogmatic, even though he knew that dogma is central to any discussion of ecumenism. Thus he posed another fundamental theological question in these words:

. . . one dogmatic point is central in this discussion. What, precisely, is the relation of the properly baptized non-Catholic toward the Church? ". . . for by a kind of communion have they been joined with us. . . ." and "who indeed have been placed near her (the Church) by baptism, but who have been separated from ecclesiastical union. . . ." How are these things which have been stated to be reconciled with the paragraphs of the encyclical *Mystici Corporis* concerning the members of the Mystical Body? . . . Cardinal Bea has said: "All who have been validly baptized in Christ, even outside the Catholic Church, have been, by the fact of their baptism, organically bound to Christ and so to His Mystical Body." The explanation of the sacrament of Baptism which has been given here, namely, as "only a beginning and source," does not seem to resolve this most delicate question fully and completely.

The Archbishop's final point concerned replacing the word "vestiges" with "values." Commenting on the sentence in the schema which read, "It is helpful and right to recognize the vestiges of Christ and the gifts of the Holy Spirit in the lives of others," he added:

The word *vestiges*, at least according to the connotation understood in many modern languages, means a small sign or trace of something which is already lost. Thus the term does not seem fit to designate those things now possessed by some non-Catholics or to describe those vital elements of Protantism which are later enumerated in the schema, namely, faith in Christ, the acceptance and veneration of the Scriptures, the sacrament of Baptism, private and public prayer and the worship of a community joined together for the praise of God. It is, therefore, suggested that the word *vestiges* become *values.*

In an intervention submitted before the discussions of the second session, Bishop Helmsing suggested that the schema should contain a declaration on religious liberty and that a conciliar decree on the Jews and the relation of Christians to them should be drafted. Finally, he said, "in this or in another schema there should be greetings to all men of good will, even to the infidels—for example, the Mohammedans, and to the pagans—for example, the Buddhists." After the closing of the session, Bishop Helmsing submitted another lengthy written observation on the subject. He argued in favor of retaining the chapter concerning the Jews as part of the schema because "the hopes of the Jewish community have been and still are very high, and to delay indefinitely a statement on this subject could be very harmful to dialogue with the Jews." He also preferred to see "grateful acknowledgment" to the World Council of Churches expressed in the schema because "ecumenism owes much to the initiative and dedication of non-Catholic Christians." Likewise, he wanted to see in the text "an explicit, but brief, statement concerning the Holy Eucharist as a sign and cause of unity" as well as a "most explicit emphasis upon the Holy Spirit—His mission and indwelling within the Church—as a principle of unity." He then returned to the same subject he had discussed in the aula, namely, the attribution of the term "church" to all Christian communities.

On April 27, 1964, Pope Paul ordered that the second version of the schema be distributed to all the Council Fathers and be placed on the agenda for the third session. The schema then consisted of only the first three chapters, with the declaration on religious liberty relegated to an appendix in the booklet and a note on the title page which declared "the other declaration, or concerning the Jews and non-Christians, will be transmitted together with a *relatio* as soon as possible." The most striking change in the new schema was the change in the title of the first chapter. It was no longer entitled "The Principles of Catholic Ecumenism," but "The Catholic Principles of Ecumenism." Significantly, the change admitted the fact that the ecumenical movement already was a reality among Protestant groups. Catholics now were not so much imposing a "new" ecumenism as recognizing and adopting the progressive movement already going on within other Christian churches.

The revised schema was returned to the Council floor during the ninety-third congregation, October 2, 1964. During the following congregation, October 5, Archbishop Joseph Martin of Rouen, France, introduced the first chapter, and the first of fourteen votes to be taken on the entire schema were cast. The first chapter was approved by a vote of 1,926 to 30, with 209 voting with reservations. The vote on the second chapter was approved by a large majority, as was the third chapter on October 8. Immediately the Secretariat returned to work examining the *modi* and soon returned the schema to the Council floor. In this series of votes, between November 10 and 14, the schema was again overwhelmingly approved. On November 19, the Secretariat approved 19 alterations in the text which were submitted "by higher authority," presumably Pope Paul. On the following day, during the final working congregation of the third session, the revised schema was approved by a vote of 2,054 to 64. On November 21, Pope Paul formally promulgated the Decree after a final vote of 2,137 affirmative and eleven negative votes. As the Fathers departed from Rome on the following day, the thought which Pope Paul had expressed in his opening address of the second session took on a new and deeper significance. He had said at that time:

> Our voice trembles and our heart beats the faster both because of the inexpressible consolation and reasonable hope that their [the observer-delegates] presence stirs up within us, as well as because of the deep sadness we feel at their prolonged separation. If we are in any way to blame for that separation, we humbly beg God's forgiveness and ask pardon, too, of our brethren who feel themselves to have been injured by us. For our part, we willingly forgive the injuries which the Catholic Church has suffered and forget the grief endured during the long series of dissensions and separations.

In many more ways than any recorder can recount, the observer-delegates of the other Christian churches made the Second Vatican Council a reality among millions of American people. They came, first of all, as somewhat uncertain spectators, but they were soon caught up in the spirit of the conciliar experience. After the ice was broken, they realized that they were among the most active and admired participants of the Council. They were not only guests and friends; much more than that, they were keen and, at times, critical observers. Their voice was heard through their weekly meetings with the members of the Secretariat for Promoting Christian Unity. Invariably one or the other member of the Secretariat would express the opinion—if you will, the intervention—of a Protestant observer on the Council floor. They were, from beginning to end, the faithful friends of the Church precisely because they knew—as the Decree on Ecumenism would intimate—that "our" Church was in some way "their" Church. They were *not* outsiders. In point of fact, they were more on the *inside* than many of the insiders.

Several American observers especially come to mind. Dr. Douglas Horton claims the admiration of Americans at the Council because he lays claim to the title of being one of the few members within the aula who resisted the temptation to leave his seat during the morning congregations. Dr. George Lindbeck and Dr. Warren Quanbeck contributed many incisive, yet at all times charitable, observations on the conciliar documents. Dr. Albert Outler was among the most active and outstanding, for even at the risk of a serious heart attack he gave himself totally, day after day, for the sake of Christian unity. Other observers from the United States, such as Dr. Douglas Steere, Dr. Robert Cushman and Dr. Frederick Grant were also conspicuous by their presence, which was an enrichment for many American participants.

During the first two sessions of the Council, Father Gustave Weigel had served as a translator, friend and counsel for the English-speaking observers. It was evident that these persons came to have a great affection for this great man. Gustave Weigel died January 3, 1964, at the editorial offices of *America* magazine. Several months before that, he had stated his philosophy in these words: "We do not know where God will lead us or when He will effect Christian unity. At the present moment we must allow ourselves to be led where God wills. This imposes upon all of us a tremendous act of hope and trust in God." Writing in *Christianity and Crisis* a month after Father Weigel's death, Dr. Robert McAfee Brown paid him the following tribute:

> The ways of providence are mysterious, but both Catholics and Protestants, confronted with the completely unexpected death of the great-hearted man whom many called "Gus," can agree that there was probably no man on either side of the divide we could less afford to spare. . . . His was an "open-door mind." This did not mean that he sat lightly to Roman dogma. Indeed, he was more conventional and orthodox in his theology than many Protestants who knew him chiefly through his hearty good spirit and broad humanity were aware. But he did not have a fixed and narrow mind; he was always open to new currents. . . . But those who knew his devotion to the possibilities of renewal that the Council has opened up can believe that he will be very close to St. Peter's, cheering the Council on from that same corner of heaven in which Pope John has been engaged in an identical enterprise.

During the time of the Council, however, ecumenism was much more than a document considered in the aula, in commission meetings and among the members of the unity Secretariat. The presence of the observers under the statue of St. Longinus in St. Peter's basilica was a constant reminder of the concern about the Council among the other Christian churches. During the first session there were 35 observers representing 17 churches; in the second, 66 from 22 churches; in the third, 75 from 23 churches; in the fourth, 93 from 28 churches.

American bishops were, for the most part, particularly eager to meet with the observers from the United States. They would be seen together in groups around luncheon and dinner tables on almost every day and in almost any place in Rome. Several American prelates interviewed observers for their diocesan papers or on tapes to be played over local radio stations back home. Bishops and observers would be seen chatting in the side aisles of St. Peter's or rubbing shoulders quite literally as they jammed into the coffee bars. What all this meant, from an American observer's point of view, has been delightfully described by Robert McAfee Brown in his book concerning the second session, *Observer in Rome.*

An integral part of this practical ecumenism carried out in the Eternal City was the receptions for the American bishops and English-speaking observers sponsored by the Paulist Fathers during the closing weeks of the last three sessions. These were important exercises in dialogue, the first such occasions many bishops and observers had for witnessing and participating in this kind of action.

One of the best addresses given by anyone throughout the time of the Council was that delivered by Dr. Albert C. Outler at the last of these receptions in 1965. He entitled his address "Reformation—Roman Style" and presented his appraisal of the Council from the point of view of a Protestant observer. His remarks were sprinkled with humor, but, more importantly, he revealed profound insights into the transformations that were underway within the Roman Catholic Church as a result of the conciliar experience. He explained the choice of his title for the address and, at the same time, put his finger on the heart of this conciliar experience in these words:

. . . the most truly unique aspect of *this* Council lies in its deliberate concern for reform within the limits of Christian community and in vital continuity with the Christian past. Vatican II has been as self-consciously a reforming Council as Constance was, or Florence, or Trent—but with a decisive difference. Typical reformers value truth above community and, having the truth, they will sacrifice community—with pious reluctance (as at Augsburg) or with pious exuberance (as with the anathemata of Trent). Standard operating procedure for the other reforming councils has been to separate the sheep from the goats and then to scape the goats and fit out the sheep with haloes. Vatican II is a very rare instance of historic change within a continuum of identity and consensus. One cannot miss the evident concern here for reform without schism in the soul of the Church—in the face of intransigence that has sometimes seemed to reach over and beyond the call of duty. This is what I mean by my corny title, "Reformation—Roman Style." Vatican II has been a Council that has dismayed the die-hards, but has not alienated them; that has damped down the arsonists without quenching their fire; that has chafed the progressives and bored the unimaginative. It has been a subtle affair, in which some of the changes are only "development" and some "developments" are real changes, where much is left open to further development and/or change—and where an adequate theory for *this particular kind* of development and/or change has yet to be developed. In my judgment, this is one of the most interesting of all the problems generated by this Council. It opens up a whole constellation of acute issues, for Roman Catholics and Protestants alike, theoretical and practical, all bearing on the vital ecumenical question of the role of the Church in history and the role of history in the Church.

The closing days of the fourth session witnessed two other significant ecumenical encounters. The first occurred on December 4 during a prayer service for promoting Christian unity in the Basilica of St. Paul's outside the Walls. Participants were Pope Paul VI, the Fathers of the Council and the observers and guests of the other Christian churches. During this service Dr. Outler read one of the two Scripture readings. An American bishop explained his reaction in these words:

> This ceremony impressed me as much as any other during the entire fourth session. If anyone had told me before this Council started that before it ended there would be a joint prayer service in St. Paul's, with the Holy Father presiding and preaching a homily while the Scripture readings were read by observers, I would have considered such a suggestion a futile dream. . . . At the point where the Holy Father introduced the Lord's Prayer in Latin and each one present recited it in his own language, I was overcome with emotion. It is the first time in a long time that I said the Our Father in tears. . . . For any bishop who is interested in doing anything at all to implement the Decree on Ecumenism, this event was an answer to a prayer. . . . It should do more to promote earnest dialogue than any amount of theoretical material in the Decree or any number of suggestions in directives.

Another ecumenical gesture of the highest significance occurred on December 7 when the Roman Catholic Church formally lifted the excommunication of 1054 against Michael Cerularius. During the public session on that day, Metropolitan Meliton represented Patriarch Athenagoras I and received the kiss of peace from Pope Paul. In Istanbul, Cardinal Shehan represented Pope Paul and received the kiss of peace from Athenagoras. In the joint declaration issued on the occasion, both Pope Paul and Patriarch Athenagoras regretted "offensive words, reproaches without foundation and the reprehensible gestures" of both sides. They also deplored "later vexing events which . . . eventually led to the effective rupture of ecclesiastical communion." Commenting on this event, Cardinal Shehan wrote: "Through this declaration of regret for past mistakes, of esteem and charity for the present, and of hope for future reconciliation, the Church of Constantinople and the See of Peter took a beautiful and promising step toward each other."

The walls of nine hundred and four hundred years were tumbling down. We have all—all together—entered upon a new era.

Decree on Ecumenism

✠ INTERVENTIONS

ARCHBISHOP AMBROSE SENYSHYN, *27 November, 1962*

The schema of the decree on the unity of the Church is generally acceptable. However, I have certain proposals to set forth for the Fathers' consideration.

First Proposal: Let this decree appear, not as in a schema published after the Constitution on the Instruments of Communication, with which it has no connection, but rather let it be placed as a corollary of the Constitution on the Church, since this is actually its logical consequence.

In this way, let us avoid repetitions of themes which deal with the same subject both in the Constitution on the Church and in the decree on the unity of the Church.

And so, in this decree let us delete all numbers from one to eight inclusive which consider the Constitution of the Church as the body of Christ, primacy, hierarchy, etc., all of which are professedly considered again in the Constitution on the Church.

On the other hand, in the same manner let us eliminate from the Constitution on the Church all those things which deal with union with those who are separated (all of number ten) since our decree on the unity of the Church expressly deals with this point.

Second Proposal: In the decree on the unity of the Church, the greater part deals—and, indeed, in a laudable fashion—with the means of unity with our separated brethren; about these things I have a few observations to make.

There is no mention in the schema about communication in religious worship specifically with the separated brethren who often feel themselves offended, since the same rigid norms for communication in worship are applied to them as to the Protestants. My observation, Venerable Fathers, concerns the sacramentology of the Orthodox which differs greatly from that of the Protestants—and I mean this without offense. For these have a true hierarchy, a true priesthood, they offer a true Mass, they recognize and have the same seven sacraments as we do. Thus it does not seem fitting that we should equate them with Protestants in this respect, as is very often done.

Thus, while we consider here the means of unity, we should direct our attention to this obstacle in the way of any approach to them, lest we impose impediments where divine law does not require this. Indeed, as I have stated, in the schema of our decree there is not a word about this matter.

While it is true that the rules which we have mentioned above for the communication in divine liturgy are considered within the schema of the Constitution on the Church, here, however, it would be fitting to consider them in their application to the Orthodox brethren under the aspect of unity.

FRANCIS CARDINAL SPELLMAN, 28 *November, 1962*

According to Catholic doctrine, there is only one Church of Christ, founded on Peter, and governed by his successors. Therefore, communion with the See of Peter is necessary, and, on the contrary, any body separated from this See does not truly pertain to the Church of Christ.

The Church of Christ, however, while necessarily upholding unity, by no means seeks uniformity. According to circumstances of place and time, it wishes to keep itself capable of serving the traditions and customs of various parts of the earth where its sons dwell and especially where the venerable Eastern Churches flourish. Such opportune diversity does not impede, but rather postulates a unique authority which coordinates, brings together and joins all things.

Those, however, should not be passed over who in good faith adhere to separate Churches and are separated from the Vicar of Christ. We say that, although these in some way are not strangers to the true Church, they are nonetheless deprived of many means of salvation which are found in the true Church. Therefore, regardless of the matter of individual salvation, it is certain that the division in the heart of Christian society brings with it serious harm and grave loss.

The Catholic Church has never ceased working for the restoration of the communion of all Christian believers. Furthermore, this Ecumenical Synod judges it to be its purpose that the minds and hearts of all who glory in the name Christian be led to this, that, joined in prayers and work, they strive for that unity which Christ the Lord pleaded for before He passed from this world to the Father. It also has used quite strong means to remove the obstacles which are present.

Many great obstacles remain which oppose Christian unity. A happy success might well be despaired of were not Christ in the Gospels heard to say that among men this is impossible, but that with God all things are possible. Therefore, it is altogether necessary that supernatural help be insisted upon, especially in prayer which ought to have an unshakable faith joined with it, and that with a more reliable faith there be prayer to the Blessed Virgin, the

Mother of God and man, whereby a great fortress of Christian unity might be divinely offered in Mary.

In this practice, all indeed can cooperate to promote unity. Other means—theological, liturgical, canonical or disciplinary, logical or practical—ought to be applied by the bishops, by the clergy and by *periti* who should apply them with all solicitude and charity.

Care must be taken, however, lest by a certain false irenicism Catholic doctrine be made to conform to or somehow accommodate the doctrine of the dissidents. The result of this irenicism would be that the purity and clarity of Catholic doctrine would suffer damage or that its genuine and certain sense would be obscured. The Catholic Church hopes for the reunion of both the Protestant and the schismatic churches; but, humanly speaking, there is less hope for the corporate reunion of the Protestant churches because of their individual differences in faith and their greater doctrinal and liturgical discrepancy. It is rather to be hoped that from these groups will come personal conversions and conversions of particular groups.

Concerning the schismatic churches it is legitimate to hope that at some time these will be restored into corporate reunion for they officially profess the doctrine of the first seven Ecumenical Councils, they have true orders, Mass and seven sacraments.

Therefore, it is rightly proposed in this schema that if, with God illuminating and helping them, the Oriental Churches wish to return to Catholic unity and the authority of the Roman Pontiff and profess faith in the usual way, they be granted the right of exercising their orders and carrying out their own discipline, omitting only those things which perhaps oppose faith and good practice. Therefore, the schema on the unity of the Church is acceptable.

BISHOP NICHOLAS ELKO, *30 November, 1962*

A lot has been said wisely and well of the schema of the decree on the unity of the Church, but some things are less accurate. To clarify some of these points, having carefully read and maturely considered all that is proposed in the decree, I think the following should be noted.

General observations: The schema of the proposed decree, as it stands, is acceptable. Why? For the following reasons:

First: because, as is clear from the whole text of the decree, the primary end of the schema, in my opinion, is none other than to give the fundamental principles on the visibility, indivisibility and the unity of the Church with and under Peter and, further, to show the way for restoring unity with our brothers separated from the Holy See, and not with other Christians separated from the Catholic Church;

Second: because this schema clearly shows a sense of reverence and sincere and fraternal charity toward our separated brothers.

Thus the schema proposes very practical matters, or, if you will, pastoral concerns about which there is no doubt. It is clear that the Commission on Eastern Churches could not surpass its boundaries in preparing this schema.

It is also a well-known fact that the separated brethren acknowledge the same seven sacraments and retain them as we do for the regeneration of souls. They also observe the Eucharistic meal and preserve it in the Christian life.

Furthermore, Venerable Fathers, we cannot deny that they also preserve the discipline of the seven Ecumenical Councils and other particular synods in the Orient before the well-known separation.

All this, Venerable Fathers, is not only worthy of due estimation and praise but should also be considered as the common patrimony of the universal Church of Christ.

In my humble, really humble, opinion, all this has been presented in the present schema and constitutes a valid basis for promoting and restoring union with these same brothers, so that finally there be "one fold and one shepherd."

Furthermore, the same schema proposes the basic principle of the jurisdictional power of the successor of Peter. This seems to me the basic principle in the schema. Bound to this are pastors and faithful of any rank and dignity, individually and together, by the duty of hierarchical subordination and true obedience not only in matters of faiths and morals, but also in matter of universal discipline for the whole Church throughout the world (cf. Vatican I, session four, chapter three).

Thus, those who say this schema wants to deceive the good will of our separated brothers are seriously wrong. No. I know from experience. What experience? My experience of a few years ago in talking with the monks of Mount Athos. From them I gather that today the obstacle to unity is not so much the doctrine of purgatory, or the doctrine concerning the *Filioque,* or the Immaculate Conception or the Assumption of the Holy Virgin Mary as the dogma of the infallibility and primacy of the Roman Pontiff.

However, Venerable Fathers, our separated brothers easily see the primacy and infallibility of Peter and his successor in seeing the discipline present in the whole Catholic Church, the discipline necessary for conserving the unity of faith and the integrity of morals. All this I learned neither from erudite dissertation nor, much less, from a special inspiration of the Holy Spirit, but from my personal experience of daily life among the separated brothers. For in the last few years in North America, in our Exarchate we had 1,121 conversions among the laity and 14 priests who returned to the bosom of the Catholic Church from Pravoslava or from the separated Church.

Why? Because they see the order, the discipline, flourishing in the whole Catholic Church.

Our most dear observers, present in this conciliar aula, are witnesses, by sight and hearing, that our Holy Father John XXIII, happily reigning (whom

God keeps safe and sound for us), that the Holy Father is not a dictator but the servant of the servants of God. Subjects always have to bow to a dictator and say "Lord have mercy! Mercy! Amen! Alleluja!" But not so in this Council. We are given free liberty in this Council, liberty of speech, of expressing our opinion, of making propositions, going out for coffee, making comments, and so on. And, dear Fathers, without danger of punishment or detention in jail.

JOSEPH CARDINAL RITTER, *18 November, 1963*

I speak for myself and other bishops of the United States.

In general the schema on ecumenism pleased us very much because it responded well to the necessity of expressing the practical consequences of the *aggiornamento* of the Church.

Theologically and historically, it means the final end of the counter-Reformation with its unfortunate polemics. Spiritually, it exhorts us to turn our charity and thoughts toward our brothers in Christ who have been separated by different doctrines. Pastorally, it urges us to hasten that day in which all will be one in Christ through prayer, study, dialogue and action.

Nevertheless, there are shallow spots in the proposed text. Joyfully we received the news of chapter five, namely, on religious liberty, and we await tomorrow's distribution. Without such a declaration, mutual faithfulness would be impossible and a serious dialogue would be precluded. Since we consider religious liberty to be the foundation and prerequisite for ecumenical relations with other Christians, we strongly urge that the tract on this subject be incorporated in the schema before a consideration of the practices of ecumenism.

Merely expedient motives should not prompt such a text as being worthy of Council deliberation and ecumenical value. Our declaration is solidly founded on theological principles. We must incorporate considerations on the freedom of the act of faith, on the dignity of the human person, and his inviolable conscience, on the total incompetence of civil laws in passing judgment on the Gospel of Christ and its interpretation. Thus, this declaration reaffirms the complete independence of the Church from any government in fulfilling her mission.

Secondly, the schema lacks an exposition of the principles of ecumenism. The Eucharistic Celebration as a sign and cause of the unity of the Church should appear more clearly. The meaning of the liturgy and its renewal in the life of the Church are of great importance in ecumenism, and this importance should appear explicitly in the text. In the text is also found the explicit affirmation of the validity of orders and the sacraments of the Oriental Church, with whom ecclesial communion was unfortunately broken.

Thirdly, as far as possible, terminology which is perhaps offensive to our separated brethren should be removed in the emendations made by the commission. Without a judgment about their orders and Eucharistic Celebration, we strenuously ask that the term "Church" not be denied to these Christian groups which in the text are called "communities."

Fourthly, whether or not the fourth chapter in the strict sense pertains to the schema on ecumenism, such a statement clearly pertains to the proposed end of the Council and exceedingly pleases us.

Fifth and lastly, ecumenism is subject to the common failings of all living movements. Ecumenism can be confused with a sugary rigidity; it can become sterile because of intellectual excesses; it can be turned into indifferentism. We sincerely place our hopes for the evolution of an effective ecumenism in the Directory on the Practices of Ecumenism. We shall give practical suggestions for the drawing up of such a directory to the Secretary.

ALBERT CARDINAL MEYER, *20 November, 1963*

This declaration is acceptable in its totality since it reaffirms the teaching of recent pontiffs, and especially of Pope John XXIII (*Pacem in Terris,* April 11, 1963) who have clarified and advanced the traditional teaching of the Church on this subject. Of course, as was true of other schemata, the present text can be improved by many individual, detailed corrections in word and phrase which will permit its doctrine to be stated with greater clarity and force. I desire, however, now to call your attention to three places in the text where a more thoroughgoing revision seems desirable.

1) Page 31, lines 29–40: *"Exercitium iurium, etc."*

Here the declaration tackles the ticklish problem of the limitations placed on the right of religious liberty by the requirements of social peace. If we consider the entire paragraph the declaration seems to make the following assertions:

a) Social peace limits the exercise of the right of religious liberty: from line 29 to the phrase *"limitatum est."*

b) However this *limitation* must be of such a nature as to be compatible with the essential dignity of the human person and with the existence of a society of free men who are liable to error: from line 30 to line 33, the phrase *"errare possunt."* This sets the bounds beyond which the limitation of religious rights is unjustifiable.

c) Limitation of this right is permitted whenever its use runs gravely counter to the end of society: lines 33 to 36.

If this interpretation of the paragraph be correct, the first sentence joins two disparate assertions into a single compound sentence. Moreover that sentence is so phrased that the reader almost necessarily takes the subject of the first part—"*Exercitium iurium*"—to be the subject of the second part as well. Really the subject of the second part seems to be a phrase like "*haec autem limitatio*," which remains unexpressed. In any hypothesis this sentence is needlessly obscure and should be revised.

My second objection to this section is that the determination of the fact that the conditions for the limitation of religious liberty have been reached is left to the discretion of the civil rulers. It is they who are to determine when religious activity "seriously contradicts the end of society" (line 34) and when the "uses" of religious liberty are "perverse" (line 39). Our experience of the subjective way in which civil rulers can decide such matters should warn us to be more prudent here. I suggest, therefore, that this section be reworked in the following spirit.

Social harmony requires that all individuals living in society exercise their right to religious liberty, with moderation, in the interest of social peace. Since positive law cannot determine all the forms of civil intercourse required for social peace, all have a moral obligation to practice the virtue of prudence in this matter. Prudence, to say nothing of charity, requires that all avoid, as far as possible, giving any unreasonable offense to their fellow men. All should respect the religious sincerity of others and not regard differences of religious belief and practice as excuses for violating the moral obligation to treat all fellow citizens with respect, justice and charity.

If these precepts of prudence be neglected, an outraged populace will naturally demand that restraints be placed on those who have abused religious liberty, and, where no other course is effective, civil rulers may accede to such demands. But, in general, such demands should be resisted by civil rulers who will find that encouragement of a sound religious education of their people is a better means than restraint to counter such abuses.

2) Page 31, line 41 to page 32 line 3: "*Contra vero . . .*"

Perhaps the phrase "*nefas est*" is too strong an expression in a world where the supreme political power is restricted to members of a definite religious society for reasons of historical culture, etc. The same doctrine could be expressed without any fear of giving offense, I believe, by a statement couched along the following lines:

> Although it is understandable that, in some countries, adherence to a particular religion, regarded as part of the people's historical culture, be required for eligibility to public office, this requirement runs counter to the principle of religious liberty as a civil right. It also runs counter to the political right of the people to choose whoever they believe will best govern them. But only the people involved, if they are free, can vindicate the religious and political rights at stake here.

3) Page 32, line 14 to page 33, line 3: "*Libertas coetuum religiosorum in societate.*"

This paragraph develops as follows:

a) The basis of the right of religious liberty for groups is given: lines 14–19.

b) The right itself is then enunciated: lines 19–24.

c) The corollaries are then drawn, the first of which concerns the Catholic Church. The rights of the Church are stated at length and with peculiar solemnity. Then lines 38 ff. make a qualified endorsement of the rights of non-Catholic Churches.

This way of structuring the paragraph may confirm non-Catholic suspicions that, when Catholics talk of religious liberty, they mean the rights of Catholics to religious liberty. This could be avoided by inserting before the corollaries on the Catholic Church and other religions a statement along the following lines:

> These principles of religious liberty and the right of religious association free from State domination are universal in scope. They vindicate the rights of all forms of religious associations, Christian and non-Christian, under all forms of political authority to carry on their missions as they conceive them. These rights are rooted in the right of free, rational, human personality, individual and social.

This insertion would involve some changes in what follows, but these would be of secondary nature.

May I suggest a much less important change as well. On page 33 and line 22 in the sentence which begins *"pacifica cohabitatio, etc.,"* the classical phase *"ut cum maxime"* occurs after *"hodie,"* the whole complex carrying the meaning "especially today." Could we not sacrifice Latinity here in the interest of clarity?

JOSEPH CARDINAL RITTER, *25 November, 1963*

Ecumenism, in the first chapter is defined or, better, described as "the movement and action directed to fostering that unity of Christians which Jesus Christ asked for by prayer." That unity, since it is the end of the movement, is, unless I am mistaken, the fundamental principle of ecumenism. Wherefore the concept of the same unity ought to be developed and spelled out. This seems to be stated in the schema when, in the first paragraph, there is a discussion on the unity and unicity of the Church. But as I see it this renders the principle less suitable. Allow me to offer my reasons for this objection, and then to propose another principle.

The fundamental principle of ecumenism as it pertains to this schema, ought to be pastoral, doctrinal and ecumenical.

First, it ought to be pastoral because this is the chief purpose of the Council. It is required therefore that the decree not only establish something which is to be done, but also that it offer impetus and motivation to do it effectively. The principle of every movement or action is the end, considered not only as a simple term of activity but as a good eminently desirable. It is not sufficient, therefore, that the schema on the unity of the Church speak speculatively; it ought to manifest Christian unity as a good of inestimable worth and Christian division as an evil of equal magnitude.

The fundamental principle ought to be doctrinal if, indeed, we seek that unity alone which Christ desired. Also the principle ought to be ecumenical. Even in its simple elements ecumenism implies common desires and actions among Catholics and their separated brethren and, therefore, it implies also a common end.

The first paragraph, as it stands, offers a concept of unity which, formally speaking, acknowledges only Catholics. Thus, another concept that is no less true is demanded. Most surely, all, both Catholics and non-Catholics, urgently and ardently desire that unity which Christ wishes. But we can and we ought to desire that same unity and actually seek it under an aspect more concrete and more specific.

Christian unity is something good and eminently desirable not only because it is according to the will of Christ, but even more because in a sense this unity is Christ himself. The ultimate end of the Church—human salvation, the salvation of men themselves and of all things—is the glory of God and Christ. On earth this glory of Christ is perfected through the Church: the good will of God is to "restore all things in Christ," and, therefore, "God has put all things under His feet and made Him head of the whole Church." This "to restore all things" under Christ the Head is the mission, life and very nature of the Church. The glory of Christ is the unity of the Church.

In its present condition the Church is far from the perfection of its nature. By its unity and holiness, the Church ought to manifest Christ, His love and His saving work to the world. But, in reality, on account of its division and imperfection, the Church is a scandal to the world. Thus the schema fittingly states: "By the division of Christians the splendor of the face of Christ is somewhat obscured, and the meaning of the divine kingdom is clouded."

All of us, Catholic and separated brethren, desire the glory of Christ—the unity of the Church. Whatever we believe about the nature of the Church, we acknowledge in agreement that this unity will be obtained when all are communicants of one Lord's Supper and all celebrate one Eucharist: "because we many are one bread, one body, who participate in the one bread."

This is the end, it seems to me, and the fundamental principle of all ecumenism which the schema ought to develop. From this principle the necessity of personal and ecclesial renewal will be agreed upon by all. From it will be manifested how evil is division and how good and desirable is Christian unity. From it will flow creative solicitude for all human beings who are brothers.

From each and everyone approaching Christ in his own proper Eucharistic

Celebration, let there be prayer that we may all be one, that we may come to a knowledge of the whole truth and that from the one bread we may be made one body.

Finally, dear brothers, allow me to add a few words which do not especially apply to conciliar business. The sudden and violent death of our beloved John Fitzgerald Kennedy now moves the Bishops of the United States of America to a very great sorrow. To you, brothers, we offer deep and sincere gratitude for all your expressions of condolence and promises of prayers. Where there is not charity and mutual consideration, hatred, whose fruit is death, easily seizes the heart of man. We pray and work in this Council so that we and our separated brethren may live together in the peace and charity of Christ always and that sometime in the future we may live in the same Christian unity.

BISHOP STEPHEN LEVEN, *26 November, 1963*

What I have to say about the first chapter can be said also about the second chapter, for I wish to speak about the principles and practice of ecumenism.

Every day it becomes clearer that we need a dialogue not only with Protestants, but also among us bishops.

For there are some Fathers who have already spoken to us frequently in the Council who speak as if the only text in the Holy Bible were Matthew 16:18: "Thou art Peter and upon this rock I will build my Church." In every intervention they argue against the collegiality of the bishops. They preach to us and chastise us as if we were against Peter and his successors or as if we desired to steal away the faith of our flocks and promote indifferentism.

They speak as if our Holy Father, John XXIII, had never cited in our day the expression of St. Augustine: "They are our brothers; they will not cease to be our brothers until they cease saying Our Father." They speak as if the whole doctrine of the freedom of conscience due every man, so clearly stated in *Pacem in Terris,* were offensive to pious ears.

Again and again in this aula they continue to chastise us as if the prelate who feels compelled by clear evidence to acknowledge the gifts of the Holy Spirit in persons of other ecclesiastical bodies were denying the faith and giving grave scandal to the innocent.

They prefer to blame non-Catholics whom, perhaps, they have never seen rather than to instruct children in their parishes. Otherwise, why are they so afraid the effects of ecumenism would not be good? Why are their people not better instructed? Why are their people not visited in their homes? Why is there not an active and working Confraternity of Christian Doctrine in their parishes?

It seems the dangers arising from ecumenism may be exaggerated. The prelates who seek a sincere and fruitful dialogue with non-Catholics are not the ones who show disaffection and disloyalty to the Holy Father. It is not our people who miss Mass on Sunday, refuse the sacraments and vote the Communist ticket.

It is not we who make little of the well known and often repeated (by word and example) desire of Pope Paul VI and John XXIII. And what of the will of God who, as St. Paul says, "wishes all men to be saved and to come to the knowledge of the truth" (1 Tim. 2:4)? Jesus said, "For he who is not against you is for you" (Mk. 9:40).

Our Catholics are good Catholics, loyal to us bishops, to holy Mother Church and to the Holy Father. We have not lost the working class. They are the foundation and the support of the Church.

Venerable conciliar brothers: I pray you, let us put an end to the scandal of mutual recrimination. Let us proceed in an orderly way with the examination and study of this providential movement called ecumenism so that, with patience and humility, we may achieve that unity for which the Lord Christ prayed at the Last Supper. St. Paul wrote: "So there abide faith, hope and charity, there are three; but the greatest of these is charity" (1 Cor 13:13).

BISHOP CHARLES HELMSING, 29 *November, 1963*

In very many respects we have praise for the third chapter, the second part of this schema, and we agree with it. We freely recognize the reasons for distinguishing and for calling the Oriental communions "churches," among which is certainly found a validly consecrated episcopacy and a valid celebration of the Eucharist. However, the unfortunate comparison between the Oriental Churches and the other so-called "communities," it if were to remain in the text, would be a grave impediment to dialogue with the Anglicans and many other Protestants. We, together with His Eminence Cardinal Ritter, ask that the title "churches" be extended to these other communities. Thus we strongly hope that, in place of the reading "communities which have sprung up since the sixteenth century," the word "church" or the words "other Christian churches" may be inserted, both for practical reasons and especially for theological reasons. Here are the reasons.

First. Almost everybody uses the word "churches" whether in daily life or in books and newspapers, scientific or popularized, Catholic or non-Catholic. Further, if we wish to enter into a true and genuine dialogue with other Christians, since they call themselves "churches" and are offended if we deny them this, then ordinary decency and politeness urge us to call them "churches."

Second. The word and notion "churches" should be noted, and it can be used neither univocally nor equivocally, but analogically.

Third. We are furnished with a better reason from Holy Scripture, where we learn that at one time a type of schism happened within the Kingdom of the People of God. At that time, the Israelites of the Northern Kingdom, although these were in schism from the seat of David which was subject to the privilege of the Divine Promise, *still* belonged to the *People of God.* And the Spirit of God never stopped inspiring them. Let us not forget that He appointed prophets and sent them word that they correct the abuses of the Kingdom of the South. As it was then, so it is now. Regardless of the sad break of the ecclesiastical union with the chair of Peter, these Christian communities belong to the People of God, and they should also be called churches without violating all the rights of the one true Catholic Church.

Fourth. Although the schema is to be praised for its positive and honest elaboration of the salvific elements found among those who are not in perfect union with the Roman See, nevertheless, it is fitting to be honestly aware that these elements are found not only individually, but also ecclesiastically. We should note the following examples:

a) It is from the confession or from him who speaks in the name of that confession that they hear the *Word of God.*

b) It is in an assembly or in a church that they profess Christ; they are baptized by ecclesiastical ministers, and it is within the context of a church tradition that the life of the gift of divine grace is fostered.

c) Not as individuals, but as people *called together* and *con-gregated,* they are united for the hearing of the Word of God and for the worship of God by public prayers.

d) It is in the function of the ecclesial community that they very often enjoy charismata and that they exercise their *diakonia* and *marturia* (service and witness), signs of the presence of the Holy Spirit which we have already recognized.

e) Can we praise their fraternal charity without admitting that it is based on that mysterious and spiritual communion, *koinonia,* "fellowship," which they experience together with others?

f) Although they lack the full reality of the Eucharist, it is within these communities, and more than communities, that the *Eucharistic signs* continue to be presented with their genuine intent to proclaim the death of the Lord until He comes, that they may foreshadow the heavenly table and the liturgy of Jesus Christ, the eternal and only Priest of all of us Christians.

Decree on Ecumenism

✠ SPECIAL ADDRESSES

DR. ALBERT OUTLER, Observer-Delegate, *6 November, 1965**

Eminences, Excellencies, Fathers and Brethren—and Sisters in Christ

Let me say quickly, simply and sincerely that I greatly appreciate this honor of speaking to you, yet once again, on this happy occasion of the Paulist Fathers' Reception. Each year, it has been one of the most gracious gatherings of the session—and our contacts and acquaintances formed or extended here have been greatly meaningful in our experience of the Council. We observers are, therefore, doubly indebted: to the Paulist Fathers for their hospitality and unstinted devotion to the ecumenical enterprise, and to the American hierarchy and their *periti* for their countless courtesies and their zealous tuition of us in the ways and mazes of the Roman Catholic Church in Council.

It has been said that there are four "parties" among the bishops, *periti* and Catholic journalists: diehards, conservatives, progressives and arsonists. *Mutatis mutandis,* one might speak of four "types" among the observers and onlookers: "Hussites," skeptics, admirers and visionaries. The "Hussites" believe that there is still time for you to revoke our safe-conduct passages and to close the Council with an auto-da-fe in the Piazza di Sant'Uffizio. The skeptics see many outward signs of change, but, knowing Rome of old, they regard these as illusions. The admirers readily admit that great things have been wrought here in Council, but they fear that, once the tumult and shouting are over, the tide of reform will ebb away, leaving only your noisemakers clamoring for what might have been. The visionaries, however, believe that you really have let the ecumenical genii out of the bottle, that you have opened Pandora's box of trouble and hope—if ever so slightly in some places—and thus have committed yourselves to at least a generation of exacting, exciting and rewarding work, trying to bring the Church thought and practice up to the level of the Council's vision. By Hussite charge and my own frank admission, I belong among the visionaries, and it is in this spirit that I speak to you today.

* This address was delivered by Dr. Albert C. Outler at a reception in the Grand Hotel, Rome, given by the Paulist Fathers in honor of the Observer-Delegates and the American Hierarchy. Dr. Outler, an observer for the World Methodist Council, is professor of theology at Perkins School for Theology, Dallas, Texas.

Now, obviously, is the time for all good men to turn in their appraisals of Vatican II and to try to keep from trading on each other's platitudes. Here we are, virtually at the end of the most epochal event in modern Church history, already in the initial stages of a new era, on the verge of the enormous undertakings (and confusions) of the post-conciliar period. Each of us has to put all this in some sort of perspective, if only to place himself in the new situation and its involvements.

And yet, just as inevitably, our best efforts at appraisals are bound to be inadequate, for at least two reasons. One is the sheer scope of the Council—far too many blind men reporting their impressions of much too large an elephant. Our other bafflement, more subtle and tantalizing, is that every appraisal is already pre-shrunk, along the bias of one's *expectations* of the Council, one's calculations of the gap between its *possibilities* (at this stage or that) and its *performance* (on this point or the other). There are, as we know, those with a fine show of prophetic fervor who complain that the Council has not ushered in the millennium, that it has not really met all the needs of a desperate world, that it has not actually accomplished the reunion of all Christians. This means, of course, that their expectations were formed of the dreamstuff that sells hair tonic.

There are others who complain, with a curious mixture of bitterness and pathos, that the Council has dared to tamper with ancient ways and notions, ratified by papal teaching and sanctified by curial administration. Obviously, their expectation of the Council was that it should confirm the *status quo.*

There are those who complain that the council has been too "churchy," too much preoccupied with ecclesiastical housekeeping, not radically involved in the exigencies and agonies of the world that huddles under the walls of the Leonine City and that stretches to the Pentagon, the Kremlin and the jungles of Vietnam. There are those who fear another Protestant Reformation and yet others who seem to think that one is overdue—as the man who, at one point in this curious affair of the indulgences, asked me if I knew where there was a handy bulletin board where he could tack up another round of theses for debate.

My own bias in this matter is historical. Thus, I keep on being astonished at how far you had to come from where you started, and I am still puzzled as to just how you made it. But I am certain that there is no hope at all of rightly estimating the achievements of Vatican II if you skip its prehistory: the successive humiliations of the papacy, first by devoutly Christian monarchs and thereafter by the two Napoleons and the secular liberals, the successive crises of revolution and anti-clericalism that turned the Vatican into a beleaguered fortress, fortified by the firm conviction that the world of *those* times was irreconcilable, the successive alienations of the European intelligentsia and the workers, the stubborn maintenance of the old Church-State theories, even while Roman Catholics in North America and the missions were discovering that they could do very well without them, the two centuries of what E. E. Y. Hales has called "that long sequence of censures (of the world) codified by Pius IX, given a philosophical basis by Leo XIII, supplied with teeth by St. Pius X and sublimated by Pius XII."

It was this prehistory that set the stance and policies of the Roman Catholic Church right up to the eve of the Council. This is why the initial odds were so slight that what has happened could have happened. For one remembers that the early preparations for the Council were made inside the beleaguered fortress, by its chief defenders; the first schemata, in the summer of 1962, were plainly dominated by their siege mentality.

It was, of course, the genius of Pope John XXIII that transformed this mood and mind-set, that flung the Church into the maelstrom of the *modern* world with an invincible goodness that even cynics were abashed by, and with a breath-taking, simple-hearted confidence that the Church would fare better in free encounter with men of good will, that Christian unity might become a live option if Rome were renovated. It was this charismatic vision, this heart-lifting demonstration of the irresistible power of Christian graciousness, that brought the Council into being and gave to it its distinctive character. It is in this sense that Vatican II is and always will be Pope John's Council.

But the fact is that its first session settled nothing really, except that the Council had to be carried on. It has been the genius of Pope Paul and others who with him had grasped the substance of the Johannine vision to guide the Council going through the complex maze it has threaded from the confused gropings of Session One to the now nearly humdrum consensus of Session Four. The pattern of this leadership is far too complex to summarize here, and I see it, naturally, through a glass darkly—but, on any accounting, it has been an extraordinary performance and still, I think, generally underestimated.

One of the most striking impressions of these four years is that this Council has regularly failed to follow its script—not any one of several that have been in readiness from time to time. Plainly, it has not turned out quite as Pope John envisaged it; it is certainly not the Council that the ante-preparatory commissions prepared for. It has not filled the prescriptions of the *immobilisti*— and yet the progressives can hardly claim that they have called the tune for every stave. The most advanced of its documents bear visible traces of *pionismo;* even the most conservative reflect something of the spirit of *aggiornamento.*

It goes with the epoch-making character of Vatican II that it is has been a Council chiefly of *characters*, of new beginnings and mandates. Far less has been accomplished than has been made possible; more frontiers have been opened up than occupied. As vast as the agenda has been, it is slight in comparison with the budget of unfinished business you have produced—for yourselves, your priests, your scholars (lay and clerical), your lay folk—and, not least of all, for us separated brethren who must now find appropriate ways to reciprocate. The real meaning of most of the conciliar documents has still to be worked out in practice—in the Church in the modern world. For example, the keystone of the *De Ecclesia* is collegiality, but what does it mean? What the text seems to say? What the *nota explicativa* seems to imply? Or something else again? Nobody knows, nor shall we until we have watched it at work over a sizable span of years, in a trial-and-error process, the first ambiguous sequences of which have already taken place. If the *collegium episcoporum* ever really gets the hang of acting collegially, the resultant doctrine will look one way; if not, the character of *De Ecclesia* will fall into desuetude. And so it will be with all the other conciliar documents that have broken new ground: ecumenism, religious liberty, Christian–non-Christian relations, etc. The real meaning of what they say has yet to be determined by their translation into the basic experiences and understandings of the People of God. Then we shall know how much is substance and how much was conciliar rhetoric.

But the most unique aspect of this Council lies in its deliberate concern for reform within the limits of Christian community and in vital continuity with the Christian past. Vatican II has been as self-consciously a reforming Council as was Constance, or Florence or Trent—but with a decisive difference. Typical reformers value truth above community and, having the truth, they will sacrifice community—with pious reluctance (as at Augsburg) or with pious exuberance (as with the anathemata of Trent). Standard operating procedure for the other reforming councils has been to separate the sheep from the goats and then to scape the goats and fit out the sheep with halos. Vatican II is a very rare instance of historic change within a continuum of identity and consensus. One cannot miss the evident concern here for reform without schism in the soul of the Church—in the face of intransigence—that has sometimes seemed to reach over and beyond the call of duty. This is what I mean by my corny title, *Reformation Roman-Style*. Vatican II has been a Council that has dismayed the diehards, but has not alienated them, that has chafed the progressives and bored the unimaginative. It has been a subtle affair, in which some of the changes are only "development" and some "developments" are real changes, where much is left open to further development and/or change—and where an adequate theory for *this particular kind* of development and/or change has yet to be developed. In my judgment, this is one of the most interesting of all the problems generated by this Council. It opens up a whole constellation of acute issues, for Roman Catholics and Protestants alike, theoretical and practical, all bearing on the vital ecumenical question of the role of the Church in history and the role of history in the Church.

This distinctive style of reformation has not been without design. Pope John's notion of *aggiornamento* was meant to imply reform and has done so— though not in the classical styles of Hus or Gerson or Savonarola. In accepting and modulating the Johannine program, Pope Paul has become the highly reflective director of an incredibly complex enterprise that is solidly conservative in doctrine and discipline, on the one hand, and vigorously progressive in policy and program, on the other. He will have no tampering with the core of traditional doctrine; yet he has already initiated more changes in traditional papal policy and practice than any pope since Pius IX.

There are, however, many changes that have been initiated by Vatican II that may not touch the core of doctrine, but that do pose a tricky problem for the tradition of invariable traditions. The *immobilisti* have often been quite right when they have complained that the new formulations of collegiality, ecumenism, religious liberty, Christian-Jewish relations have altered traditional patterns that run back for centuries. They have been wrong in their *non sequitur* that these formulations are improper *because* they entail significant change. Thus, one of the important consequences of your Reformation Roman-Style is that in it you have continued to maintain a stable community in terms of theories about that stability that now require reexamination. This, too, is an addition to your budget of unfinished business.

The main thing, however, is that thus far you have avoided many of the standard ways of mismanaging reformations. One of these has been to strike down dissent and to damn the heretics in the name of some *proprietary system* of truth.

Another: to bulldoze the conscientious minority (especially if it is more proud than pitiful!). A third: to rend the bonds of Christian community in the name of one version of the Gospel or in some perfectionist protest against the imperfect structure of the visible Church. A fourth way is for timid reformers (and most reformers are more timid than they appear) to give up after their first manhandling by the ecclesiastical housekeepers.

But Reformation Roman-Style would seem to have its pitfalls, too. The most obvious is the illusion that a reform well-launched is somehow guaranteed a successful voyage. But it is all too plain that reforms and reformers are normally better in the sprints than in the marathon—that liberals have a distressing tendency to quit too easily or to count their chickens in the incubator. One wonders and worries about the swiftly ebbing tide of the reform spirit in this Council in these last days. Something like this was due, but it has come sooner and is more precipitate than I expected. The consequences of this can be serious, now that the real work of actualizing the Council in the Church and the world is just beginning.

The other danger, also clear and present, is the excess of the special virtue of this sort of reformation. In your laudable preference for community above polemics, for progress without schism, will you settle for anything less than your own highest possibilities? In your realistic concern to bring everybody along together, will you be careful not to hobble those who run on ahead— some of whom are your ablest and choicest spirits? The good *is* the enemy of the best, and we have already had that spelled out in more ways than one. One of the strongest impressions I have gained here is of an enormous pool of talent and an immense capital fund of expectant zeal in your *periti*, priests and people—and I can't help hoping and praying that you will find ways and the will to turn this huge potential loose on the world (and in the world) in patterns that are somewhat more apostolically radical than the essentially genteel and civilized essays of Vatican II. God knows, we Protestants have no shining alternatives to cite, no Archimedian standpoint from which to press a longer lever than yours. But in a world literally perishing for redemptive love, we all have need of mutual exhortation and each the right to rejoice at all the charisms of the Spirit—now so abundant in your midst—and to hope for their full fruition.

There will be no more meetings of this sort again in our lifetime. Our ways from here lie in a thousand directions—all in God's keeping, thank God! The splendors of Vatican II—this strange interlude when we have been so strangely one—will fade and be filed in the archives of our memories. But a new advent of the Holy Spirit has happened in our world in our time—an epiphany of love that has stirred men's hearts wherever they have glimpsed it incarnated. We saw that ourselves in the extraordinary uprise of faith and hope in the city of cynics when Pope Paul visited New York. In lesser ways, is not this task of incarnating the Spirit of Vatican II a possibility and imperative of the Council as it goes into its Diaspora?

What must not fade is the clear conviction set down in *De Ecumenismo* that "there can be no ecumenism worthy of the name (nor any effective outreach to the world) without interior conversion . . . , a change of heart and holiness of life." The way to Christian unity is long and arduous—and the end is not in sight. But on such a way, as on all other providential journeys, the pilgrim People of God walk by faith and not by sight. Pope Paul has wisely warned us against a facile hope and a false irenicism that trifles with the grave issues that have so long divided us. But even this warning is full of hope and is itself a landmark on our way.

Meanwhile, the least we can do is to remember that our confidence is not in ourselves, that our vocations are not for ourselves and cannot be exercised by ourselves. We are Christ's and our mission is in and for the world for which Christ died. That mysterious high moment in the Mass, *"per ipsum, et cum ipso, et in ipso"* ("by Christ, and with Christ and in Christ"), is really the basic formula for the apostolate of the whole People of God. This, at least, is what I have come to believe is the deepest level of the truth we confess *together* in that familiar refrain that you—and now we—seem to sing with more gusto than any other of our hymns: *"Christus vincit, Christus regnat, Christus, Christus imperat!"*

DR. DOUGLAS HORTON, Observer-Delegate, *18 September, 1965*

Allow me, Your Eminence, to say a word which, though it comes from my lips, speaks the sentiment of all of us observers.

You have opened to us many doors.

To speak of the most immediate matter, you have opened to us the door which has admitted us to this charming reception. There is a modern invention called the cocktail hour which is surely as concentrated a piece of irrationality as civilized man is ever asked to face: people standing in a room too small for them, drinking they hardly know what, shouting at each other (though strangers for the most part) in voices loud enough to overcome the shouts of their neighbors, and talking of subjects in which they have no interest and which they will soon forget. But your receptions are not of this pattern. They bring together, in most attractive surroundings, people of a common interest, who enjoy each other and carry away from each other's conversations memories which linger with them long and pleasantly. For this we thank you.

But you have also opened to us the door of St. Peter's. I think that most of us, in reporting the Council, try to drop the information with light nonchalance, almost as if we did not know we were saying it, that we observers are allowed to enter the basilica by the entrance used by the cardinals. And when, on the first day, we found our way to the place of our assignment, we discovered that our seats were not good ones at all: they were simply the best seats in the hall, thanks to your door-opening magic. It is hardly surprising that one bishop, whose seat is at the eastern end of the basilica, is said to have remarked, "I am going to leave the Church and come back as an observer in order to be able to see what is going on."

But our place under the protective spear of St. Longinus is only a single illustration of your continuing and unstinted concern for us. To us comes the same literature that goes to the Council Fathers themselves; to us it is given to hear every debate in the hall, to which we listen eloquently—but if we miss the meaning of the Latin, to us it is also given to turn to translators close by and hear the truth repeated to us in the language of Trafalgar Square, the Champs Elysées, Red Square or any of several other contemporary outposts of the Tower of Babel.

And these translators, by the way, have become more to us than simple retailers of speech; they have proved to be interpreters of men and relationships, uncovering to us the inner richness, including the creative tensions, of the Council, which we could only have conjectured without them. Some of us have the advantage of living at the Hotel de luxe Castel Sant'Angelo which overshadows the Hilton for good comradeship and opportunity for illuminating discussion. We are indeed coming to know each other so well that you may be said to be responsible for a new burst of ecumenism among non-Roman Christians, And, crowning all, there is the chance for talking things over with the Secretariat at our weekly meetings. These are the spice that is added to the banquet of St. Peter's. Through these conferences we feel drawn into the heart of the Council itself. Often our ideas reappear a few days later on the floor of St. Peter's, carried there through your arrangement by some good courier of like mind. Always we are met in the conferences with open-minded candor, and we have been indeed most grateful to enter through this door.

Most of all, we are indebted to you for opening the door of your friendship.

Now there are a few differences of theology and policy which have developed between the Roman Church and the rest of us during the centuries in which we have been studying how to keep separate. We shall have to trust the generations, not to say centuries, to come, to give us opportunity to resolve them; but it is evident to all that, thanks to the friendship you have shown us, the ground is now laid out of which reconciliations can grow. As a theologian, you may call friendship a non-theological factor, but, theological or not, friendship must have a part to play in the future of the Church. The historian can easily show that unhappy non-theological factors went into the greatest divisions of the Church —economic and political rivalries and the like—and, if that is the case, then the happy non-theological factor of friendship can play its part in the reintegration of Christendom. Because you have made us your friends, nothing important to you can be unimportant to us; we shall never again be indifferent, however we may disagree, with anything in your theology, your policy, your liturgy. Let this relationship of simple human friendship be carried from the center you have created here to the boundaries of Christendom, and we have at least the beginnings of ecumenism.

I said at the beginning that, though mine was the voice speaking, the words came from all of us observers. In closing, let me add that, though my words are directed to your ears, we should not be sorry to have them reach the hearts of all your loyal aides in the Secretariat for they are intended for them as well. But please keep some of our gratitude for yourself; so far as we observers are concerned, *Beatitudo* begins with Bea.

Decree on Ecumenism

✠ COMMENTARY *by Rev. George H. Tavard, A.A.*

The Decree on Ecumenism embodies an entirely new approach, on the part of the Church, to the problems that have plagued her existence since the early days when groups of Christians found themselves conscientiously disagreeing with points of faith or discipline. On this score, its publication marks the beginning of a totally new age and a radical departure from former conceptions regarding heresy and schism.[1] A new dimension has now been opened to Catholic life and theology, the scope of which should be carefully assessed.

The attitude which used to prevail was one of condemnation of all deviations from accepted standards of doctrine. Although such a reaction to theological or doctrinal novelty was reinforced during the Counter-Reformation, it had been dominant since the early centuries of the Church. The fight of the apostolic Church against docetism and the early forms of gnosticism had the consequence that the Great Church, at the time of the Fathers, considered all separations as practical manifestations of fundamentally heretical tendencies, even when, as in the case of the Donatists, no new doctrines were involved. Heresy meant, equivalently, setting oneself, and one's private spirit, up against the unanimous consensus of the Church as expressed in the recognized councils and taught by the major episcopal sees. The Middle Ages had basically the same understanding of non-conformity in doctrine, although the area open to free exchanges of thoughts and to doctrinal disputations was much wider than it was to become in modern times.

With the separations between the Apostolic See of Rome and the Patriarchal See of Constantinople and the ensuing mutual excommunications, and with the drama of the Great Western Schism (1389–1417), a new historical fact appeared: some schisms are not separations from the Church, but lacks of communications within the Church. This was such an unwonted happening that

[1] Three introductions to, or commentaries on, the Decree of Ecumenism were published before this essay was written: the Introduction by Thomas Stransky, C.S.P., to the Paulist Press edition of the Decree, 1965; Lorenz Cardinal Jaeger, *A Stand on Ecumenism: the Council's decree*, 1965; Bernard Leeming, C.Ss.R., *The Vatican Council and Christian Unity*, 1966. The Cardinal's commentary explains the text and its genesis rather than the issues involved; Fr. Leeming explains the text and the issues with great historical erudition, but does not stress the underlying theology.

321

both sides vainly endeavored to justify the separations by docketing heretical labels on the other. The events of the sixteenth century, during which the Protestant movement came to form separate churches, made the situation still more complex. As a result of the violent polemics between the reformers and the defenders of the Roman See, Protestantism was judged to be a conglomerate of all heresies, as witness the many anathemas pronounced by the Council of Trent. According to more recent Catholic studies of the Reformation, however, the Protestant movement, in its origin and in a number of the doctrinal formulas which it adopted, was not only Catholic, biblical and traditional in intention, but furthermore was actually so. Its forms of thought, however, followed other categories and were couched in other language than prevailed in the Church at large. Only after the first efforts of the reformers were misunderstood by the leaders of the Catholic Church and her most prominent theologians did the Protestant movement stretch farther and farther away from Catholic doctrine as hitherto accepted. This more objective awareness of the historical meaning of the Reformation brings up the fundamental question: Is it possible that such a movement would have been left out of God's providence? Is it not possible that, through it, God has been leading His Church to a deeper fidelity to the Gospel? If so, is it not time to try and read the writing on the wall in order to achieve this greater fidelity?

The recent striving of the Orthodox Churches and of the Protestant Churches and Communities toward a greater concern for Christian reunion has given rise to a further evolution of the positions. The ecumenical movement has begun to replace polemics with dialogue, rivalry with cooperation, mistrust with mutual confidence, anathema with doctrinal interchange. It has united in activities Churches that are still separated in doctrine. It has attempted to present the secular world with a common Christian witness. It has started to supersede confessional and denominational loyalties with a quest for the Church universal. And this has been done in all honesty, without any discarding of conscientious beliefs by any of the Churches committed to the ecumenical fellowship.

Since the 1920's, the ecumenical movement in Orthodoxy and Protestantism has, in turn, occasioned a similar movement of thought among Catholic theologians and pastors. This Catholic contribution to the ecumenical movement was, at first, the prerogative of a few pioneers. Yet their numbers grew, as years went by, to such a point that the attention of the Holy See was attracted toward this movement on several occasions. Two notable disciplinary documents were published: on the occasion of the assemblies of Life and Work and of Faith and Order, and at the time of the first assembly of the World Council of Churches. In the first instance, Pope Pius XI published his encyclical *Mortalium Animos* (Jan. 6, 1928), in which he took a negative view of ecumenism which he considered to be a pan-protestant movement. In the second instance, the Holy Office published its instruction *De Motione Oecumenica* (1949), which cautiously, yet positively, endorsed participation by qualified Catholics in ecumenical activities. In both cases, the position of the Holy See was disciplinary; no special doctrinal statements were included or implied in these official acts, except insofar as the traditional doctrine on the unity of the Catholic Church was reexpressed.

The question of Christian unity was raised at the Second Vatican Council in entirely new terms. On the one hand, the ecumenical movement had not evolved, as Pius XI feared, in the direction of pan-protestantism, but was genuinely concerned in a universal Christian reunion which would do justice to the points of view of all the Churches, including the Catholic Church. On the other hand, the ecumenical activities of Catholics, especially at the theological level, had become an integral part of contemporary reflection on Christian unity and a source of inspiration for the ecumenical concerns of Protestants themselves. It was clear that a merely disciplinary statement would not suffice. The Church needed to take a new doctrinal look at the question of unity and at the ecclesiological status of the separated communities.

The three chapters of the Decree deal, respectively, with the Catholic *principles* of ecumenism, with its *practice,* which is carefully described, and with an *assessment of the present situation* as regards the Orthodox Churches and the separated Churches and Communities of the West. Since the history, the constitution and the doctrine of the Orthodox Churches are radically distinct from those of the Western Churches, which derive, in the main, from the Reformation of the sixteenth century, their treatment is very different. The Orthodox Churches are described in their present ethos and teaching as these pertain to a consideration of problems of reunion. The Western Churches are not described, but an attempt is made to indicate the most fruitful areas of cooperation and doctrinal dialogue with them in our present circumstances.

Since it is impossible to comment on all the points explained in the Decree, we shall focus attention on the most important items.

The Council does not provide *principles of Catholic ecumenism,* but *Catholic principles of ecumenism.* For the ecumenical movement is one. Ecumenism is neither Protestant nor Orthodox nor Catholic. It is simply ecumenism, a search for Christian unity. All Christians should search for unity, even those who, like the Orthodox and the Catholics, believe that the unity of the Church is already achieved in their own communion. For unity must always be perfected; and just as Jesus prayed to the Father for unity among His disciples, the disciples ought to pray for the same purpose and to behave in such a way that they will promote, rather than harm, unity.

The Catholic principles of ecumenism are the doctrinal principles regulating the Catholic concept of the Church. But ecclesiology, at mid-twentieth century, is not yet a fully surveyed area of doctrine. The main points have been assured for a long time; yet many shaded spots remain unclear. The considerations on ecclesiology that have been introduced into our text are naturally to be read in the light of the longer exposition made by the conciliar Constitution on the Church. These are also to be explained in the light of the developments in ecclesiology that have taken place since the First Vatican Council and of the researches made by the great ecclesiologists of our times, like Yves Congar or Charles Cardinal Journet.

In the light of ecclesiology, the first chapter epitomizes a Trinitarian approach to the Church, in which the community of the disciples is seen as participating in the community of the Three Persons in God, through the mediation of the one Mediator, Jesus Christ who, through the redemptive actions of His life, passion and resurrection, enables us to become "sons in his Sonship" and recipients of His Spirit. The College of the Twelve and the institutional aspects of the Church, which the College symbolizes and embraces, have instrumental functions relative to sharing the life of the Triune God. They are to spread the Gospel by preaching, to announce the good news of salvation until the end of the world, to initiate all men into "the mystery of the Church's unity, in Christ and through Christ, the Holy Spirit contributing the variety of his gifts" (n. 2).

Such a Church is unique. For just as there is only one community of the Three Persons, and one Mediator, there can be only one community of those who share the Trinitarian life. The Council, however, acknowledges the historical fact of the existence of separate Christian Communions, the members of which, having been born into them, cannot be accused of the sin of schism. Here lies the fundamentally new dimension of the Decree on Ecumenism. When St. Cyprian called the man guilty of schism "an imitator of Judas rather than of Jesus,"[2] he had in mind men who were personally guilty of "the crime of dissension." Before the separations of East and West, it was possible to hold a simplified view of the question, in which separation was equated with sin. The situation was still interpreted in this way in the sixteenth century. The prolongation of schism between East and West and of the Reformation, however, has introduced the new situation that multitudes of Christians in good faith have inherited separations made in the past. Actually, this is not entirely new, since it was already the case for the non-Chalcedonian Churches whose schism dates back to the aftermath of the Councils of Ephesus (431) and of Chalcedon (451). Yet it is the growing intercourse of Catholics with Orthodox and Protestants which has put this fact into focus.

If separations are not sins in those who have been born into them, what are they? This is where the Council has blazed a new path. On the one hand, it does not—and it cannot—renounce the traditional Catholic doctrine which sees the Mystical Body of the Lord as subsisting in the Roman Catholic Church. *De Ecumenismo*, n. 3, tallies with *De Ecclesia* on the same subject. On the other hand, the Churches and Communities separated from us have preserved, to an extent which would have to be defined in each case, the nature of the Church. For the nature of the Church is to be the organ of salvation. And, in the words of the Decree, "It follows that, although we believe them to suffer from certain

2 St. Cyprian, De Oratione Dominica, XXIV (PL, IV: 536).

defects, the severed Churches and Communities have been by no means deprived of meaning and of weight in the mystery of salvation. For the Spirit of Christ has not refrained from using them as means of salvation, whose value derives from the very fulness of grace and of truth entrusted to the Catholic Church" (n. 3). The conclusion that the severed Churches participate, in a mysterious way, in the true nature of the Church by being the instruments of Christ and the Spirit for the spreading of the Gospel and the salvation of mankind represents a marked advance on previous theological speculations concerning Christian disunion. Until this century, most theologians were willing to consider the relationship of the individual separated Christians to the true Church, but would not have admitted their Communities to a similar relationship. More recently, the ecclesiology developed in connection with the ecumenical movement began to introduce the notion of *vestigia Ecclesiae:* there would be remnants of the Church in the acts performed and the doctrines preached by the several Churches, insofar as these are truly conducive to faith in Christ and union with him. The notion of *vestigia Ecclesiae* was endorsed by Pius XI in a famous reference to the "gold" preserved in the Orthodox Churches.[3] Vatican II has drawn the logical consequences of this: remnants of the Church cannot survive in what would not be the Church at all. That such remnants have been recognized implies that the Church is in them. Therefore, Communities which at one time and in a certain light appeared to have totally unchurched themselves have truly preserved the essence of the Church in its core, the minimum of which would be the life of grace as an interior element and the preaching of the Gospel as an exterior one.

This ecclesiological status of severed Communities justifies the existence of, and the Catholics' participation in, the ecumenical movement. This movement is briefly but carefully described in n. 4, and its relationship to other aspects of the Church's life is indicated.

The newness of our document appears again in striking fashion in the second chapter, devoted to "the practice of ecumenism." Although this is intended to be practical, it does not go into the details of all that can be done or ought to be done in order to promote Christian unity. These details have been left to further precision on the part of the Secretariat of Christian Unity; and several decrees may be published from time to time on the implementation of ecumenism. This chapter outlines only a general view of the nature and qualities of ecumenical activity.

The new element here resides in a vision of ecumenical activity in the perspective of the spiritual life. The temptation of the ecumenical movement has always been to multiply activities. The organization of mutual services among Christians and the marshalling of resources to bring service to non-Christians, whenever this is possible and desirable, constitute important fields of ecumenical action. Indeed, one of the drives behind the World Council of Churches

[3] Address to the Italian Catholic University Federation, Jan. 10, 1927.

is the desire to proceed to a united stand, by which Christians can witness together to their belief in the redemptive love of the Lord. However, this should only be a side-issue and a side-activity, for the ecumenical concern ought to be focused mainly on the essential unity which Christ willed for His Church: the unity of man with man in Christ, the unity of man with God through the mediation of the Savior, the unity of mankind brought together into one by the power of the Holy Spirit.

In this perspective, the second chapter constitutes an appeal to "renewal of the Church," an exhortation to her members to follow "her pilgrim way," a perspective opened on "the continual reformation of which she always has need" (n. 6). The reform of the Church means, in the first place, the conversion of her members. For the Church is no abstract entity separated from the People of God. That the Church is, as the Constitution *De Ecclesia* (Ch. 2) insists, the People of God implies that what happens to the People happens to her. The Church, therefore, will not be reformed unless the People themselves change the form of their life, passing from sin to grace, from distance to nearness, from citizenship on earth to citizenship in heaven. Accordingly, the Council declares: "There can be no ecumenism worthy of the name without interior conversion" (n. 7). This entails a trust that the Spirit will lead the People to conversion and will Himself undertake the task of reforming the Church. Precisely, past separations took place because there was not sufficient faith in the action and guidance of the Spirit, because certain persons, in high places, put their confidence in the guarantee of the institution rather than in the advent of the Spirit, who "breathes where He will." There are now tokens, as the Council notes, that the Spirit is at work: "the biblical and liturgical movements, the preaching of the Word of God and catechetics, the apostolate of the laity, new forms of religious life, the spirituality of married life, and the Church's social teaching and activity" (n. 6). These are signs of the Spirit's presence in our days. Yet it remains to orient these Spirit-inspired actions toward the restoration of unity.

It remains also, and this will be the key to the whole ecumenical movement, to implement the Spirit's promises at the level of our own spiritual life. Only those who live in the Spirit can do the acts of the Spirit. Only those who are attuned to His suggestions can carry out His purposes. Therefore the Council invites us all to "newness of attitudes of mind, to self-denial and to unstinted love" (n. 7). In this connection, the Council endorses the idea, suggested a long time ago by some of the Catholic pioneers of the ecumenical movement, that the Spirit requires us to acknowledge our collective faults against unity: "St. John has testified: 'If we say that we have not sinned, we make him a liar, and his word is not in us.' This holds good for sins against unity. Thus, in humble prayer we beg pardon of God and of our separated brethren, just as we forgive them that trespass against us" (n. 7). Pope Paul had himself opened the way to this confession in his address at the beginning of the second session of the Council when he said:

If we are in any way to blame for that separation, we humbly beg God's forgiveness. And we ask pardon, too, of our brethren who feel themselves to have been injured by us. For our part, we willingly forgive the injuries which the Catholic Church has suffered and forget the grief during the long series of dissensions and separations. May the heavenly Father deign to hear our prayers and grant us true brotherly peace.

The allusion to the Lord's Prayer, in both the Pope's speech and the Council's formula, introduces this confession of sins into the liturgical setting of worship: it is only if we have been reconciled to our brother that our gifts may be brought to the altar. Thus the whole Church becomes involved in an act of repentance. Nonetheless, the Council never wishes to assert that the Church, as such, is guilty of sin. As the organ of salvation, as the channel of God's gracious condescension toward man, as the realm of redemption, as the anticipation of the Kingdom of God, the Church lives beyond the possibility of sinning, at a level where "all tears are wiped away" (Ap. 21:4). If we attribute sins to the Church, this can only be as a manner of speaking, by which the Church is taken for the People who constitute her human aspect. As such, she is subject to human bondage and is affected and hurt by the sins of the People. As People of God, endowed by God's grace, she remains sinless; as People of the earth, she has been damaged and soiled by the earthly elements of her life.[4]

"Spiritual ecumenism," mentioned in n. 8, is an expression borrowed from one of the early workers in the ecumenical vineyard, Abbé Paul Couturier (1881–1953).[5] The Council describes it as "this change of heart and holiness of life, along with public and private prayer for the unity of Christians"; it should be "the soul of the ecumenical movement." A hint is obviously given here to those who might be tempted to practice an academic ecumenism, an ecumenism for scholars, without deep participation in the life of worship and prayer of the Church as a whole. True ecumenism operates at all levels, in spiritual transformation, in common prayer, in intellectual exchange, in theological research. It is possible even to conceive of the steps toward Christian unity on the pattern of the ascent of spiritual life toward union with God.[6] The specific contribution of Paul Couturier to the ecumenical movement had been to orient Christians toward simultaneous prayer for unity mainly, though not only, through the help of the Week of Universal Prayer for Christian Unity (January 18–25). The Council could not, of course, specifically recommend this week of prayer. Other periods of the year have been advocated by others as suitable to prayer for unity, especially the ocatve of the Epiphany and the eight days before the feast of Pentecost. By using Couturier's cherished formula of

---

[4] I am entirely in agreement with Father Bernard Leeming's interpretation of this passage, *op. cit.*, pp. 127–128.

[5] See Maurice Villain, *Unity*, 1961.

[6] See *L'Angoisse de l'Unité*, Paris, 1952; also, "Tentative Approaches to a Mystique of Unity," *Journal of Ecumenical Studies*, 1966.

"spiritual ecumenism," the Council did not prefer the Week of January to other periods of prayer for unity. It simply endorsed prayer as one of the most thorough means of preparing for Christian unity. It even encouraged it to an extent that went much farther than Couturier had envisioned. For Couturier wished prayer to be simultaneous, yet not in common:[7] there should be no blurring of differences by attempting *communicatio in sacris,* forbidden by Canon 1258; there should be no "confusion."

Couturier's view on this point is dated. It belongs to a period when *communicatio in sacris* was often taken to forbid not only participation in the sacraments, but even participation in the same prayers. This, which was not the original meaning of the term, has been definitely discarded by the Council. The passage on "communication in the sacraments" (*communicatio in sacris*) should be attended to very carefully, for it constitutes an epoch-making breakthrough in canonical legislation and in the theological understanding of prayer in common in spite of separations:

> Yet *communicatio in sacris* is not to be considered as a means to be used indiscriminately for the restoration of unity among Christians. There are two main principles upon which the practice of such *communicatio* depends: first, that of the unity of the Church, which ought to be expressed in prayer; second, that of sharing in the means of grace. The unity to be expressed generally forbids *communicatio in sacris.* The grace to be obtained sometimes recommends it. The concrete course to be adopted, with due regard to all the circumstances of time, place and persons, is left to the prudent decision of the local episcopal authority, unless the Bishops' Conference according to its statutes, or the Holy See, has determined otherwise. (n. 8)

The expression *communicatio in sacris,* in the present context, is to be taken in the strict sense which it has in Canon 1258: it means participation in "sacred actions," that is ,in sacraments. The *Decree on the Catholic Churches of the Eastern Rite,* Nn. 26–29, gives it the broader sense of participation in all holy things. The proper expression for this should be *communicatio in spiritualibus,* participation in spiritual goods.

Our passage has two parts, theological and disciplinary. The disciplinary instruction leaves practical decisions to the local bishop, unless the regional Conference of Bishops in each region or the Holy See has already announced official decisions. However, these decisions should be made in the light of the theological section of the passage which explains the principles regulating the participation of separated Christians in the same sacraments and, in a broader sense, in worship. There are two such principles, the balance of which should provide the light in which a practical decision can be made.

Participation in the same sacraments, and especially in the Holy Eucharist,

[7] See Couturier, "Unanimité d'intercession sans confusionisme," in Maurice Villain, ed., *Oecumenisme Spirituel,* 1962, pp. 154–155.

expresses the unity of the Church. For the sacraments are related to the oneness of the Church in two ways. On the one hand, they are the means taken by Christ to reach man today in his body and soul, by which He makes Himself contemporary to every believer: they express the oneness of the mediator and of the Gathering of those whom Christ has reached and whom He united in His Body. This applies particularly to the Holy Eucharist, the sacrament of unity par excellence; yet all sacraments are also corporate experiences of the same divine life in the one Church. From this point of view, only those who are united in the same Church can express and manifest the unity of that Church by receiving the sacraments together.

On the other hand, as objects and occasions of faith, the sacraments do not express a divided faith, but one faith. They are a common expression of the same relationship to Christ by many members of the same body united together by being assumed in the one Body and by sharing the same tradition, the same means of grace, the same formulation of faith, the same hierarchy, the same institutional elements of the Church's life. It follows that, from the standpoint of the unity of the Church expressed by and manifested through the sacrament, *communicatio in sacris* will be ruled out most of the time.

The Council is careful not to rule it out all the time. For it does not contradict here what it says in two other places: communication in the sacraments between Orthodox and Catholics is, given certain circumstances, not only possible, but also commendable. This point is clearly made in n. 15 of our decree:

> These Churches [Orthodox], although separated from us, yet possess true sacraments, above all, by apostolic succession, the priesthood and the Eucharist, whereby they are still joined to us in closest intimacy. Therefore, *communicatio in sacris*, given suitable circumstances and the approval of Church authority, is not merely possible, but is encouraged.

The same doctrine is found in the Decree on Eastern Catholic Churches, which, however, does not explain the underlying principle so concisely and precisely as the Decree on Ecumenism:

> According to the principles laid down, the sacraments of Penance, the Eucharist and the Anointing of the Sick can be conferred on those Eastern Christians who in good faith are separated from the Catholic Church, if of their own accord they ask for them and are rightly disposed. Moreover, Catholics may seek the same sacraments from those non-Catholic ministers in whose Church the sacraments are considered to be valid, whenever there is need or real spiritual benefit, and access to a Catholic priest is physically or morally impossible. (n. 27)

What it grants as regards the sacraments, the Decree on Eastern Catholic Churches grants *a fortiori* concerning less important spiritual goods: "Similarly, in accordance with the same principles, a sharing in sacred functions, services and places is for a just cause allowed between Catholics and separated Eastern brothers" (n. 28).

The principle that common sacramental participation manifests unity opens such a fellowship to all Christians to the extent that they are united in faith and in similar sacramental and liturgical traditions. Thus, the Decree leans toward the side of the Orthodox, with whom we have a great unity in faith and liturgical tradition, more than toward that of Protestants.

However, another principle must be taken account of: prayer implies a reception of grace; the sacraments are privileged means of grace. Since it is essential to the Christian life to seek for God's grace through prayer and the sacraments, one should not neglect these channels of grace, even if this means doing it in common with Christians separated from us. This principle would seem to open the possibility of participation in the sacraments with all Christians, including Protestants. This would be true if only this principle was to be considered. But theological balance requires that both principles be held together: the latter, which orients toward all forms of intercommunion; and the former, which bans intercommunion with most separated Christians. This is where the burden of authority comes in. The bishop, who is called upon to decide what to do in concrete cases, has to weigh the scope and effects of each principle in the given circumstances of time, place and persons. At times, he may conclude that the grace to be obtained allows for an exception to be made to the principle of the expression of unity. He will then permit actions which express full unity, although full unity does not exist. At other times he may conclude, on the contrary, that the distance between the full unity expressed by communication in the sacraments and the actual lack of unity is too great to be overlooked: this will then outweigh the consideration of the grace to be obtained through common participation in the sacraments.

At any rate, the Council makes it clear that intercommunion cannot be "a means to be used indiscriminately for the restoration of unity among Christians." It thus parts with those circles in the ecumenical movement where widespread intercommunion is advocated as a means to unity. The sacraments are means of grace to be handled by God through the channels He has instituted in the Church; they are not at the disposal of men to handle the way they think appropriate, in keeping with their own conceptions of unity. *Communicatio in sacris* will, in certain circumstances, be a means of grace to which we should have recourse; it cannot be a universal means to reach unity, to be adopted *indiscretim*, that is, imprudently, without regard to the proper theological principles of sacramental theology and ecclesiology.

We should now cast a quick look at the third and last chapter of the Decree on Ecumenism. As stated before, it describes the Orthodox Churches, and indicates at the same time the attitude to be adopted by Catholics in regard to Orthodoxy. It then analyzes the most important elements for the contemporary dialogue between Catholicism and Protestantism. The section concerning Orthodoxy is most important. Yet, since this topic should already be handled in connection with the Decree on Eastern Catholic Churches, I shall avoid duplication and speak only of the first half of this chapter.

One main point arises from the difference in treatment between Orthodoxy and Protestantism (or the "Churches and Ecclesial Communities of the West"): the Orthodox and the Protestant Churches are not the Church in the same sense. If they were, there would be no ground for a separate treatment. The beginning of the Decree on Ecumenism introduced the question of the ecclesiological status of separated Communities and suggested that these Communities are, in some sense, the Church. Here, however, a clear distinction is made. The Orthodox are the Church in the full sacramental sense of the term; communion in the liturgy under the Presidency of a Mystagogue makes them the Church as the Eucharistic Gathering in which heaven is mystically present and the human life is raised, eschatologically, to participation in the Kingdom of the Saints. The Communities of the West, in general, are not the Church in this full eucharistic sense, but only insofar as they form a community of the faithful gathered for common worship in which the Word is preached. No doubt, the Protestant Communions, and especially the Anglican and the Lutheran, also believe that in them "the sacraments are duly administered." There is no doubt either that the Catholic Church gratefully acknowledges the truth of their Baptism and recognizes the sacrament of Matrimony sealed between two Protestants. Nonetheless, the barrier of the sacrament of Orders persists between the Catholic Church and the Churches issued from the Reformation.

For this reason, a delicate passage of the third chapter, section two, deals with the Eucharist:

> Although the ecclesiastical communities separated from us lack the fullness of unity with us which flows from Baptism, and although we believe that they have not preserved the proper reality of the eucharistic mystery in its fullness, especially because of the absence of the sacrament of Orders, nevertheless, when they commemorate the Lord's death and resurrection in the Holy Supper, they profess that it signifies life in communion with Christ and await his coming in glory. (n. 22)

It is not suggested, of course, that this is the sum total of eucharistic teaching in the Churches of the Reformation. The Council describes here a minimum, which all Churches seem to hold, regardless of additions each would feel compelled to make to such a description. Three points are held to have been preserved in these Churches: commemoration of the Lord's death and resurrection; communion with Christ; eschatological expectation of the Lord's return. Thus, the Protestant Eucharist is considered a memorial by which the past events of salvation are made alive in the communities during the cult; a testimony to the faith that the Holy Supper implies a symbolic participation in the life of Christ, by which one is united to Him and therefore strengthened for Christian witness and for spiritual progress; finally, an expectation of the Second Advent, in which the coming of the glory of the Lord is anticipated in hope. The Council avoids any statement that could be taken to mean that the Lord makes Himself present during these services of Holy Communion. Yet it does not wish to exclude this possibility. Whatever must be said, in fidelity to the Catholic and the Orthodox tradition, about the Real Presence of the Lord in the Holy Eucharist through the instrumentality of the priesthood, one may hope that the Lord also makes Himself present to the faith of those who seek Him in the eucharistic services of their ecclesiastical communities, even when these do not believe in or have not preserved the sacrament of Orders. If separated Christians do testify that they have experienced the presence of the Lord in the Supper, there is no theological reason to doubt the validity of their testimony. Accordingly, the Council urges dialogue concerning "the doctrine about the Lord's Supper, about other sacraments, worship and ministry in the Church" (n. 22).

Another point deserves to be noted in the Council's treatment of the subject of dialogue between Catholicism and the heirs of the Reformation: the Christian regard for the Word of God. For Word and Sacrament are, for both Catholicism and Protestantism, the two *foci* of the Christian life. The most significant text is as follows:

> A love and reverence, almost a cult, of Holy Scripture leads our brethren to a constant and diligent study of the sacred text. For the Gospel is "the power of God for salvation to everyone who has faith, to the Jew first and then to the Greek" (Rom. 1:16). While invoking the Holy Spirit, they seek in these very Scriptures God speaking to them in Christ, the One whom the prophets foretold, the Word of God made flesh for us. In the Scriptures they contemplate the life of Christ, as well as the teachings and actions of the divine Master for the salvation of men, in particular the mysteries of His death and resurrection. (n. 21)

This is not a mere analysis of the Protestant reading of the Bible. It tells what *lectio divina* ought to be, a search for God speaking to us in Christ, an adhesion to the Word made flesh, a contemplation of His life, a constant attention to, and listening for, the voice of God. Such a reading cannot be made without the active assistance of the Spirit. Here again, then, the Decree on Ecumenism urges all to a deeper awareness of the Spirit and foretells a charismatic period for the life of the Church. Admittedly, Protestant reading of Scripture does not give sufficient room to the authoritative voice of the Church through which the authentic interpretation of the Sacred Text comes down to us in the transmission of the apostolic Revelation. This is duly noted in our text. Nevertheless, the Protestant desire to be faithful to the Word written and spoken is one authentic feature of the Church which has not only survived, but even thrived in the Churches issued from the Reformation.

This passage of the Decree ought to be read in the light of the Council's Constitution *De Revelatione,* in which the conditions for reading Scripture in the Church are explained more at length. In turn, however, it throws additional light on the Constitution, for it shows that reading the Bible, the traditional *lectio divina* as practiced by the Fathers and as forming the core of medieval piety, has not been in recent centuries the privilege of Catholics. Other Christians also have found the Gospel to be "the power of God for salvation to everyone who has faith" and have been led by the testimony of the Spirit to the fountains of living water flowing from the Holy Scriptures of the Old and New Testaments. The Catholic Church finds, in the acknowledgment of this fact, more than an incentive to ecumenical dialogue: she feels a profound joy at the mystery of the mercies of God who has found ways to speak to the heart of all Christians, even those separated from the center of Catholic unity, as formerly He found ways to make His People those who were not His People.

The Decree on Ecumenism, in common with the other documents issued by the Vatican Council, heralds a new age in the history of the Church, the age of reconciliation, which we may also call the age of the Spirit, for only the Spirit can achieve reconciliation, or the age of new charisms, for such a task will require charisms unknown to the past. This ultimate purpose and meaning of the Decree is valid for the Church as a whole. No geographic, national or cultural portion of the Church on earth may claim the Decree for itself. It applies to all and invites all to the conversion of heart required for the promised reform.

Yet the Decree on Ecumenism has a special meaning for the Church in America on account of the history of American Catholicism and its past peculiar transformation in regard to ecumenical activities. The Church of the eighteenth and nineteenth centuries, headed by the great Bishops Carroll, England and Ireland, and enlivened by generous personalities like those of Orestes Brownson or Isaac Hecker, was amazingly open, and—although this word was not current then in its contemporary sense—ecumenical in spirit. Little by little, however, under the impact of the rabid anti-Catholicism of some sections of American Protestantism, and with the growing influence of uneducated Irish immigrants whose past experience did not dispose them to take a favorable view of their Protestant neighbors, the American Church narrowed its horizons and recoiled upon itself, building its own shell in which to seek protection from the outside world. This process of ghettoizing was hastened by the unfortunate polemics around the "phantom heresy" of Americanism, the condemnation of which by Pope Leo XII (*Testem benevolentiae,* January 22, 1899) clinched the efforts of the conservative wing of American Catholics to stifle more liberal voices. As a result, the ecumenical movement was dead among American Catholics when it spread in other lands between 1910 and 1950.

Only around 1950[8] and 1955[9] did ecumenical concerns start again in the United States after the pre-ecumenical activities of Father Paul Wattson (1863–1940) earlier in the century. Since then it has grown by leaps and bounds, especially after Pope John XXIII had personally encouraged it and taken bold steps to promote it. The creation of the Pontifical Secretariat for Promoting Christian Unity, which made the Decree on Ecumenism possible, marked a new age for the Church. Meditation on the Decree on Ecumenism should give depth to our ecumenical resurgence and should mark the end of the attitude of self-defense, of apology and of polemics which dominated the Church in America during the first half of our century. Here also the Decree on Ecumenism should spark newness of life, in the light of the Word better understood, in the wake of the powerful attraction of the Holy Spirit.

[8] Publication of Gustave Weigel's essay, "Contemporary Protestantism and Paul Tillich" (*Theological Studies*, 1950, pp. 177 ff), and "Protestant Theological Positions Today" (*Theological Studies*, 1950, pp. 62 ff).
[9] Publication of *The Catholic Approach to Protestantism.*

VII/DECREE ON EASTERN CATHOLIC CHURCHES

Decree on Eastern Catholic Churches
✠ HISTORICAL INTRODUCTION

No decree of the Second Vatican Council has been so little discussed and so slightly noted as this Decree on the Eastern Catholic Churches. Most commentators admit that it will neither be long remembered nor frequently cited. It may well be outdated the day the revised Code of Canon Law for the Eastern churches will be promulgated. The shortcomings of the Decree, however, are neither in the text itself nor in the conscious intention of its drafters. They are found, rather, like the other decrees that were reduced to general propositions, in the shortcomings due to the pressure of the conciliar process.

The preparatory Commission for the Eastern Churches was presided over by Amleto Cardinal Cicognani, papal Secretary of State. The Reverend Dunstan Donovan, S.A., was the only American consultor on this Commission. According to Pope John, in establishing the Commission on July 2, 1960, one of its principal purposes was to seek avenues of reconciliation with the Oriental Christians. The Commission examined the suggestions offered by the world's bishops, Catholic universities and offices of the Roman curia, and then presented their findings in a series of eleven schemata in eleven booklets.

During the third plenary session of the Central Preparatory Commission on January 18 and 19, 1962, Cardinal Cicognani presented five schemata: 1) on the diversity of rites in the Church; 2) on the dignity of Oriental patriarchs; 3) on the relations of Catholics with non-Catholic Oriental Christians in sacred ceremonies, 4) on the vernacular languages in the Oriental liturgy; 5) on the sacraments in the Oriental Church. During the fourth session, on February 27, 1962, Cardinal Cicognani presented ecclesiastical prescriptions concerning the Catholics of the Eastern rites. On May 12, the last day of the sixth session, Cardinal Cicognani presented four other schemata concerning the Eastern Churches. They were on the powers of the bishops, on religious instruction, on the perpetual calendar and the celebration of Easter, and on the Divine Office. During the seventh and final plenary session of the Central Preparatory Commission on June 16, Cardinal Cicognani again reported on a schema concerning the unity of Christians from the viewpoint of the Eastern Churches.

The Central Preparatory Commission ordered that the first ten of these

337

schemata be reduced and collated into one schema. After this had been accomplished, the schema consisted of an introduction and five chapters: 1) concerning rites; 2) concerning the discipline of the clergy; 3) concerning the discipline of the sacraments; 4) concerning divine worship; 5) concerning the Church's magisterium. The last of these preparatory schemata was revised and entitled "Concerning the Unity of the Church: That They All May Be One." These schemata were discussed on the floor of the Council from November 27 to December 1 during the first session. On the latter date, the Council Fathers resolved to combine the contents of this schema with the materials in both the proposed schema on ecumenism and the proposed constitution on the Church.*

On January 30, 1963, the Central Coordinating Commission of the Council instructed the conciliar Commission for the Eastern Churches to revise the original schema. The Commission did so, from February to April. The conciliar Commission was still presided over by Cardinal Cicognani. Two American prelates were among its members: the Most Reverend Ambrose Senyshyn, Archbishop of Philadelphia for the Ukrainians, and the Most Reverend Bryan McEntegart, Bishop of Brooklyn, New York. This revised schema was distributed to the Council Fathers, and they were requested to submit their observations on the text. The Commission also formed subcommissions with members of the Secretariat for the Promotion of Christian Unity and the Doctrinal Commission to assist in drafting the documents assigned to those two groups. Furthermore, the Commission for the Eastern Churches also profited greatly from the discussion, on the floor of the Council during the second session, concerning both the nature of the Church and ecumenism. These discussions, as well as the 140 interventions submitted directly to the Oriental commission, assisted greatly in redrafting the text of its schema.

During this period, two American prelates submitted their observations on the text. Cardinal Spellman agreed with the second paragraph of the text which declared:

> The variety of the particular Oriental Churches within the same Church in no way harms catholicity; rather it declares it; for the Catholic Church intends that the legitimate particular traditions of each nation or area remain intact and preserved, and likewise she wishes to adapt her plan of life to the various needs of time and place.

However, in order to make this statement even stronger, the Cardinal suggested that this sentence should be added: "It is earnestly recommended to the orders and congregations of the Church of the Latin rite, which assist the Oriental faithful, that for the greater efficiency of the apostolate, they establish as much

---

* Confer the chapters concerning the Decree on Ecumenism and the Dogmatic Constitution on the Church.

as possible oriental houses and even provinces." The Cardinal also held a reservation on a sentence that would later become one of the key problems of the schema. That sentence declared that "baptized non-Catholics returning to the Catholic Church are advised to keep their own rite in regions of their own rite." He asked whether the term "advised" was an order or only an exhortation. "I prefer," he wrote, "the merely exhortative meaning, lest the freedom of the sons of God who are returning to the Church be restrained without need. Perhaps it would be better to use another word." The Cardinal also felt that the schema's discussion concerning unity should be contained in the Decree on Ecumenism, and he was also happy to see that the document declared the validity of the priesthood among Orthodox clergy. Finally, he was pleased with the schema's concluding tribute to the Blessed Virgin Mary because "the Oriental churches have been most zealous in increasing and propagating the cult of the Virgin Mother of God."

In his intervention submitted on July 19, 1963, Archbishop John J. Krol of Philadelphia felt that everything in the schema was in keeping with the dignity of the Oriental churches. However, he had several observations to make on the text. His first was the same reservation that Cardinal Spellman had concerning the schema's statement that members of the Orthodox Churches must join the corresponding rite entering the Roman Catholic Church. He wrote:

> The change from one rite to another presumes a *terminus a quo* and a *terminus ad quem*. In the case of a person baptized in another rite who wishes to remain in this rite, we actually lack a *terminus a quo*. Therefore, it seems that in cases of this type, it is not a matter of transition from one rite to another. Thus the formalities established for the change of rite should not be required.

Secondly, Archbishop Krol wanted to see the text declare that when an Eastern-rite priest hears confessions in a Latin-rite church, he should secure faculties from the Latin local ordinary "lest there arise abuses and confusion."

On January 15, 1964, the Central Coordinating Commission directed the Oriental commission (as it had also directed other commissions) to reduce the text of its schema to certain fundamental points that would promote an *aggiornamento* of ecclesiastical practices, especially regarding *communicatio in sacris*. The Commission met from March 10 to 16 and redrafted the text, although, for all practical purposes, it was not drastically shortened from the previous schema. Pope Paul VI approved the revised text on April 27, and it was distributed to the Council Fathers.

On October 15 during the 102nd working congregation, Cardinal Cicognani and Coadjutor Archbishop Gabriel Bukato of Belgrade, Yugoslavia, introduced the propositions on the Oriental churches to the Council Fathers. The text was discussed by 30 Council Fathers throughout four congregations and, on October 20, of the 2,180 Council Fathers present, 1911 approved the acceptability of the text for immediate voting. The vote itself was somewhat of a surprise, because even during this brief debate it was apparent that the text suffered from several serious defects. Among these defects expressed by the Council Fathers were the patronizing attitude of the text toward the Eastern churches, the failure of the Latin Church to understand the psyche of the Eastern Churches, the lack of proper estimation for the patriarchal dignity and the insistence that a baptized non-Catholic must join his corresponding rite when he decides to enter the Catholic Church. During these discussions on the floor of the Council, two Americans expressed their views, both speaking on October 19 during the 104th general congregation.

Auxiliary Bishop Gerald McDevitt of Philadelphia echoed in his remarks the same sentiments earlier expressed by Cardinal Spellman and Archbishop Krol. He cited the revised version of the text which read: "Finally, each and every one of the faithful, as well as those baptized non-Catholics coming into the Church, retain that rite proper to whatever area they live in, and they celebrate and keep that rite with all their resources; the law of appeal in particular cases to the Holy See is preserved." Bishop McDevitt stated that in his judgment, the text was partly acceptable and partly unacceptable. He then presented two arguments why he favored changing the text, the one canonical and the other from his own personal experiences.

This text excessively restricts the liberty of those baptized non-Catholics who wish to come into the Church. I completely understand that the recourse to the Holy See of those Catholics who are already in the Church and who wish to change over to a rite different from their own is designed to preserve the various rites and to avoid difficulties and discords which could arise among the different rites, etc. But the case of the baptized non-Catholics coming into the Catholic Church seems to me as an entirely different situation. This is the case of those who stand outside and knock. I do not know why the Ecumenical Council should wish to pose the obstacle of recourse to the Holy See for the entrance of these baptized non-Catholics into the Church. Why does the Council want to change the very recent ruling contained in the new Oriental Code (1958) where it says, "Baptized non-Catholics of the Eastern rite, who are admitted into the Catholic Church, can embrace whatever rite they prefer; it is to be hoped, however, that they will keep their own rite" (Can. II). It seems to me that the prescription in the present text of the schema is against the whole spirit of this Council in which we have spoken, are speaking, and will speak so much about freedom of conscience and about the pastoral as well as the ecumenical spirit. I do not know why the Council should wish to give approval to such legislative retrogression in this matter.

For ten years I worked, in the Apostolic Delegation in Washington, almost daily over petitions for transfer of rite, and I can well appreciate how much time is required for the preparation of such appeals to the Holy See. Ordinarily six months and then again, often even a full year, are necessary to complete such appeals and to receive a decision. The imposition of such an appeal upon those who wish to come into the Catholic Church through the influx of grace is, in my opinion, something astonishing, or, should I say, something cruel. The grace of God has almost to await the outcome of this appeal.

He concluded by saying that "the good of souls, the principle of freedom of conscience and even due reverence toward all the rites of the Church" would be preserved if the text would add this sentence: "However, baptized non-Catholics who come into the Church are able to embrace whatever rite they prefer; however, it is to be hoped that they will keep their own rite."

Bishop Stephan Kocisko of Passaic, New Jersey, in general approved the schema because "it shows the love and solicitude for the Oriental rites that has always been manifested in the letters and encyclicals of the Roman Pontiffs." He expressed the hope that the mutual love of brothers in the East and the West might incline the separated brothers of the East "to the Church which proclaims such liberty, benevolence, proper and reciprocal love." He also urged that the teaching of the schema be put into practice lest it remain only so many beautifully written words. He suggested that, in order to accomplish this end, interritual bonds grow stronger in the days to come. In order to foster reciprocal esteem for various rites in the Church, Bishop Kocisko suggested in conclusion, that the following sentence be added to the text:

> Hierarchies are to provide that those who are to receive sacred orders be well instructed in the rites, especially concerning the practical norms in interritual matters and that also the laity should be instructed concerning the rites, their importance and free communion according to the norms of the universal Church.

On October 21 and 22 the Council Fathers cast seven votes on various sections of the schema. Six of the votes received a surprising two-thirds majority. The second vote, concerning precisely the matter of baptized non-Catholics joining the parallel rite when they come into the Catholic Church, failed to receive the necessary majority. This was precisely the issue that three of the four Americans who had made interventions discussed. The text was returned to the Commission for the Eastern Churches to examine more than 1,920 suggestions and, where necessary, to incorporate these emendations into the revised text. This text was returned to the floor at the final working congregation of the third session on November 20. During that session the Council Fathers again cast three ballots on the text: the first concerning articles two, three and four; the second on the manner in which the Commission for the Eastern Churches had treated the Fathers' suggestions; the third on the text as a whole. All three passed overwhelmingly and on the following day, during the solemn public session closing the third session, the Fathers again voted 2,151 to 5, in favor of the text, and the words of promulgation were accordingly uttered by Pope Paul VI.

Decree on Eastern Catholic Churches

✠ INTERVENTIONS

BISHOP GERALD McDEVITT, *19 October, 1965*

I wish to make some observations concerning number four, page six, lines 6–10, where there is a discussion about the observance and choice of rites. The present text reads as follows:

> Finally, each and every one of the faithful, as well as those baptized non-Catholics coming into the Church, retain that rite proper to whatever area they live in and they celebrate and keep that rite with all their resources; the law of appeal in particular cases to the Holy See is preserved.

This text, as it stands, is in part acceptable and in part unacceptable for these reasons:

This text excessively restricts the liberty of those baptized non-Catholics who wish to come into the Church. I completely understand that the recourse to the Holy See of those Catholics who are already in the Church and who wish to change over to a rite different from their own is designed to preserve the various rites and to avoid difficulties and discords which could arise among the different rites, etc. But the case of the baptized non-Catholics coming into the Catholic Church seems to me as an entirely different situation. This is the case of those who stand outside and knock; I do not know why the Ecumenical Council should wish to pose the obstacle of recourse to the Holy See for the entrance of these baptized non-Catholics into the Church. Why does the Council want to change the very recent ruling contained in the new Oriental Code (1958), where it says: "Baptized non-Catholics of the eastern rite, who are admitted into the Catholic Church, can embrace whatever rite they prefer; it is to be hoped, however, that they will keep their own rite" (Can. II). It seems to me that the prescription in the present text of the schema is against the whole spirit of this Council in which we have spoken, are speaking, and will speak so much about freedom of conscience and about the pastoral as well as the ecumenical spirit. I do not know why the Council should wish to give approval to such legislative retrogression in this matter.

For ten years I worked in the Apostolic Delegation in Washington almost daily over petitions for transfer of rite, and I can well appreciate how much time is required for the preparation of such appeals to the Holy See. Ordinarily six months and then again, often even a full year, are necessary to complete such appeals and to receive a decision. The imposition of such an appeal upon those who wish to come into the Catholic Church through the influx of grace is, in my opinion, something astonishing, or should I say, something cruel. The grace of God has almost to await the outcome of this appeal.

Recently many, if not all, of us bishops received—and even in places quite removed from this assembly—a private communication in which arguments against the present text of the schema were contained and in which another drafting was proposed for the consideration of the Fathers. This is the proposed version: "Finally, each and every one of the faithful should retain the rite proper to his area, and the right is preserved for baptized non-Catholics, who come into the Church, to select another rite if this is introduced by them as a necessary condition." As you see, this draft grants greater freedom than the present text of the schema, since it does not require recourse to the Holy See; but I am still not satisfied with it. The words ". . . if this is introduced by them as a necessary condition" are almost the same words which were contained in the constitution on the dignity of the Orientals of Pope Leo XIII (1894). I fail to see why we ought to revert to such a restriction or why we should impose such a burden upon the conscience of those who wish to enter the Catholic Church. The exaction in this matter of such a necessary condition always seemed to me very dangerous. If anyone should impose a necessary condition of this type for his entrance into the Catholic Church, it would be the same as saying, "I want to enter the Catholic Church, but I will not enter the Catholic Church unless it grant me the opportunity of selecting a rite other than my own." Can anyone make such a declaration or have such an intention? Such a declaration or intention seems to me sinful, and I cannot see why we should expose these souls to a danger of this type. It is a question here of the selection of rite, which, though it is certainly very important, is not a question of some article of faith or of an eighth sacrament.

Thus, I humbly present the following approach to our schema in place of the present text. It should be noted that in the text I propose, I use the words "baptized non-Catholics" without adding the words "of the eastern rite," so that it might be clearer than in the Oriental Code that Protestants coming into the Catholic Church enjoy the same freedom to select a rite different from the Latin. This is the text of my proposal: "Finally, each and every one of the faithful should retain that rite proper to whatever area they live in, and they should celebrate and keep that same rite with all their resources; the law of appeal to the Holy See in particular cases is preserved. However, baptized non-Catholics who come into the Church are able to embrace whichever rite they prefer; however, it is to be hoped that they will keep their own rite."

The present law, which seems very good to me, in this way is kept; and in my humble opinion we would preserve the principle of the good of souls, the principle of freedom of conscience and even due reverence toward all the rites of the Church.

BISHOP STEPHAN KOCISKO, *19 October, 1964*

The schema on the Eastern Churches, in general, is good. It shows the love and solicitude for the Oriental rites that has always been manifested in the letters and encyclicals of the Roman Pontiffs.

The present schema intends to have the Orientals free in all things that may help keep their heritage of the East intact. One with their brothers of the West, with whom they themselves are united, they enjoy reciprocal respect and love. Therefore, it is to be hoped that even the separated brothers of the East, free from all fear, be inclined to the Church which proclaims such liberty, benevolence, proper and reciprocal love.

It is true that in the past there arose interritual difficulties in the Church because of ignorance of the rites. Lest the teaching of this schema (which no one seriously fears) remain only in beautifully written words, announcing a happy principle, let us, insofar as we are able, put it into practice. May we, therefore, see, Venerable Fathers, that the interritual bonds, especially in regard to a praiseworthy knowledge of the rites and, indeed, related to a practical reciprocal conversation, where it is necessary or opportune, grow stronger in the days to come.

Because of this, may I propose that, on the sixth page of the schema, under number four, line six, after the words *"disciplinam efficacius tuendam,"* these words be added:

> Hierarchies are to provide that those who are to receive sacred orders be well instructed in the rites, especially concerning the practical norms in interritual matters and that also the laity should be instructed concerning the rites, their importance and free communion according to the norms of the universal Church.

From this instruction of the clergy and laity based on charity, may a reciprocal esteem of the rites and of Church rituals increase so that even relations with the separated brothers may grow better in the days to come.

Decree on Eastern Catholic Churches

✠ COMMENTARY by Rev. Melitius M. Wojnar

It is necessary to consider the changes and clarifications made at the Council regarding the Oriental Catholic Churches which are developing increasingly in the United States.

There are at present in the United States five eparchies (dioceses), two apostolic exarchies and several dozen parishes of different Oriental Catholics.

Full development has already been attained in the Ukrainian Catholic Church in its provincial organization, which consists of the archeparchy of Philadelphia, Pa. (163,439 faithful), the eparchy of Stamford, Conn. (87,620 faithful), and the eparchy of Chicago (29,601 faithful). Next in development is a group of the same rite, the Ruthenians, with two eparchies: Pittsburgh, Pa. (222,712 faithful), and Passaic, N.J. (96,085 faithful).[1] These two eparchies are separate and directly dependent upon the Holy See.

Recently the Holy See established two apostolic exarchates for two conspicuous Oriental groups: the Maronites (49 parishes), with the see in Detroit, Michigan, and the Melkites (27 parishes) with the see in Boston, Mass.[2] Other Oriental groups are under the jurisdiction of the Latin Rite bishops: Armenians (6 parishes), Byelorussians (1 parish), Chaldeans (3 parishes), Romanians (16 parishes), and Russians (5 parishes). Without their own parochial organization are Italo-Albanians (10,000) and Syrians (5,000).[3]

It is not the purpose of this article to give a full exposition of the Decree on Eastern Catholic Churches of the Second Vatican Council; that has already been done in The Jurist XXV (1965), 173–255.[4] It is the intention here to show only its application in the United States, following, however, the order of that decree.

---

[1] Cf. The Official Catholic Directory, 1966, P. J. Kenedy, New York, publishers.

[2] The announcement of the Apostolic Delegate in Washington, D.C., June 21, 1966.

[3] 1966 National Catholic Almanac (Editor, F. A. Foy, O.F.M.), Doubleday and Co., Garden City, N.Y., p. 289.

[4] Cf. Herman Aem., "De ritu in iure canonico" in Orientalia Christiana, Nr. 89, p. 106.

I. The Law by which Oriental Churches Are Obliged

The main affirmation of the Decree on Eastern Catholic Churches (n. 1) is that the Eastern Rite Churches are governed by the following principles:

A) those which affect the universal Church;

B) those given in this Decree;

C) those already made or to be made by synods of Eastern Churches;

D) those issued or to be issued by the Holy See for the Eastern Churches.

As in the past, there are ordinarily two chief lawmakers for Eastern Churches, to which the Decree commits a further legislation: "All else is remitted to the care of the Eastern Synods and of the Apostolic See" (n. 1). Here no change was made, only a clarification.

One of the consequences of this affirmation is that these lawmakers are empowered to determine precisely some canonical institutes mentioned in the Decree. It did not, however, give the last determination, e.g., the aggregation of a bishop outside the patriarchate to a hierarchy of the patriarchate.

As in the past, the discipline of the Eastern Catholic Churches was elaborated mainly in their synods, both national and provincial. (This now holds true in the United States since it is one Oriental province.) The Decree gave the norms for direction which should influence future legislation, and spoke of the preservation and accommodation of the spiritual heritage of the Eastern Churches, as shown below.

II. The Preservation of the Eastern Churches

Here we shall consider the many problems approached by the Decree on Eastern Catholic Churches in its different sections.

A) First, it must be noted that a special task of the Council was to determine the concept of the Eastern Churches in order to correct some false notions in the matter. In the West, the Latin Rite Church was often considered as a universal Catholic Church and the Oriental Churches as particular Churches. Sometimes this also had canonical consequences for the whole canonical system, e.g., the Canon Law of the Latin Church was considered as the common law for the whole universal Catholic Church, while the law of singular Oriental Churches, even pertaining to the whole Oriental Church, was a particular only in relation and comparison with the Latin. The Decree made it clear that both the Eastern Rite Churches and the Latin Rite Church are all particular in the universal Catholic Church, even though the Latin Church is numerically the largest. Secondly, in determining the concept of a particular Church, the Decree expressly requires that a group of faithful be "held together by a hierarchy" which, according to the Decree on Ecumenism, is "by apostolic succession." Since the dissident Oriental Churches hold this, they are also considered under the concept of a particular Church.[5]

B) In the problem of the preservation of these particular Oriental Churches, the Decree intends both 1) the physical preservation of these Churches, and 2) the preservation of their spiritual heritage.

1) The physical preservation includes two means: a) the erection and constitution of the ritual parishes and dioceses, and b) the prohibition of the faithful to transfer to another rite. Each of these must be considered separately.

The first step toward the preservation of a singular particular Church or rite is the erection of the first nucleus of the ecclesiastical organization, which is the parish. This is required by the Decree (n. 4) without regard for the territory where the faithful of a certain rite are, i.e., in both "Oriental regions"[6] and outside of them. The Decree says: "Means should be taken, therefore, in every part of the world for the protection and advancement of all the particular Churches and, to this end, parishes and a proper hierarchy should be established where the spiritual good of the faithful demands it." The responsibility for systematically providing the means for erecting parishes lies in the bishop of the territory where the faithful are. There is a canonical difference between the erection of a ritual parish and a national one. While the latter requires the apostolic indult (Code of Canon Law, canon 216, paragraph 4), the former, after the subjection of the faithful of the Oriental Rite to the jurisdiction of a hierarchy of the Latin Rite, does not require an apostolic indult (Motu Proprio *Cleri Sanctitati*, canon 22, paragraph 3) but rather, here in the Decree is urged to be made by a bishop of another rite.

According to the mind of the *Decree,* the proper hierarchy of each rite should be established or constituted without regard to the territory, as above, and only because of a sufficient number of parishes. According to the present law of the Decree (n. 9, 10), in the Oriental patriarchates and major archbishoprics the constitution of new bishoprics belongs to the patriarchs or major archbishops with their own synods; outside of patriarchates and major archbishoprics, Motu Proprio *Cleri Sanctitati*, canon 22, paragraph 3 is still valid.[7] No difficulties pertaining to this arise in the Latin Rite hierarchy. The difficulty, however, does exist in the establishment of the Oriental Rite hierarchy outside of their "Oriental regions." The Decree insists on the removal of this difficulty. In fact, in recent times, there have been established in different countries in the West the eparchies (as in the United States and Canada) as well as the apostolic exarchies for all Orientals (as in Brazil, Argentina and France), or for some rites only (as in Australia, England, France, Germany and the United States).

[5] Cf. The Decree on Ecumenism, chapter III, "The Special Position of the Eastern Churches."

[6] PM (*Postquam Apostolicis*), canon 303, paragraph 1, number 2.

[7] It provides for the care of faithful; but nothing is said about the constitution of the Oriental hierarchy; therefore this Decree provided for the latter.

The other very important provision in the Decree for the physical preservation of the Oriental Rites is the prohibition on the faithful to transfer to another rite without the permission of the Holy See. This problem must be seen as a whole in its present legislation and not only in the decision of the Decree, since the Decree did not abolish the existing legislation, but rather completed it in order to achieve the purpose intended by the Decree, that is, the preservation of the particular Oriental Churches or Rites. We shall, therefore, consider what the Decree did to achieve that purpose in the light of the existing legislation.

Because this matter is an interritual problem, the legislation in this matter can be given in either code, Latin or Oriental, obligatory for both sides. However, the latest legislation, as the *lex posterior*, will decide in the differences between both codes. In both codes, the faithful are expressly prohibited to transfer to another rite without the permission of the Holy See. In the Code of Canon Law, canon 98, paragraph 3 is stated: *"Nemini licet sine venia Apostolicae Sedis ad alium ritum transire, aut, post legitimum transitum, ad pristinum reverti."* Some authors present two arguments pertaining to this paragraph, which tend to limit this prohibition. The first maintains that the permission required here is only to the liceity of transfer since the text itself suggests *"Nemini licet."* The second maintains that this paragraph obliges only Catholics, since in paragraph 1 of that canon the lawmaker declares that he wants, in this whole matter, to consider only the relations between different Catholic rites (*"Inter varios catholicos ritus . . ."*) After the Code of Canon Law was promulgated, the Motu Proprio *Cleri Sanctitati*, as the *lex posterior*, ordered this matter *ex toto*. Taking into consideration the limitations made by some authors, it expressly constituted against them by stating that the permission of the Holy See for the transfer to another rite is to the validity of it (*"Nemo potest sine licentia Sedis Apostolicae ad alium ritum valide transire"*; canon 8). In the formulation of canon 6 (*"Inter varios ritus . . ."*), it intentionally omitted *"catholicos"* in order to avoid any reason for the limitation of this prohibition to Catholics only, but including in this matter all baptized persons. To special categories of baptized persons it granted the permission to transfer to another rite without permission. These three categories are: wives (canon 9), children before puberty (canon 10), and Oriental non-Catholics coming back to the Catholic Church (canon 11, paragraph 1).

The last legislation in this matter, the Decree on Eastern Catholic Churches, in substance, made only one change in this matter. It revoked the permission granted by the Motu Proprio *Cleri Sanctitati* to the Oriental non-Catholics and consequently abrogated canon 11, paragraph 1 of the Motu Proprio, as above.[8]

This is the true approach to this problem; all others are contrary not only to the intention of the Decree, as above, but also to its formulation. The positive affirmation of the Decree, that all Catholics must retain their rite, is

---

[8] Cf. Mahfoud P. *"Quel, Rite doit adopter le fidèle oriental acatholique qui rejoit l'Eglise catholique?"* in *Apollinaris*, XXXVIII (1965), p. 184.

not against the Motu Proprio *Cleri Sanctitati,* canon 8, paragraph 1, which requires that everyone who wants to transfer to another rite must have permission from the Holy See. But the similar positive affirmation, that non-Catholics, in coming back to communion with the Catholic Church, should retain their former rite, is against the Motu Proprio *Cleri Sanctitati,* canon 11, paragraph 1, because permission granted by the MP in a positive way, now in a positive way is revoked, and non-Catholics are consequently included in the general norm of the Motu Proprio *Cleri Sanctitati,* canon 8, paragraph 1 which is, as above, universal. To make the distinction here between the valid or illicit transfer of Oriental non-Catholics to another rite in coming back to the Catholic Church does not have application because what was positively permitted is now positively revoked by the contrary statement.[9]

2) Another way of preserving the Eastern Churches is the preservation of their cultural ecclesiastical treasure: their discipline, liturgy, theological system, theological expression, special spirituality, monastic life, special ecclesiastical art, etc., which constitute their spiritual heritage. The Decree imposes the obligation of this preservation at first on the Orientals themselves. They should find special application for the Decree in the future legislation of their synods. It must be understood also in regard to the accomodation of their discipline to the present time in its organic harmony with the general character of their discipline.

The Decree also obliges those who are in any way in contact with Orientals to the same preservation of this heritage. To this purpose they must also be instructed in the Oriental discipline. This disposition is in harmony with former tendencies of the Holy See in this matter, which in recent times erected the Institute for Oriental Studies and ordered the same studies in all seminaries and insisted on different publications in the matter.

III. The Diaspores of the Eastern Churches

After the aforementioned general introductory decisions on Oriental Churches, the Decree is occupied with the most characteristic institutes of those Churches, i.e., with the patriarchs and the major archbishops.

The patriarchs are presented here in their actual form as the *fathers and heads* of their rites. Above all, their old rights and privileges, which they had before the separation of the Churches, should be reinstated and accomodated to the circumstances of the present time. Now the Decree expressly acknowl-

[9] Pospishil V. J., *Orientalium Ecclesiarum.* The Decree on the Eastern Catholic Churches of the II Council of Vatican, New York 1965, pp. 16–21, introduced that distinction between the valid and illicit transfer to another rite by Oriental non-Catholics in their reunion with the Catholic Church. But Ivan Zuzek, S.J., *"Animadversiones quaedam in Decretum de Ecclesii Orientalibus Catholicis Concilii Vaticani"* in *Periodica de re morali, canonica, liturgica,* LV (1966), pp. 273–276, examined his reasons and shows the unadoptability of this distinction here.

edges their right to erect new eparchies and to appoint the bishops in the territory of their patriarchates, as well as, in general, to treat all affairs of their patriarchates (n. 8, 9). It completes their juridical figure, which was already established in the Motu Proprio *Cleri Sanctitati.*[10]

The major archbishop is considered here as the one who is the head of an entire particular Church or rite, Consequently, he is equal to the patriarch (n. 10) according to the norms established or to be established by law. In the Motu Proprio *Cleri Sanctitati* the major archbishop is considered in many matters to be equal to the patriarch (cf. *The Jurist,* XIX (1959), p. 429).

Since the United States is not an "Oriental region" with patriarchates and major archbishoprics, we shall show here what was done in the Decree to retain the relationship of the diaspores with their original mother Churches. It is true that, for the preservation of the unity and entirety of the Oriental Churches, it is necessary that the heads of rites have power over their entire Churches and rites disregarding the territory where the original Church exists, and looking, instead, on the territories where the faithful of that Church exist. Based on this principle, the patriarchs require this power over the diaspores also. It seems, however, that there are some difficulties in the inter-State relationships because the civil governments do not like any interference in their States by the citizens of other States or by those of a religious character, such as patriarchs. Therefore, these difficulties must first be removed.

The Decree has established some principles in regard to the relations of diaspores to their mother Churches.

The first principle is the admission of the possibility that a patriarch can have the power over diaspores of his Church in the definition of patriarch itself, where it is affirmed that the patriarch has jurisdiction over bishops "of his own territory or rite" (*territorii vel ritus*). Because in the Motu Proprio *Cleri Sanctitati,* canon 216, paragraph 2, number 1, the parallel definition said "*patriarchatui* seu *ritui tamquam pater et caput praesunt*" (with the identifying connotation of "*seu*"), the concept of rite was limited to the territory of a patriarchate. Therefore, the Decree, in order to avoid this misunderstanding, substituted "*vel*" for "*seu.*" The former ("*vel*") never has the sense of identification, but, rather, of an opposition. Consequently, the Decree admitted here the possibility that a patriarch can have jurisdiction also over bishops of his rite in the diaspores, i.e., outside of the territory of his patriarchate, since the rite is not bound by territory.

The second principle is the attachment of bishops "appointed outside the territorial limits of the patriarchate . . . to the hierarchy of the patriarchate" (n. 7). This is a new institute in Canon Law and, therefore, the question still remains about the canonical limits of the connection, between the mentioned hierarchy of diaspores and the patriarchate. The Council did not determine this, but left it to future legislation because the limits of connection are not

[10] See the whole canonical figure of patriarchs in *The Jurist,* XIX (1959), pp. 418–427.

necessarily the same in all circumstances. These limits can be determined by a future code or by the Roman Pontiff in regard to individual Churches.

IV. *The Discipline of the Sacraments*

The Decree on Eastern Catholic Churches starts this chapter with the general approbation of "the ancient discipline on the sacraments existing in the Oriental Churches and likewise the usage connected with their celebration and administration" (n. 12). This approbation is of great value not only in the historical view on this matter (insofar as the Oriental discipline sometimes was only tolerated), but also in the present time when there still is remarkable misunderstanding in this matter. After the promulgation of this Decree, no one can doubt about the legitimacy of this discipline in the Church and about the validity of the sacraments, if the discipline is observed on the basis of the discipline itself. But this approval was granted only for the "ancient disciplines"; therefore all innovations illegitimately introduced are not approved, and, therefore, the ancient discipline should be restored.

The question was brought out: To whom does it belong to restore that ancient discipline? In order not to create a new confusion, it is prudent that the legislative power for an entire particular Church does it, since it is evident that the Council did not intend new confusion by any bishop starting a new reform of that latinized discipline.

In regard to singular sacraments, the Decree did not intend to give their entire canonical exposition. Rather it resolved only some questions discussed by authors and accommodated their discipline to the present time.

In the sacrament of Confirmation, all Oriental priests, both Catholic and non-Catholic, are authorized to perform it validly to the faithful of all rites, including the Latin. But they should still observe the former law, both common and particular, for the licit administration of this sacrament. The Latin rite priests may do it also, in the limits of their faculties, but in this condition they can also do it validly to Orientals. For the licit administration, they should also observe the former law, both common and particular. In general, what was prohibited up to this time under the clause of invalidity of act because of lack of competence is now still prohibited, but only as illicit. The former performances of the sacrament of Confirmation, i.e., made before this Decree, should be decided according to the law that existed when the Confirmation was performed.

Regarding the Holy Eucharist, the Decree makes the following decisions:

1) The obligation to celebrate Sundays and holy days is specified
   a) for some rites by assisting at Mass;
   b) for others by assisting at any Divine Office.
2) The time to fulfill this obligation is now longer, namely, from the vigil of Sundays and holy days to the end of these days.

3) The frequent non-obligatory reception of the Holy Eucharist, especially on Sundays and holy days, is recommended for the Oriental faithful.

Pertaining to the sacrament of Penance, the Decree states that the places of exclusive jurisdiction on the cumulative territory are also included in the faculty to hear confessions granted by the hierarchy, if granted without any territorial restrictions, and the hierarchy of these places did not expressly exclude it. Former provisions in this matter were of less efficacy. Because the United States is "Oriental territory" (Motu Proprio *Postquam Apostolicis,* canon 303, paragraph 1, number 3) for four Oriental groups (Ukrainian, Ruthenian, Maronite and Melkite), it is therefore the cumulative territory for five jurisdictions (those Oriental and Latin), with the places of exclusive jurisdiction of each group (as churches, rectories, parochial schools, etc.) to which the jurisdiction to hear confessions of the faithful of any rite now is extended for priests of another rite.

In the matter of Orders two main provisions were made by the Decree: 1) regarding the reestablishment of the permanent diaconate, and 2) regarding the rights and obligations of the minor orders.

Because the institution of the permanent diaconate in many Oriental rites never was abrogated, the Decree simply expresses the desire to reestablish it, if it has fallen into disuse. Here again, in order to avoid any new confusion in the particular Church, it seems that no individual bishop should do it, but that the synod or the conference of bishops should decide on this problem.

There are several reasons why the Decree paid special attention to the minor orders in the Oriental Churches. The change of former discipline, made by the Motu Proprio *Postquam Apostolicis,* canon 310, established in the general Oriental discipline that the subdiaconate and lower orders are minor orders; while in the former discipline (before this Motu Proprio) the subdiaconate in some Oriental Churches was the major order, as with the Armenians, Ethiopians and Malabars. On the other hand, in the Motu Proprio *Crebrae allatae,* canon 62, paragraph 2, all Oriental subdeacons are bound by the diriment impediment not to marry, even though only in minor orders.[11] Therefore, the determination of their canonical position (rights and duties) was left by the Decree to "the legislative authority of each particular Church" (n. 17). In force of this decision, for example, in the Melkite Church, the patriarch with the Holy Synod (Beirut, January 8–9, 1965) decided that the subdiaconate in their community no longer constitutes a diriment impediment to marriage.[12]

Similar questions can be asked regarding, for example, the grave obligation of the Armenian subdeacons to say the Divine Office[13] for the same reason that they are now no longer in major orders.

[11] Cf. *Acta Innocentii PP. IV,* Pont. Comm. ad. redigendum CICO, Fontes, Series III, vol. IV, t. I, p. 176.

[12] *Proche Orient Chrétien,* XV (1965), p. 410.

[13] Cf. Synod of Rome 1911, nr. 740.

Still another question can arise—for example, on the permanent subdiaconate which already exists in some Oriental Churches, as in the Melkites,[14] Syrians, Chaldeans, Copts and Ethiopians.[15]

All these questions the Decree left to the decision of the aforementioned legislative authority of each Oriental Church.

A very complicated problem that occupied the conciliar Commission on Oriental Churches was the problem of mixed marriage between two Orientals, of whom one is Catholic and the other non-Catholic, and which is decided valid, even if illicit, in the case that it is concluded before a sacred minister. This sacred minister can be a deacon or any priest, either Catholic or non-Catholic, of any rite.

The canonical Catholic form of marriage established in the Motu Proprio *Crebrae allatae,* canon 85, does not oblige any more for the validity of the act in all cases when the marriage is contracted between an Oriental Catholic and an Oriental non-Catholic. That form obliges, in the force of the Decree, the Catholic party only and for liceity only, if the just and grave cause does not render its observance impossible, as it is in the case of all positive laws in general. For the validity of these mixed marriages, the presence of any sacred minister, Catholic or non-Catholic, of any community, is sufficient. Other requirements needed for the form prescribed in the Code of Canon Law and the Motu Proprio *Crebrae allatae* are not needed here for validity, as, for example, to ask and receive the matrimonial consent by an assisting priest, since it is sufficient if spouses pronounce their consent in the presence only of a sacred minister. It was such, for example, in the decree *Tametsi,* i.e., without the latter's activity or his blessing. This presence, however, of a sacred minister in that case constitutes the special matrimonial form.

By the formulation of this decision of the Decree, the Council did not canonize the Oriental canonical form of marriage in regard to both non-Catholic Orientals or in regard to one of them and a Protestant, because both canon 1099 of the Code of Canon Law and the Motu Proprio *Crebrae allatae,* canon 90, are still in force, making them free from any prescribed form.

Finally, it is evident that the Oriental apostates do not come under consideration here as Oriental non-Catholics because they are bound by the same law as Catholics.

V. *The Discipline on the Divine Cult.*

This section of the Decree on Eastern Catholic Churches has only some decisions on the divine cult. It treats sacred seasons, the Divine Office and the vernacular in the liturgy.

The Sacred Seasons. It was decided that the competent authority to deter-

---

[14] *Proche Orient Chrétien,* IX (1959), p. 282, p. 210.
[15] *The Jurist,* XIX (1959), p. 282, n. 43.

mine the transfer or the suppression of feast days common to all Eastern Churches is an Ecumenical Council or the Holy See. The transfer or suppression of other feast days (particular to each Eastern Church) is within the competence of the Apostolic See or of the patriarchal or archiepiscopal synod. Consequently, for non-patriarchal or non-archiepiscopal Churches, the only authority in this matter is the Holy See.

Another decision in this matter pertains to the establishment of Easter Sunday, which is intended by the Decree to be celebrated on the same Sunday by all Christians of the locale, area or nation. For this purpose, the Decree permits conferral also with non-Catholics (n. 20).

Still another problem of the interritual matter resolved by this Decree is the time of observance of the sacred seasons by two kinds of Orientals. The first kind are those who live outside of their own region or territory and who can follow the law of the place. In the United States, there are four groups of Orientals who have bishops of their own rite, i.e., they are outside of Oriental "regions," but not outside of Oriental "territory," and consequently, generally speaking, they should follow the law of their bishops. Thus, this decision of the Decree does not pertain to them. These four groups of Orientals are: the Ukrainians, Ruthenians, Maronites and Melkites. In regard to Ukrainians and Ruthenians, however, their particular law according to the Decree *Cum data fuerit* of March 1, 1929 (art. 36), made the same provision. All other Orientals in the United States who are subject to the Latin rite hierarchy can follow the law of the Latin rite bishop of the place on the sacred times, i.e., the celebration of feast days, abstinence and prohibited times. The second kind of Orientals, who are regarded here by the Decree as being everywhere (not only outside of Oriental regions or territory) are interritual families, both Latin and Oriental or Orientals among themselves. These families can, by proper decision, follow the law of one rite, but always the same law (n. 21).

The Divine Office. On the Divine Office the Decree has only one decision which pertains to its public celebration by Oriental clerics and religious with the devout assistance of the faithful as far as possible "in accordance with the prescriptions and traditions of their own established customs" (n. 22).

The public celebration of the Divine Office in regard to religious is now determined by the Motu Proprio *Postquam Apostolicis,* canon 157 according to which all Oriental monks and also some orders and congregations are obliged to perform it *"secundum statuta vel legitimas consuetudines."*

In regard to secular priests, this public celebration of the Divine Office must be performed by all Oriental pastors on Sundays and holy days (Motu Proprio *Cleri Sanctitati,* canon 508), as well as in the cathedral and in every city, at least in one or other church and at least on Sundays and holy days (*ibid.,* canon 401). Some Oriental Churches prescribed it in their synods (Zamost 1720, tit. 16; Mount Lebanon 1736, part IV. chap. V; Sharfeh. 1888, chap. III, art. VI, n. 2 and chap. VI, art. IV, n. 2; Lviv 1891, tit. IV, chap. III; Alexandria

1898, sect. II, chap. II, art. I, n. 4; Rome 1911, n. 741; Grottaferrata 1940, art. 283).[16]

The Vernacular in the Liturgy. The main question on this subject is this: Who will decide 1) on the introduction of the vernacular into the liturgy (partially or completely) and 2) on the approbation of the translations of liturgical texts.

The Decree gives a double answer on these questions regarding the two situations of the particular Churches.

1) If the Church is patriarchial, then this authority for the whole Church is in the patriarch and his synod. The same holds true in the Church with a major archbishop, since both the patriarch and the major archbishop have power in liturgical matters in their Churches.

2) In other Churches, the supreme authority lies with the bishops who will decide on both aforementioned questions (n. 23). It means that if there is only a metropolitan in the Church, then he will decide on it with his bishops after the report made for the Holy See (e.g., in the Greek Catholic Church or the Russian Catholic Church). It is natural that, if there is more than one bishop, then they should come together for these decisions.

VI. The New Approach of Catholics to Oriental Non-Catholics.

In the former schema, under the title *"Ut omnes unum sint,"* this part of the Decree was much larger than it is now. It included an exposition and evaluation of the different means leading to the more effective approach to the future reunion of Churches. There were presented the theological, pastoral,

---

[16] In the discussion of the personal obligation of clerics (deacons and priests) to the Divine Office, particularly in the Ukrainian Rite, Pospishil (*op. cit.*) and I hold two opposite opinions. I should like to add to the last word of the former (*op. cit.* p. 59) that the custom invoked by the synod of Lviv 1891 was not based on the error, but on the intention and task, of the Ukrainian clergy to make themselves equal to the Latin-rite clergy. This is the main reason for complete latinization, i.e., introduction of the elements of the Latin discipline into that of the Ukrainian in the Polish kingdom. To obtain equal rights with the Latin-rite clergy was the task of the Ukrainian clergy during centuries in that kingdom. This is clear from both the documents of the Polish government, as well as from the Ukrainian clergy petitions. Yet "on his way to Rome, Cardinal Isidore stopped in Bude, where the young Polish-Hungarian King Ladislaus III was preparing for a crusade against the Turks. Isidore succeeded in obtaining a charter in 1443 from King Ladislaus III which granted the Eastern Church rights and privileges equal to the Western Church" (Lencyk W., *The Eastern Catholic Church and Czar Nicholas I*, Rome, New York, 1966, p. 7). The same was promised on the occasion of the Union of Berest-Lytovkyj, 1595. As the proof of that custom *in vigore* is the very early document of the synod of Zamost 1720 (cf. *Coll. Lac.* II, col. 68). Therefore the Motu Proprio *Cleri Sanctitati* among the footnotes of canon 76 very rightly cites as the document of that law in the Ukrainian Church the aforementioned synod of Lviv.

psychological and other means to this goal. But the Council, in discussing that schema, ordered the transfer of those means to the schema on ecumenism, regarding that as the more proper place for them. Therefore, this Decree, after that transfer, retains in this part the same character as in other parts, i.e., the resolution of some canonical problems in the matter of the relationship between Catholics and Oriental non-Catholics. These solutions, which seem to be new, in general are concerned with three matters: 1) the express commitment to the Oriental Catholics in the work of the ecumenical movement for the unity of Churches; 2) the regulations in the reception of Oriental non-Catholics into communion with the Catholic Church; and 3) the regulations in the common participation in worship (*communicatio in sacris*) with Oriental non-Catholics.

1) In the express commitment to the Oriental Catholics in the work of the ecumenical movement for the unity of Churches, is the new fact that this mission of Oriental Catholics is considered their special right (*munus*). Being connected with their non-Catholic brethren by many chains, this mission seems to be for them a natural one and more effective. Before this final redaction of the Decree, there were indicated the general and ordinary means for that purpose: prayer, good example, faithfulness in observance of Oriental traditions, better knowledge of one another, mutual cooperation and brotherly respectfulness.

2) Among the regulations in the reception of Oriental non-Catholics into communion with the Catholic Church, new is the fact that they are no longer obliged to the former profession of faith, but a simple profession of faith is sufficient, e.g., the recitation of the Nicene-Constantinopolitan Creed with some such general addition as "I believe everything that the Catholic Church believes." Then the ordination of Oriental non-Catholic clerics to be received into the Catholic Church is recognized as valid. The decision, however, on the exercise of their orders is reserved to the Catholic bishops who can also issue some norms in this matter. These norms can deal with the investigation of the fact of their ordination, proof of their constancy, the place of their first assignment and the accomplishment of their priestly training.

3) The regulations on the common participation in worship (*communicatio in sacris*) with Oriental non-Catholics is reelaborated by this Decree comparative to the former discipline before the Council. The new regulations regard the participation in worship in both sacramental and extra-sacramental fields in both positive and negative forms (the positive will be if Catholics partake in the public cult of non-Catholics; the negative will be if non-Catholics are admitted to the public cult of Catholics). Finally, the positive participation can be formal or material only, depending on the intention of the Catholics to adore God by the cult of the non-Catholics. The formal, i.e., with the aforementioned intention, is prohibited by the divine law and, therefore, never can be permitted. In a parallel way, the negative can regard both formal non-Catholics and non-Catholics in good faith, depending on their persuasion that their

religion is true. The formal non-Catholics are always excluded by divine law from the sacramental field since they are indisposed for the reception of the sacraments.

The Decree builds the new law on this matter on the following principles:

1) It indicates what is prohibited by the divine law in this common participation in worship in both sacramental and extra-sacramental fields. These elements prohibited by the divine law are first of all: harm of unity, acceptance of formal error, danger of aberration in faith, danger of scandal and danger of indifferentism.

2) The Decree affirms that pastoral experience shows that all these elements prohibited by the divine law can be avoided. This affirmation has its foundation in the religious culture of modern society, especially in certain circles which make the precise distinction among different religions according to the teaching of the Church.

3) Positively considered are the different spiritual goods which can flow from the common participation in worship, e.g., salvation of souls, promotion of spiritual good, example of Christian charity, promotion of the unity of Churches and avoidance of any obstacle to salvation.

4) On the basis of these reasons, the Decree enacts a new and milder policy for the common participation in worship in both sacramental and extra-sacramental fields.

a) In the sacramental field in the negative participation, the Decree admits the non-Catholics to the three sacraments performed by the Catholic ministers; Penance, Holy Eucharist and Anointing of the Sick, under the following conditions:

(1) that there is absence of any prohibition of divine law;

(2) that the non-Catholics are in good faith;

(3) that they are asking for these sacraments by themselves;

(4) that the regulations issued by the bishops of the place are observed.

b) In the sacramental field in the positive participation, the Decree permits Catholics to receive the same sacraments performed by non-Catholic ministers, both formal or in good faith, under the following conditions:

(1) that there is absence of any prohibition of divine law;

(2) that the non-Catholic Church, from which the Catholic seeks the sacraments, has the corresponding sacrament;

(3) that there is a positive reason which permits Catholics to ask for these sacraments;

(4) that a Catholic priest is not available, either physically or morally (e.g., because access to him is prohibited by a civil power).

b) In the extra-sacramental field of common participation in the sacred functions, sacred things and sacred places, the Decree permits both positive and negative participation under similar conditions as for the admission to the sacraments. But it is natural that in this area common participation can be more easily admitted than in the sacraments.

From the post-conciliar applications of the new law in practice, we noted that the American Conference of Bishops decided not to admit non-Catholics as godparents in Catholic baptisms.[17] On the contrary, the Conference of Ukrainian Bishops, held in Rome, permitted that one of the godparents in a Catholic baptism and one of the witnesses in a Catholic marriage can be an Orthodox.[18] The reason for this difference seems to be obvious, because, according to canon 765, number 2, of the Code of Canon Law a non-Catholic cannot be a valid godparent in a baptism, and, on the contrary, in the Oriental discipline, the similar invalidating law does not exist.[19]

The Decree submitted this whole new discipline on the *communicatio in sacris* in regard to Oriental non-Catholics to the vigilance and direction of a hierarch, who in the spirit of this Decree will resolve the particular problem by his own decision. For this purpose, Catholic bishops of some area or region can have common consultations with corresponding Oriental non-Catholic hierarchs and they then can issue special regulations. The subject of these regulations will mainly be, if necessary, the determination of which sacraments of those permitted by the Decree and in what manner they may be given to non-Catholic Orientals because of the circumstances of the place. In a similar way, they may name those sacred functions, things or places which should be excluded from common participation because of the particular circumstances of the country or the place.

Conclusion:

The Decree on Eastern Catholic Churches concludes with the expression of joy for the cooperation of both Churches, Latin and Oriental, for issuing this Decree. The final, but very important, statement notes that this Decree is given for the Oriental *Catholic* Churches only, with the supposition that, in the reunion of Oriental non-Catholic Churches, a new revision of the whole Oriental discipline can be made. Consequently, in accordance with this final statement, the former title of the Decree on Oriental Churches was changed and made more specific by including the term "Catholic" in its title, although some decisions pertain also to non-Catholic Orientals.

[17] Cf. Interim guidelines for prayer in common and *communicatio in sacris, The Jurist,* XXV (1965), p. 366.

[18] *Litterae-Nuntiae Archiepiscopi Maioris Ritus Byzantino-Ukraini,* II, 1, Castelgandolfo, 1966, p. 45.

[19] It can be seen from the different Oriental synods, as well as from the decisions of Holy Office, as, e.g. *Collectanea S.C. de Propaganda Fide,* nn. 211; 355; 447; 1257; n. 4; 1495; 1831; as well as it was also in the Latin Church before CIC., cf. Sipos S., *Enchiridion iuris canonici,* 6 ed., Rome 1954: *"Hi omnes hucusque ut indigni illicite patrini adhibebantur",* p. 369.

VIII/DECREE ON THE BISHOPS' PASTORAL OFFICE IN THE CHURCH

Decree on the Bishops' Pastoral Office in the Church

✠ HISTORICAL INTRODUCTION

The Decree *Christus Dominus,* on the pastoral office of bishops in the Church, cannot be considered apart from the third chapter of the Dogmatic Constitution *Lumen Gentium.* The statements in that chapter concerning the sacramentality of the episcopacy and the nature of episcopal collegiality form the theological basis for this Decree. Rightly has Archbishop Paul J. Hallinan of Atlanta, Georgia, termed the Dogmatic Constitution on the Church the "mother schema" of this decree.

The Decree on the Bishops' Pastoral Office in the Church is in many ways the practical application of the theology of the episcopacy. In many ways the Decree is an explication of the lesson which St. Ignatius of Antioch taught the church of Smyrna when he wrote: "You must all follow the lead of the bishop as Jesus Christ followed that of the Father. . . . Where the bishop appears, there let the people be, just as where Jesus Christ is, there is the Catholic Church." At the same time, this Decree echoes the sentiments which Pope Paul expressed in his address opening the fourth session of the Council when he referred to himself and his brother bishops as "we who are no more than the companions and brothers of the people among whom we live." Finally, the Decree emphasizes the role of the bishop as the chief pastor, teacher and sanctifier appointed by God to serve His people. He is no longer a mere messenger or local functionary of the Holy See. In this Decree the bishop appears as the chief shepherd of the flock committed to his care, the bond of unity between the local and universal Church and the bridge between God and man.

The preparatory Commission on Bishops and the Government of Dioceses was charged with examining and collating the numerous suggestions of the world's bishops concerning these subjects. Paolo Cardinal Marella was president of the Commission, and two American prelates served as members: Archbishops John J. Krol of Philadelphia and Leo Binz of St. Paul. Between 1961 and 1962 the preparatory Commission had drafted seven schemata: 1) the relationship between bishops and the Roman Curia; 2) the episcopal conferences; 3) coadjutor and auxiliary bishops and the retirement of bishops; 4) the relationship between bishops and pastors; 5) the relationship between bishops and religious, especially in regard to apostolic works; 6) the partition of dioceses; 7) the principal problems concerning the care of souls. These schemata were presented by Cardinal Marella to the members of the Central Preparatory Commission during the third, sixth and seventh plenary sessions in February, May and June of 1962. The Central Preparatory Commission decided that this material should be included in two schemata, one to be entitled "Bishops and the Government of Dioceses," and the other "On the Care of Souls."

This latter schema was to be drafted in cooperation with the preparatory Commission on the Discipline of the Clergy and Christian People, presided over by Pietro Cardinal Ciriaci. On this Commission there were also two members of the American hierarchy. They were Bishop Ernest J. Primeau of Manchester, New Hampshire, and Bishop Charles P. Greco of Alexandria, Louisiana. The lengthy schema drafted by this Commission consisted of 88 pages of text divided into 202 paragraphs. The schema's five chapters were: 1) the pastoral office of bishops; 2) the pastoral duty of pastors; 3) the relationship between bishops and religious; 4) the pastoral care of specialized groups of the faithful; 5) the catechetical instruction of the Christian people.

None of these schemata were discussed during the first session. During this period, however, the conciliar Commission on Bishops and the Government of Dioceses and the Commission on the Discipline of the Clergy and Christian People were busy at work emending the original schemata. On December 6 both commissions presented the results of their work to the office of the Secretary General. This work, in turn, was examined by the newly created Central Coordinating Commission in January, 1963. At that time the schemata were returned to the two conciliar commissions with the directive to work more closely together on and to abbreviate the contents of both schemata. On March 26 the Central Coordinating Commission approved the emended work of both commissions, and the texts were presented to the Holy Father for approval. Pope John approved the texts on April 22, and the revised schemata were mailed out to the Council Fathers shortly thereafter. At this stage the schema on bishops and the government of dioceses consisted of five chapters and two appendices. These chapters were: 1) the relationship between bishops and the congregations of the Roman curia; 2) coadjutor and auxiliary bishops; 3) national assemblies or conferences of bishops; 4) the boundaries of dioceses and ecclesiastical provinces; 5) the establishment and boundaries of parishes.

Two American prelates submitted their comments in writing during the preparatory and coordinating phases of the two schemata. Writing in 1962 on the schema concerning catechetical instruction, Francis Cardinal Spellman expressed his hope that the need to discuss Christian doctrine would be realized in the Council. He was also of the opinion that "rather than one single catechism, the Fathers of the Second Vatican Council should decree that some sort of universal directory ought to be completed in which precepts and general norms are set forth which ought to be contained in the individual catechisms to be elaborated under the care of the conferences of bishops." He then explained what he felt should be the tenor of the proposed catechism:

> . . . Christian doctrine should not be expounded in a philosophical and apologetic manner, but rather as a simple explanation of truth which is contained in the words of Christ and the Apostles and in the deposit of faith entrusted to the Church. This warning is obviously derived from the very purpose and nature of catechetical instruction. Nevertheless, in view of present-day conditions, some apologetic instruction must not be forgotten. A Christian is made a soldier and witness of Christ by the sacrament of Confirmation. According to the decree for the Armenians, the effect of the sacrament of Confirmation is "that therein the Holy Spirit is given for strength, just as he was given to the Apostles on Pentecost, so that evidently the Christian might boldly confess the name of Christ." To all Christians according to their various conditions and ages—and not only to those who are *ex professo* teachers of religion and catachists—some suitable apologetic instruction must be given so that they might be able to profess the Christian faith and Catholic religion prudently and intelligently before all men. This instruction is indeed necessary, especially in those regions where a large segment of the population is not Catholic.

The Archbishop of New York made another proposal. He felt that the schema should "encourage the local ordinaries to take special care that Catholic theology and the true perennial philosophy, the handmaid of sacred theology, are taught to youths attending non-Catholic or State high schools and universities."

On July 19, 1963, Archbishop Krol submitted his observations on the schema concerning the care of souls. He felt, in general, that "words are used which are more rhetorical than legal" and thus such "usage will only increase the confusion that naturally accompanies a discussion of rights and obligations." Regarding the schema's discussion about associations of lay Catholics, he wrote:

> It could be that lay associations, whose purpose is non-ecclesiastical, harm the Church. Lay associations quite often include the name of the Church in some way or even the name of some saint in their title. Wherefore, their actions are often presumed by the uninformed to be approved by the authority of the Church. If the permission of the local ordinary is demanded by law before the establishment of an association of this type, then the bishop would be able to urge the use of another name in the title and the inculcation of stronger discipline.

Archbishop Krol also took exception to the suggestion in the schema that pastors be entitled to enjoy at least three weeks of vacation each year.

Dissensions can arise out of this. The abrogation of the ordinary's ability to diminish the length of a parish priest's vacation can cause some troublesome effects. If the parish circumstances are such that the flock is suffering detriment through the absence of a parish priest even for a month, the ordinary is unable to force the parish priest to cut his vacation short, since he no longer enjoys that faculty.

During the first session two Americans were elected to the Commission on Bishops and the Government of Dioceses, and another was appointed by the Pope. James Cardinal McIntyre of Los Angeles and Archbishop Karl Alter of Cincinnati were elected, and Archbishop Leo Binz was appointed. At the same time two other Americans, Joseph Cardinal Ritter and Archbishop Lawrence Shehan were elected, and Bishop Charles Greco appointed by the Pope, to serve on the Commission for the Discipline of the Clergy and Christian People.

Archbishop Alter was assigned to the subcommission dealing with diocesan boundaries. During the preparatory phase he was also a member of the Central Preparatory Commission. He felt that the most crucial aspect of his work on the Commission was the statement that bishops "teach, sanctify and rule the flock committed to their care not by delegation of authority, but by reason of their succession of the Apostles through the sacrament of their own episcopal consecration." He was also of the opinion that one of the lasting results of the Commission's work was the establishment of a clear, definite and mutual relationship of responsibility between the bishops and the supreme pontiff.

Archbishop Binz, who served on both the preparatory and conciliar Commission on Bishops and the Government of Dioceses, made six journeys to Rome and served as a member of the subcommission charged with the second section of chapter three, which treated of the cooperators of the diocesan bishop in his pastoral ministry. He felt that "the emphasis on the pastoral office, rather than on the government of dioceses" could be the most crucial aspect of the Commission's work. For him, one of the satisfying aspects of working on the Commission was Pope Paul's specific mention of the Commission on Bishops and the Government of Dioceses in his address announcing the formation of a synod of bishops. Archbishop Binz stated that "the formation of episcopal conferences and the synod of bishops will make perhaps the greatest difference in the history of the Church." He also spoke words of praise for Cardinal Marella who kept the Commission's work well divided among all the members.

Bishop Greco also served on both the preparatory and conciliar Commissions for the Discipline of the Clergy and the Christian People. He made 21 trips to Rome to carry out his duties on the Commission and attended 225 individual meetings. This represented for him some 775 hours of work in Rome. He served as chairman of the subcommission charged with the treatment of the catechetical instruction of the Christian people. After the work of the Commission was reassigned, Bishop Greco found himself a member of the subcommission dealing with the decree on the ministry and life of priests. He was especially happy to see that through his efforts the decree contained the admonition to bishops to "see to it that, under the vigilance of the hierarchy, sufficient provision is made for an appropriate program of preventive medicine and so-called health benefits, and for the necessary support of priests burdened by infirmity, ill health or old age." He was equally pleased to find, through his insistence, the specific mention of the Confraternity of Christian Doctrine in the Decree on the Bishops' Pastoral Office in the Church. "There was much opposition to this," he wrote, "and I had a sustained battle, but finally succeeded."

The only American expert assigned to work with the conciliar Commission on Bishops and the Government of Dioceses was the Right Reverend Monsignor John S. Quinn. As *officialis* of the Archdiocese of Chicago, he was most suitably prepared to render service both to the preparatory and the conciliar commissions. He served also as chairman of the *ad hoc* committee of American experts that was organized during the second session. Those who knew Monsignor Quinn and watched him throughout the four sessions of the Council continually marveled at his inexhaustible supply of energy as well as his constant manifestation of magnanimous charity.

According to Monsignor Quinn there were 112 opinions submitted by the Council Fathers on the first schema concerning bishops and the government of dioceses which he termed "a very juridical and rigid type of document." Seven American Council Fathers submitted proposals for the clarification and improvement of this text.

Cardinal Spellman also wanted clearer ideas on the suppressing and changing of personal and national parishes into territorial parishes. Cardinal Ritter wanted a better treatment of the nature of the episcopacy and called for a development of the theology of the episcopacy. He said that the schema treated auxiliary bishops in a purely juridical point of view. Further, he wanted to do away with taxes assessed by the Roman Curia, suggested that there be an annual tax or assessment on every diocese. Finally, he wanted a complete reconstruction of the Roman Curia and submitted a whole outline for this.

Archbishop Krol of Philadelphia, while bringing out the thought that Peter and his successor had full and supreme power in the Church and even possessed the immediate power to intervene directly in all churches, thought, nevertheless, that great changes were needed for the governing of the Church because of the changing conditions of people, times and circumstances. He thought that the local bishops understood the actual conditions better. The faculties, therefore, should be highly amplified and restrictions removed. He also offered specific recommendations for changing words in all five of the chapters. Bishop Charles Helmsing wished that the Curia would be reorganized. He also wanted the method and system of taxation of the various congregations to be completely changed. Bishop Loras Lane of Rockford, Illinois, had five observations. He pointed out the problems of coadjutor bishops and also brought out the difficulties that can arise between an ordinary in his relationship with his auxiliary and his coadjutor bishops. Archbishop Shehan of Baltimore had nine observations and minor corrections in various chapters. The main thing he wanted was the elimination of any report of a bishop who acted against his episcopal conference. He saw no need of any report to the president of the conference. Archbishop Alter submitted eight pages of suggested changes in wording and material.

The schema on bishops and the government of dioceses finally reached the floor of the Council on November 5, 1963, during the sixtieth general congregation. It followed the preceding month's discussion of the schema on the Church and, as many participants had expected, there were immediate repercussions. Cardinal Marella was defensive in his introductory remarks. His statement that "the Roman Curia has accurate and precise knowledge of each diocese" was received by the Council Fathers with sentiments of consternation. Bishop Luigi Carli of Segni, Italy, added to the stir by admitting in his introduction to the schema that the text was the product of curial officials who, according to one observer, "had not bothered to consult the other members of the commission."

Bishop Giuseppe Gargitter of Bressanone, Italy, a member of the conciliar Commission, led the attack against the schema. He stated flatly: "The text as we have it now is certainly not the one drawn up by the preparatory commission. It expounds its doctrine under the one-sided light of insistence on the rights and the central organs of the Roman Curia." He was echoed in his criticism by Bishop Jean Rupp of the principality of Monaco who called the text "a shining model of Roman brevity." He said the original text "was much more complete . . . but in the meantime it has undergone several surgical operations, with the result that we no longer have that clear and definite version which was the fruit of the preliminary discussions of the Commission."

At the regular weekly meeting of the American hierarchy that same afternoon, a lively discussion took place concerning the subject of episcopal conferences. Archibishop Alter introduced the subject, and comments were offered by Cardinals Ritter and McIntyre, Archbishops Binz and Krol, and Bishop Philip Hannan. The general feeling of the Americans at the meeting was that they should vote in favor of the schema as a basis for discussion, even though it would require many emendations. Their reason for voting approval of the schema, according to one American present, was that it would take too much time for the Commission to draft another schema.

The commotion did not end on November 5. On November 8 came the celebrated encounter between Cardinal Frings of Cologne and Cardinal Ottaviani of the Roman Curia. The story has been recounted by many authors, and there is no need to retell it here except mention that it was the high point of the second session. The New York *Herald Tribune,* on November 9, captured the spirit of the congregation in its headline: "Holy Office 'Harmful,' Cardinal Charges." The Rome *Daily American* was by no means exaggerating when it proclaimed in its headline, "Hot Words Fly at Council." According to the report of one American prelate, Cardinal Frings went to the Vatican on November 9 to see a functionary close to the Holy Father. This man told the Cardinal that the Holy Father was "highly pleased" by his intervention and complained about the harmful activities of the Holy Office.

The Frings-Ottaviani encounter highlighted the glaring deficiencies in the schema. It was obvious to all that the schema would stand, but would be thoroughly revised. The discussions on the floor of the Council continued from November 5 to November 18, throughout ten congregations, with 149 Fathers addressing their remarks to the contents of the schema. A total of more than three hundred Fathers submitted their observations for improving the text. During this period six Americans addressed the Council Fathers.

On November 5, Cardinal McIntyre vehemently opposed the juridical status of an episcopal conference. He warned of the great dangers that might arise from such an institution.

> The introduction of a juridical effect excepting the power of the ordinary of the place is neither necessary nor desirable in any way. The bishop has the power of jurisdiction in his own diocese; if many bishops decide to act in unity in a certain way, the same effect is obtained, and a juridical sanction is not required. Thus, a local *coetus* is a purely voluntary gathering among many dioceses with the same problems. If the problems require regulations besides the general law, permission can be obtained by petitioning the Holy See and with apparent satisfaction.
>
> Therefore, it is better to give these conferences recognition, but without juridical status. A juridical status can introduce and create psychological consequences which could greatly disturb some bishops and some dioceses. It is clear from history that the unity of the Church often has been impeded because of juridical impositions which were not for the convenience of the local community.

On the following day, Bishop Joseph H. Hodges of Wheeling, West Virginia, spoke in the name of "some of the bishops of the United States." He criticized the schema because it did not seem to show any relationship to the doctrine of the episcopacy as stated in the schema on the Church. He argued, first of all, that the first chapter of the schema should treat of the relationship between bishops and the Supreme Pontiff because the Council Fathers have already shown their approval of the principle that "the body or college of bishops, together with its head, and never without that head, exercise full and supreme power in the whole Church." He then suggested that the second chapter treat of the congregations of the Roman Curia.

> In this chapter the nature and principle of the authority of these congregations ought to be stated precisely because they depend upon the Supreme Pontiff, because they are created and perdure through his good

will, because they do not exist for themselves, nor is there in them any supreme power by divine institution. These congregations exist for the purpose of helping the Supreme Pontiff and the bishops in the government of the Church. There ought also be explained the meaning of the words "Holy See" or "Apostolic See." The words, "they fulfill their duty in his name and authority," should be explained.

Cardinal Ritter spoke on November 7, in the name of many other American bishops and advocated that the actual necessities of the Church "demand that the powers of resident bishops in many matters be amplified."

This amplification must be completed not through concessions and faculties, as the schema proposed, but through the abrogation or derogation of those laws which have restricted episcopal powers. Let no faculties or indults be given; but let the episcopal powers by divine right, which indeed from just causes have hitherto been withheld, be reinstated.

The Archbishop of St. Louis admitted that this would be a most difficult matter and that it would be perfected only in the revision of the Code of Canon Law. Then, speaking in his own name, he made another observation concerning the relationship that exists between bishops and the Roman Curia. He said that "the Roman Curia exists only because it is delegated by the Roman Pontiff," and, therefore, the title of the chapters should be changed so that it would treat primarily of matters between the bishops and the Roman Pontiff.

On November 11, Cardinal Spellman spoke "only in my own name." Once again he had his eye on the public and declared that, since the discussions in St. Peter's are being reported in newspapers and journals, "I clearly see that the discussions are being interpreted without a clear understanding of things, especially with regard to the collegiality of bishops, resulting in a great disturbance of minds and to the detriment of souls." Obviously the Cardinal was referring to the public airing of the Frings-Ottaviani encounter which had received a great deal of space in the German press. Cardinal Spellman's remarks concerning the Roman curia also reflected the typical curial reading of Pope Paul's address to the Curia shortly before the opening of this second session.

As is completely clear to us from the doctrine which we have already learned in school and which we believe with a firm heart, the authority of the Supreme Pontiff is supreme and full in itself. It is not necessary that he share it with others, even if they are bishops, whose collaboration in governing the universal Church can be asked for by the Supreme Pontiff himself, but is neither necessary nor essential.

That which pertains to the Roman Curia, because it is the important executive arm of the Supreme Pontiff himself and elected by him, is neither up to us to judge nor to reform, but pertains only to the Supreme Pontiff himself. In a certain address to the Roman Curia, he himself stated that he is not of a mind toward any reforms, having given the matter careful consideration.

Cardinal McIntyre, on November 12, reiterated his previous stand concerning episcopal conferences. His remarks were brief and to the point.

> Regional conferences of bishops are good and must be advocated! However, the introduction of a juridical element is not necessary; in fact, it is also useless! The goal of the conferences can be reached in the same manner without the introduction of a juridical element.
>
> The jurisdiction of the regional conferences is restricted to the members and the territories of the conference. All in the region are obliged to keep the laws and regulations which they have determined. If there are some who do not agree, it would be better if the obligation were moral rather than juridical.

On the same day, two other American cardinals, Meyer and Ritter, presented their views concerning episcopal conferences. Cardinal Ritter maintained that episcopal conferences "seem necessary for an effective ministry." He then described the utility of an episcopal conference in these words:

> Many times—and this is evident enough without needing proof—many times a unanimity both of voice and action is required on the part of the national body of bishops in order to attain a common goal. For unanimity will manifest authority and strength to decrees, undertakings and decisions. Unanimity will give firmness and fortitude to every bishop in pursuing the end. Who will be able to deny that such authority and fortitude are often necessary in those things which pertain not only to the salvation of souls, but also to moral and social problems? And what will be able to manifest the required unanimity securely, unwaveringly and at opportune times if not the episcopal conferences?

Cardinal Ritter said also that a strong episcopal conference would help in making the Roman Curia more international as well as make "an authentic and effective representation to the Holy See" possible. He then asked his colleagues to "constitute national episcopal conferences having juridical status and strength" and then, almost as a direct answer to Cardinal McIntyre's position, he offered this argument in favor of his own position:

> Who will be able to say that the institution of such conferences is contrary to the monarchical nature of the episcopacy? The institution of conferences says nothing, implies nothing, of the nature of the episcopacy. It offers a more efficacious and more ordered way in which the Roman Pontiff can

exercise his monarchical primacy. While the legislative force of the conferences comes forth from the recognition of the Roman Pontiff or from the Ecumenical Council, it is falsely said that the institution of conferences puts another authoritative body between the Roman Pontiff and the individual bishops.

Albert Cardinal Meyer took a position between the two enunciated by the Cardinal of Los Angeles and the Cardinal of St. Louis. He termed the section dealing with the decisions of an episcopal conference "an article that can be called the core and heart of this chapter, perhaps, indeed, of the entire schema." He pointed out the necessity of an episcopal conference in modern times and, at the same time, the importance of safeguarding the authority and freedom of the residential bishop. In order to strike a balance, Cardinal Meyer proposed two amendments to the text. First, he wanted to see this sentence inserted into the text: "The presiding officer will be elected by a secret, written ballot for a period of time to be fixed by the conference itself, unless special statutes prescribe otherwise." He was, secondly, in favor of restricting the juridical nature of decisions approved by the episcopal conference only to those which are part of the common law of the Church or of special mandate of the Supreme Pontiff. He made this suggestion, which was finally incorporated into the final decree, to ward off "that great danger of a new form of centralization that is too extensive and too complicated. A juridical obligation," he added, "ought to be imposed only when absolutely needed to carry out the will of the supreme authority in the Church." Throughout his intervention, Cardinal Meyer insisted upon preserving "the freedom of a bishop to act according to his own conscience."

In a written intervention, Bishop Ernest Unterkoefler of Charleston, South Carolina, agreed with Cardinal Meyer's observations. He thought it would be dangerous to the authority and jurisdiction of the local ordinary to insist upon the juridical nature of decisions of the episcopal conference. He wanted to limit the items in which episcopal conferences would have jurisdiction to two, namely, in matters described in common law or in a special mandate of the Apostolic See and the decree and declarations of an ecumenical council.

On the following day Cardinal Spellman presented his ideas concerning the episcopal conference. He favored episcopal conferences, but did not approve of giving the conferences a juridical nature. "It is necessary," he said, "for bishops to remain completely free in the government of their dioceses although morally —not indeed juridically—it would be fitting that in matters that pertain to the whole nation they agree with the rest of the bishops." He felt that legislation with juridical force should be left to plenary and provincial councils presided over by papal legates.

On November 13, Auxiliary Bishop Gerald McDevitt of Philadelphia spoke on the schema's statement concerning auxiliary bishops. "Although I speak in my own name," he began, "I hope that I express the mind of many of the bishops who, as I, are *merely* titular bishops." He was opposed to the text which allowed "a titular bishop only the possibility of belonging to the conference of bishops in his own country." He expressed his reason in these words:

Recently the most eminent moderators proposed various propositions to the Council Fathers with the view in mind of throwing open the disposition of the congregation about the proposed issues through a vote. The completed votes showed that the Fathers were pleased to write a schema stating that episcopal consecration establishes the highest level of the sacrament of orders; that each bishop legitimately consecrated, etc., is a member of the body of bishops; that the body or college of bishops, in the tasks of evangelizing, sanctifying, and in governing succeeds the College of Apostles and that it, together with its head, the Roman Pontiff—and never without this head, etc.—exercises the fullest and highest power over the entire Church; that this power belongs to the college of bishops united with its head by divine right.

After having said these things, I would immediately wonder how we can use the word *merely* with relation to titular bishops. If these votes manifest the mind of the Fathers and if this will be the mind of this Council for the future, then the word *merely* should be dropped from this article and from all the documents of this Council. It is the very episcopal consecration itself which has the power, and nothing else.

Bishop McDevitt then proposed three suggestions for the schema: first, that the word "merely" in reference to titular bishops be struck and used no more; secondly, that all titular bishops living and serving in any capacity in a country be members of the episcopal conference; thirdly, that all these titular bishops enjoy a deliberative vote in the national conference. He concluded:

Many titular bishops, and I am no exception, have sees situated in some deserted spot, but it does not follow from this that we ought to be voices crying in the desert. Unless I am mistaken, we are rather voices crying in this Council, and we should also be voices crying in the national conferences of bishops.

Writing in *Commonweal* shortly after this time, the Reverend Gregory Baum, O.S.A., called Bishop McDevitt's remarks "a truly parliamentary speech" and, "as far as form of delivery is concerned, the best intervention on the floor." Father Baum continued:

Bishop McDevitt convinced the Fathers that this was not simply a matter important to auxiliaries, but that it touched the very notion of episcopacy. I believe that this single speech, which was interrupted by applause, not only brought about the correction of the text, but also gave the Fathers a more intelligent and practical grasp of the meaning of collegiality.

At the end of the second session it was obvious that the schema on pastoral office of bishops needed drastic revision. The Central Coordinating Commission, in a letter of November 29, 1963, directed the Commission to reduce the contents of the schema according to the pastoral nature of the Council. In another letter, dated January 23, 1964, the Central Coordinating Commission instructed this Commission to incorporate into the schema the salient points discussed in the schema on the care of souls. The task was committed to the charge of five subcommissions whose work was examined and approved by the Central Preparatory Commission in March, 1964. The revised schema was approved by Pope Paul VI on April 27 and distributed to the Council Fathers. The schema then consisted of three chapters: 1) bishops in relationship to the universal Church; 2) bishops in relation to local churches and dioceses; 3) the common action of bishops cooperating for the good of all the churches.

At the beginning of the third session, those parts of the schema that included material from the schema on the care of souls were discussed on the floor of the Council. From September 18 to 23, during the eighty-third to the eighty-sixth general congregations, 39 Council Fathers directed their observations to this material. At this time two American prelates made their suggestions concerning the Confraternity of Christian Doctrine. On September 18 the forceful Archbishop of San Antonio, Texas, Robert E. Lucey, lamented the fact that "in many places the faith is weak and almost dead because the office of teaching is performed negligently if not entirely forgotten." He defended the Confraternity of Christian Doctrine which, he pointed out, "acts as a canonical congregation *through* and *because* of the laity for the purpose of restoring all things in Christ as far as it is possible and under the command of their own Ordinary." He then cited this fourfold program of the Confraternity:

> *First:* The religious education of children who attend public grade schools in which supernatural truths are rigorously excluded.
>
> *Second:* The religious instruction of youths of both sexes in secular universities and colleges of higher studies, and also youths who have been dismissed or have left school.
>
> *Third:* The religious instruction of adults by means of discussion groups in which men and women of individual parishes participate and in which lay apostles for the parish confraternity are instructed.
>
> *Fourth:* The instruction of parents, in which they are especially educated in their duty toward their children and in particular the duty of sharing and imparting Christian doctrine to their children.

Archbishop Lucey continued to speak glowingly about the work of the Confraternity.

> In our times a vast multitude of men throughout the world do not know the eternal truths and the doctrines necessary for salvation. The apostolic

function of the Confraternity consists in the imparting of knowledge and love of Christ to that "vast number" who make up the nucleus of the "turning-point" spoken of by the eminent Pius X in brilliant eloquence. The Confraternity sets up for itself the task of founding, under clear parochial leadership, the riches of intellect, good will and firm piety which the laity possess and of turning these riches into a Catholic faith which must be propagated among the above-mentioned multitude. With the greatest faithfulness it can be affirmed that the Confraternity can by no means be terminated, since it brings forth the neglected vast intellectual and moral works which the faithful laity now offer to the holy Church of God.

Unfortunately the Archbishop was interrupted by the moderator. Cardinal Döpfner of Munich, Germany. On July 21, 1965, the Archbishop recalled the incident in the following words:

I did not have any particular trouble getting on the list to speak to the Council Fathers, but Bishop Charles Greco, Chairman of the Episcopal Committee for the CCD in the United States, came near not getting on at all. Since the European Bishops have not the slightest idea of what the Confraternity of Christian Doctrine is, they saw no reason for wasting time listening to speeches about it. As a matter of fact, just before Bishop Greco rose to speak about the Confraternity, Archbishop Krol of Philadelphia, at the request of one of the four Cardinal-Moderators, went down to the Bishop's place in the bleachers and conveyed to him the request from the Moderator that he make his speech short and that, in fact, he give a brief introduction, leave out most of the body of the speech and then give the conclusion.

Anyone familiar with the Church in the United States and the place of honor held by the Confraternity as the best means of teaching religion to the masses of the people would consider such action as fantastic. All kinds of queer speeches were made by the brethren, and the audience seemed to stand up pretty well under a great deal of punishment, but when a subject and an organization that are greatly needed in Europe and Latin America were discussed, certain Princes of the Church had no time for such things.

As a matter of fact, I got some rough treatment from Cardinal Döpfner of Munich who, just like all of the European bishops understood the Latin words that I was using, but couldn't figure out what I was talking about. At one point in my speech the Cardinal interrupted and said that what I was saying was not *ad rem*. In view of the fact that I organized the Confraternity of Christian Doctrine in Los Angeles, California, in 1925, I think I know something about the Confraternity. . . . After all this the good Cardinal, being perfectly innocent of any knowledge of the Confraternity, told me that what I was saying was not *ad rem*. Just as I was approaching the conclusion of my speech, the Cardinal again interrupted to say, "Most Excellent Archbishop, all that you are saying is very fine, but which paragraph of the schema are you discussing?" The treatise on the Church covered at least one hundred fifty printed pages, and I was supposed to remember which paragraph referred to the Confraternity. Incidentally, we had to work like Trojans to get the phrase "Confraternity of Christian Doctrine" into the schema at all, because the Europeans did not know what kind of organization it was, and they kept throwing it out.

When the good Cardinal pulled that one on me, I was thoroughly disgusted and, since I was practically at the conclusion of my speech, I simply said, *"Dixi."* Two thousand bishops, including Cardinal Döpfner, were stunned, but I thought it was the best way to handle an impossible situation.

On September 23, Bishop Charles P. Greco delivered his intervention "in the name of the National Conference of Bishops of the United States of America on behalf of the Confraternity of Christian Doctrine." The specific point he made was summarized in his last sentence: "The omission of the Confraternity of Christian Doctrine in this schema is a denial of its great assistance to bishops and priests in the task of teaching, and it is a kind of contempt for the popes and sacred congregations which, even up to this time, have strongly ordered and especially recommended the Confraternity of Christian Doctrine." He also observed that the conciliar commission dealing with the subject of catechetical instruction had unanimously voted that the Confraternity of Christian Doctrine be mentioned in the schema. His major objection was that "the schema seems cautiously to avoid mention about that most distinguished lay Confraternity which the Church itself founded and which by the firm and timely voice of the popes it commanded to be established—and it still so commands—in order that bishops and priests may be helped in their duty of teaching." He called the Confraternity "indispensable for the life, vigor and extension of the Church in these modern times" and "the most fitting, efficient and opportune means for imparting Christian doctrine." He then stated his request:

> I do not have enough time remaining to mention the great number of Council Fathers who recognize and foster the Confraternity in their dioceses, but I am absolutely certain that I express their mind when I most humbly ask the most excellent Council Fathers to favor the insertion of the name of the Confraternity in the schema and that they also introduce it and foster it in their dioceses, if they have not already done so.

In another written intervention, Bishop Henry Grimmelsman wanted to give to the ordinary the power to transfer pastors according to his own judgment about the needs of a parish. He thought the stability of pastorates was very often undesirable; it favored inertia and lack of obedience. Bishop Charles Helmsing of Kansas City said he liked the section on the relationship between priests and bishops, but he would like to have the collegiality of the priesthood shown more specifically in order to bring out the unity needed among priests for the universal care of souls. He also wanted to bring out the point that great prudence was needed in describing methods for the spiritual care of immigrants. National parishes in the United States, according to pastoral experience, had often led to ghettos and divisions in civil society. He made a further point that bishops should not issue so many pastoral letters because they impede the necessary homily that would be the best instruction for people. People should be urged to read not only the New Testament, but select parts of the Old. He thought that it was good to emphasize catechetics, but that this should not be the only stress. There should be a complete reordination of catechetical material. Finally, he thought that the episcopal curia should be reconstructed.

Archbishop Krol praised the document, but thought that there was too much rhetorical language in it. Juridical words would be preferable, he said because clearer concepts could be drawn from such language. The subjunctive mood and ablative absolutes were not clear enough. Moreover, too little was left to the judgment of the local ordinary in many parts of the schema. He wanted to bring out the fact that because the Church is different in different regions, many of the sections ought to have the provision "unless the ordinary of the place provides otherwise." Furthermore, he pointed out, many items that would pertain to the revision of the Code of Canon Law—for example, the removal of vicars forain, the subject of the diocese of incardination instead of the diocese of origin. He saw no need of a diocesan office for social pastoral care as a universal need. In many places—for example, in the United States—there already are offices for Catholic Charities and Catholic Youth Councils. The words *valide* and *licite*, he said, should be more widely employed in the document to give greater clarity. Cardinal Ritter thought that the text was deficient because it did not say anything about the doctrine of collegiality of priests. The ideas on catechetics should be reexamined in the light of present-day pastoral requirements.

Archbishop Alter had various opinions on textual changes and wordings. Bishop Whealon wanted the ordinary to have authority to dismiss religious from parishes when the needs of the diocese no longer required their services. Cardinal Shehan thought that priests who do not belong to a religious congregation ought to be called diocesan rather than secular. He wanted also to eliminate personal jurisdiction for immigrants and make all jurisdiction territorial since national parishes do not do well in the United States. Finally Cardinal Spellman wished to remove the ideas on the distribution of the clergy from this schema. The great differences in persons and places warranted that the question should remain experimental. Put this matter and the question on the renovation of the clergy in the schema on clerics and leave the judgment to the ordinary, he said.

After the discussion the schema was returned to the commission to make emendations according to the wishes of the Fathers. On October 30 the commission returned the emended text to the floor and on November 4, 5 and 6 the Council Fathers, in a series of 21 votes, expressed their opinions concerning the present text. The commission again returned to the work of cataloguing and evaluating the text according to the wishes of the majority. The third session ended without the text returning to the floor for a final vote.

During the 138th, 139th, and 140th congregations, from September 29 to October 1, 1965, the Council Fathers again cast a series of 16 votes on the revised draft of the schema. Finally, on October 6, the schema received an overwhelmingly favorable vote. Of the 2,181 Fathers present, 2,167 voted in favor of the text and only 14 signed *non placet* ballots. The Decree on the Bishops' Pastoral Office in the Church was promulgated during the seventh public session of the Council on October 28, 1964, with 2,319 Council Fathers voting approval and only two voting their disapproval. The Decree, entitled *Christus Dominus,* will in many ways, like the Dogmatic Constitution on the Church, reshape the image of the Church of tomorrow. Subsequent events, however, have borne out the cautiousness expressed by one American bishop who wrote in his diary on October 28:

> I do not see why it will require all this time from October until the end of June to set up certain norms on this point. Of course, we suspect that the Curia wanted a good long time to study this whole matter [of collegiality] and work out procedures that will whittle down the impact of the document as much as possible. But I do hope that at least they will maintain the principle that by virtue of collegiality the ordinaries will be recognized as having ordinary jurisdiction for the government of their own dioceses by divine right. . . . It is, of course, obvious that, for practical reasons of administration, certain things must be kept directly under the supreme authority of the Holy Father if proper order is to be maintained in the Church. But the thing that the Council Fathers have been fighting for is to get rid of the tremendous burden which curialism places upon the bishops of the world.

This same Council Father, throughout the four sessions, had a favorite expression: *"Videbimus"*—"We shall see." No Council document depends so utterly upon the future as this Decree on the Bishops' Pastoral Office in the Church. Many men at the present time are saying to themselves, *"Videbimus."*

Decree on the Bishops' Pastoral Office in the Church

✠ INTERVENTIONS

JAMES CARDINAL McINTYRE, 5 *November, 1963*

The proposed plan to institute national or regional conferences is nothing new. Benefits increase when the circumstances of time and place are coordinated. The effect is similarity of action and the consequent unity of action. The intention of these conferences is a reasonable and coordinated operation. They pertain to human activities as applied to the administration of the Church. Thus, they are useful and desirable especially in growing communities.

But the question arises: Why should juridical status be given to them? It is said in the relation of this schema that these conferences which are to be instituted are not identified with plenary or provincial councils which are treated in Canon Law.

The practical end of these conferences is to treat of the necessities and advantages of the circumstances which are peculiar to a certain region or a number of dioceses. The decisions of such conferences generally do not have, nor should they have, universal application. They should be applied only in a particular and definite region and according to the judgment of many bishops, with the approbation of the Holy See.

The introduction of a juridical effect excepting the power of the ordinary of the place is neither necessary nor desirable in any way. The bishop has the power of jurisdiction in his own diocese; if many bishops decide to act in unity in a certain way, the same effect is obtained and a juridical sanction is not required. Thus a local *coetus* is a purely voluntary gathering among many dioceses with the same problems. If the problems require regulations besides the general law, permission can be obtained by petitioning the Holy See, and with apparent satisfaction.

Therefore, it is better to give these conferences recognition, but without juridical status. A juridical status can introduce and create psychological consequences which could greatly disturb some bishops and some dioceses. It is clear from history that the unity of the Church often has been impeded because of juridical impositions which were not for the convenience of the local community.

BISHOP JOSEPH HODGES, *6 November, 1963*

I speak in the name of some of the bishops of the United States of America.

The schema on bishops and the government of dioceses seems to us to contain a good deal of material which could be the basis for further discussion. We thank the commission for its labors. Nevertheless, the arrangement of this schema does not seem to show a connection with the doctrine of the episcopate as it appears in the schema on the Church. This gap is not the fault of the commission, which prepared the schema, but now must supplement it.

1) In this aula, the Council Fathers have clearly shown their attitude toward the proposition: "The body or college of bishops, together with its head, and never without that head, exercise full and supreme power in the whole Church." It seems logical to me that this schema, which deals with the pastoral ministry and jurisdictional power of bishops, ought to have as its first chapter, "The relationship between bishops and the Supreme Pontiff, the head of the body of bishops." In this chapter would be treated the exercise of the double form of supreme power in the Church.

In this chapter also could be explained the meaning of the words, "the many faculties reserved to the *Roman Pontiff*" (which is something different than the term "Apostolic See"), which are mentioned in the introduction. In this chapter could be stated how ultimately supreme power remains in Christ, the Son of God, who gave the full and supreme power to rule the Church to Peter and the Apostles, and to their successors, the Supreme Pontiff and the bishops.

2) When the relation between the double form of supreme power has been stated, then, in the second chapter, could be treated "The Congregations of the Holy Roman Curia." The division of this chapter could be somewhat like this:

a) Their relation to the Supreme Pontiff.
b) Their relation to the body of bishops.
c) Their relation to the bishops dispersed throughout the world.

In this chapter, the nature and principle of the authority of these congregations ought to be stated precisely because they depend upon the Supreme Pontiff, because they are created and perdure through his good will, because they do not exist for themselves, nor is there in them any supreme power by divine institution. These congregations exist for the purpose of helping the Supreme Pontiff and the bishops in the government of the Church. There ought also to be explained the meaning of the words "Holy See" or "Apostolic See." The words, "they fulfill their duty in his name and authority," should be explained (cf. page seven, 1, 4).

It is proposed, therefore, that the first chapter be "The Relationship between the Bishops and the Roman Pontiff, the Head of the Body of Bishops," and the second chapter be "The Relationship between the Sacred Congregations of the Roman Curia and the Supreme Pontiff, the Body of Bishops, and Individual Bishops." Other chapters could take up and amend the course of the discussion.

In my opinion, and in that of many other bishops of the United States, this deficient and limping schema must be kept under discussion.

JOSEPH CARDINAL RITTER, 7 *November, 1963*

I speak in my name and in the name of many other bishops of the United States of America. The amendment which we propose is very simple, but it is necessary to explain its reasons.

In the third paragraph, lines 18 and following, it states: "Resident bishops have all faculties by common right, which demands the more apt and expeditious exercise of their ordinary and immediate power." However, by divine right, the ordinary and immediate jurisdiction of resident bishops already by itself offers all that is required for effective exercise. Most certainly, this jurisdiction must be exercised only "under the jurisdictional primacy of the Roman Pontiff." But it must be remembered that it is not the primacy of the Roman Pontiff itself that restricts the episcopal jurisdiction, but the exercise of it through legislation.

The actual necessities of the Church, as the schema itself acknowledges, demand that the powers of resident bishops in many matters be amplified. This amplification must be completed not through concessions and faculties, as the schema proposes, but through the abrogation or derogation of those laws which have restricted episcopal powers. Let no faculties or indults be given; but let the episcopal powers by divine right, which, indeed, from just causes have hitherto been withheld, be reinstated.

Hence we propose that the beginning words of the first chapter be so changed as to read:

The Holy Synod believes that the opportune and most useful thing for the good of souls will be made if, excepting the rights and privileges of the Oriental Church, in the future the exercise of their jurisdiction (in many cases hitherto from just causes was reserved to the Apostolic See or the Oriental Patriarchs) be restored to the bishops.

We propose also that the whole chapter be so reorganized that it may conform to this spirit and prospect.

Venerable Fathers, we humbly admit that this is a most difficult thing. Similarly, we admit that this will be perfected only in the revision of the Code of Canon Law. There will be neither less nor enough; nothing less in our judgment will be worthy in order to complete the already accepted doctrine of the episcopacy. Most certainly, this Council will not be able to accomplish all things. However, it will be able to indicate and, indeed, list the matters in which the canons will have to be rewritten.

I wish to propose something else. But in this I speak for myself only. The title of this first chapter, in my opinion, needs to be changed. The communications matters or relationships that exist between the bishops and the Roman Curia are not primary and *in se* fixed, but secondary and derivative. The Roman Curia exists only because it is delegated by the Roman Pontiff. Hence, the title, as also the chapter, must primarily treat the matters between the bishops and the Roman Pontiff. Thus, I propose that the title be changed to "Concerning the Relation between the Bishops and the Roman Pontiff" or "Concerning the Matters between the Bishops and the Apostolic See."

FRANCIS CARDINAL SPELLMAN, 11 *November, 1963*

I speak only in my own name.

Since there have come to my attention many notices from newspapers and journals, particularly of other nations, I clearly see that the discussions which take place in this Council are being interpreted without a clear understanding of things, especially with regard to the collegiality of bishops, resulting in a great disturbance of minds and to the detriment of souls.

As is completely clear to us from the doctrine which we have already learned in school and which we believe with a firm heart, the authority of the Supreme Pontiff is supreme and full in itself. It is not necessary that he share it with others, even if they are bishops whose collaboration in governing the universal Church can be asked for by the Supreme Pontiff himself, but is neither necessary nor essential.

That which pertains to the Roman Curia, because it is the important executive arm of the Supreme Pontiff himself and elected by him, is neither up to us to judge nor to reform, but pertains only to the Supreme Pontiff himself. In a certain address to the Roman Curia, he himself stated that he is not of a mind toward any reforms, having given the matter careful consideration.

Wherefore, we feel that we must be careful not to propose anything in this Council which contradicts and opposes principles already stated by the Roman Pontiff or by other Ecumenical Councils.

JAMES CARDINAL McINTYRE, *12 November, 1963*

Regional conferences of bishops are good and must be advocated! However, the introduction of a juridical element is not necessary; in fact it is also useless! The goal of the conferences can be reached in the same manner without the introduction of a juridical element.

The jurisdiction of the regional conferences is restricted to the members and the territories of the conference. All in the region are obliged to keep the laws and regulations which they have determined. If there are some who do not agree, it would be better if the obligation were moral rather than juridical.

ALBERT CARDINAL MEYER, *12 November, 1963*

I should like to speak on the third article of this chapter, where there is question "Of the Decisions of a Conference," an article that can be called the core and heart of this chapter—perhaps, indeed, of the entire schema.

A rather serious problem can arise from this article. On the one hand, the schema sets forth an objective of the greatest importance, one that is particularly necessary in modern circumstances, namely, that "all the bishops of the same region, meeting together and taking common counsel, advance Catholic interests more effectively in their entire territory" (cf. n. 17). On the other hand, the authority and, therefore, the freedom of a residential bishop to follow his conscience in dealing with the diocese entrusted to him must be most firmly safeguarded. In order better to reconcile these two necessary aims, I propose the following emendations to the text offered us:

First: In number 20 of chapter 3, I propose that a new paragraph be introduced, to follow immediately after the words "let these be determined within each conference." This paragraph should run somewhat along these lines: "The presiding officer, who will be elected by a secret, written ballot for a period of time to be fixed by the conference itself, unless special statutes warn against this."

The reason for this emendation is this: The office of presiding officer of a conference is of such importance that the manner of his election ought to be determined by the Council itself. I propose the method which most fully accords with the full freedom of all the bishops, namely, a secret and written ballot. Extraordinary circumstances can be provided for by adding this clause: "unless special statutes warn otherwise."

Second: I propose that number 22, i.e., the general principle be done over and, indeed, somewhat in this fashion:

With proper regard for number 24, let the common deliberations of the bishops legitimately united in a national conference have this principal objective, that the individual residential bishops, after an exchange of information in a fraternal spirit, may better tend, according to their consciences, their own parts of the flock of the Lord and, at the same time, remain in communion with the bishops of the same region.

The reason for this emendation consists principally in this: The general principle, as it is now expressed in the schema, seems to be set forth too juridically and to restrict the rights of bishops in an undue way. For, as it now stands in the schema, the principle speaks only "of decisions set forth by the bishops, which each bishop will receive with proper reverence and carry into effect." On the basis of experience with the national conference which has existed for many years already in the United States, the new version of the text which I have proposed seems better suited to foster the goal of common collaboration without introducing a double peril, namely, undue interference in the government of the diocese entrusted to a residential bishop, and likewise the peril of some new centralization that would be too extensive and complicated.

Third: In the same spirit, and for the same reasons, I propose that number 23, "On a bishop acting against decisions," be entirely dropped.

I propose this, I state, for practically the same reasons. Now, as this number presently reads, there is placed on a bishop, practically speaking, an obligation that is more than a moral one, and thus the freedom of a bishop to act according to his conscience is not sufficiently protected, and there exists danger of a new form of centralization that is too extensive, indeed sometimes hateful.

Fourth: I propose the dropping of subsections (b), (c), and)d) of number 24. If these deletions are made, the decisions which bind bishops with juridical force will be limited to those which seem necessary and sufficient, namely, to those which are listed under (a). Let the text of this subsection (a), however, be emended more or less in this way:

When there may be question of particular matters which will have been entrusted to the national episcopal conference for discussion and decision, whether in virtue of common law, or by special commission of the Supreme Pontiff or of the Ecumenical Council.

The reason why, in my opinion, cases involving juridical forces ought to be strictly limited to those listed under (a) derives precisely from that great danger of a new form of centralization that is too extensive and too complicated. Hence, a juridical obligation ought to be imposed only when absolutely needed to carry out the will of the supreme authority in the Church. However, this will of the supreme authority in the Church is expressed only by the Supreme Pontiff, an Ecumenical Council and common law. By substituting, moreover, the words

"Supreme Pontiff" and "Ecumenical Council" in place of the phrase "Apostolic See," the seat of supreme authority is more clearly described.

If some national conference thinks juridical force should be extended to those cases listed under (b), (c), and (d), it can certainly obtain authorization in this sense from the Supreme Pontiff. A decree of the Ecumenical Council, however, ought not to place so great a burden on all national conferences.

Finally, in this same number 24, it seems to me entirely necessary to provide precise and fixed norms as to how the required majority is to be obtained, namely, through secret and written ballots, in some manner similar to that provided for our decisions in the *Ordo* of the Ecumenical Council. The text as it now reads requires a two-thirds majority. Although such a majority seems sufficient to me, serious consideration should be given to the reasons advanced by those who would require a greater plurality.

JOSEPH CARDINAL RITTER, *12 November, 1963*

With few exceptions, I like the third chapter of this schema.

Above all, the episcopal conferences to me seem necessary for an effective ministry. And I speak, not of the conferences with which the prescriptions of paragraphs 22 and 23 are concerned, but of those which possess a truly juridical position and strength as are described in paragraph 24.

Many times—and this is evident enough without needing proof—many times a unanimity both of voice and action is required on the part of the national body of bishops in order to attain a common goal. For unanimity will manifest authority and strength to decrees, undertakings, and decisions. Unanimity will give firmness and fortitude to every bishop in pursuing the end. Who will be able to deny that such authority and fortitude are often necessary in those things which pertain not only to the salvation of souls, but also to moral and social problems? And what will be able to manifest the required unanimity securely, unwaveringly and at opportune times if not the episcopal conferences?

Will conferences of this kind, possessing truly juridical status and strength, advance decentralization quickly? For, as is already provided whether for laws or for the juridical body, the necessity and right in order that superior authority might intervene through legislation are precluded indeed by a sort of preemption according to the principle of subsidiarity. Similarly, the conferences will serve those ends which look hopefully to the Roman Curia becoming more international. For where the bishops of some nation stand united authoritatively in some action or decision, there an authentic and effective representation toward the Holy See is rendered possible. The representation will be the most efficacious means, on the one hand, for explaining the special relations of the Holy

See to each and every nation and, on the other hand, for obtaining special and useful changes of common law.

Further, this Ecumenical Council taught us what it is to care and regulate for the universal Church. In this dimension of deliberation we daily teach many things of the greatest importance about understanding others' problems and making decisions which truly provide for the common good. This ruling can be, and must be, carried out best and effectively in episcopal conferences.

On the other hand, the schema treats soundly and prudently of instituting conferences. Certainly it is imbued with a universal spirit. Restricting itself to generic considerations, it leaves specific and particulars to each body of bishops themselves. Thus, paragraph 18 decrees that each and every conference determine its fundamental laws and its own mode of procedure, that it constitute its own method of electing officials and so on.

Above all, the schema is very prudent in instituting obligation. Thus, paragraphs 22 and 23 exclude every obligation of positive law where the Holy See will not have intervened previously. Where it treats of imposing obligations, the schema requires that the decisions "be passed by two-thirds of the voters and also recognized by the Apostolic See." All these things are most pleasing to me. Others, doubtless, want other rulings. Nevertheless, Council Fathers, I ask and urge you that, changes having been made, you support the substance of paragraph 24—that you constitute national episcopal conferences having juridical status and strength.

Who will be able to say that the institution of such conferences is contrary to the monarchical nature of the episcopacy? The institution of conferences says nothing, implies nothing, of the nature of the episcopacy. It offers a more efficacious and more ordered way in which the Roman Pontiff can exercise his monarchical primacy. While the legislative force of the conferences comes forth from the recognition of the Roman Pontiff or from the Ecumenical Council, it is falsely said that the institution of conferences puts another authoritative body between the Roman Pontiff and the individual bishops.

Finally, I would like to propose one change only in the schema. In the nineteenth paragraph, the second article, the same status should be given to auxiliary bishops in the conferences which is conceded to coadjutors in the preceding paragraph. Let it state that auxiliary bishops pertain to the national conference of bishops by right and with deliberative vote.

FRANCIS CARDINAL SPELLMAN, *13 November, 1963*

Episcopal Conferences which already exist in all, or almost all, nations are certainly very useful because clear lights from them attract all to solve various common questions. Nonetheless, in my judgment, it would not be good to give the conferences the power of deciding matters with a juridic obligation for each bishop.

It is necessary for bishops to remain completely free in the government of their dioceses although morally—not, indeed, juridically—it would be fitting that in matters that pertain to the whole nation they agree with the rest of the bishops.

Decrees with obligatory force would be left to the plenary and provincial councils over which an apostolic legate presides. Nor can these same decrees be promulgated before they would be approved by the Holy See.

If the episcopal conferences would enjoy the right of juridic decision, that is, with obligatory force and without the presence of an apostolic legate, they would have authority superior to the authority of Councils, which would not be harmonious.

BISHOP GERALD McDEVITT, *13 November, 1963*

Although I speak in my own name, I hope that I express the mind of many of the bishops who, as I, are *merely* titular bishops. The observations which I make are directed to chapter three, article nineteen, page fifteen, where there is a discussion of matters pertaining to the national conference. In the first number of this article it is established that all local ordinaries and coadjutors belong to the national conference of bishops, both as a matter of law and with a deliberative vote. Truly this is fitting and just. But in number two of this article there is an attempt to decide what should be done with those bishops who are *only* titular. Out of true kindness it decided that these bishops *could* join the national conference of bishops; and, if they do join in, they *can* have a deliberative vote or only a consultative vote.

All of these things strike me as inharmonious. Why? Recently the most eminent moderators proposed various propositions to the Council Fathers with the view in mind of throwing open the disposition of the congregation about the proposed issues through a vote. The completed votes showed that the Fathers were pleased to write a schema stating that episcopal consecration established the highest level of the sacrament of orders; that each bishop legitimately consecrated, etc., is a member of the body of bishops; that the body or college of bishops, in the tasks of evangelizing, sanctifying, and in governing succeeds the College of Apostles and that it, together with its head, the Roman Pontiff—and never without this head, etc.—exercises the fullest and highest power over the entire Church; that this power belongs to the college of bishops united with its head by divine right.

After having said these things, I would immediately wonder how we can use the word *merely* with relation to titular bishops. If these votes manifest the mind of the Fathers and if this will be the mind of this Council for the future, then the word *merely* should be dropped from this article and from all the documents of this Council. It is the very episcopal consecration itself which has the power and nothing else. No distinction is discovered in these propositions and votes, nor should we make any.

For these reasons, that is, because the Fathers approved of those proposals, I cannot understand in the least how this article can give a titular bishop only the possibility of belonging to the conference of bishops of his own country. Is it the mind of the Council that it should be easier to join with the college of bishops than with the national conference of bishops? However, although a bishop by right of his episcopal consecration becomes a member of the college of bishops, according to this article he does not become a member of the national conference of bishops. And even if the titular bishop should join the conference of bishops, the question still remains concerning the status of the vote which he would enjoy. Titular bishops according to the Code of Canon Law do not have the right of participation in an Ecumenical Council unless they should be invited—this regulation, in my humble opinion, also should be changed; but, if they are invited, the Code of Canon Law grants them a presumptive vote in deliberation, unless something else has been provided for. We even noticed here that titular bishops could more easily participate in the Ecumenical Council than in the conference of bishops in their country. If all bishops by reason of their legitimate episcopal consecration become members of the college of bishops and in this college, united with their head, exercise full and supreme power over the entire Church, then it is almost inconceivable that there could be a possibility that the titular bishops be excluded from the national conference of bishops. I have to admit that I cannot understand the reason for the action of some of the Council Fathers, no exception being made for the most eminent cardinals. They work and speak so much on behalf of the collegiality of all the bishops in governing the whole Church together with their head. In this respect I completely concur. But, at the same time, these same Fathers are unwilling to grant the titular and auxiliary bishops any participation in the government of the diocese or in the conference of bishops. In my opinion, this point flows from the principle of the college of bishops.

And so, first of all I propose that the word *merely* in reference to titular bishops be struck from this article and be used no more; secondly, that all titular bishops living in a country and, note this well, serving in any capacity in the country as, for example, auxiliary bishops, legally belong to the national conference of bishops; thirdly, that all these titular bishops described above enjoy a deliberative vote in the national conference, at least in the sense in which the Code of Canon Law grants it to them for an Ecumenical Council.

In conclusion, my observations are not directed against the concept of a national conference of bishops, which generally pleases me and is in accordance with the mind of the eminent Cardinal Meyer, nor are these ideas contrary to the National Conference of Bishops in the United States of America, in which all bishops are members and even have a deliberative vote. But if article nineteen stays as it is, I am afraid lest future changes take place, perhaps even in the United States.

Many titular bishops, and I am no exception, have sees situated in some deserted spot, but it does not follow from this that we ought to be voices crying in the desert. Unless I am mistaken, we are rather voices crying in this Council, and we should also be voices crying in the national conferences of bishops.

ARCHBISHOP ROBERT LUCEY, *18 September, 1964*

Allow us to say a few words.

There is an already vast and ever-increasing number of those who are entirely ignorant of religion or who have such a notion of God that they live in an idolatrous fashion. Indeed, how many are there who—not boys, but adults and very old—are plainly ignorant of the principal mysteries of the faith! From the fact that the faith of people of that age is weakened to the extent that in many it is half dead, we can rightly conclude that the office of teaching the necessary truths is either negligently performed or entirely passed off.

What kind of man spoke these words? Is he not a Communist? A Socialist? Perhaps an enemy of the Church? By no means, for these words were spoken by St. Pius X. It is clear that in many places the faith is weak and almost dead because the office of teaching is performed negligently, if not entirely forgotten (cf. *Acerbo nimis*, 1905).

Let the similar words of Pius XII, of happy memory, be heard:

The Body of Christ, which is the Church, is at a great turning-point not only because of hostile powers from without, but because of weakness within. This growing weakness, this process which is drawing off vital powers, proceeds from ignorance of Christian doctrine." (*Radio Address to the Catechetic Congress of Boston,* 1948)

Nor by any means can we forget the words of John XXIII, of holy and immortal memory. He wrote concerning the sacred office of catechetics as follows in *Pacem in Terris:*

We think that the fact that among the faithful today a religious faith is more and more separated from reasonable action arises from the insufficiency of those things which cultivate Christian mores and the institution of Christian doctrine. Therefore, necessity demands that the education of youth be complete, be continuous, be handed down in such a way that the nurturing of religious things and the formation of the mind proceeds in step with scientific knowledge and the daily progressing skills.

There is no one who does not recognize that it is the right and the office of the bishops of the world to preach the Gospel, instruct and form the faithful, both by their own words and writings and by the work of the priest and the laity. For St. Peter says, "And He commanded us to preach and bear witness to the people that it is He who is constituted judge of the living and the dead by God" (Acts 10:42). And, in Luke's Gospel, Jesus Christ Himself proclaims the words of Isaiah: "The spirit of the Lord is upon me; because He has anointed me; to bring good news to the poor He has sent me" (Lk. 4:17). St. Paul also, in his Epistle to the Corinthians: "For Christ did not send me to baptize, but to preach the Gospel" (I Cor. 1:17). "Woe to me if I do not preach the Gospel" (I Cor. 9:16).

Now someone comes along and asks: "Why do you refer this to the Confraternity of Christian Doctrine? It is certain that neither St. Peter nor St. Paul taught anything about an institution of this sort. Jesus Christ Himself preached; the Holy Apostles preached; Saint Anthony was a magnificent preacher. Forget the Confraternity!"

What shall we say? Time and customs have changed. In these days the faithful work at knowing, teaching, spreading the Holy Gospel not because it is the whim of priests, but because it is the will of God. The Confraternity of Christian Doctrine acts as a canonical congregation *through* and *because* of the laity for the purpose of restoring all things in Christ as far as it is possible and under the command of their own ordinary.

It is advantageous to remember the words of St. Luke:

Now after this the Lord appointed seventy-two others and sent them two by two before His face into every town and city where He was about to come. And He said to them: "Cure the sick and say to them, 'The kingdom of God is at hand for you.'"

How happy will that time be when the faithful of the world, although unbelieving and confused, cry out with one accord the words of exultation and salvation under the authority of their bishops: "The kingdom of God is at hand for you!"

Specifically, what is the purpose of the Confraternity? It is sufficient to enumerate four parts of this apostolic function.

First: The religious education of children who attend public grade schools in which supernatural truths are rigorously excluded.

Second: The religious instruction of youths of both sexes in secular universities and colleges of higher studies, and also youths who have been dismissed or have left school.

Third: The religious instruction of adults by means of discussion groups in which men and women of individual parishes participate and in which lay apostles for the parish confraternity are instructed.

Fourth: The instruction of parents, in which they are especially educated in their duty toward their children and in particular the duty of sharing and imparting Christian doctrine to their children.

It is evident that no canonical congregation can be found which possesses all the necessary and useful means for the religious instruction of the faithful adult or child except the Confraternity of Christian Doctrine.

In our times a vast multitude of men throughout the world do not know the eternal truths and the doctrines necessary for salvation. The apostolic function of the Confraternity consists in the imparting of knowledge and love of Christ to that "vast number" who make up the nucleus of the "turning-point" spoken of by the eminent Pius X in brilliant eloquence. The Confraternity sets up for itself the task of founding, under clear parochial leadership, the riches of intellect, good will and firm piety which the laity possess and of turning these riches into a Catholic faith which must be propagated among the above-mentioned multitude. With the greatest faithfulness it can be affirmed that the Confraternity can by no means be terminated since it brings forth the neglected vast intellectual and moral works which the faithful laity now offer to the holy Church of God.

BISHOP CHARLES GRECO, *23 September, 1964*

I speak as president and in the name of the National Conference of Bishops of the United States of America on behalf of the Confraternity of Christian Doctrine.

1) We all know that no duty in the Church is as grave, as necessary and as fundamental to the life of the Church and the salvation of souls as the duty of teaching Christian doctrine. Many excellent things are said about this responsibility in the schema on the pastoral duty of bishops, especially numbers twelve, thirteen, fourteen, and seventeen. There is even a brief mention in number fourteen about the preparation of teachers of catechetics for the job of teaching doctrine. But the schema says altogether nothing about the unfortunate lack of catechetic teachers which troubles the Church and affects it with great sorrow and the gravest anxiety. The schema neither poses nor suggests any solution for this problem. Further, the schema seems cautiously to avoid mention about that most distinguished lay *Confraternity* which the

Church itself founded and which, by the firm and timely voice of the popes, it commanded to be established—and it still so commands—in order that bishops and priests may be helped in their duty of teaching. As we all know, this lay association is called the Confraternity of Christian Doctrine. The Church has prescribed a solution—would that it might be accepted!

2) By inserting the name of this association of laymen in this schema, the Second Vatican Council would place this inestimable source of catechists in honor, strength and activity everywhere in the world for the solving of the lack of teachers, for the great growth and joy of the Church and for the copious salvation of souls.

3) This Confraternity, so long commanded by the Church and which alone has been ordered by the Church for this duty, is a parish assembly of laymen who are joined together by a cleric and who are prepared in mind and heart for everything having to do with the task of teaching Christian doctrine. It has programs for every age and for every need to foster religious instruction, beginning with the parents of the new-born and reaching to Catholic children, especially those who frequent non-religious schools, or public schools, as they are called. It even concerns itself with Catholic adults who need religious instruction (as do almost all), with non-Catholics and fallen-away Catholics who are led to Christ and the Church, or who are at least kindly disposed toward the Church. Truly it is of the greatest help in completing the task of conversion.

4) Since the number of priests, brothers and sisters decreases day by day (especially when we consider the daily increase of the Christian faithful), and since religious instruction is the basis for faith and salvation, every one sees that the lay Confraternity of Christian Doctrine is indispensable for the life, vigor and extension of the Church in these modern times.

5) This Confraternity is now especially widespread in each of the dioceses of the United States of America, in Canadian dioceses and in very many dioceses of Latin America, Africa, India, the Philippine Islands and in quite a few of the dioceses of Europe.

6) As president of the episcopal association for the Confraternity in the United States of America, I have contacts with many bishops in many regions. Very many bishops have told me that they could not have governed their diocese nor could they have carried out any program with success, especially in the duty of teaching, without the help of the Confraternity.

7) The Confraternity, thus proved and known, can easily declare that it is the most fitting, efficient and opportune means for imparting Christian doctrine. It is also easy to understand why the bishops and priests who know the Confraternity and who carefully use it declare that the future of the Church is in the hands of the Confraternity of Christian Doctrine, that is, in the help which the members of the association offer to bishops and parish priests.

8) Since this Confraternity of laymen is the greatest remedy for the lack of teachers and is thus necessary in the Church, it is not to be wondered that

the popes (even from the sixteenth century), especially at the present time, have recommended and even ordered the establishment of the Confraternity in every parish of the world.

a) Time does not permit me to read from more than Pope Pius X who, in the decree *Acerbo Nimis*, issued the following order: "The Confraternity of Christian Doctrine is to be established canonically in every parish of the world as the first among all societies. In the Confraternity, parish priests discover a great help for catechetical instruction from the lay people . . ." The prescriptions of this decree have afterwards been inserted in the Code of Canon Law, especially in canons 711 to 720. The other popes of this century, and recently the most Holy Father happily reigning, Pope Paul VI, and the Sacred Congregation of the Council, published a great deal both in praising and prescribing the Confraternity.

10) Venerable Fathers, from the decrees, letters and recommendations of the popes and the sacred congregations, and likewise from the glorious fruits of the Confraternity in many dioceses and parishes where it thrives and flourishes, it cannot be doubted that it is the mind and will of the Church that the Confraternity of Christian Doctrine by ecclesiastical mandate be established in every diocese and parish as the greatest aid to bishops and parish priests in the important responsibility of teaching Christian doctrine and making conversions.

11) It can be added that the conciliar commission, which recently discussed catechetical instruction, voted unanimously that the Confraternity of Christian Doctrine be named in the schema.

12) I do not have enough time remaining to mention the great number of Council Fathers who recognize and foster the Confraternity in their dioceses, but I am absolutely certain that I express their mind when I most humbly ask the most excellent Council Fathers to favor the insertion of the name of the Confraternity in the schema and that they also introduce it and foster it in their diocese, if they have not already done so.

The omission of the Confraternity of Christian Doctrine in this schema is a denial of its great assistance to bishops and priests in the task of teaching, and it is a kind of contempt for the popes and sacred congregations which, even to this time, have strongly ordered and have especially recommended the Confraternity of Christian Doctrine.

Decree on the Bishops' Pastoral Office in the Church

✠ COMMENTARY by Rt. Rev. Monsignor John S. Quinn

This Decree on the Bishops' Pastoral Office in the Church should help to bring about the concept of Pope John XXIII that this "pastoral Council" renew the inner life of the Church, because it brings it more into line with the pastoral needs of the People of God as they are today involved in the modern world. The Decree dovetails very closely with the Constitution on the Church which was promulgated at the end of the third session of the Council. The Constitution on the Church was a doctrinal description made up of eight chapters on the nature of the Church and the elements in it. One of its principal elements is, of course, the authority and direction of the Church involving popes and bishops. This is treated in the third chapter of the Constitution on the Church. It was a key problem to be answered and considered by the Second Vatican Council because it was a problem which has remained from the teaching of the First Vatican Council (1869–1870).

In that First Vatican Council the doctrine of the primacy of the Pope and the definition of his infallibility in proclaiming a doctrine of faith or morals brought forth loud protests, particularly in Germany and France. These protests claimed that the doctrine of primacy was downgrading the very office of the bishop and constituted him a mere agent of the Pope. They decried the fact that the bishop would, because of such a concept of primacy, be restricted in his office merely to carrying out the orders of the Pope. From time to time during the century between the First Vatican Council and the Second, such objections concerning the downgraded office of the bishop were voiced. Immediately after the announcement that the Second Vatican Council was to be held, these same objections came forth and were presented during the preparatory stage. The third chapter of the Constitution on the Church addressed itself to this problem and set forth a clear teaching on the nature of the institution of bishops in the Church. It presupposed the establishment, perpetuity, power and nature of the sacred primacy of the Roman Pontiff and his infallible teaching authority, but it went on to draw forth this doctrine on the teaching and ruling authority of the Church a step forward by making a universal confession and proclamation of the Church's teachings about bishops.

Bishops are depicted in this third chapter of the Constitution on the Church as successors of the Apostles. As such, they control the household of the living God. Joined with the Pope as successor of St. Peter and head of the visible Church in its entirety, they form one body or college. By the Lord's established promise, St. Peter and the other Apostles constitute a single apostolic college. In like manner, the Roman Pontiff, as Peter's successor, and the bishops, successors of the Apostles, are linked together.

The character and nature of the order of bishops is shown forth in the ancient practice whereby bishops, established all over the world, maintained communion with each other and with the Roman Pontiff in the bond of unity, charity and peace. This is shown clearly by the assembling of Councils. These Councils are held in order that more important matters might be decided in common and greater weight given to their decisions by the deliberation of the whole number. This membership forms one body or college. Its consequent association and combined action is described as the doctrine of collegiality. Every bishop shares in this by reason of his consecration. When the preparatory commissions were established, the competency or subject-matter assigned to the preparatory commission for bishops and dioceses was twofold. It was to treat, first, of bishops and their ruling of dioceses, and, secondly, of the care of souls. Hence the preparatory commission, in pursuing its work, invited the bishops of the world to send in their opinions on these two areas of the life of the Church, and during the work of the preparatory commission these two subject-matters were kept in distinct categories. The final efforts of the preparatory commission brought forth two drafts, or booklets: one on bishops and the rule of dioceses, and the other on the care of souls. The first decree or schema had five chapters. The first chapter had to do with bishops and their relationship to the Roman congregations; the second chapter dealt with coadjutor and auxiliary bishops; the third chapter treated of the national conferences of bishops; the fourth had to do with establishing boundaries for dioceses and ecclesiastical provinces; and the fifth had to do with the establishment and delineation of boundaries for parishes. Attached to this document were two appendices. The matters contained in the appendices were not for discussion on the floor. The first appendix had to do with the manner or method for bishops in treating with Roman congregations. The second appendix had to do with the manner or method of the Roman congregations in treating with bishops. The first appendix went on to describe at length the faculties of bishops. The second appendix described the manner in which a bishop was to address a request to the Sacred Congregation.

How this Decree will affect the Church, the People of God in practice, especially in the United States, remains to be seen. As it is implemented, it will make changes on the national, diocesan and parochial levels.

About the national level, the Decree says, "In these days especially, bishops frequently are unable to fulfill their office effectively and fruitfully unless they develop a common effort involving constant growth in harmony and closeness of ties with other bishops." The instrument to achieve this aim is an association of bishops from the same nation or region that will meet at fixed times, share and exchange views and merge energies in the service of the common good of the churches. This is called an episcopal conference. The conference has its own statutes. By a two-thirds majority vote in matters assigned by the common law, it can make binding laws for the territory.

The Episcopal Conference of the United States of America will reorganize in accord with this Decree of the Council. Most probably it will have vitally functioning committees for the various areas of the Church's life that were treated in the Council. Already it has a functioning committee for the liturgy. This committee studied the Council's Constitution on the Sacred Liturgy, made reports for its use in the United States, conducted meetings and obtained the necessary majority to make the changes we have experienced. It continues to work for greater education of the people in the field of liturgy and for more changes in the structure of the Mass and other forms of liturgy and Church music. Another commission for ecumenical affairs has been active. It already has eight subcommittees.

No doubt, other committees for Christian education, seminaries, religious, the lay apostolate, the pastoral office of bishops and social communications will be constituted in the near future. A committee on the pastoral office of bishops is sorely needed to study questions on the size and condition of dioceses, the need to have new dioceses and the division of present dioceses. This would have to be done in the light of scientific, religious and sociological research. Such a committee should develop methods and ways for selecting the best possible candidates for the office of bishops, with the intent of employing democratic processes. These should strive to include all members of the People of God—bishops, priests and laymen. Such information gathered by the committee would be invaluable for the Holy Father in his actual appointment of a bishop.

On the diocesan level, the decree describes a new type of collaboration for the diocesan bishop, namely, an "episcopal vicar." The usual offices of coadjutor and auxiliary bishops and vicar general remain. The episcopal vicar enjoys the same authority which the common law grants the vicar general, but only for a certain part of the diocese, or for a determined type of transaction or for the faithful of a determined rite. Episcopal vicars would help a great deal, especially in large dioceses, for they could serve as direct channels of communication with the diocesan bishop. In many of the large dioceses, the diocesan bishop is so overburdened with many problems that he finds it difficult to know, let alone solve, the difficulties and to serve the needs of his priests, religious and faithful.

Furthermore, the Decree requests that the diocesan curia be organized as a proper instrument not only for administration of the diocese, but for carrying out the works of the apostolate. Most curias or chancery offices today are engaged practically full time in solving personnel problems, marriage cases, building and fund-raising needs. Hence the promotion of the positive apostolate suffers.

The Decree expresses the hope that each diocese will have a pastoral commission presided over by the bishop personally and made up of specially chosen clergy, religious and lay people. The scope of this commission will be to investigate and weigh pastoral undertakings and to formulate practical conclusions regarding them. Help of this kind will be invaluable to the spirit of the diocese and the spread of the Christian message.

With changes on the diocesan level, made in the spirit of the Decree, changes will necessarily come about in parishes. First and foremost should be the establishment of a parish council which would work very closely with the diocesan pastoral commission. Members of the parish council should be the pastor, the assistant priests, the superior and first counselor of a religious group (for example, nuns that might be engaged in the parish school) and the presidents of the lay organizations—men and women—in the parish. The statutes of such a council ought to provide for frequent rotation, the members cooperating with the pastor and priests for a period, say, of three or five years. This type of directing effort should emphasize the community spirit of a parish and the need for community action, which has been so stressed in the whole of the Second Vatican Council.

IX/DECREE ON PRIESTLY FORMATION

Decree on Priestly Formation
✠ HISTORICAL INTRODUCTION

Shortly before the beginning of the Council, Giuseppe Cardinal Pizzardo, prefect of the Sacred Congregation of Seminaries and Universities, cited statistics that revealed the extent of the "vocation crisis" in the Church. In the 1,100 dioceses associated with this Congregation, there were 228,653 priests serving 418,000,000 Catholics in a total population of 692,000,000 people. In order to achieve a proportion of one priest for every thousand Catholics, 190,000 more priests would be needed, and, to arrive at a proportion of one priest for every thousand people, 470,000 more priests would be required. The "vocation crisis," however, is much deeper than mere statistics reveal. As Auxiliary Bishop Fulton J. Sheen of New York pointed out in his written intervention on the subject, the cause of the crisis is the fact "that the legislation of the Church which pertains to seminaries has remained unchanged from the time of the Council of Trent up to the present day." "Since the alterations and changes which have been made in the world in the past four centuries are known to all," he asked, "do you not think we should consider the adaptation of seminaries to modern times?"

That was precisely the question which the preparatory Commission on Seminaries, Universities and Catholic Schools faced. This Commission, under the presidency of Giuseppe Cardinal Pizzardo, listed three Americans among its members. Archbishop John P. Cody was a member, and Archbishop Patrick A. O'Boyle and the Right Reverend Monsignor Rudolph G. Bandas of St. Paul were consultors. The Commission examined the 557 suggestions submitted by the bishops of the world, by Catholic universities and by congregations of the Roman Curia. These suggestions were arranged under three general headings: 1) the selection and formation of seminarians; 2) the administration of seminaries; 3) ecclesiastical studies. Early in 1962 the Commission had completed its work of drafting two schemata, one on fostering religious vocations and the other on the formation of seminarians. The latter contained six chapters dealing with the general administration of seminaries, the spiritual, disciplinary, intellectual and pastoral formation of seminarians and the continuing formation of priests after completion of their seminary studies. On February 22, 1962, the Central Preparatory Commission ordered that the schema on vocations be incorporated into the second schema.

As a member of the Central Preparatory Commission, Francis Cardinal Spellman of New York submitted his observations on this original text. He felt that such a document was necessary so that "the instruction of seminarians might conform more safely to the mission of Christ the Eternal High Priest in the dangers of satisfying this age of progress." In general, he was pleased with the balance between the Church's venerable traditions and recent progress. Again he insisted on the rights of local ordinaries and episcopal conferences when he wrote:

> The traditional practice of the Church in this matter of greatest importance must not be tossed aside, but must be adapted to the special conditions of our age. Certainly it should be noted that it is the duty of the Ecumenical Council to decree certain laws to be followed by the whole Church. The particular norms which ought to be consulted in conditions of time, place and persons should rather be established by the local ordinaries or by the conferences of bishops, according to the spirit and letter of the decrees published by the Vatican Council and according to the instructions of the Apostolic See.

His reservations on psychological tests were similar to the same reservations he had made on the decree concerning religious. He wrote:

> What is said is good, that, in the conducting of scrutinies to form a firm judgment on the positive fitness of students, sometimes it is appropriate to seek the advice of a skilled doctor who is of a Christian frame of mind. It would hardly seem to be useless, however, to admonish him explicitly that in his psychological investigations he may not violate the natural right of a person who does not manifest any hidden problems. Such a warning would not exclude the investigations of experienced psychologists, but it would exclude the abuses and dangers which could arise from an immoderate or imprudent use of the opinions of skilled men.

Cardinal Spellman also praised the schema for its statement concerning the internal disposition of mind whereby the authority of the superior is freely accepted by seminarians because it "correctly refutes the errors by which the meaning and force of sound discipline are extenuated or ultimately destroyed." He felt, too, that the Council should stress the importance of "appropriate pastoral instruction in all the seminaries of the whole Catholic world," but he was opposed to extending the course of studies and spiritual formation after ordination. Rather than have young priests return to the seminary, he suggested that perhaps "young priests could come together twice a month for a full day,

in some predetermined place where they would receive instruction and formation under the direction of experienced and prudent teachers."

When members were chosen for the conciliar Commission on Seminaries,
Universities and Catholic Schools, Archbishop O'Boyle and, later, Bishop
Loras Lane of Rockford, Illinois, were elected by their colleagues, and Arch-
bishop Cody was appointed by the Holy Father. The conciliar Commission
examined the preparatory Commission's schema, entitled "On the Formation
of Seminarians," during February, 1963, in the light of the observations submitted by the members of the conciliar Commission. On March 25 the Central
Coordinating Commission approved the text as did Pope John on April 22.
During May the schema was distributed to all the Council Fathers. In March,
Cardinal Spellman again submitted his observations on the text to the Central
Coordinating Commission. Again he objected to the proposal in the schema
that would recall young priests, after a certain number of years, to the
seminary or similar house for continued study and formation. He wrote:

> When similar suggestions were first made by the preparatory commission
> in the schema on the decree on the sacrament of Holy Orders, all the
> cardinals and the president of the Bishops' Conference of the United States
> of America sent letters to the Central Preparatory Commission in which they
> expressed their votes as totally against such suggestions. By such sugges-
> tions, if they should be put into practice, our dioceses would be deprived of
> priests necessary for the salvation of souls, and the pastoral work of the
> bishops would be hurt. The proper pastoral and spiritual instruction of
> young priests can be posited without such a great deprivation of the daily
> pastoral assistance of these men, which is so necessary for the good of
> souls. . . .
>
> Furthermore, it is of the greatest importance to note that in the United
> States of America the custom of common life among the clergy prevails
> everywhere in dioceses. The young priest leads his life in common with the
> pastor, as his assistant, and often with one or two other assistants. Therefore,
> he begins his priestly and pastoral life in truly healthy circumstances in
> which the perils of the age are avoided as well as this is possible with human
> precautions. Newly ordained priests receive a totally practical pastoral
> instruction, in an apprenticeship that is really *de facto* pastoral, from priests
> more advanced in experience and age with whom they engage in a com-
> mon life and work under the same roof and near the parish church.

On July 19, Archbishop John J. Krol of Philadelphia sent his observations
to the Commission. He praised the schema for three reasons: first, because it
recognized the variety of conditions in different regions; secondly, because it
cautioned against ignoring practical problems in seminary training; thirdly,
because it warned that modern theological and philosophical opinions should

be discussed and subjected to examination. The Archbishop also had a reservation about applying the term "prophet" to priests because, even though the Savior was a prophet, "this aspect of His activity is not necessarily found among priests." He continued:

> Thus the charism of prophecy is not given only to priests, although every charism ought to submit itself to the authority of the holy hierarchy.
>
> Besides, the full power of orders is had only by bishops who govern a certain part of the People of God. Although seminaries should also form future bishops, no one ordinarily considers this to be the office of the average regular seminary.
>
> Also it can be noticed, and perhaps it should be, that men not enhanced with the priesthood had a part in governing the Church, in sanctifying people, and also in the position of teaching. For the sake of example, think of the deacons and the old cardinal deacons of the Holy Roman Church.

During the second session of the Council, the Commission was divided into three subcommissions charged with examining the many observations submitted by Council Fathers. The work of the subcommissions was approved during a plenary session of the commission, with the result that the schema was changed. It was now entitled "The Formation of Students to the Priesthood" and consisted of an introduction and six chapters. As in the case of other schemata drawn up by other conciliar commissions, the Central Coordinating Commission, on January 23, 1964, instructed this Commission to reduce its schema to a series of propositions that would contain only the essential principles. Other material already approved by the Commission would be turned over to the Commission for the Revision of the Code of Canon Law and to the post-conciliar commission charged with drawing up a directory for seminaries. The members of the Commission, accordingly, returned to their work, meeting from March 3 to 11, and were guided by the firm conviction expressed in the *relatio* attached to the series of 19 propositions: "If the great work of the Council and the spirit of renewal it has generated is to permeate the world, it is the seminaries that must become the real bridge to the future of the Church."

The new schema of propositions was approved by Pope Paul on April 27 and distributed to the Council Fathers. The schema was now entitled "On Priestly Formation," and, after more emendations from the Council Fathers were incorporated, it was increased from 19 to 22 propositions. Bishop Giuseppe Carraro of Verona, Italy, introduced the text on the floor of the Council on November 12, during the 121st general congregation.

Albert Cardinal Meyer of Chicago was the first to speak on the schema. He was especially pleased to see the general principle laid down at the very beginning that the program of priestly training be established by episcopal conferences. "With this principle," he said, "a real possibility exists that priestly education may always respond to the pastoral needs of those areas where they are going to exercise their ministry." He wondered, however, "whether our present schema in these few propositions really treats so excellent a theme sufficiently." He then made two observations; the first on the unity of the priesthood; the second on the fundamental humanity of the priest.

The text's assertions that all priests are, by nature, men and that their task is to be mediators between God and men, continued Cardinal Meyer, "constitute the foundation of *all* seminary formation." Asking what is the unity of the universal priesthood, he replied:

> According to traditional teaching, this unity consists in the mediation in which the priest is engaged in the sacrifice of the Mass and his prayer life (Heb. 5:1). Thus, the unity of the priesthood indicates also the unity of whatever apostolate the priest has, whether the priest is regular or secular, whether in the active ministry or in contemplative life, or whether he is occupied in the ordinary ministry or in the extraordinary ministry. Every priest should also be an apostle, as St. John Eudes says, "a priest on account of souls." The source of this apostolate for each priest ought to be his interior life, proceeding especially from the principal act of every priest, namely, the Sacrifice of the Mass, according to the saying of some holy priest, "as the Mass is, so is the priest *and* apostle." The end, therefore, of all seminary formation is the apostolate, however this apostolate is going to be exercised.

Secondly, the Cardinal felt, the schema does not "insist sufficiently that the priest is already, as a Christian man, obligated to the same perfection to which all who belong to the People of God are called." He explained his reasons:

> The priesthood, although conferred in a sacrament, is, first of all, a grace given freely to an individual *for the good of the Church*. Whether one uses this grace worthily or unworthily depends on his human cooperation which, with the help of grace, should stand forth. No one can prudently take upon himself the obligations of a priestly life unless he has previously shown the human capacity to bear these obligations and to persevere in fulfilling them. In a few words, the priest will not be truly effective in his ministry unless he has cultivated in himself truthfulness, sincerity, fortitude and justice. In a word, before anyone can go forth a good priest, it is necessary for him to be a good man and a good Christian, according to that saying of Pius XII: "For anyone to be a perfect priest, he must in some way first be a perfect man."

Perhaps these things seem obvious. But it is to be feared that they are not obvious to all candidates for the priesthood. Experience shows that there are seminarians who look to the priesthood not so much as to a freely given grace with which they must cooperate with all their power, but as a healing grace by the power of which they hope to satisfy the demands of Christian life more appropriately. . . . Undoubtedly the priesthood, as looked forward to, ought to determine seminary formation no differently from the way the future profession of a doctor determines his formation. But somewhere in the schema there should be brought out the necessity of things which are demanded of the seminarian in the area of ethics and which are indeed demanded not only in preparation for the priesthood, but already belong to formation under the true name of Christian. Only in this way can it be avoided that seminarians hope that their natural talents will be, as it were, magically transformed through ordination. And only in this way can there likewise be inculcated the necessity of striving with every power, and with the help of the grace of God, in the formation of that personality which constitutes the natural foundation of sanctity and priestly effectiveness.

Three other American prelates submitted their observations in writing. In the same intervention cited earlier, Bishop Sheen said that he would like to see the following paragraph incorporated into the text:

The time for vacations seems to us to be too long, therefore: the theological course should be prolonged to ten months; during the scholastic year, once or twice a week, the seminary directors should see to it that the students visit and aid the sick, the poor, non-Catholics, fallen-away Catholics, young people, those in jail, laborers, etc. During the summer vacation, seminarians, with the consent of the ordinary of the place, should be sent to give spiritual aid in those places where there is a great need of priests, so that they learn from the time of their formation to bear "the burden of the day and the heat."

Auxiliary Bishop George Speltz of Winona, Minnesota, speaking from his own experience as a rector of a seminary, submitted his observations concerning the education of priests, especially regarding philosophy and the last two years of classical studies. "I am moved to do so," he wrote, "because I find among not a few priests of my acquaintance little esteem for philosophy." First, he wanted to see the schema recognize the possibility that seminary education be associated more closely with the entire system of Catholic higher education. "In the United States," he wrote, "this would, in certain instances, be greatly facilitated by a change from the traditional minor-major seminary divisions to the so-called four-four-four plan corresponding to our high school, college and university divisions." In this arrangement philosophy would be taught within the four-year liberal arts college. He continued:

Such a structuring of seminary training would have many advantages; it would allow a more homogeneous age-grouping than is now possible in the minor seminary; it would facilitate accreditation of our seminaries and teacher preparation. Also it would be mutually advantageous both to philosophy, the humanities and science. The intellectual atmosphere resulting from the association of faculty members and students of these academic branches would furnish the developing philosopher with needed intellectual stimulation and subject-matter for philosophizing. In this setting, the impact and errors of modern systems of philosophy will more readily be understood. By the same token, the student of the humanities will be matured by his association with the philosophy faculty and students. The traditional stress of the propaedeutic relation of philosophy to theology in the seminary curriculum too little takes into account the close relation of philosophy to the liberal arts. As a consequence, we have not realized in our seminaries the formative value of this subject. Properly taught, philosophy can be a decisive influence in the liberal formation of the priest in Christian humanism who will be qualified, by reason of his human and intellectual attainment, to know men and the times and to win the respect of all.

Bishop Speltz suggested also that the schema should recognize the limitations of Latin manuals and should urge that they be supplemented by readings from other sources. He added:

Too often, in the United States and possibly elsewhere, excessive dependence upon Latin manuals has absorbed all the student's time to the virtual exclusion of collateral reading in philosophy and cognate branches, with the result that he has acquired only a verbal knowledge of philosophical definitions, principles and technical expressions. This method of presenting philosophy has been a factor in causing it to be little esteemed by many priests; and it has dulled their scholarly interests.

Bishop William P. O'Connor of Madison, Wisconsin, wrote that he wished "to present one particular example" and hoped "that the example of our own new diocesan Holy Name Seminary will already show the principles in action in such a concrete way as to test what the Council Fathers wish to say." He suggested that "our judgment of the propositions should be sharpened by such particular cases, to prevent our proposals from becoming too theoretical." He then described Holy Name Seminary:

It has been the good fortune of the young Diocese of Madison to build a seminary during these challenging times. The edifice itself and the daily administration of our minor seminary are based upon "the unit system." To keep a close relationship between faculty and students, between priests and seminarists themselves, the seminary has eleven residential units. Each unit has its own priest moderator, family lounge and facilities. Thus, each priest is in intimate and immediate contact with a small number of students.

This unit system has multiple advantages in the minor seminary. Adolescents are not totally removed from home. Their spiritual, moral and intellectual formation is personalized: "I know mine and mine know me." Their social development is under natural, healthy circumstances.

Students of the same age advance together. Each level is treated distinctively. As the boys grow older, they are freed from minute restrictions, so that they discipline themselves and recognize that they bear responsibility for their own actions.

More than thirty years of experience in seminaries also prompted the Bishop of Madison to furnish each seminarian with his own room. To maintain individuality and to develop personal responsibility, each student has his own small room, a cubicle with desk, bed and wardrobe. Traditional dormitories and study halls have been purposely omitted. Instead, the cubicles serve to develop that self-reliance and independence which should characterize the diocesan priest. At the same time, through the convenient-sized unit and the unit moderator, the young men relate to others spiritually and emotionally.

Smaller groups also make it possible to personalize day-to-day discipline, almost as a family does, without great masses of petty rules which irritate young men today. The words of St. Paul seem to apply: "Fathers, do not rouse your children to resentment, or you will break their spirits" (Col 3:21). The seminary professor and student become less apt to think of seminary training as a sort of passive formation. The student also forms himself more easily by personal initiative through the positive influence of the moderators and his fellow students.

Several Fathers of the Council have remarked that seminaries are not supposed to be "little monasteries." The pastoral formation of diocesan seminarians especially calls for a life within the seminary walls which is more akin to the life the seminarians lead before and after their training. It is impossible for seminarians to practice later in the pastoral ministry what they have no opportunity to practice among themselves.

Thirty-two Fathers spoke on the schema from November 12 to 17, during the 121st to 125th general congregations. On November 17 and 18 the Council Fathers, in a series of seven votes, overwhelmingly approved the schema of propositions, the highest number of reservations being 319. The text was returned to the Commission so that it could take into consideration the opinions of the Fathers. This was done during the following March, April and May in meetings of the subcommissions. During the fourth session, on October 11 and 12, the Council Fathers in a series of 15 votes again overwhelmingly approved various sections of the text. On the following day, by a vote of 2,196 to 15, the schema was approved. The schema had profited immensely from the conciliar discussions which had preceded it. The various drafts of the schema had advanced from an excessive juridical aspect to an open, alert statement on the necessity of preparing priests to meet the needs of a renewing Church in a changing world. Its first paragraph, stating that episcopal conferences should draw up a program of priestly formation is, as one commentator has observed, "a key implementation of the spirit of the Council." Acknowledging the necessity of decentralization, this paragraph alone assures the success of Pope John's *aggiornamento*. During the seventh public session, on October 28, 2,318 Council Fathers voted their approval of the text, and only three cast their vote negatively. Pope Paul, in promulgating the Decree, declared:

> Each and every one of the things set forth in this Decree has won the consent of the Fathers of this most sacred Council. We, too, by the apostolic authority conferred on us by Christ, join with the Venerable Fathers in approving, decreeing and establishing these things in the Holy Spirit, and we direct that what has thus been enacted in synod be published to God's glory.

Decree on Priestly Formation

✠ INTERVENTION

ALBERT CARDINAL MEYER, *12 November, 1964*

1) *Introduction*

This schema undoubtedly contains many useful things on the effective formation of seminarians. Especially pleasing is the general principle laid down in
the first section, according to which "in individual countries or rites a special
estimate of priestly education may be made, to be set up by bishops' conferences, and at certain times to be recognized and approved by the Apostolic
See." From this "estimate," universal laws may be adjusted to the special
limitations of time and place. With this principle a real possibility exists that
"priestly education may always respond to the pastoral needs of those areas
where they are going to exercise their ministry." Therefore, this principle, it
seems to me, truly corresponds with the pastoral intent of this Council.

Yet, it can be doubted whether the principles are sufficiently explained
which are truly common to all areas and all priests and, indeed, which can be
legitimately diverse.

The importance of this schema is such that it can scarcely be exaggerated.
Thus it seems to me that much of what was so admirably said in the hall by
many Fathers on the schema "on the Priestly Life and Ministry" can also be
applied to this schema. For the formation of seminarians tends precisely to be
a preparation for the priestly life and ministry. We may, on that account,
doubt, just as with the former schema, whether our present schema in these
few propositions really treats so excellent a theme sufficiently, especially when
we take account of what has been brought out by recent pontiffs in their
encyclical letters. The question can even arise whether one schema should not
perhaps be made from these two, or at least that, in the drawing up of distinct
schemas, the closest possible collaboration between the two commissions
should not obtain.

Having made these introductory remarks, I should like to say that it is not
my intention to touch on all points since, in other interventions by other
Fathers, many other excellent things have already been said and are going to

be said. I should like only to call attention to two general observations which, it seems to me, underlie many propositions already contained in the schema and which suggest that the schema should perhaps be more developed and elaborated.

2) *First General Observation*

The essential qualities of the priesthood are summed up in the famous definition of Paul: "Every high priest is taken from among men and appointed their representative before God, to offer gifts and sacrifices" (Heb. 5:1). This text makes two special assertions: first, all priests are by their nature men; second, their job is to be mediators acting between God and men. These two assertions, therefore, constitute the foundation of *all* seminary formation.

The schema says admirably: "Priestly education, on account of the very unity of the Catholic universal priesthood, is necessary for all priests of any rite whatever." Yet, one may ask: What is this unity of the universal priesthood? According to traditional teaching, this unity consists in the mediation in which the priest is engaged in the sacrifice of the Mass and his prayer-life (Heb. 5:1). Thus, the unity of the priesthood indicates also the unity of whatever apostolate the priest has, whether the priest is regular or secular, whether in the active ministry or in contemplative life, or whether he is occupied in the ordinary ministry or in the extraordinary ministry. Every priest should also be an apostle, as St. John Eudes says, "a priest on account of souls." The source of this apostolate for each priest ought to be his interior life, proceeding especially from the principal act of every priest, namely the Sacrifice of the Mass, according to the saying of some holy priest, "as the Mass is, so is the priest *and* apostle." The end, therefore, of all seminary formation is the apostolate, however this apostolate is going to be exercised.

From this identity and unity of the apostolate, there does not follow an identification of seminary formation altogether. And this distinction does not clearly shine out in our text. It is said in any case that this diversity is unknown in a reckoning of priestly living by saying "in referring suitable matters to the suitable persons," but it does not seem that the matter can be discussed in sufficient detail in these names or labels. For the norms set up in the schema seem to impose on the universal Church that which looks only to the formation of clerics in the Latin Church who are occupied in the active ministry under the bishop's leadership. If the schema intends this, it ought to establish it clearly. But, if the discussion is of the education necessary for all priests in general, the schema should be either restricted to what is truly essential or should give an account of the principles of various methods of exercising the priesthood. This latter alternative, namely that the schema should give an account of the formal diversity of the apostolate, seems preferable to me, so that we might have a schema elaborated in all respects, just as very many Fathers wanted to have in the schema on the priestly life and ministry.

3) *Second General Observation*

The schema, in section eleven, admirably indicates that the norms of a *Christian* education are to be scrupulously preserved in seminary formation. Yet it does not seem to me to insist sufficiently that the priest is already, as a Christian man, obligated to the same perfection to which all who belong to the People of God are called. The priesthood, although conferred in a sacrament, is, first of all, a grace given freely to an individual *for the good of the Church.* Whether one uses this grace worthily or unworthily depends on his human cooperation which, with the help of grace, should stand forth. No one can prudently take upon himself the obligations of a priestly life unless he has previously shown the human capacity to bear these obligations and to persevere in fulfilling them. In a few words, the priest will not be truly effective in his ministry unless he has cultivated in himself truthfulness, sincerity, fortitude and justice. In a word, before anyone can go forth a good priest, it is necessary for him to be a good man and a good Christian, according to that saying of Pius XII: "For anyone to be a perfect priest, he must in some way first be a perfect man."

Perhaps these things seem obvious. But it is to be feared that they are not obvious to all candidates for the priesthood. Experience shows that there are seminarians who look to the priesthood not so much as a freely given grace with which they must cooperate with all their power, but as a healing grace by the power of which they hope to satisfy the demands of Christian life more appropriately. Therefore, it seems entirely necessary that the norms of spiritual formation do not look exclusively to the future priest as the end of section eleven simply says: "Let the whole rationale of the seminary, imbued with an eagerness for piety and silence, be so ordained as to be already a certain initiation into the future life the priest will lead." This is, indeed, the best principle, but it deserves much more discussion, for it does not sufficiently indicate that seminarians are already obligated to Christian perfection in virtue of Christian morality. From the principle enunciated in section eleven in so general a way, the danger can exist that there may arise in seminarians the idea of a future priestly life which is entirely different from the simple Christian life. Undoubtedly the priesthood, as looked forward to, ought to determine seminary formation no differently from the way the future profession of a doctor determines his formation. But somewhere in the schema there should be brought out the necessity of things which are demanded of the seminarian in the area of ethics and which are indeed demanded not only in preparation for the priesthood, but already belong to formation under the true name of Christian. Only in this way can it be avoided that seminarians hope that their natural talents will be, as it were, magically transformed through ordination. And only in this way can there likewise be inculcated the necessity of striving with every power, and with the help of the grace of God, in the formation of that personality which constitutes the natural foundation of sanctity and priestly effectiveness.

4) *Conclusion*

Among the other statements that are certainly going to be made by other Fathers, these things are offered on our schema which ought to be more elaborated and refined in order that we may have a new impulse in the spirit of renewal of the Council of Trent for the formation of those men who truly bear in themselves, in great part, the hope of those fruits that we all look to from this Council.

Decree on Priestly Formation

✠ COMMENTARY by Bishop James A. Hickey

In the twenty-two articles and almost three thousand words of the Decree on Priestly Formation, the Council gives us neither a mere updating of Canon Law nor an untried program of highly theoretical reform. The Decree seeks rather to present a series of positive, well-balanced objectives for seminaries, objectives that would mirror the theological positions taken in the Constitution on the Sacred Liturgy and the Constitution on the Church. These goals for priestly training reflect the pastoral orientation of the Council and are designed to furnish the Church with zealous ministers of the Word, real priests of Sacrifice, and competent, Christ-centered, fully human guides of souls. These broad objectives are not restricted to any particular rite nor to the diocesan clergy. They are as broad as the Church and apply, with proper accommodation, to the religious and diocesan clergy alike of East and West.

1) It is in the very first article of the Decree that the greatest administrative innovation is found. For it commits to the several national hierarchies the basic responsibility for drawing up the programs of priestly formation in their countries. These programs must take into account the universal needs of the Church and her general laws, yet also give due regard to the diversity of local needs and conditions. The decisions of the episcopal conferences, in turn, will be submitted to the Holy See for approval. This procedure, as is obvious, is a considerable departure from present practice which centralizes the planning and administration of seminary programs in the Sacred Congregation for Seminaries and in corresponding congregations for the missions and for the Oriental rites.

This principle of decentralization, so broadly applied in the final draft of the Decree, was earlier proposed only with regard to the program of studies. Obviously, diversification of scholastic programs was needed in view of the differing educational patterns throughout the world. It soon became clear, however, that the culture, modes of thought and aspirations of regions and nations must necessarily reflect themselves in the patterns established for the formation of the clergy. This grant of basic and proper responsibility to the bishops was warmly praised in speeches from the Council floor.

It is clear, of course, that these local adaptations must be within the spirit and framework of the conciliar decree. National hierarchies are not empowered

414

to reverse a position taken by the Council: for example, the necessity of major seminaries in the training of priests. Nor is there a question of imposing an absolute uniformity upon all the diocesan and religious seminaries of a given country. The individual needs of dioceses and religious families will be remembered, and a national policy will be established with sufficient flexibility to accommodate them.

This same principle of decentralization also creates a good climate for well conceived and carefully controlled experimentation. The discipline of scientific educational research can be employed, and the results more easily incorporated in a national seminary system.

In the United States we may expect implementation of this portion of the Decree through appointment of a committee of bishops charged with the responsibility of reviewing seminary formation in accordance with the conciliar documents. The recommendations of such a group would be presented to the national body for its approval; these, in turn, would be forwarded to the Sacred Congregation for Seminaries and Studies.

2) In the preparatory phase of the Council there was a special draft-decree dealing with vocations and the means to encourage young men in the fulfillment of an attraction to the priesthood. A decision of the Central Commission caused that draft to be incorporated as an early article of the Decree on Priestly Formation.

The document carefully avoids any theoretical consideration of a vocation, its definition or the obligation of following a vocation when known. Instead, the article dwells on the duty of promoting vocations and lays great stress on the family and parish as the real seedbeds of a call to the priesthood. Methodical planning and all the resources of modern psychology and sociology are commended, but only as considerations secondary to prayer and penance performed by the entire Christian community. The role of the parent, the pastor, the teacher and the directors of youth is underlined. This essentially personal and human approach has particular relevance in the United States where we may be tempted to rely overly much on mass-selling techniques.

3) Under the same general heading of means to increase vocations, the Council recognizes minor seminaries as a proper and suitable means of fostering vocations. The preparatory phases of the document vary in their approach to this institution. Since minor seminaries do not exist all over the world, there was some doubt about including them in a document of universal application. On the other hand, it was recognized that large numbers of candidates for the priesthood are currently students in such seminaries, and that the minor-seminary system is necessary and fruitful in many countries. The present text, therefore sets forth positive norms, largely based on the exhortation *Menti Nostrae* of Pius XII and correlated with the over-all pastoral goal of forming a whole and complete man for the service of God.

Appropriate spiritual direction, a milieu of fatherly concern, suitable psychological contact with family and peers and, finally, studies fully equal to those of their contemporaries summarize the chief points stressed for minor seminarians. Much also of what is said concerning major-seminary training (e.g., training of teachers, Christocentric spirituality, etc.) is to be applied to minor seminarians also, but always in accord with the purpose and structure of the minor seminary.

It should be evident from the above that the Decree does not abolish or criticize in negative fashion the basic concepts of minor-seminary training. It seeks, rather, to encourage an intensive spiritual, intellectual, psychological and apostolic experience in which the candidates may grow into Christian manhood, fostering and developing their initial aspiration to serve the Church as priests.

Legislation for minor seminaries in the United States may well be expected to follow these basic outlines. The development of a suitable religious experience, with neither too little nor too much spiritual direction and formal exercises of devotion, should be a real concern. The question of a suitable routine and apt psychological contacts will be solved on a more local level in accordance with particular needs. Certainly the development of day-school seminaries on a secondary level is of considerable interest in metropolitan areas, but almost impractical in more rural sections. Imaginative and creative administration will be required to achieve more integration of our seminaries with the diocesan high school and college systems. At the same time, in order to achieve a suitable level of academic studies, it would seem that the Decree calls for seminaries to enjoy the benefits of State and regional accreditation. Such accreditation, however, is a bare minimum. The minor seminary must seek an educational program of constant enrichment; it must make continual efforts to develop men of broad interests and sympathetic understandings; it must impart a humanistic tradition and a real appreciation of today's culture.

The next four articles of the Decree deal with the establishment of major seminaries. In view of the much-discussed topic of seminary education, it is interesting to note that, in the very last version of article four, the sentence was added to establish this principle: "Major seminaries are necessary for priestly formation."

4) The basis of all seminary training is laid in the formation of real pastors of the Church—men who will resemble Christ in the role of teacher, sanctifier and counselor to the people. This pastoral role is characteristic of Vatican II, and, indeed, the Decree here reflects the teaching of chapter three, number twenty-eight, of the Constitution *Lumen Gentium* and numbers six and seven of the Constitution on the Sacred Liturgy. This pastoral insistence is constantly present in the other numbers of the Decree. It is the norm for the spiritual formation (Nn. 8–9), the intellectual formation (Nn. 14–16) and is most obviously the basis of the numbers which deal with apostolic and pastoral training (Nn. 19–22). In all of this is reflected the anxiety of the bishops that candidates for the priesthood be well-balanced personalities, truly competent in their field of caring for souls.

5) The Decree also insists on the appointment of the best men to seminary work, men with suitable pastoral experience and special training for their work. This presupposes a psychological ability for the work, a desire to engage in it and a continuous program to enrich their professional knowledge and skill. These chosen men are urged to live in a familial spirit with their rector and with the bishop.

The practical application of this article in the United States could be found in the establishment of a special institute in conjunction with some major Catholic university which would specialize in the training of professors for the major and minor seminaries. Residing at a central house of studies, the future professors could take the general graduate courses needed for their teaching fields and take specialized courses in spiritual direction, seminary counseling, seminary administration and similar subjects. Institutes of adequate time and professional depth could also be furnished in the summer months. These permit the professors to be abreast of the latest developments in their particular fields and also in the spirit and methods of seminary education. Another possibility is the creation of an agency, appointed by the Bishop's Commission on Seminaries, to certify professors for seminary teaching. Certification would be issued on the basis of proven professional competence and psychological suitability. Whatever form this preparation of teachers may take, it is abundantly clear that some formal system must be established which will insure truly competent teachers in all seminaries of the country.

6) In treating of the selection of candidates for the priesthood, there is the customary insistence on right intention, free choice and moral and intellectual suitability. The concept of physical and psychological health is recalled together with the over-all ability to be leaders and servants of God's people. Candidates who are not qualified are not to be considered as failures, but as Christians to be guided to a suitable form of the apostolate which is theirs by Baptism.

These notions are thoroughly in accord with testing procedures currently in use in many American seminaries. Certainly the reference to psychological health should reassure those who fear to use qualified persons in determining the psychological adequacy of candidates.

7) Another instance of the decentralization of authority regarding seminaries is found in the authorization for bishops to establish interdiocesan or regional seminaries and to govern them directly. Formerly this type of activity was under the direct control of the Holy See (Canon 1357). In the general area of seminary administration one can expect to see the American bishops give formal approval to the 4-4-4 system which corresponds so well with our national educational system. In the question of consolidation, it would seem that the seminary high schools would lose certain values if, in the interest of great size, they were to be too far removed from the families and the immediate locale which they serve. On the college level there will undoubtedly be much discussion of joining existing seminaries in units of larger educational oppor-

tunity. It may be hoped that such groupings of colleges will avoid provincialism and the perpetuation of needless isolation. Certainly, on the level of theological schools, it may be hoped that there will be great consolidation of existing facilities. There are hopeful tendencies toward large regional and national groupings which will utilize common libraries, teacher resources and the disciplines of adjacent universities of the highest quality.

At the same time the Decree expresses real concern for the dehumanizing potential of the very large seminary. In the formation of the priest there is a real need for a truly personal contact between students, professors and spiritual counselors. There must be real community interaction, and to achieve this there is the suggestion of dividing the students into smaller groupings to provide better for their personal formation.

It may be of interest to note that a proposal was offered whereby major seminaries would, where feasible, be located in connection with existing universities. While the suggestion has great merit in many parts of the world, conciliar enunciation of this principle could have caused difficulty in some areas where proximity to the existing universities is not in the present best interest of the Church. While not accepted into the text, this placement of seminaries is by no means forbidden by it.

Five articles of the Decree are devoted to the necessary spiritual formation of candidates for the priesthood.

8) The main theme of this spiritual training is that it must be Christ-centered. The students must establish a close relationship between doctrine and their spiritual life; they must learn to live as the friends and colleagues of Jesus. Their spirituality must be closely related to the Word of God, to the Eucharist, to the bishop and to those to whom they are sent to minister. The traditional exercises of piety are commended, but the spiritual formation must not be thought of as consisting merely in these alone. Prayer must become a real part of their personality, something flowing from their calling. In a word, their spirituality should not be conceived as something imposed from without, but rather as the logical development of the call to be a Christian and the call to the priesthood of Orders, a development of their relationship with Christ.

9) A deep sense of the Church must be created in the students. This is to involve deep reverence for the Holy Father, the bishop and their fellow priests. This sense of unity involves a proper concept of obedience and the exercise of self-denial.

10) One of the most beautiful paragraphs in the text deals with the concept of priestly celibacy. Stressing the biblical concept of renouncing marriage for the sake of the kingdom of heaven and of bearing witness to the resurrection of the world to come, the practice of celibacy is set forth as a means for the practice of perfect love whereby the priest can become all things to all men in the priestly ministry. Celibacy is recognized both as a command and as a gift

of God and, as such, is to be esteemed. Without underestimating either the dignity of Christian marriage or the difficulties of sacerdotal chastity, stress is to be laid on the positive value of this sacrifice as achieving a deeper mastery of soul and body and a more perfect sharing in an evangelical reward.

11) Coupled with the previous notions of spiritual training is the insistence on the sound psychological principles which are to be employed in the development of the whole man. On this point Cardinal Meyer laid great emphasis on the good priest as being, first of all, a good man, strong in the virtues of veracity, sincerity, courage and justice. This consideration is mirrored in the text. To be acceptable priestly witnesses to Christ, the candidates must be well-balanced, mature individuals. They must be men able to govern themselves, to use liberty wisely, to exercise initiative, to work with their associates and with the laity and to be possessed of the natural virtues expected in their contemporary society. Discipline must necessarily form an important element of the priestly character, but it is to be a well-motivated and inward self-discipline based on an ideal of Christian and priestly living. It must be the discipline of a person who realizes his goals and endeavors to achieve them in a manly and purposeful way.

12) So that the student may achieve a more mature decision with regard to the priestly vocation, the individual bishop may institute a special period of spiritual formation which would be a type of novitiate or periods away from the seminary itself to engage in some form of pastoral activity. Along this same line, the bishop would be fully empowered to grant a leave of absence for a suitable period of lay activity if the circumstances of the individual warranted. The bishop of a diocese may also decide to ordain his students only at an age beyond that of the common law or to require that a candidate spend some time in the diaconate before ordination to priesthood.

Dioceses in the United States have long made use of the summer vacations for the purposes mentioned in the Decree, and it would appear that there is no pressing national reason why the period of testing should be prolonged. Certainly, however, an individual bishop may see fit to test his seminarians in one or other of the ways outlined.

The organization of seminary studies occupies six articles of the Decree.

13) There is presupposed in the candidates for philosophy and theology a previous training in humanistic and scientific studies. Included in this is a knowledge of Latin which will enable the student to understand and make use of the sources needed in his purely ecclesiastical studies. No reference is made to oral Latin or to the detailed provisions of *Veterum Sapientia*. Special mention, however, is made of the proper language of one's rite and of the biblical languages. Implicit, of course, to the concept of suitable training is the development of an openness and interest in the intellectual life. There must be a sense of logical thinking, a willingness to share ideas, a willingness to hear the ideas of others and an ability to evaluate. And surely, also, the stu-

dents must be trained in at least the elementary tools of scholarship and in an intelligent use of library resources.

14) In presenting Church studies, the Decree wisely calls for the establishment of a frame of reference according to which all the subjects are to be considered: the mystery of Christ. To achieve this, the Council calls for an introductory course wherein all the themes of philosophy and theology can be related to the basic mystery of salvation and can demonstrate the pastoral purpose in all the facets of the education to come. Within the framework of a four-year college this introductory course could well take place in the freshman or at least in the sophomore year. This would obviate the difficulty of those students who often take courses in philosophy without any notion of their relation to the Christian message.

15) The teaching of philosophy must aim at a solid, coherent understanding of man, the world and God. The students are to become well versed in philosophy, relying on a patrimony "which is perennially valid," and likewise taking account of successive philosophical thought. There has been great uneasiness in some circles that the text is not sufficiently vigorous in insisting on a study of scholastic, and precisely Thomistic, thought. The wording, as revised by the commission, was certainly intended to call for a thorough grounding in scholastic philosophy (the *philosophia perennis*); interpretations to the contrary would disregard the clear explicative note given to the Fathers of the Council at the time of the voting. However, without in any way renouncing the rich philosophical heritage of the past which provides us with so many useful and necessary concepts, the Decree urges the students to a rigorous and contemporary search for truth.

16) Theological studies, the very heart of the preparation of the priest, are to be strongly biblical in content. Indeed, Bible studies are to be the very soul of all theology. With this in mind, the seminarian must be carefully trained in exegesis and be thoroughly conversant with the great biblical themes.

It is these same scriptural themes that are to be the first consideration in the teaching of dogmatic theology. Dogma is also to be taught through patristic references and through a study of the history of dogma. In penetrating more deeply into theological matters through the help of speculation, seminarians are to have St. Thomas as a guide. The role of St. Thomas was sharply debated in the conciliar discussion, and the present text may well be called something of a compromise between a position that would refrain from naming any single theologian and a strongly Thomistic position which would have imposed the conclusions of the Angelic Doctor. The specific reference is to questions of theological speculation, and it speaks of St. Thomas as a guide. This by no means limits the student to Thomistic conclusions, but rather commends to the inquirer the same courageous and original pattern of speculation which St. Thomas himself so often employs. Apropos of the insistence on Bible studies, the Decree insists on the renewal of moral theology, Canon Law and other ecclesiastical disciplines on the basis of greater scriptural formation.

Specific mention is also made of ecumenism and the knowledge of other religions, especially those prevalent in one's own region.

17) There is much insistence likewise on the basic reformation which must take place in the pedagogy of ecclesiastical studies. All the resources, techniques and possibilities of modern education must be employed. On the American scene, with the great variety of pedagogical tools which are at our disposal, seminary authorities have a clear obligation to be thoroughly abreast of these potentialities. The days of the memorized manualist and of the mesmerizing lecturer should be gone forever. Likewise rejected is the unwise multiplication of courses and the planning of a schedule which leaves little or no time for real personal study.

18) Related also to the question of ecclesiastical studies is the reminder that special institutes and schools of a higher scientific level must be provided to care for the development of Church studies.

19) As might be expected from this essentially pastoral treatment of priestly training, the Decree emphasizes in detail the types of activity with which the student is to be made conversant. The sacred ministry of catechesis and preaching, liturgical worship, sacramental administration, works of charity, direction of souls, ability to help and counsel religious men and women—these are all detailed as pastoral concerns which must be thoroughly taught, not merely taken for granted! All of these activities must coalesce in an ability to speak to the modern world, to know its problems and to have an ability to communicate with it.

20) All of the above implies an interest in all phases of God's People. The student must know much of psychology, sociology, pedagogy and all other suitable means for the apostolate. Coupled with these must be a largeness of heart and a realization of the total needs of the Church.

21) Most interesting in this section on pastoral training is the evident desire of the Council to promote a type of internship program whereby the students could actually engage in some forms of the ministry while still continuing their seminary studies. In the United States this has long been practiced in specially supervised summer projects and in programs for newly ordained priests. Internship programs for students in their deacon year have also been developed. This work, of course, must be done under careful supervision and with real concern that it become a genuine learning experience.

22) The final number of the Decree deals with post-seminary training and is not strictly within the scope of the document. It takes care, however, to require that episcopal conferences employ some suitable means for continuing education after ordination. Pastoral institutes, diocesan conferences and special study courses for the younger clergy will help to insure a more thoroughly trained and pastorally orientated priest.

In summary, we may characterize the Decree on Priestly Formation as (1) an indication of the pastoral zeal of the Council in seeking the best possible spiritual, intellectual, humane and pastoral formation for its priests; (2) an exemplification of the desire of the bishops to assume national responsibility for training men in accordance with regional needs; (3) a clear pledge of the Fathers that the work of renewal, initiated in the Council, will be carried on in the seminaries through the education of responsible, well-informed and solidly religious young men. That was surely the hope and prayer of the Holy Father and the bishops of the world on October 28, 1965, as this Decree was voted and promulgated as the basic law governing the seminaries of the world.

X/DECREE ON
THE APPROPRIATE RENEWAL
OF THE RELIGIOUS LIFE

Decree on the Appropriate Renewal
of the Religious Life
✠ HISTORICAL INTRODUCTION

The preparatory Commission on Religious was charged early in 1960 with drafting a conciliar text based upon the suggestions submitted by the Catholic bishops of the world, the faculties of Catholic universities and the congregations of the Roman Curia. These suggestions were summarized in a series of 558 propositions and under three principal headings: 1) the religious state; 2) religious institutions; and 3) the government of religious communities. The preparatory Commission was under the presidency of Valerio Cardinal Valeri. Three Americans served on this Commission: the Reverend Edward Heston, C.S.C., as a member, and the Reverend Romaeus O'Brien, O.Carm., and Charles Corcoran, C.S.C., as consultors.

The Commission had prepared a schema on states of acquiring perfection and submitted this text to the Central Preparatory Commission during its fourth, sixth and seventh plenary sessions in 1962. The subjects discussed in this schema were lay religious congregations, secular institutes, religious vocations, the formation of candidates to the religious life, collaboration between religious communities and the diocesan ordinary or—the general subject of exemption—the privilege by which some religious depend directly on the Holy See rather than on the bishop of the place. During the fifth plenary session of the preparatory Commission, Gregorio Pietro Cardinal Agagianian, as president of the preparatory Commission on the Missions, presented the subject of religious in mission areas.

During the opening days of the Council, the Fathers elected members to the conciliar Commission. Valerio Cardinal Valeri remained as president of the Commission on Religious, and two Americans were elected to serve on the Commission. They were Bishop Edward Daly of Des Moines, Iowa, and Bishop Joseph McShea of Allentown, Pennsylvania. Bishop Daly lost his life in the fatal air crash at Rome's Fiumacino Airport on December 9, 1964. Father Heston remained a consultant to the Commission and, during the second session, assumed the duty of being the English-speaking press officer of the Council.

At this time Cardinal Spellman submitted in writing his observations on the preparatory Commission's schema concerning the states of acquiring perfection. He directed his remarks to chapters 16 to 25 of the schema, concerning the education of young people in acquiring perfection. He was strongly of the opinion that spiritual directors and professors should be "men of proven virtue, endowed with solid doctrine and adequate experience." He was also in favor of regional or interdiocesan seminaries because in such institutes "moderators, professors and spiritual directors can be had more easily who are properly selected, prepared and free from other duties or cares, so that they may exercise their office properly and fittingly." On the subject of the education of religious, the Cardinal wrote:

> Without doubt, all students of the state of perfection, whether they are men or women, should be presented with adequate religious, intellectual and even aesthetic instruction accommodated to their situation. A solid and adequate instruction should be imparted to cloistered monks as well. As St. Augustine says, "No one can love what he does not know." According to St. Thomas, the study of the liberal arts is fitting for the religious "in two ways in respect to that which is proper to the contemplative life: in one way, by directly aiding contemplation by the enlightenment of the intellect, as it were. . . . In a second way the study of the liberal arts helps the contemplative life indirectly by removing the dangers of contemplation, namely, the errors which, in the contemplation of divine things, occur to those who do not know the Scriptures." Because of the nature of the cloistered life of monks and also because of the poverty of many of the monasteries of monks, their instruction is not without difficulties.

The Archbishop of New York also raised "a necessary caution in conducting psychological investigations of candidates." He suggested that religious superiors

> should consider not only the conclusions of scientific investigations by skilled men, but also the other conditions of the person. Furthermore, the Council Fathers might wish to make an explicit admonition that in these investigations the natural right of a person should not be violated if he does not manifest some hidden problem. In Canon 530 of the Code of Canon Law all religious superiors are strictly forbidden in any way to persuade those subject to them to give an open manifestation of their conscience to them. Even if candidates for the postulancy or novitiate are not included under the protection of this canon, it still seems totally against the practice of the Church to require some open and public manifestation of conscience as a condition without which the candidates are not admitted to the postulancy or novitiate. Such a warning would not exclude an investigation by experienced psychologists, but it would exclude the abuses and dangers which

could arise from an immoderate or imprudent use of the opinions of skilled men.

The conciliar Commission on Religious held its first meeting on November 26, 1962, and during this meeting the schema prepared by the preparatory Commission was presented to the members. In this preliminary meeting the members had their first opportunity to become acquainted with one another and to hear from Valerio Cardinal Valeri, president of the Commission, a summary account of what had been accomplished by the preparatory Commission. On December 9, 1962, the Council Presidency issued directives for the reduction of Council documents in the period between the end of the first session and the beginning of the second session. These directives naturally had marked repercussions on the work plans of the Commission on Religious.

The month of December, 1962, and January, 1965, can be termed the inchoative phase of the commission's activities. The instructions emanating from the Council Presidency had directed that the fourthcoming document on religious should be restricted to the following points: (1) the states of perfection in general; (2) religious vocation; (3) the adaptation and renovation of the religious life; (4) the formation of candidates and their admission to profession and to orders. In the treatment of these themes the Commission was directed to discuss only general principles, leaving aside specific questions not pertinent to the subject. Material dealing with the future revision of the Code of Canon Law was to be referred to the competent commission, and details were to be left to the future post-conciliar commissions. At the same time announcement was made of the organization of a new commission charged with coordinating the work of the various commissions.

The Commission on Religious met again on December 5, 1962. To expedite its procedure, it set up a subcommission of seven members to work out a reduced text in the light of the foregoing directives. The Commission members were instructed to submit their suggestions to this subcommission by the end of January, 1963.

It was finally agreed that the desired abbreviation of the schema submitted by the preparatory Commission could be best achieved by eliminating certain sections and referring others to the Commission for the Revision of the Code of Canon Law or to post-conciliar pontifical documents. Just when this work was getting under way, everything was brought to a standstill by the announcement that new instructions would be forthcoming from the recently constituted Central Coordinating Commission.

The second phase of the Commission's work was finally launched and extended over the months of February and March, 1963. From February 8 to February 13, 1963, a special group of members designated by the Cardinal President held meetings to study ways and means of executing these latest directives. At this point it became necessary also to consider certain allied drafts, such as the chapter on the religious life in the Dogmatic Constitution on the Church, the section on the relationships between bishops and religious engaged in the apostolate in the Decree on the Bishops' Pastoral Office in the Church and the passages dealing with religious in the Decree on the Church's Missionary Activity. Three subcommissions were appointed, one for the study of each of the previously named topics.

From February 20 to March 1, 1963, the third plenary meeting of the Council Commission worked at the abbreviation of the schema already under study. Fifteen Council Fathers were present, aided by a group of *periti*, for a total of nine meetings during which they examined all the observations sent in by the Commission members. In the last of these meetings an editorial subcommission was appointed. This group held five meetings from March 1 to March 7, deciding ultimately to change the title of the document to "On Religious." On March 9, 1963, this new text was submitted to Amleto Cardinal Cicognani, president of the Central Coordinating Commission, with an explanation of the method and principles that had guided the work of revision. A later communication from Cardinal Cicognani expressed warm praise for the Commission's faithful execution of the instructions received, at the same time suggesting a deeper study of certain detailed points that seemed likely to give rise to heated discussion when the schema would ultimately reach the floor of the Council.

A further revised schema was sent to the Central Coordinating Commission on April 23, 1963, after three meetings of the reduced commission under the presidency of Valerio Cardinal Valeri. Further meetings of this same group were held in late April and early May for a careful study of certain concrete suggestions proffered by Julius Cardinal Döpfner who was in charge of the schema on religious in the meetings of the Central Coordinating Commission. The text presented to this latter Commission on April 23 was gone over by a specialist in Latin style and sent back to the Commission on Religious for the preparation of the final draft.

On May 8, 1963, a definitive text was turned over to the General Secretary of the Council. It was printed and sent out to the bishops of the world by the end of the month, with instructions to return observations before the end of July.

In the meantime Pope John XXIII died on June 3, 1963, causing the suspension of the Council. A little more than a month after the death of Pope John XXIII, the commission for religious was in mourning for its president, Valerio Cardinal Valeri, who died on July 22, 1963. He was succeeded by Ildebrando Cardinal Antoniutti both as prefect of the Congregation of Religious and as president of the Commission.

During the period from July to October, 1963, the main work of the Commission was to revise the text in the light of the observations sent in by hundreds of Council Fathers. Since not all of these suggestions had been received by the deadline of July 31, they had to be presented to the Commission members in stages: 135 mimeographed pages on September 12, followed by 60 pages more on October 5, which were later supplemented by pages 61–108. Further observations arrived even as late as January and February, 1964, and were duly transmitted to the Commission members for study. A compendium of the examination of these texts was distibuted to all the Council Fathers at the beginning of the third session.

Just prior to the opening of this session, a further plenary meeting of the Commission was convoked for September 23, 1963, for a study of the schema on the adaptation and renewal of the religious life as well as of the documents from other commissions touching on various aspects of the life and activities of religious institutes. The discussion in this meeting centered mostly on the chapter in the Dogmatic Constitution on the Church dealing with the vocation of all the members of the Church to sanctity. At this time it became evident that lack of time would prevent the document on the religious life from coming before the Council in its second session. Hence, the work of the Commission was temporarily suspended while awaiting new directives from the Control Coordinating Commission on the further condensation of the schema.

In November, 1963, and January, 1964, these new norms were transmitted to the Commission. A fifth plenary meeting of the Commission had been called on December 3, 1963, which had designated six subcommissions, replacing the four previous ones, each put in charge of a special aspect of the schema. At this time also, a meeting of the Commission's coordinating subcommission was decided on for the end of January. This subcommission met from January 27 to February 4, 1964, and concerned itself particularly with carrying out the directives recently received from the Central Coordinating Commission.

According to these instructions, the text, which had already been pared down to what appeared to be an absolute minimum, was to be condensed still further, its contents being formulated in a series of propositions as several other commissions had been directed to do with their material. This proved to be no easy task. The document already prepared had been worked over very carefully, and words and expressions had been the result of well-considered decisions. Already packed with content and significance, it seemed almost impossible to compress the text satisfactorily into brief and dry "propositions." But higher orders were dutifully carried out, even though the net result pleased practically no one. Not a few Commission members and consultants declared frankly that they were ready to discard these jejune propositions and settle for the excellent theological treatment of the religious life in the sixth chapter of the Constitution on the Church.

A further plenary assembly of the Commission met on March 4, 1964, with available consultants likewise in attendance. It studied further editing of the document on religious life, especially the chapter concerning religious in the apostolate as contained in the schema on the pastoral office of bishops. With the text worked out in final form after all the vicissitudes of the previous two years, the Commission appended to it a detailed report on all the aspects of the procedure followed. Thus, at last, the text on the adaptation and renovation of the religious life was ready to be put on the agenda for the third session.

The schema on religious was introduced on the floor of the Council on November 10, 1964, during the 119th congregation. Bishop McShea was the member of the Commission who introduced the schema, and Cardinal Spellman was the only Father who spoke that day on its contents. In general, he was pleased with the schema, although he admitted that it needed certain modifications and definite clarifications on some fundamental points. He insisted that the appropriate renewal of the religious life "is a question of adaptation only of external forms and accidentals," but "no question of changing the nature of the religious life." The Cardinal then explained his concept of the religious life as

a life of entire dedication to God and the things of God; it is a life of prayer and union with God; it is a life of sacrifice and self-abnegation; it is a public testimony that the Kingdom of God is not of this world (John 18:36), a testimony of which the Church has special need today. It is a serious error, then, to think of the religious life as though it were nothing more than a kind of lay apostolate, differing from the ordinary lay apostolate only by the fact that religious take vows. This would be to confuse two testimonies—the testimony of the baptized Christian who lives and acts in the world and the deeper testimony of the religious who, even when acting in the world, must be seen to transcend it.

The Cardinal also expressed his concern over the confusion that is being stirred up among religious by writers who overlook the special witness which the religious life, as such, gives. "Suggestions," he said, "have been made for modernizing religious life which tend to deprive it of its specific nature, which tend, in fact, to destroy it." He continued:

Religious life must be modernized—though the need for this can be exaggerated—and religious orders must adapt their special apostolate to cope with modern needs, but nothing must be suggested and nothing must be done in the name of modernization or of apostolic efficiency which would prevent religious from bearing their essential witness to Christ by their vows, by their life of union with God, by their detachment from the world and the things of the world, by their wholehearted spirit of abnegation and self-renunciation which unites them to Christ in His Redemption.

Certain things which have been said and written, Venerable Fathers, have not been merely inadequate in theory, but, I say with all possible conviction, they have been seriously harmful in practice. In not a few cases they have disturbed the mind and spirit of religious men and women, indeed of whole religious communities, causing them to doubt whether their life of dedication, of poverty, of chastity and obedience, of prayer and penance in its present form is of value for the Church. Not a few have been so disturbed that they have desired to leave religious life.

The Archbishop of New York then paid tribute to the religious working in his archdiocese where " there are over 5,000 religious women alone." He said these men and women have borne excellent witness to Christ, have labored faithfully among Catholics and have gained the admiration and reverence of non-Catholics as well. Without them, he said, his archdiocese would be poorer spiritually, for "no amount of lay Catholic activity, however excellent in itself, could compensate for this loss." He concluded by saying that he was mentioning these things because "I owe it as a public tribute to the religious men and women of my diocese and as an acknowledgement of their profound religious spirit."

On the following day the Very Reverend Joseph Buckley, Superior General of the Marists, addressed the Council Fathers. He praised many things about the schema, but frankly stated that it contained many defects. He specifically cited three of these. First, he said, the schema contained no gesture of friendship toward the diocesan clergy.

> Bishops want to exercise a greater authority over the religious in their dioceses. Religious are worried about this. But we religious may as well face up to the fact that some of our habits irritate the diocesan clergy; for example, our inclination to talk as if we were the only ones in the state of perfection.
>
> It is time we recognized that diocesan priests have their own sound spirituality. There is much in common between them and religious. In many places they live in community. They observe the same chasity as we do. They all have to obey their bishop, and assistants have to obey their pastors. Their poverty is often not much different from ours. They carry out the same kinds of apostolic ministry in the same way. It is safe to say that religious priests of the active life are closer to diocesan priests than they are to contemplative religious.

Father Buckley next wanted to see the distinction between religious orders and religious congregations removed. He said that religious congregations have long since proved their value and that now is the time to stop thinking of their members as second-class religious. Thirdly, he took exception to the schema's propositions concerning religious obedience since it "might be all right for monks, but it is not what the active-apostolic religious needs today." He explained his criticism in these words:

> Some superiors are always talking about the crisis in obedience. My opinion is that the crisis is with the superiors, not with the subjects. The

truth is that today's young people don't swallow archaic formulas like "The will of the superior is exactly the same as the will of God."

Nothing is said in the schema about the obligation of superiors to consult their council—local, provincial or general. There are many superiors, particularly among the nuns—among the men, too—who do not understand even the proper and efficient procedure for running a council meeting. I suggest that renovation of religious life is more a matter of the formation and efficiency of superiors than of greater obedience in the subject.

He concluded by asking for another revision of the schema "still more favorable to *aggiornamento*," adding that he felt this could be achieved only by adding new consultors to the Commission.

During this time two other Americans submitted interventions in writing on the schema. Bishop Robert Tracy of Baton Rouge, Louisiana, submitted his observations on October 12, 1964. He proposed:

> Since actually religious institutes in nowise are merely associations for the exercise of the apostolate, but they are primarily ordered so that the Christian faithful may imitate Christ through a profession of the evangelical counsels and that they may become more closely united with Him, then in procuring the renewal of any religious institute, the principal parts must always be allotted to the spiritual life of the members. Never must that false opinion gain prominence which says that chief concern should be given to external works, and only secondary concern to the study of interior perfection as if this were demanded by the characteristics of this age and the needs of the Church.

Among other suggestions, Bishop Tracy also wanted to see the work of the teaching brother recognized in the schema because

> a) everybody recognizes that they, with the apostolate of education, for the zealous and fruitful exercise of which they have even forsaken the joys of the priesthood, have their own part in the pastoral cares of the Church, and
> b) that their ministry, which has determined the specific end of their institute, is retained by all as a "holy ministry entrusted to them by the Church and which is to be carried out in her name."

Auxiliary Bishop Stanislaus J. Brzana of Buffalo, New York, also submitted his observations in writing. Concerning the title of the schema, he made this observation:

> All of the schemata of the Council deal with the accommodation and renewal of the life of the Church. "*Aggiornamento*" is a characteristic note for the whole Council. The titles of the other schemata are simply "On the

Priesthood," "On the Institution of the Priesthood," "On the Lay Apostolate," etc. In conformity with this method of action, a preferable title for our schema is simply "On Religious."

The Bishop wanted also to see the propositions expanded and explained in greater detail and that exempt religious be admonished to show obedience and cooperation to the local ordinary in all necessary affairs. "Women superiors," he wrote, "should be admonished against abusing their authority and against the reduction of their charges to the state of children. Religious women should be treated as mature women."

Following the standing vote to close the debate on the schema on November 12, Bishop McShea in the name of the Commission summarized the discussion. He expressed the Commission's gratitude for the Fathers' observations on its schema and assured the assembly that these suggestions would be seriously considered by the Commission in redrafting the schema. He reminded his listeners that the theological aspect of achieving the state of perfection had been treated in the Constitution on the Church, with the result that the present schema appeared predominantly juridical in its tone. He reviewed the Fathers' criticism of the text and concluded his *relatio* with these words:

> . . . it should be observed that, if we speak of the renewal and adaptation of the religious life and labor, it is not because religious institutes everywhere need some sort of reform, as if they were deficient in their proper vocation to sanctity and the apostolate. It is, rather, to consolidate and perfect their double vocation and to make it better suited to the conditions of the times. In such a way the institutes will always be equal in merit to what they have been, and they will continue to carry on their mission in the Church, with the fruits of sanctity and progress, in the days to come.

The Commission returned to its work, examining the 26 oral and 19 written interventions of the Fathers. Upon the close of debate on November 12, the Fathers decided, 1,155 to 882, to vote on the individual propositions.

None of these propositions were rejected outrightly, the highest number of *non placet* votes on any given proposition being 77. The introduction and the first 13 propositions were approved *juxta modum,* i.e., with reservations to be inserted into the text. Propositions 14–20 were approved by a more than two-thirds majority of the voting Fathers.

On November 19, 1964, the Commission immediately began work on the almost fifteen thousand *modi* submitted in the voting—the same *modus* being sometimes submitted by groups of several hundred—in order to edit a final text for presentation to the Council. Groups of consultors were at work in subcommissions in the period from February 12 to 23, 1965. Their recommendations were then submitted to a subcommission of Council Fathers which met at Rome with the consultors from March 9 to 12. Finally, a plenary meeting of the Commission members and consultants was held in Rome from April 27 to May 1, and a definitive text was accepted to be voted on by the Council Fathers in the Fall. The 1964 text was considerably expanded, especially in the introduction, and the 20 previous propositions grew to 25 in compliance with the *modi* of many Council Fathers who desired the specific treatment of particular points. The propositions that were added dealt mainly with the following points: the monastic life; the completeness of the vocation of the lay religious; secular institutes; a final exhortation.

The final voting by the Council on the document on the appropriate renewal of the religious life took place on October 7th and 8th. Following the usual procedure this voting was not on the text itself, but on the way in which the commission had handled the *modi* submitted by the Council Fathers in 1964. October 11, 1965, brought the definitive vote on the whole of the text. Of the 2,143 Fathers present, 2,130 approved the document and only 13 registered disapproval. Pope Paul VI also approved the text and decreed that it should be submitted for solemn vote and promulgation in the public session on October 18, 1965.

Decree on the Appropriate Renewal of the Religious Life

☩ INTERVENTIONS

FRANCIS CARDINAL SPELLMAN, *10 November, 1964*

In general terms, the schema meets with my approval. With certain modifications and definite clarification on some fundamental points, it can be accepted by the Council and used as a basis of sincere renewal of religious life in the Church.

This schema is important, Venerable Fathers, since, in the words of Pope Paul VI, "the Church receives a great part of her power in the world from the flourishing condition of the religious life. . . . The work of religious institutes is wholly necessary for the Church in these days" (*L'Osservatore Romano,* May 24, 1964). Therefore, this schema deals with matters of no less vital interest for the welfare of the Mystical Body of Christ than those which we have been discussing in the Council up to the present.

A renewal of religious life, both as regards its internal constitution and its external apostolate as well as an adaptation to modern conditions, is necessary in many instances. This work of *aggiornamento* has been going on for many years and will gather momentum from the encouragement which we give it in this Council. But this *aggiornamento* presupposes that the true nature of religious life and its essential function in the Church is both appreciated and safeguarded. There is question of adaptation only of external forms and accidentals. There is no question of changing the nature of the religious life. We must beware "lest our youth, becoming confused while thinking of their choice of a state of life, should be hindered in any way from having a clear and distinct vision of the special function and immutable importance of the religious state within the Church" (Pope Paul VI).

The religious life is a life of entire dedication to God and the things of God; it is a life of prayer and union with God; it is a life of sacrifice and self-abnegation; it is a public testimony that the Kingdom of God is not of this world (John 18:36), a testimony of which the Church has special need today. It is a serious error, then, to think of the religious life as though it were noth-more than a kind of lay apostolate, differing from the ordinary lay apostolate only by the fact that religious take vows. This would be to confuse two testimonies—the testimony of the baptized Christian who lives and acts in the world, and the deeper testimony of the religious who, even when acting in the world, must be seen to transcend it. "The profession of the evangelical vows is a super-addition to that consecration which is proper to Baptism. It is, indeed, a special consecration which perfects the former one, inasmuch as by it the follower of Christ totally commits and dedicates himself to God, thereby making his entire life a service to God alone" (Pope Paul VI).

Now, certain things have been said and written regarding the religious life and its adaptation to modern conditions which seem to involve this confusion: they seem to overlook and almost deny the special witness which is given to Christ by the religious life. Suggestions have been made for modernizing religious life which tend to deprive it of its specific nature, which tend, in fact, to destroy it. Religious life must be modernized—although the need for for this can be exaggerated—and religious orders must adapt their special apostolate to cope with modern needs; but nothing must be suggested and nothing must be done in the name of modernization or of apostolic efficiency which would prevent religious from bearing their essential witness to Christ by their vows, by their life of union with God, by their detachment from the world and the things of the world, by their wholehearted spirit of abnegation and self-renunciation which unites them to Christ in His redemption.

Certain things which have been said and written, Venerable Fathers, have not been merely inadequate in theory, but, I say with all possible conviction, they have been seriously harmful in practice. In not a few cases they have disturbed the mind and spirit of religious men and women, indeed of whole religious communities, causing them to doubt whether their life of dedication, of poverty, of chastity and obedience, of prayer and penance in its present form is of value for the Church. Not a few have been so disturbed that they have desired to leave religious life.

In my diocese there are over 5,000 religious women alone. These excellent religious have borne and bear their own special testimony to Christ, and that testimony has been fruitful among the Catholics of my diocese and has excited the admiration and reverence of non-Catholics as well. Without the testimony of these religious men and women, my diocese would be much poorer spiritually; no amount of lay Catholic activity, however excellent in itself, could compensate this loss. Yet even in my diocese not a few religious have been disturbed by confused writings and speeches on the modernization of religious life in the Church.

I must, therefore, ask that the Council in its statement on religious life emphasize its special nature and insist on the special testimony that it gives to Christ in the Church. This Council should hold up before the world the essential values of genuine religious obedience, religious poverty and consecration to God by chastity; it should make clear the necessity of the lives of sacrifice, of prayer, of self-abnegation and penance which genuine Religious lead. The work of modernization and adaptation should proceed under proper guidance, but nothing must be done under the plea of *aggiornamento* which empties the religious life of its purpose and significance. We must hold up the religious life for what it is, and not condone, or seem to condone, any ideas which confuse it or would reduce it to the level of other forms of Christian life in the Church, however excellent.

This plea I make in the deepest sincerity since I owe it as a public tribute to the religious men and women of my diocese and as an acknowledgement of their profound religious spirit.

VERY REV. JOSEPH BUCKLEY, S.M., *11 November, 1964*

I should like to begin by thanking the 130 Council Fathers who signed my request to speak.

There are some good aspects of this latest schema on religious. It insists on the renewal which is the chief aim of this Second Vatican Council. It expressly pursues the adaptation which the Sacred Congregation of Religious began as far back as 1950 and has continued to promote ever since.

But there are many defects in the schema:

1) For instance, there is no gesture of friendship toward the diocesan clergy. It can be objected that this kind of gesture does not belong to a schema on the renewal of religious life. But the disagreements between religious and bishops and diocesan priests are a serious difficulty to the Church.

Bishops want to exercise a greater authority over the religious in their diocese. Religious are worried about this. But we religious may as well face up to the fact that some of our habits irritate the diocesan clergy; for example, our inclination to talk as if we were the only ones in the state of perfection.

It is time we recognized that diocesan priests have their own sound spirituality. There is much in common between them and religious. In many places they live in community. They observe the same chastity as we do. They all have to obey their bishop, and assistants have to obey their pastor. Their poverty is often not much different from ours. They carry out the same kinds of apostolic ministry in the same way. It is safe to say that religious priests of the active life are closer to diocesan priests than they are to contemplative religious.

Even though we have to make a canonical distinction, we do not have to insist on it in practice. "What unites us is more important than what separates us" is good philosophy.

I put these ideas to Pope John in an audience. With that spontaneity of his, he replied immediately, "*Adesso c'intendiamo*"—"That's what I think, too."

2) The same principle of removing unnecessary differences suggests

another step in renewing religious life: remove the distinctions between orders and congregations.

Congregations have already proved their worth in the Church. It is time to stop thinking of their members as second-class religious, poor relations—*"dei parenti poveri."* We are very grateful to the Holy Fathers John XXIII and Paul VI that the superiors general of congregations are members of the Council, provided they have a thousand priests in their congregation. On the other hand, superiors general of orders that do not even have one hundred priests are members of the Council, not to mention bishops with less than one hundred diocesan priests in their diocese.

It seems to me that a step in the renovation of the congregations, at least the congregations of men, is to grant them power of jurisdiction and faculties for the exercise of the sacred ministry in their own houses for their own subjects without the obligation of continually asking for indults.

3) Number eight of the new schema is on religious obedience. This seems to apply to all religious a concept of obedience which might be all right for monks, but it is not what the active-apostolic religious needs today.

Some superiors are always talking about the crisis in obedience. My opinion is that the crisis is with the superiors, not with the subjects. The truth is that today's young people don't swallow archaic formulas like "the will of the superior is exactly the same as the will of God."

Nothing is said in the schema about the obligation of superiors to consult their council—local, provincial or general. There are many superiors, particularly among the nuns—among the men, too—who do not understand even the proper and efficient procedure for running a council meeting. I suggest that renovation of religious life is more a matter of the formation and efficiency of superiors than of greater obedience in the subject.

For these reasons, and others there is no time for now, it appears to me that the present schema does not give us a full response to the modern problems of religious life.

Another revision, still more favorable to *aggiornamento*, is called for. I doubt if it can come from the Commission, unless new *periti* are added to it.

Decree on the Appropriate Renewal
of the Religious Life

✠ COMMENTARY by Rev. Edward Heston, C.S.C.

It was not easy for the Ecumenical Council to face up to the task of producing a degree on the *aggiornamento* of the religious life in the modern world. Throughout the Church there are well over a million souls living a life of total consecration to Christ either within the framework of the religious life or in the more recent structure of secular institutes. In these ranks we find priests or clerics, brothers and sisters. Some offer their witness within the limited confines of the contemplative life, making their contribution to the Mystical Body by lives of prayer and sacrifice.

Legions of religious dedicate their lives to God and neighbor in the almost infinite variety of apostolic works in the Church: teaching, care of the sick and the poor, manual and professional activities, the apostolate of the press and all other activities which reflect the vitalizing presence of consecrated souls wherever the Church is in need. Many religious are carrying on their work in surroundings which favor and welcome their contribution to human welfare, while others must carry on in the face of stubborn opposition and even of outright persecution. It is easy to understand the problems involved in trying to edit a document which would be universally applicable and which would, nevertheless, not run afoul of the stern rules of brevity laid down by Council authorities.

But this was exactly what had to be done because of the incalculable importance of religious in the Church. The over-all preparation of the Decree on the Appropriate Renewal of the Religious Life covered three phases: the ante-preparatory period (June, 1959–July, 1960); the preparatory period (July, 1960–October, 1962); and, finally, the conciliar period (October, 1962–December, 1965). This present study is limited to the preparatory and the conciliar periods, the only ones on which specific detailed data are available.

Strange as it may seem, religious had to wait until the twenty-first Ecumenical Council of the Church before any Council document undertook to formulate the theological and spiritual foundations of their mode of life and its organic place in the structure of the Church. Four hundred years earlier, the Council

439

of Trent (1545–1563) had only touched upon a few disciplinary points in order to counteract crying abuses. The next Council, Vatican I (1869–1870), had the subject of the religious life on its agenda, but the brusque transformation of the political scene by the Italian invasion of Rome and the seizure of the Papal States by Vittorio Emmanuele II prevented the Council from taking up this point.

The Holy See has issued numerous decrees, constitutions and other documents dealing with the religious life. Leo XIII's Constitution *Romanos Pontifices* (May 8, 1881), addressed to the Bishops of England, clarified the relationships between religious and the hierarchy in the apostolate. In a further Constitution *Conditae a Christo* (December 8, 1900), this same Pope confirmed the full religious status of religious with simple vows. Pope Pius XI reminded all religious of the essential role of their founder in the life and activity of every religious institute (*Unigenitus Dei Filius*, March 19, 1924). More recently Pius XII's Apostolic Constitution *Sedes Sapientiae* (March 25, 1957), with its accompanying directives, was a first practical step toward the deepening and strengthening of all religious formation to meet the needs of modern times.

Thus it is clear that the religious life had not been entirely neglected. Nevertheless, no Council or other document had ever been issued with a thorough exposition of the authentic foundations of the religious life or of its proper place in the framework of the Church. This void has now been filled with Vatican II's Decree on the Adaptation and Renewal of the Religious Life.

From the very beginning of the preparatory discussion on religious in November, 1960, there was rather wide disagreement as to just how the question of religious in the Church should be treated. The question was within the competence of two preparatory commissions, namely, the Commission on Religious and the Doctrinal Commission. The Commission on Religious wanted a special dogmatic constitution on the religious life. In the Doctrinal Commission it was felt that religious, if they were to be treated at all as a distinct group, should be included in the Dogmatic Constitution on the Church. A third tendency would have excluded any special mention of religious at all. The reasoning of this group was that since, by Baptism, all members of the Church without exception are bound to strive after the perfection of the Christian life, any special attention to religious as a group would inevitably favor the erroneous impression that religious are the only ones in the Church pursuing perfection, and this would entail a downgrading of the dignity of Christian life in general. This group would have been satisfied with simply mentioning religious as one of the groups composing the great body of the People of God, all vowed to perfection by virtue of their Baptism.

In the early stages of the discussion it seemed for a while that this latter school of thought might eventually prevail. Nevertheless, after prolonged and detailed discussion in joint commissions and joint subcommissions of the

Doctrinal Commission and the Commission on Religious, it was decided to incorporate the Council's treatment of religious into the Dogmatic Constitution on the Church rather than draw up a special dogmatic constitution. In this way, for the first time in conciliar history, an Ecumenical Council would discuss the place of religious in the general constitutional structure of the Church.

But this decision left another phase of the original question still unanswered. In this Dogmatic Constitution on the Church, would a separate chapter be dedicated to religious, or would they be merely discussed in the chapter on "The People of God" or in the chapter on "The Laity"? After lengthy discussion had failed to bring about any fruitful meeting of minds, it was jointly decided by the two interested commissions to have the matter settled by a vote of the Council Fathers themselves. The result of this vote in the third session was that religious should have a separate chapter in the Constitution on the Church. It is now the sixth chapter of this epoch-making document. The basic principle underlying this decision was that, although all members of the Church are obligated by Baptism to strive constantly toward the fullness of the perfection of the Gospel, nevertheless religious constitute a special category in the Church because their entire life is geared to perfection *through the practice of the evangelical counsels.* In other words, although the *goal* of perfection is the same, the *means* of achieving this goal are different. This difference of *means* confers on religious life its special character in the Church.

It is quite generally agreed that the treatment of religious in the sixth chapter of the Dogmatic Constitution on the Church is a splendid piece of work. After careful discussion and re-working in numerous joint commission meetings, this chapter was formulated in its definitive form by the Doctrinal Commission. It is a profound and rich theological presentation of the nature and purpose of the consecrated life of religious and others professing the counsels. The general consensus of opinion is that, in its succinctness, it is easily the most meaningful document ever to issue from the Holy See or any Council on the theological and scriptural foundations of the religious life and its proper place in the framework of the Church.

The task of the commission on religious was thus narrowed down to producing a document which, whatever its technical title might eventually be, would set off in clearer relief the main juridical and canonical aspects of the religious life. The commission eventually submitted a lengthy printed document entitled "Schema on the States for Acquiring Perfection." Because of the undesirable connotations of a monopoly on Christian perfection by religious, the title became "On Religious." Since, however, its scope was to lay down principles for all categories of those aiming at the achievement of perfection, including secular institutes, which are not, strictly speaking, religious institutes, this second title was subsequently abandoned in favor of the first. Finally, largely because of the difficulty of translation into modern language, the earlier title "De Statibus Perfectionis Acquirendae" was definitely rejected and "De Religiosis" was once more adopted. A still further change took place later, which will be mentioned in its proper place.

Inasmuch as the sixth chapter of the Constitution on the Church had already treated extensively of the religious life under its theological and scriptural aspects, the commission on religious dealt only with the juridical and canonical aspects. But since most of the details connected with these problems would later be on the agenda for the commission appointed to revise the Code of Canon Law, it had been important to forestall needless repetition. Hence the commission had decided to concentrate its attention on the elements of renewal and adaptation which were already such marked characteristics of the Council. This explains the new title under which these twenty propositions were submitted to the vote of the Council: "The Adaptation and Renewal of the Religious Life."

Long and complex as was the evolution of the Council decree on religious, nevertheless it does not represent the sum-total of what the Council has done for the enriching and the strengthening of the religious life. The splendid sixth chapter of the Constitution on the Church lays down the basic principles, the theology of the religious life. The Decree on the Bishops' Pastoral Office in the Church considers religious in their relationships with the hierarchy, with emphasis on the responsibility of the hierarchy for the apostolate in the Church and for religious, as also the responsibility of religious and their cooperation in the hierarchical apostolate—two responsibilities mutually distinct, but not separate. The Decree currently under study recalls the theology set forth in the sixth chapter of the Constitution on the Church and insists vigorously on *renewal* under its twofold aspect, namely fidelity to authentically unchangeable values and, at the same time, fidelity in facing up to new situations, as has so often been the case in the history of the religious life. The Decree on the Church's Missionary Activity stresses the apostolic dimensions of the religious life under its most visible and most important aspect, i.e., the birth and the growth of new churches. Conjointly the Decree on Priestly Formation and the Decree on The Ministry and Life of Priests are applicable likewise to religious, of whom many are priests. These two decrees present a synthesis of the riches found in the hierarchical mission of the priesthood and also of those contained in their own charismatic mission as religious. In all of these documents the religious life stands out in clear and unmistakable light. It is beheld as a reality representing not only certain immutable values, but also the dynamic values of fecundity which share in the divine mission of the Church. Thus, even a superficial study of religious in the teaching of Vatican II leads to the conclusion that religious have fared exceptionally well.

It would be difficult to single out from among the twenty-five propositions constituting our Decree, any salient points which might be said to have particular significance for the Church in the United States. By its very nature the entire text of the Decree is of special interest wherever religious are at work in the

Church. It might be observed, however, that the Council Decree bases the importance of religious in the Church less on their valuable contributions to the apostolic ministry of bishops and priests than on their special role as *witnesses* of the supernatural through a life centered on the observance of the evangelical counsels as special means for achieving the perfection of the Christian life. The Council declares that its intention in the formulation of the Decree is to emphasize the outstanding value of a life consecrated by profession of the counsels and its necessary role in the world of today. Thus it does not aim to go into details, preferring to leave such items to the competent post-conciliar commissions and future directives of the Holy See.

It will be noticed also that the title given to the Vatican Decree on the religious life is not a literal translation of the Latin original, "*De Accommodata Renovatione Vitae Religiosae.*" A direct translation would be next to impossible. "Accommodated renovation" would be meaningless. But since the real meaning of the various derivatives of the Latin *accommodare* always includes the element of adjustment or adaptation, and since the renovation demanded by the Council deals not with the abstract, but with the concrete milieu in which religious must live and work, many translations have preferred to use the two substantives "adaptation" and "renovation" in order to render the two key ideas clearly and forcefully.

The Decree takes up, at the very outset, the crucial question of the adaptation and renovation of the religious life. This process demands a continuous return to the sources of all Christian life, to the original inspiration of institutes and then the adaptation of these elements to the changed conditions of modern times. The basic principles of this adaptation and renovation are: 1) All institutes are to regard the following of Christ as their supreme norm since the ultimate norm of the religious life is the following of Christ as set forth in the Gospel; 2) The interests of the Church call for institutes to have their particular nature and role. Hence they are to recognize and preserve the spirit of the founder and his ideals as also those sound traditions which are their patrimony; 3) All institutes must share in the life of the Church and, each according to its own character, must follow the directives of the Church in the biblical, liturgical, dogmatic, pastoral, ecumenical, missionary and social fields; 4) Institutes must see to it that their members be well acquainted with men and their times and with the needs of the Church in order to enable them to judge modern times in the light of faith and thus be the better equipped to minister to men with genuine apostolic zeal; 5) Since the chief aim of the religious life is that its members should follow Christ and be united with God through the profession of the evangelical counsels, it must be remembered that necessary adaptations must spring from *spiritual renewal*, which must always be foremost even in the works of the external apostolate.

Emphasis is placed on the need of bringing an institute's program of life, prayer and work into harmony with the physical and psychological background of the members, also taking into account, where necessary, the needs of the apostolate. Worthwhile adaptation requires the wholehearted collaboration of all members, although decisions on the kind and degree of adaptation belong to superiors.

The Decree stresses the spiritual significance of religious profession and the fact that it entails a perfect consecration of one's self to God. This emphasizes the need of combining some degree of contemplation with apostolic love. Religious are exhorted to a deeper spirit of prayer, to familiar acquaintance with Holy Scripture and to fervent devotion to the Holy Eucharist, thus assuring them of twofold nourishment from the table of the Law and from the table of the Eucharist. Esteem is expressed particularly for the witness value of the contemplative life in the midst of a turbulent and distracted world, and the Council also declares that the monastic life has a vital role in the Church today.

An important article insists that the lay religious state, whether for men or women, constitutes in its own right a complete state of profession of the evangelical counsels. This declaration is important in the face of a certain tendency to regard religious brothers only as individuals unable to achieve the priesthood.

Attention is paid also to secular institutes and to their special vocation of witnessing to the Gospel *in* and *from* the world.

The Decree urges all those making profession of the evangelical counsels in whatever way never to lose sight of the positive supernatural ideals required by their consecration to God. On the question of obedience the Council stresses the reciprocal responsibilities of both superiors and subjects, and it sees in the vow of obedience a means whereby a Christian offers the complete dedication of his own will as a sacrifice to God and is thus more firmly and more securely united to the divine salvific will.

As for the religious habit, the Council wisely preferred not to go into details: "The religious habit, as a sign of consecration, should be simple and modest, poor and fitting, and, in addition, in keeping with the requirements of health, circumstances of time and place, and the requirements of the apostolate." Habits, whether of men or of women, which do not meet these requirements, shall be changed.

The Decree urges great care in the formation of candidates, restraint in the foundation of new institutes, the development of the missionary spirit, the organization of federations among institutes belonging to the same spiritual family or engaged in similar activities and the establishment of conferences of major superiors.

Lastly, we find a special article on vocations to the religious life and the means of promoting them, with a closing exhortation which urges all religious to carry on in integrity of faith, love of God and neighbor, love of the Cross and the hope of future glory, helping to spread the good news of Christ throughout the world and to give to the world the kind of witness whereby God may be glorified. The Decree concludes with a final prayer for the blessing of the Virgin Mother "whose life is a lesson for us all" (St. Ambrose).

The twenty-five propositions of the Decree on The Appropriate Renewal of the Religious Life are so many signposts, indicating the various directions which this adaptation and renewal are to take. The Decree makes no pretense to provide solutions for all the varied problems of twentieth-century religious life. For numerous reasons the Council had to limit itself to general principles. Further directives from the post-conciliar commissions, as also instructions emanating from the Holy See, will show how specific goals are to be attained. Perhaps greatest of all, however, is the responsibility of each individual institute to undertake courageous adaptation and unhesitating renewal in its own modes of life and activity. The Council has only pointed out the road. Progress on that road can come solely from religious themselves, all members collaborating wholeheartedly with their superiors to make Christ ever more richly present in the Church.

Decree on the Apostolate of the Laity

✠ HISTORICAL INTRODUCTION

In one of his works the late Jules Cardinal Saliége of Toulouse, France, declared, "The wretched theologians! They have forgotten two things—the laymen and the Holy Spirit." To the undying credit of the Fathers of the Second Vatican Council, neither the laity nor the Holy Spirit were overlooked. Theirs was the first Ecumenical Council to treat specifically the role of the laity in God's Church. Their Council, too, was the first to invite representatives of the laity to be official observers of the proceedings. They were also the first to be addressed during a regular working congregation by members of the laity. Although the Second Vatican Council was in most aspects a "bishops' council," it nonetheless paved the way to making, perhaps, the third or fourth Vatican Council a "layman's council." The groundwork was laid in the Decree entitled *Apostolicam actuositatem*, and, even with its imperfections, this Decree will serve as a solid foundation for future generations to construct a more suitable and perfect structure.

More than a little stir was caused on September 15, 1963, when Pope Paul announced that he was inviting representatives of the laity as observers to the Council. Eleven laymen were appointed observers during the second session, including James J. Norris, assistant to the executive director of the Catholic Relief Services—National Catholic Welfare Conference, and president of the International Catholic Migration Commission. During the third session the number rose to 28 lay auditors, and this time seven women were included in the group—the first time in history when women were so recognized. In the fourth session the number of lay auditors rose to 41 and included two other Americans, Martin Work, executive director of the National Council of Catholic Men, and Mrs. Catherine McCarthy, president of the National Council of Catholic Women. The lay auditors were gradually organized into a special group, with regular weekly meetings and briefings, and given ready access to all the documents of the Council. At the same time, the lay auditors contributed a great deal to the formation of the Decree on the Apostolate of the Laity through their personal contacts with members of the hierarchy and especially through the suggestions they submitted to the conciliar Commission charged with drafting the Decree. Many, in fact, were appointed consultants to one or another commission.

Six members of the group addressed the Council Fathers. At the end of the second session Jean Guitton and Vittorino Veronese, personal friends of both Pope John and Pope Paul, spoke to the assembly. During the third session Mr. Patrick Keegan, president of the International Catholic Worker's Movement, spoke to the Council Fathers in English during the one hundredth general congregation on October 13, 1964. He received enthusiastic applause from the Council Fathers who were seemingly delighted to be addressed by a member of the laity. Mr. Norris addressed the assembly during the fourth session. In yet another way, through press conferences and speeches to various groups of national hierarchies, the lay auditors performed a distinct service in the drafting of the Decree which so intimately concerned them and the members of the laity whom they represented. On October 8, 1964, Martin Work took part in a panel discussing the schema on the lay apostolate that was sponsored by the information office of the hierarchy of England and Wales. In answering the question of what laymen wanted from the Council, he distinguished between the indifferent layman who "just wants to be left alone and thinks that everything is just fine with the Church" and the other laymen who have a personal mystique apart from the mainstream of the Church and the organized lay apostolate. This latter group, he said, "want nothing but the freedom to conceive and execute their own apostolate and might be a little uncertain about belonging to the People of God." He continued: "This is a great body of intelligent, active laymen looking for a full opportunity to exercise a mature mission in the Church and in the world. This is the important group; from it will come the leaders of tomorrow, the real leaven in society." He then spelled out these eight propositions which he felt this group of laity wanted to see enunciated more clearly in the Decree on the Apostolate of the Laity:

1) Support and encouragement in his mission.
2) Release from excessive clerical direction and interference.
3) Increase of spiritual guidance and motivation from the clergy.
4) Greater communication with the clergy and hierarchy.
5) Opportunity to express the apostolate of public opinion, to be heard and at least be given an intelligent response.
6) General recognition, on the part of the clergy, that the layman has a legitimate interest in the Church.
7) A document that will not smack of juridical and clerical terminology.
8) A document that will be post-conciliar rather than pre-conciliar.

The influence of Martin Work and his colleagues among the lay auditors will never be able to be evaluated fully. Their influence, in a word, left its mark upon the final Decree. Their work, so effective and efficient and productive, stood in striking contrast to the carping and negative criticism voiced by another segment of American observers at the Council. When one such critic voiced his sentiments in a leading Catholic journal, James Norris felt obliged to answer him. In his letter to the editor of this journal, Mr. Norris wrote:

> It may be true that there was little, if any, lay participation in the original preparatory work of the Council and in the activities of the first session. The organizers of the Council followed the pattern of previous councils in confining participation to bishops and *periti*. From the beginning, however, numerous bishops requested the participation of laity in one form or another.
>
> As a result of this pressure, twenty laymen were invited to Rome for a period of three days in the spring of 1963, to work on a draft of the schema on the Church in the modern world. At that meeting there was one other American layman besides myself. There was full and free discussion among the bishops, *periti* and laymen, and a revised proposed draft resulted from these meetings.
>
> Since the appointment of the first ten Catholic lay auditors in September, 1963, they have received all Council documents and have been asked to submit comments and proposals to the commissions. Lay auditors have frequently sent written "emendations" to the commissions, and laymen and laywomen have taken an active part in discussions at meetings of the commissions on the lay apostolate and the Church in the modern world.

In the same letter Mr. Norris pointed out that the lay auditors participated in the work of the subcommissions dealing with the schema on the lay apostolate and acknowledged that "the bishops on the subcommissions in which we participated were not just 'polite,' but rather accepted the laymen as full participants in the discussions." He pointed out that on the subcommission on which he served there were five bishops, five clerical experts, two laymen and one laywoman and that they met twice each week for two and a half hours over a period of five weeks. Concluding his letter, Mr. Norris made this pointed observation:

> As a further indication of the progress made in the participation of the laity in the Council, I cite my own experience in being invited to speak to the Council on the problem of world poverty. My remarks were distributed to the bishops as an official *relatio* introducing the chapter on human solidarity of the schema on the Church in the modern world.
>
> There may be some bishops who keep laymen at arm's length. . . . But in fairness to the large number, ever increasing, of bishops who welcome the participation of laymen, I feel that the description of the role of the layman at the Council as "more that of a Hollywood extra than of a supporting actor" refers to a group of people who get second-hand information

at coffee bars along Via dellà Conciliazione and not to the lay people who are taking an increasingly active part in the work of the Council.

The deficiencies of the Decree on the Apostolate of the Laity can be easily explained when one examines its history. Bishop Francis Hengsbach of Essen, Germany, one of the great guiding spirits of the document, admitted this in his *relatio* of September 23, 1965, calling the drafting of the schema "a long, difficult and perilous journey." The original schema prepared by the preparatory Commission was a detailed and intricate document consisting of two parts; the first considered the apostolate of the laity in general; the second considered the apostolate of the laity in particular forms. It was readied by the preparatory Commission under the presidency of Fernando Cardinal Cento according to the sentiments expressed by the bishops of the world, the faculties of Catholic universities and the Roman congregations. The original schema was overlaid with juridicism and clericalism. It was introduced on the floor of the Council during the seventy-ninth general congregation, on December 2, 1963, but no action was taken. Instead, the Council Fathers were invited to submit their observations on the text in order that the Commission might emend the document according to their wishes. At this time three American prelates were members of the commission: Archbishop Martin J. O'Connor, rector of the North American College; Archbishop William Cousins of Milwaukee; Bishop Allen Babcock of Grand Rapids, Michigan. One of the more vocal experts serving the commission was the Right Reverend Monsignor George G. Higgins, director of the Social Action Department, National Catholic Welfare Conference.

At this time seven episcopal conferences, 85 Council Fathers as a group and 74 Council Fathers individually had submitted their written observations concerning the text. The commission had already been instructed by the Central Coordinating Commission, as of January 23, 1964, to reduce the text to its essential points—an instruction, incidentally, that the commission never carried out. Nonetheless, the heart of the schema had already been removed during the discussions on the conciliar statement concerning the Church. That document had already incorporated the theological heart of the schema on the lay apostolate in its fourth chapter. At the same time another major segment of this schema had been transferred to the mixed commission dealing with the schema on the Church in the modern world, and another part of the schema had been transferred to the commission dealing with the revision of the Code of Canon Law. This decree must be studied in the light of chapter four of the Dogmatic Constitution on the Church.

The preparatory Commission, under the presidency of Fernando Cardinal Cento, consisted of 39 members, 11 bishops and 29 consultors representing 26 nations of the world. The Commission was divided into three subcommissions: the first was concerned with the general principles of the apostolate of the laity; the second was concerned with the promotion of the lay apostolate in works of charity; and the third was concerned with the lay apostolate in the area of social action. At this stage no representatives of the laity were present in the meetings of the preparatory Commission. This Commission had prepared four distinct schemata, dealing with the lay apostolate in general, its religious, social and charitable activities. The schemata never were presented to the consideration of the Council Fathers. The conciliar Commission on the Lay Apostolate radically redrafted the schema, condensing the original four schemata into one and referring the theological consideration of the laity to the commission drafting the schema on the Church. During the Commission meetings in March, 1963, many members of the laity assisted in redrafting the original schema. In April of the same year the Central Preparatory Commission examined the work of this Commission and approved it. This text was finally approved by Pope John on April 22, 1963, and distributed to the Council Fathers.

Even this text failed to be introduced on the floor of the Council during the second session. Nevertheless, many Council Fathers submitted their observations on this text, so that in January, 1964, the five subcommissions charged with redrafting the text were able to present a new schema according to the wishes of the Council Fathers. This new text consisted of five chapters: 1) the apostolic vocation of the laity; 2) communities and situations; 3) the aims to be achieved by the lay apostolate; 4) associations of the laity; and 5) the fundamentals of well-established lay organizations. This text was approved by Pope Paul VI on April 27, 1964, and distributed to the Council Fathers.

On the following July 19, Archbishop John J. Krol of Philadelphia submitted his observations on the text. He cited 16 corrections that should be made in the text concerning its grammatical construction and "some typographical mistakes that should be corrected." His general observation was one of pleasure with the text of the schema because it "reveals that the Church truly stands in need of an apostolate of the laity at the present time; it reveals the fields in which the Christian faithful can labor apostolically . . . so that lay collaboration with the hierarchical apostolate may be fruitful." He then wrote:

It is truly comforting for the Christian faithful that part of the schema exhorts all the clergy to recognize the dignity and responsibility of the laity in the Church. At the same time they are exhorted to remember always that they must work with the laity in the Church and for the Church and that they should show great concern for lay people working in the apostolate; that they should entrust resources confidently to the hands of the laity for the service of the Church.

On October 6, 1964, during the ninety-fifth congregation, Cardinal Cento presented the text of the schema on the apostolate of the laity for the consideration of the Council Fathers. On the following day Bishop Hengsbach presented a more detailed report on the schema. Not as sanguine about the document as Cardinal Cento, he said that he welcomed the criticisms the Council Fathers would offer. The Fathers of the Council heeded the admonition of Bishop Hengsbach. Immediately Cardinal Ritter took the floor as the first speaker to address the Fathers about the schema. He criticized the schema for its lack of order and admitted that "in its actual form the schema cannot be accepted as a definitive decree." He then cited some of the weaknesses of the schema that should be eliminated in order to strengthen it and to introduce a new ordering of the material. In regard to eliminating its weaknesses, Cardinal Ritter said:

> There are three main faults: clerical spirit, juridicism and, as I would say, favoritism. The schema is too *clerical* because it speaks in a patronizing manner to the laity about the laity; because it presumes that the highest apostolate of the laity is the assistance of clerics; because it hardly acknowledges the talent and capacities of the laity in a practical manner. The *juridicism* of the schema is evident in those paragraphs which treat of the revision of the Code of Canon Law and of the relationship of the laity to the hierarchy. All of this is extraneous to a pastoral decree. Finally, the schema is guilty of *favoritism* in praising Catholic Action in a singular way and, by so doing, the schema truly and wrongly disparages other forms of the apostolate.

In order to strengthen the values of the schema, the Archbishop of St. Louis said that "all the elements dispersed here and there in the schema [should] be brought together in a logical way." Finally, he said, "holiness, or the spirituality of the laity, should be explained according to the principles of the chapter concerning the laity in the Constitution on the Church." In regard to introducing a new ordering of the schema, Cardinal Ritter had this to propose:

> A preface should be selected from the chapter on the laity in the Constitution on the Church. The body of the decree, which ought to be very short, should consist of three paragraphs: first, on the essence of the apostolate; second, on the different forms of the apostolate; and third, on the sanctity of the laity as the essential element of the apostolate.The conclusion would be written in the manner of a pastoral exhortation which would call all of Christ's faithful to engage in the apostolate.

A total of 56 Council Fathers expressed their observations on the schema on the floor of the Council, and another 90 Fathers submitted their observations in writing. The second American prelate to give voice to his opinion on the floor of the Council was Auxiliary Bishop Stephen A. Leven of San Antonio, Texas. Speaking on October 8, he remarked that "the apostolate of the laity is of the essential nature of the Church" and "not something conceded and mandated to the laity by the bishop or the pastor, but the working out in practice of the gifts of the Holy Spirit." He conceded that "it is the duty of those who receive the charismata of authority and administration to moderate and guide the apostolate of the laity, but they may not suppress it." He then suggested that the schema should advocate "a real and meaningful dialogue between the bishop and the pastor and the laity." Bishop Leven admitted that there is no true dialogue "if the laity are only invited to listen" or if "the bishop listens only to individuals, such as his doctor or his housekeeper." He then concluded with the following appeal:

> Obviously the laity cannot do in the Church the things that require the powers of orders or jurisdiction. Obviously the bishop cannot engage in conversation with every layman in his diocese. Obviously there are some fanatic and unbalanced people with whom the bishop should not lose much time. But of all the desires of an intelligent and well-instructed and dedicated laity, the first is for true and meaningful and respectful dialogue. The post-conciliar commission is earnestly asked to include in its directory the setting up of machinery through which every reasonable suggestion from the laity may reach the bishop, receive consideration and be given an honorable acknowledgement.
>
> Our laity look to us for acceptance as full and mature members in the Body of Christ. They ask only to be allowed to exercise the charismata the Holy Spirit has given them.

Five other American prelates submitted their observations in writing. Auxiliary Bishop Fulton J. Sheen of New York urged his observations on the laity in light of the universal priesthood of Christ. He argued that the hierarchical priesthood "was constituted *not* over the Church but *in* the Church," and, therefore, "if the 'service' of the priesthood is considered together with 'authority' and not separately, both the primacy of bishops and priests and the priesthood of the laity can be maintained." In support of his argument, Bishop Sheen wrote:

> To understand this, let it be kept in mind that there are three stages of "service": (1) the beginning of "service" which is had in Baptism; (2) the strengthening of "service" which is obtained through Confirmation (for in this sacrament the baptismal vows are renewed); (3) the representation of "service," which is conferred in the sacrament of Orders.
>
> If now in the place of "service" we put the word "priesthood," we will see that the sacrament of Baptism is the "beginning" of the priesthood, the sacrament of Confirmation is the "strengthening" of the same priesthood, and the sacrament of Orders offers the "representative aspect" of the priesthood. By the representative aspect of the priesthood, that priesthood is

meant in which power is had to offer to God the desires and sacrifices of the people. Therefore, the sacrament of Orders only confers the representative priesthood.

Auxiliary Bishop Stanislaus J. Brzana of Buffalo, New York, also submitted his observations on this schema, insisting that "the individual responsibility of each disciple of Christ in the lay apostolate ought to be considered more important" than the special associations and societies in general. He wanted to see the schema stress the importance of the daily labor as well as the importance of the apostolate as an essential characteristic of all those who are part of the people of God. He said, too, that "the cooperation of laymen with the bishop or pastor should be so stressed that spontaneous action, energy, initiative and mature activity are neither limited nor extinguished."

In another written intervention, Auxiliary Bishop Philip Hannan of Washington, D.C., urged that bishops should encourage Catholics to work actively in organizations of charity and social welfare not under the direction of the Church. He offered four reasons for this statement. First, he said, Catholics should act in such a way because there is "a persistent suspicion that Catholics are not greatly interested in those outside the household of the faith and are willing to work only in their own organizations and institutions—which is obviously false." Secondly, he said:

> Such participation in works of charity and social welfare would show clearly our deep respect for the great virtue of those outside the Church. This is of enormous value in encouraging works of charity. It must be recalled that the vast majority of institutions of charity and social welfare in many countries are the result of the virtue of Protestants and Jews. We should always generously and truthfully praise such accomplishments.

Such cooperation, continued Bishop Hannan, would bind together the community in a cordial spirit and, finally, would also benefit Catholic organizations because they would learn other methods of performing charitable works.

During this period Bishop John J. Wright of Pittsburgh also submitted an intervention supported by about fifty other American bishops. This intervention pleaded that

> the Decree on the Apostolate of the Laity recognizes unequivocally that the *apostolate of the laity*, in its authentic sense, is a participation *in the saving mission of the Church;* that the priestly work of the laity, as laity, should be thus *directly* defined in terms of the work of the Church itself; and that, therefore, the concept of the lay apostolate in terms of "Catholic Action" ("participation of the laity in the work of the hierarchy") should be treated separately on the grounds that "Catholic Action," so understood, is a

tertium quid—neither apostolate of the hierarchy nor apostolate of the laity —but a joint work involving both, but defining neither.

The final American intervention was submitted by Cardinal Spellman on April 10, 1965, after the conciliar Commission had submitted its revised text to the Central Coordinating Commission. The Cardinal admitted that "in our days a truly apostolic life which is better informed is altogether necessary for all who are designated as the People of God." He approved of the revised text because it so well established the "principles and norms of the Church's doctrine." The Cardinal remained insistent, however, upon the rights of local authority to carry out the application of general directives. He wrote:

It is pleasing that the Commission happily cautions that the apostolic structure, which perhaps for some places seems opportune and even necessary, is not to be imposed without detriment to every part of the whole Church. With the variations from place to place in mind, it seems better that many things are not commanded, but left to bishops and episcopal conferences. Sometimes the same end can be reached by quite diverse means, and it is wise to leave a place for such healthy diversity. Means which are found suitable in one place can be found less suitable in another place or even harmful. Therefore, the Commission proceeds cautiously and prudently lest too many specific adaptations result rather in injuring the good of the community.

All in all, however, Cardinal Spellman was quite pleased with the revised schema and gave it his wholehearted approval.

The schema was brought back to the floor of the Council on September 23, 1965. Throughout three general working congregations it was voted on by the Council Fathers and, although it was generally overwhelmingly approved, nonetheless there were more than 700 suggestions submitted for improving the wording of the text. Again the Commission began work, incorporating these suggestions, when necessary, into the text. On November 9, the Commission returned the emended text to the floor of the Council. Once again the Council Fathers were asked to cast their ballots in a series of six distinct votes on the revised text. Again a consensus was achieved. On November 10, 1965, the Council Fathers overwhelmingly approved the text of the schema, with 2,201 voting approval and only two registering their disapproval of the text. During the eighth public session, on November 18, 1965, Pope Paul, together with his brother bishops, solemnly promulgated the Decree with 2,340 Council Fathers voting their approval and, again, only two registering their disapproval.

The Decree on the Apostolate of the Laity in the Church had suffered a great many vicissitudes since its inauguration in the early days of 1960. Nonetheless, the document, as it now stands, represents a turning point in the history of the Church. That turning point was enunciated by Philip Scharper early in 1966 when he declared that "most lay people want neither to be simple nor sheep." Mr. Scharper continued:

> We do not have too much time to make this translation [between the Church and the world] and to do it well, but at least honest efforts are being made. I do think enough of it will come through to warrant the belief that we are really on the threshold of a great new age of the Church. I am convinced that Pope John's prayer that the Council will usher in a new Pentecost has been heard.

Mr. Scharper's comments are a fitting commentary on the Decree on the Apostolate of the Laity in the Church. They are an echo of a prophetic voice heard by but a few at the turn of the century when, in 1900, Léon Bloy had written:

> Present events are certainly hideous, but not vulgar as to their tendencies. . . . I therefore again think that we are at the prologue of an extraordinary drama, the likes of which has not been seen for twenty centuries, and I invite you to a certain degree of recollection.

Decree on the Apostolate of the Laity

✠ INTERVENTIONS

JOSEPH CARDINAL RITTER, 7 *October, 1964*

The schema on the Decree on the Apostolate of the Laity, as it seems to me, contains almost all that is required to plan an apt and effective decree. However, in its entirety, it minimally attains its pastoral end. Its principal faults are found in the distribution of the material and in a lack of order, for those things of real value that it contains are dispersed here and there and are mixed with extraneous and useless elements. Most certainly, in its actual form, the schema cannot be accepted as a definitive decree. Nevertheless, by eliminating the extraneous and useless parts, by strengthening whatever is of value and by introducing a new order, we would be able to compose a decree from the elements here presented that would respond eminently to the needs of our time. It would be easier and more expeditious to accept this schema as a basis than to draw up another new document. Thus, in my humble judgment, the proposed schema should be accepted as a basis for discussion.

Permit me to indicate briefly some weaknesses to be eliminated, the valuable parts to be strengthened and the new order to be introduced.

First, in regard to eliminating weaknesses: There are three main faults: clerical spirit, juridicism, and as I would say, favoritism. The schema is too *clerical* because it speaks in a patronizing manner to the laity about the laity; because it presumes that the highest apostolate of the laity is the assistance of clerics; because it hardly acknowledges the talent and capacities of the laity in a practical manner. The *juridicism* of the schema is evident in those paragraphs which treat of the revision of the Code of Canon Law and of the relationship of the laity to the hierarchy. All of this is extraneous to a pastoral decree. Finally, the schema is guilty of *favoritism* in praising Catholic Action in a singular way and, by so doing, the schema truly and wrongly disparages other forms of the apostolate.

Second, in regard to strengthening values: There are three points clearly and distinctly stated and well and effectively formulated: the very nature of the apostolate, its different forms and the specific spirituality of the laity. An *essential* exposition of the apostolate requires that all the elements dispersed

459

here and there in the schema be brought together in a logical way; that the rights and duties of the laity in the exercise of the apostolate, whether individually or collectively, be clearly and distinctly pointed out; and that the apostolate of the laity be manifested in its essential relation to the life of the Church. The different *forms* of the apostolate have been explained individually and in their mutual relations; they should be distinguished from one another, not as related to the hierarchy, but generally according to various ends and, specifically, according to the various means used to attain the same end. Finally, *holiness*, or the spirituality of the laity, should be explained according to the principles of the chapter concerning the laity in the Dogmatic Constitution on the Church.

Third, in regard to introducing a new order: A preface should be selected from the chapter on the laity in the Constitution on the Church. The body of the decree, which ought to be very short, should consist of three paragraphs: first, on the essence of the apostolate; second, on the different forms of the apostolate; and third, on the sanctity of the laity as the essential element of the apostolate. The conclusion would be written in the manner of a pastoral exhortation which would call all of Christ's faithful to engage in the apostolate.

Venerable Fathers, at this time it is for us to decide not only whether this schema should be accepted, but certainly whether we wish to discuss the apostolate of the laity in these days or not. It seems to me that now is the acceptable time for we do not know whether another occasion will present itself. Therefore, notwithstanding its faults and shortcomings, I advise and I urge that the proposed schema be accepted as the basis for discussion on a subject of such great importance.

BISHOP STEPHEN LEVEN, *8 October, 1964*

That there should be a schema on the apostolate of the laity is certainly pleasing. This Sacred Synod which, for the first time in conciliar history, has spoken of the laity in a positive way, calling them the People of God, which teaches us again to think of the Church not as an organization held together by authority and Canon Law, but as the Body of Christ structured by the sacrament of the episcopacy and living by the charismata given by the Holy Spirit to each member according to His mysterious will, rightly turns its attention to the laity as part in the apostolate.

The schema should, therefore, say more plainly and forcefully and fully that the apostolate of the laity is of the essential nature of the Church. The apostolate is not something conceded and mandated to the laity by the bishop or the pastor, but the working out in practice of the gifts of the Holy Spirit. It is the duty of those who receive the charismata of authority and administration to moderate and guide the apostolate of the laity, but they may not suppress it. If Jesus said in the parable of the talents that it is a sin to wrap one's talent in a napkin and bury it, can the bishop or the pastor who, by his ineptitude, causes the entire body of the laity to keep their charismata fruitless be without fault?

What the schema says of the apostolate, it says too repetitiously and timidly. It should be streamlined and shortened and given more strength.

The schema should emphasize more the necessity of a real and meaningful dialogue between the bishop and the pastor and the laity. This is especially true where there is an educated laity. There is no dialogue if the laity are only invited to listen. Nor is there a dialogue if the bishop listens only to individuals, such as his doctor or his housekeeper, rather than to truly representative laymen and laywomen.

If the schema cannot set out a detailed method of dialogue, because it is concerned only with general principles and specific details are left to a post-conciliar commission, then we, as Council Fathers, should instruct such a commission to make adequate plans for a sort of parliament, perhaps on the order of the rumored senate of bishops to assist the pope. Obviously the laity cannot do in the Church the things that require the powers of orders or jurisdiction. Obviously the bishop cannot engage in conversation with every layman in his diocese. Obviously there are some fanatic and unbalanced people with whom the bishop should not lose much time. But of all the desires of an intelligent and well-instructed and dedicated laity, the first is for true and meaningful and respectful dialogue. The post-conciliar commission is earnestly asked to include in its directory the setting up of machinery through which every reasonable suggestion from the laity may reach the bishop, receive consideration and be given an honorable acknowledgment.

Our laity look to us for acceptance as full and mature members in the Body of Christ. They ask only to be allowed to exercise the charismata the Holy Spirit has given them.

Decree on the Apostolate of the Laity

✠ COMMENTARY by Martin H. Work

The first thing to be said about the Decree on the Apostolate of the Laity is that it has no precedence in the history of the Church. It is the first conciliar statement issued on the subject in two thousand years. This must be said first not to stress its uniqueness, but rather to help understand the character of the document itself. The pre-conciliar preparatory commission responsible for developing the first draft was faced with the formidable task of developing not only a comprehensive statement on the role of the layman in the mission of the Church, but one that would have universal validity for all the world. Members of the commission began this work at a time when there was not even an official theology of the laity to serve as a doctrinal basis. The fourth chapter of the Dogmatic Constitution on the Church had not yet reached a first-draft stage. At hand for the work were the Gospels, a collection of papal references, the writings of a few theologians and the actual experiences of the lay apostolate in action throughout the world.

It was clear from existing theological writing and the experiences of the apostolate that the laity shared in the whole apostolic life of the Church, save in those functions reserved exclusively for the ordained priesthood. This meant to the preparatory commission that any document on the lay apostolate would have to treat comprehensively every aspect of the apostolate of the Church in which laymen had a role to play. As a result, the first draft produced by the preparatory commission was about five times as long as the final Decree and was based, not on the theology as finally set forth in *De Ecclesia*, but upon the then current theological writings. By the time the Decree on the Apostolate of the Laity was proclaimed on November 18, 1965, its theological basis had been adjusted to reflect the new official conciliar theology on the laity. In addition, its scope and depth of treatment of various aspects of the apostolate had been limited to essentials by the transference to other decrees, such as the Pastoral Constitution on the Church in the Modern World, of much of its substance. On the other hand, it was one of 13 documents that survived the cutback from the original 70 that was directed by the coordinating commission of the Council in the period following the first session.

It is necessary to relate this much of history in order to understand the present and final form of the Decree. It says all that need be said to guide the development of the lay apostolate, but not all that could be said nor, indeed, all that was said by the Council concerning the layman's role in the mission of the Church. Well over half the documents produced by the Council refer to the laity either substantially as in the Dogmatic Constitution on the Church, the Pastoral Constitution on the Church in the Modern World or, incidentally as in the Decree on Ecumenism and the Decree on the Church's Missionary Activity.

This Decree will be disappointing to anyone who approaches it, looking for an exclusive confirmation of a single approach to the apostolate, whether it be in terms of an organizational formula, a program objective, a training method or a simple answer to the question "How much freedom or dependence is there for the laity in exercising their apostolate?" It is as nearly as possible a universal document, universal in its comprehension of the needs of the Church, universal in the truths that it sets forth and universal in the norms and guidance that it gives. Each nation, each apostolic organization and each individual will have to examine and study it to determine what it says for them.

Implicit in this examination will be the determination of the necessity for renewal, sometimes radical, that must take place in all forms of the lay apostolate. This "agonizing reappraisal" is essential in the United States. It is apparent that our lay organizations, in the massive whole, need to be "aggiornamentoed" in the light of the Decree. During the Council many organizations began this renewal, but many did not—notably those at the parish level. The whole pastoral life of the Church in the United States will be undergoing a rapid evolution, if not revolution, due to the final decisions of the Council. The lay apostolate will be caught up in this renewal, and lay structures will either become a part of the renewal or be left "by the side of the road." The Decree itself makes an indirect reference to this when, in speaking of "dispersion of effort," it says, "This happens when new associations or projects are promoted without sufficient reason, or if antiquated associations or methods are retained beyond their period of usefulness."

Although, in general, the Decree maintains a comprehensive balance throughout on such questions as the value of the individual as compared to the organized apostolate, or the apostolate "in the Church" as against the apostolate of the "Christian in the temporal order," I think it is safe to say that the importance of the organized apostolate received marked emphasis, especially those organizations that possess the four marks of Catholic Action that are listed in paragraph 20 of this Decree.

On the other hand, the primary position given to such statements as "modern conditions demand that their apostolate be broadened and intensified" and "the areas of the lay apostolate have been immensely widened, particularly in fields that have been for the most part open to the laity alone," as well as to such statements as "the laity must take up the renewal of the temporal order as their own special obligation," provide considerable evidence that the Council has definitely underscored the secular world order as the primary area of the lay apostolic efforts.

The sensitive question of the freedom of the apostolate is discussed in the fifth chapter on external relationships. It calls for harmony and apostolic cooperation on the part of clergy, religious and the laity. It requires of the hierarchy the promotion of the apostolate, the provision of spiritual principles and support, direction for the common good of the Church and the preservation of doctrine and order. It then calls attention to the fact that

> the lay apostolate admits of different types of relationship with the hierarchy in accordance with the various forms and objects of this apostolate. For in the Church there are many apostolic undertakings which are established by the free choice of the laity and regulated by their prudent judgment. The mission of the Church can better be accomplished in certain circumstances by undertakings of this kind; therefore, they are frequently praised or recommended by the hierarchy. No project, however, may claim the name "Catholic" unless it had obtained the consent of the lawful Church authority.

Essentially, what the document says in this respect is simply that the lay apostolate is "lay" in that it is carried out and managed by the laity, that the direction of the hierarchy will vary from merely the authentic teaching and interpreting of moral principles in temporal affairs and that the judgment as to the conformity of matters to moral principles is up to the immediate direction of the actual activities of the laity, such as in the teaching of Catechism in mission countries.

However, it also seems clear that the laity have the right to organize apostolic undertakings privately, and to do this in their own prudent judgment without asking permission of the bishop or pastor, providing they do not bear a specifically Catholic name. Obviously, however, courtesy and prudence would indicate that the bishop or pastor should be informed of such developments. The main point of this matter is not to establish "freedom for its own sake," but rather to stimulate the initiative of the laity and to free them from unnecessary inhibitions in the pursuit of the apostolate.

The lay-apostolate schema joins with the chapter on the laity in *De Ecclesia* in establishing what I call the "Apostolate of Public Opinion" in the Church. The first chapter of the Decree on the Laity, "The Vocation of the Laity to the Apostolate," speaks of the special gifts that the Holy Spirit gives to the faithful: "From the acceptance of these charisms . . . there arise for each believer the right and the duty to use them in the Church and in the world for the good of men and the building up of the Church, in the freedom of the Holy Spirit, "Who breathes where he will." This statement, with even the more explicit reference in *De Ecclesia*, encourages among other things, the expression of opinion on matters related to the welfare of the Church, especially through "organs specifically erected for this purpose." Other documents of the Council, e.g., the Decree on the Bishops' Pastoral Office in the Church, also refer to the necessity of lay consultation for the good of the Church. Out of this concept there will undoubtedly arise a variety of consultative structures in the Church in the United States (some of which now exist) that will make it possible for the laity to offer their opinions to the parish, to the diocese and to the national conferences on many matters of Church welfare.

The concern of the Council for cooperation and unity in the apostolate is expressed in many places. However, it comes to a point in the specific suggestion in paragraph 26 of the Decree which recommends a "council" at the parish, interparochial and interdiocesan and national and international level to "promote the mutual coordination of various lay associations and enterprises." In the United States we have the basis for such "councils" in the National Council of Catholic Men and the National Council of Catholic Women, with their diocesan and parochial counterparts. However, both of these Councils, established some 45 years ago by the bishops, have realized for some time that adjustments are needed in their program and organizational formula if the principle of unity and coordination on which they were founded is validly to meet the growth in diversity of the apostolate that has taken place in the last decade. The National Council of Catholic Youth, although of later origin, would also seem to qualify in some respects as a useful pattern for the councils called for in the Decree.

It would seem to me that we can look forward to the establishment of a variety of formulas for "councils" at the parish and diocesan level. They will have several common characteristics; e.g., their membership will be representative of the total parish, both those engaged in the individual apostolate in the temporal order and those in apostolic organizations; they will be consultative to the pastor; they will also share in some decision-making processes; and they will be primarily apostolic in their activities.

The International Secretariat for the Lay Apostolate, called for by the Decree, is an exceedingly interesting development that will serve many purposes. Basically, it will give status to the laity and the apostolate at the Holy See, and it will enhance the "dialogue" at the international level as well as provide an authoritative stimulus to the apostolate throughout the world.

The laity in the United States, and the clergy too, now have not only a conciliar yardstick to measure the present effectiveness of the apostolate, but also a charter to guide the laity in the future direction which the Church wishes to see the apostolate take. It will take careful reading, study and experimentation to read the yardstick accurately and completely and to interpret the principles of the charter into actual programs of action. However, it would be most unwise to read and study only the Decree on the Apostolate of the Laity in determining the full mind of the Church. There are many important and often essential references to the laity in other documents.

XII/DECREE ON THE MINISTRY AND LIFE OF PRIESTS

Decree on the Ministry and Life of Priests
✠ HISTORICAL INTRODUCTION

The preparatory Commission for the Discipline of the Clergy and Christian People was charged with drafting a schema concerning the priesthood. In those early days of 1960–61, the Commission set to work, undoubtedly with the best of intentions, but with results, unfortunately, that were far from satisfactory. Perhaps the original intention of the members of this preparatory Commission and the actual achievement of the conciliar Commission reflect in this conciliar document more dramatically than any other the gulf between the juridical nature of the preparatory Commission and the pastoral achievement of the Council. The same reason might be adduced for the many revisions of this schema from its beginning until its promulgation on December 7, 1965, during the ninth public session. The four negative votes out of the total 2,394 votes cast reflect also the consensus achieved among the Council Fathers because of their conciliar experience.

The preparatory Commission set to work examining the 768 suggestions submitted in writing by the bishops of the world. From these suggestions the Commission culled 17 general subjects which were printed in 17 booklets. These subjects covered such topics as the pastoral ministry, financial offerings at Mass, priestly ordination of non-Catholic ministers, provisions for establishing parishes, pious donations, distribution of the clergy, ecclesiastical benefices and clerical tonsure. Later the preparatory Commission, under the presidency of Pietro Cardinal Ciriaci, condensed these suggestions to these six schemata: 1) the sanctity of the clerical life; 2) ecclesiastical goods; 3) the distribution of the clergy; 4) clerical dress and tonsure; 5) the obligation of pastors; 6) the obligations of pastors in regard to the care of souls.

These schemata were presented to the Council's Central Preparatory Commission during its meetings from February 22 to May 5, 1962. However, these schemata were never presented to the Council Fathers for their vote; as a matter of fact, the subject of the priesthood was not even introduced during the first session. After the experience of the first session, it was readily agreed that these schemata were too juridical in their presentation and entered into too many details.

Cardinal Spellman, however, as a member of the Central Preparatory

Commission, submitted four observations on these schemata. In 1961 he had commented on another schema prepared by the Commission on the Discipline of the Sacraments concerning the Sacrament of Orders. The Cardinal was opposed to adding another year to the course of priestly training as well as the reestablishment of a permanent diaconate and other clerical orders. Although he granted that the ancient practice might assist bishops in missionary areas, he felt it "would offer great inconvenience to local ordinaries, at least in the United States." He then painted the following picture of how young priests in the United States receive their pastoral training as curates.

It is very important to note that in the United States of America the custom of the common life among clerics thrives in almost every diocese. Never do priests live with families, but they dwell always in a parish house or in an ecclesiastical building. A priest is named pastor only after many years. The young priest leads the common life with the pastor as his co-worker and quite often together with one or another curate. Therefore, he begins the priestly and pastoral life under truly salubrious circumstances in which secular dangers are well warded off, as far as human means can have it. New priests receive an altogether practical pastoral education in their training, namely, as a matter of fact, from priests more advanced in experience and age, with whom they lead a common life and labor under the same roof and near the parish church.

The following year Cardinal Spellman submitted three further written observations to the Central Preparatory Commission. In the first he commented on priests who had given up their priestly ministry. He approved the first part of the proposed schema, especially that section concerning "the most holy and most salutary law of ecclesiastical celibacy from which the greatest part of the strength and glory of the Church flows." He was, however, more cautious in extending the causes for granting a dispensation from the obligation of celibacy, He remarked:

How great a bewilderment for the faithful, if not a scandal; how great a consolation or diabolical hope there will be for the enemies of the Church; and likewise how great an occasion for the falling away of priests who are in danger of their celibacy and chastity if the whole world will be informed tomorrow of the norms of the Second Vatican Council by which dispensation from the obligation of celibacy is granted to those who have validly and licitly received the order of the presbyterate with the possibility, even at that time, of not sustaining the burdens connected with that order!

In another written observation on the subject of promoting to orders those who were once non-Catholic pastors, Cardinal Spellman directed his comments to this sentence in the schema: "There are many non-Catholic pastors or ministers who would be converted to the true Church of Christ if they would be allowed to receive Holy Orders and to exercise their care of souls." He felt that these words might lend themselves to "some false interpretation" by non-Catholics and imprudent Catholics. He preferred that "in individual cases of this type, a concession can be prudently made by the Apostolic See." He did not, however, overlook the ecumenical nature of this proposal, and thus wrote as follows:

> The Fathers of the Second Vatican Council have proposed that all things must be done to foster true unity of Christians. The words of the decree which is proposed in this schema could easily be twisted around by some who are hostile to this true unity. In such a way the cause of Christian unity would suffer. This possibility would not be a sufficient reason why the Council Fathers ought to hold back from publishing any decree, however, if that decree were otherwise necessary or useful for the good of the Church and of souls.

Regarding Mass stipends, the Cardinal felt that "there is no need of profound changes." With a nod to the press, he continued: "Since the words of the decrees of this [Second Vatican] Council will certainly receive ample publication in the press and other public communications media, there is an opportunity for teaching both Catholics and non-Catholics the reason for the offering or stipend which the faithful pay the ministers of the Church on the occasion of their assistance at Mass." He felt also that in the future "no pious founded Masses should be received with the obligation to have one or more Masses celebrated forever or for longer than thirty years." He seemed reluctant to accept the proposal that a Mass offered once or twice a week in a parish church for all the deceased of the parish, with all the offerings freely made by the faithful, be retained as a single stipend for that Mass. "This proposal," he said, "might become an occasion for abuses or the astonishment of the people."

On December 3, 1962, the conciliar Commission for the Discipline of the Clergy and Christian People held its first plenary session. Pietro Cardinal Ciriaci remained as president and Joseph Cardinal Ritter (the only American member of the Commission) was one of the two vice-presidents. At this meeting the Commission examined the schemata presented by the preparatory Commission as well as the 295 observations submitted by the Fathers of the Council. This meeting resulted in the drafting of a completely new schema, now entitled "Concerning the Clergy" and consisting of 26 pages. This schema was composed of three chapters: the first on the perfection of the priestly life; the second on pastoral zeal and knowledge; the third on the universal distribution of the clergy.

This schema was completed during a Commission meeting held in Rome, February 12–23. On March 9 the schema was presented to the Council's Central Coordinating Commission and was approved on March 25. Pope

John XXIII approved it on April 23 and ordered that its text be distributed to the Council Fathers. The following month it was mailed to all the Council Fathers throughout the world. Between July and October the Commission received 464 written observations on the text of this schema from 237 Fathers.

Two American prelates submitted observations on this schema: Cardinal Spellman and Archbishop Krol. In March, Cardinal Spellman submitted one intervention and, on April 22, two further interventions. All three interventions approved the schema in general, even though Cardinal Spellman advocated that the schema be shortened. He espoused the cause of the common life for the parochial clergy; he was opposed to an additional one-year pastoral course; he asked for greater recognition of the magisterium; he warned of the danger of laicism; he cautioned against a superiority complex among the clergy.

Concerning the perfection of the priestly life, the subject of the first chapter of the revised schema, the Cardinal wrote:

> Our experience in the United States of America teaches us the great advantage of the customary common life among clerics. Furthermore, very many bishops have told me how great a good comes to the Church of God and her priests from this custom. Perhaps in this number it should be stated more forcefully: "The common life among clerics should be renewed as much and as fast as it can possibly be."

He approved also of the second chapter which laid down the general principles on sacred and profane studies, and he proposed that the section be strengthened.

> The knowledge and recognition of the Church of Christ essentially brings with it a sincere reverence toward the ecclesiastical magisterium. Without this reverence *true Christian wisdom* cannot be acquired. Therefore, in my judgment, there should be a more explicit mention of the need for reverence and respect toward the magisterium, both extraordinary and ordinary, of Holy Mother Church.

The Cardinal's earlier opposition to a fifth year of pastoral theology for the seminarian was repeated in all three of these interventions in these and similar words:

> It is proposed . . . that young priests, after completing their theological curriculum of studies, complete a pastoral course of one year. All the cardinals and presidents of the Conference of Bishops of the United States have strenuously spoken against this proposal in the letter, which I mentioned before in my observations on the schema of this constitution and on

the points for the instruction of forming students of religion. This proposal is altogether unacceptable to us since thus our dioceses would be deprived, without any need and without any great advantage, of priests necessary for the good of souls. The end of this Second Vatican Council is to foster the pastoral work of the bishops. From this proposal, if it is enacted everywhere in the world, that care of souls would suffer a loss.

The Archbishop of New York felt also that the third chapter, on the use of goods, was still too long and that "it seems enough to recall general principles" and "leave the individual cases and the particulars to the Commission for the Revision of the Code of Canon Law." He referred to the role of the layman in this sphere:

That knowledgeable laymen have a part in the administration of goods is acceptable to me. But care must be taken lest the freedom of the Church be put in danger in this way. Ecclesiastical history teaches us the dangers which can arise from this practice. The norms should be so established that knowledgeable laymen have a part in the administration of the temporal affairs of the Church and that dangers of this kind are avoided.

Finally, in discussing the proper distribution of clergy throughout the world, Cardinal Spellman made the following suggestion:

The words in the schema, "of other persons or groups whose members enjoy either a weak social condition or who lack all culture and the required formation," should be omitted or radically changed lest we offend the national sense of the peoples in Latin America, Africa and Asia. Because of these words, some enemies of the Church could say that the Council Fathers are imbued with a spirit of pride among those who regard "new" peoples as inferior or "colonials."

The other American prelate who submitted observations on this schema was Archbishop John J. Krol of Philadelphia. He wrote that "the greatest portion of this schema is a recapitulation and amplification of the duties proper to clerics as already clear in the Code of Canon Law." On the subject of laymen assisting in the administration of Church goods, The Archbishop raised the following warning:

. . . laymen, even if they are the most experienced, are used *only* if the bishop provides for it and thinks that such a participation will be *absolutely necessary*, and then only with a consultative vote—never with a deliberative vote. Otherwise, the danger remains and will always remain that these laymen gradually inject themselves without reason into the administration of the *ordinary* goods of the Church. From experience we know that laymen who set up the *Trustee System* many years ago in these areas (especially in the Archdiocese of Philadelphia) were a great impediment in the administration of the goods of the Church and could still be even to this time.

During the second session the Commission was not idle. It met in a plenary session on October 7–8, and each member, as well as twenty *periti* assigned to the Commission, received a volume containing the further observations submitted by the Fathers. Throughout the session four subcommissions examined each of the observations in meetings lasting from October 15 to November 10. Other plenary sessions were held on November 18 and 25–27, during which gatherings all the members of the Commission examined the work of the subcommissions.

On January 23, 1964, the Central Coordinating Commission, striving to expedite the work of the Council, decreed that the schema "Concerning the Clergy" be reduced to its essential points and presented in the form of propositions. Accordingly a special subcommission met on January 28–30 and acted with this end in view. The title of the schema was changed again, this time to "On the Priesthood." Its text was submitted to all the members and *periti* of the Commission for their examination, and they, in turn, suggested 48 modifications. These were carefully considered during the Commission's plenary session on March 3–4 and finally reduced to ten propositions. On March 16 the new schema of propositions was presented to the Central Coordinating Commission which approved it on April 17.

This new schema was prefaced by a reference to the Constitution on the Church where, it stated, "the theological nature and mission of the presbyterate is discussed." This fact should be mentioned, for the Constitution on the Church did have a decided influence on the priesthood schema.

During the Council's discussions concerning the chapter on the episcopate in the second session, not a few Council Fathers made excellent observations concerning the presbyterate. During nine congregations, from October 4–16, nine Fathers directed their remarks to the subject of the presbyterate. Archbishop Ermenegildo Florit of Italy stressed its sacramentality, and Archbishop William Conway of Ireland, pleading for a new chapter in the schema on the Church dealing with the presbyterate, said:

The text devotes nine pages to the episcopate and seven pages to the laity. But only half of one page is devoted to the priesthood, and then not to the priesthood directly and immediately, but only in its relation to the episcopate. The text should undertake to put the dignity of the priesthood in bolder relief.

During the same congregation, October 9, Archbishop Denis Hurley of South Africa scored the same point.

The priesthood is treated too casually in this schema. The fact of the matter is that very often the bishop will have no contact with his people except through his priests, because the bishop remains a remote and unknown figure. The priest is the hands and feet, the eyes, ears and very voice of the bishop, and this should bring him greater attention in this discussion on the structure of the Church.

The result of these and similar remarks is found in number 28 of the Constitution on the Church. Therein priests are called "prudent cooperators with the episcopal order" and "bound together in an intimate brotherhood" and are to be regarded by bishops as "sons and friends." In a way, this digression on the presbyterate during the discussion on the episcopate was a forewarning of what would happen to the schema "On the Priesthood" if and when it reached the Council floor. That, however, was not to happen before another year and until another Council session was convened.

During this second session, nonetheless, the Council Fathers did attempt to present a message to all the priests of the world. It was divided into three sections, the first concerning the unity of the priesthood, the second on the unity of the same divine mission, and the third on the unity of the same type of holiness. *Le Figaro* reported that the message was drafted by Bishop Alexandre Renard of Versailles. It was distributed to the Fathers on Friday, November 29, with the General Secretary announcing they would be asked to vote on its approval or rejection on the following Monday, December 2. Over the weekend, however, more than two hundred suggestions had been submitted by the Fathers, thus necessitating another announcement from the General Secretary that further consideration of the document would be postponed indefinitely. That was the last to be heard of the message on the Council floor. It was never published as a message from the Council.

Finally, during the one hundredth congregation, October 13, 1964, the schema "On the Priesthood" arrived on the floor of the Council. It was introduced by Archbishop François Marty of Rheims who might rightly be called the "father" of the priesthood decree. He guided the document along every step of its sometimes faltering way. A good fighter and a brilliant scholar, he stood by the various drafts of the schema, through both its good and bad days. The schema remained the object of 41 critical interventions during the congregations of this session. It was doomed, however, the moment the first speaker had finished his address. That speaker was Albert Cardinal Meyer.

"In all sincerity," the late Cardinal of Chicago began, "I should confess that the schema of propositions in all it encompasses is not very satisfactory . . . because proper discussion is not given to what is of such great importance, as was done in the schema on the pastoral office of bishops and the schema on the apostolate of the laity." Cardinal Meyer's comments on this occasion might well be called devastating. His criticisms can be summarized as follows:

1) This schema "does not offer much comfort to our priests or encouragement for the fulfillment of their obligations."

2) "It is indeed true that the priest is appointed for men, but in those thing which are for God. Let him, therefore, be a man of God before he is a man among men."

3) "It is not very satisfactory that . . . the greatest work and the greatest source of the apostolate, namely, the Sacrifice of the Mass, in which action the priest's greatest dignity also shines forth, be mentioned in so few words." Cardinal Meyer then concluded in the following unequivocal words:

It is my wish that we might have the whole schema broken down almost like the schemata that treat the apostolate of the bishops and laity. This wish will, I am convinced, correspond better both with the eminently pastoral purpose of this Council and with the expectations of very many priests who continue to rely upon this purpose.

During the same congregation Auxiliary Bishop John Donovan of Detroit spoke on proposition four in the schema concerning the care of priests. With great compassion he made the following observations:

In keeping with the role of a solicitous father and kindly pastor of pastors, a bishop must be willing to expend not only his strength, but also the material means available to him from diocesan sources—if they are needed —in order to provide the most skillful medical and therapeutic care for his priests. It is only after all medical arts have been patiently and generously but unsuccessfully engaged, that a bishop can in good conscience begin to consider that a specific illness of one of his priests is incurable. . . . I have in mind, in particular, certain psychological and neurological sicknesses which have of late become vastly more widespread in our society—especially since the last world war—and unfortunately include among their victims an ever-growing number of priests. These victims, truly priests of the New Testament according to the image of Christ, the Eternal High Priest (as the conciliar treatise on the Church has described them), sometimes become a stumbling block for the faithful, even though in a certain sense they may not be completely responsible for their abnormal behavior.

In these unhappy circumstances, bishops often impose canonical penalties on such unfortunate co-workers and also isolate them from society by confining them to a special type of sanitorium or even to what is looked upon as an ecclesiastical jail. It is in this kind of a situation that bishops should, on the contrary, be ready not only to exhaust their own personal powers of assistance, but also to spend funds generously so that such sick priests may regain their health. These men are tragic figures, so mentally and emotionally disturbed, so obsessed with guilt and misgivings, that they know only despair in their day-to-day struggle with life. Despite their sad conditions, they still remain chosen to bring Christ's saving graces to the people of God.

During the 104th congregation, the Council Fathers, by a vote of 1,199 to 930, sent the schema back to the Commission for complete revision. The Commission went to work at once examining the 455 observations that were submitted by the Fathers, both orally and in writing. On November 20, the eve of the closing of the third session, the Commission had resolved upon a new title for the schema. Henceforth it would be called the schema on "The Ministry and Life of Priests." The Fathers were urged to submit further observations on the schema during the coming weeks.

In April, 1965, the Commission met again in Rome for redrafting the schema in the light of the 523 observations submitted by more than 200 Fathers from 30 different nations after the closing of the third session. The revised schema was extended to 19 paragraphs and consisted of an introduction and two parts: the first part concerned the ministry of priests; the second concerned the life of priests. It was approved by the Central Commission and by Pope Paul VI on May 28 and mailed to the Council Fathers.

On October 13, 1965 (coincidentally, exactly one year to the day from the first introduction), the schema was introduced on the Council floor, again by Archbishop Marty. For the next five congregations the schema was debated by 54 Fathers. However, preceeding Archbishop Marty's introduction, Pope Paul sent a letter to the Council Fathers on the subject of the priesthood which Archbishop Felici, on October 11, read to the Council Fathers.

In his letter addressed to Cardinal Tisserant, the dean of the College of Cardinals and first of the council presidents, the Holy Father informed the Council that he not only intended to preserve the ancient law of celibacy for the clergy of the Roman rite, but also "to reinforce its observance." The Pope stated that he was aware that several Fathers had indicated a desire to speak on this delicate subject, but he requested that those who still wished to do so should submit their observations on the subject in writing. These observations should then be given to the Presidency of the Council to be transmitted, in turn, to the Pope personally for his examination. "Without impeding in any way the liberty of the Fathers," the Pope said he wanted to express his own opinion. That opinion he stated in the following words:

Public debate is not opportune on this subject which is so important and which demands such profound prudence. Furthermore it is our intention not only to maintain this ancient, sacred and providential law with all the force of which we are capable, but also to reinforce its observance, calling on priests of the Latin Church to recognize anew the causes and reasons why today, especially today, the law must be considered most suitable. Through it priests are able to consecrate all their love completely to Christ and to dedicate themselves exclusively and generously to service of the Church and souls.

During the 149th congregation the Fathers opened their discussions on the schema. On the following day Auxiliary Bishop Stanislaus Brzana of Buffalo was the first American in this session to speak on the subject. He asked to see a more detailed treatment of humility in the text, calling it "not merely an aid to the spiritual life; rather, it is the fundamental virtue." Humility, he continued, "promotes the true development and maturity of personality in the spirit of the Gospel." In his second observation of his intervention, Bishop Brzana pleaded for a more kindly policy toward fallen priests. The apostolate in favor of priests who have proven unfaithful to their obligations, he observed, demands sincere effort and effective cooperation on the part of all priests, because the entire Church has some share in responsibility for this work. The path to reconciliation, urged Bishop Brzana, should be made broader.

On the following day, October 16, Auxiliary Bishop Stephen Leven of San Antonio rose and said, "I wish to speak for the forgotten man of this schema, the assistant pastor." He then went on to describe the life of the curate:

> In larger archdioceses and dioceses, far more than half of the active priests are assistants. Certainly they do more than half of the work. Yet the assistant has no juridical status and almost no rights. Everyone laughs when it is said that the assistant has no rights except that of Christian burial. It is not a joke to the assistant.
>
> The assistant is often spoken of as a child and treated as a child. But he is not a child. He is a mature man. He may be twenty-four or forty-two or older. If all the parish clergy live together, he is like a guest, and his life like that of a seminarian. If he is in a diocese where each priest lives in a house apart, he is often isolated and poor. . . .
>
> In many parishes in European countries and in my own, I have asked assistants who complain of nothing worthwhile to do, "Why do you not visit your people in their homes? Why not organize study clubs for adults and catechism classes for children?"—only to be told: "The pastor does not believe in such novelties and forbids them." Let no one deny that the trauma of frustrated assistants is serious in the Church. Our present, almost universal, system of inefficient utilization of personnel prevents them from exercising their charisma now and unfits them to do so when, and if, they become pastors.
>
> Would modern technology and industry spend so much time and money to train men and use them so poorly? Modern successful managers have learned that treating grown men as individuals worthy of personal reverence and trust and confidence increases effectiveness and does not lessen authority. In the Church this lesson is far from being universally known.

On the same day Lawrence Cardinal Shehan praised the schema for its "dynamic treatment of the priesthood" and said that it should be accepted as a basis for discussion. However, he made two observations which he felt would strengthen the text. First, he thought the emphasis on the role of the priest as mediator was too one-sided, citing it as "a lack of balance in the schema's treatment of the *full* ministry of the priest." He continued:

. . . [the priest], after the image of the One Mediator, is a mediator between God and men. This mediation has a twofold direction: toward God and toward men. In my opinion, the Godward movement is too sparsely treated in the schema, which results in its being excessively anthropocentric—for example, there is only passing mention made in it that the priest is consecrated to God for *His* glorification and service. Configuration to Christ, which is effected in the sacrament of Orders, is a union with Christ in the real and ontological order. By it, the priest is made sacred, consecrated to God for the praise and glory of God. Whenever the schema speaks of the priest's consecration, it says that he is consecrated to preach the Gospel, to serve the brethren, and so on.

The Cardinal felt also that the schema labored "under a certain imprecision regarding the fundamental basis of the relationship between bishops and priests" and thus failed in "its very purpose of putting an end to the unfortunate separation of priests from their bishops and of fostering a true union between them." He made the following observation:

Bishops and priests both, but in their proper order, share in the one mission of Christ because they share in the one priesthood and ministry of Christ, although bishops fully, and priests less fully. The priest can act in the person of Christ fundamentally because he shares in the priesthood of Christ, and consequently he shares in the episcopal mission, which is the mission of Christ.

In an intervention submitted in writing about this time, Bishop Ernest J. Primeau of Manchester made observations similar to Bishop Leven's. "I would like to speak," he wrote, "about the brotherhood and cooperation among priests, especially among pastors and their assistants." He recalled how Cardinal Meyer often commented on this problem which arose "from the fact that priests do not become pastors for many years, sometimes even twenty or thirty years." Consequently, he observed, "the relationship between pastor and assistant especially in the large cities is almost feudal." In such a situation, he continued, few curates "remained sincere and upright; but gradually their zeal is lessened, their enthusiasm is extinguished, their strength destroyed, and their capabilities, since they lack efficacy, are little by little weakened." Bishop Primeau then proposed the following solution:

Sometimes the solution lies in the establishment of parishes of smaller size or in the reorganization of the larger parishes. It would also help solve the problem to determine that age at which pastors should retire from office. In the same way it would be no small step to give bishops the faculty of removing pastors from office who treat their assistants unjustly; instances of appeal might also be established for the benefit of the junior clergy. In any event, the commission established to revise the Code of Canon Law can see to it that the human and Christian rights of assistants are clearly defined and safeguarded. This same commission should clearly spell out the duties of pastors toward their curates.

Another American prelate to speak on the floor of the Council concerning the priesthood was Archbishop Thomas A. Connolly of Seattle, Washington. On October 25 he addressed himself to the crisis of obedience in the Church, making the following points:

> . . . it seems to me that the virtue of obedience, especially in this day and age, should be brought into clearer focus. There is a crisis in obedience that seems to have developed here and there as the result of a false notion of freedom and independence, of a new atmosphere generated by this Vatican Council II. There are priests, pseudo-existentialists, who denigrate authority as such. Each one seems to be a law unto himself, and the result is invariably scandalous. . . .
>
> Hence, if priests are to be true co-workers and helpers of the bishops, if they are to act as real sons and friends, they will need a deep spirit of obedience. The Roman Pontifical asks obedience of them in the very rite of ordination. The Constitution on the Church has already mentioned that priests who share in the priesthood and mission of the bishop should look upon him as their father and should reverently obey him. In the present schema on the ministry and life of priests there is, however, but brief mention made of priestly obedience. Yet, this is so necessary for the ministry of the priest and so central in his life that I feel the notion of priestly obedience should now be further developed and the reasons for it treated far more profoundly.

Four other American prelates submitted written interventions on the schema during this session. Cardinal Spellman felt the revised schema "will contribute much, now and in the future, to the sanctity and effective ministry of priests." He suggested, however, four observations which he would like to see emphasized in the text. First, he said,

> there should be more attention given to the importance and influence of the Blessed Mary, the Mother of Christ and His Church, in the life and ministry of His priests. The humble example of the Immaculate Virgin and her

total consecration offer a most sure remedy against the spirit of pride which endangers a true love of Christ, His Church, and the people of God. . . . May Christ, the great Eternal High Priest, live in His priests through Mary.

Secondly, the Cardinal said, "more explicit mention should be made of the necessity of obedience and reverence toward the magisterium of the Church." This thought reiterated his earlier observations on the same subject. Thirdly, he suggested, the schema should include "a special word of encouragement to these our brothers" who are suffering persecution today. Finally, he was amazed that the schema did not stress more emphatically that all clergy should frequently receive the sacrament of Penance. "Even now," he said, "there are those who diminish and attenuate the estimation of frequent confession. For this reason, it is absolutely necessary that the Fathers of the Council speak explicitly of the importance of the sacrament of Penance as a means of fostering the interior life of priests."

Bishop Leo T. Maher of Santa Rosa, California, submitted an intervention concerning the threefold role of the priest as liturgist, teacher and member of the civil community. In fulfilling these roles, he observed, the relationship between the bishop and his priest should be stressed since "the priest owes the bishop not only reverence and obedience, but even his very sacerdotal existence." Developing this thought, Bishop Maher continued:

It is fitting, then, that the priesthood of priests be defined as that manifold office as a mediator which Christ Himself exercised through His life and which communicates itself through the episcopacy. St. Paul seems to attest to this essential connection between the office of the bishop when he exhorts the presbyters of Ephesus: "Take heed to yourselves and to the whole flock in which the Holy Spirit has placed you as bishops, to rule the Church of God which he has purchased with his own blood" (Acts 20:29). These words have suggested that the Apostle communicated the power of orders to his successors in a lesser and dependent way since the Holy Spirit, by the grace of orders, made them helpers of the Apostolate. The old prayer of the Roman Pontifical supports this interpretation: in the rite of ordination to the sacred orders of the diaconate and priesthood, after the imposition of the hands, there is no mention of the power of the ordained in relation to the Eucharistic Body of Christ. Rather, there is a clear statement that they are co-workers of the bishops "in the second merit." For this reason, Holy Scripture and the oldest traditions of Holy Mother Church plainly show that the priest, because of the power of orders, is the fellow helper of the bishop in the extension of redemption throughout the earth.

One of the most touching interventions submitted by any American prelate was that of Bishop Thomas J. Drury of Corpus Christi, Texas, on the care which a bishop should exercise toward a priest who had forsaken the ministry. He began with the following observation:

> This is a pastoral Council. It has addressed itself to the world—Christian and non-Christian—in a spirit of humility, proffering to the world love, understanding and hope. It must now do no less for those who should always be the special object of the Church's solicitude, namely, those men who are signed with the priestly character, but who, because of sickness or human frailty, are outside the active ministry. Here we should recall the example of Christ Himself when He was denied and deserted by Peter and the Apostles. Peter was forgiven with a glance charged with mercy and love, and to the other Apostles, Christ, after His resurrection, brought peace and forgiveness: "Peace be upon you; it is myself, do not be afraid."

The Bishop cited the complex nature of this problem and regretted that "little or no scientific study has been made." He expressed his opinion that such priests are sick, and pointed out that "sickness of whatever sort is not a sin and should not be stigmatized as such in any way." He concluded by making the following appeal to the Fathers of the Council:

> Venerable Brothers, this Council, in my humble opinion, should exhort national hierarchies to begin at once to attend to this important task of caring for the priest who is outside of the ministry. Adequate facilities and personnel, trained not merely in the psycho-therapeutic sciences, but also in the spiritual life must be provided. Adequate financial aid must be made available on a regular basis to those already engaged in this work.
>
> Moreover, where medical and spiritual healing has been completed and there is moral certainty that the required cure has been effected, unnecessary or overly strict canonical requirements must not be added so as to prevent the return of the prodigal to his father's house. Otherwise it will be said that the Church itself is the last to forgive its wayward sons. Finally, let this Council, proud of the fine record of the Catholic priesthood, place the work of rehabilitating the priests who are outside the ministry under the protection and care of Him who, "Son of God though he was, learned obedience in the school of suffering and now his full achievement reached, he wins eternal salvation for all those who render obedience to him" (Heb 5:8–9).

After discussion of the schema had been completed on the Council floor, the Commission returned to its work of redrafting the schema in the light of the observations presented. In the meantime, however, two events took place of particular interest among the Americans in Rome.

On October 27, during the 154th general congregation, the Reverend Thomas Falls addressed the Council Fathers in the name of pastor-auditors who had been invited to the Council during the previous session by Pope Paul. Father Falls, a former professor of patristics at St. Charles Seminary, Overbrook, Pa., and currently pastor of Sacred Heart parish, Havertown, Pa., was one of the five American priest-auditors. The others were Monsignor Joseph Emmenegger of the Archdiocese of Milwaukee, Monsignor Gerard Frey of the Archdiocese of New Orleans, Monsignor Walter Tappe from the Diocese of Santa Rosa and the Reverend Joseph Shimek of the Diocese of Winona.

Father Falls spoke in the name of the pastor-auditors as well as of the Catholic clergy of the world. He thanked the Fathers for their wise observations on the priesthood schema and thanked Pope Paul VI for inviting pastors to be present at the council. In his opening remarks he expressed his pleasure with what the schema had to say on priests living a community life, on priests celebrating Mass every day on the demand that "priests be given proper sustenance and that their salary be such that they will be able to lead a life in accord with the locality in which they work." He also expressed pleasure in what was stated about clerical celibacy, "with all due reverence to our brothers of the Oriental Church." He then stated what he believed the schema should express more clearly, namely, that a priest can be aptly called "another Christ," that the sacerdotal priesthood is a participation with the college of bishops, that the spirituality of priests be delineated more precisely and, in the case of diocesan priests, suited to an active life among men. He concluded his remarks with the following pledge:

> After this ecumenical Council has ended, it will be the task of the bishops to implement its decrees and constitutions. In carrying out this work, all of us pastors and other priests will have to be of great help to our own bishops by making clear to the people the true meaning of the Council's provisions. We pastor-auditors, in our name and in the name of all priests, promise that we will dedicate all our energies to fulfilling this task.

Following Father Falls' address, one American bishop made the following entry in his diary:

> Father Falls' delivery of his paper was just about perfect. He spoke with self-assurance, clearly and without the "American accent" which Council fathers from other countries complain about. His speech was not merely a polite formality with obsequious platitudes. . . . He pulled no punches when he added that the schema should spell out in detail the concrete obligations of the bishop to guarantee a decent living wage to every priest of his diocese. . . . Father Falls received a most enthusiastic applause from the Council Fathers at the close of his speech.

Prior to the Council's discussion on the priesthood, the American *periti* held one of their somewhat irregular meetings on October 12. As a group, they were dissatisfied with the text of the schema and felt that their opinions should be voiced. Thus under the chairmanship of their president, Monsignor John S. Quinn of the Archdiocese of Chicago, the group convened in the Sala Transportina with approximately twenty members of the American hierarchy present. Three American priests served on the panel: the Reverend Frank Norris, S.S., discussing the dogmatic aspects of the schema; the Reverend Francis X. Murphy, C.SS.R., commenting on the active ministry of the priest; the Reverend Barnabas Ahern, C.P., speaking on the spiritual life of the priest. Monsignor Alfred Horrigan of the Archdiocese of Louisville was drafted as chairman of the panel.

In his opening remarks Father Norris cited two principal defects in the schema. The first he expressed in the following words:

> On the one hand, there is now the clear teaching of the sacramental nature of the episcopate and the derived and dependent way in which the presbyter participates in the priesthood of Christ as it is fully possessed (in the sacramental order) by the bishop. The priest is not an independent agent. He is a sign not directly of Christ the Priest, but of his bishop, who alone is the direct and immediate sign of Christ to his flock. Theoretically, were the bishop able to fulfill all of his pastoral duties to his flock by himself in a satisfactory way, he would have no reason to ordain presbyters. It is precisely because he cannot be everywhere at once and see to the building up of the Church by himself that he has a corps of co-workers who are his "extensions" and who teach, hallow and rule in his name.

> On the other hand, the priest is a mature person and a fully initiated Christian. He, too, shares in the freedom of the sons of God. He personally feels grave responsibility for the good and the growth of the Church, both in view of his baptismal initiation and of his sacramental ordination. Hence the understandable tension between two factors of priestly existence that are not always easily reconciled and kept in proper balance.

With somewhat the voice of a prophet, Father Norris observed that "the problem of priestly initiative is one that is uppermost in the minds of many priests today and will become even more acute in the future." He suggested that it would be of great value if the Council would first recognize this problem and, secondly, offer guidelines "according to which concrete patterns of the priest-bishop relationship could be worked out." The second defect of the schema, he said, is the overall ecclesiological approach of the text, especially in the light of the constitution on the Church. In offering this criticism of the text, he said:

> The Church in *Lumen Gentium* is a growing, developing community in the midst of and in intimate relation with the whole Family of Man. The Church

in this schema appears as an established entity, a community apart from the "world." If it is awaiting a parousia at all, it is simply treading water until it takes place. Furthermore, the almost endless use of subjective exhortations in the text serves only to weary the reader. I am afraid that the present text will strike many a priest as being pretty much "the same old thing" that he has heard about the priesthood for years and that he will fail to see and to appreciate the new insights that the text does possess.

The second speaker, the Reverend Francis X. Murphy, directed his remarks to the active ministry of the priest. He felt, first of all, a division of the schema into the categories of ministry, life and sanctification was unreal. He felt, secondly, that priests in specialized work, such as hospital, institutional and military chaplains, were given scant attention. Finally, he criticized the schema because of its preoccupation with the subject of priestly vocations which had already been treated in another schema. Thus he said:

It seems, likewise, that perhaps too much space is given to the fostering of priestly vocations—not that this is not an all important concern, but because it is handled with considerable length in the schema on priestly education. It would be just as well here to insist that the image of the priest created in the mind of young boys and men in the parish or school is usually the spark of a vocation—and then drive home the fact that if the priest is truly Christlike in all things, this will impress youths, and the priest will have the opportunity to counsel and encourage vocations.

In conclusion he remarked that the schema could be given more force and concreteness by stressing a priest's "competence in execution of pastoral tasks along with a fundamental stress on his knowledge and spiritual motivation." Father Barnabas Ahern opened his remarks with the observation that many will find in the second part of this schema "the tried and true directives of a typical nineteenth-century manual on priestly holiness." He said it lacks "the fullness of vision and dynamic power to inspire the priest of today." He then cited two fundamental defects in the schema.

. . . priestly holiness is not seen within the context of the holiness of the People of God. The theme of what a man is bound to as a priest obscures the theme of what he is bound to as a Christian. Somehow or other, the truth has been overlooked that a priest is personally pleasing to God not because of the *gratia gratis data* of his priesthood, but rather because of the *gratia gratum faciens* which he shares with all the holy members of the family of God. Although it is true that the sacramental character of priesthood gives a definite form and tonality to the spiritual life of the priest, the fact remains that a priest's holiness must be fully Christian, following the pattern and alive with the virtues of all sanctity in the Church of God. . . .

Secondly, the schema seems to envisage the spiritual life and practices of the priest as something he develops and safeguards in spite of the pressures and activities of his ministry. While providing for the necessary spiritual exercise of priestly life, these are seen as something to be cherished and preserved in, away from the initiative, the planning and the labors of the priest's work-a-day activities. Even a casual reader of the schema will sense that its treatment of the spiritual life merely continues the dichotomy of departmentalization and the tension between spirituality and action.

Father Ahern, however, did praise the first part of the schema and cited the following "three genial themes" as worthy of praise and further consideration. He stated these themes as follows:

1) The priest, like all his fellow Christians, belongs to the family of God.

2) The priest's life of service is, above all, a ministry of the Gospel.

3) The crowning theme of a priest's life is his relation to the Eucharist in the life of the Church. It is "the center and source" and "the root and hinge" of priestly holiness.

Immediately following this meeting, Archbishop Hallinan suggested that these suggestions be drawn up in the form of an intervention and submitted to the conciliar commission. On the spot he secured a dozen American bishops to sign their names to this intervention, among whom were Bishops Ernest Unterkoefler, Henry Soenneker, George Speltz, Raymond Hunthausen, Sylvester Treinen, Lambert Hoch, Leo Dworschak and Leo Byrne. Commenting on the meeting, Bishop Dworschak called it "a most enlightening discussion." He said, "Father Barnabas Ahern did a marvelous job, and I hope that his suggestions will be accepted."

The schema was back in the hands of the commission for emendations according to the criticisms and suggestions of the Fathers. Many of the American bishops' observations were incorporated in the revised text which was returned to the *aula* on November 12 for voting. Again it was introduced by that veteran advocate, Archbishop Marty, who insisted that the text should be called a "decree" rather than a "constitution" because it dealt only with the pastoral exercise of the ministry of priests and the nature of priestly life. He added that "the doctrine of the presbyterate has already been stated in the dogmatic constitution *Lumen Gentium*."

During the following two congregations the Council Fathers voted on 15 propositions concerning this schema. All 15 votes received an overwhelming affirmative approval. During the 166th congregation the final drafting of the schema was presented with the *modi* included in the text as suggested by the Fathers. At this time Archbishop Marty called attention to the fact that the text made no change in the reference to celibacy among priests. He said that the revised text first stresses the priest's consecration to Christ, verified through celibacy, and, secondly, that the value of celibacy is accentuated as both a symbol and a witness of priestly virtue.

On December 2, during the 166th congregation, the Council Fathers voted 2,257 to 11 in favor of the final text of the schema. At that point it was submitted to the pope who decided that it should be proposed for a solemn vote in the public session of December 7. On that day the schema became the decree which now stands as a guide and directory for priests of the coming generations. It is a document worthy of so much labor.

Decree on the Ministry and Life of Priests

✠ INTERVENTIONS

ALBERT CARDINAL MEYER, *13 October, 1964*

1) In all sincerity, I should confess that the schema of propositions, in all that it encompasses, is not very satisfactory. I am saying this not because single propositions are not generally good in themselves, but rather because the precise purpose of this schema is not easily brought out. According to the *relatio*, this purpose is that "an accurate account may be had of the pastoral needs of the Church and of the conditions of the priestly life and apostolate in today's world—and that more positively than negatively." But from the things we heard in the debates on the apostolate of the laity, it does not seem to me that in these few propositions we "have an accurate account of the pastoral needs which truly belong to the life and work of priests." For many things which were said of the apostolate of the laity are even truer of priests and should be said in our schema because of the dignity and importance of their apostolate.

2) The schema of propositions, therefore, is not very satisfactory because proper discussion is not given to what is of such great importance, as was done in the schema "On the Pastoral Duty of Bishops" and in the schema "On the Apostolate of the Laity."

Priests are, indeed, as the schema well says, the "provident cooperators" in the task of the bishop, and bishops greatly depend on the work and pastoral zeal of priests in the proper performance of their own task. Besides this, even the apostolate of the laity depends in many ways on the apostolate of the priests. Certainly the greatest cooperation between priests and laity is desired, as we have already heard from a lay speaker today. This fact is well, though briefly, illustrated in the first number of the schema.

It is fitting, in my opinion, for the whole schema to illustrate these truths at greater length. It is also fitting that the Council Fathers preserve the truth in such a way that their very close bond with all priests may be manifested.

I say "with all priests," for the schema should, in my judgment, also reflect the principles enunciated in the sayings of Pope Pius XII "on the ordinary ministry and the extraordinary ministry" of priests, or, according to the terminology of Pope John XXIII, "on the direct ministry and the indirect ministry."

3) The schema of propositions, as it now stands, does not seem to maintain a good balance, and it seems to me that the account in it ought to be laid aside because it is reduced to these few propositions.

a) So, the schema of propositions speaks almost exclusively of the varying obligations of priests, and does not offer much comfort to our priests or encouragement for the fulfillment of their obligations.

Therefore, I should like something said, at least in the preface, about the dignity, the necessity and the high mission of the priest in the whole complex of the Church's mission. It is true that the preface, as it now reads, briefly recalls what is said of priests in the schema, *De Ecclesia*. But these things should be recalled at somewhat greater length under the pastoral aspect.

b) I ought to confess that it is not evident to me whether the schema, as it now stands, wants to set up norms to be followed now or wants only to indicate some general norms which should be considered in the revision of Canon Law.

c) It is not easily understood why, after the preface, a sudden transition is made to "conversation of priests with laity." It is indeed true that the priest is appointed [*constitui*] for men, but in those things which are for God. Let him, therefore, be a man of God before he is a man among men.

d) It is not very satisfactory that in number three the greatest work and the greatest source of the apostolate, namely, the Sacrifice of the Mass, in which action the priests' greatest dignity also shines forth, is mentioned in so few words: "may they value greatly the cult of the most holy Eucharist."

e) What I said above about the balance not being well maintained seems to me to be especially valid in the case of number 2 (the priest's life should follow the pattern of the Gospel) and of number 3 (which ought to shine forth in the priestly ministry). It could likewise be said of number 9, at least in this sense, that the matter there treated, especially in the last part of that number, will have had its only mention in a conciliar document.

f) Number 12, where it speaks of "a certain common mass," as it reads in the text, is not at all satisfactory, because a general norm, as it were, will not truly correspond in different areas bordering on one another.

4) *Conclusion.* It is my wish that we might have the whole schema broken down almost like the schemas that treat the apostolate of the bishops and the apostolate of the laity.

This wish will, I am convinced, correspond better both with the eminently pastoral purpose of this Council, and with the expectations of very many priests who continue to rely upon this purpose. I have finished.

BISHOP JOHN DONOVAN, *13 October, 1964*

In number four of this treatise dealing with the life and ministry of priests, bishops are reminded of their duty to provide for the health of their priests. I am happy to find in a conciliar document this recognition of a pressing episcopal responsibility. However, since it happens at times, if not often, that bishops fail to discharge this duty well, their responsibility must be pointed up more forcefully and in greater detail. In addition, whatever is said in this fuller development of the subject should be clearly directed as well, and in its own proper context, to major religious superiors since they have the same responsibility as bishops for the priests under their jurisdiction.

In keeping with the role of a solicitous father and a kindly pastor of pastors, a bishop must be willing to expend not only his strength, but also the material means available to him from diocesan sources—if they are needed —in order to provide the most skillful medical and therapeutic care for his priests. It is only after all medical arts have been patiently and generously but unsuccessfully engaged, that a bishop can in good conscience begin to consider that a specific illness of one of his priests is incurable. In this regard, all of us are aware that illnesses of a mental, emotional and neurological nature very frequently require longer care and more skillful medical treatment.

I have in mind, in particular, certain psychological and neurological sicknesses which have of late become vastly more widespread in our society— especially since the last world war—and unfortunately include among their victims an ever-growing number of priests. These victims, truly priests, of the New Testament according to the image of Christ, the Eternal High Priest (as the conciliar treatise on the Church has described them), sometimes become a stumbling block for the faithful, even though in a certain sense they may not be completely responsible for their abnormal behaviour.

In these unhappy circumstances bishops often impose canonical penalties on such unfortunate co-workers and also isolate them from society by confining them to a special type of sanitorium or even to what is looked upon as an ecclesiastical jail. It is in this kind of a situation that bishops should, on the contrary, be ready not only to exhaust their own personal powers of assistance, but also to spend funds generously so that such sick priests may regain their health. These men are tragic figures, so mentally and emotionally disturbed, so obsessed with guilt and misgivings, that they know only despair in their day-to-day struggle with life. Despite their sad condition, they still remain chosen to bring Christ's saving grace to the people of God.

These sick priests can in most instances be cured if bishops would put them in touch with skilled scientists in the field of psychiatry, clinical psychology and neurology, for these experts are achieving more and more success these days in the treatment of abnormal human behavior in our society. It is true that this charitable effort, which has its roots in justice, will take patience, time and money; but of what particular value are such requirements when compared with the rehabilitation of those who really have a vocation and hence continue to share with bishops the power to celebrate the mystery of Our Lord's death, to preach the Word of salvation and to care for souls?

Is it not true that, in accordance with the very words used in other treatises already approved by this conciliar body, bishops are to treat their priests as sons and friends? They are to treat their priests with paternal charity, being solicitous about their welfare. They are to look out for priests who are in any kind of trouble with an all-pervading and never-ending mercy.

Our schema must recognize this absolutely modern reality of which I speak and treat it in more detail, so that, insofar as it is possible, every priest may possess at all times, or once again as the case may be, a sound mind in a healthy body.

For the rest, the text is too juridical in certain places and thus hardly corresponds to the pastoral nature found in other schemata dealing with the priesthood, namely the Constitution on the Church and the Decree on the Bishops' Pastoral Office in the Church.

Let it be left to the post-conciliar Commission for Revising the Code of Canon Law to handle all the juridical elements, especially what is said about studies in number six and about benefices in number ten.

In number four, line 21 to the end of the number, the recommendation of common life for all priests needs clarification. Clearly, many join the diocesan clergy because they do not want a community life as found in religious communities. If the words *"vita communis"* mean some association of friendship among priests in order to avoid overwhelming and dangerous solitude, let the text say so clearly.

What is said in number nine about church goods and their correct use should be directed not only to priests, but also and even primarily should be extended openly to bishops. Should not bishops, the highest grade of the priesthood, be mindful in a very special way to bind themselves "to giving an example of holiness in charity, humility and a simple life"?

BISHOP STANISLAUS BRZANA, *15 October, 1965*

The revised text of our schema describes clearly the dignity, ministry and life of the priest. It corresponds suitably to the needs of our day, and, upon the completion of debate and amendments, it merits strong approval. Allow me to make observations on two points.

First Observation

Many virtues are aptly recommended in our schema, especially the evangelical counsels. Although not every virtue can be cited along the lines of a treatise on ascetics, I propose that more be said about the virtue of humility. It is true that humility is cited twice and is directly recommended in a phrase in number eleven, where there is a discussion about the means for developing the interior life. However, humility is not merely an aid to the spiritual life; rather, it is the fundamental virtue. According to St. Augustine, the higher the temple of holiness is to be built, so much deeper must the foundation of humility be dug. Genuine humility is completely necessary in order that the priests be able to conduct themselves in the sublime dignity of the priesthood in a fitting manner. Humility is necessary for the priest to be able to develop the virtues explicitly recommended in this schema and in others, namely, to adore God, to love their neighbor, to respect the personal worth of every man, to offer perfect obedience to superiors, to minister joyfully to others and to lead their lives according to the example of Christ. The Lord Jesus Himself said, "Learn from me for I am meek and humble of heart" (Mt. 11:29).

May the younger priests not fear that humility will inhibit the so-called "development of personality." On the contrary, humility promotes the true development and maturity of personality in the spirit of the Gospel.

It is fitting that I have this opportunity to speak today on humility on the Feast of St. Teresa of Avila, who wrote so many beautiful things about this very same virtue. According to her, humility is pleasing to God inasmuch as it is nothing else than truth.

Therefore, I propose, and humbly so, that in number eleven or in some other place humility be more strongly recommended to priests in a short paragraph or sentence.

Second Observation

It states in number seven: "Indeed, by reason of that same brotherhood and communion within the priesthood, priests should realize that they are also obligated towards those who may have fallen in some matters, and they should therefore attend to them with mercy and great love."

We greatly rejoiced in these words which express the concern of the Church toward those brothers who have fallen away.

The task of restoring these unfortunate priests—a task in which the Church has grave responsibility—is not an easy one, because of various difficulties even on the part of the fallen priests themselves. However, in many cases this arises not from bad will, but from human weakness. Certainly penitence and cooperation are needed on the part of the fallen priest. Some priests can accomplish much in this matter as friends, as classmates of the seminary, as brothers who were ordained together. Often a path lies open to these priests which would not be evident to others. It is opportune, therefore, that all the priests are admonished by the Council to receive their unfaithful brothers not only with compassion and great love, but also to pursue them actively.

Likewise, local ordinaries and all prelates are advised, notwithstanding the difficulties, to attend to their unfaithful priests with "painstaking mercy" as has been said in the schema of the decree on the Pastoral Duty of Bishops.

There are some who fear that such a more moderate method of procedure in these cases might offer an opportunity for others to follow their unfortunate example. Due caution observed, however, this will not be true. I have never heard about a priest who was scandalized because mercy was shown a penitent brother. Everybody knows the parable of the prodigal son who was received most lovingly by his father; everyone remembers the words of the Lord on the need to forgive sins seventy times seven.

LAWRENCE CARDINAL SHEHAN, *16 October, 1965*

The revised text of this schema on the life and ministry of priests is, in general, satisfactory, and certainly should be accepted as a basis for discussion. It presents the matter in a dynamic fashion—although not without some hesitancy —thus remedying a defect in previous drafts of the schema and especially of the list of propositions presented in the preceding session. Certainly, too, it is more worthy of the priests, diocesan and religious, on whom the *aggiornamento* will depend. As Pope John once said in a discourse to seminarians in Rome, "the *aggiornamento* will depend, above all, on holy priests." However, this present schema can be still further improved. For this improvement I should like to offer two observations and submit several emendations in writing.

First Observation

Although the pastoral orientation of the schema is very laudable and emphasis is placed on the priest's ministry to the people of God and to all men, there is a lack of balance in the schema's treatment of the *full* ministry of the priest who, after the image of the One Mediator, is a mediator between God and men. This mediation has a twofold direction: toward God and toward men. In my opinion, the Godward movement is too sparsely treated in the schema, which results in its being excessively anthropocentric—for example, there is only passing mention made in it that the priest is consecrated to God for *His* glorification and service. Configuration to Christ, which is effected in the sacrament of Orders, is a union with Christ in the real and ontological order. By it, the priest is made sacred, consecrated to God for the praise and glory of God. Whenever the schema speaks of the priest's consecration, it says that he is consecrated to preach the Gospel, to serve the brethren, and so on.

In the schema of the Decree on Priestly Formation (page 7, lines 3 and 4), in speaking of vocations to the priesthood, it is said: ". . . by the sign of the Holy Spirit they [priests] are consecrated for the worship of God and the Church's service." Thus are expressed the idea of priestly consecration and the two-directional movements of priestly mediation, namely, toward the worship of God *and* toward the service of the Church.

Likewise, in the Constitution *Lumen Gentium,* when speaking of the common priesthood of the faithful, we find the ideas of their consecration and offering as a living sacrifice, pleasing to God—for example, numbers 10, 31, 34, 40. When this same Constitution speaks of the ministerial or hierarchical priest-hood, the same idea is found—for example, numbers 10 and 28.

Since a renewed consciousness on the part of priests of their consecration to God and to Christ, as well as of their dedication to the service of men, is important for the renewal of the priestly life and ministry, I should desire that a theocentric orientation be more strongly presented in the schema in order that a more balanced theology of the priesthood result. For the glory of God and the good of souls—this is the purpose of the priesthood and constitutes the *recta intentio* of priestly vocation.

Second Observation

In my opinion, the revised text, in its general tone and especially in some particular numbers, labors under a certain imprecision regarding the funda-mental basis of the relationship between bishops and priests. As a result, the schema may defeat its very purpose of putting an end to the unfortunate separa-tion of priests from their bishops and of fostering a true union between them. This lack of clarity should be remedied for two reasons: 1) the same theology of the priesthood which is so beautifully taught in the Constitution *Lumen Gentium* must be faithfully adhered to in this schema; 2) for the sake of a renewal of the union in the mission, work and life of bishops and priests, any-thing smacking of "episcopalism" should be avoided, so that priests do not look upon their bishops as authoritarian employers rather than fellow priests, fellow workers in the same ministry and mission of Jesus Christ, preserving always the distinction of orders (that is, priests of the first and priests of the second order).

According to the theology of the priesthood expounded in the Constitution *Lumen Gentium* (Ch. III, number 28), the basic bond between bishops and priests is their *participation* in one and the same priesthood—that of Christ Himself. It is clearly stated in the Constitution that priests are truly subordinate (*secundi ordinis*) to bishops precisely because they share in the priesthood of

Christ less fully than bishops, but they are *united* with bishops in sacerdotal dignity by reason of the power of the sacrament of Orders of which the bishop is the minister. It is through the sacrament of Orders that bishops hand on to priests their proper participation in the one priesthood of Christ, in which the bishops also participate but in a more complete way than priests of the second rank.

This doctrine was clearly expressed in the previously emended text (on the left side of the schema, page 13, lines 24–38). Note well the wording found there. The revised text changes this wording and, in my opinion, changes the doctrine (page 13, lines 1 and 4–6). It is one thing to say, as does the previously emended text, that *because* priests have a special participation in the Priesthood of Christ and are configured to Christ, the Head, in a subordinate way, *therefore* they share in the episcopal mission which is the apostolic mission, the mission of Christ Himself. It is another thing to say, as does the revised text, that "the priesthood of the presbyterate needs a special sacramental initiation, by which the priest is configured to Christ in a particular way, so that, *having been made a sharer of the episcopal mission,* he can act in the person of Christ, Head, Teacher, Pontiff and Ruler."

Bishops and priests both, but in their proper orders, share in the one mission of Christ because they share in the one priesthood and ministry of Christ, although bishops fully, and priests less fully. The priest can act in the person of Christ *fundamentally* because he shares in the priesthood of Christ, and *consequently* he shares in the episcopal mission, which is the mission of Christ.

In the New Testament no one was given the title *sacerdos* except Christ Himself. Actually, Christ conferred on the Apostles and their successors a *ministerium,* and it was in the context of *ministerium* that the hierarchical rank and distinction of bishops, priests and deacons developed. Thus, *ministerium* becomes identified with *sacerdotium.* To say, then, as does the revised text (number 22, line 19) that priests share in the *ministerium* of the bishops is to say that they share in the *sacerdotium* of the bishops, but bishops share in their own way, as do priests in their own way in the *sacerdotium unicum Christi.*

Conclusion

Because priests have a special participation in the priesthood of Christ, although less fully than the bishops, *therefore* they share in the episcopal mission, which is the Apostolic mission and the very mission of Christ. It is according to this theology that our schema should treat of the relationship between bishops and priests, both as regards their unity of mission and as regards their dependence in obedience and in other ways on the bishop.

In view of this, I propose certain emendations which I shall submit to the Secretariat.

BISHOP STEPHEN LEVEN, *16 October, 1965*

I wish to speak for the forgotten man of this schema, the *vicarius cooperator*, or the assistant pastor.

The Sacred Council has said many beautiful things of the status of bishops, even auxiliaries; it has said much of pastors, of religious, of our separated brethren and of non-Christians. Yet, this schema concerning the ministry and life of priests says nothing of the role and the apostolate of assistants. Can this Holy Synod pass them over in silence? Is their place not important or their status not worthy of examination and correction?

In larger archdioceses and dioceses, far more than half of the active priests are assistants. Certainly they do more than half of the work. Yet the assistant has no juridical status and almost no rights. Everyone laughs when it is said that the assistant has no right except that of Christian burial. It is not a joke to the assistant.

The assistant is often spoken of as a child and treated as a child. But he is not a child. He is a mature man. He may be twenty-four or forty-two or older. If all the parish clergy live together, he is like a guest, and his life like that of a seminarian. If he is in a diocese where each priest lives in a house apart, he is often isolated and poor.

According to Canon Law, the pastor alone has juridical status and responsibility for the affairs of the parish. Too often in large dioceses a priest becomes a pastor only after his years of vigor and energy have passed. In Canon Law this is even called being awarded a benefice, with the connotation that it is a prize to be enjoyed rather than a task to demand all one's energies. The ministry of such parishes becomes depersonalized and dehumanized, and then the people of God suffer.

In many parishes in European countries and in my own, I have asked assistants who complained of nothing worthwhile to do, "Why do you not visit your people in their homes? Why not organize study clubs for adults and catechism classes for children?"—only to be told: "The pastor does not believe in such novelties and forbids them." Let no one deny that the trauma of frustrated assistants is serious in the Church. Our present, almost universal, system of inefficient utilization of personnel prevents them from exercising their charisma now and unfits them to do so when, and if, they become pastors.

Would modern technology and industry spend so much time and money to train men and use them so poorly? Modern successful managers have learned that treating grown men as individuals worthy of personal reverence and trust and confidence increases effectiveness and does not lessen authority. In the Church this lesson is far from being universally known. This schema should assist in teaching it.

Assistants form one moral person with the pastor. Theirs is the same priesthood, theirs the same task, to lead and feed the people of God. The pastor should, therefore, involve his assistants in parish affairs, respect them and listen to them.

Decision-making in the parish, as well as in any other complex circumstances, involves four steps: 1) the assembly of all pertinent data for a certain course of action; 2) the consideration of all possible alternatives and their probable effects; 3) the logical conclusion as to which action is best in the circumstances; 4) the decision that this particular course of action rather than another is to be followed. Only in the last stage is authority involved. Authority is never lessened when its proper role is understood and observed.

Paragraph six of the schema, beginning at line 40, piously says that, after the Council, we must have a body of priests better organized than it is now. I request that it be explicitly said that younger clergy, especially assistants, be included in due proportion to their numbers in such an organization. This should likewise be done in the pastoral council recommended in the schema on the pastoral role of bishops.

Secondly, this schema should specifically recommend that modern machines and methods be used in the priestly ministry; for example, what pastor of a parish of 30,000 souls or 3,000, can know his parishioners personally according to the word of the Good Shepherd, in John 10: 14, "I know my sheep"? But there are modern machines whereby the individuals can be listed with their qualifications and charismata, their needs, their status—for example, religious education, whether married *coram ecclesia* or not—by the skillful use of which a pastor can know his flock.

It may be objected that special skills are requested for this. Let them be acquired, or let trained laymen be employed to assist the priest in this matter. It may be objected that this costs too much, that another priest on the parish staff could do it more cheaply. But, first, no number of added priests can do this adequately, and, secondly, machines and laymen are available; priests are not.

ARCHBISHOP THOMAS CONNOLLY, 25 *October, 1965*

The text of this decree, as reviewed and revised, appears to be more or less satisfactory. However, it seems to me that the virtue of obedience, especially in this day and age, should be brought into clearer focus. There is a crisis in obedience that seems to have developed here and there as the result of a false notion of freedom and independence, of a new atmosphere generated by this Vatican Council II. There are priests, pseudo-existentialists, who denigrate authority as such. Each one seems to be a law unto himself, and the result is invariably scandalous.

In the Constitution on the Church (chapter three), the Fathers of this Ecumenical Council spoke at some length on the hierarchial nature of the

Church and on the heavy responsibilities of bishops who "by divine institution have succeeded to the place of the Apostles as shepherds of the Church (so that he who hears them, hears Christ, and he who rejects them, rejects Christ and Him who sent Christ) (number 20). The Holy Spirit is so conferred on these successors of the Apostles (by the imposition of hands and the words of consecration) that in an eminent and visible way they sustain the roles of Christ Himself as teacher, shepherd and high priest, acting in His person (number 21).

However, to fulfill, in the particular Church, Christ's role (as teacher, shepherd, and high priest) the bishop, with the care of a diocese, needs the help of other men, who (by the grace of God and the imposition of a bishop's hands) have obtained the *"secundi meriti munus."* As prudent cooperators of the episcopal order and associated with the bishop in a spirit of trust and generosity, these priests will make the bishop present in a certain sense in the individual local congregations and take upon themselves, as far as they are able, his duties and the burden of his care (number 28).

Since these priests share in the priesthood and mission of the bishops, they (as the Constitution on the Church suggests) must be regarded by the bishops as co-workers, sons and friends, just as Jesus Christ called His disciples *now not servants, but friends* (number 28). In the text of the schema now under discussion (*De Ministerio et Vita Pres.*, n.6) we are again happily reminded that priests are the true helpers and counselors of the bishops in the ministry, and we gladly note that, according to a form and to norms to be determined by law, provision will be made for them to help the bishop more efficaciously in the rule of the diocese.

However it is the bishops, "as vicars and ambassadors of Christ," who "govern the particular churches entrusted to them by their counsel, exhortations, example, and even by their authority and sacred power . . . which they personally exercise in Christ's name. In virtue of this power, bishops have the sacred right and duty before the Lord to make laws for their subjects, to pass judgment on them, and to moderate everything pertaining to the ordering of worship and the apostolate" (*De. Eccl.*, n. 27).

Hence, if priests are to be true co-workers and helpers of the bishops, if they are to act as real sons and friends, they will need a deep spirit of obedience. The Roman Pontifical asks obedience of them in the very rite of ordination. The Constitution on the Church has already mentioned that priests who share in the priesthood and mission of the bishop should look upon him as their father and should reverently obey him (number 28). In the present schema on the ministry and life of priests (number 6, paragraph 2), there is, however, but brief mention made of priestly obedience. Yet, this is so necessary for the ministry of the priest and so central in his life that I feel the notion of priestly obedience should now be developed further and the reasons for it treated far more profoundly.

I am aware that, at all times, priestly obedience can be, to some extent, a burden. Has not each pope of this century, for example, felt himself impelled to speak out forcefully on the subject and the necessity of this virtue? In our days, when the value of obedience itself is questioned by some, this possible burden can weigh even more heavily on our priests unless their minds are enlightened to see its real value and their hearts are moved to accept it willingly. Even the *aggiornamento* of the Church can make it more difficult for a priest today to obey an order whose wisdom for the apostolate he does not personally see, and, in these days of ferment, priests are more apt to have their own opinions on many important matters. Consequently, our love for our priests and for the Church demands that this schema present priestly obedience in a fuller and richer light.

Obedience has its ultimate root in the divine will. We obey because God wishes us to obey. In the light of this truth, we understand that the reason for obedience is neither the worthiness nor the benevolence nor the wisdom of those we obey. The reason is the intrinsic moral value of obedience, and ultimately it is conformity to the divine will. On the whole, one never obeys merely a man; one obeys God; this obedience becomes meritorious before God and eventually turns into love.

The obedience to his bishop that is asked of a priest is, of course, not a mere juridical burden that God imposes to try His priests, nor is it a mere matter of utility. As the present schema indicates, it is required by the very nature of the priestly office in the Church. The obedience of the priest, moreover, is intrinsically connected with the unity of the Church, the sanctification of souls, and the personal holiness of the priest himself.

1) The unity of the Church demands that a priest be obedient to his bishop. This unity of the Church, of course, will be realized in its perfection only on the last day when those who are perfected will completely give themselves to God and to one another in utter freedom and spontaneity. But until then, the manifestation of the unity of the Church requires the visible direction provided by God in the establishment of a visibly exercised authority. To express, at the present time, the unity that Christ willed for His Church, men must now be united to their bishops in the only way possible: by union of mind and will, which is obedience. This is supremely true for the priest who has freely accepted the role of a collaborator of the bishop and who is the very extension of the bishop into the local community. If the priest is not united to the bishop by bonds of obedience, the unity of the Church is not manifested there, and the unity of operation of the Church is destroyed.

2) The obedience of a priest to his bishop is also necessary for the good of souls. For the People of God, the Church, to move toward its common destiny, unified activity around the bishop is imperative, for where the bishop is, there is the Church. "Whoever is not in union with the bishop, is not in union with the Church," said St. Cyprian. If a priest should refuse obedience to his bishop, even for what seems to him the laudable motives of the apostolate, he rends the seamless garment of the Church and destroys that

unity which is vitally necessary for the true apostolate. Priests should be helped to understand that even if a bishop, through a mistake in judgment, should command something that may not be the wisest course to follow—and this should not be easily presumed—the welfare of souls is better served by obedience. A short-term improvement in the local apostolate at the expense of the unity of the Church can never promote the ultimate realization of the Kingdom of God as does obedience which preserves that unity and promotes the good of souls.

3) Finally, it is through obedience to his bishop that the priest in large measure realizes that perfection of charity, that holiness which the priestly office demands. Holiness, for the priest as for every man, means the complete response of his whole being to God, as God comes to him in all the circumstances of his life. Since, for the priest, these circumstances consist basically in his relationship to the bishop, and with and in the bishop to the rest of the People of God, priestly obedience is the core of his freely given submission to the will of God manifested in the circumstances of his life, and it is at the heart of priestly sanctity. This point is of special concern to the bishop who is the father and shepherd of his priestly co-workers.

Pope Leo XIII wrote:

Let the authority of their superiors be sacred to priests; let them know for a certainty that the priestly ministry, unless it be exercised under the direction of the bishops, cannot be either *holy* or fruitful or deserving of commendation.

Pope Pius XII exhorted the clergy:

At a time like the present, when the principle of authority is imprudently called into question, it is absolutely essential that the priest should keep a firm hold on the precepts of his faith, and regard and duly accept authority not only as a bulwark of religion and society, but as the foundation of his own *personal sanctification.*

Pope John XXIII said this statement should be kept firmly in mind:

The holiness of each individual life and the efficacy of the apostolate are based and sustained, as on a solid foundation, on a constant and faithful subjection to the sacred hierarchy.

What these Popes have taught, I have also learned by experience: priestly obedience is the necessary foundation and condition for priestly holiness.

Pope Paul VI, now happily reigning, recently told the seminarians of the North American College:

Here in the seminary you have order and discipline . . . we know your young spirits rebel at times at what seemingly is a brake on your initiative. Remember that obedience is most necessary in any well-ordered society and that it is a most basic virtue. Without it, chaos would result. This spirit creates the continuity and unity of action that is so necessary if apostolic undertakings are to be brought to their successful conclusion.

As a Council Father, I now feel a heartfelt desire to have obedience treated in greater depth in this schema on the ministry and life of priests. Reflecting the teaching of these Popes, the schema should show its relationship to priestly holiness, as well as to the unity of the Church and the good of souls.

The very brief treatment of priestly obedience in the present schema could somehow imply that obedience is less important for the priest of today. A failure, then, to develop the notion of obedience would be a disservice to our priests, if not a tragic mistake. We should put this virtue in its proper light and so help our priests to see its value and necessity in their labors for the Kingdom of God as our co-workers, sons and friends. For, like Pope John, I am confident that "when clerics are sufficiently aware of the force and beauty of this virtue, they will more zealously desire it."

Decree on the Ministry and Life of Priests

✠ COMMENTARY by Rev. John McCormack, S.S.

1) In the very first sentence of the Preface to the Decree on the Ministry and Life of Priests we are reminded that priests had already received attention in earlier documents of the Council; the relevant note cites the Constitution on the Sacred Liturgy, the Constitution on the Church, the Decree on the Bishops' Pastoral Office in the Church and the Decree on Priestly Formation. As a matter of fact, for a while it seemed that priests were to be the forgotten men of the Council who would have to depend on isolated references in other documents to catch the Council's mind on the nature of their life and work. There was definite need of a separate treatment, and the present document, growing out of a "proposition" introduced on October 13, 1964, fills that need. The Introduction, given in this volume, furnishes the full story of the Decree's development.

After making it clear that the Decree applies to all priests, secular and religious, the first paragraph of the official Latin text gives us, succinctly but completely, the sources of the priest's power and the ways in which he exercises those powers. By ordination he is assimilated to Christ the Priest and gains a share in the unique priesthood that is Christ's and, therefore, in the powers of Christ the Priest; but it is by the mission given him by his bishop, who alone is the direct and immediate sign of Christ to his flock, that he exercises his ministry of teaching, sanctifying and ruling the holy People of God. The priest, therefore, depends upon the bishop for his power of orders and, through the bishop's mandate, for the exercise of his priesthood; he thus becomes an extension of the bishop.

In concluding the brief Preface, the Council faces the fact that, because of the many changes of all kinds brought about in our modern age, the delineation of the priesthood and the guidelines for the ministry and life of priests must be brought up to date. The image aimed at is the modern priest, the priest of the second half of the twentieth century.

In accomplishing its task, the Decree begins by placing the priesthood within the whole framework of the Church's mission. In its second chapter it sets forth the ministry of priests by describing the priest's functions; his relations with the bishop, with his fellow priests, and with the laity, and it terminates the chapter with a discussion of the practical problems of recruitment and distribution of priests. The third chapter treats of the priestly life, discussing in detail both the spiritual and material aspects. A brief conclusion and exhortation bring the document to a close.

CHAPTER I / THE PRIESTHOOD IN THE MISSION OF THE CHURCH

2) The priest of the New Law must not be studied in a vacuum. It cannot be said of him that he is "without father, without mother, without genealogy" (Heb. 7:3*); he is, rather, "taken from among men" (Heb. 5:1 *C*)—and this Decree is at pains throughout to keep the priest in this proper setting. Before he receives the sacrament of Orders and is thus set apart by a special character to exercise a public priestly office among and for men, he is already a member of a holy and royal priesthood, that priesthood which is common to all members of the Mystical Body. By his Baptism and Confirmation he has been initiated into this priesthood and, along with all the faithful, he has had a part in the mission of the whole Body, the Church. In becoming a priest, however, a man is answering a call to join those ministers who, by reason of sacred ordination, exercise a special function in the Church, offering the Eucharistic sacrifice, remitting sin and, in general, performing the priestly office publicly for men in the name of Christ, continuing on earth His role of Teacher, Priest and King. As Christ had been sent by the Father, so Christ sent the Apostles and, through them, the bishops and, through the bishops, priests who would carry out the ministry of the bishops in a limited degree. The threefold office of Christ is, therefore, continued from the Master Himself down to the most recently ordained priest, and it rests on the sacraments of Baptism, Confirmation, and Holy Orders. There is only one eternal priesthood and one mission.

By his office of teacher, the priest, proclaiming the Word of God, the Good News of salvation, draws together the People of God. Thus drawn together and sanctified by the Holy Spirit, they offer themselves as "a sacrifice, living, holy, pleasing to God" (Rom 12:11 C), the spiritual sacrifice which they are empowered to offer to God by their initiation as Christians. This spiritual sacrifice the priest takes and brings to perfection in union with the sacrifice of Christ which he, by his special consecration in Holy Orders, offers in an unbloody and sacramental manner. Thus, all are brought together, priest and people, in union with Christ to form one body, to give glory to God the Father.

In stressing the glory of God the Father as the purpose which priests pursue in their ministry, the Decree is not minimizing the priest's objective of serving the people. All that the priest does for and among the people gives glory to God and helps to expand His kingdom on earth.

3) Echoing the familiar words of the Epistle to the Hebrews (5:11), the

---

* C: *Holy Bible,* Confraternity Edition. Copyright 1962 The Confraternity of Christian Doctrine and reprinted by permission.

Decree emphasizes the fact that the priest must deal with other men as brothers. He was taken from among them not to be set on a pedestal or to have his head in the clouds, not to be a member of an untouchable priestly caste; rather is he appointed *for* men, and, therefore, he must be truly and deeply involved in all that concerns them not only in their relations with God, but in the many details of their life which are connected directly or indirectly with salvation. The example of Christ Himself and of the Apostles and St. Paul is cited as a model. Like the Apostle to the Gentiles, the priest must become "all things to all men that he might save all." At the same time a warning is sounded against conformity with the world. Our Savior, in the beautiful prayer He uttered on the night before He died, petitioned the Father: "I do not pray that thou take them out of the world, but that thou keep them from evil." We hear a great deal currently about the secularization of the ministry, the need of using to the full the means the world offers in order to save men. As long as the priest keeps the proper perspective and exercises the virtue of prudence, this secularization can be truly effective. But we must be on our guard lest it turn into secularism. If the priest gets too completely in step with the world, he may easily become just another layman, with a layman's heart and a layman's outlook on life. He must, indeed, know that heart and know that outlook, else he will not be able to render to men the service his office demands. But he must be conscious of his higher call by priestly ordination.

In any discussion of secularization of the ministry, a frequent topic is that of clerical dress, although the Decree does not introduce it. Here custom has been the chief and sure guide. But some wonder whether it would not make for greater effectiveness in our dealings with our fellow men to be less distinctively dressed, even wearing collar and tie and perhaps reducing the peculiarly priestly trappings to a simple cross on our lapel (for our Christian military chaplains this cross on the lapel is the only distinguishing mark, nor is there any further distinction for Catholic chaplains). With such a change, black would probably yield quickly to other colors, but presumably the priest would keep to a fairly sombre shade. Already concessions have been made in tropical climes permitting the wearing of a white suit, but still with the so-called Roman collar; in some places, I believe, where the summer is insufferably hot, a white sport shirt and black trousers are permitted. These are seasonal concessions, to be sure, but they may point the way to more general future changes. Americans have always felt that the European custom of wearing the cassock always and everywhere in the priestly round of duties has raised a real barrier to anything like human communication, and we welcome the new trend toward the dress called "clergyman" in France and even in Italy. What the future holds in store we cannot conjecture, but the prudent priest will be guided by the customs and regulations approved by his Ordinary.

No matter what his prescribed dress, the priest must always be attuned to the ways and the needs of the people whom he serves. His divine mission imposes this obligation upon him.

In concluding the first chapter, the Decree reminds us of those natural virtues which are too often forgotten among us, but which are essential in our dealings with men. In the earlier text this sentence came in the section on the priest's relations with the laity, but in the revision was fitted into the more general picture of the priesthood in the mission of the Church.

CHAPTER II / THE MINISTRY OF PRIESTS

I. *Priestly functions*

4) Remaining true to the new emphasis on the Word of God brought out, time and again, by the Second Vatican Council since its very first document, the Constitution on the Sacred Liturgy, this Decree straightforwardly says that "priests, as co-workers with their bishops, have as their primary duty the proclamation of the gospel of God to all." "Faith depends on hearing, and hearing on the word of Christ" (Rom. 10:17 C). The ministry of the priest is seen as beginning with the proclamation of the Word, for it is thus that the people are drawn from unbelief to an acceptance of the mystery of Christ and to initiation into the Mystical Body by Baptism. It is only after this assembling of the People of God by the preaching of the Word that the priest can apply his sacramental ministrations and join the spiritual sacrifices of the faithful to his offering of the Eucharistic sacrifice. It is obvious that the Decree is speaking not only of what we may call pulpit preaching, but also of the various channels of communication available to the priest for the spread of the Word, including the liturgy of the Word in which the priest's ministry of the Word reaches its culmination.

The emphasis here placed on the proclamation of the Word implies an increased need to stress preaching during seminary training. There is, indeed, in recent times a renewed interest in this subject, and the importance now given to the homily in the liturgical life of the Church serves to underline the need of homiletic training.

5) The proclamation of the Word is but the first step in the priest's ministry. By it he becomes a fisher of men. But, having caught men in the tender meshes of God's Word and initiated them into the mystery of Christ by Baptism, he must continue to nourish them with the Word and with the sacramental graces which he is appointed to channel to men. By the proclamation of the Word, the priest fulfills and extends Christ's and the bishop's office of teacher; by the administration of the sacraments he shares in the office of sanctifying men.

This area of his activity is centered on his offering of the Sacrifice of the Mass for, as the Decree tells us, "The other sacraments, as well as every ministry of the Church and every work of the apostolate, are linked with the holy Eucharist and are directed toward it. For the most blessed Eucharist contains the Church's entire spiritual wealth, that is, Christ Himself, our Passover and living bread. . . . the Eucharistic Action is the very heartbeat of the congregation of the faithful over which the priest presides." The faithful, already marked by Baptism as a royal priesthood capable of offering a spiritual sacrifice to God and strengthened in their faith by Confirmation, are joined fully to the Body of Christ through their reception of the Eucharist. When they succumb to the world's allurements and turn from Christ either wholly or in part, they are drawn back to Him in the sacrament of Penance.

In all this ministry the priest must himself be a man of prayer and he must instill the spirit of prayer in his people lest their worship of God become a set of external acts which fail to pervade their being. Their sacramental and prayer life must be the driving power which enables them to fulfill God's purpose for them in the world to the degree and extent of which they are capable.

In his own prayer the priest will give the primary place to his careful and prayerful recitation of the Divine Office. He will not consider it a burden, but an opportunity to act as public and official spokesman for all his people and for all the People of God and for the whole world.

As the Decree nears the end of its treatment of the priest as sanctifier, it reminds the priest of the obligations he assumed when he was ordained a porter in the House of God, the chief center of his Eucharistic activity. He must see to it that the church is well kept and always suitable for sacred functions. We may also add further reminders of constant fidelity to duty and punctuality in service to our people.

If the priest is to be truly effective in his sacramental ministry, he must know the liturgy. There is no longer any excuse for ignorance of the liturgy or for a misunderstanding of it. In the past, many priests have nourished a spirit of opposition to the liturgy simply because they have not understood its true nature. Unfortunately, the terminology of textbooks and of seminary catalogues helped to perpetuate the misunderstanding. Too many looked upon it as a sort of ecclesiastical "Emily Post," the great authority on how we should act when engaged in ceremonies. Rubrics were mistaken for liturgy. But with the help of Pius XII and his *Mediator Dei*, and in view of the great step made toward the participation of the faithful in his Instruction of September 3, 1958, we were well prepared for the beautiful unfolding of the liturgy in the Constitution promulgated by Paul VI on December 4, 1963. This document must be the priest's *vademecum*. He must put aside former prejudices and see the changes as vast strides forward in the people's intelligent worship of God. He will see how the grant of the vernacular has made the rites of the Church so much more meaningful. He may disagree with this or that translation, but he will realize that we are going through a period of transition and experimentation, and he will exercise patience. But he simply must know the liturgy in all the facets shown in the Council's Constitution and apply it, if his ministry is to lead his people to give more adequate "praise to God, the Father and the Son and the Holy Spirit."

6) In treating of the priest's shared office of ruling, the Decree carefully avoids any suggestion of the priest's lording it over his flock; it stresses rather the relationship of father to those whom he or another like him has begotten through Baptism. Indeed, whatever authority he has is derived from the bishop and is exercised in the bishop's name. Conscious that he is another Christ, he will have Christ as his model in his dealings with men. He will try to direct all, the good and faithful, the wayward, the poor and lowly in a special way, the young and the married to true Christian maturity; the sick and the dying he will console and strengthen. There must be no patronizing air about his ministrations; in all his dealings he must be the Christlike shepherd, kindly and loving.

An especially important responsibility will be the formation of a genuine Christian community, the parish, for the priest's ministry is not confined to individuals. This community will avoid a narrow parochialism; it will be outgoing in its interests and activities, contributing to the spiritual and civic welfare of the larger community in which it resides, and going beyond that to the problems of the Church universal and of the world; it will manifest a missionary zeal. Its common basis and source of power will be in the celebration of the Holy Eucharist. By charity, prayer, example and works of penance—the penance which we need so sorely in our affluent and materialistic society—this Christian community can be a powerful force for the extension of God's kingdom. The priest, in all this work, must carefully shun the political arena.

II. *Priests as Related to Others*

7) The Decree points out in this section the very close tie that binds bishops and priests together. The priest has received his consecration at the hands of the bishop; his mission likewise comes from the bishop. Thanks to the Council's Constitution on the Sacred Liturgy, this unity can now be manifested in a most excellent way in concelebration of the Mass where, in close resemblance to the gathering of the Apostles around the Master at the Last Supper, priests gather around the immediate source of their powers and their mission to perform the highest action of their lives. It is incumbent on bishops to acknowledge priests as their necessary helpers and counselors in the ministry and in the task of teaching, sanctifying and directing the People of God. The bishop alone simply cannot fulfill all his duties to his flock; he must have these helpers. This point is brought out more than once in the rite of ordination. In the preface, which follows the essential act of the imposition of the bishop's hand (the matter of the sacrament), the bishop says, "Having appointed bishops to rule Thy people, Thou didst choose, as their companions and helpers, men next in rank and dignity. Thus, in the desert, didst Thou spread the spirit of Moses by means of the wisdom of the seventy elders, through whose assistance he governed with ease countless multitudes of Thy people. . . . So also, O Lord, didst thou associate with the Apostles of Thy Son teachers of the faith, through

whom they have filled the whole world with their successful preaching. Wherefore, we beseech thee, O Lord, grant us also the same helps to our weakness, which, inasmuch as it is greater than theirs, stands so much the more in need of such assistance. . . . May they be prudent fellow-workers with us." The bishop, therefore, should look upon his priests as brothers and friends; he should have at heart their material and especially their spiritual welfare. The Decree places a special obligation on the bishop with regard to continued spiritual formation of the priest. Hence, the bishop must, first of all, know his priests; he must know the milieu in which he is placing them. He must arrange for an annual retreat which will be a truly fruitful period of spiritual rejuvenation. He should encourage those who seek, from time to time, a period of closed retreat when they can more truly give themselves over to prayer, recollection and self-examination. He will likewise make available periodic days of recollection when his priests, freed from duty for the day, can enliven the spirit of their priesthood.

Very importantly, for ease of relationship as well as for the material and spiritual benefit of the priest, there must be a fatherly openness on the part of the bishop in order that there may be that open channel of communication for which there is such a clamor nowadays on every level in the Church and in the world at large. The Decree recommends here the establishment of a group or senate of priests. Already, in this country, a number of bishops have set in motion the organization of such representative bodies. Doubtlessly we shall see this organization take many forms. In some dioceses a number of assistants, elected by their fellows, are added to the board of diocesan consultors. Presumably, these men will meet with all or a large number of their fellow priests from time to time, so as to know and to be able to voice at the consultors' meetings the opinions of the whole group. Frequent "seminars" might be held in which, through free dialogue, complaints and criticisms may be aired in a spirit of Christian charity and where suggestions and solutions of problems may be proposed. It must be remembered always that this "communication" is a two-way street: the bishop must have his opportunity to voice his own complaints and criticisms, and he should have a right to expect a respectful hearing and hearty cooperation. Nor must he consult all his priests on all problems. There are times, indeed, when the bishop, by reason of circumstances, must carry certain burdens alone and make certain decisions alone. On these occasions he has a right to the trust and confidence of his priests. Generally, this trust will be shown according to the measure of the bishop's customary openness with his priests.

On their part, priests, as Christian gentlemen marked in a special way with the seal of the Holy Spirit, must respect in the bishop the authority of the chief Shepherd, Christ. In charity and obedience—an obedience which today is customarily a reasoned and reasonable yielding of one's own will—they will support their bishop and cooperate with him. The goal we all have in common of spreading the Kingdom of God on earth is too vast and far too important for us to risk failure by petty carping and criticism and by undercutting the authority of those to whom we owe our priesthood and on whom our mission depends.

8) By ordination all priests are intimately joined in a sacramental brotherhood. We are priests of the universal Church, but, for most, the exercise of the priestly ministry is confined to a particular diocese. This ministry takes on many forms: most priests do their work in parishes; some are engaged in scientific research, whether it be in the sacred or profane sciences; for many the classroom is their parish; still others must work for the glory of God behind a desk; and so through countless forms of the priestly apostolate. At this point the Decree makes an interesting reference to priests who by manual labor share in the lot of the workers themselves—"if there seems to be need for this and competent authority approves." Here we have conciliar approval of an apostolate which has had its difficulties and dangers and which has created considerable controversy. The Decree emphasizes the fact that extra precautions are necessary in this form of apostolate. Whatever the form of apostolate, the priest must never forget that he is a priest and that in his own way he is building up Christ's Body.

With the idea of brotherhood always in mind, priests must keep and foster an unexceptionable *esprit de corps*. At ordinations, priests welcome the newly ordained by imposing hands after the bishop; they also now have the opportunity to concelebrate, a most impressive sign of the unity of the priesthood. These symbols of unity must be constantly realized as priests live out their ministry in a bond of charity, prayer and cooperation, religious and diocesan alike, shoulder to shoulder in the great task that is theirs.

In any consideration of priestly brotherhood, an inevitable topic is the relationship of the old with the young, of pastors with assistants. Here we meet very real problems, problems which at times admit of no easy solutions; the fault often lies on both sides. The new breath of air blowing in the Church today should help to solve many of these problems; at the same time we are obliged to admit that the present changes in the Church enhance some of these problems. Pastors should take a paternal interest in the young priests who are sent to them; they should guide them in their first steps in the ministry, not patronizingly, but with wisdom and delicacy. It is not too much to say that a young priest can be made or broken by his first pastor. Unfortunately, some older priests have forgotten the years of their own apprenticeship, have become set in their ways and look upon the new assistant as a threat to their popularity and to their consecrated way of doing things. On his part, the young priest should defer to the age and experience of the pastor, seek his advice and follow his directions. As between bishops and their priests, so, too, between pastors and their assistants there should be free and steady communication. Assistants should not forget that pastors have also served their period of apprenticeship and have experienced much the same trials that they are now experiencing. Forbearance must be the slogan on both sides.

In large dioceses where assistants must see the hope of a pastorate deferred until middle age and beyond, there is an inevitable feeling of frustration. How good it would be if we could all know ourselves well enough to lay down the burden when we can no longer carry it effectively and make way for a younger and stronger successor. This is a knotty problem and, involved as it is with human sensitivities, it cannot be easily solved.

One of the priest's most effective helps is to be found in association with fellow priests. Without prejudice to a cordial and humane relationship with the lay people whom he serves, the priest should regularly seek his recreation with fellow priests. The Decree recommends some form of community life, a suggestion which is realized or can be realized among us in rectory life as we have it in this country. It is the priest who drifts away from his fellows who causes concern, particularly if he becomes a "loner." His fellow priests should immediately reach out to him, to make him feel wanted and to protect him with all the graces and advantages of the brotherhood. For those who have already defected from their priesthood there should be the fellowship of prayer; moreover, an effort should be made "to keep in touch," due awareness being given, where marriage has been attempted, to the danger of risking civil lawsuits. Frequent gatherings for discussion of priestly topics and problems are also suggested. With the superabundance of printed material on every aspect of the Church's life available today in books and reviews, it is physically impossible for a priest to keep abreast. Would it not be fruitful for priests to organize into some kind of "journal club" in which individuals would accept the responsibility for covering certain specified journals or reviews of books, so that in the general meetings there could be a pooling and sharing of the information? Discussion could then be nourished with up-to-date thinking to the benefit of all concerned.

9) The Decree now turns to the priest's relations with the laity. In his dealings with the People of God the priest is at once a brother and father and teacher. As a baptized Christian, a member of the royal priesthood of the laity, the priest is a brother among brothers; as one who has received the further consecration of Holy Orders, he is set to lead his people as father and teacher. In both functions his watchword must be service: he is appointed *for* men, not for his own aggrandizement. Moreover, if his service is to be effective and if he is to join the laity to himself in the common task of upbuilding the Body of Christ, he must realize here, as in his other relationships, the absolute need of open communication. We would all have to agree that the vast potential of the laity has hardly been tapped. Only now, with the guidelines set down clearly in the laity's own Decree (on the Apostolate of the Laity) do all of us have the unmistakable mandate before us. Already the Constitution on the Sacred Liturgy is making its own contribution in a greater participation in the worship of God by the laity as a whole and as individuals. These beginnings will undoubtedly open the way to greater understanding and to a more fruitful use of the many talents and charisms to be found among the people. There are many

details of the priestly ministry in parishes for which many a priest is ill-prepared: details of real estate, construction, the handling of finances, various legal problems; at the same time, he will generally have specialists available in his own flock who can be of untold help and who can save him from many a mistake. With such aid he can intensify his more truly apostolic efforts.

By example, above all, the priest will lead his people. But he will try to know them better as individuals that he may minister to their particular needs. The day of "the parlor-call priest" has long since passed; the priest must go out to his people, seeking those who have fallen away, caring for the poor and the sick in body and mind. Their problems must be his problems. He should be able to make his own the words of the Good Shepherd: "I know mine and mine know me" (Jn. 10:14 *C*).

The cordial interfaith atmosphere created by the Council's Decree on Ecumenism adds further possibilities to the priest's ministry, and he should take every advantage of them. Nor will he close his heart to the non-Christians with whom he comes in contact. He will be guided in all these relations by his Ordinary's directives.

If the priest observes a free and open communication with his people, there will be little difficulty about receiving a trusting response from them. Their respect and cooperation will truly mean a common shouldering of the common task.

III. *The Distribution of Priests and Priestly Vocations*

10) Although the priest's ministry will be regularly and normally centered on his work in the parish or on his particular assignment in the diocese, he must not be narrowly parochial in his outlook. He must have a concern for the needs of the Church universal. This concern will have to be developed henceforth in the seminary, where the young aspirant's gaze will be directed to the priest-starved areas of the Church. The Church in America is under a heavy debt to the Europeans who laid firm foundations for the flourishing structure we know today. Now that we have come of age, we must show a recognition of that debt by being sincerely missionary-minded. Happily, many an American diocese already has representatives abroad, most of them in Latin American countries. Dioceses and even parishes are adopting missionary parishes. Some of the details which will govern this new situation will be left to the commission entrusted with the compilation of a new Code of Canon Law; other details will remain to be worked out by the relevant authorities in Rome; still other recommendations, in the realm of the practical, are brought out by this Decree: the sending of at least two or three priests to a new field of labor; the absolute need of adequate linguistic and cultural preparation; concern for their spiritual life as well as for their mental and bodily health.

11) The Decree, at the conclusion of Chapter II, turns its attention to vocations, a topic also treated in the Decree on Priestly Formation. The same point

is made in both documents, namely that the task of fostering vocations devolves on the whole Christian community. This responsibility demands, first of all, that the community live in a fully Christian way, for it is chiefly in such an atmosphere that vocations will flourish. Priests, by their ministry of the Word and by their dedication to service in a spirit of paschal joy, will bespeak the excellence and necessity of the priesthood. It is their example, above all, that will attract aspirants from the young men in their charge. They should carefully look for the marks of a vocation and gently direct those who manifest these signs. They should be ready with spiritual direction, nor should their interest in the aspirants lag once the young men are in the seminary. As the seminarian advances, the priest should encourage him in brotherly fashion. Parents and teachers should also make a real contribution. Never should parents raise obstacles to the pursuit of a priestly or religious vocation.

CHAPTER THREE/THE LIFE OF PRIESTS

I. *The Priestly Call to Perfection*

12) Before his ordination to the priesthood placed special demands upon him, the priest was already called to perfection by his initiation through Baptism as a member of the Christian community. It was not to future priests alone, but to all His disciples that Christ said, "You therefore are to be perfect, even as your heavenly father is perfect" (Mt. 5:48 C). But, since the priest represents the person of Christ Himself, the challenge is all the greater for him, and he is enriched with special grace to answer that challenge. Their everyday sacred actions and their entire ministry direct them toward perfection of life. Holiness of life is essential if their priesthood is to be really effective. The Council, through this Decree, urges priests to use the appropriate means endorsed by the Church to attain that sanctity which will make them increasingly useful instruments in the service of all God's people. A note in the official text reminds us of the classical documents issued by the popes of this century regarding priestly holiness. It cites St. Pius X's "Exhortation to the Clergy" (*Haerent animo*), which stands as a great gift to priests on the occasion of the saintly Pontiff's golden jubilee of priesthood; it refers to Pius XI's *Ad catholici sacerdotii* of 1935; it recalls Pius XII's detailed exposition of the development of priestly holiness in his *Menti nostrae* of 1950; and it lists, finally, John XXIII's *Sacerdotii nostri primordia* of 1959. The contents of these documents has not become outmoded; their clear words of advice and exhortation should form a part of the modern priest's spiritual reading and furnish material for his mental prayer.

13) It is, above all, in and from the very exercise of their ministry that priests should develop holiness of life. As preachers of the Word of God, they should themselves be imbued with the lessons which that Word teaches. Their prayerful study of the Word will enrich their own contemplation as they prepare

the message for their people. Their celebration of the Sacrifice of the Mass should be the center of each day and the source of daily Christian living. "Imitate what you handle," priests were told on ordination day; the rest of their lives should be a fulfillment of that advice. A quotation of some length from Paul VI's encyclical *Mysterium Fidei* occurs at this point as a note in the official text, urging fidelity to the daily celebration of Mass whether the faithful are present or not, for "no Mass is a private thing; it is an act of Christ and the Church. . . . The fact is that every Mass which is celebrated is offered not for the salvation of ourselves alone, but for the salvation of the whole world."

In their sacramental ministry priests are joined with the intention and love of Christ. The Decree adds here a word of exhortation toward a generous readiness on the part of the priest to hear confessions as often as the faithful reasonably request it. There should be more than "office hours" on Saturdays and eves of holy days.

By the recitation of the Divine Office the priest not only nourishes his own prayer life, but he acts as spokesman for all his people and all humanity; he makes himself one with Christ who "lives always to make intercession for us" (Heb. 7:25 C).

Service must be the byword for the priest. His people will come first in his thoughts, prayers and actions; their convenience, not his, will be the dictating principle.

14) The Decree acknowledges the feverish activity of modern life and sees the priest involved in the same vortex as his fellow men; it realizes that the priest, in seeking an interior life, will have difficulties of adjustment. It offers a solution by pointing to Christ Himself whose food was to do the will of Him who sent Him to accomplish His work. Doing the will of the Father and dedicating himself wholeheartedly to the flock committed to him will be the priest's surest path to perfection.

Throughout his ministry the priest will act always in union with his bishop and with his brother priests. By this loyalty to the Church he best shows his loyalty to Christ; he will find the unity of his own life in the very unity of the Church's mission.

II. *Special Spiritual Needs of the Priestly Life*

15) In this section the Decree singles out three specific needs in the priest's life: humble obedience; celibacy; a spirit of poverty. If, as the Decree pointed out in the preceding section, God's will is to be the guiding light of the priest's life and ministry, the priest must acknowledge that will as it is interpreted for him by his lawful superiors. As a priest, he is part of a hierarchical community; his ministry is not his own, but the ministry of the Church herself. "Therefore pastoral love demands that acting in this communion (with the whole Church), priests dedicate their own wills through obedience to the service of God and their brothers." In practice this means obedience to the Sovereign Pontiff, their

own bishop or other superiors. Obedience does not rule out the open communication mentioned earlier, but it demands ultimate acceptance of the judgment of those who exercise the chief responsibility for governing the Church of God.

16) The Decree now broaches the subject which has recently been debated in the public prints: celibacy. In a letter addressed to Cardinal Tisserant, the senior president of the Council, and read on October 11, 1965, Pope Paul VI informed the Council that he intends not only to preserve the ancient law of celibacy of the clergy of the Latin-rite Church, but also "to reinforce its observance." Thus, in effect, the Pope removed the subject of celibacy from the competence of the Council. The Pope said that he wanted to express his own opinion "without impeding in any way the liberty of the Fathers." Although he wrote that "Public debate is not opportune on this subject which is so important and which demands such profound prudence," he left the way open for Fathers still wishing to express their views to submit them in writing to the Council's Presidency for transmission to him personally for his "attentive examination before God." The papal announcement was met with prolonged applause, a manifestation of the agreement of the vast majority with the Holy Father's stand. Commenting on the treatment of celibacy in this Decree, Archbishop Guilford C. Young, of Hobart, Tasmania, writes in *The Documents of Vatican II*, edited by Walter M. Abbott, S.J., published by Guild Press, New York: "To a world cynical of man's capability of virtuous sex, and cynical even of its desirability, the Church calmly restates the high value she places on the centuries-old tradition of perfect continence for her priests" (p. 530). The Decree is careful to exclude the Eastern Churches, in which the discipline is different. It acknowledges that celibacy is not demanded by the very nature of the priesthood, but recalls that perfect and perpetual continence for the sake of the Kingdom of Heaven was recommended by Christ and has been gladly embraced and praiseworthily observed down through the years and in our days, too, by many Christians. Thus priests are consecrated to Christ in a new way. They more easily hold fast to Him with undivided heart.

Much has been written on celibacy in recent months. Much of what has been written against its requirement for Latin-rite priests has been colored with emotionalism, romanticism or unrealism. Marriage is presented often as paradise on earth without any advertence to the very real sacrifices demanded of the married couples. The sexual aspects are magnified beyond all proportion and the priest is pictured as love-starved, unfulfilled, really only half a man. Although figures are quoted which are calculated to give the impression that the vast majority of priests are straining to break the bonds of celibacy, the experience of many priests is that they do not meet these thousands who allegedly are groaning under their burden. That there is a problem for some, and perhaps for many, cannot be denied, but that the general abolition of celibacy in the Western Church is the answer is not clear. One tends to think that the yen for freedom which makes some priests wish to be relieved of the burden of celibacy will, in time, make these same men yearn for freedom from the marriage bond.

At all events, the Holy Father has made the question merely academic at this time. Hence the Decree exhorts priests to hold fast to sacred celibacy magnanimously and wholeheartedly. They are urged to make use of all the supernatural and natural helps available to remain faithful. It likewise asks the prayerful help of all the faithful that God may always lavish this gift on His Church abundantly.

17) The Decree now moves on to a discussion of the spirit of poverty and detachment from the world. The treatment is positive and realistic, recognizing the right use of the world and its goods, but emphasizing the priest's obligation to keep himself free from the allurements of our material and affluent world. The objectives of the priest's life will determine his attitude toward temporal goods. He will also be careful of the Church's goods, availing himself in their management of the help of laymen experienced in financial affairs.

The Decree recognizes the right of priests and bishops to a decent livelihood and to an adequate compensation for their services, but it warns against the use of ecclesiastical office for personal profit or for the advantage of one's own family. It is interesting to note that the Fathers of the Council included themselves in this section, lest they seem to be imposing demands on their priests which they themselves were not ready to meet.

Priests must not attach their hearts to riches; they must avoid all greediness and carefully abstain from any appearance of merchandising.

It happens at times that a priest, because of a legitimate anxiety about old age and infirmity, will begin to save his money. From praiseworthy prudence he may move on to miserliness, until the saving of money becomes an obsession. He may "play the market." Soon his heart becomes as hard as the gold he is hoarding. The cares and needs of his people fade from his view, and he becomes wrapped up in self. His priestliness is gone and his effectiveness becomes nil. Although not frequent, this development can occur and must be recognized as a danger.

The Decree recommends voluntary poverty. It also recalls the communion of goods of the early Church, described in the Acts of the Apostles.

The section is concluded with a general reminder, again to bishops as well as priests, to avoid whatever would offend the poor in any way. Specifically mentioned is the kind of dwelling they should have, the kind that will appear closed to no one and which no one will fear to visit, even the humblest.

III. *Aids to Priestly Life*

18) The Decree, in its discussion of aids to priestly life, turns first to "those means, common and particular, new and old, which the Spirit of God never ceases to stir up in the People of God and which the Church commends and, indeed, at times commands for the sanctification of her members." It emphasizes immediately the two great sources of spiritual nourishment: the Word of God and the Eucharist. These two poles of the Church's life, already recog-

nized as all-important, have been given even greater significance in Vatican II. That they are essential to the priest's spiritual life needs no elaboration.

Although the priest's sacramental ministry is primarily for the benefit of the faithful in his charge, he is reminded that he himself must never overlook the graces of the sacraments for himself. This reminder is needed particularly with regard to the sacrament of Penance for, as Pius XII warned priests in *Menti nostrae*, it can easily happen that the minister of reconciliation may himself grow careless about the reception of this sacrament.

In two paragraphs of the official Latin text at this point, the Decree includes all the spiritual exercises, with one exception, which are laid down for clerics in Canons 125 and 126 of the Code of Canon Law: frequent confession; daily mental prayer; daily visit to the Blessed Sacrament; daily examination of conscience; annual retreat. The one exception is daily recitation of the rosary, which is omitted obviously because, in the Eastern Churches, Our Lady is honored by other prayer forms (the Decree, of course, is intended for the priests of the whole Church). Priests are urged, however, to make the Blessed Virgin Mary their model and to show the devotion and veneration of sons to this mother of the Supreme and Eternal Priest, this Queen of the Apostles and protectress of their ministry.

Spiritual reading as a means of nourishing faith, mental prayer, various forms of private prayer and conversation with Christ in daily visits of personal devotion to the Most Holy Eucharist are stressed as great helps to priestly living, but nowhere does the Decree express a preference for any one school of spirituality.

19) Here we have an acknowledgment of the importance of study for the priest. Emphasis is first placed on the study of the sacred sciences, Scripture and theology, and the necessity of being well acquainted with the documents of the Church's teaching authority, the Councils and the Roman Pontiffs; but the Decree urges likewise that priests keep abreast of developments in human affairs. They must be able to undertake discussions with their contemporaries.

Lest this whole area of intellectual advancement be left to chance, the Council places a responsibility on bishops to provide opportunities for priestly study: the establishment of courses or congresses, of centers of pastoral study, of accessible libraries and so on. They should also be concerned with the training of genuine theologians for the continued education of seminarians and priests and to have experts who can, among clergy and laity, serve for the advancement of theological knowledge.

20) Very practical matters engage our attention as the Decree nears its conclusion. Even given the spirit of detachment and the voluntary poverty which the Decree earlier recommends, it still remains that the priest must live. The responsibility rests generally on the faithful, and bishops are obliged to remind them of this duty. There should be equitable remuneration, more, surely, than just enough for the priests to eke out a living; he has others whom he must reimburse for their services, and he should be in a position to help the

needy. The priest is likewise entitled to enough for a reasonable vacation each year.

A call is made for the reform or abolition of the system of benefices, a system that is alien to our American customs, but which still obtains in some places in the Old World.

21) Once again the Decree recalls the example of the early Church where "they had all things in common" (Acts 4:32 C) and "distribution was made to each according as anyone had need" (Acts 4:35 C). An appeal is made to that practice of charity within a diocese or among dioceses which will make for the establishment of common funds, an arrangement whereby wealthier parishes or dioceses can help parishes or dioceses in need. The application of this suggestion would be tangible evidence, indeed, that we had reached Christian maturity.

Social security is mentioned. In this country priests are eligible for social security. They should inform themselves regarding the benefits and the procedures to be followed. Moreover, in these days of frightening medical and hospital costs, priests should know and take advantage of available medical and hospitalization insurance plans; older priests should enroll in Medicare. The Decree itself considers, more particularly, diocesan or interdiocesan organizations for the various forms of clergy relief and asks the cooperation of priests in support of these projects. In this country today, however, it is difficult and perhaps unnecessary for such ecclesiastical organizations to compete with professional or governmental agencies. In practice, priests will be guided by suggestions or instructions from the Chancery office. At all events, anxiety about the future, referred to earlier, can be fairly well eliminated, and the priest can be free to dedicate himself wholeheartedly to the welfare of souls and to practice the voluntary poverty recommended by the Decree.

CONCLUSION AND EXHORTATION

22) In concluding, the Decree takes an honest look at the world about us. It acknowledges the difficulties which beset a priest with the rapidly occurring transformations in economic and social conditions and even in the customs of men. It recognizes that a priest can become depressed in the face of modern obstacles blocking the faith and can feel that his past labors have come to naught. He may feel a bitter loneliness from his difficulty or even inability to communicate with this changing world. The Decree takes an optimistic view: in spite of its many sins, the world is not all bad; there is a vast amount of good will abroad in the world and an array of talents which can be used for the building up of God's Church. And the priest is not alone. He has his brother priests and he has the faithful, his own and those of the whole world. With the eyes of faith he will look beyond the material things that tie men down to earth to the great hope of what is to come.

The Council "rejoices that the earth has been sown with the seeds of the Gospel and now bears fruit in many places under the influence of the Spirit. He it is who fills the whole earth and has stirred up a true missionary spirit in the hearts of many priests and faithful. For all of these blessings, this most holy Synod gives most loving thanks to all the priests of the world."

XIII/DECREE ON THE CHURCH'S MISSIONARY ACTIVITY

Decree on the Church's Missionary Activity
✠ HISTORICAL INTRODUCTION

The schema on the missionary activity of the Church holds the distinction of being the only document of the Council that was introduced to the Council Fathers by the Holy Father himself. During the 116th general congregation, on November 6, 1964, the discussion on the Church in the modern world was interrupted, and Pope Paul VI took a precedent-shattering action. He entered St. Peter's basilica, assisted at the celebration of the sacred liturgy in the Ethiopian rite and took his place at the table of the Presidency to introduce the draft document on the missions. He said he was doing so because of "our most ardent desire to be present at an assembly of the ecumenical Council" and introduced the missionary schema with these words:

> Examining the schema which you have in your hands, in which this subject is treated, we have found many things worthy of our praise, both as to the contents as well as to the order of their presentation. We believe, therefore, that the text will be easily approved by you even after having noted the necessity of final improvement.

The Holy Father was the victim of some very bad counsel. Little did he know at that moment the great dissatisfaction among the Council Fathers over the truncated document. On the following day Bishop Daniel Lamont of Umtali, Rhodesia, delivered his famous "dry bones" speech in which he expressed the sentiments of many Council Fathers concerning the schema. He declared:

> We looked to the Council for a pentecostal light which would illumine the minds of men throughout the world—they have lighted this little candle for us! We asked for modern weapons against the fiery darts of paganism—they offered us in this schema bows and arrows. We asked them for bread and they gave us, I do not say a stone, but a few cold propositions from a tract on missiology.

Throughout three congregations 28 Council Fathers spoke on the schema, voicing an almost unanimous criticism of the text. Most of the speakers criticized its failure to grasp the essential missionary aspect of the Church itself; for perpetuating an untheological distinction between the Church and the missions, for the proposal to establish a central missionary commission under the Congregation for the Propagation of the Faith. One Father suggested that even the title of that congregation should be changed and called, rather, the Congregation for New Churches.

Auxiliary Bishop Fulton J. Sheen of New York was the final Council Father to speak on the subject. Speaking on November 9, he suggested that, instead of posing the theological question regarding the nature of the missions, "we turn to the practical question: 'Where are the missions?'" He pointed out "that the doctrine of the collegiality of bishops imposes on us a missionary responsibility, not only for territories which were defined as missionary three hundred years ago, but also 'for the salvation of the whole world.'" He added that bishops "must not enter into a dispute about what is a missionary territory and what is not, or who belongs to this congregation or to that congregation." He then expressed his own pleasure with the establishment of a central commission for spreading the Gospel, calling it "the true Catholic solution to this problem of the diversity of mission." The second part of his intervention was an eloquent plea for the Church to identify itself more closely with poverty. He said:

> I beg you most earnestly, Venerable Fathers, that the notion of poverty be strongly affirmed in this Council.
>
> Put your finger on the 30th Parallel; run it around a globe of the earth, lifting it slightly above China. What do you find?
>
> Practically all of the prosperity is above the 30th Parallel, and the greater part of the poverty of the world is beneath the 30th Parallel, that is, in Africa, Asia and Latin America.
>
> As chastity was the fruit of the Council of Trent, and obedience the fruit of the First Vatican Council, so may the spirit of poverty be the fruit of this Second Vatican Council.
>
> We live in a world, in which 200 million people would willingly take the vow of poverty tomorrow, if they could live as well, eat as well, be clothed as well, and be housed as well as I am—or even some who take the vow of poverty.
>
> The greater number of bishops in this Council are living in want or in persecution, and they come from all peoples and nations.
>
> As only a wounded Christ could convert a doubting Thomas, so only a Church wounded by poverty can convert a doubting world.

During the 118th congregation, the Secretary General, Archbishop Felici, posed the question that the majority of the Council Fathers had been waiting for since the very day the schema was introduced. He asked them to vote on whether or not the schema should be returned to the Commission for revision. The response was 1,601 in favor of so doing, and only 311 against it. Thus the document went back to the Commission which had already spent countless hours in preparing a text.

On October 24, 1960, the preparatory Commission on the Missions was established and immediately the members were divided into five subcommissions. Gregorio Pietro Cardinal Agagianian, the prefect of the Congregation for the Propagation of the Faith, was the president of both the preparatory and conciliar commissions on the missions. The members and consultors of the Commission performed much of its work at home because of the great distances many of them would have to travel to meet together. Among this group were two American consultors: the Reverend Timothy L. Bouscaren, S.J., and the Reverend Amand Reuter, O.M.I. Nevertheless, the preparatory Commission met in two plenary sessions, once from April 17 to 26, and again from November 20 to 30 in 1961. The Commission had drafted seven schemata which were presented to the Central Preparatory Commission during its fifth session, from March 28 to 31, 1962. The subjects of the seven schemata were: 1) life in the missions; 2) liturgy in the missions; 3) discipline of the clergy; 4) discipline of the Christian people; 5) missionary cooperation; 6) seminary studies; 7) missionary members of religious communities. The Central Coordinating Commission returned the missionary schemata to the Commission for emendation.

On this original schema, Cardinal Spellman, as a member of the Central Preparatory Commission, submitted his observations in writing. He praised the schema in general and singled out for special merit the request in the introduction that there be fewer cases seeking recourse to the Holy See. He said this was well stated for two reasons: "lest mission rule be harmfully impeded as a consequence of immoderate delay, and lest the Sacred Office be burdened by too much work often of lesser importance to the detriment of the business of the whole Church." He also favored the schema's suggestion that faculties of the missionary ordinaries be increased.

He did, however, have several reservations concerning the matter in the schema. While approving the granting of the faculty to missionary bishops to use the vernacular in their dealings with the Holy See, he wanted to see the same faculty extended to ordinaries in all parts of the world. "Great difficulty and loss of time," he wrote, "is had in making translations in mission lands, and these same reasons are scarcely altogether lacking elsewhere, especially because of the immense daily bulk of work in the courts of dioceses with a great number of people and because of the customary lack of clergy for pastoral work." The Cardinal also objected to the suggestion in the schema that, in missionary dioceses, a third of the diocesan consultors are to be selected by priests of every rank. He called the proposal "simply unacceptable" and added:

Is this not a question of whether the bishops are able to nominate, as their consultors, priests who are distinguished by their piety, behavior, teaching and prudence? Although, perhaps, it complies with some spirit of democracy, the possible most unfortunate consequences of this innovation can give place to dangers even outside of missionary dioceses.

During the opening days of the Council, Bishop Sheen was elected to serve as a member of the conciliar Commission on the Missions. This group met for the first time on November 28, even though at the time no definite procedures were determined. After Pope John had published his directives for carrying on the work of the Council between the sessions, the Commission on the Missions met in plenary session in Rome from March 20 to 29, 1963, to revise the previous schemata. At this time a new text was prepared containing an introduction, a concluding exhortation and two parts. The first part consisted of three chapters: 1) the general principles concerning the missions; 2) the sacred ministry in the missions on the part of both clergy and laity; 3) the government of the missions both regarding its relation to the Holy See as well as internally. The second part of the schema also contained three chapters: 1) promotion of the missionary obligations; 2) cooperation among bishops, priests, and religious; and 3) cooperation among the laity. This text was presented to the Central Coordinating Commission, was examined by it in June, 1963, and was returned to the Commission for emendations.

At this point it was announced that the Theological Commission had prepared a special section concerning the missionary nature of the Church for the Dogmatic Constitution on the Church. This text was examined by the Commission on the Missions and approved by it. During this time it was also decided by the Commission to leave the theological foundations concerning the mission of the Church to the schema on the Church. The text concerning seminary training was also submitted to the Commission on the Missions for its suggestions and approval. Thus the missionary schema underwent another revision and was approved by 23 of the members of the Commission, with one voting disapproval, on December 3, 1963. The new schema consisted of an introduction and four chapters: 1) doctrinal principles; 2) the general notions of the missionary apostolate; 3) missionary formation; and 4) missionary cooperation. The Central Coordinating Commission approved this schema, distributed it to the Council Fathers and asked that they submit their observations on the text of the schema by March 31, 1964. Sixty-seven Council Fathers submitted their observations: 17 from Europe, 13 from America, 16 from Africa, and 20 from Asia.

On April 23, 1964, the commission was informed by the Secretary General of the Council that its schema should be reduced to a few essential propositions. The task was a staggering one, for the members of the Commission had a book of 283 pages of observations submitted by the Council Fathers on the previous text. Nonetheless, the task was performed chiefly under the direction of the vice-president of the Commission, Bishop Stanislaus Lokuang of Tainan, China, and on May 13 it received the unanimous vote of the Commission's members.

This text, consisting of an introduction and 13 propositions, was the one rejected by the Council Fathers during the third session.

Bishop Sheen was an active member of the Commission. He attended every Commission meeting, which occasioned at least three and sometimes four trips each year to Rome. He felt that the most significant work of the Commission was "enlarging the concept of missions beyond territories under the Propaganda and making the missions the burden of the *whole* Church." In the long view of history, he felt, the establishment of an international commission on the missions or an internationalization of the curia would be the most enduring contribution of the Commission's work. He felt also that the emphasis in the conciliar decree that bishops are consecrated *first* for the world and secondly for their own diocese will be one of the most lasting fruits of the Commission's efforts.

During this time Bishop Sheen also submitted five written interventions on the missionary schema. In one intervention he cited the statement in the schema declaring that "bishops are consecrated for the salvation of the whole world rather than for a particular diocese." He then added:

> Because of this, we will no longer consider the world as having a population explosion, but rather offering a "soul-explosion." The missions are not to be considered as orphans left abandoned at our doorstep, but as loving sons seated with us around a table.
>
> Let us not be like Jonas, who refused his mission to the Ninevites, lest we are forced to learn love for the missions in the stomach of a whale.
>
> What God has joined together—namely the Church and the missions— let no schema put asunder.

Suggesting that Christians consider the world, Bishop Sheen continued:

> We see a world in which there are millions of people who have not even heard of Christ or the Blessed Virgin. If these people would pass by in front of this basilica in single file, day and night, constantly, how long would it take for all of them to pass by? Thirty years!
>
> If all the hungry in the mission countries were to stretch out in a single file how many times would they encircle the world? Twenty-five times!
>
> In the world in which we live, there are 200,000,000 poor who would willingly take the vow of poverty tomorrow morning if they had the opportunity of eating, dressing and living as well as I do, and some of those who have taken the vow of poverty. From this it follows that the mission not only finds its origins in Christ, but also in the pains and sorrows of our brothers. With this spiritual and material poverty, a certain irony is detected in the second number of the schema, where missionaries are exhorted to be poor. Poor! They are submerged in poverty! They are members of the Church of the Poor! A great number of the bishops in this assembly live in poverty or under

persecution. If we were to add up the years spent in prison by bishops here today, for the defense of the faith, it would amount to hundreds.

In another written intervention, Bishop Sheen proposed that the title of the Sacred Congregation of the Propagation of the Faith should be changed because it "seems to obscure the end for which the Sacred Congregation is intended." He was against the present name for these reasons:

In the Western world (which reflects an English character) an entirely new meaning is given to the word propaganda. In the modern sense, propaganda is entirely different from evangelization.

Today the word propaganda denotes the imposition of ideas or of a certain erroneous ideology, while evangelization means the presentation of truth which is acceptable to all minds and hearts. According to Tertullian the mind is naturally Christian.

The use of the word propaganda which the Church uses is not much different from the ideological indoctrination by communists in free countries. Communists also use the word propaganda to intimate that certain counter-propaganda should be involved. . . .

Also it should be noted that the word propaganda has a certain offensive political meaning for Eastern people today. Propagation of the Faith of Christ is considered by many as an importation by the westerners of a certain religion or foreign ideology; these things are contrary to the nationalistic spirit growing in these regions.

To protect the sensibility of all people and to preclude the possibility of rejection of the Gospel, it would seem very opportune that a new title be attributed to the Congregation of the Propaganda of the Faith which would help it to eradicate divisions coming from nationality or color.

Congregation of Charity seems to us to be very appropriate. . . .

Bishop Sheen also submitted three interventions concerning the cooperation of bishops, priests and religious in the missionary activity of the Church. Concerning the missionary nature of the episcopacy, he wrote:

In apostolic times, there is no such thing as a missionary society in the Church, one which is distinct from the Church.

At this time there is only one society in the Church, namely, the Mystical Body of Christ.

The bishops were the missionaries, first, because they were consecrated for the whole Church, and then because of the divine mandate, of which they were the immediate heirs, to preach to all nations.

Nowhere in the New Testament is any mention made of a distinction between the Church and its missionary activity. The Church, in its every essence, is missionary. If, in the Church, any organization is given to the

Church, such an organization is ordained for fulfilling the mission of the Church throughout the whole world.

It is the obligation of the universal Church to offer help to the apostolate, and this must be explained independently of any historical cause, since it inheres in the episcopal office itself.

The bishop is consecrated for the whole world, and only by reason of jurisdiction is he committed to a small part of the world.

He then proposed that ordinaries in other than missionary lands send one diocesan priest for every hundred into the missions and that ordinaries of wealthy dioceses "should join together with other bishops in the episcopal conference and decide where donations are necessary to alleviate the indigence of other members of the Mystical Body of Christ." Finally, Bishop Sheen suggested the many pontifical societies engaged in soliciting donations for the welfare of the universal Church should all "be coordinated into a single society, namely, the Society for the Propagation of the Faith."

Concerning the missionary nature of the priesthood he wrote:

Priests are ordained for the ministry of the Church, just as bishops are consecrated for the whole Church, even if, because of law, they are assigned to a particular diocese. . . .

The distinction between "missionary" and "non-missionary" priests is merely geographical. Every priest, and, in fact, every bishop, is a missionary!

Therefore, the sacrifices demanded from the clergy to help the Pontifical Missionary Works, and also to sustain the missions he selects on his own, do not seem to suffice. The priest who is prepared for this ought freely to offer himself to the ordinary of the place in order to help those missions throughout the world which especially need clergy.

Bishop Sheen suggested that religious communities with members working in the missions submit an annual financial statement to the Congregation for the Propagation of the Faith "in order that there might be equity in the distribution of aid to those missions which are in need." He also suggested that religious communities in the missions should cooperate more closely in the educational and social apostolate in mission lands. He then wrote:

All religious societies or institutes, whether they be expressly missionary or simply religious, have been ordained for the good of the whole Church.

Just as the offerings of the faithful must be directed toward helping those members of the Church who suffer poverty, so also the members of all religious institutes must be prepared to fulfill the mission of the Church throughout the world.

Lest the merit of voluntary offerings be taken away, the Sacred Synod recommends that out of one hundred, at least ten members of every non-missionary institute be placed under the direct authority of the Supreme Pastor of the Church, to fulfill in far-off lands that mission which is deemed of great importance by the Sovereign Pontiff.

The Commission on the Missions returned to its work of drafting a new schema on November 13, 1964. At this meeting the members unanimously decided that an entirely new and complete schema should be drafted according to the recommendations of the Council Fathers. The new schema was drafted by a subcommission under the presidency of the Very Reverend Giovanni Schütte, S.V.D., Superior General of the Society of the Divine Word. The subcommission met from January 12 to 27, 1965, in the College of the Divine Word in Rome and redrafted the text according to the observations. This text was distributed to the members and consultors of the entire Commission who studied it before returning to a plenary session from March 29 to April 3, during which the new schema received its definitive form. The new text was, as Bishop Lamont would admit during the fourth session, "no longer a naked series of frigid propositions, but a solid body of doctrine." The thirteen propositions were expanded to 39 paragraphs in a booklet of 40 pages. It was by no means a perfect document, and yet, profiting greatly from the doctrinal content of the Constitution on the Church, it was a document superior to its predecessor.

The new text was approved by Pope Paul on May 28, 1965, and distributed to the Council Fathers through the mails. It was introduced on the floor of the Council again during the 144th congregation on October 7, 1965, by both Cardinal Agagianian and Father Schütte. The latter mentioned that it was drafted in the light of the 193 interventions submitted by the Fathers which were printed in a booklet of approximately 550 pages. Throughout the next four congregations it was discussed by 49 Fathers in the aula. During this period, no American prelate spoke on the document; however, three of them submitted their observations in writing.

Cardinal Spellman was most pleased with the revised schema because "the description of the missionary activity of the Church which is drawn from the perception of the Church as the 'sacrament of universal salvation' is most fruitful." He felt, however, that the treatment of the missionary vocation was still weak. "If the decree," he added, "is able to present more specific ideas about the nature of the missionary vocation and the psychological formation of missionaries, the whole Church will be greatly helped."

On October 12, the last day on which the schema was discussed in the Council, Lawrence Cardinal Shehan of Baltimore submitted his observations on two sections of the schema, the one dealing with the missionary duty of bishops, and the other with the missionary duty of the laity. He admitted that the bishops are the first missionaries in the Church and, as successors to the Apostles, have an obligation to assist the missions. He admitted, too, the urgency of the demand to send more priests and financial aid to the missions.

But the purpose of his intervention was to insist as well on the necessity "for trained lay helpers in the various fields of sociology, economics, technology and the like." The reasons for the need of lay helpers he explained in these words:

The Church's mission is primarily a spiritual mission, but she cannot ignore the fact that the men whom she sets out to evangelize live in a specific cultural environment, which *must first be prepared to receive the good news of salvation.* The end of missionary activity is to establish the local Church, which must be a particularization of the universal Church. The establishment of the local, visible Church demands a *relative social* and *economic strength* in order to survive, to carry on and to expand her apostolic ministry. Every missionary knows the difficulty of establishing the Church in an undeveloped or defective social system.

New emphases in the mission of the Church are evoked by the immediate needs and crises which arise in the society in which she is working. The Church grows up together with society, not outside it. . . . If those to be evangelized are one day to assume the total responsibility for the full life of the Church, they must achieve an economic, social and technical level compatible with such an objective.

In evolving societies the Church cannot afford to give the impression that she is indifferent to their temporal aspirations. She cannot and may not ignore these aspirations and surrender the realization of these hopes to materialistic and secularistic forces. The new nations are determined to acquire in a short time what has taken the western world centuries to achieve. In their zeal these nations are made susceptible to the seductions of a scientific and technical teaching which is often the tool of Communist subversion.

As these evolving societies struggle to industrialize and expand, many new moral and social problems are being created. Is the missionary Church prepared to offer solutions to these problems? Or must she stand off and watch while men pass by her in their fascination for the promises of immediate economic well-being. Must the missionary Church not get involved because her mission is primarily supernatural? Or must she keep in the forefront, having before her eyes always that "the building of the earthly city is founded on the Lord and is directed towards him" (*Lumen Gentium*, n. 46)?

The Church, then, has the duty to offer these new communities of God's People the substantial richness of her doctrine and her life as the "animator of a Christian social order" (Pius XII, *Fidei Donum*). Any delay in fulfilling this obligation could have serious consequences, for the Church could well witness in these new lands the alienation of the masses from her, as she had witnessed and is still witnessing in other parts of the world.

The Cardinal admitted that the major responsibility for this work rested upon governments and international agencies. He nonetheless insisted that missionaries, "and I speak principally of the lay missionaries whose proper task this is," should cooperate in every such venture and, where there exist no such programs, "they themselves will have to inaugurate such programs of social change." He praised the schema for commending the layman's cooperation in the establishment of institutions which aim at improving the fundamental structures of social life in mission countries. "But who," he asked, "is to organize, to recruit, to train such laymen?" His answer was the conclusion of his intervention:

> The section on the missionary duty of bishops should correlatively stress the need for the "home bishops" to train experts in the social, economic and technical fields for work in the missionary apostolate of the Church. This should be one of the express tasks of the various episcopal conferences: to discover from the conferences in the mission Church what are their needs, and then to train experts in the various fields to fill these specific needs.
>
> The missionary Church cannot escape involvement in the social and cultural development of its people. These are necessary for building up the strength of the local Church. The best guarantee of an intensive and integral missionary effort is the awareness of the collegial responsibility for the evangelization of the non-Christian world.

Bishop Sheen submitted a final intervention on the final draft of the schema. It is a significant intervention for several reasons. First of all, it is the longest single intervention submitted by any American on any schema, consisting of 61 double-spaced typewritten pages. Secondly, it is the most detailed of any American intervention, taking the text of the schema, chapter by chapter, verse by verse, and almost literally word by word. It would be impossible here to give a detailed analysis of the document; a few of its many salient points must suffice.*

First of all, Bishop Sheen suggested that the title of the schema be changed for these reasons:

> a) because this title makes "mission" a certain function of the Mystical Body, rather than its essential nature;
>
> b) because in the title it is assumed that "missionary activity" is *elective*, dependent upon the good will of the members, and not *prescriptive*, that is, founded upon our union with Christ;
>
> c) because it smacks of a pre-conciliar and juridical notion, that is, missionary activity is considered as that activity pertaining to a certain congregation rather than to the collegiality of the bishops and to the People of God. Finally, it is far from the idea of the Church found in the Acts of the Apostles where the Missions and the Church are one and the same.

* It is this writer's intention to make a comparative study of this intervention by Bishop Sheen and the text of the Decree in a future publication.

He said that he much preferred calling the schema simply "Concerning the Missionary Church" because

a) The Church has no mission except the mission of Christ, and the mission of Christ is directed to the world: "God so loved the world that he gave his only begotten Son" (Jn 3:16).

b) Such a title would manifest the truth of the assertion: "What God has joined—namely the Church and missions—no man can separate."

Later in his intervention, Bishop Sheen urged the Council to establish a World Council of Missions which would have three objectives: "to avoid the scandal of division and the multiplication of organizations; to affirm the responsibility of the *whole* Church for the *whole* world; to foster the ecumenical spirit." He then suggested that such an organization would have the following functions:

1) It will coordinate and unify missionary activities which are now separated as regards geography, rite and historical traditions.

2) It will promote efficient cooperation and united action in the evangelization of the world among churches, episcopal conferences and other Christian communities.

3) It will unify collections for alms for the aid of the missions and their distribution.

4) It will decide when some churches no longer are "missions" and when other churches become "missions" either through direct divine action, persecution, political changes or other circumstances.

5) It will elaborate a single strategy for the evangelization of the world which will be concretized through the union of persons and material and distinguished leaders to serve the entire Church.

At the end of his intervention, Bishop Sheen proposed adding a sixth chapter to the schema concerning the subject of ecumenism and the missions. Among other suggestions, he felt that this chapter should include this proposition:

The missionary should recognize that a) the Church, as the Mystical Body of Christ, is also present where ecclesial unity and visible organization is not yet present;

b) God acts in history through non-ecclesial ways;

c) He dispenses His grace through other extra-sacramental media, and "He rewards those who seek him" (Heb 11:6);

d) The Church does not exclude natural religions, but includes that good which she finds in them;

e) In heaven there are people "from every tribe, language, and nation."

The missionary, recognizing this, should begin a dialogue with all people, so that their potential union with Christ might be manifested in act, the union of all humanity with the Head.

Toward the end of this section, Bishop Sheen summarized in his own distinctive manner the best type of ecumenism. "Well ordered charity and the holiness of daily life," he wrote, "are two efficacious means which alone, apart from any dialogue, lead others to Christ the Savior and His Mystical Body. We never convince others of the Redemption quite so well as when we act as redeemed men."

During the 157th congregation, on November 10—one year and one day from the negative vote on the missionary propositions presented in the third session—Father Schütte brought back the revised schema to the floor of the Council. On this and the following day, in a series of 20 votes, the Council Fathers expressed their opinion on the revised draft. Five of the six chapters of the text were overwhelmingly approved by the assembly; chapter five, however, received 712 reservations out of the total number of 2,153 Fathers who voted. It thus failed to receive the necessary two-thirds majority and was remanded to the Commission. This chapter dealt with the coordination of missionary activity and specifically with the delicate subject of establishing a commission of missionary bishops and leaders and the nature of its relationship to the existing Congregation for the Propagation of the Faith.

On November 30, Father Schütte introduced the revised text on the Council floor, and this time the entire schema was approved by a vote of 2,162 in favor and only 18 opposed. Article 29, which contained the reference to the establishment of the new international group of missionary bishops and leaders was approved this time by 2,112 of the 2,169 Council Fathers. On December 7, 1965, during the ninth public session, the decree on the missionary activity of the Church was approved by 2,394 Council Fathers (with only five negative votes) and was duly promulgated by Pope Paul VI.

Commenting on the significance of the decree while still in its drafting stages, the Reverend Ronan Hoffman, O.F.M.Conv., wrote:

It must be borne in mind that no other Council in the history of the Church has ever taken up the topic of the missionary activity of the Church. Even though this is but the beginning, it should not be underestimated. . . . In bringing together the concepts of "Church" and "missions," therefore, this present Council has taken a big step towards laying the dogmatic foundation of the missionary activity of the Church. Nothing offers greater hope for practical mission success in the long run than the development of the theology of the missionary action of the Church.

Decree on the Church's Missionary Activity

✠ INTERVENTION

BISHOP FULTON SHEEN, 9 *November, 1964*

Paul the Sixth, reigning as a missionary pontiff, has suggested to the Council that our schema be polished and developed. Let us do this, at the same time granting to every member of the Commission the right to choose his own "expert."

First Observation

In place of the theological question, "What are missions?" I would suggest that we turn to the practical question: "Where are the missions?" or "Are the missions also in those regions where there are few priests, few churches and great poverty?" The simple answer to this question is: The missions are both.

I am a servant of the missions under the Propaganda. But during three sessions of this Council, many bishops who are living in great poverty come to my seat in the Council hall. They come from territories which are not under the Propaganda, but from areas where there are only seven to ten priests to care for 50,000 square miles.

I ask: Is it Christian, is it Catholic, is it worthy of the charity of Christ to say to them: "You do not belong to mission territory"?

Is it not true that the doctrine of the collegiality of bishops imposes on us a missionary responsibility, not only for territories which were defined as missionary three hundred years ago, but also "for the salvation of the whole world"? (Confer number four of the Schema.)

Why does Paul the Sixth, reigning as a pastor, in his encyclical letter *Ecclesiam Suam* so rarely use the word "mission"? What other words does he use in its place? Dialogue. And he uses that word 77 times. To him, dialogue is the showing of the love and charity of Christ to all men.

We bishops in this Council must not enter into a dispute about what is a missionary territory and what is not, or who belongs to this congregation or to that congregation, saying: "I am one of Paul's men," "I am one of Apollo's"

533

or "I am one of Cephas' "; while some one else says, "I owe my faith to Christ alone." What are you saying? Is there more than one Christ? (1 Cor. 1:12)

Let us not be like the priest and the levite, in the parable of the Good Samaritan, who passed by the wounded man saying, "He does not belong to our congregation." In the Body of Christ there are no "new churches," there are no "old churches," for we are all living cells in that Body dependent on one another. It is souls, not territories, which make the missions. The missions must not be the one aspect of life of the Church which admits of no *aggiornamento*.

What God has joined together—the Church and the missions—let no schema separate.

The true Catholic solution to this problem of the diversity of missions is to be found in number four of the schema, where there is proposed a "Central Council for Spreading the Gospel." This Council transcends all juridicial distinctions about congregations and gives flexibility to missionary effort, according to diverse circumstances.

Let no one fear that he will receive less aid if some help is given to a needy brother. In the early Church, just as soon as there was "one heart and one soul," then they began to "consider all property in common" (Acts 3:32). Furthermore, if we share, then as we read in the Epistle to the Corinthians: "He that gathered much had nothing over, he that gathered little had no lack" (2 Cor. 8:15).

Second Observation

One of the conciliar Fathers has asked that all reference to poverty be taken out of this schema.

I beg you most earnestly, Venerable Fathers, that the notion of poverty be strongly affirmed in this Council.

Put your finger on the 30th Parallel; run it around a globe of the earth, lifting it slightly above China. What do you find?

Practically all of the prosperity is above the 30th Parallel, and the greater part of the poverty of the world is beneath the 30th Parallel, that is, in Africa, Asia and Latin America.

As chastity was the fruit of the Council of Trent, and obedience the fruit of the First Vatican Council, so may the spirit of poverty be the fruit of this Second Vatican Council.

We live in a world, in which 200 million people would willingly take the vow of poverty tomorrow, if they could live as well, eat as well, be clothed as well, and be housed as well as I am—or even some who take the vow of poverty.

The greater number of bishops in this Council are living in want or in persecution, and they come from all peoples and nations.

As only a wounded Christ could convert a doubting Thomas, so only a Church wounded by poverty can convert a doubting world.

Conclusion

If we show an ecumenical spirit to brothers that are outside the Church, then let us show an ecumenical spirit to brothers who are inside the Church. Let us be charitable about the missions, remembering that the Lord who said, "Go teach all nations" (Congregation of the Propaganda) is the same Lord who bewailed, "I have mercy on the multitudes" (Latin America).

Decree on the Church's Missionary Activity

✠ COMMENTARY by Rt. Rev. Monsignor Luigi G. Ligutti

I know the missions quite well, and I love them the more. I listened to most of the discussion on the floor of the Council and heard triumphal paeans on the subject as well as bitter criticism bordering on the uncharitable and evidently sarcastic.

The Decree coursed the gamut of a race with handicaps, barriers and pitfalls. The original evidently had the backing of the authorities, but it was voted down. So it reappeared later in a considerably changed form. I believe that such an event and the result were all to the good.

The Decree is now much more complete in its general outline and detail. Its six chapters are logically arranged; the basic theology is expressed succinctly, but fully. There is perhaps less verbosity and rhetoric than in most *acta* of the Council. Any formalism and pomposity reduced to a lower key, *ad usum Delphini,* can always be appreciated.

Its first chapter is basic. It is Christocentric, as it should be, not unmindful, however, of the triune God and of man's nobility and his eschatological destiny.

It is good to see that in the opening chapter we are told that new times demand new measures and new men.

The suggestion made in number 40 amounts to this: Constitutions were made for men, and not men for the constitutions, so, if need arises, let's bring them up to date.

Throughout the six chapters of the Decree, one may find some repetitions here and there, but actually a thought may be stressed over and over when applied to the various units in the mosaic of the Decree. Thus the expression that unity in mutual love and esteem should be an aim and a positive work; avoiding unhealthy rivalry is found in numbers 6 and 15.

Personal as well as official cooperation with fellow countrymen should be extended, as mentioned in numbers 15 and 21. We hope that this will mean the end of the ghetto mentality so traditionally evidenced by the mission compounds of yesteryear. Such cooperation should be extended by an interest in the international organizations and in many other common endeavors for the good of society.

It is clearly set forth in numbers 10, 11, 12 and 22 that all God's gifts to man and the man-made additions to God's gifts (culture, traditions and the like) should be known, appreciated and used.

In all this work the missions must lend themselves with a spirit of giving, not of receiving, with service as the paramount end, and not to achieve political or other advantages (confer number 12 and, *passim*, the encylical *Ecclesiam Suam*).

An interesting note is introduced in number 13 about using worrisome wiles in making converts.

When we speak of missions, we use juridical and institutional terms. However, it is really man we must think about. It is the man with a calling for the mission field as an integral man, body and soul, his abilities and disabilities, that concerns us. To be a real missionary, one must be different. There is a special gene in the makeup of a missionary. He must be imaginative, enthusiastic, zealous and completely self-effacing. Above all, he must possess a most solid base in the natural virtues, cardinal and otherwise.

The above remarks do not pretend to do anymore than to touch the high spots of the well-studied and exhaustive treatise. And now, for a few criticisms and suggestions. Your best friend is one who, in all honesty, even though mistakenly, questions some of your actions, criticizes you or suggests possible alternatives. So here I come as *amicus curiae*.

1) The sixth chapter contains excellent suggestions on the duty of the well-established Church to assist the nascent Church with personal and material means. It never hurts the local Church to be generous with the missions, and it never hurts the missions when generosity is exhibited toward other causes. The age-old traditional methods of collections might well be brought up to date. Stamps to redeem pagan babies is a slightly out-of-date method for aiding the missions.

2) Self-supporting missions are barely hinted at. I personally believe that the idea of responsible stewardship is not a difficult idea to put across to converts. Its basic tenet is found in the Decree on the Apostolate of the Laity:

They should constantly develop an appreciation of their own diocese, of which the parish is, so to speak, a cell, ever ready at their bishop's invitation to give their support to diocesan projects. Indeed, to respond to the needs of cities and rural areas, they should not limit their cooperation to parochial boundaries, but strive to extend it to interparochial, interdiocesan, national, and international fields, all the more so because the daily increase in mobility of populations, reciprocal relationships, and the ease of communication no longer allow any sector of society to remain an isolated unit. Thus they should be concerned about the needs of the People of God spread throughout the world. They should especially make missionary activity their own by giving material or even personal assistance. It is a duty and honor for

Christians to return to God a part of the good things that they receive from Him.

The Seventh Day Adventists and Jehovah's Witnesses have proven that it can be done and that it builds up loyalty and responsibility.

3) In our missiology courses a thorough study should be made of other groups' training of future missionaries, of their refresher courses, their financial systems, security and so on. There is so much to be learned from others within the Church and out of the Church.

4) The missionary should also know the working of the international organizations. They are very important, and they can be very helpful.

5) The plea on behalf of the catechists and deacons is indeed praiseworthy. Nothing much is said in praise of the lay brothers who have done so much for the missions.

6) There is a complete lacuna in the Decree on the very important item of living conditions, diet, medical care and rest periods for all mission workers. A missionary represents a big-money investment, and his service is very valuable. If he is unable to function in his work, it is also a financial loss to the community. More is spent on a jeep for upkeep and repairs than on one of our missionaries.

7) There is an urgent and absolute need for reliable research on all phases of mission endeavors. Let us begin with the questionnaires for annual reports. What do we want to know? What is the emphasis to be? Some very alarming situations would be revealed.

Decisions on mission policies must be based on facts, not on fancies and not on mere impressions or impersonal quotations. The Truth is God, and the Truth will make us free. Let us face it.

8) We come now to the touchiest of topics. The following remarks are made with all respect for authority and with great admiration for the dedicated workers in Propaganda Fide.

a) Even though Romanity does furnish a most valuable background, it does not *ex opere operato* give omniscience and infallibility. Officials of the Sacred Congregations should have the highest possible training not only in the Roman office, but in the field. They should be personally acquainted with the missions with which they deal daily. This experience should be gained by actual work in the mission country not as an attaché to a nunciature or delegation, but as an assistant missionary or a helper to a native bishop. They should know what it means to cross swollen streams, to battle with mosquitoes, to do their own cooking or to face miles and miles of dirty roads astride an over-age motorcycle.

b) Most assuredly the priest to be appointed vicar apostolic or bishop must have had pastoral mission experience. There have been times when a priest, residing thousands of miles away, was appointed bishop in mission territory. Perhaps now and then, with the assistance of the Holy Spirit, such a move does work, as when Dr. Mannix of Maynooth became the Bishop of Melbourne. He had never set foot on Australian soil. At the end of his hundred years of life, he could rightly be called "the greatest Australian of them all." The exception proves the rule.

c) Preparing candidates for the priesthood for service in their native surroundings in diocesan or regional seminaries is emphasized and rightly so. This advocacy seems to contradict the age-old practice of the Propaganda Fide Seminary for undergraduates in Rome. What will six or eight years away from their native land do for them? Certainly Rome should be a most desirable location for postgraduate work of the native clergy.

Conclusion

My deep love for the missions of the Church has prompted me to make these observations. I make them in the light of first-hand observations gained through frequent visits to the missions. They also, I believe, reflect the thinking of most of the missionaries whom I have met in my travels throughout the past decade. These observations are made by one who has striven to be a servant of that Church which we now see in these post-conciliar days as, above all else, a Servant Church.

XIV/DECLARATION ON CHRISTIAN EDUCATION

Declaration on Christian Education

✠ HISTORICAL INTRODUCTION

"Pardon me," said Archbishop John P. Cody of Chicago in his speech on November 17, 1964, "if I dare to mention the United States of America. The Declaration approved by the Council will bring sincere joy to our 45 million Catholics who support 13,655 Catholic schools, which receive ten and a half million students in every grade of education, directed by 191,126 priests, brothers, sisters and lay teachers." The Archbishop's remark was but one of many indications of the American interest in this Declaration. The presence, as members of the Commission on Seminaries, Universities and Catholic Schools, of three American prelates—Archbishop Cody, Archbishop Patrick O'Boyle of Washington, D.C., and Bishop Loras T. Lane of Rockford, Illinois —as well as of three American consultants—the Right Reverend Monsignors Rudolph G. Bandas, John Steinmueller and Mark J. Hurley—was another indication.

The preparatory Commission on Seminaries, Universities and Catholic Schools had examined 81 propositions on the subject presented by the world's bishops, Catholic universities and the Roman congregations. These consisted of 61 propositions concerning the right of the Church and scholastic education, 12 propositions concerning ecclesiastical colleges, and eight concerning the establishment of special institutions. In March, 1962, the Commission had prepared a schema entitled simply "On Catholic Schools," and in June of the same year the Central Preparatory Commission suggested that all this material should be presented in one schema to be entitled "On Catholic Schools and Academic Studies."

After the election of the conciliar Commission on Seminaries, Universities and Catholic Schools, the material was refined in even greater detail, with some subjects being referred to the Dogmatic Constitution on the Church and others to the Dogmatic Constitution on Divine Revelation. Accordingly, the Commission drafted a new schema in March, 1963, entitled simply "On Catholic Schools." This schema was approved by Pope John on April 22 and dispatched to the Council Fathers. On July 19, Archbishop John J. Krol of Philadelphia submitted his observations on this schema, declaring that it "treats very clearly everything that pertains to good school administration in our age and should be altogether accepted." He felt, too, that "the description of the qualities of a truly Catholic school is appropriate and sufficient." Finally, he wrote, "The Catholic university increases in importance day by day as a greater number of youths enroll in its courses and as the number of the courses themselves grows."

During the second session the members of the Commission examined the many suggestions of the Council Fathers and produced another schema very similar in many respects to its predecessor. On January 23, 1964, the Central Coordinating Commission instructed this Commission to reduce its "Constitution" on Catholic schools to a *votum*—a recommendation to the Council Fathers of what might be directed to subsequent organs concerning Catholic education. This suggestion, however, was resisted by the Commission, and resisted so strongly that the Central Coordinating Commission acceded to calling the document a declaration.

The Commission did, however, follow the Central Coordinating Commission's recommendation that a major part of its document be referred either to the Commission for the Revision of the Code of Canon Law or to a post-conciliar commission on education that would be charged with drafting a directory. The Declaration, as finally approved by Pope Paul on April 27 and distributed to the Council Fathers, consisted of an introduction and a series of 17 propositions. Again, through the insistence of the Commission that drafted the document, rather than settling for a mere vote on the propositions, the Central Coordinating Commission agreed to allow a brief discussion on the text in the fourth session.*

The Declaration was introduced on the floor of the Council by Bishop Jules Daem of Antwerp, Belgium, on November 17, 1964, during the 124th general congregation. On that very day three Americans spoke concerning the text. Cardinal Spellman praised the Commission for excellently setting forth "certain fundamental principles." Recognizing the existence of the question concerning the support of schools as "a difficult and complicated one" in many nations, he felt that the text should be so clarified that the rights of children and their parents be not confused with the seeking of public money for religious schools. He therefore proposed the following amendment to the text:

> Parents should be free to choose the schools they wish for their children. They should not, in consequence of their choice, be subject to unjust economic burdens which would infringe upon this freedom of choice. Since it is the function of the State to facilitate civil freedom, justice and equity

* There is no need here to enter into a lengthy history of the document since it has already been discussed at great length by Mark J. Hurley, a consultant to the commission, both in his commentary on the text later in this volume as well as elsewhere. Cf. *Declaration on Christian Education of Vatican Council II,* Paulist Press, Glen Rock, New Jersey, 1966.

demand that a due measure of public aid be available to parents in support of the schools they select for their children.

Moreover, if these schools serve the public purpose of popular education, the fact that they may be religious in their orientation should not exclude them from a rightful measure of public support.

The Archbishop of New York then returned to his frequent theme that many items should be left to the discretion of the local ordinary or episcopal conferences. He felt that "no commission can decide all the particular norms for the whole world or give definitive answers to the schools of all nations and their problems." He therefore commended the Commission upon proposing "the establishment of a special post-conciliar commission to study further the intricate problems of Christian education." This commission, he said:

. . . must not only have representation from the major areas of the world, but as well have truly expert members from all phases of education and include laymen along with priests and religious men and women. I commend the suggestion, also, that the practical application of these general principles be placed in the hands of the conferences of bishops around the world in accord with the instructions of the Holy See.

On the same day Joseph Cardinal Ritter of St. Louis said he was extremely pleased with the schema. He admitted the practical problems associated with the drafting of this text:

Indeed, Christian education, associated so intimately with the mission of the Church to teach all nations, deserves a fuller and more careful consideration. However, this seems impossible for this Council because of the great implications of the subject. Christian education, just in itself, to the preclusion of all others, is a very difficult subject to treat since it demands not only a theology and philosophy of education, but also that the pedagogical arts and sciences be understood. Upon consideration of the circumstances of this time, this work becomes almost impossible. Discrepancy of culture, different stages of wealth, various modes of living—all these things which differentiate one nation from another stand in the way of a declaration which might contain specific principles of education. The size of the labor becomes more evident when we consider the diversity which characterizes the relationships between Church and State in each country.

Secondly, the Cardinal said, he was greatly pleased with the new title of the schema "since the educational concern of the Church embraces far more than the building and administering of schools; it should extend itself to those individuals who seek an education in non-Catholic schools." He felt also that the schema should mention those "who spend themselves in giving a Christian education to those who remain outside of Catholic schools." The Cardinal expressed his approval of the schema's encouragement of freedom within the field of education:

> ... the schema should more clearly and distinctly follow up those things which are mentioned in paragraph nine about the freedom of scientific inquiry. For if the Church teaches that truth is one, and if she believes that all truth leads to God, and if she professes that truth makes men free, then Catholic schools and universities should be examples of that true freedom which greatly benefits students and teachers.

The Cardinal's final point was that the purpose of Catholic schools should be delineated more clearly.

> Our schools are not established in order to separate Catholics from all others or to guard our boys and girls from the life outside; rather they are set up so that parents, priests, religious, and lay Catholics, of their own free will and with great sacrifice, might better serve both God and mankind, Church and family. For Catholic schools should be of great service for the communities in which they live and for human society itself. Otherwise, they would be unworthy of the name "Catholic schools."

Archbishop John Patrick Cody, a former priest of St. Louis and then Coadjutor Archbishop of New Orleans, was the next American speaker during this congregation. He spoke eloquently in defense of the schema, both as a member of the Commission, as well as the chairman of the subcommission charged with drafting norms for the revision of the Code of Canon Law. He spoke, too, not only in the name of the bishops of the United States and in the name of many missionary bishops, but also as president of the National Catholic Education Association. He said that "the Commission has wisely suggested that after the acceptance of the present schema as a *Magna Carta* of Christian education, a post-conciliar commission examine more broadly and more exactly all aspects of the problem." He felt such a procedure would be the best "both on account of the present shortage of time and on account of the complexity of the problems which need accurate study."

The Archbishop was obviously defending the schema against the many who felt it should be discarded because of its inadequacies. He presented his argument:

> It seems to me, moreover, that the Second Vatican Council cannot deny approval to this Declaration which is so closely connected with the schemata already examined in this Council. For education is intimately connected with the schemata of "The Church in the Modern World," "The Apostolate

of the Laity," "The Missionary Activity of the Church," etc. If the Council does not act on Catholic education, there is no doubt that this will be a cause of great surprise and sorrow, since the principles pertinent to Catholic education are the foundation of the previously mentioned schemata and also of the apostolic mission and of the sanctification of the Church in the whole world.

It is also proper to note that if the Council does nothing on Catholic education, it will bring certainly serious offense to innumerable lay Catholics who, not rarely, with great sacrifice generously sustain the Church in the exercise of her magisterial office, whether in Catholic universities or in primary schools, both parochial and abbatial, in secondary schools and colleges, which schools indeed have often been built by the Christian people not without tears or blood.

Finally, he appealed for the passage of the schema "since it seems a solid basis for the happy exercise of the pastoral office so very often desired by this Council."

On the following day, November 18, 1964, Auxiliary Bishop James Malone of Youngstown, Ohio, presented one of the finest interventions of all on the subject of Christian education. He suggested a fundamental proposition to undergird the treatment of education, namely, the clear and explicit distinction between society and State, which is society's political instrument. "The schema," he said, "must go deeper and put into perspective the delicate and complex relationships among all those agents with rights in education. We cannot," he added, "rest our case simply on the affirmation of rights." He continued:

Consequently, the full schema must include the fundamental distinction between society itself and the State. Society is a social concept which describes the community itself; society means "the people"—as we say in English, "we the people"—whereas, in contrast, the State is a political concept, much narrower in meaning. The State, or the government, is an instrument of society, the political arm of society, and its functions and specific duties must be determined by the consent of the people, i.e., by society itself. Society, then, must be distinguished from the State, or government, precisely because it is not co-terminous with either in extension or in fundamental rights.

Contrary to some prevalent theories of the State, the government is not and must not become the master of the people, but rather its servant. In the field of education, the government must not be the official teacher and arbiter of religion, science, art, literature, music or culture. Rather, the State must be the servant of the expressed will and consent of the people with its unquestioned right to see to it that its citizens are fully equipped to fulfill their obligations as citizens and members of the body politic within the field of its proper competence.

Bishop Malone concludes by saying that

> this basic distinction between the people and its political arm, the State, will go a long way toward clearing up confusion in the field of education. We plead, therefore, for the freedom of man in the field of education and, indeed, as a prime test of the freedom of religion.

Auxiliary Bishop Fulton J. Sheen of New York also submitted three interventions in writing. The first concerned Catholic universities.

> When the human body is separated from the soul, it dissolves and divides into almost innumerable molecules. This also happens when Catholic universities, neglecting the spiritual goal to which they are ordained, divide and dissolve into many and disparate courses. To avoid this, it seems to us to be truly proper that Catholic universities be reduced to the principal and fundamental courses, and the other courses, if there is a reason for retaining them, be considered as a complement to the fundamental studies.

His second intervention concerned trade schools. "Up until now," he wrote, "the schools of higher learning have been more heavily emphasized." He continued, "We suggest that not all young people are fit for higher learning. Therefore, Catholics who are conspicuous in industry and trade schools should be urged to create practical schools which will prepare youth according to the industrial life of modern times." His third intervention touched upon the very basis of Christian education.

> Education, in order to be complete, must touch the whole man and his faculties. Therefore, there are three ends to education, as we consider the various human faculties. Thus, if education is referred to the intellect, its end will be truth; if to the will, the end of education will be the good; if to action, the scope of education will be testimony.
>
> Since there are three principal faculties of man, it would be wrong to extol truth and goodness too much, to the detriment, as it seems to us, or neglect of action, whose object (i.e., testimony) is attained more gradually than the object of the intellect or will.
>
> Our Lord Jesus Christ did not say, whoever knows my doctrine will be saved, but "he that doth the will of my father who is in heaven, he shall enter the kingdom of heaven."

Bishop Hugh Donohue of Stockton, California, also submitted his observations on the schema in writing. He echoed the sentiment of Cardinal Spellman in his opening words:

. . . parents do have the primary and inalienable right to choose the schools they wish for their sons and daughters. Furthermore, since parents are also citizens, they are entitled to equal and equitable treatment in this choice of schools under the laws of their country and do not at all forfeit their right by reason of the religion they profess or the type of school they choose for their children. Similarly, as the State and government must, the Catholic Church, too, stands willing to help parents fulfill their obligations in education.

However, in its zeal to assist the family, the Church must not forget the schools themselves. It is not at all sufficient to put the label "Catholic" upon a school, its administration and teaching corps; it is equally necessary that the mark of excellence be the goal and first purpose of the school, its administration and teaching staff. The Catholic Church must not be mesmerized by the mere numbers of schools or of children in them, but strive to conduct schools of superior character and excellence. Quality of education must never be sacrificed to quantity or to the tyranny of numbers. Achievement is not necessarily proved by statistics.

In the same vein, the schools of the Church are not defensive weapons existing to shelter and protect children from the world and the market place like so many hot-house plants. Rather these schools serve the family and children precisely by preparing students to take their rightful place in the world, to be witnesses to Christ not only without fear and with confidence, but as well with intelligence and knowledge.

Bishop Donohue went on to advocate expanding the notion of Catholic education as a true apostolate, to include others than only those who teach in Catholic schools. He pleaded for recognition of those "devoted laymen and laywomen who are teachers in State-conducted and other schools." If we are going to speak of parental rights and lay participation, he said, "then we must be prepared to accept the role of parents in the determination of policy in Catholic schools. We must also be prepared to accept laymen not only as teachers but, indeed, as administrators and presidents of our Catholic institutions of learning." His fourth point echoed the sentiments that Bishop Ernest J. Primeau had expressed earlier in his intervention concerning the laity. Said Bishop Donohue:

While we rightly insist on freedom for the schools chosen by parents, it is necessary that these schools *within their own walls* be models of Christian freedom. Proudly and confidently do we assert that our schools are dedicated to the truth, precisely as Christ called Himself the Truth. We assert quite correctly that truth is one and whole and cannot be found in contradiction to itself. Consequently, there must be no fear in the pursuit of learning, in the pursuit of truth, for we seek the truth which the Gospel tells us will make us free.

Auxiliary Bishop Clarence E. Elwell of Cleveland, Ohio, submitted the lengthiest American intervention on the subject of Christian education. He spoke from a background of many years of experience as a diocesan superintendent of schools. He was, first of all, pleased that the Council should recognize the pastoral importance of Catholic schools and said that the schema was well planned and accommodated in many ways to present necessities. Nonetheless, he proposed five general suggestions for improving the text. He felt, first of all, that the text should more carefully distinguish instruction, "which is concerned primarily with the intellectual virtues, from education, which includes instruction, but adds to it the proper formation of the will and the formation of good moral habits by means of the moral virtues." Secondly, he felt, the schema should "assert for the Church not only a supernatural right to educate, but also the right of any society in the natural order to form its members in accordance with its purpose." He then went on to praise the Catholic school system in the United States:

> In view of the extraordinary benefits which have accrued to the Catholic Church in the United States because the Plenary Councils of Baltimore of the nineteenth century have urged and even prescribed that every parish should have its own parish elementary school, would it not be good for the Council to consider whether it can formulate a directive applicable to the entire world which would urge the necessity of parishes and dioceses supplying integral Catholic education for all children.
>
> Ordinarily, the only place where a Catholic child will receive systematic instruction in all the essentials of his religion, together with parallel habit formation in the habits and virtues and practices of a Christian life, is in a Catholic elementary school. Also it is only in Catholic schools that the teacher has the freedom and the opportunity to apply to every subject-matter field or secular instruction the corrective and directive influence of the principles of sound philosophy and correct moral and dogmatic theology, e.g., in literature, in history, in science, etc. A Christian child can hardly be formed to the mind of the Church without such systematic and basic religious instruction.

Bishop Elwell felt also that all Catholics, regardless of whether they have children of school age or not, should support the Catholic school system. He suggested that the Commission for the Revision of the Code of Canon Law should "so change the law that poor schools in poor parishes can be aided by the ordinary from the income of richer parishes, so that a common standard of education can be maintained for all children, the poor included." Finally, he suggested, Canon Law should be changed in such a manner concerning the status of exempt religious that the ordinary of a diocese can provide adequate secondary education for all the young people in his diocese. "The legislation should be such as to enable a bishop," he wrote, "to establish a system of secondary education which meets the spiritual, vocational and other needs of his young people in the entire diocese, the slow as well as the bright, the poor as well as the rich, those bound for college and university as well as those who are not."

Bishop Elwell then proposed 23 specific emendations to the schema. Of these, three are especially noteworthy. First, concerning the necessity of the Catholic school and its value he wrote:

> In the present circumstances it is only in the truly Catholic school that it is possible to impart to our children a complete, adequate and systematic knowledge of and habituation in their holy religion and its practices as well as to show the relation of religion to all other subjects and all of life.
>
> Most parents are unable to do this. Religious instruction once or twice a week is completely inadequate to prepare the child of today to cope with the enormous amount of secular knowledge he acquires in school or to secure the guidance he needs in an often highly secularized world. It is, therefore, the wish of the Holy Ecumenical Synod that Catholic schools be established where they do not exist or that they be brought into keeping with the principles and norms here established as well as those found in the encyclical *Divini Illius Magistri.* This encyclical should be explicitly referred to by the Council as the enchiridion for education.

Secondly, concerning the preparation of teachers for Catholic schools, Bishop Elwell wrote:

> There is such great diversity among the religious communities, especially of women, in determining the length, nature and content of the postulancy, novitiate and juniorate years that it is impossible for any college or university to arrange a schedule of classes which will maintain the sequence and selection of courses which is required by the State, accrediting associations and common sense.
>
> The Commission will, therefore, do Catholic education a great favor if it requires all religious communities in a given nation to follow the same schedule for postulancy and novitiate as regards length, times of beginning and ending, secular and religious subjects which can be taken in these years, etc.
>
> Or the Commission can give the national or regional conference of bishops the authority, in cooperation with the religious superiors, to work out a satisfactory and praiseworthy arrangement and solve this problem. Without such an arrangement, many communities will continue to be very weak in the calibre of teachers they supply. This will harm Catholic education and its good name.

Bishop Elwell's final point concerned the exempt status of religious.

A complete review of the matter of the exemption of religious as regards secondary education is required. This secondary education is becoming universal in some countries and widespread in many others. It pertains to basic education in the more advanced nations. The bishop of the diocese, therefore, needs and should be given unhampered power to set up a diocesan system of education which will meet the spiritual and other needs of his subjects. Many kinds and types of secondary schools are needed for this; complete control of the qualifications of teachers is also required. (Perhaps exempt religious should supply proof that their teachers meet State and diocesan requirements as regards preparation.) All lay teachers even in exempt schools should be certified by the diocesan school office.

During the discussion of schema 21, speakers made their observations on the floor of the Council, and many more submitted theirs in writing. On November 19 the Council Fathers voted 1,457 to 419 to accept the Declaration on Christian Education. In a series of four votes on various sections of the schema, they also approved the contents of the schema by large majorities. It remained only for the Commission to incorporate the Fathers' suggestions into a revised text that would be presented during the coming session.

On October 6, 1965, the revised text was distributed to the Fathers, and on October 13, during the 148th general congregation, Bishop Daem explained the manner in which the Commission had accepted the suggestions of the Council Fathers and asked that they give their vote of approval to the revised text. This the Council Fathers did in a series of nine votes, and, on the following day, by a vote of 1,912 to 183, they approved the complete schema. During the seventh public session of October 28 the Declaration on Christian Education was approved by a vote of 2,290 to 35 of the Council Fathers. Pope Paul VI duly promulgated it along with four other Council documents on the same day.

The Declaration is not the final word on Christian education. It is a beginning and, in the minds of its drafters, was meant to be no more than that. The Americans involved in the drafting of the text brought the pragmatic experience of their own nation to bear on the text. Without saying it, they did, in effect, echo the sentiments of their thirty-fifth president who said, "Let us begin."

Declaration on Christian Education

✠ INTERVENTIONS

FRANCIS CARDINAL SPELLMAN, *17 November, 1964*

If one considers the purpose of this schema as it is set forth in its preface, namely that of proposing "certain general principles" dealing with Catholic schools, we are compelled to say that the Commission has achieved this purpose remarkably well.

However, I do propose one change in wording so that the Council's intention may be seen more clearly in the text itself.

For the direct intention of this schema is to affirm the rights of parents and children and not necessarily to seek public funds for the maintenance of religious schools. On that account, I propose that section six of the schema read as follows:

> The rights of parents, distributive justice and the very good of society itself demand that public monies destined as means or helps for the support of schools ought to be allotted to every educable child in the nation. Moreover, this ought to be done without any discrimination among persons as long as the children attend schools which are not harmful to the common good.

I propose this change in phrasing in order that the intention of the Council may be revealed more clearly; and, in this way, I hope that in the future we may avoid fruitless disputes over the schema's meaning.

Proposals for Catholic Schools

There remains, however, a more fundamental question. Is it really possible that this Council or any post-conciliar commission or even the Commission for Revising the Code of Canon Law will be able to apply these general principles to the actual problems of Catholic schools and Christian education? After considering how these schools vary from place to place, with a consequent diversity of problems, it is my opinion that no commission is able to establish

553

all the particular norms on a worldwide scale, nor is it able to address itself to the schools of all nations in their difficulties.

In these present proposals, the Fathers of the Council acknowledge the very great importance of education in the modern world; they defend the rights of parents and children as founded in the dignity of the human person. This schema pleases me, although, perhaps, some changes are desirable as far as modes of expression are concerned. Finally, I hope that all specifications and practical applications will be left to the episcopal conferences of the individual nations so that they may be able to reduce to particular norms the general principles of this schema and other instructions of the Holy See.

JOSEPH CARDINAL RITTER, *17 November, 1964*

I am extremely pleased with the schema of the declaration on Christian education. Many things about it are truly praiseworthy, among which I should like to mention the following.

First of all, *in general:* The schema restricts itself within bounds of practical possibility. Indeed, Christian education, associated so intimately with the mission of the Church to teach all nations, deserves a fuller and more careful consideration. However, this seems impossible for this Council because of the great implications of the subject. Christian education, just in itself to the preclusion of all others, is a very difficult subject to treat since it demands not only a theology and philosophy of education, but also that the pedagogical arts and sciences be understood. Upon consideration of the circumstances of this time, this work becomes almost impossible. Discrepancy of culture, different stages of wealth, various modes of living—all these things which differentiate one nation from another stand in the way of a declaration which might contain specific principles of education. The size of the labor becomes more evident when we consider the diversity which characterizes the relationships between Church and State in each country.

Thus, justly and rightly, the schema avoids the easy, but erroneous, path of compromise which would help no one, would profit no one, but which might, on the contrary, endanger its very freedom. The schema asks two things:

a) The establishment of a special post-conciliar commission which, once the necessary and proper studies are completed, might further discuss the principles set forth here and might prepare a more detailed declaration.

b) The freedom of assemblies of bishops to determine particular issues.

Secondly, I should like to mention a few things which in my opinion deserve *special* praise. I am greatly pleased with the new title, since the educational concern of the Church embraces far more than the building and administering of schools; it should extend itself to those individuals who seek an education in non-Catholic schools. Next, the schema should make special mention of those who spend themselves in giving a Christian education to those who stay outside of Catholic schools.

I am glad that the schema encourages, in various ways, freedoms within the educational field. However, in treating of the right of parents freely to select schools, the schema should also declare the right and obligation which parents have in school administration. In like manner, the schema should more clearly and distinctly follow up those things which are mentioned in paragraph nine about the freedom of scientific inquiry. For if the Church teaches that truth is one, and if she believes that all truth leads to God, and if she professes that truth makes men free, then Catholic schools and universities should be examples of that true freedom which greatly benefits students and teachers.

In conclusion, I propose that the schema more explicitly and broadly consider the nature and limits of Catholic schools. Our schools are not established in order to separate Catholics from all others or to guard our boys and girls from the life outside; rather they are set up so that parents, priests, religious and lay Catholics, of their own free will and with great sacrifice, might better serve both God and mankind, Church and family. For Catholic schools should be of great service for the communities in which they live and for human society itself. Otherwise, they would be unworthy of the name *"Catholic schools."*

Thus, Venerable Fathers, with the deepest conviction I recommend the present schema to your consideration and acceptance. I am satisfied both with the general principles established in it and with the proposal for the establishment of a post-conciliar commission which might develop these principles further.

ARCHBISHOP JOHN CODY, *17 November, 1964*

I speak in the name of the bishops of the United States of America and also in the name of many bishops who work in the mission fields, and also as president of the association which is called the National Catholic Education Association.

Since the question of Catholic education is so difficult and so complicated especially in our times, on account of a certain evolution in the methods of teaching, both because of the human element and because of technical systems, the Commission has wisely suggested that after the acceptance of the present schema as a *Magna Carta* of Christian education, a post-conciliar commission examine more broadly and more exactly all aspects of the problem. It is certain that this cannot happen in a few weeks or even in a few months, and it must not be done by a post-conciliar Commission *a priori;* but, first, the various problems must be treated by episcopal conferences in each nation—with the help of various experts, either religious or lay—which must produce a certain program according to the principles established by the Declaration; it must then be submitted to the post-conciliar commission for the purpose of coordination with the diverse programs of other nations.

Let me say that such a method of procedure seems the best, both on account of the present shortage of time and on account of the complexity of the problems which need accurate study. Therefore, when it has been approved, the Declaration will offer the opportunity to all the bishops to examine the serious problems of education better and more at ease, in the light of the special conditions of each nation, and there to give suggestions which appear more useful for the solving of questions, afterwards to be examined by a post-conciliar commission which will represent every episcopate.

Two questions especially occupy the minds of the heads of State: namely, defense and education. On the one side, there are those who, always fearful that war will break out, invest huge sums of money in the building of armaments; on the other side, however, since citizens are continually increasing in number, governments are compelled to build, in greater numbers every day, classrooms for students, universities, and so forth. The Church indeed, following the example of her divine Founder, always and efficaciously has exercised her office of teaching; however, nothing seems more useful to me now—especially if we heed the pastoral and the ecumenical spirit of the Council—than the approval of this Declaration which brilliantly demonstrates to the whole world the desire of the Church to cooperate, either nationally or internationally, in solving such grave problems of our times. For only if men are thoroughly instructed can they understand the difficulties of others, know well the desires and the aspirations of peoples, and foster their own good and, indeed, that of society, care for and promote it.

It seems to me, moreover, that Vatican Council II cannot deny approval to this Declaration which is so closely connected with the schemata already examined in this Council. For education is intimately connected with the schemata of "The Church in the Modern World," "The Apostolate of the Laity," "The Missionary Activity of the Church," etc. If the Council does not act on Catholic education, there is no doubt that this will be a cause of great surprise and sorrow, since the principles pertinent to Catholic education are the foundation of the previously mentioned schemata and also of the apostolic mission and of the sanctifying Church in the whole world.

It is also proper to note that if the Council does nothing on Catholic education, it will bring certainly serious offense to innumerable lay Catholics who, not rarely, with great sacrifice generously sustain the Church in the exercise of her magisterial office, whether in Catholic universities or in primary schools, both parochial and abbatial, in secondary schools and colleges, which schools indeed have often been built by the Christian people not without tears or blood.

If we do not speak about Catholic education, Venerable Fathers, how can we join ranks with the many priests, religious, sisters and laity, daily increasing in number, who expand their energy generously for Catholic education? Our Declaration, accurately worked out by the Commission, will spur the souls of the laity to the assistance and defense of the Catholic schools; it will be a consolation and a solace to the priests, religious and laity who not rarely think that their apostolate is not sufficiently esteemed; it will be an incentive to the lay teachers whose help daily more and more we need in our schools; and this Declaration will finally be a solemn confirmation that the Church of our time, perhaps more than ever before, wishes to fulfill the divine mandate to "teach all nations."

Pardon me, Venerable Fathers, if I dare to mention the United States of America. For the Declaration approved by the Council will bring sincere joy to our 45 million Catholics who support 13,655 Catholic schools, which receive ten and a half million students in every grade of education, directed by 191,126 priests, brothers, sisters and lay teachers.

The Declaration, which urges the building of Catholic schools wherever possible, will be of great assistance to the missionary activity of the Church. Lay teachers, whose help we need in order that many of our schools may live and flourish, priests, brothers and sisters would feel that they are indeed participants in the apostolic mission of the Church and provident cooperators of the bishops, as indeed it is stated in the Decree on the Pastoral Office of Bishops in the Church:

> Bishops must see to it that they use the various means which are at hand to announce Christian doctrine in today's world, to wit, preaching and catechetical instruction which indeed always hold the principal place, but also the teaching of doctrine in the schools, in academies, conferences, etc., by which it is entirely fitting that the Gospel of Christ be announced.

Venerable Brothers, having heard the reasons given by His Excellency, the Relator, for the preference of this Declaration over the propositions which had been prepared before, and having before our eyes the importance of the question of Catholic education in the world of our time, I make bold to suggest that the Declaration produced by the Commission on Seminary Studies and Catholic Education be accepted by the Fathers, since it seems a solid basis for the happy exercise of the pastoral office so very often desired by this Council.

BISHOP JAMES MALONE, *18 November, 1964*

Within the limits of its reduced form, this Declaration on Christian education "placet." All will concede that the Declaration must be amplified, enlarged upon, and expanded into a full document, as the Commission which drew up the schema suggests. Thus we suggest a fundamental proposition to undergird and to support our treatment of education, namely that a clear and explicit distinction be elucidated between society itself and the State or government which is society's political arm or instrument.

It is not sufficient simply to affirm the rights of the Church in education, to proclaim the rights of the family, to delineate the rights of the State and its correlative duties. It is equally necessary to give the reasons why these rights and corresponding duties are what they are; to present both a theological and philosophical basis for the claims we make; to fashion a coherent synthesis that makes sense not only to our people, but to all men of good will.

Our document justly affirms the rights of parents to choose the schools they wish for their children; their right to equal treatment under the laws of a nation in the matter of education; and equally rejects all monopoly of education as contrary to these parental rights. But the schema must go deeper and put into perspective the delicate and complex relationships among all those agents with rights in education: Church, State, family, private associations, schools, teachers and administrators and the students themselves. The respective relationships put into focus in modern times by Pope Pius XI in his great encyclical on education, *Divini Illius Magistri*, must be developed further. We cannot rest our case simply on the affirmation of rights.

The school is not *"simpliciter"* the extension of the home or family; the teachers are not *"simpliciter"* delegates of the parents or even of the Church. Neither is the school *"simpliciter"* the agent, much less the servant of the State. Each agent in education has a proper and legitimate interest in the education of its children, but each from its own point of view and within the limits of its own competence.

Consequently, the full schema must include the fundamental distinction between society itself and the State. Society is a social concept which describes the community itself; society means "the people"—as we say in English, "we the people"—whereas, in contrast, the State is a political concept, much narrower in meaning. The State or the government is an instrument of society, the political arm of society, and its functions and specific duties must be determined by the consent of the people, i.e., by society itself. Society, then, must be distinguished from the State or government precisely because it is not co-terminous with either in extension or in fundamental rights.

Contrary to some prevalent theories of the State, the government is not and must not become the master of the people, but rather its servant. In the field of education, the government must not be the official teacher and arbiter of religion, science, art, literature, music or culture. Rather, the State must be the servant of the expressed will and consent of the people with its unquestioned right to see to it that its citizens are fully equipped to fulfill their obligations as citizens and members of the body politic within the field of its proper competence.

Having made this fundamental point, the schema may then proceed to the general principles in education which concern man in the exercise of his highest faculties and in his dignity as a free person. The right of a family to equal treatment under the laws of a State or Nation, the repudiation of all monopoly in education as an offense against the dignity of a parent to choose the school he wishes for his children; the right of equal justice in relationship to government subsidies in pluralistic societies; the duties of the Church and the State alike to foster and assist parents in their task and duty; all these will be brought into clearer focus.

The confusion in education today in most countries of the world, whether of the Occident or Orient, stems largely from a confusion of the bases upon which each agent in education vindicates its rights and duties.

The theory of State monopoly in education is based upon the total identification of society and the State. We cannot answer that monopoly with a theory of family monopoly, or Church monopoly, in the twentieth century.

This basic distinction between the people and its political arm, the State, will go a long way toward clearing up this confusion in the field of education.

We plead, therefore, for the freedom of man in the field of education and indeed as a prime test of the freedom of religion.

Declaration on Christian Education
☩ COMMENTARY *by Rt. Rev. Monsignor Mark J. Hurley*

Americans from the United States, by reason of the "school question" which has remained a major problem through the entire life of the Republic, brought to the Vatican Council their own experiences and their own hopes for solution. Two chief questions occupied their mind and attention: first, the relationship of the Church school to the State, with all its attendant circumstances of freedom of choice for parents, monopoly of education by the government, financial support and distributive justice; and secondly, the total educational effort of the Church in perspective, which involves the Catholic schools as such and the broader question of Catholic education, especially of those Catholics in the State and private schools and universities.

The contribution of the Americans at the Council must be measured not only by what appeared in the document or was spoken in debate, but equally by what did not appear in the texts and what was excised from the various drafts of the schema on education by reason of American intervention. In this sense, then, this contribution was both positive and negative, as the American conciliar Fathers proposed and opposed a variety of suggestions from all over the world.

The preparatory Commission, which began its work some two years prior to the presentation of the first drafts on "Catholic Schools" and on "Colleges and Universities," stressed a very defensive role for Catholic education. Schools were to be instruments of evangelization; Catholic people were to be informed of their rights and obligations in education, especially in relationship to the State; the Church must be vigilant and warn its people against the pernicious errors and false doctrines. Co-education was to be condemned, at least in principle, with exceptions allowed at the discretion of local bishops.[1]

The conciliar Commission, which was elected by the Fathers of the Council and which replaced the preparatory Commission, rejected this original draft almost entirely.

In contrast, many bishops from the new and emerging states of Asia and Africa especially, faced with the threat of "socialist" take-over of Catholic

[1] Mark J. Hurley, *Commentary on the Declaration on Christian Education at Vatican Council II*, Paulist Press, Glen Rock, N.J., 1966, p. 17.

schools, pleaded for a strong statement on freedom of education and its corollary, financial equality under distributive justice. They saw the mission schools threatened by many governments which considered them "relics of colonialism," and by others who, in the name of "socialism," would nationalize the mission schools.

The American reaction to this point of view sought to soften both the language and tone of this demand for a powerful statement, while at the same time supporting the basic position. One American priest-expert from the Commission on Education addressed the African hierarchy at their weekly meeting in Rome to the effect that "a hard line," a peremptory demand, a unilateral vindication of rights, would both be unwise as a practical approach to the solution of the problems and would becloud the issue not only in Africa, but over the world, and especially in the United States of America where the Johnson administration was striving to work out solutions on a pragmatic level. If the basic theory of the Catholic position on schools was sound, he argued, then it would commend itself to the governments of good will over the world.

The problematic of the bishops of northern Europe, where Catholic schools in so many countries are State schools and State supported, concerned the colleges and universities, especially cooperation in freedom of research in higher learning. The Council Fathers of the United States stood in support.

The swift-moving events in the United States had their influence upon the positions taken by the American bishops. President Kennedy's opposition to "across-the-board" federal aid to Catholic elementary and secondary schools, his support for aid to all colleges and the outspoken opposition of Cardinal Spellman to the President's position left their marks on the consciousness of the American hierarchy. In contrast, the Anti-Poverty and the Aid-to-Education bills of the Johnson administration, which modified the government's position *vis-à-vis* Catholic and other non-public schools, encouraged the bishops to seek a viable solution on theoretical as well as practical grounds. A clarification of the philosophy of Catholic education, particularly with reference to the place of the Catholic school in a pluralistic society, became a prime target of the American hierarchy, and this objective was clearly reflected in their interventions on the floor of St. Peter's Basilica.

A second problem, more internal in nature, demanded special attention. While the Council was working in Rome, widespread and, at times, acrimonious debate was taking place in the United States on the worth of Catholic schools. Was the Church spending too much of its resources in time, talent and treasure on Catholic schools to the detriment of the wider fields of Christian education? What of those students not in Catholic schools? What of the schools of religion of the Confraternity of Christian Doctrine? The Newman apostolate? The Young Christian Students? Adult Education? Were Catholic colleges and universities worth the great sacrifices demanded to keep them operating?

The elected members of the Commission on Christian Education from the United States were Archbishop Patrick A. O'Boyle of Washington, D.C., Archbishop John P. Cody of New Orleans (Chicago in 1965), and Bishop Loras Lane of Rockford, Illinois.[2] They reflected in their speeches and discussions three chief concerns which might fairly be judged to have been "majority thinking" among the American hierarchy.

First, the Council must lay the foundation for a coherent statement of the position of Catholic schools in society, with a view toward a solution of Church-State problems in the field. Secondly, the Church must reaffirm its determination to keep and strengthen Catholic schools as well as the other structures of Catholic education in the broader sense. Thirdly, the great 1929 encyclical of Pius XI on "The Christian Education of Youth" should be up-dated and significant advances in thought and content made.[3]

The 1963 Text

During the waning days of the first session of Vatican II, on December 3, 1962, the elected members of the conciliar Commission met for the first time. The Prefect of the Sacred Congregation of Seminaries and Universities, Joseph Cardinal Pizzardo presided. Archbishop Dino Staffa of the same congregation and vice-president of the Commission, was given the role of chairman.

The text of the preparatory Commission did not reach the floor of St. Peter's during the first session. The new Commission spent the first meeting organizing itself, particularly in nominating priest-experts (*periti*) and forming subcommissions to study elementary and secondary education, higher education and the possible effects of each study on the proposed new Code of Canon Law.

In February and March, 1963, the full Commission met in Rome to revise the initial text. Severe criticisms had been sent to the Commission by bishops, and more were heard in Rome. But the subject of education still lay a long way off in the future debates of the Council.

The new text of 1963 attempted to meet these criticisms. It was more positive in tone, less concerned with canonical limitations and more in line with the spirit of Pope John. It refrained from condemnations and censures, seeking a pastoral tone.

One topic of some concern to the American members at this juncture was the proposal to condemn co-education and to "tolerate" the practice at the discretion of local bishops. The American delegates on the subcommission on schools argued successfully that the "exception" allowed would constitute a case of "the tail wagging the dog," for far more children are in co-educational schools in the United States, both public and private, than in separated schools. The full Commission accepted the objection of the Americans and resisted all later suggestions to include the subject in the text.

[2] The *periti* (priest-experts) on the subcommission for schools were the present author, Right Rev. Mark J. Hurley of San Francisco, Right Rev. Rudolph Bandas of St. Paul, and Right Rev. John Steinmueller of Brooklyn, New York.

[3] Cf. *America*, October 16, 1965. Bishop Robert Tracy of Baton Rouge, La., proposed a new encyclical on education.

The subcommittee on schools further requested that the text avoid needless controversies, be free of sharp language and avoid a literary style that might be considered contentious, if not pugnacious, in tone.

The hierarchy of the United States, at their special meeting in Chicago during August, 1963, discussed the school text among other documents. Archbishop O'Boyle of Washington, D.C., presented a critique of the text and asked for support in Rome from the bishops in his efforts to modify the text.

The role of the State in education cannot be made clear, he asserted, until proper distinction is drawn between society, as such, and the State as its political arm. Nor without such a base can the demand for equality of treatment for all parents and pupils be seen in a coherent synthesis.

Catholic schools, he declared, are dedicated to the service of society, the State, the home and the pupils, not simply for the good of the Church. Furthermore, much greater attention must be given to the matter of religious education of those not in Catholic schools; positively, he requested conciliar support for the Confraternity of Christian Doctrine, the Newman Apostolate, the Young Christian Students.

A sweeping paragraph which urged a centralized control by the Holy See not merely over universities and faculties in a general way, but even over courses of study to "determine accurately the *ratio studiorum*" evoked negative criticism.

As the second session of the Council came to its conclusion, Pope Paul spoke to the American hierarchy during a special audience. Significantly he told the bishops: "Tell the sisters of the United States of America never to give up Catholic schools."

The 1964 Texts

By the fall of 1963 it had become apparent that the Council was beginning to run out of time, that the ambitious plans for 64 documents could not be realized and that some administrative surgery would have to be performed in the interest of concluding the Council.

At one time the schema of the Constitution on Christian Education—the highest category at Vatican II—was reduced to a *votum*—the lowest category of a conciliar document. Later it was changed to a series of 17 propositions which, by plan, were to be voted upon on the floor of St. Peter's *without debate* in the 1964 session.

Upon receipt in February, 1964, of the directive that the text would be reduced to a *votum*, Archbishop O'Boyle of the subcommission on schools submitted what he considered five irreducible points to be included in the text. These were:

1) The Church recognizes the importance of Catholic schools in the apostolate of the Church.

2) The Catholic school must serve the common good and a public purpose in society.

3) The Council must clarify the concepts "society" and "State" as essential for a solution of the "school question" around the world.

4) The Council must call for justice in the support of schools.

5) The Council must urge the laity to exercise their God-given roles in the apostolate of Christian education both inside and outside of Catholic schools.

Archbishop O'Boyle's written intervention to the commission summed up the American problematic rather well and illustrated what the United States bishops, by and large, sought from the Council in the field of education.

The appearance of the 17 propositions brought immediate reaction from the United States. In a circular letter addressed to the American hierarchy, the Educational Association of the U.S.A. wrote, "Under no circumstances should this series of propositions be published by the Council as its statement on Catholic education."

But this warning was unnecessary. The members of the Commission on Education at its first plenary session in September, 1964, voted unanimously to scuttle the propositions. Archbishop O'Boyle was the first speaker. In a sweeping critique of the propositions as "utterly inadequate," he said that they were scarcely defensible. Furthermore, he continued, there must be a debate in St. Peter's on education, so that the "mind of the Council" would become known. A new text, even at this late date and contrary to the directive of the Central Coordinating Commission, must be written, he concluded.

A new text, brief and concise, with a new title, "Declaration on Christian Education," was hastily composed by the subcommission on schools. It became the basis for conciliar debate.

At issue in this new text was the matter of State subsidy for schools. Should the State support *schools* or *parents* in their choice of schools? The question was anything but academic to the United States with its theory of aid-to-the child rather than direct aid to schools. Previous texts had directly demanded subsidy for Church schools without qualification.

An American *peritus* addressed the Commission in plenary session on this point. He said:

> Catholics, by reason of their religion, can claim no special favors from the State, nor do they lose their rights as citizens. Consequently, Catholic parents and the institutions which serve a public purpose do have a right to equal treatment in the laws of the State: the denial of this right is, in itself, an unjust form of coercion against both parents and children and constitutes unjust discrimination.

The intervention concluded in the following words:

> We respectfully submit that the shorter, simplistic and brief statements suggested in previous printed texts will raise more questions than they will

solve. What is needed is a much more sophisticated and qualified statement which will allow for proper distinctions, avoiding a doctrinaire secularism on the one hand and an arrogant demand for money by the Church on the other.

The Final Text

The subcommission on education met April 26–May 3, 1965, to draft the final text. No American served on this subcommission. The text was neither published nor sent to the Council Fathers prior to the opening of the fourth session. It was not surprising, then, that some opposition to the text from Americans arose when it appeared in Rome in late September.

Bishop Robert Tracy reported "behind the scenes, a certain restlessness" with the text. Circulars in French, Latin and English were distributed to the conciliar Fathers, asking for the defeat of the document.[4]

The new text had quite ignored the fundamental distinction between "society" and "the State" as its political arm; it had reverted to an earlier formula on State aid calling for "distributive justice"; and, finally, it had been loosely written in many spots. The criticism had some results.

Three "last minute" additions were made: A prudent sex education was favored; mention was made of "society as a whole" in contradiction to "civil society"; the name of St. Thomas Aquinas was included in the paragraph on research in higher education.

In general, the American bishops saw their views on education sustained. The text recognized the import of both the Catholic school and the school of religion for those not in Catholic schools. It affirmed the rights of parents in education, but in formulae less sophisticated and differentiated than many had advocated. It just barely gave mention to the fundamental points necessary for the enunciation of a viable philosophy of Catholic education.

Most bishops at the Council were not at all reluctant to vote for the education text precisely because it had a "safety valve" built into it. The Declaration gave only some general principles, but left further elucidation explicitly to the post-conciliar commission on education. Moreover, national conferences of bishops were empowered to put these principles into practice within a given country or territory.

The text stands now as a challenge to the United States bishops and *periti* who are on the post-conciliar commission and to the National Conference of Bishops to implement the principles and directives adumbrated in the Declaration.

[4] The author criticized the text at the commission's final meeting for its omission of the distinction between society and the State.

XV/DECLARATION ON THE RELATIONSHIP OF THE CHURCH TO NON-CHRISTIAN RELIGIONS

Declaration on the Relationship of the Church to Non-Christian Religions

✠ HISTORICAL INTRODUCTION

The Declaration on the Relationship of the Church to Non-Christian Religions has its origin in the unique personality of Pope John XXIII. Even before he had charged Cardinal Bea and the newly-established secretariat for unity with the task of drafting a text on the Church and the Jewish people, Pope John pointed the direction he wished his Council to follow. Cardinal Spellman, speaking in April, 1964, before the American Jewish Committee, recalled the first incident in these words:

> The beloved Pope John taught the world a lesson which I pray it will neither ignore nor forget, when in greeting a delegation of Jewish visitors to the Vatican in 1962 he opened wide his arms and said, "I am Joseph, your brother." In that one simple gesture, springing from his great heart, he proclaimed to the world the true meaning of the Christian spirit.

On another occasion, at this same time, Pope John addressed the leaders of the B'nai B'rith: "You of the Old Testament and we of the New must come closer and closer, as brothers under God, to work for peace throughout the world."

Early, during the preparatory phase of the Council, the Jewish historian Jules Isaac had an audience with Pope John. He expressed the hope of the Jewish people that the Council would place on its agenda a discussion of the Christian's relationship to the Jews. His wish was fulfilled on the day Pope John committed the drafting of such a statement to the secretariat for unity.

Strangely, the statement was not even so much as mentioned during the meeting of the Central Preparatory Commission, nor was it even discussed during the first session. Some observers had pointed out that Cardinal Bea felt the time was not propitious, even though the schema was completed in May, 1962. The German Jesuit cardinal, however, was not idle. His secretariat was working quietly behind the scenes for two years in preparing this draft.

Even calm men, known for their sober approach to problems, became emotionally involved in this discussion about the declaration on the Jews. On June 29, 1963, following an address in Atlantic City, Dr. M. Delott Garber asked the Reverend Gustave Weigel, S.J., whether he thought the Ecumenical Council would produce a statement on anti-Semitism or any statement dealing with the Jews or Judaism. Father Weigel replied that, although such a statement had been drafted during the first session, it was not presented to the Council Fathers "for the very simple reason that they were very much afraid of the Arab identification of this matter of moral principle with a political interest." At the same time Father Weigel stated that, in his personal opinion, "there would be definitely a readiness on the part of the whole Council of bishops to make a declaration on anti-Semitism, but this political obstacle would incline them rather to say nothing."

The Jesuit's remark prompted a reply from an official of the secretariat for unity that "no authorization whatever had been given to making statements like the one attributed to Father Weigel." This exchange, which was reported in the *New York Times,* occasioned a further statement by the Jesuit theologian: "I expressed it as my personal guess without instruction from anyone and representing no one, that it would probably be avoided in the second session. Gladly do I accept information from those in a better position who can give a contrary prognosis." During the second session Father Weigel admitted that he realized he had fallen into a trap nicely laid out for him by a journalist. At the same time, he felt, his remark had stirred things up and would, in the end, contribute to the passing of the Declaration.

Only during the second session did many Council participants come to realize that such a draft was in the making and that it would be distributed as part of the schema on ecumenism. The reason for its being incorporated as part of the draft on ecumenism was, perhaps, best presented by Bishop Charles Helmsing of Kansas City-St. Joseph, Mo., when he wrote in one of his interventions:

The "schism" between the Church and the Synagogue is a kind of prototype for all the other tragic divisions which have followed in the course of history. Ecumenical theologians are aware of this and frequently return to this consideration in their writings and discussions. . . . The proposal to include a statement on the Jews within the schema on ecumenism has already been made known to the world. The Jewish community has expressed its pleasure and looks forward longingly to this statement. To exclude all references to the Jews from this schema could well be interpreted as an attempt to exclude Jews from the ecumenical dialogue. Catholics, non-Catholic Christians, as well as Jews, are aware of the distinctions that must be made when Jews are included within the ecumenical dialogue; but once these distinctions are accepted, the unique relationship of the Jewish people with this dialogue still remains and should be recognized by all.

On November 8, 1963, the original text of this Declaration was distributed to the Council Fathers. At that time it was a text of 339 words and entitled chapter four of the schema on ecumenism. Its title was "The Relation of Catholics to non-Christians and especially the Jews." The second schema, called the "Arricia text," was approved on July 3, 1964, by the secretariat and entitled "Concerning the Jews and Non-Christians." The third version, distributed during the closing days of the third session—and the one actually discussed on the floor of the Council—was simply a "declaration" and entitled "The Relationship of the Church to non-Christian Religions." This same title survived in the fourth version which was voted upon during the fourth session. It remains the title of the finally promulgated Declaration which was expanded from the original 339 words to 1,117 words. The change in the title of the Declaration reflects, according to the judgment of some observers, a spirit of compromise seeking consensus among the Council Fathers. Other observers, however, are quick to point out that the final title reflects a broadening and deepening awareness on the part of the Council of the entire world and its religions.

This point was emphatically made by Father Thomas Stransky, C.S.P., a secretary of the secretariat for unity and one who had a key role in the final passage of the Declaration. Speaking at the United States Bishops' press panel on the afternoon of October 14, 1965, Father Stransky made the following observation:

Most of us forget that the subject of Jewish-Catholic relations is only one chapter of the document because of the specific problems with the Jews in our tradition. We tend to forget in our narrow, western way that two-thirds of the world is neither Jew nor Christian. Perhaps future historians will hail this document not so much for the chapter on the Jews, but for what the entire document says about all religions.

If you study conciliar history in the Church, you will recognize that this is the first time a Council looked not only to the Jews, but the Hindus, Moslems, Buddhists and even to its enemies, recognizing and praising the workings of God among these people. This Council is telling Catholics to get out of their ghetto, or their Christian-Jewish ghetto, and leap out towards all men and try to dialogue with them and cooperate with them when it is possible.

Nonetheless it was imperative that the Council direct its attention to the problem of Catholic-Jewish relations. Some of the statements uttered on the very floor of the Council were proof that a great deal of latent anti-Semitism was still at work in the thinking of Catholics. The spate of "hate" literature circulated during the time in which the Council was in session was still another proof. Such pamphlets as "The Council and the Assault of the Central European Bloc," "The Jews and the Council in the Light of Holy Scripture and Tradition," "The Jewish-Masonic Activity in the Council" and several anti-Semitic letters to the American hierarchy were but a few examples. The relationship of Italian political-economic life to the Middle East was also a factor not to be overlooked.

The insistence on the part of the Jewish community for such a text was personified in two representatives of Jewish groups who spent a great deal of time in Rome during the Council. They were Dr. Joseph L. Lichten of the Anti-Defamation League and Dr. Zacariah Schuster, European director of the American Jewish Committee. At a press conference sponsored by the Divine Word News Service on November 12, 1963, Dr. Schuster hailed the distribution of this schema on the previous November 8 as "one of the greatest moments in Jewish history. Jews of this generation," he continued, "will feel fortunate to have witnessed this historic step on the part of the Church." During this same press conference, John Cogley expressed the sentiments of an average American Catholic as well as his own feelings about the original text of this schema. He said:

I am an American and I was brought up on the doctrine of the brotherhood of man, and my teachers and my family instilled in me, early, the lesson of tolerance. But the awfulness of the Hitlerian persecution and the ugly doctrines put forth there demanded more than goodwill slogans in the language of tolerance that I was used to. It was then that I realized, I think for the first time, that there was a religious, a theological dimension to the Jewish-Catholic relationship. It was then I realized for the first time that there was a sense, some sense at least, in which every Catholic is also a Jew because we share so much of the same religious heritage. At the time, Pope Pius XI, replying to the outrages of the anti-Semites of the 1930's, said in his famous remark: "Spiritually we are Semites." I think the Pope meant, of course, that spiritually we are Jews. We call the Old Testament our own. We speak of our father Abraham. The Jewish prophets and the lawgivers are our prophets and our lawgivers. Our Lord and His disciples and His first Christians were all Jews. Our liturgy has its roots in the synagogue. We are, in fact, from morning till night drenched in Judaism. Without the Jews we would be nothing. Everything of which we are proud, for which we are grateful, has its source in the people of God, the people God chose long ago as His own. What He has planned for them in the future we don't pretend to know. . . . Now, when a Catholic meditates on these questions, his reverence for the Jewish tradition extends far beyond our tolerance or secular brotherhood. Anti-Semitism becomes an abomination, unspeakable abomination. . . . It seems to me that the importance of this statement released by the Vatican strikes an historic note because at long last it is focused correctly on the theological relationship between Catholic and Jew. It strikes deep at the Christian conscience. It is not merely a warning against bigotry or hatred, but a positive affirmation of the brotherhood, a brotherhood that extends even above and beyond the unity that joins us with all other men. The theology is not new, but the emphasis given to it is new.

Dr. Lichten, writing in *The Catholic World* between the second and third sessions, stated what he felt the Jewish people desired to see the Council propose. He went further and explained three reasons why this desire was so urgent at the present time.

First: we are persuaded that anti-Semitism is partly rooted in Christian traditions. Please note that I say *traditions*, for those of us who have examined the basic teachings of Christianity know full well that they contain no justification for anti-Semitism.

Second: we know that our sufferings are too often looked upon, even today, as God's righteous punishment for the alleged guilt of the Jewish people for the death of Christ.

Third: we see our beliefs and our solidarity as a people used against us, persistently and harmfully, to exclude us not only from the respect of other religious groups, but also from civic and social benefits.

During the third session Dr. Lichten presented a preliminary report on a research project sponsored by the Anti-Defamation League. His report was distributed through the Dutch Documentation Center and received a most favorable response among Americans. He concluded his report in the following words:

In sum, it seems reasonably clear that a majority of Roman Catholics interpret the Crucifixion story in ways which are not prejudicial to their conceptions and relations with their Jewish neighbors. Given the Church's concern to foster brotherhood among peoples, it can take justifiable pride in this evidence of the considerable progress which has been made. Nevertheless, there remains a significant minority of American Catholics who reveal anti-Semitic prejudice. Not all of this prejudice can be attributable to these Catholics' understanding of the Crucifixion story. Perhaps for as many as five million American Catholics (out of a total of over 44,874,371), however, if we project our figures to the national population, such an attribution is warranted. These Catholics continue to see the Jews as principally responsible for the death of Jesus, and they are led thereby to negative assessment of the contemporary Jew. The fact that those who believe and feel this way tend to go to church more frequently underscores the need for the

Catholic Church to intensify its efforts, if it hopes to win all Catholics to the principles of brotherhood which it espouses.

The role of the Arab countries, particularly in the pressure they exerted upon the Catholic minorities in their lands, was also a factor to be considered. "Nasserism," wrote one observer, "was built on anti-Semitism as a keystone." This same writer, explaining the reasons why the document was not presented in the first session, stated: "So well organized was the opposition to this document, so well orchestrated the voices from the Secretariat of State, Vatican City, and obedient Apostolic Delegates in the Near East, that Bea was forced to withdraw the document from the first session and bide his time."

Cardinal Bea's time, however, came during the seventieth general congregation on November 19, 1963. On that day he introduced the text for the consideration of the Council Fathers. He said the schema was undertaken by "the express command" of Pope John and added at the very outset: "There is no national or political question here. Especially, there is no question of acknowledging the State of Israel on the part of the Holy See." In the course of his introduction he stated the purpose of this document:

the aim of this very brief decree is to call to the attention of Christ's faithful these truths concerning the Jews proposed by the Apostle and contained in the deposit of faith, and to do this so clearly that in dealing with the children of that people the faithful will act in no other way than did Christ the Lord and His Apostles Peter and Paul. . . . The point, therefore, is not in any way to call into doubt—as is sometimes asserted—the events which are narrated in the Gospels about Christ's consciousness of His dignity and divine nature or about the manner in which the innocent Lord was unjustly condemned. Rather that, with these things kept fully in mind, it is possible and necessary to imitate the gentle charity of Christ the Lord and His Apostles with which they excused their persecutors.

Subsequent events, unfortunately, revealed that some of the Cardinal's listeners neither heard nor understood the meaning of his eloquent presentation. The formulation of the Declaration was one of the stormiest of all the debates on conciliar documents. If, as has been charged, the conservative theologians, the Italian political situation and the pressure of the Arab countries combined to make this true, responsibility for the turbulent route of the Declaration must also be borne by the petulance of some Jewish groups as well as the pressures exerted in some segments of the American press. If, as some observers point out, only these last two groups helped in keeping the document alive, they also assisted in forming opposition groups which did succeed in securing the compromises contained in the final text of the Declaration.

An American observer-delegate, Dr. Douglas Horton, viewed these concluding days of the second session in a much more dispassionate manner. Writing in his *Vatican Diary 1963* under the date of December 2, Dr. Horton made this observation:

> Some of the brethren are terribly disappointed that Bishop Helmsing's suggestion that the chapter on the Jews and on religious liberty be voted on before the end of the session has not been taken up. Some even feel that there has been dirty work at the crossroads by the conservatives to prevent discussion. But I wonder. I am not sure that the Americans, who have been especially eager to have the two chapters accepted as a basis for subsequent debate, are aware of the depth of the ocean of anti-Judaism with which the establishment of the State of Israel has engulfed the eastern end of the Mediterranean and the consequent necessity of talking the whole subject through without the presupposition of an adopted text—and the chapter on religious liberty is linked to that on the Jews, at least psychologically. At any rate, I believe Cardinal Bea when he says there is not enough time for adequate discussion and rely upon his promise that the two important subjects will be brought up next autumn.

Although Cardinal Bea introduced the text in the closing days of the second session, it did not come up for discussion on the floor of the Council at that time. The Council Fathers, however, did submit many observations on the text. These ware carefully considered during the plenary meeting of the secretariat for unity held from February 27 to March 7, 1964. According to a press release issued by the secretariat for unity, this plenary meeting agreed upon the following four points: 1) The schema on ecumenism, strictly so-called, will, as is logical, discuss only the question of unity among Christians. 2) The revised chapter on the Jews will be retained both for internal reasons and for its importance and because of the universal expectation which it has aroused. 3) Because of the special bonds uniting the people of the Old Covenant with the Church, the document on the Jews will be an appendix to the text on ecumenism, but not a chapter since, strictly speaking, ecumenism deals only with relationships among Christians. 4) This same appendix will touch on the relationships of Christians with non-Christian religions, with special emphasis on Islamism. As we have seen, the new text was approved by the Holy Father on July 3, 1964.

Throughout this period between sessions, fears were expressed concerning the fate of the Declaration. *The Pilgrim* made its appearance and expressed haunting doubts on almost every other page about the future of this schema. The *New York Times'* correspondent in Rome filed stories that were disturbing to many. Obviously, pressures were being exerted from every side.

Cardinal Spellman, as a member of the central coordinating commission and one of the presidents of the Council, was attuned to these anxieties. He acknowledged receipt of the Declaration on the Jews and non-Christians in an intervention submitted and dated June 13, 1964. Since, he wrote, the Declaration "will not be discussed for the next meeting of the committee for the coordination of the works of the Council [June 26]," he wanted to tell Amleto Cardinal Cicognani, Papal Secretary of State, "how many people have accepted the rumors of newspapers and other means of communications which state that this Declaration has been weakened in much of its significance and that it distinctly has left out any statement freeing the Jews from the guilt of deicide." The Archbishop of New York then continued:

> Having considered the publicity and the opinions of the men of this nation, it befits me, Your Eminence, to inform you of the consequences which will most certainly follow if the text of the definition will not clearly proclaim that the Jewish people themselves are not to be held guilty for the crucifixion of the Lord. From the very beginning, very many in the Jewish community held that the public profession of the Church about this innocence of the Jews was an essential aspect of the whole Declaration on the Jews. They necessarily believe that the omission has been calamitous and that it is very important that it be restored. I include an account in yesterday's *New York Times* [June 12], which speaks of a "widespread but trustworthy" Roman source, that expresses this same interpretation in describing the amended Declaration as "muted." I also send a copy of a statement I recently gave before the American Jewish Committee in order to illustrate that it seems to us that the Jewish people ought to hear from us if true harmony is to be sustained and strengthened.

In conclusion, Cardinal Spellman said that he felt it was his duty to inform His Eminence "that it is desirable that the words 'or of deicide' in the last paragraph of this section of the schema be reinserted. I also hope that this reinsertion can be so submitted as to compensate for the adverse tendency of the published accounts of its suppression."

The text finally came up for discussion during the eighty-ninth congregation, on September 28, 1964. It was discussed throughout three congregations with thirty-two Fathers making their voices heard on the floor of the Council. The fears of the Near East bishops were most eloquently expressed by Patriarch Maximos IV Saigh of Antioch. The reservations of the conservative theologians were voiced by such spokesmen as Ernesto Cardinal Ruffini of Palermo and Bishop Luigi Carli of Segni. The liberal and open attitudes were expressed by the five American prelates who voiced their sentiments on September 28 and 29. Richard Cardinal Cushing of Boston was the first American to speak and proposed three amendments. He asked, first, that the statement be "more positive, less timid, more charitable. Surely," he continued, "we ought to indicate the fact that we sons of Abraham according to the spirit must show a special esteem and particular love for the sons of Abraham according to the flesh because of this common patrimony. As sons of Adam, they are our brothers; as sons of Abraham, they are the blood brothers of Christ."

Secondly, the Archbishop of Boston declared,

In this Declaration in clear and evident words we must deny that the Jews are guilty of the death of our Savior, except insofar as all men have sinned and on that account crucified Him and, indeed, still crucify Him. And especially we must condemn any who would attempt to justify inequities, hatred, or even persecution of the Jews as Christian actions.

All of us have seen the evil fruit of this kind of false reasoning. In this august assembly, in this solemn moment, we must cry out. There is no Christian rationale—neither theological nor historical—for any inequity, hatred, or persecution of our Jewish brothers.

In his third point the Cardinal said that we should "confess humbly before the world that Christians too frequently have not shown themselves as true Christians, as faithful to Christ, in their relations with their Jewish brothers."

The second American to speak was Albert Cardinal Meyer of Chicago who said the schema was "satisfactory in this sense that we do have a schema dealing with this matter." He felt, however, that "the earlier text given to us last year dealt with the question of the Jews in a better and more ecumenical fashion." Among the five points he made, his second was the most insistent. He said:

It is not sufficient, in my judgment, to say that the Church decries and condemns hatred and persecution of the Jews for the simple reason that "it severely repudiates wrongs done to men wherever they appear." Justice demands that we give explicit attention to the enormous impact of the wrongs done through the centuries to the Jews. The particular afflictions which the Jewish people have undergone make it imperative that we add a special condemnation of every form of anti-Semitism, as was done in the earlier text when it stated: "Thus it all the more decries and condemns with maternal sentiments the hatred and persecutions inflicted on the Jews, whether of old or in our own times."

In his fourth point Cardinal Meyer advocated returning to the text of the previous schema in these words:

These lines, as they stand, admonish Christian people never to speak of the Jews as a reprobate race, and "not to blame the Jews of our day for what happened in the passion of Christ." The Cardinal Relator has already pointed out to us in his *relatio* the difficulty of finding an apt formula, but he has also invited us to take this part of the schema and once more "place it under scrutiny and discuss it." Indeed, our schema appears to say far too little in this place. Briefly, but in a better manner, in my view, the earlier text had stated on this point: "wrongly nevertheless would they be styled as an accursed people, since they remained most dear to God because of the fathers and the gifts given to them (cf. Romans 11:28), or a deicide race, because it was the sins of all men, which were the cause of the passion and death of Jesus Christ, that the Lord atoned for in His passion and death."

During the same congregation Joseph Cardinal Ritter of St. Louis said that he eagerly awaited "this Declaration which both directly and aptly responds to a modern need." He felt the Declaration made "a good beginning," but could be improved. He expressed one of his suggestions in these words:

> The Declaration should speak more fully and explicitly about the religious patrimony which the Jewish people and the Christian people once and even today share. The promises made to Abraham by God, which do not fail nor are able to fail faith, pertain now to the Jews. Divine love itself is extended in a special way to Jews and Christians, and because of this there ought to grow between us and them the sharpest unity of love and esteem. And so, this spirit of love, which was found in the original schema, should also shine forth even more in this Declaration. Our debt and witness before the Jews, which in this schema are acknowledged hesitantly and somewhat forebodingly, should be proclaimed with great joy.

He suggested, in conclusion, that the final paragraph of the schema should be couched in the following language:

> Therefore all should be careful lest they represent the Jewish people as a rejected people, cursed, or in any way as deicides; lest they impute to the whole Jewish people then living, nor *a fortiori* to the Jews of our time, what was perpetrated in the passion of Christ. All these things actually should be imputed to all sinful men and especially to Christians who live willfully in sin.

On the following day Auxiliary Bishop Stephen Leven of San Antonio addressed the Council Fathers. He likewise objected to the omission of the word "deicide" from the text and advocated its return in the following words:

> To paragraph 32, line 22 should be added, "The Jews must never be called a deicide people." This *monitum* was set forth plainly in the first version of this document, that is, in chapter four of the schema on ecumenism given to us last year. It was said in that text that the Jews were not guilty of deicide. Now this statement is not in the present text.
>
> Some say this statement was suppressed because the word "deicide" is philosophically and theologically absurd, *per se* contradictory, and therefore not worthy of a conciliar document.
>
> Fathers of the Council, we are not dealing here with some philosophical entity, but with a word of infamy and execration which was invented by

Christians and used to blame and persecute the Jews. For so many centuries, and even in our own, Christians have hurled this word against Jews, and because of it they have justified every kind of horrible excess and even their slaughter and destruction. It is not up to us to make a declaration about something philosophical, but to reprobate and damn a word which has furnished so many occasions of persecution through the centuries. We must tear this word out of the Christian vocabulary so that it may never again be used against the Jews.

Archbishop Patrick O'Boyle of Washington, D.C., also spoke during this nintieth congregation. His remarks were summarized by the Vatican Council press bulletin in the following paragraph:

Certain amendments are called for lest the aims of the Declaration be misinterpreted by Jews. The spirit of the text is ecumenical, and the Declaration will be carefully studied by Jews. Hence we must speak in a manner intelligible to them. Our motive is not false irenicism, but only the desire to be precise and exact and to be inspired by wisdom and charity. Every Jew will interpret our words in the context of history, and our text does not show sufficient respect for the sensibilities of the Jewish people. Any even remote suggestion of "conversion" will recall the sufferings of the past and the forced conversions which were imposed on the Jews. Rightly they want no part of any similar proselytism. The text should be changed in the part dealing with the responsibility of Jews for the death of Christ. It should include Jews both today and at the time of Christ. We must give the whole truth, in keeping with the traditional teaching of the Church against opprobrium heaped upon the Jewish people in the past. The charity of Christ urges us.

Bishop Charles Helmsing, who was elected by his colleagues during the preceding session to serve as a member of the secretariat for unity, submitted two written interventions concerning the Church's relationship with the Jewish people. In a lengthy document treating many aspects of the Decree on Ecumenism, one of his points concerned the Jews. He wrote:

With regard to the relationship of the Church to the Jews, however, it can well be argued that such a treatment belongs in this schema. Although a statement on the Jews could well be assigned to another schema, the reasons presented by His Eminence, Cardinal Bea, in presenting the *relatio* on Chapter IV merit the greatest consideration, and this chapter could well remain as part of the schema on ecumenism. The hopes of the Jewish community have been and still are very high, and to delay indefinitely a statement on this subject could be very harmful to dialogue with the Jews.

Whether this statement remains in the present schema or not, it should be treated by the Council.

In another written intervention, Bishop Helmsing presented another argument when he wrote: "According to the spirit of the encyclical letter *Pacem in Terris,* in this or in another schema there should be greetings to all men of good will, even to the infidels, for example, the Mohammedans, and to the pagans, for example, the Buddhists."

Auxiliary Bishop Fulton J. Sheen also submitted his written observations on this schema. He argued that both the Old and New Testament prove that the Catholic's relationship to the Jew should be one of love and brotherhood. Addressing his remarks to the charge of condemning the Jews he wrote:

> If Christ Himself prayed to the Father for the Jews, "Father, forgive them, for they know not what they do" (Lk. 23:34), we are not given the right to condemn them. That a whole race should be condemned for a few is not just!
>
> The Jews were not only our fathers, but also they will be our future offspring. "I do not want you to ignore this mystery, that partial blindness has come upon Israel, to last until all the nations have come in, and then, *all Israel will be saved*" (Rom 11: 25–26).
>
> How, therefore, can we condemn those who will be our deliverers in the future? In condemning them, we condemn ourselves!

Finally, he concluded with an argument from the present situation in the world.

> A certain "polarism" seems to be truly necessary today. "Polarism" is here understood as that quality by virtue of which two or more extremes, opposite and remaining separate, tend to one and the same end.
>
> Since no one denies the existing necessity today of forming a certain coalition between the different religions of the world in order to fight atheism, Jews joining together with Catholics and other religions must be united by a chain of charity and peace.

The discussions on the schema were concluded during the ninety-first congregation, September 30, and the document was returned to the secretariat for unity for emendation. The revised text was distributed to the Council Fathers on November 18, during the 125th congregation. It escaped the tragic finale of the Declaration on Religious Freedom during these concluding dark days of the third session only by the fact that it was submitted for a vote of approval or rejection. The vote was both a victory for the Declaration and the secretariat for unity. Of the 1,996 Council Fathers who cast their votes, 1,651 approved, 242 approved with reservation, and only 99 voted disapproval of the Declaration.

There was, again, an air of disappointment among many of the Council Fathers over the failure to act definitively on this Declaration. In some ways, however, this disappointment was a failure to distinguish between the lack of a vote on the Declaration of Religious Freedom and this Declaration. Many failed to realize that the vote of November 20 placed the Declaration squarely on the docket for the next session. It achieved the legal status of being "in possession."

Between the third and fourth sessions the secretariat for unity set to work again revising and amending the text of the Declaration according to the suggestions offered by the Council Fathers. Once again the world press voiced its doubts about the safety of the document. Rumors from Jerusalem to New York to Rome were again rife. The propaganda mills were busily grinding out their versions of what was happening to the schema. The secretariat for unity was besieged from all quarters concerning the status of the declaration. A prominent American conciliar consultant used his own offices to urge Ambassador to the United Nations, Arthur J. Goldberg, to intercede with Vatican officials on behalf of the Declaration. It was reported that emissaries from the Arab countries were busily at work in exerting their pressures on Vatican offices. All these rumors and counter-rumors can be documented only by a future historian. One intervention, however, was submitted by the Cardinal Archbishop of New York. Writing to the central coordinating commission during this time, Cardinal Spellman made the following statement:

> Since we are aware of the publicity and concern this matter has aroused, we must see to it that the greatest care be taken lest the Council appear to consider the question on the Jews of little importance. Because the deliberations undertaken in the Council's second session have become public knowledge, many people have awaited firm and certain testimony of the Council, stating that the Jews of our time are not personally responsible for the death of Our Lord. Without doubt, therefore, any weakening or change whatsoever of the present text will lend itself to the worst possible interpretation.

During the intersession the Council Fathers received no revised text of the Declaration. Only after they had been present for almost a month at the fourth session did they finally receive the "amended" text of the previously "approved" text. Immediately they turned to page nine and there discovered that, in spite of the many interventions submitted, the word "deicide" was omitted. On the same page they also discovered that the verb "condemns" was also missing from the sentence in which the Holy Synod "deplores and condemns hatred and persecution against the Jews." These omissions caused great discussion among the Council Fathers, the press representatives and the Jewish organizations. The reasons presented by the secretariat for unity, namely, that "deicide" was an untheological word and "condemnations" were not consistent with the pastoral nature of this Council, offered meagre solace. In a last-ditch stand, Auxiliary Bishop Stephen Leven circulated a memo to the American bishops. The text of his memo was as follows:

> There can be no doubt that in general the paragraph (No. 4) on the Jews in the Declaration of the Relation of the Church to non-Christians is stronger than its predecessors. However, in one significant point it has been made weaker and much less acceptable. This is the change which in the new text appears on page 9, line 3 to line 9, which reads: "Although the Church is the new People of God, the Jews should not be presented as rejected by God, or accursed, as if this follows from the Holy Scriptures." This replaces what in the former text read: "May they never present the Jewish people as one rejected, cursed or guilty of deicide."
>
> The sixth question on page 38 asks if the bishops approve this change. Unless two thirds approve the change, the former text will stand.
>
> The word "deicide" was invented by Christians and has been hurled at the Jews for centuries to justify persecutions and pogroms. It seems fitting that this Sacred Council should specifically reject it.
>
> You are respectfully asked to consider voting "non placet" on the sixth question so that the former and *approved* text may remain.

Unfortunately, Bishop Leven's valiant crusade was mounted too late. At this stage of the conciliar process the status of the question had resolved itself into one of two positions: acceptance of the declaration totally or total rejection. During the 149th and 150th congregations the Council Fathers were presented eight votes on the Declaration. All of them passed overwhelmingly. The ninth vote, on the Declaration as a whole, passed by a vote of 1,856 to 243. At this point the Council had arrived at a consensus, even if it was achieved by way of compromise.

This same afternoon, Bishop Francis P. Leipzig of Baker, Oregon, appeared at the United States Bishops' press panel as chairman of the subcommission on Catholic-Jewish relations of the United States Bishops' Commission on Ecumenism. At this time he announced the members who would serve on his subcommission, with Monsignor George G. Higgins as secretary. The membership, which he said would be expanded in the coming years, included Monsignors John M. Oesterreicher of Seton Hall University; Mark J. Hurley of the Archdiocese of San Francisco; Daniel Cantwell of the Archdiocese of Chicago; Francis J. Lally of the Archdiocese of Boston; Reverends Raymond Bosler of the Archdiocese of Indianapolis; Edward Flannery of the Diocese of Providence; Elmo L. Romagosa of the Archdiocese of New Orleans, Gerald F. Van Ackeren, S.J., of St. Mary's College, Kansas; Roland Murphy, O.Carm., of The

Catholic University of America; Edward Duff, S.J., of Holy Cross College, Worcester, Mass.; and Donald Campion, S.J., of Fordham University, New York. During this same press panel Bishop Leipzig made the following statement:

> I am delighted at the approval of the Declaration on non-Christian religions by the Council. The whole Declaration is of great significance. To me, of course, the section on the Jews is most important. I am sure it will usher in a new era of friendship and cooperation with our Jewish brethren, for the benefit of all men.
>
> It is true the Declaration has a few—in my opinion, minor—imperfections. But so have some other documents issued or to be issued by this Council. The commission charged with the preparation of conciliar texts seeks to get the greatest possible consensus. They must also try to avoid misunderstandings, here and there. The consequences of this are, at times, some weaker expressions than one would wish. But the individual expressions or sentences carry less weight than the entire document. What count are the over-all text and the over-all spirit.
>
> This spirit is one of kinship, reverence and determination. The Fathers of the Council are conscious, lovingly conscious, of the heritage the Church shares with the Jews. They are filled with reverence for the people of God selected for this special purpose. They reject the notion that the Jewish people is collectively guilty of the death of Jesus or that it is excluded from the grace of God. On the contrary, the Council Fathers honor the Jews as a people He holds most dear. The bishops are determined that, as far as they are concerned, all manifestations of anti-Semitism—like all hatred, all persecutions, all discrimination of whatever kind—must disappear from the face of the earth.
>
> I look forward to the time when the Council's wish for more deepened conversations with our Jewish brethren will be implemented, and I pledge my whole-hearted support toward that important purpose.

The discussions that accompanied the Declaration on the Relationship of the Church to Non-Christian Religions produced two very important Vatican secretariats. The one, established on May 17, 1964 by Pope Paul VI, is the Secretariat for Non-Christian Religions under the presidency of Paolo Cardinal Marella. One of the members of this secretariat is Archbishop John F. Dearden of Detroit. The purpose of this secretariat was explained by one of its consultors, Father Joseph Spae, C.I.C.M., in these words:

> It proposes to create a climate of cordiality, sincerity and charity between Christians and the followers of other religions, be they considered institutionally or as individuals. It does not aim at convert-making through discussions of doctrinal problems, apologetics or polemics. Nor does it intend

to take over from missionaries the task of preaching the Gospel and the care of souls.

Rather, its attention goes toward setting up contact with non-Christians regarding questions of common human interest. The secretariat intends to dissipate prejudices against, and ignorance of, the Catholic Faith by opening our own eyes to those prejudices and ignorance in ourselves which may prevent our fruitful contact with others.

The Secretariat for Non-Believers was created by Pope Paul shortly afterwards, before the beginning of the fourth session. Its president is Franziskus Cardinal König of Vienna. Its first full meeting, with 23 member-bishops from throughout the world, was held on November 13, 1965. The keystone for both these secretariats will be the Declaration on the Relationship of the Church to Non-Christian Religions. The Declaration was solemnly promulgated on October 28, 1965 by Pope Paul VI after a vote on the part of the Council Fathers, with 2,221 approving and only 88 casting a negative vote.

The final text of the Declaration was recognized by everyone as a compromise, a consensus. "A Council document," wrote Father John B. Sheerin, C.S.P., editor of *The Catholic World,* "to be a sweeping success needs a consensus. The Council's motive in changing the wording was to produce a truly effective weapon in the war against anti-Semitism."

Summing up the Declaration from another viewpoint, Rabbi Marc H. Tanenbaum, who was invited to the Council by Cardinal Lawrence Shehan, a member of the secretariat for unity, said, "The intent is clear. It is an unambiguous mandate to the Catholic people to remove the roots of anti-Semitism from the whole culture, both religious and secular." In an excellent essay entitled "The Council's Statement on the Jew," Dr. Lichten made the following acute and accurate observation:

> The Declaration cannot be discussed apart from the purposes of Vatican II and the historic exigencies weighing upon it. The document cannot be viewed independently of other schemas, which also encountered difficulties and which some also consider to be not altogether perfect. The final draft of every conciliar decree represents the confluence of various opinions, theological interpretations, outside pressures—in brief, the reality in which the Catholic Church of our time lives and works. Now that the historic four-session meeting has ended, and the 2500 bishops, cardinals and *periti,* or experts, have returned to their homelands all over the world, it is helpful to realize that the doctrines they propounded were the best which were possible in consideration of all the influences present: influences of history, of cultural contexts, of races, of nationalities, of social concepts, and, most important, of religious legacy. From this viewpoint, the Declaration on non-Christian religions, whatever its infelicities or shortcomings, emerges as a milestone in the history of the Church.

The Declaration on the Relationship of the Church to non-Christian Religions is now an official teaching of the Roman Catholic Church. History, unfortunately, records the sometimes tragic distance between teaching and practice. This Declaration will achieve its objective only when all Christians make part and parcel of their lives these words of the Declaration:

We cannot truly call on God, the Father of all, if we refuse to treat in a brotherly way any man, created as he is in the image of God. Man's relation to God the Father and his relation to men his brothers are so linked together that Scripture says, "He who does not love does not know God."

Declaration on the Relationship of the Church to Non-Christian Religions

✠ INTERVENTIONS

RICHARD CARDINAL CUSHING, 28 *September, 1964*

The declaration on the Jews and non-Christians is acceptable, in general. Through this Ecumenical Council the Church must manifest to the whole world, and to all men, a concern which is genuine, an esteem all embracing, a sincere charity—in a word, it must show forth Christ. And this schema *De Ecumenismo,* with its declarations on religious liberty and on the Jews and non-Christians, in a certain sense does just that. I would propose, however, three amendments specifically on the Jews.

First: We must make our statement about the Jews more positive, less timid, more charitable. Our text well illustrates the priceless patrimony which the new Israel has received from the law and the prophets.

And it well illustrates what the Jews and Christians share in common. But surely we ought to indicate the fact that we, sons of Abraham according to the spirit, must show a special esteem and particular love for the sons of Abraham according to the flesh because of this common patrimony. As sons of Adam, they are our brothers; as sons of Abraham, they are the blood brothers of Christ.

The fourth paragraph of this declaration should manifest this and our obligation of special esteem as a conclusion which logically flows from the first section.

Secondly: On the culpability of the Jews for the death of our Savior, as we read in Sacred Scriptures, the rejection of the Messiah by His own people is a mystery: a mystery which is indeed for our instruction, not our exaltation.

The parables and prophecies of Our Lord teach us this. We cannot judge the leaders of ancient Israel; God alone is their judge. And, most certainly, we cannot dare attribute to later generations of Jews the guilt of the crucifixion of the Lord Jesus or the death of the Savior of the world, except in the sense of the universal guilt in which all of us men share.

We know and we believe that Christ died freely, and He died for all men and because of the sins of all men, Jews and Gentiles.

Therefore, in this declaration, in clear and evident words we must deny that the Jews are guilty of the death of our Savior, except insofar as all men have sinned and on that account crucified Him and, indeed, still crucify Him. And we must especially condemn any who would attempt to justify inequities, hatred or even persecution of the Jews as Christian actions.

All of us have seen the evil fruit of this kind of false reasoning. In this august assembly, in this solemn moment, we must cry out. There is no Christian rationale—neither theological nor historical—for any inequity, hatred or persecution of our Jewish brothers.

Great is the hope, both among Catholics and among our separated Christian brothers, as well as among our Jewish friends in the New World, that this Sacred Synod will make such a fitting declaration.

Thirdly, and finally, I ask, Venerable Brothers, whether we ought not to confess humbly before the world that Christians too frequently have not shown themselves as true Christians, as faithful to Christ, in their relations with their Jewish brothers? In this our age, how many have suffered! How many have died because of the indifference of the Christians, because of silence! There is no need to enumerate the crimes committed in our own time. If not many Christian voices were lifted in recent years against the great injustices, yet let our voices humbly cry out now!

ALBERT CARDINAL MEYER, *28 September, 1964*

The schema is satisfactory in this sense that we do have a schema dealing with this matter. For, in speaking on ecumenism, the Council rightly treats in a special manner and by name of the Jews, as the Cardinal Relator has just abundantly proved in his relation. We know, indeed, in the light of divine revelation that the Jews had and still continue to have a special role in the economy of salvation.

Moreover, it is a fact of history that many Christians have not always properly acknowledged this role of the Jewish people in the economy of salvation—in fact, at times they have demeaned it. It is our task to remove the cause of this failing and to remind the faithful of Sacred Scripture's unambiguous teaching about this people. Thus, the demands of religion and of the charity of Christ prompt us to deal in particular and by name with the Jews. The importance, therefore, of this declaration has already been fully set forth in every aspect by the Cardinal Relator, and there is no need for me to repeat the very copious reasons advanced by him, but simply to state that I heartily support them all.

The schema as it stands, however, is satisfactory only after a fashion [*juxta modum*]. In my opinion, the earlier text given to us last year dealt with the question of the Jews in a better and more ecumenical fashion. In order that this may be true of our present text I wish to recommend some emendations.

1) It would be better to place lines 14–16 of number 32 before lines 11–13. In this way the logical order of the Pauline text is preserved (Roman 9: 4–5). If these two paragraphs are thus arranged, they can be readily rounded off with an explicit statement that the faith of the Church drew its beginning directly from those Jews who were the first, under the movement of God's grace, to open their spirits to the Gospel of Christ and to share the Good News with others. With this in mind, I propose a new draft of the text for lines 11–16, which, for brevity's sake, I shall not read, but submit in writing:

> The Church ever has and will have before its eyes the words of the Apostle Paul concerning the Jews, "to whom belong the adoption of the sons and of glory, the covenant, the law, service and promises, and the fathers, from whose number came Christ according to the flesh, who is God over all things" (Romans 9:4–5). Neither does the Church forget that from the Jewish people were born Christ's mother, the Virgin Mary, and the Apostles, the foundation and pillars of the Church, and those many early Christians who first gave the teaching of Christ to the world.

2) *Lines 20–22 of the same number 32:* It is not sufficient, in my judgment, to say that the Church decries and condemns hatred and persecution of the Jews for the simple reason that "it severely repudiates wrongs done to men wherever they appear." Justice demands that we give explicit attention to the enormous impact of the wrongs done through the centuries to the Jews. The particular afflictions which the Jewish people have undergone make it imperative that we add a special condemnation of every form of anti-Semitism, as was done in the earlier text when it stated: "thus it all the more decries and condemns with maternal sentiment the hatred and persecutions inflicted on the Jews, whether of old or in our own times."

3) *Lines 23–27 of the same number 32:* What is contained in this paragraph certainly has a base in the clear teaching of St. Paul (cf. Romans 11:25). The question here is only whether it is not impossible in a document that in all other places treats of ecumenism to explain this a little more fully, more or less according to the spirit of the principles set forth in number 4 of the first chapter of this entire schema "On Ecumenism." If this is not possible, it is to be feared, in my opinion, that this declaration of ours will furnish an occasion for a false interpretation of our true intention in making it.

4) *Lines 28–32 of the same number 32:* These lines, as they stand, admonish Christian people never to speak of the Jews as a reprobate race, and "not to blame the Jews of our day for what happened in the passion of Christ." The Cardinal Relator has already pointed out to us in his *relatio* the difficulty of finding an apt formula, but he has also invited us to take this part of the schema and once more "place it under scrutiny and discuss it." Indeed, our

schema appears to say far too little in this place. Briefly, but in a better manner, in my view, the earlier text had stated on this point: "wrongly, nevertheless, would they be styled as an accursed people, since they remained most dear to God because of the fathers and the gifts given to them (cf. Romans 11:28), or a deicide race, because it was the sins of all men which were the cause of the passion and death of Jesus Christ, that the Lord atoned for in His passion and death."

Is it not true, on this point, that our task is rather to set forth the whole truth about the Jews, more or less according to the mind of St. Thomas (ST III, q. 47, art. 5, *in corpus*), as was done in the earlier text? For St. Thomas, on the basis of Sacred Scripture, laid down these two points: 1) None of the Jews of the time of Christ was formally and subjectively guilty of deicide since all were ignorant of Christ's divinity. This ought to be said explicitly in our text. 2) The mass of the Jews must be absolved of all formal guilt because they followed the leaders out of ignorance. In proof of this, St. Thomas advances the words of St. Peter: "I know that you did this out of ignorance, as did your leaders" (Acts 3:17).

Finally, something will have to be stated about where the true cause of the sufferings of Christ is to be sought: "He died for us and for our salvation!"

5) *With respect to the second part of our declaration* (nn. 33–34): What is contained in these numbers is certainly of the greatest importance, and it is by all means necessary that the Council, even though it be only briefly as here, treat of these two points, namely, of the divine fatherhood with regard to all men, and of the condemnation of all brands of discrimination.

Some Fathers perhaps think that these teachings ought better to be dealt with in Schema 13 where there is question of the Church in the modern world. The question of where a topic is to be treated seems to me to be a matter of less importance, and, in my opinion, the topic is rightly included in our declaration.

Two points, however, in the text presented us seem worthy of mention:

a) The reasons given in the text for a special mention of the Muslims apply equally well to other non-Christian communities. Thus, there ought to be an explicit reference to them together with the Muslims; or merely a general mention of all those who "are monotheists and joined by cultural bonds with us" would be sufficient.

b) Quite rightly and deservedly ought we to speak out against every brand of discrimination—whether on grounds of religion, or of race, color or human status. Nevertheless, since discrimination because of color, race or human status is truly one of the gravest problems confronting the world today, I should like to see the teaching of the Church against this form of discrimination set forth more at length and in more positive fashion, so that the image of the Church may shine forth by glowing example in every area in accord with the most sacred words of our Lord: "In this may all men know that you are my disciples, that you have love one for another."

JOSEPH CARDINAL RITTER, *28 September, 1964*

I am speaking on the schema which treats of the Jews and specifically about paragraph 32. I eagerly await this declaration which both directly and aptly responds to a modern need. The need of which I am speaking is not to avoid or conciliate political or ethnic pressure or to seek the favor of men, but simply to repair an injustice of the centuries.

We Christians, for many centuries now, have been guilty of error and injustice against the Jews. We, as many others, have been assuming that God has abandoned this people. Christians, even in Church documents, have been accusing the Jewish people of the passion and death of Christ. In prayers they have been called "the perfidious people," "the deicide people" who "upon themselves have once called the blood of the Savior." The opportunity now presents itself today that we, gathered in an ecumenical Council, reject and repair such errors and injustices.

The schema offers a declaration which makes a good beginning toward this end. But the schema can be improved, and it demands, it seems to me, certain amendments among which, I propose the following:

1) The declaration should speak more fully and explicitly about the religious patrimony which the Jewish people and the Christian people once and even today share. The promises made to Abraham by God, which do not fail nor are able to fail faith, pertain now to the Jews. Divine love itself is extended in a special way to Jews and Christians, and because of this there ought to grow between us and them the sharpest unity of love and esteem. And so, this spirit of love, which was found in the original schema, should also shine forth even more in this declaration. Our debt and witness before the Jews, which in this schema are acknowledged hesitantly and somewhat forebodingly, should be proclaimed with great joy.

2) In lines 23 to 27, the manner of treating of "union of the Jewish people with the Church" by pointing out their errors sounds like *conversion of the Jews,* especially because neither the Moslems, pagans nor man in general is so treated Nevertheless, the mission of the Church, as also the Mystery of Christ, embraces all men in Christian hope. It would be better, in fact almost necessary, conforming to the nature of the Church and as less offensive to all, to transfer these lines to the end of the whole declaration on non-Christians in a universal manner which includes all men.

3) The last article in paragraph 32 pleases me least. It does nothing to correct errors or repair injustices. On the contrary, by reason of the last sentence in which only the Jews of our time are exonerated, both the error and the injustice are compounded.

Venerable Fathers, we should erase this error which makes a people guilty of a crime committed by individuals which imbues even in the hearts of infants a spirit of hatred for a people so loved by God. This last article should be removed, and in its place should be inserted this paragraph or something similar:

> Therefore, all should be careful lest they represent the Jewish people as a rejected people, cursed, or in any way as deicides; lest they impute to the whole Jewish people then living and *a fortiori* to the Jews of our time, what was perpetrated in the passion of Christ. All these things actually should be imputed to all sinful men and especially to Christians who live willfully in sin. Also, as the Catechism of the Council of Trent most clearly mentions: "It is judged that all are held by this guilt who habitually live willfully in sin. For since our sins struck Christ the Lord so that He underwent the humiliation of the cross, truly those who continue in shameful actions and heinous deeds—because He is in them—crucify in themselves the Son of God."

BISHOP STEPHEN LEVEN, *29 September, 1964*

In general, the declaration is satisfactory, but I wish to propose three emendations. Proposing the first and second, I speak in the name of nearly all the archbishops and bishops of the United States; proposing the third, I speak in my own name.

1) To paragraph 32, line 22 should be added, "The Jews must never be called a deicide people." This *monitum* was set forth plainly in the first version of this document, that is, in chapter four of the schema on ecumenism given to us last year. It was said in that text that the Jews were not guilty of deicide. Now this statement is not in the present text.

Some say this statement was suppressed because the word "deicide" is philosophically and theologically absurd, *per se* contradictory, and therefore not worthy of a conciliar document.

Fathers of the Council, we are not dealing here with some philosophical entity, but with a word of infamy and execration which was invented by Christians and used to blame and persecute the Jews. For so many centuries, and even in our own, Christians have hurled this word against Jews, and because of it they have justified every kind of horrible excess and even their slaughter and destruction. It is not up to us to make a declaration about something philosophical, but to reprobate and damn a word which has furnished so many occasions of persecution through the centuries. We must tear this word out of the Christian vocabulary, so that it may never again be used against the Jews.

The Council of Trent declared that all men and their sins were the cause of the death of Christ. Therefore, we are all guilty and must confess that we have sinned and procured the death of Christ. This death is not to be attributed to any one people.

There is another reason why this sentence should be restored in the text of our declaration. The whole world knows the history of anti-Semitism among Christians. So many horrible things have been perpetrated against the Jews. Now the world awaits and expects an absolute and irrefutable sign of our good faith in this matter of justice. We must repudiate the Machiavellian spirit by which we should demand justice for ourselves alone. We, as Fathers of the Council, must seek justice for all men according to the necessities of situation and time. Our time and our situation now demand this repudiation and reprobation. Precisely because this was in the earlier document does its omission here seem a refusal of the justice we must render to the Jews.

2) My second emendation: in paragraph 32 after line 32 should be inserted, "Not all the Jews of the time of Christ are to be blamed for the death of Christ."

Obviously, many of the Jews of the time of Christ, especially in the diaspora, never heard of Him, nor could they have consented to His death. It is as absurd to accuse all the Jews of the time of Christ of His death as it would be to blame all the Romans of that time for His death because the Roman Pilate delivered Him up and Roman soldiers nailed Him to the Cross.

3) The third and final emendation I make in my own name. To paragraph 33, line two there should be added an expression of our eschatological hope that all men of every race and people, Jews and Gentiles, will be gathered together with God, as St. Paul wrote (I Tim. 2:4): "It is the will of God that all men should be saved and come to the knowledge of the truth." Thus also we shall apply in this context the beautiful words of the Constitution on the Church, chapter one, paragraph two, lines 10–15, "But at that time, as we read in the holy Fathers, all the just from the time of Adam, 'from Abel the just even to the last of the elect,' will be gathered together with the Father in the universal Church."

ARCHBISHOP PATRICK O'BOYLE, 29 *September, 1964*

Speaking about the declaration concerning Jews and non-Christians, I should like to propose certain changes. These are prompted by practical reasons which arise quite naturally in the mind of a bishop in whose country live a larger number of Jews than in any other nation in the world and who presently have definite objections against the contents of this declaration.

It is true that this declaration is proposed as an expression of the Catholic bishops and it is directed primarily to Catholics. However, the spirit of this declaration is ecumenical, and the things it finally enunciates will be studied diligently by the Jews since it deals primarily with them. Hence, the spirit, the style and the words of this declaration must be ecumenical by orientation. The charity of Christ impels us to express our thoughts in such a way as to avoid any occasion for offense and to speak in a way which would be intelligible to the Jews and in harmony with the hopes and aspirations of the Jewish mind.

This does not mean that we should hide the truths of the Catholic faith by a false "irenicism." On the contrary, it means that our words must be very precise and exact and must be guided by wisdom or by "knowledge animated by charity" which takes into consideration the historical context in which our words are going to be understood by each and every Jew. I have fear that the declaration, as it is, in some respects does not conform with this norm. In fact, in some places the declaration deflects from the truth and fails to pay attention to the great sensitivity which history has occasioned in the hearts of the Jewish people.

The first example is found in number 32 from the 23rd to the 27th line. The phrases "the union of the Jewish people with the Church" and "the drawing of this people . . . to the fullness of the People of God" suggest immediately to a Jewish mind a vehement desire of Catholics for "the conversion" of the Jews. This term "conversion" immediately recalls to the mind of the Jews the persecutions, the suffering and even the forced rejection of all the truths by which subjectively, and in good faith, a Jew sincerely lives. Thus, when a Jew hears of the desire of Catholics for his conversion, he thinks of the renewal of the "proselytism" which for many centuries violated his rights and personal dignity.

To be sure, a conversion of the Jews and of all other peoples to the Catholic faith is the hope of all Catholics. But, as St. Thomas stated, "a hope concerning one's neighbor must be governed by a sense of moderation." We must not forget that a hope for the conversion of the Jews is no certainty for a happy ending. The fate of the Jewish people depends entirely on the disposition of Divine Providence and the grace of God. Therefore, when we express our hope in words which lead the Jews to interpret them as a definite and clear intention to work for their conversion, we construct another high wall separating us from a holy and fruitful dialogue with the Jewish people.

Furthermore, in expressing the hope for the conversion of the Jews and of all other people, the declaration, from the 23rd to the 27th line, oversteps the precise boundaries of Catholic teaching. In fact, the text of St. Paul's letter to the Romans (Rom 11:25) is quoted in the declaration. In this passage the Apostle uses words so vague and mysterious that Catholic exegetes themselves propose very different interpretations. It would be better, therefore, if we accepted the limitations of our knowledge and the unknown ways of Divine Providence. It would be better if we expressed hope for the conversion of the Jews in such a way that the Jews themselves would perceive our respect for their sincerity and our humble recognition of the truth that the mysteries of salvation depend not on us, but on the action of God. Hence, I propose that the following words be used in place of the paragraph in question:

It is well to remember that the union of the Jewish people and of our own people is part of our Christian hope. This union, which the Church ardently hopes for with undaunted faith, will be accomplished by God in His own time and in a manner known to Him alone. (cf. Rom 11:25–26)

Likewise, out of consideration for truth and charity, I am compelled to repeat the opinion of His Eminence Cardinal Meyer that the statement contained in number 32, from the 28th to the 32nd line, be totally changed. In the present text, as it reads now, the declaration proposes only half the truth and most certainly it will offend the Jews. Speaking of the role of the Jews in the death of Christ, the declaration states that all the things committed in the Passion of Christ are not to be imputed to the Jews of our times. This expression differs from the statements contained in the *Catechism of the Council of Trent* and in the *Summa Theologica* of St. Thomas (III, 47, a.5). Namely, that none of the Jews at the time of Christ was formally and subjectively guilty of deicide and that the greater part of the Jews of those days were not formally and subjectively responsible for the injustices surrounding the death of Christ. By these changes we shall be presenting the full truth which the Jews expect and hope for. Only this proposition will free the Jews of the hatred placed upon them over the period of many centuries. The charity of Christ impels us to incorporate such a statement.

Declaration on the Relationship of the Church to Non-Christian Religions

✠ COMMENTARY by Rt. Rev. Monsignor John M. Oesterreicher

There is something uncommon about this Declaration. No conciliar document has been opposed as much—political powers even tried to scuttle it. But as pressure mounted, interest mounted too. Without that tension, its message might have remained a small voice; through that tension, it became a trumpet summoning Catholics to a fuller view of the mystery of salvation. Involuntarily, the antagonists of the Declaration have thus helped enrich the Church.

Shortest of the conciliar documents, it is one of the most far-reaching. This is its marvel: it speaks of those "outside" the Church with sincere respect; lovingly, it points to the various treasures that are theirs. As if this were not enough, its tenor even suggests that those outside her immediate range help her fulfill her task among men. For the co-existence of the Christian and non-Christian world amounts to a dialogue. More than that, it is a challenge compelling the Church to ever greater fidelity.

When the bishops first arrived in Rome, the complex of problems involved in this Declaration was puzzling to them and unfamiliar to most Catholics, many of whom may have thought: "Here are we, the members of the Church, and across an abyss there are the 'others,' going nowhere." When the Council ended, the bishops had in hand more than another printed statement; they had awakened within the Church a new concern for the "others," for the men and women who have not heard the Gospel—the god-spell, the authentic and full "God-story"—but are nonetheless on the way to the living God, even close to Him. Over and above this, a new bond had been fashioned with them.

Antecedents

In the order of its making, the Declaration has two parts: one on the Jews; another on various religions and Islam. The first, originally meant to stand by itself, was later proposed as a chapter of the Decree on Ecumenism, then as a passage in the Constitution on the Church, until it received its present position as the climax of the whole document. The second was added after the great debate on the document during the third session. The preamble and conclusion were formulated at the same time. Since this book deals in particular with American participation in Vatican II, it seems germane to begin with a record of American suggestions during the earliest stage of the Council.

As for the second part. At the end of 1963, Dr. Barry Ulanov, a fellow of the Institute of Judaeo-Christian Studies, drew up a statement on what he called "a heartfelt celebration of the multiplicity of human experiences" as well as "of their essential unity." The Church was entrusted, he held, with a joyful celebration "of every just act, of every just man, of every act of charity, of every man of charity, of every open motion of the soul toward God, no matter how slight, which proclaims the loving kindness of God and man for each other." In recognizing the religious experiences outside her pale, he went on, the Church is not insensitive to the great differences between herself and those who do not believe in Christ. But in acknowledging the work of the Spirit wherever He breathes, "she can deepen her own asceticism and piety, her own compassion, her own unceasing prayers." At the same time, she proves herself the faithful companion and intercessor of those who seek ultimate peace. In February, 1964, the Institute forwarded Dr. Ulanov's statement as the expression of its own mind to the Secretariat for Christian Unity and to several American bishops.

As for the first part of the Declaration. Soon after the announcement of the Council, all bishops and pontifical universities were requested to submit their ideas. Although it belonged to neither category, the Institute of Judaeo-Christian Studies made bold to draw up a petition. It was signed by Bishop John J. Dougherty, the president of Seton Hall University, and by the author of this paper as director of the Institute, in their own names and in the names of the following priest-associates: Monsignors Myles M. Bourke, Edward G. Murray and William Ryan; the Fathers Gregory Baum, O.S.A., Joseph P. Brennan, J. Edgar Bruns, Edward H. Flannery, Isaac Jacob, O.S.B., Ambrose Schaeffer, O.S.B., Quentin L. Schaut, O.S.B.

Encouraged by the solemn utterance of Pope Pius XI, "Spiritually, we are Semites," by the allusion of Pius XII, at the opening of the Holy Year, 1950, to the messianic character of Jewish existence and by the loving care with which Pope John had several liturgical prayers cleansed of expressions hurtful to Jews, the associates of the Institute made the following suggestions: First, that any definition of the Church's nature by the Council should "proclaim that the call of Abraham and, again, Israel's exodus from Egypt were part of the Church's genesis." Second, that God's continuous dealings with man be brought into greater relief; that His unbroken saving design, "so often contemplated in the prayers that accompany the administration of the sacraments, be given further liturgical expression" by extending the feasts of St. Abraham, St. Moses, St. Isaiah and other just men of the Old Covenant, as now celebrated in the Patriarchate of Jerusalem, to the universal Church. Third, that regrettable expressions, particularly in the lessons of the Divine Office, be altered, so that no undue offense be given and the true teaching of the Church be not misunderstood; further that, should the Council "turn its attention to contemporary problems, the Church denounce once more, as she has done in the past, the hatred against the people 'from whom is the Christ according to the flesh, who is over all things, God blessed forever, Amen'" (Rom. 9:5).

In those early days, none of the preparatory commissions had been established, only a pre-preparatory body; neither were the Council's program or procedure known, except in very general terms. Thus it was difficult to decide what points the petition ought to contain and to whom it should be addressed. Under consideration for months and deliberately kept to a minimum of requests, it was given its final shape in the late spring of 1960. This writer handed it to Cardinal Bea during his first visit to the United States, on June 9, 1960, the very week his appointment as President of the Secretariat for Christian Unity was made public. This proved to be providential.

Vanity is no small factor in history. Thus men who have in the course of the last five years visited the Secretariat's premises, written to it, or spoken to one of its members tend to think that theirs was a decisive influence. There developed among publicity enthusiasts a little game of who carried the day. I have no desire to join it by claiming a monopoly or even a "first," although a simple comparison between the Council's text and the Institute's petition shows that the latter was not without weight. Anyone who wishes to honor reality must gratefully admit that many had a part in shaping the Declaration, from Pope John to the last Council bishop. Even a quick glance at the reports on the interventions of the Council Fathers in the aula of St. Peter during the third session shows how persuasive they were.

The recommendations of the American hierarchy were so numerous that it is impossible to record them here. Reference to contributions by two European bishops, however, prove my thesis that the basis of the Declaration was far wider than the ground upon which a single man or group can stand. The first sentence of the section on the Jews, "As this Sacred Synod probes the mystery of the Church, it remembers the spiritual bond that ties the people of the New Covenant to Abraham's stock," echoes a thought Cardinal Lercaro of Bologna expressed at the third session. The final reminder, "Sent to preach, the Church is, therefore, bound to proclaim the cross of Christ as the sign of God's all-embracing love and as the fountain from which every grace flows," takes up an utterance of Franziskus Cardinal König of Vienna during the great debate on the Declaration.

The initial request that the Council consider the bond between the Church and the people of Israel may well have been that of the Pontifical Biblical Institute. Among its proposals was one entitled *De antisemitismo vitando*, "On Avoiding Anti-Semitism." The Latin has the matter-of-factness of a legal brief. Transposed into the pastoral tone of the Council, it may be read as: "There must be no traffic with anti-Semitism." The unnamed author—the style suggests the pen of Père Stanislas Lyonnet, S.J.—expresses the hope that a conciliar clarification of the "Israelite dignity" of the Church (Easter Vigil) would deepen the Christian attitude toward Jews. Again, that a rejection of the notion of collective guilt and of the subsequent myth of the wandering Jew, together with other theological pronouncements, would strip hostility against the Jews of some of its pretexts.

In addition to the petition of the Institute of Judaeo-Christian Studies, there were others. Space permits only the mentioning of one. In August, 1960, laymen and priests from various European and American countries who had made work toward a new encounter between Church and Synagogue their lifetask, met in Apeldoorn, the Netherlands. There they formulated a detailed position paper which was later presented to the Secretariat for Christian Unity.

In Concert

Preparing the Declaration, no less than other documents, was thus the work of a community, a community wider than any committee charged with the actual wording. The whole Declaration reflects the insights of prophetic thinkers and of scholars prior to the Council. To name but a few who have brought about a deeper appreciation of the major non-Christian religions: Otto Karrer, Thomas Ohm, Franziskus Cardinal König, Jacques A. Cuttat, Raymond Pannikar, Karl Rahner, Joseph Ratzinger, Matthias Vereno, Heinz R. Schlette, and Yves Congar. Cardinal Lavigerie and his White Fathers, Charles de Foucauld and his Little Brothers and Sisters, the Dominican Institute of Oriental Studies in Cairo, the Benedictine monks at Tiouliline in the Atlas Mountains of Morocco and their protector Louis Massignon, among others, have contributed to a new esteem for Islam. The fresh vision of the role of the Jewish people in the scheme of salvation was helped by these reviews: *Die Erfullung* (Vienna) *La Question d'Israël* and *Cahiers Sioniens* (Paris), *Freiburger Rundbrief* (Freiburg, Germany), *The Bridge* (Newark, New Jersey); men as different as Léon Bloy, Friedrich W. Maier, Charles Cardinal Journet, Jacques Maritain, Paul Démann, Karl Thieme, Kurt Schubert and Gregory Baum were among its champions.

The thought of these and other pioneers converged at the Council as did that of many Christians who seemingly had no say. It is one of the happy characteristics of the Council, often gone unnoticed, that many problems secretly stirring the hearts of alert Christians were given voice in the *aula* of St. Peter. Issues that had rarely been aired in public clamored their way into the conciliar assembly, so that in the end many heard their own unspoken, even unformed, aspirations expressed by this or that Council Father.

I have touched on the prehistory of the Declaration for one important reason. Just the fact that it was in the making for years, even before the Council was thought of, voids journalistic claims like that of *Look* magazine in its patchwork article, "How the Jews Changed Catholic Thinking" (Jan. 25,

1966). Without wishing to deny to the public mind all force or consequence, neither the memoranda of Jewish organizations nor the entreaties or protests by individuals—some dignified, others forward or frantic—really determined the course of the Council. In the words of Father Gregory Baum, "The contacts which the Jewish persons mentioned in the [*Look*] article had with the Secretariat for Christian Unity were altogether marginal in the whole story of the Council."

A newsman may think differently, for his perspective is limited. His eyes are perforce held by a single incident or by some exciting detail which keeps him from grasping the totality of events. Yet, the Declaration must be seen in the context of the Church's inner life and of her growth through the centuries. In our day, a fresh appreciation of Scripture has given her a new impetus to look up to God, "the Lord and Lover of life" (Wis. 11:26), and to look about her where men's souls are "livid with the hue of death" (Mary W. Shelley) or gay with the color of life.

The Yeast of Understanding

It is impossible to trace this development in so brief a chapter. A few strokes may suggest its depth and its bearing on our theme. For us, truth is a judgment, stated or unstated, that conforms to reality or the sum total of things, facts and events that comprise the universe. In Scripture, however, God's truth is His fidelity, the fidelity that saves. Salvation, in turn, is "not a punctual, unrelated, vertical event" (Oscar Cullman), but unfolds in history, *is* history—a scandal to ancient as well as to modern minds. Revelation, too, is not a communication of ideas or a set of propositions, although it can certainly be so translated; it is the disclosure of God's plan for men and of His dealings with them.

Thus the Lord reveals Himself to Moses as Yahweh, a mysterious name that has often been rendered as "the One who is." No doubt, He *is* the One who is, but the voice coming from the burning bush discloses Him as the Ever-present, ready to come to the rescue of His chosen ones. The God of Israel walks, therefore, with His people as guide and companion, going ahead of them in their pilgrimage (Ex. 13:21).

In Christ Jesus, God's faithfulness soars like a never-dying flame. He is "the Amen, the faithful and true witness," the prime source of God's creation (Ap. 3:14). No neutral or ambiguous blend of "Yes" and "No," He is the divine "Yes." In Him every one of God's promises is affirmed, which enables us to shout "Amen" (2 Cor. 1:19–20). In Hebrew, *Amen*, "so it is," *emuna*, "trust," "faith," and *emet*, "truth," "fidelity," are kindred words, having the same root. As the great Amen, Christ seals God's covenant with His people and, in doing so, opens it to all nations. In assuming the flesh that is the nature of a man, He made all men His brothers (cf. Pius XII, *Mystici Corporis*, 94). With His coming, the inner structure of the world, too, was remade. When

He rose from the dead, the entire cosmos was summoned to newness. "In Him the world is risen, in Him heaven is risen, in Him the earth is risen" (St. Ambrose, PL 16:1403).

In this vast perspective, reduced here to the smallest possible size, the Church in Council could rethink the nature of her bond with the people from whom she sprang and the peoples among whom she lives. She could examine her relationship to the world of men among whom she is placed, for whom she yearns and whom she is sent to serve. Since man is, at one and at the same time, a person and a communal being, her care extends not to individuals in isolation, but to individuals who are members of religious bodies and hence to the bodies themselves.

In speaking first of the variety of man's religions, then of Islam and, finally, of Judaism, the Council did not aim at completeness. Anyone who comes to the Declaration expecting a handbook that gives the entire history of these religions, describes their tenets, their rites, their strong and weak points, even examines the theological ramifications of the Church's relationship to them, will be keenly disappointed. But the fault is not with the Declaration; it is not a scientific treatise, but a pastoral document. It is like a *fervorino*, exhorting and encouraging the faithful to put an end to all triumphalism, to any false sense of achievement, as if the Church had completed her pilgrimage. Humbly the Council urges that Christians and Muslims forget their past quarrels and hostilities so that both can work for mutual understanding and the promotion of justice, peace and freedom. Even though unexpressed, the same entreaty for friendship is directed to all religious men. In short, the Declaration marks the beginning it calls for.

The Ministry of Reconciliation

In her yearning for unity and love among men, the Church focuses this Declaration on "what men have in common and what draws them to fellowship." Their origin is one, and so is their ultimate goal, God. The human condition is the same everywhere. Basing itself on the Augustinian insight into the restlessness of the human heart seeking its rest in God, the Declaration maintains that all men are stirred by the same unsolved riddles:

What is man? What is the meaning, what the purpose of our lives? What is the moral good, what is sin? What is suffering, and what end does it serve? Which is the road to true happiness? What are death, judgment, and retribution after death? What, finally, is that ultimate, inexpressible mystery which, encompassing our existence, is its source as well as its destiny?

No matter what air men breathe, these questions are the same. The answers, however, often differ with varying cultures. Far from being discouraged by such variety, the Council sees God's finger at work in the religions of the nations. Although He does not move in them with the full glory that is the mark of the biblical revelation, He is, nevertheless, there. Otherwise, the Council could not have bowed in respect to all those who believe, worship and live according to the lights of their native religions. On October 28, 1965, the day of promulgation, the Church paused in public wonder at men's earnest gropings for the Absolute, convinced that whenever a man seeks the Fountain of all being and stands in awe before the Mystery of mysteries, there something of the living God is glimpsed.

It was a decisive moment when an ecumenical gathering of bishops proclaimed that the Church scorns nothing that is real and good in the various spiritual traditions of mankind. "The Catholic Church rejects nothing that is true and holy in these religions" is a key sentence of the Declaration. Some timid souls fear that, in saying this, the Council Fathers have come dangerously close to indifferentism. How absurd! Far from asserting that it makes no difference what a man holds true and dear, the bishops expressed an insight altogether, if not uniquely, Catholic: No matter who utters a truth, his thought and word are gifts of the Spirit.

The relativistic view has it that all traditions are right and, at the same time, that none are right; in other words, that each tradition is true for its bearer, and only for him. So little does the Council's appreciation of the values in non-Christian religions flow from this notion that it calls upon Christ as guarantor. He is obviously the road, the truth and the life of all who follow Him, but, in a hidden way, He is also the power of those who do not yet know Him. In Him, God reconciled all things to Himself (2 Cor. 5:19). The openness of the Council, then, has no other source than Christ's work of reconciliation.

When the Apostle rejoiced in the fact that, in Christ, God reconciled the world to Himself, he also rejoiced: "God has entrusted to us the ministry of reconciliation" (2 Cor. 5:18). It is as ministers of this redemptive work that the bishops have acknowledged the deep longing in Hinduism and Buddhism, their search for freedom from the anguish of the human condition or from the fleetingness of things. It is as servants of this reconciliation that they value Islam's adoration of God who made heaven and earth and has spoken to men; that they recognize the Abraham-like submission to God's will by devout Muslims, and that they ask all of us to go beyond the past so that peace may reign.

The Church's Ministry

Four hundred years ago, the Church condemned frightening notions like these: All works of "infidels" are sins, and the virtues of philosophers are vices; vice-ridden, then, pagans, Jews, heretics, and others are lumped together in doom; they are outside the Church, and outside her no grace is granted (D 1025, 1925, 1379). The present Declaration goes far beyond a mere dismissal of this dejected mood, which is ultimately distrust in God. Joyfully, the Church states that she

> regards with sincere reverence those ways of action and of life, those precepts and teachings which, differ though they do in many aspects from the ones she holds and sets forth, nonetheless reflect a ray of that Truth which enlightens all men.

If divine power scales the wall that separates the Church from the non-Christian world, if there are communities outside, moved in one way or another by the Spirit of God, do they remain strangers, are they unrelated to her? Or does the Church, her well-defined boundaries notwithstanding, extend her presence to all the habitations of men? An enclave of mercy and prayer in the world, she is somehow one with it. The world lives by her *diakonia,* her service, as she lives thanks to the *diakonia* of the great Servant, Jesus Christ, who represents God to man and man to God. The Church continues this representative and salvific function on behalf of all humanity. As the communion of the faithful, she is chosen to interpret the ministry of Christ, the Mediator, not only through her preaching, but through her existence and activity, so that she represents it in history, that is, between the Ascension and the Parousia (Joseph Ratzinger, Johannes Feiner).

Without knowing it, the non-Christian world has some part in this ministry. No doubt, the Buddhist longing to be freed from the burden of existence is alien to the biblical mind. But what Christian would dare consider it altogether negative, particularly when he contemplates the serenity of the statues of the smiling Buddha? What Christian would see in the thousands of devout Hindus who annually repair to their sacred river, in order to wash away their sins, nothing but dupes? What Christian would be foolish enough to hold that a Muslim's repeated call to Allah goes absolutely nowhere? Among Muslims, every significant deed is done in His name who is merciful and compassionate. The Koran itself opens with this eulogium:

> In the name of Allah, Compassionate and Merciful,
> Praise be to Allah, Lord of creation,
> The Compassionate and Merciful,
> Master of the Day of Judgment.
> You alone we worship, you alone we beseech for help.
> Guide us on the right path,
> The path of those whom you have favored. . . .

The role which this prayer plays among Muslims is comparable to that of the "Our Father" among Christians. As a matter of fact, it is an offspring of biblical spirituality; in it, the voice of Revelation resounds.

The Christ-ed World

Jewish and Christian influences on Islam are unquestionable. But what is the value of signs and prayers like those mentioned above that have had no such sponsorship? Are they empty or has Christ's dwelling among men made them, too, aids on the road to God? In His sovereign mercy, God has not chained His grace to prayers which the Church received from Christ, Israel's psalmists, or her own poets, nor to the sacraments, those wondrous arms of Christ, dispensers of His gifts. As the scholastics put it: *Deus virtutem suam non alligavit sacramentis:* God did not bind His power to quicken and hallow to the sacraments (cf. S.Th., III, 64, 7). In some measure, then, non-Christian religions have a sanctifying, even a salvific function, sharing as they do, although not knowing it, in the same grace of Christ that is at work in the Church, day and night. This function "challenges" the Church because it reminds her, time and again, that all she is and has she owes to God's goodness. Thus the non-Christian world becomes, in a way, her helper—indeed, the servant of the servant Church.

Some will see in the Council's vision of non-Christian religions a symptom of capitulation. Nothing could be farther from the mark. A sign of renewed vigor, this vision has nothing to do with the widespread spiritual fatigue of today and the passion for noncommitment. "The kingdom we are given is unshakable; let us therefore give thanks to God and so worship Him as He would be worshipped, with reverence and awe; for our God is a devouring fire" (Heb. 12:28 f). These words are as true today as they were yesterday, and they will be true tomorrow. Idolatry is still an abomination (cf. Dt. 7:25; 27:15). Outright murderers and idolators are still "shut out" (Ap. 22:15). The curse of prophets and apostles has not been withdrawn, nor has the Church suddenly become irresolute and made its peace with wickedness. What has happened and is manifest in the Declaration is the overwhelming recognition that, although very far from having been Christianized, the world has been Christ-ed. Christ has entered the world, and no one can undo this merciful event. All men are His images—images, however faint, of the eternal Logos-made-flesh. To all, whether they know it or not, a share in the divine life is offered. All are infinitely loved and have their being in that love alone. Thus God's footprints are everywhere, and we must open our eyes to them.

Although they are never spelled out, reflections like these underlie the Declaration. They owe much to Karl Rahner, yet their substance is far from novel. As Henri de Lubac puts it:

Without closing our eyes to the miserable state of many who are "in the shadow of death," we consider, nevertheless, with St. Irenaeus, that the Son, from the very beginning and in every part of the world, gives a more or less obscure revelation of the Father to every creature, and that he can be the

"Salvation of those who are born outside the Way." We believe, with St. Cyprian, St. Hilary and St. Ambrose, that the divine Sun of Justice shines on all and for all. We teach, with St. John Chrysostom, that grace is diffused everywhere and that there is no soul that cannot feel its attraction. With Origen, St. Jerome and St. Cyril of Alexandria we refuse to assert that any man is born without Christ. And, lastly, we willingly allow, with St. Augustine, the strictest of the Fathers, that divine mercy was always at work among all peoples, and that even the pagans had their "hidden saints" and their prophets.[1]

The Council has given these often forgotten vistas new strength, but we must not rest content with their magnificence. The Declaration challenges us to a deeper knowledge of the ways of God and the ways of men. The more we learn of the beliefs and practices of non-biblical provenance, the more we shall perceive His delicate, almost shy, movements everywhere, even in the jungles, the mountains and the temples not yet marked by the Cross. Today, the centers of modishness resound with the pretentious chatter that "God is dead." The framers of the Declaration gave the self-appointed pallbearers of faith no thought, yet they gave them the perfect answer: Hidden though His ways may be, the true God is never absent from this world.

Lasting Ties

While the first two major sections pay tribute to God's omnipresence, the third—on the Jews—celebrates His faithfulness. It is the nucleus around which the rest of the Declaration grew, and its theological center. The very beginning of the section proves it. At the outset, the Declaration as a whole ponders a world changed, a world become small; not so the section on the Jews. It, too, could have based itself on a changed world. It could have pointed to a new civic structure, that of the pluralistic society; it could have mentioned the psychological repercussions caused by Hitler's war of annihilation against the Jews, the deepened insights into Jewish existence by increased study of rabbinical literature, the altered image of the Jewish people through the creation of a Jewish state. Yet it spoke of a "sameness," that is, of the continuous dealings of God with the people of Israel, of the lasting ties between the Church and Abraham's stock. Convoked to examine her role in the modern world, the Church in Council was impelled to take a look at her past. She could not understand her mission of today unless she understood her roots in the ancient Israel.

Few conciliar passages are so frequently misinterpreted as is the section on the Jews. To give two instances: It has been seen as a not altogether satisfactory rejection of anti-Semitism. Basically, it is not a condemnation, weak or strong, although it does decry "hatred, persecution, and displays of anti-Semitism," not

[1] The exact patristic references can be found in the French edition of de Lubac's book, *Catholicisme*, at the beginning of Chapter VII, "*Le salut par l'Eglise.*"

only those by pharaohs or emperors, by a Hitler and Stalin, but those "staged against the Jews at whatever time in history and by whomsoever." In the minds of the framers of the Declaration, the latter clause is an unmistakable reference to the infernal events of our age, on the one hand, and to contempt and bloodshed by Christians on the other. Still, the conciliar statement is not an angry denunciation of others, but, beyond everything, an examination of, and appeal to, the Christian conscience. Another misunderstanding construes the Declaration as a chilly attempt to remind Jews that they are, at best, the *old* people of God. As a matter of fact, it abounds with titles of honor, with signifi- cant appellations bespeaking God's favor heaped on Israel, not the least of which is "beloved": "Now as before, God holds them most dear, for the sake of the patriarchs." In short, the Declaration does not remind Jews of their status before God or of anything else, for it is not addressed to them. It—and this cannot be stressed too often or too vigorously—serves the inner reform of the Church, the spirit of renewal among Catholics.

Renewal of the Church

There can be no renewal, the Declaration implies, without an awareness that Christians are sons and daughters of Abraham. But what does a Christian of today have to do with "that sheep and cattle breeder" of long ago? He has been described by the sociologist Max Weber as good-natured and sly, as a mere peaceable figure. There is truth in this description. Although his military strategy should not be despised (Gen. 14:8–16), he was no Alexander the Great, interested in conquering the world. For the most part, his life as des- cribed in Scripture was, in the eyes of a man of the twentieth century, unevent- ful. But it was imbued with a new experience, brought about by a seed planted in his soul: trust in the one, living and holy God.

Possibly Abraham had to witness how the members of his tribe, dissatisfied with life on the outskirts, longed to be part of the city's mainstream, how they were lured away from their ancestors' primitive worship to more sophisticated ways. When he decided to cut himself off from their life, to look for new ground whereon to graze his flocks, he detected in his plans and movements the hand of God. He heard a call; it sounded like "Go forth. . . ." Thus—it matters little whether suddenly or step by step—the search for pastureland, the flight from a world of saturation and unrest, was changed into a pursuit *by* the Lord.

St. Augustine saw in Abraham's call an *articulus temporis,* "a hinge of time," a turning point (PL 41:492). So much so, that, from then on, "go forth" be- came one of the central themes of God's dealings with men. Variations are heard at the exodus from Egypt or at Israel's return from exile, while its full volume is reached in the "Come, follow me" of the gospels. No longer are kinship, milieu and inheritance roads to God; He speaks to the one ready to be trans- formed. Detachment, separation from clan and country, as well as the things they stood for, a journey into unstaked territory—such was Abraham's way.

Essentially, to move toward his destiny is still the Christian's mode of perfection. On October 17, 1963, when the non-Roman observers of the Council paid their first visit to Pope Paul, the Lutheran professor Kristen E. Skydsgaard of Denmark was their spokesman. In response to his greeting, the Pope said:

> If we are truly to possess divine truth and live it to the fullest, we must spare no pains to deepen our understanding. "Seek that you may find, and find that you may seek further." These words of St. Augustine, which we just had the pleasure of hearing Professor Skydsgaard quote, concern us all. A true Christian does not stand pat [*un vrai chrétien ne connaît pas l'immobilisme*].

The wayfaring Abraham is not only the model of the individual Christian; he is also the Church's guide and companion. He and, with him, the entire history of his people remind her that she has not yet arrived at her destination, that she is still *en route*, that hers is the humble glory of the people of God in pilgrimage.

In biblical thought, ancestor and offspring are one; they are, in the words of H. Wheeler Robinson, "a corporate personality." The life of the patriarch anticipates that of his descendants, while their history repeats the great lines of his story. To a large extent, then, the root of a tree shapes trunk, branches and top. Thus the Declaration can say that the Church "draws sustenance from the root of that well-cultivated olive tree onto which the wild shoots of the Gentiles have been grafted" (Rom. 11:17–24). What ought to capture our attention is the shift in tenses. In the previous sentence, the Declaration says that the revelation of the Old Testament *came* to the Church through the medium of the Jewish people. Here, however, as in a few other instances, the present tense is used, although one might expect the past. The formative influence of ancient Israel upon the Church is not a matter of mere historical record; it is a living source.

The dowry given to the Church at her birth can never be exhausted; indeed, it grows. What she learned from the patriarchs, prophets, poets and princes will always work in her and for her. The genius of the Old Testament stamps her life in more ways than one. The people of the Old Covenant experienced God as the Lord of history, as the God who acts and speaks, and so does the Church. Thus Israel's writings impart to her a sense of time, of its sacredness and sacramentality. From them she learned the art of prayer, particularly its highest form: praise. A passion for justice, too, a hope in the triumph of mercy, and the conviction that the service of God demands love of neighbor and respect for the stranger are among Israel's legacies (Lev. 19:13–18). Grounded in that inspired tradition, the Apostle James can declare that punctiliousness in outward observance is not religion. Genuine worship, a flawless religion before God, requires that the devout "go to the help of widows and orphans in their distress" (Jas. 1:27). The nourishment the Church once received from her native soil she continues and must continue to absorb. Without it she would not be the Church of Christ. Without it she would not be able to give the service that she is called to give and that the world needs. This is only one of several ways by which the Declaration can vigorously contribute to an inner reform.

"The Christ-Killers"

Other contributions to the reform of the Christian life are the attempts to clarify "Jewish responsibility" for the crucifixion as well as the place of present-day Israel before God. The insistence of the Council that, no matter what the wrong of the Jerusalem authorities may have been, the whole Jewish people must never be charged with the murder of Jesus is meant to repair the injustice done to Jews by the frequent invective, "assassins of Christ." Like every invective, this one falls easily from the lips of men who have not mastered their inner conflicts or conquered their own hostilities, although it should, more than any other, stick in a man's throat—even if it were true. But it is not. Once the Council's leaven has worked itself into the public consciousness, it will, by the grace of God, heal a deep-seated trauma of Jews. No less will it, by His grace, free Christians from a drag: whether they know it or not, the unparalleled accusations that have so often been hurled at the Jewish people retard spiritual ascent.

The conciliar statement frees preachers and catechists, moreover, from the snare of arrogance. There is no more deadly pitfall for Christian spirituality than to point, in the presence of the suffering Christ, an accusing finger at His people. It is a horror and a farce. If "He bore *our* infirmities and endured *our* sufferings" (Is. 53:43), if "we were healed" because "He was pierced for *our* offenses [and] crushed for *our* sins" (53:5), how can we possibly turn around and smite *others?* Yet, Christians have done so, not once, but again and again. Unwittingly, their "punishment" of the Jews sought to annul the work of Christ. I do not wish to imply that, in the past, the side-by-side existence of Christians and Jews through the centuries was one of unrelieved abuse and enmity, although it often appears that way. There was occasional evidence of true neighborliness. There were those who protected the Jews against the mobs. There was a fruitful exchange of ideas on the philosophical and theological levels. Still, enough was said and done to chill our blood. The Council wishes to put an end to all injustice of the past with that glorious finale of its statement on the Jews:

> Christ underwent His passion and death freely and out of infinite love because of the sins of all men, so that all may obtain salvation. This the Church has always held and holds now. Sent to preach, the Church is, therefore,

bound to proclaim the cross of Christ as the sign of God's all-embracing love and as the fountain from which every grace flows.

All this is a far cry from the newspaper headlines, "Council Absolves Jews from Murder of Christ." These headlines found their way into sermons, speeches and editorials. Journals like *The New Statesman* and *Nation, Conservative Judaism* and *The Reconstructionist,* and men as different as Dr. Eugene Carson Blake, then Stated Clerk of the United Presbyterian Church, and Rabbi Maurice Eisendrath, President of the American Hebrew Congregations, accepted this canard. The first warned that God is the judge of men and "that any usurpation of His prerogative of judgment is as great a sin as any it would presume to absolve." The second, making an editorial of the *Christian Century* his own, charged the Church with committing "a crime against the Jews [and] a sin against God." With the same magazine, he cried out: "What monstrous arrogance is this which assumes that Christians have the right and power to forgive or not forgive the Jews for a crime of which they are not guilty!"

There is not the least foundation for this censure. If men and magazines of this caliber can so misread the words and meaning of the Declaration, is it surprising that Christians of the past often misread the New Testament as one big indictment against the Jewish people? I ask this question, not because I want to whitewash the past, but because I fear that its errors will not be righted nor the torn fabric of Christian-Jewish co-existence mended if all do not take meticulous care to be just and truthful. The pacification sought by the Council will not be realized unless everything that could poison the atmosphere is avoided. What a blessing it would be if those who maligned the Council made amends, as Christians must do for the wrongs done to Jews.

Christian and Jewish Hope

The rejuvenation of the Christian life requires that Catholics do their utmost in responding to the Council. We must examine our thoughts as well as our writings on the Jews and eradicate from them every false idea: for instance, that the Jews are a "castaway," an "obsolete people," a "relic of the past," in Toynbee's language "a fossil." Contrary to the opinion of many, this is not the official doctrine of the Church, even though Christian writers and speakers frequently gave that impression. The Council's teaching on this matter is neither ambiguous nor obscure. It invites brotherly conversations and encourages a deeper mutual knowledge and respect. This is ample proof: One does not converse with a corpse, nor does one draw near a people that has "seen its day" and is now "on the dunghill of history."

In calling the Jewish people "most dear for the sake of the patriarchs," the Council acknowledges the unity of that people, the oneness I mentioned before between generation and generation, the bridge that links past, present and future. Thus it cannot but look forward, with prophet and Apostle, to the—

possibly far away—day when "all peoples will address the Lord in a single voice and 'serve him with one accord' " (Soph. 3:9; cf. Is. 66:23; Ps. 65:4; Rom. 11:11–12). This, too, has been misunderstood as if here the Church engaged in a cheap proselytism. In reality, the Church honors the Synagogue by clothing her own eschatological hope in the language of the Jewish tradition.

Another, somewhat later, oracle proclaiming the same hope for the universal acknowledgement of the one living God is that of the prophet Zechariah: "And the Lord shall be King over all the earth: On that day shall the Lord be one and His name one" (14:9). Obviously, it could not have entered the mind of the prophet to deny, ahead of its revelation, the triune nature of the Lord, but rather does he emphasize the uniqueness of the God of Israel, peerless and sovereign. His saying is, in the words of the late chief rabbi of the British Empire, Joseph H. Hertz,

> one of the fundamental verses of the Jewish conception of the Kingdom of Heaven. It proclaims the Providential care of God for all mankind, and the future recognition of the true God by all mankind. It closes all synagogue services.

The frequency of its recitation gives it a role similar to that of the Exordium of the Koran quoted earlier and, beyond all, to the Lord's prayer with which it shares the ardent desire for the complete unfolding of God's kinship.

It goes without saying that the Jewish and Christian concepts of the age-to-come differ and that no Council would wish to gloss over that difference. But it ought not to go unnoticed that the Council wished to bridge the gap in an unusual way. Traditional Judaism foresees a time when the nations of the earth will become part of the people of Israel and submit to the Law of God as written in the Torah; Christianity's hope, however, is that in the end all will turn toward the Way that is Christ. As the Council quotes one prophetic utterance and implies another with which the Jewish liturgy resounds, it points to an age when words, far from losing their meaning, will reveal their full wealth, when they will no longer separate, but unite, when the reality-to-come will far surpass our present stammer.

Judaism

It is not only at the end that the Jewish people will again live in and for God. At this very moment, the worshipping community of Israel is alive to Him. The synagogal morning service, for instance, contains a prayer that seems to have originated around 450 A.D. when a Persian ruler, persecuting both Christians and Jews, forbade the latter to keep the Sabbath or recite the *Shema* in public. Though insisting that all things pass, even the highest, the prayer does not lead the pious Jew to despair at the finite world, rather to rejoice in God:

Sovereign of all the worlds!
Not because of our virtues
do we bring our prayers before You,
rather because of Your abundant mercy.

What are we?
What is our life?
What our love?
What our righteousness?
What our victory?
What our strength?

What are we to say in Your presence,
Lord our God and God of our fathers?
Are not the mightiest as nothing before You,
the men of fame as if they had never been,
the learned as if without knowledge,
the wise as if lacking in understanding?
For most of their works are void,
and the days of their lives but vapor in Your sight.
What advantage has man over the beast?
For all is futility.

Nonetheless, we are Your people,
the sons of Your covenant.
We are the children of Abraham, Your friend
to whom You gave Your promise on Mount Moriah.
We are the seed of Isaac, his only son
who was bound upon the altar.
We are the community of Jacob, Your firstborn
whom You called Israel and Jeshurun,
for You lavished Your love on him and took delight in him.

We must, therefore, give thanks to You,
praise and glorify you, bless and sanctify Your name. . . .
Happy are we
who, early and late, morning and evening,
twice each day declare:
> *Shema Yisrael: Adonay Elohenu,*
> *Adonay echad.*
> Hear, O Israel: The Lord our God,
> the Lord alone.

Gladly does the pious Jew acknowledge his utter dependence on the Lord's mercy. Is not the spirituality expressed in this prayer akin to Christian spirituality? Does it not have that breath a Christian calls evangelical? Still, Christ separates the Jew from the Christian, and this neither can ignore. But the difference does not end their confrontation. For the one God, living and thrice holy, binds them together in a bond that, no matter how often it was cruelly severed, may still become one of friendship.

The Future

This book is concerned with American participation in the Second Vatican Council. Given the force of that participation, it is more than appropriate to conclude this chapter on a note of hope. The work of American bishops on the Commission that prepared the Council's Declaration on The Relationship of the Church to Non-Christian Religions was impressive; particularly moving was their support of the section on the Jews. So, too, were their interventions in the aula of St. Peter. Courageously they faced the sins of the past and looked ahead toward a renewed vision of the mystery of Israel. Their commitment and openness bodes well for the future. The forthrightness of the Council days will—must—stay with us. There is good reason to be confident that the Church in this country will be in the vanguard of those who seek to convert the Declaration into a living reality.

Some problems, not dealt with explicitly in the text of the Declaration, but very much a part of its concern, press to be solved. One of the most vexatious is the use of the term "the Jews" in the many liturgical pericopes taken from the Gospel according to St. John; the Gospel for the first Sunday after Easter, for instance, tells that the disciples had locked the doors of the room in which they had assembled "for fear of the Jews" (Jn. 20:19). As the sentence stands, it may lead to misunderstanding and antagonism. It may reinforce the false notion of collective guilt. Since the disciples were Jews themselves, "the Jews" they feared could only have been the Jewish authorities because of the latter's opposition to Christ and hence to the apostles as His followers. What can be done, many will wonder, since it is hardly legitimate to rewrite the Gospels? Far be it from me to suggest that liberty be taken with the words of the Evangelist. Our translations, however, are far from untouchable. The original, that is, the Greek text, says *Judaioi* which means "Judaeans" as well as "Jews."

The same point was recently made by Father Francis X. Weiser, S.J., in the March, 1966, issue of *Eucharist*. Part of a series called "Gospel Gleanings," his meditation urges on the reader the importance of the true Lenten spirit: Without occasional retreat into spiritual solitude and the renewal born of it, no full Christian life is possible. Father Weiser bases his plea on the Gospel verse that tells of Jesus' withdrawal from the public eye during the last few weeks before His passion. Most English versions, Father Weiser goes on to say, render John 11:54 as:

"he went no longer openly among the Jews"; this, however, is not a correct translation, since Jesus did not leave the country of the Jews. He stayed among His own people, but withdrew only from the Judaeans, the rulers in Jerusalem. The confusion is caused by the fact that the Greek word *Judaioi* means either "Judaeans," or (in Roman usage) the whole people of the Jews (including Galileans, Transjordanian Jews and Jews in the Diaspora). St. John here—and in many other places of his Gospel—obviously speaks of the *Judaeans,* not of the Jews as a whole nation. We have a similar twofold meaning in our word "Yankees," which sometimes means the Puritans of New England, and sometimes *all* Americans. May the Holy Spirit guide our scholars not to use the word "Jews" in Gospel translations whenever the sacred authors clearly mean the "Judaeans."

What makes this statement remarkable is that it comes from the pen, not of a professional Scripture scholar or of a man actively engaged in the work of reconciliation between Christians and Jews, but from that of a priest moved by pastoral concern and, above all, by a sense of justice. It is also a pleasure to record that, years before Father Weiser's appeal, the editors of *The New English Bible* translated the Johannine verse in question the following way: "Accordingly [that is, from the day on which the High Priest and the men subservient to him began to plot His death] Jesus no longer went about publicly in Judaea, but left that region for the country bordering on the desert. . . ."

Historically, the use of *Judaioi* for the opponents of the Christian message is, no doubt, rooted in the conflict between the Church of the Evangelist's time and the Judaism of his day. But why did he pick this term, and no other? A remote psychological reason, that is to say, one antedating the Gospel's composition, could possibly lie in the frequent tensions between northerners and southerners—in this case, between Galileans and Judaeans, or in the general aversion of the citizens of a given country for the inhabitants of the capital, particularly the rulers. Thus the *Judaioi* of St. John could well be the equivalent of the subject in St. Paul's phrase "the people of Jerusalem and their rulers did not recognize Him nor understand the utterances of the prophets which are read Sabbath by Sabbath; indeed, they fulfilled them by condemning Him . . . [and by asking] Pilate to have Him executed" (Ac. 13:27f).

A much more likely source of the Johannine terminology is that of the Dead Sea Scrolls. Hans Kosmala, a Swedish Lutheran scholar who is presently director of the Institutum Delitzchianum in Jerusalem, has drawn attention to the fact that the community of Qumran saw itself as "Israel" or "Jacob" or "Ephraim," while its opponents were called "Juda" or "the house of Juda," even "the land of Juda." The Damascus Document, for instance, speaks of the priests who are sons of Zadok and thus the rightful ministers of the Temple as the "penitents of Israel who went out of the land of Juda" (CD iv 2). While most commentators seem to take this departure from Juda literally as forced emigration and exile, Kosmala, as well as Gaster, understands it figuratively as a spiritual withdrawal of the early Covenanters from those who, in their eyes, had forsaken God's Covenant and chosen their own pleasure, going astray in the stubbornness of their hearts. Thus the Damascus Document is able to say that, when the present era is completed, "there will be no more uniting with the house of Juda but each must stand within his own stronghold. 'The fence will be rebuilt, and the bounds be far-flung' (cf. Mi. 7:11)" (CD iv 11–12).

As far as I can see, the deepest interpretation of the Evangelist's use of "the Jews" rather than "adversaries" or "plotters" for the opponents of Jesus has been offered by another Scandinavian scholar, Nils Alstrup Dahl. Danielou and Démann, among others, have taken a similar stand. According to Dahl, the term "the Jews" does not designate the people of the Jews, rather does it represent "the world in its hostility to God," in the words of the Evangelist, the world—the very one He created—that failed to recognize Him (Jn 1:10). "The essential nature of this world," as the Evangelist sees it, "is the self-assertion over against God, the vanity to assume that life and liberty are man's own possession, so that he does not need the gift of Christ."

The idea of Israel's representative character did not originate with the New Testament; only the use St. John made of it is new. According to Jewish tradition, Jerusalem, and in particular Mt. Zion, is the center of the universe. In the days-to-come, the rabbis hold, Jerusalem will be the mother-city of the world. For the prophets before them, messianic Jerusalem was to be the place to which the nations stream and from which instruction and the word of God go forth (Is. 2:2–3). Hence, the city is the center of salvation, the focus of grace, the home of faith. For the Evangelist, Jesus' mission in Israel is really a mission to the entire world; it is there that He fulfills His ministry to all mankind. To this, however, St. John adds a negative aspect: he sees the world's opposition brought together at Jerusalem whose officialdom gives concentrated expression to man's hostility toward His Redeemer. Thus, the authorities there, "the Jews," become the representatives of the ubiquitous and constant resistance to the divine offer of renewal. All in all, the use of "the Jews" in St. John's Gospel is a literary device for expressing the profound theological realization of man's lack of response to God's revelation in Christ.

It is for scholars to argue the validity of these and other theories. Still, it will not be enough to carry even the best of them to the people in the form of footnotes to Bibles, Missals, and Missalettes. A new translation is needed, particularly for the many instances when a pericope is read aloud in which the term "the Jews" occurs. In my opinion, "Judaeans" has the advantage of not forcing any one interpretation on the listener but of making him sit up and take notice. Without explanation he will sense that the expression bespeaks mystery rather than abuse.

As the Declaration challenges exegetes and other theologians, so it summons priests, teachers and all the faithful to make its letters alive. The message needs to be implemented in the pulpit, in the classroom and the home. We must all learn to tell Israel's story anew, God's inexplicable favor to her, the marvel of the Covenant and, no less, the vicissitudes of her history. We must learn to tell, particularly, the events of the Gospel in a language that takes into account all the knowledge of the time of Jesus newly acquired in this century and the last, a language, moreover, that does justice to Israel's mysterious destiny. The nature of Judaism, with all its complexities, needs to be a prominent part of the seminary curriculum. High schools and colleges, parishes, too, with their discussion groups ought to make Judaism the object of study, each in a way appropriate to its own possibilities and needs. To a certain degree, the same holds true for all non-Christian religions.

In view of our overburdened curricula, this looks like an impossible or, at least, a most difficult task. It is indeed difficult but, at the same time, most rewarding. A genuine acquaintance with the faith and worship of non-Christians, especially with the beliefs and practices of Jews to whom we are tied by many affinities, can only strengthen our obedience, while a nodding one may be confusing, even disturbing. A confrontation with the religious experiences of others can, if our hearts are delicately tuned, enrich our own; it can bring freshness into our lives, make us humble before God and man and thus enable us to live a life of fullness. Only the humble are truly alive.

All this is especially true of the Christian's acquaintance with the ways of the ancient Israel and those of first-century Judaism. Apart from the fact that a knowledge of them helps immensely in the proper understanding of the sayings, signs and the saving work of Jesus, they summon us to greater fidelity, to an authentic following of Him. The vision of God at work everywhere, but superbly and uniquely in His Church, can only confirm our belief in the God who is love. In no way does the Declaration intend to have us "swept off [our] course by all sorts of outlandish teachings" (Heb. 13:9). Rather does it help us realize that the reach of Jesus the Christ, who "is the same, yesterday, today, and forever" (Heb. 13:8), is vaster than we often imagine, that His presence is not confined to one place but is everywhere.

XVI/DECLARATION ON RELIGIOUS FREEDOM

Declaration on Religious Freedom

✠ HISTORICAL INTRODUCTION

"The achievement of the Declaration on Religious Freedom," said the Reverend John Courtney Murray, S.J., "was to bring the Church, at long last, abreast of the consciousness of civilized mankind, which has already accepted religious freedom as a principle and as a legal institution." The American bishops endorsed the declaration so wholeheartedly that it came to be known as "the American document." The Declaration on Religious Freedom is, beyond a shadow of a doubt, the specific American contribution to the Second Vatican Council.

That approach was reflected in the publication of "Questions Proposed to the Preparatory Commissions of the Second Vatican Ecumenical Council." In this opuscule the subject of religious freedom was not even mentioned. It was only obliquely touched upon in the proposed ninth chapter of the schema on the Church. There, in five pages, the general subject of relations between Church and State and religious tolerance were discussed.

During the final meeting of the Central Preparatory Commission, however, Cardinal Bea in the name of the Secretariat for the Promotion of Christian Unity presented a schema on religious freedom. His presentation, on June 19, 1962, immediately followed Cardinal Ottaviani's presentation of the ninth chapter of the schema on the Church. The subject of religious freedom, as it was outlined in both these drafts, however, never came up for discussion on the floor of the Council.

The subject of religious freedom did not reach the floor of the Council during the first session. The text of chapter five of the schema on ecumenism which dealt with religious freedom was distributed to the Council Fathers during the seventieth congregation, on November 19, 1963. Since the preparatory phase the subject had been transferred into the hands of the unity secretariat. This body had successfully argued that any meaningful discussion of ecumenism must include a statement on religious freedom, since this was precisely one of the issues that caused bitter feelings among the separated brethren.

Early in the Council, Albert Cardinal Meyer of Chicago stressed the ecumenical dimensions of a conciliar statement on religious freedom. Speaking in

Chicago, he said, "Both Protestant and Catholic ecumenists are convinced that the ecumenical movement cannot be securely founded until a clear statement on the subject of religious liberty is fully developed." Writing in the January, 1964, *Presbyterian Life,* Dr. Robert McAfee Brown stressed the importance of such a document from the Protestant viewpoint. "Whether we like it or not," he wrote, "it is clear that when it comes to religious liberty, the Catholic Church is not yet fully trusted by the non-Catholic world." He then cited the following three reasons for his statement.

1) There is the whole legacy of *past Catholic history* in which there have been notable instances of persecution of non-Catholics, particularly when the Church was in a position of political power. . . .

2) There is also the fact of *present Catholic practice* in certain parts of the world today. . . . The residual non-Catholic fear is that, as the Church gains numerically and politically elsewhere, these repressive measures will follow in its wake. . . .

3) Finally, there is the fact that there are relatively *few authoritative pronouncements* by the Church on religious liberty. . . . If the Catholic Church *really* believes in religious liberty, why doesn't it say so authoritatively, once and for all?

On November 18, 1963, during the sixty-ninth general congregation, Bishop Emile De Smedt introduced chapter five of the ecumenism schema. The chapter was entitled simply "On Religious Freedom." It consisted of but seven numbers and a brief introduction. Bishop De Smedt's introduction was eloquent, perhaps the most eloquent address delivered on the floor of the Council at any time.

On November 21 the Secretary General announced that voting would take place on the first three chapters of the ecumenism schema, and a vote on the last two chapters would occur in a few days. The second session ended with neither a vote nor a discussion of chapters four and five of the schema.

During the intersession the unity secretariat returned to work, examining and studying the 380 suggestions submitted in writing by the Council Fathers on the last two chapters. At this time the secretariat drafted a "prior declaration" which was subtitled "Concerning the Right of the Person and Communities to Freedom in Religious Matters." It was much longer than the original text, and its paragraphs were now numbered in sequence (25–31) with the concluding paragraph of chapter three of the ecumenism schema.

On September 23, 1964, during the eighty-sixth congregation, the subject of religious freedom was presented, again by Bishop De Smedt, for the discussion on the floor of the Council. During the next four congregations, 43 Fathers spoke in the aula on the subject. Upon completion of the discussion, the text was returned to the unity secretariat for revision according to the suggestions presented by the Fathers. The secretariat completed its assignment and presented its revised text to five members of the doctrinal commission for their examination. Later the full membership of the theological commission voted upon the text and approved it. Nonetheless, the text remained unduly long in the hands of the theological commission, and a sense of apprehension filled not a few members of the unity secretariat and others.

Finally, the emended text was distributed to the Council Fathers on November 17, during the 124th congregation. At the same time it was announced that five votes would be cast on the text, and then the entire text would be voted upon; furthermore, at that time the Fathers might cast a vote "with reservations." This was to take place during the 126th congregation, November 19. The events of that dramatic congregation, called by some "Black Thursday," can best be recounted in the words of one American bishop who penned this eyewitness account:

> I had come to the aula this morning, taking it for granted that after the vote on the complete text of *De Ecclesia* we would proceed immediately to the vote which was announced yesterday by the moderators and members of the Presidency to determine whether we proceed with the vote on religious liberty or whether, in response to the petition of "some" Fathers, the vote be delayed to the next session. Since the mind of the Council Fathers on the question of religious liberty was quite clear there was no question in anybody's mind what the outcome would be. In fact, I was a bit amused by the fact that three Italian bishops directly ahead of me were feverishly busy preparing *modi* to be used when the voting on the Declaration began. Each had a fist full of at least a dozen of such *modi* which he kept arranging and signing as soon as the session opened. They also had a list indicating that they were to vote *Non Placet* on all ballots where votes *iuxta modum* were not called for.

> All of a sudden it dawned on me that they were proceeding with the debate on Christian Education and called for one more balloting. Four Fathers spoke, which took us up to 10:45 when cloture was voted. Then three men spoke (Fernandez among them, of course) with the support of 70 Fathers so that he [Fernandez] could speak after cloture. Fernandez was called for going over time, but he paid no attention to this and went right on to the end, this in spite of the fact that there was loud applause when Doepfner called him.

> Now I knew that something was up; in fact, I have a note written at this point in which I wrote: "There is something funny going on. For some reason they are not bringing the Declaration on Religious Liberty to a vote. They kept droning along on Christian Education without a move to begin the balloting which had been announced yesterday."

> When the time went past eleven, I was sure. Finally, when they had disposed of Christian Education on the floor, Tisserant was introduced by Döpfner and made the following announcement: The petition by some

Council Fathers to have the vote on Religious Liberty postponed to the next session so as to permit of more time for its study had been considered. The Presidency has decided that the General Assembly is not competent to make the final declaration on a procedural matter of this kind. Therefore, the Presidency has decided that the petition will be granted and that the vote will not be taken until the next session. Council Fathers who wish to intervene on this subject must have their interventions in the hands of the Secretariat for the Promotion of Christian Unity on or before January 27, 1965.

This was a bombshell which exploded at 11:05. Cardinal Meyer was instantly on his feet and went to Tisserant to protest this action. He reminded Tisserant that there had been no meeting of the Presidency. The reply was that Tisserant called on the individual members of the Presidency and all the others agreed, so there was no need to refer to Cardinal Meyer. The latter went into action without delay, and the bishops in the aula and especially in the side nave near the coffee bar went into action immediately. By 11:30 a petition signed by more than 800 Council Fathers from many different countries had been gotten together. Cardinals Meyer, Leger, Ritter and, I believe, Alfrink went to the Vatican immediately to deliver the petition to the Holy Father. Whether they got to see the Holy Father and what, if anything he did, I do not know at this writing. But I am sure no petition ever gathered so many names in such a short time in or out of the Council.

Following these lightning-swift, disruptive events, Bishop De Smedt went through the motions of reading his introduction to the revised text of the declaration. The text of his introduction had been previously distributed, and the Bishop of Bruges did not depart from his text. Nothing, he said, was inserted into this text beyond what the Council Fathers had suggested in their interventions, and, therefore, the present draft actually is familiar to all who paid any attention to the debate. It represents, he said in conclusion, what the unity secretariat felt to be the mind of the Council Fathers.

Bishop De Smedt's delivery was a masterpiece in itself. Beginning in a low voice, he created the impression that he was deeply moved and on the verge of tears. Several times during his address he was interrupted with long applause, and at the end it was like thunder rolling through the huge vaults of St. Peter's. Not even the Holy Father had received such an ovation at any of his appearances at this third session. Nonetheless, those who were opposed to the schema were, in fact, on valid legal ground according to the rules of the Council. As a matter of fact, it was a *new* schema that had been presented to the Council Fathers.

The subject ended during this session with Cardinal Tisserant's announcement that "the Fathers can examine the document at their leisure and send their observations to the secretariat by January 31, 1965." What, in general, the Americans felt at this stage was best expressed by one bishop: "I must confess that, as I walked out of the Porta Santa Marta that day, I did not much care whether I ever got back to the Council again."

The general sentiment of Americans in these dark November days was expressed by Father John B. Sheerin, C.S.P., the editor of *The Catholic World*. He wrote his weekly column for the Catholic press aboard the Alitalia flight bringing American bishops and priests back to the United States. With a heavy heart he wrote:

> . . . the thought of returning for an American Thanksgiving is pleasant. For the Americans are heartsick. The temporary defeat of the religious liberty document rankles. It is not so much the postponement of the vote that hurts as the manner in which it was done. (For the ultimate approval of religious liberty is beyond question.)
>
> Time after time in these three sessions we have heard "juridicalism" and "legalism" condemned. To Americans, the decision to postpone voting on religious liberty was a supreme example of "legalism," something that conforms to the rule of the Council and yet is altogether unjust and unfair. The document had been ready for a vote for many days, but it was sidetracked until time was so short that the Council Presidency could rule with juridical legality that the vote would have to be put off until the fourth session.

Father John Courtney Murray had not lost heart. Before an overflowing audience at Georgetown University shortly after the session closed, he expressed the conviction that the delaying tactics of the obstructionist minority might produce an even better text on religious freedom. He expressed this same conviction in an article in the January 9, 1965 issue of *America*.

What was unhappily delayed was happily perfected. The unity secretariat met again during the winter and spring of 1965 and examined the 218 suggestions which had been submitted in writing by the Council Fathers since the close of the third session. The schema was strengthened rather than weakened. On May 11, 1965, the Central Coordinating Commission approved the revised schema and, on the following May 28, the Holy Father ordered that the revised text be sent to the Council Fathers.

The fourth session opened on September 14 with the customary address by the Pope. On the following day the Council Fathers immediately launched into the discussion of religious freedom. During the next five congregations, 62 Fathers addressed themselves to the text, with the revelation that the obstructionist minority was making a do-or-die, last-ditch stand to scuttle the document. On September 20, Josef Cardinal Beran of Prague, recently released from prison, delivered his address. Many observers felt that his words won many over to the cause of adopting the schema. Speaking from the depths of a wisdom gained through suffering, the Cardinal made the following observation:

From the very moment in which freedom of conscience was radically restricted in my country, I witnessed the grave temptations which, under such conditions, confront so many. In my whole flock, even among the priests, I have observed not only grave temptations to faith, but also to lying, hypocrisy and other moral vices which easily corrupt people who lack true freedom of conscience. . . .

Everywhere, and always, the violation of liberty of conscience gives birth to hypocrisy in many people. And, perhaps, one can say that hypocrisy in the profession of the faith is more harmful to the Church than the hypocrisy of hiding the faith, which, anyway, is more common in our times. So in my country the Catholic Church at this time seems to be suffering expiation for defects and sins committed in times gone by in her name against religious liberty, such as in the fifteenth century in the burning of the priest John Hus and during the seventeenth century the forced reconversion of a great part of the Czech people to the Catholic faith under the rule "the people of a territory follow the religion of its ruler."

At 10:45 on the morning of September 21 during the 132nd congregation, the Secretary General, speaking in the name of the Council moderators, called for a vote in these words: "Does it please the Fathers that the already amended text on religious freedom should be taken as the basis for a definitive declaration, after further amendment in the light of Catholic doctrine on the true religion and amendments proposed by the Fathers in discussion, which will be subsequently approved according to the norms of Council procedure?" The result was a victory for the unity secretariat, the American hierarchy and the lovers of religious freedom—and, incidentally, for Pope Paul who reportedly wanted the text approved before he made his appearance at the United Nations on October 4. Of the 2,222 Fathers voting, 1,997 voted in favor of accepting the text and only 224 voted against it.

The significance of that vote was instantly realized by all participants. One observer-delegate, Dr. Robert Cushman of Duke University Divinity School, Durham, North Carolina, expressed his own feelings on that day in a sermon delivered a month later to the students of Duke University.

Perhaps we do not fully comprehend it yet but on that day, September 21, 1965, a very ancient order of things—at least in principle—passed away. In principle, the era of Constantine—over sixteen hundred years of it—passed away. It was the era of the official establishment of the Christian religion. The Declaration on Religious Liberty is, in principle, disestablishment and, with it, the largest segment of Christendom ventured forth into an unknown future of ultimate risk, supported, henceforth, only by faith in the truth of the Gospel of Jesus Christ. This is the magnificent risk which a minority of Catholic bishops made every possible effort to evade and avoid. But this ultimate risk Paul VI forced, and the Council overwhelmingly approved it. It was, I believe, the most powerful blow at the policy of institutional self-maintenance which has been struck since Luther's Reformation in Germany and its legitimate successor.

The text was returned to the Secretariat for emendations according to the suggestions presented by the Fathers. It returned to the Council floor again on October 26. During the following three congregations eleven votes were taken on this revised text. Each vote received approval, and those votes of approval with reservations were carefully considered in the following weeks by the members of the secretariat. The declaration was returned to the Council floor again on November 19 for the final voting in a general congregation. At this time it was approved by a vote of 1,954 to 249.

During the ninth public session, on December 7, 1965, Pope Paul VI formally promulgated the Declaration on Religious Freedom after a final vote of 2,308 Council Fathers approving and 70 disapproving. It was a delightful victory for the American hierarchy. Richard Cardinal Cushing of Boston summarized their collective sentiments when he wrote:

I come home happy and satisfied that the voices of American Catholics have been heard and respected at the Ecumenical Council. We Americans, I feel, by the fact that we have lived in peace and harmony in a pluralistic society, offer to the world a practical lesson of the deeper significance of religious liberty.

The realization that the document was "*the* American issue at the Council" was verbalized by Archbishop Robert Lucey of San Antonio in the Spring of 1963: "It would be entirely appropriate that the American hierarchy should take the lead of a decree proclaiming authentic and universal freedom of religion, made permanent and unbreakable by constitutional guarantees." As a matter of fact, that lead had already been given in the second session of the Council through the pleas for a statement on religious freedom by the Americans who spoke during the discussions on ecumenism. That initiative, too, had been exhibited from the very beginning of the conciliar experience by the interventions submitted by Archbishop Karl Alter in 1959 and Francis Cardinal Spellman in 1960 for a clear conciliar declaration on religious freedom. Their sentiments were many times expressed by the American members and consultors of the unity secretariat, as was evidenced by Bishop Charles Helmsing's spontaneous remarks at the close of his intervention during the final days of the third session.

The American press also played no small role in fostering a healthy public opinion in favor of the document. From beginning to end, the press followed this document more closely than any other conciliar statement. It was, time after time, through every session of the Council, a constantly recurring subject for discussion at the American Bishops' Press Panel.

Stating this record, however, is not in the least intended to make it appear that the Declaration was the product of *only* the American participants in the Council. Many others from many nations also played an important role in the drafting and passage of the Declaration. Among those deserving of special mention are Bishop Jan Willebrands of the secretariat for unity, Auxiliary Bishop Carlo Colombo of Milan, Canon Charles Moeller of Louvain University, Dominican Fathers Yves Congar and Jerome Hamer, and Monsignor Pietro Pavan.

The Declaration, however, should not be interpreted as the end of a discussion that has been carried on within the Church during the time of the Council. "My conviction," wrote Bishop Ernest J. Primeau of Manchester, New Hampshire, "is that the Council's Declaration on Religious Liberty will not be the final position of the Catholic Church on this subject. There will be continued development of the theology of religious freedom and its implications."

The American prelate who, perhaps, was most intimately associated with the Declaration was Bishop Primeau. Bishop Primeau was elected a member of the Secretariat for Promoting Christian Unity by his colleagues in the November, 1963, vote of the Council Fathers. Immediately he was appointed by the Secretariat's president, Cardinal Bea, to serve on the subcommittee dealing with religious freedom. As such, he made four special trips to attend meetings in addition to the regular meetings held by the subcommittee when the Council was in session. As one of the few American bishops who was most intimately associated with the activities of the Council, he was also the American representative, along with Bishop Christopher Weldon of Springfield, Massachusetts, to serve on the International Committee of Bishops throughout the time of the Council. Before the Council convened, he had served on the Preparatory Commission on the Discipline of the Clergy and Faithful. All told, from the preparatory to the concluding phase of the Council, he made 17 round trips to Rome.

Bishop Primeau felt that the most significant work of the unity secretariat was "the ultimate success it garnered in fields that had never been considered by other Councils." He stated that the work which the Secretariat did on "the thorny problem" of religious freedom was "almost virginal, given the compromises that are inevitable in any document produced by a large body of representatives." He called the Declaration on Religious Freedom a "basic document" which will offer Catholics a "platform from which we can conduct the dialogue of ecumenism with other Christian religions and with non-Christian religions, not to mention atheists and pagans." He evaluated his particular association with the Secretariat for Promoting Christian Unity in these words:

> . . . it is my considered opinion that the most significant document for the future is that of religious freedom. Perhaps I am talking as an American. But it seems to me that entire new vistas are being opened for the Church,

within and without. This document may cause some difficulties at first, but, in time, balance will be established and the net results for the Church and the world will be enormous.

As a group, however, the American bishops wasted no time. Father Sheerin's observation that "the American bishops will make stronger efforts between now and the fourth session to insure the approval of the document" was absolutely correct. After returning home from what they felt was a setback at the end of the third session, the Americans flooded the unity secretariat with observations on religious freedom. They pleaded even more vocally than at any time before or later, for the passage of a statement on religious freedom now. Only time will tell how many of the six thousand suggestions to the unity secretariat on this subject were submitted by Americans.

Upon returning to the fourth session, the Americans—given much more than a gentle assist from the American press—were more determined than ever to secure the passage of the document. Almost to a man, they made their own the observation that Father John Courtney Murray had uttered many times—and once more, with great feeling, as he spoke to the American bishops during their regular Monday meeting on September 17, 1964:

One must have in mind that it will be the duty of the Council to establish the formula "religious freedom" within the Christian vocabulary, to define or describe its full sense and meaning, and to do this in such a way that there may be at least general agreement among Christians.

Those who have criticized the apparent failure of the American bishops to organize did not account for their work in the passage of this document. The subject of religious freedom was keenly discussed at the Chicago meeting of American bishops hosted by Cardinal Meyer in the summer of 1963. Upon their return to the third session in 1964 the American bishops had already formed a committee to coordinate their presentation of the matter on religious freedom, under the chairmanship of Archbishop Lawrence Shehan of Baltimore. During their very first Monday evening meeting at the North American College, on September 21, 1964, the Archbishop of Baltimore reported to the assembly that the following American prelates had agreed to speak in the Council chambers on the subject: Cardinals Cushing, Meyer and Ritter, Archbishops O'Boyle, Alter and Shehan, and Bishops Primeau, Hannan and Carberry. In this case the Americans had agreed upon a *modus operandi*.

As a matter of fact, a surprising number of Americans did speak on the subject. Of the 105 speeches delivered orally on the Council floor, fourteen were by Americans. Over and above the number of American bishops who spoke on the floor of the Council, there were also the more than twenty Americans who submitted written interventions.

Eight Americans spoke on this subject during the third session. The first three to speak were Cardinals Cushing, Meyer and Ritter during the eighty-sixth congregation on September 23, 1964. The Cardinal Archbishop of Boston spoke "not only in my own name, but also in the name of almost all the bishops of the United States." He said "it is most gratifying to us that at long last a full and free discussion on this subject will take place in this Council hall." By so doing, he added, "this Ecumenical Council will manifest, if I may quote words famous in our American history, 'a decent respect for the opinions of mankind.'" He argued that "in this declaration the Church must show herself to the entire modern world as the champion of liberty, of human liberty and of civil liberty, specifically in the matter of religion." He then said that the whole question could be reduced to two propositions, which he stated in the following words:

> Throughout her history the Catholic Church has ever insisted upon her own freedom in civil society and before the public powers. She has fought for the freedom of the pope and of the bishops to teach and govern the people of God, who have the right to live in civil society according to the dictates of Christian conscience without interference. The first proposition, therefore, is contained in the traditional formula, *"libertas Ecclesiae."*
>
> The second proposition is this: That same freedom in civil society which the Church has ever insisted upon for herself and her members, she now, in this our age, also champions for other churches and their members, indeed for every human person.

A keen observer of the Council, Abbé René Laurentin recorded for *Le Figaro* the following observations on the Archbishop of Boston's address:

> A vision remains with me—following me around—from this second week of the Council. It is that of Cardinal Cushing, Archbishop of Boston, speaking in the name of all the American bishops and defending the schema on "Religious Liberty." From his first words, the power of his voice and the unusual oratorical style brought me, with many others, to the edge of the section reserved for "periti." And I was fortunate enough to capture, in the luminous circle of a borrowed pair of binoculars, the tall, purple figure with white hair.
>
> He was there, he spoke Latin, this fabulous man who had gone back home shortly after the beginning of the first session because he did not understand this language and was wasting his time. . . . He had promised to come back after the installation of a simultaneous-translation system. He had promised to pay the bill. A million lire did not daunt him. The installation could not be undertaken, but he had come to take first place in pleading for a great cause, one to which American Catholicism owes its prodigious development and vitality. . . . He evoked that basic conviction that reciprocal tolerance and respect for the liberty of others are a primary value

in the concrete life of men and nations, the very earth in which Catholicism has grown, loyally and without bickering in his country.

He had come, and he spoke uniquely, syllable by syllable, that Latin which his invincible reflexes sometimes telescoped on final syllables, in spite of enormous effort and fierce concentration. There he was, one foot out in front of him, his tall profile leaning toward the microphone in the posture of a man who is saying good-by. An energy radiated from his whole being; the loudspeakers vibrated at the limit of their power.

Why did I smile, then, like so many others? Was it the desperate effort of this American throat to form the stubborn syllables, the struggles of this living man to come to grips with a dead language? Was it (for once) the thing that Bergson speaks of, the imposition of the mechanical on the real?

Yes, I smiled, and yet I shared, more deeply than I thought at the time, the emotion of this fighter defending the cause of liberty. And now when this image, this warm voice comes back to my memory, all that remains is the emotion and an admiring sympathy for this great, grey man, doing himself violence to defend an idea for which, obviously, he would give his life.

The second American speaker who addressed his remarks specifically to the subject was Albert Cardinal Meyer of Chicago. He said that the Declaration appeared to be especially "needed at this time" for the following reasons:

1) Men of our day long for the Church to promote rather than to fear religious freedom. This longing rises from a certain common experience by which, on the one hand, they have noted religious persecutions wherever the unlimited power of the State prevailed, and, on the other, they have observed religion flourishing in regions where peaceful coexistence of various religious groups is allowed.

2) By affirming the innate freedom of the human person in religious affairs, the Church will set an example to the governments of the world on how to conduct themselves in this delicate area.

3) By affirming religious freedom, the Church will caution its faithful that true religion consists essentially not so much in the display of external belonging to a religion, but rather and more especially to conscious, free and generous submission of a man to the will of his Creator.

4) This affirmation of religious freedom will be of no little importance for the Church's apostolate, since in this fashion all will learn that men cannot be brought to the truth in a free competition of religions, nor by force, nor by mere passing missionary efforts, nor by considerations that do not go to the heart of the matter, but by the fullness of truth alone and the sincerity of the charity men sense in the words and life of missionaries.

5) Finally, this affirmation of religious freedom is essential for fruitful dialogue with non-Catholics. For unless it is perfectly clear to our separated

brethren that we sincerely acknowledge their freedom, their personal dignity, the profound religious convictions, that same freedom, I say, and that same personal dignity, and those same profound religious convictions which we claim for ourselves, all of our efforts to deal with them will rightly be suspect.

The final speaker on that historic day was Joseph Cardinal Ritter. He said that the schema pleased him, but with these reservations: first, he would like to see all argumentation removed from the schema; secondly, that the schema do no more than declare that religious liberty be stated and advocated as "the innate right of all who come into this world." His principal argument was this:

Religious liberty, how and when it is declared in the schema, is an innate right of all men founded on human nature. This is a certain truth which seems to be admitted by all. For God, in his very gift of human liberty, concedes to all men a certain immunity from human coercion not only in religious matters, but also in all the affairs of life. No one has the moral power of coercing others to act or of prohibiting them from acting, unless the common good of society requires it, for no authority is given except to promote the common good. And so religious liberty, when and where it is described in the schema, is not something special and transcendent, but an aspect or part of this very human liberty.

On the following day, September 24, two more American spokesmen rose in defense of the schema. The first was the Very Reverend Joseph Buckley, S.M., Superior General of the Marist Fathers. The right to liberty, he said, is based on the principle of a "call from God. According to this principle, every sincere conscience, even if mistaken, is a call from God: a divine vocation." The gist of Father Buckley's argument is stated in his own words:

I suggest as the foundation of religious liberty not some divine vocation, but the obligation of conscience: the categoric imperative of conscience itself, under God. *Under God* for those who believe in God, but for all men the categoric imperative of conscience.

The right to religious liberty, like all other rights of man, springs from an obligation. In created things no right exists which is not founded in a prior obligation.

If a man feels that he should worship God in a particular way, he has a right to fulfill this obligation. If a man, as a social person, judges that he is obliged to worship God socially, he has a right to social worship. There is no authority superior to the individual conscience under God, unless it is an authority sincerely perceived by the conscience itself. This is how Catholics accept the authority of the Church over them.

Bishop Ernest J. Primeau rose on the same day to discuss "the very concept of religious liberty." Stating that he wished to address his remarks to "the connection between internal personal religious liberty and external social religious liberty," he then went on to make the following point:

> From this accurate metaphysics of the human person a very important conclusion can be drawn for the present material. It certainly follows that we cannot concede to man freedom of conscience and, at the same time, deny him the free exercise of religion. The same freedom exists in the same moment, so that the connection between them is inviolable. The internal freedom of the person and his external social liberty share the same origin. They are coequal and coordinate. By the same right they pertain together to the dignity and integrity of the human person. Thus, any attempt to separate these two freedoms would be a type of Kantianism. It would certainly separate the juridico-social order from the moral-personal one. This is anathema in Catholic philosophy.

Seizing the opportunity of the moment, Bishop Primeau said he also wanted to discuss the nature of religious freedom "as a true and strict right." Thus he continued:

> By "right" we mean a type of moral faculty. This moral faculty can be duplex. It is a faculty for action and a faculty for demanding that our action be not impeded by others. One affirms immunity in action; the other affirms a positive command to act. In our subject, confusing the two senses involved in the notion of right would give rise to endless confusion. In its contemporary technical sense, well understood by experts, religious liberty is a true right in the sense that it is a true juridic immunity from any legal or social force in religious matters. In this modern sense the Declaration proclaims the right of all and of all Churches to religious liberty in society. By this proclamation we do not by any means say that all men and all Churches have from the all-good God the positive mandate to spread their doctrine and worship. This would involve accepting religious indifferentism.
>
> Anyone reading this Declaration on Religious Liberty in such a way as to see in it a touch of indifferentism confesses that he has completely misunderstood the matter under discussion.

On the following day two other American prelates spoke on the same subject. Archbishop Karl Alter, who was the first American to request that this subject be discussed at the Council, rose to speak not only for himself, but "for many bishops of the United States." He stated that this subject "was diligently considered by the American bishops" and was "almost unanimously approved in its general format." However, he did want to make the following distinction:

We are not speaking of any kind of liberty, or of undetermined religious liberty, or of liberty understood in the wider sense. We are speaking precisely of that right of a human person to immunity from all external force in religious matters, whether induced by civil power or any other power. In the second session of the Council the very excellent "relator" brought to light this distinction between true religious liberty and all other false types. The right of a person to teach errors or perpetrate evil has never been affirmed in any way. The human right to immunity from external force in religious matters has been confirmed only as a social and juridical right before civil power and the temporal order; by no means has the right of a person to religious freedom before God been affirmed.

Archbishop Alter's concluding remarks returned to the theme that this declaration would foster a genuine ecumenical spirit. He said:

In the modern context, the question of religious liberty—it seems to me—must be solved primarily in the practical order, secondarily in the speculative. The liberty of the Church in carrying out her function is the principal and foremost good and, therefore, must be maintained as *the* good not only in certain areas and in particular circumstances, but also in the universal order and in all circumstances. In my opinion there is no doubt but that, if the declaration of full personal freedom in religious matters was solemnly promulgated in the Synod, it would ultimately profit greatly both the Church and society, and it would especially foster ecumenism among our separated brethren.

During this same congregation, Cardinal Suenens, the acting moderator, called for a standing vote to terminate discussion on the subject. It was overwhelmingly approved. On the following Monday, however, during the eighty-ninth congregation, four speakers had obtained 70 signatures to allow them to speak on religious freedom. One of them was Bishop John Wright of Pittsburgh, an important American member of the doctrinal commission. Bishop Wright delivered a brilliant address on "the question of religious liberty and its exercise" and how it "ultimately touches the question of the common good." "The defense of religious liberty," he said, "ought to take into account the nature and protection of that common good which, in a way, constitutes the very *res publica* and thus must be promoted by the directors of the State." He then spoke of the common good:

The common good involves a certain order of things and qualities; certainly it includes peaceful relations among citizens. But the concept of the common good should never be compared to that kind of impassive order or conformism which would be pleasing, perhaps, to the totalitarian or police State, but which would in no way befit a truly human society of persons created in the image of God and responsible finally to God. . . .

A common good worthy of persons always presupposes a moral, intellectual and spiritual element as essential and fundamental. Obedience and conformity to the moral law, divine and positive, ought always to be present in the common good and among other virtues. But such obedience, if it is to nourish a true common good, must be a virtue, the *virtue* of persons acting with knowledge and consent and, consequently, acting *freely* in a spirit of justice. . . . *For the common good is always something living, ethical, spiritual, intellectual, and, therefore, fully humane.* . . .

Hence, it seems to follow that the common good of mankind, to the extent that it is ethical and moral, demands and presumes religious faith, true and whole, strong, fruitful and, therefore, a reasonable assent to truth freely accepted and freely professed. But also, and equally as a matter of justice, it follows that the common good demands the necessity of liberty from external coercion in the matter of religion, if the common good is not to lose its very soul which is virtue, and especially the virtue of justice.

Bishop Wright concluded his remarks in a most extraordinary manner. "As a matter of fact," he said, "and this should be acknowledged openly, religious liberty is often more complete in other countries than it is in America; this is certainly the case in England with regard to school rights, and it also is so in Holland." The Americans were, quite frankly, not ready for this twist to their traditional argument!

Religious freedom, as we have already seen, had been unfortunately scuttled during the third session. It returned at the fourth session as the opening subject on the agenda. Again the "old faithfuls" of the American hierarchy were back in Rome to defend the "American schema." Conspicuously absent was Albert Cardinal Meyer whom death had claimed in April, 1965. The subject was reintroduced on the floor of the Council during the 128th congregation on September 15, 1965. During that congregation two American leaders rose in defense of the re-emendated schema. Francis Cardinal Spellman was the first. He said the revised schema was "most praiseworthy" in the light of the fact that "the greatest possible consideration must be given to the dignity, rights and duties of the human person divinely created and redeemed." He concluded with the following strong ecumenical endorsement:

Actually, according to the mind of the Church, it is wrong for the civil power to impose on its citizens the profession of one determinate religion as a condition for full and perfect participation in civil and national life. In religious matters, the Church wishes the State to be impartially benevolent toward all.

The propositions in the present Declaration are helpful to true ecumenism and will greatly assist those believers and their pastors who live among peoples of different cultures and religions. I feel that any major emendation or change of the present text of the Declaration will cause people to doubt the sincerity of the Church when she speaks of religious liberty. The Declaration ought to stand in its present form.

During the same congregation Cardinal Cushing stood before the microphone (which he really did not need) and cast his vote in favor of the revised schema. He said he had two things to say: "First of all, the doctrine on the right of man for freedom in religious matters is solidly based in Catholic teaching. Secondly, the promulgation of this teaching over the entire world is today a pastoral necessity of the first order." He then added that the entire schema was based on two propositions which he explained in the following words:

First, because the schema teaches that the *foundation of the right* to freedom in religious matters is this truth: namely, the dignity of the human person which demands that man should act with his own counsel and responsibility, so that he freely acts from a consciousness of duty and not because of external coercion. This truth concerning the dignity of man is not only the foundation for all human rights, but it is also the basis for the whole social order. It is also the foundation for religious freedom.

Secondly, the schema teaches that *the object of this right* is a good: the good of freedom or immunity from force. That good is especially due to man in society, for it is a good necessary for the human person in order that he be not forced against his conscience nor impeded by others, even by the public authority, when he acts according to his conscience.

Therefore, as regards both the foundation of the right and the object of this right to religious freedom, the teaching of the schema is based not in an altogether subjective order, as some have said, but in the objective order of truth and, therefore, in sound moral philosophy.

On the following day Cardinal Ritter again rose in defense of the schema. He expressed his great joy over this text and said that the labors of the unity secretariat "leave nothing to be desired—nothing, so to speak, but approval without delay and its promulgation at the opportune time." Even more urgently he added, "Neither love nor justice nor fidelity permit us to delay or refuse." He concluded his appeal in these words:

Finally, unless we will have approved a firm and clear Declaration on Religious Freedom, many things in the conciliar Constitution on the Church and in the Decree on Ecumenism, which have already been promulgated, will remain without meaning, value or truth. Faith, or fidelity, which must be preserved for us and others, does not allow that we be indifferent in this matter. For the Constitution on the Church teaches that the Holy

Spirit in all nations and at all times grants grace and works out salvation.

Another day passed, and again Americans seized the opportunity. During the 130th congregation, on September 17, two more Americans spoke on the subject. Archbishop Paul J. Hallinan of Atlanta, Georgia, said that the text was "very satisfactory." He then said he wanted to add a few words on one point, "the extension and limits of public authority in religious matters." On this subject he made the following observation:

It must finally be noted that where the civil law of religious liberty, based on constitutional law, really thrives, the State does not profess a religious indifferentism, a false neutrality or an agnosticism in religious matters.

Rather, where religious liberty is secure, the State simply acknowledges its own limitations over human rights which cannot be *relinquished* ("inalienable"). In other words, the State recognizes that it has no right to constrain the exercise of liberty *except in the case of civil crimes*.

The State in this concept acknowledges also the social value of religion to be of the first importance. Therefore it must promote this social value of religion, but in a manner distinct and proper to itself. The State, therefore, best fosters religion when it fosters the free exercise of it.

On the same day Bishop Charles Maloney, Auxiliary Bishop of Louisville, said that he would turn his prepared text over to the unity secretariat "in the interest of saving time." He then asked for "just three minutes" and proceeded to speak for five minutes. Propounding an *ad hominem* argument, he observed that some contradictory statements had been uttered on the floor of the Council, and thus some of them had to be false statements. By what right, then, asked Bishop Maloney, did those speak erroneously? And he answered, "Certainly their right to speak did not flow from the error they propounded," but rather "from their identity or personality as Council Fathers." He then proposed the following question to the Council Fathers:

The question before the Council is simply this: Does any person, or group, or the State have a right to force a man to act against his conscience when he is in error in matters of religion, or to prevent him from acting in accordance with his conscience so long as he does not violate the rights of others or seriously disturb public order in the community?

Finally, Bishop Maloney gave voice to the sentiments of the lay auditors in these words:

Yesterday the auditors of the Council, lay men and lay women, held a meeting and discussed this matter of religious liberty. This morning they asked me to announce their unanimous resolution: "All the auditors of the Council approve the doctrine proposed in the treatise on religious liberty. Moreover, they strongly urge that it be promulgated by the Council."

For my part, I heartily endorse their resolution.

The weekend came and went, and the Fathers returned to the 131st congregation. They had yet to hear another American speaker on the subject of religious freedom. Even by now, however, there was not a shadow of a doubt among the Council Fathers that the Americans were one hundred per cent in support of this schema. Lawrence Cardinal Shehan rose from his chair behind the table of the Presidency and declared that "the schema on religious liberty has my wholehearted support and, in my estimation, merits the approval of the Fathers." He thereupon launched into a history of the doctrinal development of the subject, referring to Cardinal Urbani's statement that the schema represents a doctrine "whose seeds are found in the Church's teaching on the dignity of the human person and whose support is drawn from the Sacred Scriptures." His concluding words, in more ways than one, summarized the whole body of arguments that the Americans—and the unity secretariat itself—had proposed throughout the past two years.

It is obvious that the whole world expects of this Council a declaration on religious liberty. The world needs such a declaration, for without the recognition of the right to religious liberty, there can be no true and lasting peace among men. The Church, too, needs such a declaration, for only through the recognition of religious liberty can the Church be revived in those countries where her life has been virtually stamped out; only through recognition of religious liberty can the Church be free in those countries where she is in shackles; only in an atmosphere of religious freedom can the Church flourish in those new and developing nations which hold out so much promise for the future. The doctrine of religious freedom in our schema is a sound doctrine, in full harmony with the body of the Church's traditional teaching. It is to be hoped, therefore, that this schema will receive overwhelming approval from the Fathers.

By this time the discussion on religious freedom was closed. The discussion, however, continued in the meetings of the Secretariat for Promoting Christian Unity. Helping them to form decisions all during this time, as well as in the preceding years, were the 20 written interventions submitted by 17 American prelates. These had started to arrive on the desk of Cardinal Bea as early as Archbishop Alter's intervention in August, 1959. They did not cease until Bishop Robert Tracy's intervention of September 17, 1965.

Cardinal Spellman, in the preparatory stage, had submitted two written interventions on the subject. In the first, on the relations between Church and State, he enunciated the traditional Catholic teaching on religious tolerance.

While granting that the State could never champion the cause of religious indifferentism, he did admit that the Church "completely accepts modern civil societies when, in practically ordering civil life, they resolve to grant the followers of each religious liberty and political equality." In the same statement the Cardinal of New York helped to chart the course of future conciliar discussion in these words:

Civil society should also grant that same religious freedom which it recognizes for its citizens, because of the social nature of the human person, to religious communities and to the other societies which the citizens make up, as long as their activities agree with the needs of public order and common good. Nor should such freedom be contained in the constitution of civil society as a mere changing concession; rather it should be sanctioned firmly in law and expressed with civil equality for religions. Although the juridical statute which sanctions religious liberty can assume different forms according to the different historical circumstances, nevertheless it is very desirable that the Catholic Church receive help from civil society in her activities which serve the common good, inasmuch as is allowable in accordance with the State's constitution. In any case, this help should likewise be granted proportionally and within the limits of the public common to communities which are not of the Catholic faith.

About the same time Cardinal Spellman submitted further observations on the principles and action of the Church in promoting the good of society. In these early, formative days of the Council he wisely made the following observation concerning the question of religious tolerance. He wrote:

Because of the pastoral object of the Council and the expectation of many Catholics as well as non-Catholics, this question, too, should be accurately considered. But again there is a question as to where such a consideration may be found and when could we see it. Since some things are proposed in the present schema on civil liberty, perhaps some things on religious freedom could also be proposed here.

Once the schema on ecumenism was submitted to the Council Fathers, the American bishops submitted their observations. Archbishop Alter argued for a statement on religious freedom in these words:

Among many Catholics as well as non-Catholics there still exist doubts as to whether the Catholic Church recognizes full religious freedom for all citizens. There is a question whether the freedom to worship God both privately and publicly, individually as well as joined in assemblies, according to the right conscience of the individual, is recognized for Catholics only or also for others. It is fitting to dispel these doubts, that Christian unity, according to the mind of Our Lord Jesus Christ, may be promoted and that both truly fraternal charity and good relations may increase, day by day, among Catholics and non-Catholics. However, in order that the doctrine of the Catholic Church may clearly come to light in the minds of all, it is necessary to have a solid basis in the principles of Catholic theology and in natural law.

About this same time Bishop Primeau submitted his suggestions "about the scope and method of the schema." His principal suggestions, in a rather lengthy intervention, were expressed in the following words:

. . . it would indeed be better if the schema would deal with the whole Catholic theology of liberty, and especially in a properly theological fashion. It should begin, therefore, with revealed doctrine, and then fill this doctrine in from the resources of human reason. Such an exposition would have four chapters, arranged approximately as follows: first, let there be a consideration of Christian liberty, inasmuch as we are Sons of God, of how there can be any participation in the liberty of the Holy Spirit by whom, within salvation history, the Sons of God "are led" (cf. Rom. 8:14) to the Father through the Incarnate Son; secondly, there should be an exposition of the liberty of the Church, in what way is there any partaking of the liberty of Christ Himself to whom all power in heaven and on earth has been given (cf. Mt. 28: 18); thirdly, we should discuss how the act of faith is free so that it might be understood in what great esteem the liberty of man is held by God; fourthly, common religious liberty should be explained in its modern sense according to which it is a right based essentially in the dignity of man and verified by human reason.

Bishop Charles Helmsing, also a member of the unity secretariat, stated his observations with the introductory remark, "I am confident that the bishops of the United States unanimously agree on the importance of this statement on religious liberty." Then drawing from the American experience, he made the following point:

Our experience in these United States has been unique under a form of government which guarantees religious freedom. Certainly the progress of the Church since the Constitution and the inauguration of the American hierarchy in the following year, 1790, gives eloquent testimony to the fact that the truth, when freely proclaimed, can and will win men of good will.
It seems to me that the lack of experience under such a system paralyzes the bishops of some countries into the fear of consequences, should this statement be made. Is not acting on this fear the type of expediency that negates the freedom of the Council itself?
From my conversations with bishops from mission territories in Asia and

Africa, I am confident that a poll of these bishops would result almost unanimously in an affirmative vote for the statement. While the statement on religious liberty might cause local problems, it seems to me to be vital for the welfare and the progress of the entire Church throughout the world.

Throughout these months, six other Americans submitted their observations on the religious-freedom schema. They were Bishop Marion F. Forst of Dodge City, Kansas, Auxiliary Bishop Fulton J. Sheen of New York, Bishop Leo T. Maher of Santa Rosa, California, Auxiliary Bishop Philip Hannan of Washington, D.C., Bishop Joseph H. Hodges of Wheeling, West Virginia, and Auxiliary Bishop John F. Whealon of Cleveland. All of them advocated the adoption of a declaration on religious freedom and argued from the American pluralistic experience. "From a practical point of view," wrote Bishop Forst, "it has certainly been the experience in the United States of America that a strong position taken by the Church on religious liberty has, rather than harmed, actually strengthened the faith of Catholics and promoted a true ecumenical spirit."

Viewing the subject in a more philosophical light, Bishop Sheen made the following distinction:

> Between the liberty to do what one pleases and the liberty to do what a dictator orders, there is that which is called "moral" liberty, namely, the liberty to do that which is to be done; that is, whatever is required by the rational and moral order. In this sense, liberty is not condemned by the Church, but rather it is praised, as liberty confers merit on the actions of men. "Before man is life and death, good and evil. That which he chooses will be given to him" (Ecl. 15:18).

Bishop Leo Maher expressed an ecumenical sentiment in his intervention. He asked "to see the spirit of Blessed Innocent XI towards the revocation of the edict of Nantes by Louis XIV in the year 1685 pervade the chapter." Then he continued in the following ecumenical vein:

> We would point out again that an enforced "faith" is a contradiction in terms, and, while praying and working for the gift of faith for our separated brethren, we may not deny them the freedom to practice their religion or presume that, because they do not accept the truth we profess, they are deliberately rejecting the light.

Bishop Philip Hannan's comment was terse and to the point:

> The concern of the Church is the liberty of all men, a right which includes religious liberty. Obviously men cannot be led to the service of God unless they have the recognition of their liberty, and the Church must vindicate

the right of every man to liberty as an endowment of God whether or not every man uses that liberty to serve God fully.

Bishop Hodges commended the secretariat for the document even though, "like all original documents, it can be improved." So he wrote on January 30, 1964, and he urged that it be accepted "as a basis for discussion in the next session of the Council." In his observations Bishop Hodges then pointed out a fact that pertained especially to Catholics.

Man indeed enjoys religious liberty according to the plan of God. We have much to gain and nothing to fear from an unambiguous proclamation of this truth. The obligation to embrace the true faith remains intact, but man must embrace it freely and according to a right conscience. Otherwise it is of no avail. We will have to preach the word of God strongly, more clearly, more intensely; but this difficulty, this labor, cannot in the least stand in the way of the truth which we know.

The final intervention in this series was written by Bishop Whealon on September 27, 1964. Short and to the point, it made the following proposal:

It would be better if the Declaration were presented in two parts:
First part—The declaration itself on religious liberty, expressed in clear and simple concepts and words, without explanations or arguments, and intelligible to all men. I think that this declaration should certainly be legal and philosophical, akin in spirit and word to the encyclical *Pacem in Terris*.
Second part—There should be a pastoral exhortation—for Catholics, leaders of States and all men. In this part it is mentioned that the Catholic Church is the true religion and that all men have an obligation to avoid error and to embrace the truth.

In the following year, 1965, the secretariat received nine more suggestions from American bishops, six of them being dated during the month of January. Bishop John Franz, writing on January 2, gave voice to a common sentiment among the Americans in these words: "Many Bishops and others are truly disturbed by the decision by which the Presidency of the Council has revoked the promised support of the schema on religious liberty. Therefore," he continued, "we ardently beg that the text of this schema, a declaration essential to all, be preserved and as quickly as possible be presented again to the fourth session of the Council."

"With great urgency," Archbishop Alter wrote in the same vein on January 13, "I plead that the schema on religious liberty, in the form in which it was presented to the conciliar Fathers at the close of the third session, be admitted immediately at the beginning of the fourth session for discussion and prompt action." The Archbishop of Cincinnati then included his two previous interventions on the subject and added: "Unless there is universal religious liberty, that is, for all men, the liberty of the Church itself is denied in practice, and the divine mission of the Church would in effect be defeated." He then concluded with this tribute to Father John Courtney Murrary, S.J.:

> The above arguments have been well stated and futher elaborated by Father John Courtney Murray, with whose intervention I am in complete agreement. Briefly, as he states: No man is to be forcibly constrained to act against his conscience; and no man is to be forcibly restrained from acting in accordance with his conscience—presupposing always the need of protecting the good of public order. The thesis advanced is operative in the temporal order and is fundamentally juridical. It has, it is true, doctrinal implications, but these are consistent with Catholic teaching and the historical development of doctrine.

On the same day, January 25, 1965, two other American prelates submitted their observations on the schema. Archbishop Joseph McGucken of San Francisco wrote: "I heartily agree with the Declaration on Religious Freedom as it now stands, both as regards its method and its structure." He then proposed thirteen suggestions for improving the text, most of them concerning the addition or deletion of a word or phrase. His most lengthy observation was expressed in these words:

> . . . the words "which exigency is entirely consonant with reason and worthy of man" should be suppressed, and in their place should be written the following words or something similar to them: "Indeed, the personal dignity of each and every person in today's civil society demands that he be free in religious matters for the safety of the public good, so that his conscience will not be subjected to the judgment of civil power or another social power, or that he be prevented by any force from acting according to his conscience." The reason for this is that man simply does not have an *absolute* right to follow an erroneous conscience. Man's right in this matter is a relative right, i.e., in the context of civil society, in accord with the temporal order that has been ordained, as that society acts beyond its limits when it hinders acts of religion, even when these acts are external—always preserving the safety of the public good.

The other American who submitted his observations the same day was Auxiliary Bishop John F. Whealon of Cleveland. He made twelve particular suggestions concerning words and phrases in the text. His general observation was:

> The text, as it stands, is acceptable and should be retained. I especially approve of the brilliant presentation of religious liberty as a human right

which must be legally confirmed. I praise the legalistic method of presentation, the difference between this internal freedom and external freedom, and likewise the concept of immunity from coercion. I hope that the present text is not to be rejected.

On the following day Bishop Albert Fletcher of Little Rock, Arkansas, submitted his observations on the schema which he said is "of the greatest importance and I sincerely hope that some practical and, at the same time, true declaration will be approved in the Council." In his lengthy statement he posed serious questions of a philosophical nature concerning the text. Bishop John King Mussio of Steubenville, Ohio, submitted his observations during the same month in a letter to Cardinal Bea. He stated that "without such a strong declaration on religious liberty, much of the accomplishment of the entire Council will be handicapped by the suspicion that the Church seeks only her own advantage at the expense of others." He concluded with this plea:

Without a strong declaration on religious liberty, nothing that the Council can say or do will be strong enough to overcome the charge of those who hold that the Church is interested only in strengthening her own position to the detriment of others. This is not true, and nothing we do should be permitted to favor such a false picture of the true nature of the Church and her aims.

In May, 1965, Cardinal Spellman submitted another intervention on the subject of religious freedom. The Cardinal wrote:

The propositions in the present declaration are helpful to true ecumenism and will greatly assist those believers and their pastors who live among peoples of different cultures and religions. I feel that any major emendation or change of the present text of the declaration will cause people to doubt the sincerity of the Church when she speaks of religious liberty. The declaration ought to stand in its present form.

The following month Bishop Tracy submitted his observations on the same subject. He declared that the declaration was "greatly pleasing" and praised it for three reasons. Several months later, on September 17, he submitted another intervention stating that "the schema makes a good start by declaring that the right to religious liberty is truly based upon the very dignity of the human person; that men in our day are becoming more and more conscious of this subject; and the subject is altogether consonant with truth and justice." In defense of man's right to worship, Bishop Tracy observed:

God gave man freedom together with the right to direct himself with his own conscience. For this reason, no human authority can justly deprive man of this good which has been conferred upon him by his Creator, nor can it force him to act against his conscience without violating justice.

The rights of conscience, among which we have the right to divine worship, whether private or public, belongs to each man, and it also belongs to these same in assemblies or in united moral bodies, since men are naturally social, and religion of its nature is social.

Civil powers, since they exist to protect and nourish human rights, have the obligation to recognize the rights of their citizens in religious matters and fully to protect these same in the exercise of their religion.

Most American prelates followed the voting on the schema on religious freedom with more than keen interest during the fourth session. Many of them submitted their observations in writing or delivered them on the floor of the Council. One American bishop, however, had the distinction of making his view heard over Vatican City Radio when, on November 5, 1965, Bishop Robert Dwyer of Reno, Nevada, was heard discussing the schema on religious freedom. His words can serve as a fitting summary to this chapter.

He called the Council "the crowning experience of our life as churchmen. "Never again," he continued, "shall we feel that 'first, fine careless rapture' that was ours when we responded to the summons of the beloved Pope John XXIII to inaugurate the *aggiornamento* of the Church as the People of God working out the mystery of salvation in the world of today." Then he continued:

> What will history record as the outstanding achievement of the council? As the definition of the Trinity was the work of Nicaea; and the dual nature, divine and human, of Jesus Christ, Son of God, Son of Mary, was the accomplishment of Chalcedon; as the doctrine of justification by works, no less than by faith, was the hallmark of Trent; and as the clarification of the infallible teaching office of the Church as exercised by her head, the vicar of Christ, was the triumph of the First Vatican Council, what will be celebrated as the supreme contribution of the Second?
>
> For our part, and without any false modesty as one less wise (though we are assured of the agreement of the vast majority of the Council Fathers), we would answer, without a moment's hesitation, the Declaration on Religious Freedom. Other dogmatic and liturgical definitions of the Council unquestionably have high importance, and it is with no thought, certainly, of downgrading such towering monuments as the schema on the Church or that on divine revelation or the Constitution on the Sacred Liturgy, that we suggest that they will have less of an immediate impact upon the thinking and believing world, and that they will assume less prominence in the perspective of history.
>
> For there is something epoch-making about this Declaration which exalts it to the stature of one of the great landmarks of religious history. It

could mark more clearly than anything else, even more sharply than the two great personalities which have been identified with its formulation and promulgation—we mean, of course, Pope John XXIII and Pope Paul VI— the beginning of a new era in the religious understanding of mankind.

Bishop Dwyer's closing words would surely be endorsed by every American bishop and priest at the Council. He said:

Freedom absolves no man from his personal responsibility to truth, nor does it dispense him from the search for the truth which God has revealed to mankind in the person of His Son, our Savior, Jesus Christ. This solemn reminder is part of the Council's Declaration on Religious Freedom, spelled out as plainly as the language permits. But the whole document is monumental. Surely, in time to come, men will say of the Second Vatican Council that it wrote the charter of man's spiritual freedom as a child of God. It is something for any bishop, however obscure, to have played some part, however microscopic, in the framing of such a charter.

Declaration on Religious Freedom

✠ INTERVENTIONS

RICHARD CARDINAL CUSHING, 23 *September, 1964*

The Declaration on Religious Liberty, in general, is acceptable. In saying this, I speak not only in my own name, but also in the name of almost all the bishops of the United States.

It is most gratifying to us that at long last a full and free discussion on this subject will take place in this Council hall. For in our time this is a practical question of great importance, both for the life of the Church and for the social and civil life. It is also a doctrinal question. For the doctrine of the Church on religious liberty in modern civil society has not yet been declared clearly and unambiguously.

This clear declaration is owed to the whole world—both Catholic and non-Catholic—which is indeed awaiting it. Therefore, in making this Declaration, this Ecumenical Council will manifest, if I may quote words famous in our American history, "a decent respect for the opinions of mankind."

As His Excellency, the Relator has said, the text of the Declaration, as it stands, needs amendment here and there. But it is earnestly hoped that the amendments be such that the Declaration be stronger in the meaning it already expresses and not weaker. For the substance of the doctrine as we have it here is true and solid. And it is aptly appropriate for our times. Therefore, the Declaration must remain intact as to its essential meaning.

One thing is of the greatest importance. In this Declaration the Church must show herself to the entire modern world as the champion of liberty, of human liberty and of civil liberty, specifically in the matter of religion.

On the one hand, this whole question of religious liberty is somewhat complicated. On the other hand, it seems to me, the question is simple. The whole matter can be reduced to two propositions.

First: Throughout her history, the Catholic Church has ever insisted upon her own freedom in civil society and before the public powers. She has fought for the freedom of the Pope and of the bishops to teach and govern the People of God, who have the right to live in civil society according to the dictates of Christian conscience, without interference. The first proposition, therefore, is contained in the traditional formula, *"libertas Ecclesiae."*

The second proposition is this: That same freedom in civil society which the Church has ever insisted upon for herself and her members, she now, in this our age, also champions for other Churches and their members, indeed for every human person.

Let me present some reasons, briefly, for this statement. They are taken from the encyclical letter, *Pacem in Terris,* of Pope John XXIII, of most blessed memory.

For Pope John said in his encyclical that every well-ordered society is grounded in truth, in justice, in love, in liberty. Now, in the first place, equal and universal religious liberty is demanded by that fundamental truth according to which all men, insofar as they are human persons, are of equal dignity—equally endowed with the same human rights, among which Pope John specified the right to religious liberty.

Secondly, religious liberty is demanded by love. For nothing is more violently destructive of unity and civic concord than coercion or discrimination, either legally or illegally, because of religious reasons.

Thirdly, religious liberty is demanded by the very principle of civil liberty. For as Lord Acton said, speaking in the tradition of Christian civilization: "Freedom is the highest political end." Now, as the highest political end, civil liberty is also the means necessary to attain the higher ends of the human person. And this is the mind of Pope John. In particular, religious freedom—or the immunity from all coercion in religious affairs—is a necessary means by which man, in a manner which is human and willed by God, can seek God, can find Him, can serve Him.

There are other arguments for the validity of the human and civil right to religious liberty in society, and these are stated in this declaration, which as I say, in general is acceptable. And so I praise and approve this Declaration.

ALBERT CARDINAL MEYER, *23 September, 1964*

My intervention is given, not only in my own name, but also in the name of almost all the bishops of the United States of America. The proposed declaration as a whole seems to be deserving of acceptance insofar as it reaffirms the teaching of more recent pontiffs—in particular of John XXIII, of happy memory, in the encyclical *Pacem in Terris*—who have clarified and carried forward traditional teaching of the Church on this matter.

This Declaration [on Religious Liberty] appears to be especially needed at this time for these reasons:

1) Men of our day long for the Church to promote rather than to fear

religious freedom. This longing rises from a certain common experience by which, on the one hand, they have noted religious persecutions wherever the unlimited power of the State prevailed, and, on the other, they have observed religion flourishing in regions where peaceful coexistence of various religious groups is allowed.

2) By affirming the innate freedom of the human person in religious affairs, the Church will set an example to the governments of the world on how to conduct themselves in this delicate area.

3) By affirming religious freedom, the Church will caution its faithful that true religion consists essentially not so much in the display of external belonging to a religion, but rather and more especially in conscious, free and generous submission of a man to the will of his Creator.

4) This affirmation of religious freedom will be of no little importance for the Church's apostolate since, in this fashion, all will learn that men cannot be brought to the truth in a free competition of religions, nor by force, nor by mere passing missionary efforts, nor by considerations that do not go to the heart of the matter, but by the fullness of truth alone and the sincerity of the charity men sense in the words and life of missionaries.

5) Finally, this affirmation of religious freedom is essential for fruitful dialogue with non-Catholics. For unless it is perfectly clear to our separated brethren that we sincerely acknowledge their freedom, their personal dignity, their profound religious convictions, that same freedom, I say, and that same personal dignity, and those same profound religious convictions which we claim for ourselves, all our efforts to deal with them will rightly be suspect.

It is clear, moreover, that this text's manner of presentation can be improved here and there. A major revision of the text seems called for in three places:

1) On page 29, number 26, lines 8 and 9, I propose that the words "let them follow the will of the Creator and Savior in religious matters" be changed to "let them seek and, insofar as they know it, let them follow the will of the Creator and Savior in religious matters." These are the reasons:

a) The text, as it stands in the rest of line 9, derives the right of all men to religious freedom from the universal duty of men to do the will of the Creator in religious matters according to the dictates of conscience. If some, therefore, because of an erroneous conscience do not follow the true will of God, the words of the text seem to suggest that they do not have the right to act according to their own religious convictions. Thus, the conclusion of the text, as it reads, could extend beyond its premises.

b) The proposed emendation broadens the premises by taking into account two points which must be considered in establishing a universal right to religious freedom, namely, on the one hand, the natural duty of all men to worship God and, on the other, the possibility of carrying this out in a true and complete manner, something that is impossible without the gift of Christian faith.

2) On page 31, lines 38 to 40: This section seems to me to be susceptible of grave abuses. For it leaves to the discretion of civil rulers the determination of whether a violation of religious freedom shall have taken place and how such a violation is to be restrained. Our experience of the subjective manner in which civil rulers act in such matters ought to caution us to be most prudent in this regard. Therefore, the Council should appeal to the nations of the world to enact laws in this sensitive area, wherever they have not already done so, that will accord with the principles laid down in lines 29 to 37 of this Declaration.

3) With respect to the section running from page 32, line 14 to page 33, line 3, the arrangement of materials could be improved. The section in the text, as prepared, is as follows:

a) In the first place, there is laid down a foundation on which the religious freedom of groups rests.

b) Then the right itself is set forth.

c) Finally, corollaries are given, the first of which concerns the Catholic Church and is expressed at length and with special solemnity. Then, after the paragraph "With these thoughts in mind"—about which immediately—there follows a qualified approval of the rights of non-Catholic Churches. This way of handling the matter could have confirmed non-Catholics in their suspicion that when Catholics speak about religious freedom they do so only to defend their own rights.

Now this difficulty can easily be avoided by inserting before the corollaries on the Catholic Church and other religious groups, the matter set forth on page 32, lines 33 to 37, where there is a vindication of the rights of types of religious associations, Christian and non-Christian, under any form of government at all, to pursue their own missions just as they conceive of them.

May I be permitted, in closing, to speak again of the immense importance of this document. One might almost say: If the Second Vatican Council shall not have made this Declaration, few, indeed, of the other statements which we hope will issue from the Council will win a hearing from men of our age.

JOSEPH CARDINAL RITTER, 23 *September, 1964*

There are two things in the schema of the Declaration on Religious Liberty which seem to me to require diligent and accurate consideration: first, the very liberty whose existence and extension are declared; secondly, the reasons and arguments upon which this same Declaration is founded. These two things, which are intimately connected in the document, are separable and, in my humble judgment, are worthy of distinct consideration.

Religious liberty, how and when it is declared in the schema, is an innate right of all men founded on human nature. This is a certain truth which seems to be admitted by all. For God, in His very gift of human liberty, concedes to all men a certain immunity from human coercion not only in religious matters, but also in all the affairs of life. No one has the moral power of coercing others to act or of prohibiting them from acting, unless the common good of society requires it, for no authority is given except to promote the common good. And so, religious liberty, when and where it is described in the schema, is not something special and transcendent, but an aspect or part of this very human liberty.

Secondly, something should be said about the reasons and arguments upon which the Declaration in the schema is based. The arguments of this Declaration have neither simplicity, clarity nor certitude. A Declaration restricted to a simple affirmation and advocation of religious liberty by omitting all argumentation would be much better. And I say this for the following, among many, reasons:

First reason: The very nature of the Declaration is not to demonstrate and prove but to propose and simply declare.

Second reason: A simple and brief document were it more to the point, would have a greater and better effect.

Third, and most important, reason: The reasons and arguments which are found in the schema invite endless controversies and discussions. It is feared lest long and extensive arguments would arise not about its substance, but only its accidents, and thus the Fathers, by rejecting the reasons, could ultimately reject the very Declaration.

Venerable Fathers, this Declaration on Religious Liberty is valid and certain, even if the reasons are weak or even invalid. We should consider the substance and accidents of the Declaration separately and according to the merits of each. I urge that the eminent moderators, inasmuch as it is possible, separate these two elements for voting.

The schema pleases me *juxta modum*. And the *modus* is: First: That all which pertains to argumentation be removed from the schema. Second: The schema, as it now proposes religious liberty, simply declare, advocate, and also, if it seems opportune, legislate that it is the innate right of all who come into this world.

VERY REV. JOSEPH BUCKLEY, S.M., *24 September, 1964*

This intervention of mine is dictated by two main considerations. First, I am concerned that this Ecumenical Council should issue a declaration of the inalienable right of man to follow the dictates of a sincere conscience, especially in matters of religion.

In the second place, I am concerned that the Council's affirmation of religious liberty should be set forth on a firm foundation—one that is also understandable and congenial to men generally.

While in the text which is now before us a number of ameliorations seem desirable, let me deal with just one which appears to merit public review, namely the very foundation of personal liberty in the religious order.

Throughout the document, repeatedly, the right to liberty of a sincere conscience [*conscientia recta*] is based on the principle of a "call from God" [*vocatio divina*]. According to this principle, every sincere conscience, even if mistaken—erroneous—is a call from God: a divine vocation. Calling an erroneous conscience a divine vocation, even from the viewpoint that it is written in the "heart of nature," constitutes the ultimate point attained thus far in a most unhappy evolution of the concept of divine vocation.

Originally in the New Testament, a divine vocation was a call to follow Christ (Mark 3: 13); to the Christian faith (2 Thess. 1: 11); to heaven (Heb. 3: 1); and to the holiness which befits those who are so privileged (1 Thess. 4:7).

In the New Testament the priesthood is also called a divine vocation (Heb. 5: 4).

This is not a suitable occasion for a discussion of the idea of a divine vocation to the priesthood, but spare me, venerable Fathers, if I recall to mind for you a tendency to speak as if the call of God to the priesthood was recognizable to each of us in the human psychological order, as if each of us knew that he was called by God.

From the evolution of the idea of divine call it has become customary to speak also of a divine vocation even to the married state. So far has the term "divine vocation" been extended that we now read and hear of a divine vocation to become a doctor, a lawyer, an engineer, a nurse.

Finally, in the document before us, we have the *reductio ad absurdum* of this entire unfortunate evolution: the imperative of a conscience, right but erroneous, is a *divine vocation*.

This way of speaking is a long way from the teaching of the Common Doctor, St. Thomas, in the *Summa Theologica* (Ia IIae, q. 19, a.10), where he asks: "For the human will to be good, is it necessary that it agree with God's will in the thing willed?" St. Thomas answers: ". . . in individual matters we are ignorant of what God wills. Hence in these things we are under no obligation of trying to make our will agree with God's."

Most talk of divine vocation and finding out of God's will is a lot of pseudo-mysticism.

I suggest as the foundation of religious liberty not some divine vocation, but the obligation of conscience: the categoric imperative of conscience itself, under God. *Under God* for those who believe in God, but for all men the categoric imperative of conscience.

The right to religious liberty, like all the other rights of man, springs from an obligation. In created things no right exists which is not founded in a prior obligation.

If a man feels that he should worship God in a particular way, he has a right to fulfill this obligation. If a man, as a social person, judges that he is obliged to worship God socially, he has a right to social worship. There is no authority superior to the individual conscience under God, unless it is an authority sincerely perceived by the conscience itself. This is how Catholics accept the authority of the Church over them.

The exercise of the right of an individual or association can be limited by society, but only inasmuch as the exercise infringes on the rights of others. Such a conflict of obligations and of rights should not be supposed too readily.

It is only on this solid basis that I hope to see the Declaration on Religious Liberty erected by the Council.

Liberty is most precious to all men. Whatever we priests may like to think, the Catholic Church does not enjoy a very high reputation in the world generally for its sponsorship of liberty. Still, such is the esteem of the world for the Church that it welcomes any earnest indication that the Catholic Church is on the side of liberty. Witness the enthusiastic reception universally given to the encyclical of Pope John XXIII, *Pacem in Terris*.

The Council must not disappoint the world!

BISHOP ERNEST PRIMEAU, *24 September, 1964*

I am in full accord with the bishops of the United States who, as was already stated, are generally, in fact particularly, pleased with the Declaration on Religious Liberty.

I want to talk about the very concept of religious liberty, which appears in paragraph 26, page 28 and elsewhere in the declaration. Two things must be said in order to explain and defend our Declaration.

The first question concerns the connection between internal personal religious liberty and external social religious liberty. In contemporary quasi-technical language, the first is called liberty of conscience, the other the free exercise of religion which is carried out in many ways. In the general conscience of modern man, the connection between both liberties, internal and external, is unbreakable.

The right to the free exercise of religion should not be seen as a logical deduction from the right of liberty of conscience. Such a deduction would be based on a certain tacit, false premise. It would presuppose the rationalistic and individualistic concept of man which was prevalent in the nineteenth century. According to this conception, man is primarily an individual and becomes a social being only in a later moment. This is a false concept of man.

According to the true metaphysics of the human person held by Catholic philosophy, human existence is essentially social and historical. In one and the same instant the human person is an individual, an *ego*, and also a social being, an *ego* with and directed toward others in the world. Thus, we cannot allow a type of dichotomy in the human person, that is, between his personal interior existence and his social historical one.

From this accurate metaphysics of the human person a very important conclusion can be drawn for the present material. It certainly follows that we cannot concede man freedom of conscience and, at the same time, deny him the free exercise of religion. The same freedom exists in the same moment, so that the connection between them is inviolable. The internal freedom of the person and his external social liberty share the same origin. They are coequal and coordinate. By the same right they pertain together to the dignity and integrity of the human person. Thus, any attempt to separate these two freedoms would be a type of Kantianism. It would certainly separate the juridico-social order from the moral-personal one. This is anathema in Catholic philosophy.

With these words, I wholeheartedly agree with the Relator who, in his comments on page six, lines 10 and 13, proposed an emendation in paragraph 26 of the Declaration (page 29, line 9). In place of "Thus there arises," "with which it is connected" or something similar should be stated. This would better express that the free exercise of religion is inseparable from freedom of conscience.

If it were clearly taught that the free exercise of religion is not a sort of logical inference from the freedom of conscience, the answer to the objection raised against the teaching of the Declaration would become clearer. According to this objection, the doctrine of the right to free exercise of religion involves an illegitimate transition or inference from the subjective order of conscience to the objective order of rights. In fact, no such inference is made. On the contrary. The true concept of religious liberty as containing two inseparable elements, the internal and the external, is reached not by an inference from the rights of conscience to social religious rights, but by a simple analysis of the human person. It is one subject of one right having two aspects, namely, freedom of conscience and the free exercise of religion.

My second question concerns religious liberty as a true and strict right. By right we mean a type of moral faculty. This moral faculty can be duplex. It is a faculty for action and a faculty for demanding that our action be not impeded by others. One affirms immunity in action; the other affirms a positive command to act. In our subject, confusing the two senses involved in the notion of right would give rise to endless confusion. In its contemporary technical sense, well understood by experts, religious liberty is a true right in the sense that it is a true juridic immunity from any legal or social force in religious matters. In this modern sense, the Declaration proclaims the right of all and of all Churches to religious liberty in society. By this proclamation we do not by any means say that all men and all Churches have from the all-good God the positive mandate to spread their doctrine and worship. This would involve accepting religious indifferentism.

Anyone reading this Declaration on religious liberty in such a way as to see in it a touch of indifferentism confesses that he has completely misunderstood the matter under discussion.

ARCHBISHOP KARL ALTER, 25 *September, 1964*

I speak not only for myself, but for many bishops of the United States. On the 17th of this month the Declaration on Religious Freedom, which is elaborated in this schema, was diligently considered by the bishops, assenting in a group, and almost unanimously approved in its general format. We, however, wish to append certain observations.

First, we are not speaking of any kind of liberty or of undetermined religious liberty, or of liberty understood in the wider sense. We are speaking precisely of that right of a human person to immunity from all external force in religious matters, whether induced by civil power or any other power. In the second session of the Council, the very excellent Relator brought to light this distinction between true religious liberty and all other false types. The right of a person to teach errors or perpetrate evil has never been affirmed in any way. The human right to immunity from external force in religious matters has been confirmed only as a social and juridical right before civil power and in the temporal order; by no means has the right of a person to religious freedom before God been affirmed.

Secondly it seems especially desirable to us and, even more so, necessary for promoting peace and harmony in civil society that this question should be treated in clear and unambiguous language in this schema on ecumenism of the Second Vatican Council. For this is expected by almost everyone and especially in those regions where a pluralism of religion flourishes.

Among both many Catholics and non-Catholics, doubts still exist as to whether the Catholic Church recognizes the full religious liberty of all citizens. For there is a question as to whether the freedom of worshipping God, in private according to the right conscience of each man, or in public in determined groups or singularly, is recognized as for Catholics only or for all men.

It is to be remembered that there is no lack of those who reproach Catholics for behaving in religious matters with a certain ambiguity, if not dishonesty. For, they say, where the Catholics constitute the political minority, they uphold the right to full religious freedom; but where they make up a political majority, they do not recognize the right of others to exercise a liberty in religious matters. For this reason, these doubts and suspicions must be eliminated in such a way that many difficulties might be removed from the public life of Catholics.

Thirdly, many important changes in the structure and extent of civil power have been made in the course of time. Public authority in modern times no longer passes judgment or establishes spiritual goods. Today, almost everywhere, citizens take for themselves the right of judging independently of civil power especially in spiritual matters. They deny the competence of the State in this area, and rightly so, for if the foundation whereby the Republic exercised authority is investigated, it becomes clear that this foundation does not enable it to make judgments as to the merits of religious matters. This type of authority is exercised in the use of the democratic principle of majority. It would, therefore, be entirely incongruous if truth, the value of divine doctrine, and Church discipline had to be submitted to majority vote.

Fourthly, *on religious liberty in relation to the Church.*

a) Because of her divine institution and solemn command to teach all nations, which was given to her by Christ, the Church enjoys absolute rights in fulfilling her mission, that is, she is entirely independent of temporal authority or commands. Moreover, in order to secure her end, the Church must be immune from all external force or pressure. The Church has constantly defended this liberty from apostolic times. And it is not without difficulty that she has maintained it throughout history.

This liberty of the Church would be vain and meaningless if each member did not have the same freedom from external pressure in religious matters. In order to be efficaciously practical, this freedom must include the same immunity for all peoples—anywhere in the world. For if this liberty is not seen as a universal principle, valid for all men, then the Church would be foolish to maintain it for herself in the eyes of world opinion.

b) The Church and her members undergo many grave evils today where in many regions the State, or civil power, unjustly blocks religious freedom and falsely assumes for itself the right of directly guiding faith and religious practice. The right of determining faith and its exercise belongs solely to God and His Church which He instituted for this purpose. The State does not enjoy this right in any way. If civil power assumes the direction of religion and faith, by this very act it exceeds its jurisdiction. The common good of society in the public order and the rights of others must be preserved, but national unity, e.g., in the temporal order, although it is of great importance, must nevertheless be subjected to the greater spiritual good of the universal Church in accord with the principle of subsidiarity. National unity must be subordinated to the common good of all society.

In conclusion: The argument based on the nature of faith and the nature of man, which brings out the fact that the human person seeks his ultimate end in the fullness of free will, seems to us to be valid and exceedingly agreeable. There are, however, other valid arguments based either on the modern juridical constitutions of many nations, or on the evident incompetence of civil power in the religious sphere, or on the social necessity of keeping peace and harmony among the citizens, or on the example of Our Lord Jesus Christ who used only spiritual means to promote the faith.

In the modern context, the question of religious liberty—it seems to me— must be solved primarily in the practical order, secondarily in the speculative. The liberty of the Church in carrying out her function is the principal and foremost good and, therefore, must be maintained as *the* good not only in certain areas and in particular circumstances, but also in the universal order and in all circumstances. In my opinion there is no doubt but that, if the declaration of full personal freedom in religious matters was solemnly promulgated in the Synod, it would ultimately profit greatly both the Church and society, and it would especially foster ecumenism among our separated brothers.

BISHOP JOHN WRIGHT, *28 September, 1964*

I have asked special permission to speak because I fear that our question has been discussed thus far with excessive pragmatism. The report itself speaks too sparingly and cautiously, perhaps, of the connection between religious liberty and that common good which would put the discussion on the level of principle.

All sides agree that the question of religious liberty and its exercise ultimately touches the question of the common good. Therefore, the analysis and defense of religious liberty ought to take into account the nature and protection of that common good which, in a way, constitutes the very *res publica* and thus must be promoted by the directors of the State.

There are those who strongly assert that the defense of religious liberty, even for those who set forth errors contrary to Catholic truth, disrupts or damages the common good, which indeed can scarcely be denied at times. On the contrary, there are those who affirm, from another angle, that paradoxical though it be, the denial of recognition to religious liberty, in its own way and often to a far worse degree, harms the common good, because the common good by its very nature positively demands and presumes as an integral and essential element such liberty and its recognition by the civil power. It is on this point that I have a few things I should like to say.

The common good involves a certain order of things and qualities; certainly it includes peaceful relations among citizens. But the concept of the common good should never be compared to that kind of impassive order or conformism which would be pleasing, perhaps, to the totalitarian or police State, but which would in no way befit a truly human society of persons created in the image of God and responsible finally to God—to God "who has made of one all mankind, causing them to dwell together on the whole face of the earth . . . that they should seek God, if haply they may grope after him and find him," according to St. Paul (Acts 17: 26–27).

Now in these words of St. Paul is suggested a hint of the necessity of religious liberty among those elements of the common good shared by the whole human race, dwelling over the whole face of the earth, called to seek God and dimly grope after Him and perhaps find Him, even though at times such liberty gives rise to the danger of controversies and contentions as a result of the very seeking after God.

A common good worthy of persons always presupposes a moral, intellectual and spiritual element as essential and fundamental. Obedience and conformity to the moral law, divine and positive, ought always to be present in the common good and among other virtues. But such obedience, if it is to nourish a true common good, must be a virtue, the *virtue* of persons acting with knowledge and consent and, consequently, acting *freely* in a spirit of justice.

The common good is not just a certain physical or mathematical accumulation of material goods which citizens share. Certainly, it includes civil services, public highways, firefighting equipment, police protection and other such things, lest turmoil break out among the populace. But all these things do not constitute the common good. Nor is it a mere treasury of acquired goods, technical machines, artifacts and objects such as are preserved in museums but which are nothing more than booty or spoils, such as might unite thieves, rather than a common good, if they are not *ethically* acquired and cherished. *For the common good is always something living, ethical, spiritual, intellectual, and, therefore, fully humane.*

The Christian philosopher Jacques Maritain has written to our point:

> The common good is something *ethically* good. And in this common good is included, as an essential element, the greatest development possible *hic et nunc* of human persons, of those persons who make up the united multitude and thus constitute a people bound together by ties not only of force, but of justice.

Hence, it seems to follow that the common good of mankind, to the extent that it is ethical and moral, demands and presumes religious faith, true and whole, strong, fruitful and, therefore, a reasonable assent to truth freely accepted and freely professed. But also, and equally as a matter of justice, it follows that the common good demands the necessity of liberty from external coercion in the matter of religion, if the common good is not to lose its very soul which is virtue, and especially the virtue of justice.

A certain non-Catholic professor once said to me: "You can well say that the idea of religious liberty should justify itself pragmatically to Catholics in the light of the way it seems to have worked out in regions where the Church is obviously flourishing under a system of just such liberty." But this pragmatic argument is less than satisfactory because it is really not worthy of the subject. It is far better to recognize, with all Christian simplicity, that the idea of religious liberty corresponds to the *truth,* to the truth not only about the nature of the person, but also about the nature of the common good itself.

Therefore those who seek the common good in its full and true sense—and according to authentic Catholic teaching with the philosophical and theological principles to which our *practice* ought to conform and not *vice versa*—those who defend such a common good will wish to strengthen, foster and extend as far as possible all truly human liberties, especially religious liberty, that is, the liberty to learn, to meditate and to worship the Supreme Good, God, the source and author of all goods. Such religious liberty can be worked out even in a State favoring some particular religion for historical reasons—as it does in England, where a Protestant Church (the so-called Established Church) traditionally enjoys special privileges, but where now, at least, all, except the King and Queen (unless I am mistaken), have full religious liberty. The case of Ireland is also pertinent, for there the Catholic Church is held in special esteem by the Constitution and in certain customs, but all enjoy full religious liberty. As a matter of fact—and it should be acknowledged openly—religious liberty is often more complete in other countries than it is in America; this is certainly the case in England with regard to school rights, and it also is so in Holland.

There can be no doubt that Catholics—and especially the pastors of souls—will pray and work tirelessly to the end that all men will use their liberty to advance to the full and perfect knowledge of the one true God and Him whom God sent, Jesus Christ. We will be witnesses to Him to the very ends of the earth, witnesses by word and by deed. We will debate, we will implore, we will rebuke in all patience and in the light of true doctrine, so that error may have no *place,* whether or not it has any *right;* but we shall do this always recognizing the rights of any who are in error. *We* will fulfill our right and duty with the help of the grace of Christ, in the light of the Gospel, by the power of the Holy Spirit and armed with the spiritual might of the Church, neither fearing nor exploiting the constraining power of the kingdoms of this world. Whatever may be said of times past and of political cultures once, perhaps, more consistent with the work of the Gospel, but now obsolete, it is now, in the present order, necessary that Christians ask of the civil power only that it respect in justice our right to fulfill the commands of Christ; that it assist in justice our efforts to play our rightful and necessary part in furthering the common good through our work in behalf of education and peace; and that it leave inviolate, as a matter of justice, the religious liberty of all those for whom the message of the Gospels and the grace of Christ are destined, namely *all men.*

God, who gave us the duty, right and liberty to preach, gave those to whom we preach the duty, right and liberty of hearing and believing as a means to that religious perfection which the civil power can neither give nor take away, and which, therefore, it should scrupulously respect, especially as regards its liberty.

We, the successors of the Apostles, men of God, bishops of the Catholic Church—we ought to be foremost and fearless leaders among the heralds of liberty, because historically we are the heirs of liberty in matters religious acquired almost in every case and almost in every nation only through the blood and tears of our fathers. Thus we know from the experience of our own history how dear and how fruitful liberty is. Much more, supernaturally we are heirs of an even greater liberty, the liberty by which Christ has made us free by His own free obedience—a free obedience which we will freely imitate, always in the hope and with the purpose of freely persuading our neighbors and brothers to a similar free obedience—a liberty that is saving because it is obedient, an obedience that saves because it is free.

FRANCIS CARDINAL SPELLMAN, *15 September, 1965*

This Declaration on Religious Liberty is particularly fitting, especially since modern circumstances demand that the dignity of the human person as created and redeemed by God, together with his rights and duties, be treated with the greatest consideration. For sometimes it happens that not only non-Catholics and non-Christians, but even the faithful themselves, form only a partial or even an erroneous idea concerning the Church's view on the person who errs and on his right to religious liberty. Therefore, it seems most opportune that the Church present, in some systematic fashion, a defense of such liberty. The declaration admirably propounds the dignity of the human person and his social right to liberty in religious matters and of one's freedom from all external force in this regard. Likewise, the schema properly takes note of the fact that the right to exercise only this liberty of conscience is valid and ought to be recognized everywhere. All these facts are most true, and all the Christian faithful who live among people of different cults and religions will rejoice at such statements.

Most useful, also, is the Declaration's teaching on the cooperation of Catholics with those who are not Catholics and on the relationships existing between the Church and civil society. For in this or in the above-mentioned matter, many men are totally unaware that the Church approves those modern civil societies where, in the practical organization of civil life, the State declares that religious liberty and political equality belong to each religion. Some are even unaware that, according to the mind of the Church, the civil State is not able to impose on its citizens the profession of one religion as a condition for exercising their full and integral rights in national and civil life. Truly, the Church desires the

State to be impartial and benevolent toward all who obey the dictates of their conscience in religious matters.

The Declaration has already been amply discussed. The opinion of this Council has been clearly expressed and, because of the modern media of communications, is known everywhere both to Catholics and non-Catholics. I am afraid that any further change in the text will be a cause of doubt, to say the least, concerning the Church's sincerity when she talks of religious liberty. The Declaration as discussed and approved in this hall ought to stand unchanged.

RICHARD CARDINAL CUSHING, 15 *September, 1965*

I have two things to say about the schema. First of all, the doctrine on the right of man for freedom in religious matters is solidly based in Catholic teaching. Secondly, the promulgation of this teaching over the entire world is today a pastoral necessity of the first order.

I speak, first of all, on the teaching of the schema.

Indeed I am not a philosopher of great renown; nevertheless, I am acquainted with the common Catholic teaching on rights. It is: every right should be based on some truth, and every right ought to have some good for its object.

It is clear that the whole schema has been based on these two propositions. *First,* because the schema teaches that the *foundation of the right* to freedom in religious matters is some truth: namely, the dignity of the human person which demands that man should act with his own counsel and responsibility, so that he freely acts from a consciousness of duty and not because of external coercion. This truth concerning the dignity of man is not only the foundation for all human rights, but it is also the basis for the whole social order. It is also the foundation for religious freedom.

Secondly, the schema teaches that *the object of this right* is a good: the good of freedom or immunity from force. That good is especially due to man in society, for it is a good necessary for the human person in order that he be not forced against his own conscience nor impeded by others, even by the public authority, when he acts according to his conscience.

Therefore, as regards both the foundation of the right and the object of this right to religious freedom, the teaching of the schema is based not in an altogether subjective order, as some have said, but in the objective order of truth and, therefore, in sound moral philosophy.

Now I speak about the schema in light of the pastoral duty of the Church.

The preaching of the Gospel especially belongs to this responsibility. This Gospel which we teach is not only the Gospel of truth, but also of liberty by which men have been called to freedom by God.

This liberty, however, is twofold: from the gift of grace (inasmuch as we have become sons of God the Father), and from the right of nature (inasmuch as we have been created to the image of God). In the present order of salvation, the right of man to freedom in society is, for him, a part of his vocation to liberty which has been announced in the Gospel. Therefore, this Holy Synod exercises its pastoral responsibility when it declares the right of man for religious freedom.

It is known, however, according to modern experience, that in many regions of the world the dictatorial power excessively restricts man's freedom, especially in religious matters. For this reason, the Gospel of freedom should be more strongly preached today than in the past, since, when man is denied the right to religious freedom, very frequently he is also denied more civil rights, so that the society almost ceases to be human.

I conclude. However in these days of ours, in accordance with the spirit of the Apostle Paul and even with the spirit of our most beloved Pope Paul, the Church should proclaim: "I am not afraid of the Gospel to the extent that it is a Gospel of freedom."

The dangers of freedom are quite often indicated by the Church. But in the life of the Church, as in the life of St. Paul, dangers are everywhere. But today there is the greatest danger lest the Church preach the Gospel of Christ to deaf ears.

The value and good, which modern man follows with anxious mind, is the good of liberty and its freedom in human life. Thus, on behalf of our pastoral duty, we should preach the whole Gospel of the freedom of Christ, so that the ears of men are opened by the true word of God. This Declaration of ours on religious freedom will be this kind of beginning for this proclamation.

Therefore, may God see to it that the preaching of this human liberty may everywhere excite in the hearts of men the beginning of a faith in the Gospel of the truth of Our Lord Jesus Christ!

JOSEPH CARDINAL RITTER, *16 September, 1965*

I should like to express my great joy on behalf of the document which we are now considering. We express deep gratitude to those of the Secretariat who have labored most diligently in order that we might receive a strong, clear, and precise affirmation of religious liberty. Their labor leaves nothing to be desired —nothing, so to speak, but approval without delay and its promulgation at the opportune time!

Everybody in this great assembly knows that the whole world is watching Rome and awaits a document which brings joy to the hearts of very many and eases their lives. Neither love, nor justice, nor fidelity permits us to delay or refuse.

First of all, "the love of Christ urges us" to approve the document which has already been accepted. In many regions men suffer persecutions almost without number only because they try to lead sincere lives according to faith and their own consciences. Beloved Brothers, without any difficulty, and almost with one word, we can grant to many, if not all men, that they find the peace in which they can worship God according to their consciences and can share more abundantly in the life and truth of Christ. Since this is the case, can love permit silence?

Further, I speak sincerely and openly, justice demands that we present men with the Declaration on Religious Liberty in a thorough presentation. For in some Catholic countries, our brothers in Christ—separated, but still our brothers —suffer many things because of sincere and even Christian consciences. At least in some cases, these religious persecutions had their origin in ecclesiastical regulations. Should we not repair these unjust conditions which result from our doing? No one says that these conditions have not resulted, at least in part, from the quasi-official action of Catholics.

Finally, unless we shall have approved a firm and clear Declaration on Religious Liberty, many things in the conciliar Constitution on the Church and in the Decree on Ecumenism, which have already been promulgated, will remain without meaning, value or truth. Faith, or fidelity, which must be preserved for us and others, does not allow that we be indifferent in this matter. For the Constitution on the Church teaches that the Holy Spirit in all nations and at all times grants grace and works out salvation.

> Divine Providence does not deny the helps which are necessary for salvation to those who, without fault, have not yet arrived at an express knowledge of God and who strive to follow a correct life not without grace. Whatever good or truthfulness is found in them, this is regarded by the Church as an evangelical preparation and has been given by Him who enlightens every man that he may have life at last.

Further,

> The Spirit raises up a desire and activity among all the disciples of Christ that all men may be *peacefully* united in one flock and under one Shepherd in a way established by Christ.

So, most beloved Brothers, it seems to me that all religious persecutions militate against the Spirit and His activity and grace. Is not the promotion of religious liberty the fostering of that peace in which men can better hear the voice of the Spirit and more promptly respond to it? Therefore, let us approve this Declaration on Religious Liberty lest we deserve by our negligence to be counted among the enemies of the Gospel.

BISHOP CHARLES MALONEY, *17 September, 1965*

In the interest of saving time, I shall turn my prepared manuscript over to the Secretariat and I ask that you give me your attention for just three minutes.

First, I should like to offer an *ad hominem* argument, but I do this in genuine charity. In this very hall, some exactly contradictory statements have been made. Of necessity, therefore, some false statements have been made. I ask you now by what right did those speak who uttered erroneous statements? The answer is this: Certainly their right to speak did not flow from the error they propounded, for it is admitted that rights can only be grounded in truth. Their right to speak flows from their identity or personality as Council Fathers.

Similarly, beyond the Council hall, a person who expounds religious errors does not derive his right from these errors. Rather, by reason of his dignity as a human person endowed with free will he has the faculty of speaking and acting.

These two ideas are poles apart: The right to act (or decline action) on the one hand, and, on the other, the right to be free from coercion in acting or attempting to act. It is this latter right which we desire to affirm in matters of religion.

From God we have the power to act freely. And God will reward or punish us according to the use we make of this freedom which refers to the morality of our actions.

The question before the Council is simply this: Does any person, or group or the State have a right to force a man to act against his conscience when he is in error in matters of religion, or to prevent him from acting in accordance with his conscience so long as he does not violate the rights of others or seriously disturb public order in the community?

A large majority would like to answer in the negative (people, groups, states cannot force a man against his conscience) but it is a tedious task to word this statement in such a way that it will not be misinterpreted.

Considering all that has been said in the Council hall, it seems to me that one obstacle to the reconciliation of the various opinions is this: not everyone here is in agreement that we treat this particular aspect of religious liberty. A great majority of the Council Fathers desire that we discuss a right which we have in common with our separated brethren and the entire human family. It is for this reason that the majority prefers to speak of man's right to be immune from physical force or coercion in matters of religion, within due limits.

This is in accord with the Decree on Ecumenism which praises the joint efforts of Christians, or of all men, which tend to promote the common good, or uphold public morality or foster peace.

Moreover, we should like to put forth evidence which will have at least some appeal to the "secularists." For these reasons the majority prefers to discuss and approve a right which is discerned in an analysis of the dignity of the human person rather than the rights which are due to the revealed word of God.

To conclude, it is of prime importance that I should note the following:

Yesterday the [Catholic] auditors of the Council, lay men and lay women, held a meeting and discussed this matter of religious liberty. This morning they asked me to announce their unanimous resolution: "All the auditors of the Council approve the doctrine proposed in the treatise on religious liberty. Moreover, they strongly urge that it be promulgated by the Council."

For my part, I heartily endorse their resolution.

ARCHBISHOP PAUL HALLINAN, *17 September, 1965*

My Brothers in Christ:

1) The present text of the declaration on religious liberty is very satisfactory (*valde placet*). I wish only to add a few words on one point—*the extension and limits of public authority*, that is, of the State, in religious matters.

2) This teaching, contained in the schema, is *solid* in itself, and it is precisely *suited* to our times. For it depends upon the doctrine of the Church, recently evolved, concerning the juridical State, or, as we say in English, "constitutional government." Pope Pius XII developed this doctrine and was followed by Pope John XXIII. Both Popes brought about an *authentic development* (*progressus authenticus*) of Catholic doctrine in this matter.

3) Moreover, the schema corresponds not only to the truth, but to the deep aspirations of people all over the world, especially in those nations which recently have happily achieved their own independence.

4) The root of this concept on the State is the dignity of the human person which is, as Pius XII said, "the subject, the foundation and the end of social life." It follows, then, that the *common good consists in the full preservation of the rights and duties of the human person*. Further, it follows that this public authority—the State—is circumscribed by certain *limits* which are, first of all, determined by the State's office of protecting and cultivating human and civil rights.

5) This general teaching is *well applied* in the schema on religious liberty. For since the right of religious liberty is clearly proved to be a right based on the dignity of the person, the public authority is bound to assure an effective safeguard for this right.

6) The care of religious *liberty* rightly pertains to the public authority, but not the care of religion itself. For religion, as the schema shows from the teaching of Pope Leo XIII, is of a *higher order* which the State cannot touch.

7) It must finally be noted that where the civil law of religious liberty, based on constitutional law, really thrives, the State does not profess a religious indifferentism, a false neutrality, or an agnosticism in religious matters.

8) Rather, where religious liberty is secure, the State simply acknowledges its own limitations over human rights which *cannot be relinquished* ("inalienable"). In other words, the State recognizes that it has no right to constrain the exercise of religious liberty *except in the case of civil crimes.*

9) The State in this concept acknowledges also the social value of religion to be of the first importance. Therefore, it must promote this social value of religion, but in a manner distinct and proper to itself. The State, therefore, best fosters religion when it fosters the free exercise of it.

LAWRENCE CARDINAL SHEHAN, 20 *September, 1965*

The schema on religious liberty has my whole-hearted support. I particularly commend the remarks which His Eminence Cardinal Urbani has made on the development of the schema's doctrine—a doctrine whose seeds are found in the Church's teaching on the dignity of the human person and whose support is drawn from Sacred Scripture, notably from the way God has dealt with man and from the words and acts of Jesus Christ and His Apostles. Here I intend to speak only of the modern development of this doctrine.

The first stages of this development are found in the many writings of Pope Leo XIII whose name has occurred so often in our discussion. No one holds that the doctrine of this schema is found explicitly in the writings of Pope Leo. But the teaching of Leo already presents to us a notable development over the doctrine commonly held during the Middle Ages and during the post-Reformation period. Furthermore, in his teaching, Pope Leo took the first steps along that path, followed by subsequent popes, particularly Pius XI, Pius XII and John XXIII.

It would be a mistake to see Leo's doctrine on toleration as the central point of his own teaching or as the final and unchangeable teaching of the Church on religious liberty. The doctrine of Leo, itself a development, in no way prevents us from going on, in the light of experience and a deeper understanding of the dignity of the human person, to find religious liberty properly understood, as a universal human right.

It would also be a mistake to say that Leo's master idea, in what concerns the public care of religion, was the exclusive right of truth and the denial of all right to error. He does insist that truth and error, right and wrong, do not enter the juridical order on an equal title, which was a sophism of the rational-ists. What is true and good may receive positive juridical authorization; what is false or evil may receive only juridical toleration. This is the only concrete juridical sense that can attach to the otherwise unhelpful abstraction that error has no rights; and no sensible man would quarrel with this concrete sense. But, strictly speaking, rights inhere in persons; they cannot inhere in abstractions.

There are two central ideas in the teaching of Leo: 1) the clear distinction between the authority of the Church and the authority of the State; and 2) the freedom of the Church.

Leo emphasized in a new way the transcendence of the Church both as a spiritual authority and as the People of God who are ruled by His law revealed in Christ. He also emphasized in a new way the relative autonomy of the People Temporal who are ruled by civil law, under civil authority, whose powers are limited by a higher order of law which is not of its own making.

But the heart of Leo's teaching was the freedom of the Church. Implicit in his teaching on this point was a declaration of the freedom of the people, once the people had fulfilled the conditions of freedom, i.e., growth of per-sonal and political consciousness. And implicit in the freedom of the people is religious freedom as a juridical institution correlative with constitutional gov-ernment. By his central emphasis on the freedom of the Church, Leo has caused the recognition that this freedom includes freedom of the human person and, hence, religious freedom as a legal institution within a system of constitu-tional government.

Thus Leo opened the way to the teaching of Pius XI who, in *Non abbiamo bisogno* (1931), undertook "to fight the good fight for freedom of conscience"; who, in *Firmissimam constantiam* (1937), stated, "The faithful have a right to live in a civil society according to the dictates of reason and conscience"; who, in *Mit brennender sorge* (1937), declared, "The man of religious faith has an inalienable right to profess his faith and practice it in appropriate ways."

Pius XII took a further step toward our doctrine of religious freedom. In his radio message of 1942, among the "fundamental rights of the person which are to be recognized and promoted" he included "the right to public and private worship of God including also religious actions of a charitable kind." Religious freedom, as a juridical notion which required legal recognition, has emerged into the open. From the vast corpus of Pius XII's letters and speeches it is possible to assemble all the principles which underlie the doctrine in our schema. It is true the Pope does not systematize these principles, and he does not explicitly draw our conclusions. But the principles are there, and they point in the direction of the explicit teaching of this proposed "declaration."

The teaching of Pope John XXIII, particularly as contained in *Pacem in Terris*, carrying the development of religious liberty one step further, is too recent and too well known to need repetition.

We do not deny that there are passages in the writings of Pius XI and Pius XII which can be cited in favor of mere toleration rather than true religious freedom. But it is clear that Leo XIII had already opened the door, and Pius XI, Pius XII and John XXIII directly contributed to the doctrine of this schema whose seeds were in the Church's teachings from the beginning.

In his address to a seminar of the United Nations more than a year ago, Pope Paul VI said:

The Church also is busy with a problem that is not without affinity with the present object of your research. It is the problem of religious freedom. The importance and the amplitude of the question are so great that it has claimed the attention of the Ecumenical Council. It is legitimate to expect the promulgation of a text on this subject that will be of great import not only for the Church, but also for all those—countless in number—who feel that an authoritative declaration on the subject is a matter of concern to them.

It is obvious that the whole world expects of this Council a declaration on religious liberty. The world needs such a declaration, for without the recognition of the right to religious liberty there can be no true and lasting peace among men. The Church, too, needs such a declaration, for only through the recognition of religious liberty can the Church be revived in those countries where her life has been virtually stamped out; only through recognition of religious liberty can the Church be free in those countries where she is in shackles; only in an atmosphere of religious freedom can the Church flourish in those new and developing nations which hold out so much promise for the future. The doctrine of religious freedom in our schema is a sound doctrine, in full harmony with the body of the Church's traditional teaching. It is to be hoped therefore, that this schema will receive overwhelming approval from the Fathers.

Declaration on Religious Freedom

✠ SPECIAL ADDRESS

BISHOP ROBERT DWYER, 5 *November*, 1965, Radio Address over Vatican City Radio

The Second Vatican Council is already passing into history. For those of us, the bishops of the Church universal who have participated in all its four sessions, listened to and shared in its discussions, and voted its chapters and Constitutions according to our conscientious convictions, it has been the crowning experience of our lives as churchmen. Never again shall we feel that "first, fine, careless rapture" that was ours when we responded to the summons of the beloved Pope John XXIII to inaugurate the *aggiornamento* of the Church as the People of God working out the mystery of salvation in the world of today. Never again shall we realize so intimately and personally what it means to be the successors of the Apostles under the primacy of Peter in the person of Pope Paul VI.

Yet time is inexorable; the Council moves to its climax and its solemn conclusion, and thereafter we return to our homes and dioceses, there to implement as fully as possible its mandates and to communicate to all men of good will the ecumenism of its spirit.

Now the mantle of the prophet is the most evanescent of garments. All too often it turns out that the would-be prophet finds himself, like the emperor in the story, wearing no clothes at all. Yet the temptation is not to be resisted.

What will history record as the outstanding achievement of the Council? As the definition of the Trinity was the work of Nicaea; as the dual nature, divine and human, of Jesus Christ, Son of God, Son of Mary, was the accomplishment of Chalcedon; as the doctrine of justification by works no less than by faith was the hallmark of Trent; and as the clarification of the infallible teaching office of the Church as exercised by her head, the vicar of Christ, was the triumph of the First Vatican Council—what will be celebrated as the supreme contribution of the Second?

For our part, and without any false modesty as one less wise (though we are assured of the agreement of the vast majority of the Council Fathers), we would answer, without a moment's hesitation: the Declaration on Religious

Liberty. Other dogmatic and liturgical definitions of the Council unquestionably have high importance, and it is with no thought, certainly, of downgrading such towering monuments as the schema on the Church or that of divine revelation or the Constitution on the Sacred Liturgy that we suggest that they will have less of an immediate impact upon the thinking and believing world, and that they will assume less prominence in the perspective of history.

For there is something epoch-making about this Declaration which exalts it to the stature of one of the great landmarks of religious history. It could mark more clearly than anything else, even more sharply than the two great personalities which have been identified with its formulation and promulgation —we mean, of course, Pope John XXIII and Pope Paul VI—the beginning of a new era in the religious understanding of mankind.

It is not, indeed, that religious liberty, as proclaimed by the Council document, is something new in Catholic doctrine or in Catholic practice. Liberty is a Catholic word. It is fundamental to the Christian view of salvation that no man can be redeemed against his will, no man can be tricked into heaven. There is a very true and exact sense in which the Church has always been the most strenuous proponent of freedom of conscience, just as she has been the indefatigable defender of freedom of the will when all the philosophers were busy denying it and all the politicians were busy destroying it. But in the concrete historical setting, in the actuality of time—especially of times past, the Middle Ages, the Renaissance, the rise of nationalism and imperialism— the Church (or should we not more accurately specify churchmen?) was beguiled by the illusion of a Christendom where religion and politics were merged into one and where the interests of the Church were hopelessly entangled with the interests of the State. How gravely the cause of religion has suffered over the centuries by reason of the fatal attractiveness of this dream (which still has its dreamers and its adepts) we can only guess. Its worst effect has been the limitation of religious freedom by the imposition of political, economic or social sanctions upon any species of non-conformity.

It serves no purpose to comment that the illusion was not confined to the Catholic imagination, that it was shared by religious men of all persuasions and by most statesmen. The final judgment upon it is that it has always failed to achieve justice, just as it has always failed to secure religious conviction. The brutal force of this reality is as obvious in the history of the various Marxist tyrannies of the twentieth century as in the Wars of Religion back in the sixteenth and seventeenth centuries.

It was time that the Church should rid herself, once for all, of the medieval dream of the Two Swords, which might better be called "the theory of the crutch." It is necessary in an age when freedom is seen ever more clearly as the essential ingredient of humanity, the very stuff of which human dignity is made, that the Church should reaffirm her basic commitment to religious liberty in terms both succinct and eloquent. Here she does no violence to her past; rather, she probes more deeply into her spiritual heritage. She disentangles the essential from the nonessential, and whereas, even as late as a century ago, the then reigning pontiff, Pius IX of holy memory, still found it difficult to formulate the doctrine of religious liberty in contradiction to the then popular and fallacious notions of Liberalism (often the very opposite of genuine freedom), the issues now have attained that degree of clarity whereby the Church, with entire confidence, can take the lead in proclaiming "liberty to all the land, to all the inhabitants thereof," and of summoning all men to be worthy of "that freedom wherewith Christ hath made us free."

There is, it goes without saying, a sharp distinction between liberty and license, between religious freedom and religious indifferentism. Freedom absolves no man from his personal responsibility to truth, nor does it dispense him from the search for the truth which God has revealed to mankind in the person of His Son, our Savior, Jesus Christ. This solemn reminder is part of the Council's Declaration on Religious Liberty, spelled out as plainly as language permits. But the whole document is monumental. Surely, in time to come, men will say of the Second Vatican Council that it wrote the charter of man's spiritual freedom as a child of God. It is something for any bishop, however obscure, to have played some part, however microscopic, in the framing of such a charter.

Declaration on Religious Freedom

✠ COMMENTARY by Rev. John Courtney Murray, S.J.

During the Council the schema on religious freedom was often called the "American schema." The adjective would be quite inappropriate with regard to the final form of the schema, the Declaration itself. It was approved by a definitive vote of 2308 to 70. It was, therefore, an act of the universal Church, like all the other conciliar documents. However, during the long course of its legislative history, the schema had the solid and consistent support of the American bishops, and their numerous interventions had considerable influence in determining its substance and language. There were those who said that the American bishops supported the schema simply for pragmatic reasons. But this is an inadequate view. Undoubtedly, the support derived its basic inspiration from the American experience, from which the Church has learned the practical value of the free-exercise clause of the First Amendment. At the same time, American Catholics have understood that the practical value of this constitutional provision derives from the truth of the principle that it embodies. It is apparent from their interventions that the American bishops made important theoretical contributions toward the illumination of the principle.

This study of the relation between the Declaration and the First Amendment must be a bit rapid. There will be, for instance, a minimum of citation from constitutional sources. It is a matter of considering the object or content of the right to religious freedom, its foundation, and its extension, the argument for the validity of the right and the norms that limit its exercise.

The object or content of the right to religious freedom, as specified both in the Declaration and in the American constitutional system, is identical. An authority in the matter, Mr. Mark de Wolfe Howe, has emphasized the importance of the distinction between a right as an immunity and a right as a positive claim. When it is forgotten, he says, "we begin to use the word 'rights' and the phrase 'civil liberties' in misleading ways. Our rights, as the framers conceived them, were essentially certain specified immunities. They were not claims on, but assurance against, the government." The right to religious freedom is essentially an immunity. Moreover, as Mr. Justice Roberts pointed out in the *Cantwell* case: "The constitutional inhibition of legislation on the subject of religion has a double aspect. On the one hand, it forbids, forestalls, compulsion by law of the acceptance of any creed or the practice of any form of worship. . . . On the other hand, it safeguards the free exercise of the chosen form of religion." In the equivalent terms of the Declaration, religious freedom means "that all men are to be immune from coercion on the part of individuals or of social groups and of any human power, in such wise that no one is to be forced to act in a manner contrary to his own beliefs, nor is anyone to be restrained from acting in accordance with his own beliefs. . . ." Nowhere in our Constitution, much less in the Declaration, is it implied that a man has a right to do what is evil or to say what is false, as if error and evil could be the object or content of a right. That would be moral nonsense. The constitutional content of freedom of religion is freedom from coercion in matters religious.

In the American view, religious freedom is, in the first instance, an assurance against government; in this sense it is properly a civil liberty. In the second instance, it is an assurance against coercions attempted by other powers in society; in this sense, it is a social freedom which will be vindicated by government. Some of the conciliar Fathers seemed unwilling to accept this conception of the problem. They wished to attribute the primacy to the social freedom. Hence they required that the definition of religious freedom, cited above, should read: ". . . and of any human power," rather than: ". . . and of government." The reasons were various. Earlier versions of the schema had been criticized on the ground that they manifested "too much preoccupation with government" or even "hostility to government." The criticism, however, seemed to reveal a reluctance or a failure on the part of some of the Fathers to grasp the true theoretical, as well as practical, position of the problem.

It belongs to the very definition of religious freedom to say that it is, in the first instance, an immunity against restrictive use of the power of government (the aspect of immunity from restriction is the more crucial of the two aspects noted above). If there be any human power which has the right to restrict the scope of religious freedom, this rightful power can reside only in government, which possesses a monopoly of coercive force in society to be used for the common good. In its very concept, therefore, religious freedom includes the understanding that government has no such right (unless its existence can be proved in the particular case, as will be said). Only in these primary terms, as an assurance against government, can religious freedom, as an immunity from coercion, be properly defined.

This view of the matter is implicitly recognized elsewhere in the Declaration, where it is question of the care of religious freedom by government. In its definition, however, the Declaration is not as correct and clear as the Constitution on the central issue that the statute of religious freedom is essentially a self-denying ordinance on the part of government. For whatever reasons, certain bishops were too concerned to put forward the notion of religious freedom as social freedom. This concern was related to a disposition to shy away from the formally political aspects of the problem—a disposition to which reference will later be made. To note this nuance of understanding is not, of course, to imply a weakness in the Declaration. The notion of religious freedom as a properly civil right is altogether clear.

The second question concerns the extension of the right to religious freedom. In the *Cantwell* case, as often elsewhere, the Supreme Court made clear that the First Amendment "embraces two concepts—freedom to believe and freedom to act." The same distinction appears in the Declaration. It emphasizes "one of the major tenets of Catholic doctrine that man's response to God in faith must be free; no one therefore is to be forced to embrace the Christian faith against his own will." Or more broadly: "The act of faith is of its very nature a free act," a statement which holds true of any act of ultimate religious commitment, even one that is atheist in tenor. (The Declaration does not explicitly advert to the atheist, despite the wishes of some conciliar Fathers that it should; nevertheless, its definition and doctrine of religious freedom clearly extends to him.) The principle of freedom of belief—what is correctly called freedom of conscience—inspires the strong condemnation of the "wrong" that is done "when government imposes upon its people, by force or fear or other means, the profession or repudiation of any religion. . . ."

The more critical aspect of the question concerns freedom to act. In the American constitutional tradition, the free exercise of religion is conceived in the broadest possible terms, even to the defense of sheer religious eccentricity. The terms of the Declaration are generous, although they naturally lack the fullness of detail that litigation has produced in the United States since *Terret vs. Taylor* in 1815. The Council affirms that a man must be free to act according to his beliefs, "whether privately or publicly, whether alone or in association with others." Moreover, corporate religious freedom is adequately described under use of a distinction—a bit blurred in the final text but still discernible—between the internal autonomy of the religious community and its external freedom of public action. This latter chiefly includes "public teaching and witness to their faith, whether by the spoken or by the written word."

Furthermore, the Declaration is careful to bring within the scope of religious freedom various forms of religiously motivated utterance and action. In the words of John Coleman Bennett, religious freedom "should be the liberty of public teaching not only about religious matters in the narrow sense, but also about all social, economic, and political concerns about which there is a religious judgment." The Declaration says the same thing more briefly: "In addition, it comes within the meaning of religious freedom that religious communities should not be prohibited from freely undertaking to show the special value of their doctrine in what concerns the organization of society and the inspiration of the whole of human activity." Even contemporary history affords only too many examples of the readiness of governments to claim that religious teaching is politically subversive. The Declaration disallows this claim. Finally, religious freedom includes the social freedom of assembly, "the right of men freely to hold meetings and to establish educational, cultural, charitable, and social organizations, under the impulse of their own religious sense."

After defining the object or content of the right to religious freedom, the Council declares that the right "has its foundation in the very dignity of the human person, as this dignity is known through the revealed word of God and by reason itself." The right is therefore inalienable. In consequence, it must be "recognized in the constitutional law whereby society is governed," and thus obtain the legal status of a "civil right." The dignity of the person is not a legal or political principle; it is the foundation of all legal and political principles. So it is presented in the Declaration of Independence upon whose conception of man the whole of the American constitutional system is erected: "We hold these truths to be self-evident, that all men are created equal, that they are endowed by their Creator with certain unalienable rights. . . ." A fair generalization is made by Joseph Costanzo, S.J., in his book, *This Nation under God:* "The substantive and procedural rights of the American Bill of Rights and of the Fourteenth Amendment are historical reassertions and juridical securities of man's personal dignity. . . ." Happily, British history rather than French revolutionary theory lies behind the Bill of Rights. As the Supreme Court said in 1897, these rights are "guarantees and immunities which are inherited from our English ancestors." It is true that even after the Glorious Revolution had overturned royal absolutism, our English ancestors notoriously failed fully to recognize that special immunity which is religious freedom. But this was an aberration in the organic development of the liberal tradition of the West, whose matrix was the Christian and medieval doctrine of man. "This medieval doctrine," as Otto von Gierke said, "was already filled with the thought of the inborn and indestructible rights of the individual" which derive from his personal dignity as disclosed by the Christian revelation. The development was again set on its right course, and fuller formulation was given to the right to religious freedom, by the American constitutional system. Caught in the more disastrous aberrations derivative from the French Revolution, the Church long failed to recognize the validity of the American development of what was, in fact, her own tradition. The Declaration accords the belated recognition. The right to religious freedom is not the creature of expedience or even of history alone. It is not a gracious grant of government in concession to social circumstances. It is a requirement of the dignity of the human person.

In order to make clear this point—that religious freedom is a matter of principle—the Declaration mounts a brief argument. It is not cast in the American style. In his classic study, *The American Commonwealth,* first published in 1888, Lord Bryce stated the terms of a problem which was felt, although never fully faced, in the drafting of the Vatican schema:

> The abstention of the state from interference in matters of faith and worship may be advocated on two principles, which may be called the

political and the religious. The former sets out from the principles of
liberty and equality. It holds any attempt at compulsion by the civil power
to be an infringement on liberty of thought, as well as on liberty of action,
which could be justified only when a practice claiming to be religious in so
obviously anti-social or immoral as to threaten the well-being of the community.

In contrast:

The second principle, embodying the more purely religious view of the
question, starts from the conception of the church as a spiritual body existing for spiritual purposes and moving along spiritual paths. . . . Compulsion
of any kind is contrary to the nature of such a body, which lives by love and
reverence, not by law.

He adds:

Of these two views it is the former much more than the latter which has
moved the American mind. . . . When the question arose in a practical shape
in the early days of the Republic, arguments of the former or political order
were found amply sufficient to settle it.

American constitutional history gives extensive evidence of the centrality of
the principle of equality before the law as the essential basis of religious freedom. In another classic nineteenth-century work, *Treatise on the Constitutional
Limitations Which Rest Upon the Legislative Power of the States of the American Union,* the famous Judge Cooley asserted that the central intention of
American state constitutions was "to guard against the slightest approach
toward the establishment of an inequality in the civil and political rights of
citizens which shall have for its basis only their difference of religious belief."
Thereafter, he adds, "the general voice has been that persons of every religious
persuasion should be made equal before the law." In the *Schimpp* case in
1963, Mr. Justice Clark recalled a century-old unpublished opinion of Mr.
Justice Alphonso Taft in the *Minor* case, which affirmed the constitutional
principle of the "absolute equality before the law of all religious opinions and
sects." (Cooley is more exact when he speaks of "persons," not of "opinions
and sects.") Citations could be multiplied. And their common supposition is
always clear. Apart from equality before the law, political freedom loses its
meaning—and political freedom is the essence of the American proposition.
Therefore, religious freedom, which is the first form of political freedom, finds
its foundation in the principle of equality before the law—an equality, evidently, which rests on the deeper ground that "all men are created equal."
    In contrast, the appeal of the Declaration is to arguments that may fairly be
characterized as religious in some broad sense—the moral obligation to seek

the truth, the function of conscience in mediating the divine law, the social nature of man (which establishes a necessary link between the internal moral imperative and the external religious act), and the transcendent nature of the religious act. From these heights the argument descends to the political order only in the laconic statement that government "would clearly transgress the limits set to its power, were it to presume to command or inhibit acts that are religious."

There were reasons why the Council followed this line. There was the view that it was not fitting for a Council to make "political" arguments— despite the fact that papal encyclical literature is full of them, as may be gathered from the title, "Documentos politicos," of Volume II of *Doctrina Pontificia*, a valuable Spanish collection of papal statements from Pius IX to Pius XII. An intrinsically more valid reason lay in the fact that a serious effort to make the political argument for religious freedom would have carried the Council into the problem of "Church and State," so called, a much broader and more complicated problem which the Council wisely wished to avoid. Finally and decisively, there was the dark spectre that brooded over the conciliar debates—the historical and doctrinal spectre of religious indifferentism. The American constitutional principle of the equality before the law, in its application to freedom of religion, carries no connotations of this theological error. This fact was never attended to, or understood, by the apostolic hierarchy of the nineteenth-century Church in Europe. It may be doubted whether a general understanding of the fact prevailed at Vatican Council II. In any event, there is no question that vast confusion and opposition, compounding confusion and opposition already existent, would have arisen if the major political argument for religious freedom—from the principle of equality before the law —had been pressed. Minds and emotions conditioned by the Continental experience of nineteenth-century laicism would surely have seen it as a concession to, if not an outright embrace of, the indifferentist principle of the equality of all religions before God.

As a matter of fact, trouble enough was occasioned by the Declaration's statement: "Finally, government is to see to it that the equality of citizens before the law, which is itself an element of the common good, is never violated, whether openly or covertly, for religious reasons." The inclusion of this cardinal principle—as a principle in itself, and especially as constitutive of the common good—was due to Anglo-American interventions, from bishops who had an understanding, whether sophisticated or intuitive, of the common-law tradition. The statement was opposed by bishops from the tradition of the Iberian peninsula. Its inclusion was altogether happy for at least two reasons. First, the principle is sound. Second, the commentator on the Vatican Declaration can find a footing in the text from which to enlarge its argument and to make a more balanced and convincing case for religious freedom by appealing to political as well as to religious or moral principle. To do this is entirely in order. It was not the intention of the Council to make the full case, but simply to indicate lines of argument whose fuller development would be left to theologians, political philosophers and constitutional historians.

The right to religious freedom is itself inalienable. Its exercise, however, is necessarily subject to limitation in particular cases. "Conduct," said the Court in the *Cantwell* case, "remains subject to regulation for the protection of society." Or, in the words of the Declaration, society "has the right to defend itself against possible abuses committed on pretext of freedom of religion. It is the special duty of government to provide this protection." Government, however, is "not to act in an arbitrary fashion or in an unfair spirit of partisanship" (one may see here a veiled reference to governments which consider the Party to be the People). Its action must be governed by "juridical norms that are in conformity with the objective moral order." American courts have never found it easy to define these norms. But the effort is constantly made.

A leading definition, frequently cited, was given in the case of *Watson vs. Jones* in 1872: "In this country the full and free right to entertain any religious belief, to practice any religious principle, and to teach any religious doctrine, which does not violate the laws of morality and property, and which does not infringe personal rights, is conceded to all." In *Davis vs. Beason* in 1890, the last of these limiting norms is again laid down, in the statement that action in the name of religion may claim protection only when it is "not injurious to the rights of others." In the same case—one of the famous Mormon cases—the moral norm is also adduced: "Bigamy and polygamy are crimes by the laws of all civilized and Christian countries. . . . To call their advocacy a tenet of religion is to offend the common sense of mankind." The application of these two norms in the concrete case may be difficult; but their validity as norms is beyond question.

Other norms of less well defined tenor have also been used. In one of the Jehovah's Witnesses' cases, *Jones vs. City of Opelika* in 1942, the Court refers to the "preservation of peace and good order" as norms limiting religious efforts at what is called "the enlightenment of the community." Again, in the *Cantwell* case the Court defends the right of a state to "safeguard the peace, good order, and comfort of the community." And in the same case, the Court attempts a definition of the elusive concept of the public peace: "The offense known as breach of the peace embraces a great variety of conduct destroying or menacing public order and tranquility. It includes not only violent acts, but acts and words likely to produce violence in others. . . . When clear and present danger of riot, disorder, interference with traffic upon the public streets, or other immediate threat to public safety, peace or order appears, the power of the State to prevent or punish is obvious." These citations, and others available, reveal some imprecision of concept and vocabulary. In particular, "peace" and "order" are used with seeming synonymity or equivalence. At the same time, they reveal the felt judicial need for a norm which will cover a "great variety of conduct" which cannot be permitted, for the valid reason that it entails some manner of "violence" done to the public.

The Declaration makes an effort at synthesis and precision. "Public order" is made the generic concept. In order to give it a firm moral basis, it is first related to the higher and more inclusive concept of the common welfare of which it is the "basic component." So basic is the value of this component that it may and must be protected, if necessary, by the use of coercion. The indispensable requirement of society is that it should be a civilized order in which crime is met by prevention or punishment. The further conciliar intention was to give a substantive content to the concept of public order. It includes three elemental social "needs," three indispensable social values—juridical, political, and moral. The juridical need is for "effective safeguard of the rights of all citizens," the political need is for "an adequate care of the public peace," and the moral need is for "a proper guardianship of public morality." When there is serious trespass upon one or other of these basic social values, coercive repression of the trespass is legitimate.

There was objection, notably by the Polish hierarchy, against the use of the concept of public order as being liable to abuse by governments hostile to religion. On the other hand, the concept has status in constitutional law, even though it is more often used than defined. It was therefore adopted, and the effort was made to surround it with qualifications that would preclude abuse, as far as possible. A similar effort to preclude abuses of governmental power has constantly been made in the American constitutional tradition. Both the Declaration and the Constitution have in common the intention of laying down strict and narrow criteria for the limitation of freedom of religion, since the exercise of a human right is at stake. Here a comparison is interesting.

In the Declaration it is simply specified that public order is to be "just," that its exigencies must be in accord with justice. The trouble is that the concept of justice, like that of order, is liable to abuse, as we know full well today. The Declaration is concerned to state the moral requirement without further detail. The American constitutional tradition is more satisfactory. Public order, or the public peace, will be just if their demands are enforced in accord with the requirements of the Fourteenth Amendment—that due process of law be observed and that the equal protection of the laws be extended to all. These procedural safeguards are matters of justice. Moreover, public order will be just in a substantive sense if it remains always an order of due and rightful freedom. Freedom always remains the supreme value protected by the First Amendment: "In every case the power to regulate must be so exercised as not, in attaining a permissible end, unduly to infringe the protected freedom" (*Cantwell*). There is no real clash of claims here. On the contrary, the higher principle always holds that the primary thing due in justice to the people is their freedom.

The Declaration stops short of these matters of procedural and substantive moment. Fortunately, however, it lays strong stress on freedom as a protected value in society, together with the value of justice, even though the two values are not explicitly related. The conclusion of the paragraph on the regulation of the free exercise of religion reads: "For the rest, the usages of society are to be the usages of freedom in their full range; that is, the freedom of man is to be respected as far as possible and not to be curtailed except when and in so far as necessary." This is the traditional rule of jurisprudence in the liberal tradition of politics. It is also the basic principle of the free society—the highest principle that controls the action of "free government." From the point of view of the American tradition, the significance of its inclusion is obvious. But its significance is even more weighty from the standpoint of the universal Church and of human society in general. For the first time, in terms even stronger than the precedental terms of *Pacem in Terris,* the Declaration on Religious Freedom, by its statement of this principle, aligns the Church firmly and irrevocably with the movement of the historical consciousness of contemporary men— with "those desires in the minds of men" which are "greatly in accord with truth and justice," from which this epochal document takes its start.

INDEX

Abbott, Walter M., 514
Abraham, 572, 596
Ackeren, Gerald F. Van, 582
Adam, 89
Aem, Herman, 346n
Agagianian, Gregorio Pietro, 193, 425, 523, 528
Ahern, Barnabas Mary, 25, 103–104, 484–486
Alfrink, Bernard Jan, 8, 95, 620
Alter, Karl J., 209, 219, 286, 366, 368, 377, 623, 625, 629–630, 638, 651–653
Ambrose, St., 444, 600, 604
Ammann, Joachim, 26
Ancel, Alfred, 187
Antonelli, Ferdinando, 132
Antoniutti, Ildebrando, 428
Apollo, 203
Aquila, 202
Aquinas, St. Thomas, 71, 217, 223, 245, 254, 257, 420, 426, 565, 593–594, 648
Athenagoras I, Patriarch, 300
Augustine, St., 115, 124, 245, 257, 291, 310, 426, 492, 604–606

Babcock, Allen J., 452
Balducci, Ernesto, 263–264
Bandas, Rudolph G., 104, 410, 543, 562n
Bartholme, Peter W., 13
Baum, Gregory, 373, 596, 598–599
Baum, William, 293
Bea, Augustin, 95–96, 98, 108, 110, 285, 292–293, 295, 320, 569, 574–575, 579, 597, 617, 624, 634
Beaudouin, Lambert, 120, 130
Begin, Floyd L., 6, 208–209, 244–247
Beran, Josef, 621
Bergson, Henri, 627
Bethune, André J. de, 193

Binz, Leo, 363, 366, 368
Blake, Eugene Carson, 608
Blomjous, Joseph, 188
Bloy, Léon, 598
Boland, Thomas A., 104
Bosler, Raymond, 582
Boudreaux, Warren L., 6, 212
Bourke, Myles M., 596
Bouscaren, Timothy L., 523
Brady, William O., 7
Brennan, Joseph P., 596
Brown, Robert McAfee, 273, 298–299, 618
Browne, Michael, 22
Brownson, Orestes, 333
Burns, J. Edgar, 596
Brzana, Stanislaus J., 218, 228, 432–433, 456, 478, 491–493
Buckley, Joseph, 11, 31, 51–53, 431, 437–438, 647–649
Bugnini, Annibale, 130–131
Bukato, Gabriel, 339
Burch, Thomas K., 193
Busch, William, 130
Buswell, Charles A., 133–134
Butler, Christopher, 21, 95, 98, 121
Byrne, Leo C., 486

Campion, Donald, 583
Canisius, St. Peter, 121
Cantwell, Daniel, 582
Caprile, Giovanni, 190
Carberry, John J., 625
Carli, Luigi, 368, 576
Carraro, Giuseppe, 404
Carroll, John, 333
Castellano, Ismaele Mario, 274
Cataline, 276

PACE UNIVERSITY LIBRARIES
MORTOLA STACKS BX830 1962.A514
American participation in the second Vat

3 3061 00061 3803

BX   Vatican Council.
830   American participation in
1962.   the second Vatican Council.
A514

PACE COLLEGE WESTCHESTER
LIBRARY
Bedford Road, Pleasantville, N. Y.
914 ROgers 9-3200

Books may be borrowed for two weeks.
Identification card must be presented each time
books are borrowed.
A charge of 5 cents is made for each day a book
is overdue.
A charge of 25 cents is made for each day a re-
serve book is overdue.

PRINTED IN U.S.A.